ds

Baedeker's

NETHERLANDS

Imprint

256 colour photographs (credits at end of book)
33 town plans, 17 drawings, 16 ground-plans, 9 general maps, 6 special maps, 6 layout plans,
1 table, 1 large map of the Netherlands (list at end of book)

Text: Vera Beck (Practical Information), Astrid Feltes (introductory chapters, The Netherlands
from A to Z), Prof. Wolfgang Hassenpflug (climate)
Consultant: Herman Brinks
Editorial work: Baedeker-Redaktion (Astrid Feltes)

Cartography: Gert Oberländer, Munich; Mairs Geographischer Verlag, Ostfildern-Kemnat
(large map of the Netherlands)

General direction:
Dr Peter Baumgarten, Baedeker Stuttgart

English language edition:
Alec Court

English translation:
James Hogarth

To make it easier to locate the various sights listed in the "A to Z" section of the Guide, their
coordinates on the large map of the Netherlands are shown in red at the head of each entry.

Following the tradition established by Karl Baedeker in 1844, sights of particular interest are
distinguished by either one or two stars.

Only a selection of hotels and restaurants can be given: no reflection is implied, therefore, on
establishments not included.

The symbol ⓘ on a town plan indicates the local tourist office from which further information
can be obtained. The post-horn symbol indicates a post office.

In a time of rapid change it is difficult to ensure that all the information given is entirely accurate
and up to date, and the possibility of error can never be completely eliminated. Although the
publishers can accept no responsibility for inaccuracies and omissions, they are always
grateful for corrections and suggestions for improvement.

1st English edition

© Baedeker Stuttgart
Original German edition

© 1992 The Automobile Association
United Kingdom and Ireland

© 1992 Jarrold and Sons Ltd
English language edition worldwide

US and Canadian Edition Prentice Hall Press

Distributed in the United Kingdom by the Publishing Division of The Automobile Association,
Fanum House, Basingstoke, Hampshire, RG21 2EA.

The name *Baedeker* is a registered trademark
A CIP catalogue record for this book is available from the British Library.

Licensed user:
Mairs Geographischer Verlag GmbH & Co., Ostfildern-Kemnat bei Stuttgart

Printed in Italy by G. Canale & C. S.p.A. – Borgaro T.se – Turin

ISBN 0–13–063611–8 US and Canada
    0–7495–0405–6 UK

Contents

The Principal Sights at a Glance

The places listed above are merely a selection of the principal sights in the Netherlands – scenic attractions and towns and other places of interest. There are of course innumerable other sights, to which attention is drawn in the A to Z section of the guide by one or more stars.

Preface

This guide to the Netherlands is one of the new generation of Baedeker guides.

These guides, illustrated throughout in colour, are designed to meet the needs of the modern traveller. They are quick and easy to consult, with the principal places of interest described in alphabetical order, and the information is presented in a format that is both attractive and easy to follow.

This guide to the kingdom of the Netherlands – commonly, if in Dutch eyes improperly, known as Holland – is in three parts. The first part gives a general account of the country, its topography, its perpetual fight against the sea, its cultural landscapes, climate, flora and fauna, population, educational system, government and administration, economy, history, famous people, art and culture. A selection of quotations and a number of suggested itineraries provide a transition to the second part, in which the country's places and features of tourist interest – towns, provinces, regions, rivers – are described. The third part contains a variety of practical information. Both the sights and the practical information are listed in alphabetical order.

The new Baedeker guides are noted for their concentration on essentials and their convenience of use. They contain numerous specially drawn plans and colour illustrations; and at the end of the book is a large map making it easy to locate the various places described in the "A to Z" section of the guide with the help of the co-ordinates given at the head of each entry.

Facts and Figures

This guide is concerned with the European territory of the Kingdom of the Netherlands, including its continental heartland, the islands and peninsulas of Zeeland (Zealand) in the south-west and the IJsselmeer (now enclosed by a dyke and partly poldered) and six West Frisian islands to the north-west.

The self-governing overseas territories of the Netherlands in the Caribbean – the Union of the Netherlands Antilles, with the islands of Curaçao, Bonaire, part of Sint Maarten, Sint Eustatius (Statia) and Saba, and the island of Aruba, now seeking independence – are described in the AA/ Baedeker guide to the Caribbean.

General

The Netherlands lie on the western edge of the European mainland between latitude 50°45' and 53°12' north and between longitude 3°21' and 7°13' east. They have a natural frontier in the north and west, with a long and much indented coast on the North Sea, and are bounded on the east by Germany (630km/390 miles; *länder* of North Rhine–Westphalia and Lower Saxony) and on the south by Belgium (450km/280 miles; provinces of Liège, Limburg, Antwerp, East Flanders and West Flanders).

Situation

Much of the Netherlands lies below sea level (hence the name Netherlands, "Low Countries") and has been won from the sea over the centuries by the construction of dykes to reclaim land from the water. As a result the country's coastline has been reduced from over 1100km/685 miles to less than 500km/310 miles.

In addition to their land area the Netherlands include large areas of water such as the Waddenzee, the IJsselmeer and the waters of the province of Zeeland. (In Dutch the term *meer* is applied to a freshwater lake or lagoon, *zee* to a saltwater sea.)

The area of the Netherlands is reckoned in a number of different ways:

(a) Total area, including arms of the sea and coastal waters: 41,864 sq.km/16,164 sq. miles.
(b) Area under local government administration: 37,334 sq.km/ 14,415 sq. miles.
(c) Area excluding waters over 6m/20ft wide: 33,934 sq.km/ 13,102 sq. miles.

As in other countries bounded by the sea, the land area cannot be exactly determined, since the action of the tides is constantly altering the coastline. In the Netherlands, where the tidal movement on the North Sea coast and in the funnel-shaped river estuaries is very considerable, areas are calcu-

◀ *Stadskanaal: a typical moorland village*

lated on the basis of the mean level of the Nieuw Amsterdams Peil (New Amsterdam Water-Mark). The area of the Netherlands has, of course, been constantly increased over the centuries as the coastline has been pushed farther seawards by the reclamation of land from the sea and large areas of inland waters have been drained.

Topography

The Netherlands are excellently situated from the point of view of communications and transport. The estuaries of the Rhine (Rijn), the Maas (Meuse) and the Schelde (Scheldt), reaching deep inland and navigable by ocean-going vessels, open up communications with inland economic centres, and a network of natural and man-made waterways provides connections with the inland regions of Europe.

Although the sea and the navigable rivers provide a basis for the country's economic development they are also a constant hazard, for behind the continuous chain of dunes which extends along the whole coast, from Friesland in the north to Zeeland in the south, lies a broad belt of low-lying land, much of it below sea level – the *marken* (marches) or *polderland*. Since the first settlement of the country around 1000 B.C. human life has been constantly under threat from the great rivers flowing down from the interior and the often stormy sea with its strong tidal movement. The people of the Netherlands have had to fight an unremitting battle with the waves. Periods during which land was laboriously won back from the sea have been repeatedly interrupted by sudden and catastrophically destructive floods. Even modern technology is sometimes helpless to prevent disasters of this kind, as the devastating intrusions of the sea in 1953 demonstrated. Overall, however, the people of the Netherlands have been victorious in their battle with the sea, though at the cost of great sacrifice – providing an impressive example of human mastery over the forces of nature.

Surface topography

The highest point in this low-lying country is the Vaalser Berg (321m/1053ft) at the south-eastern tip of Limburg. Other areas where the land rises are in Gelderland (Veluwe, up to 107m/351ft), Overijssel (Salland, 77m/253ft, and Twente, 68m/223ft) and Utrecht (Utrechtse Heuvelrug, 69m/226ft).

Most of the area of the Netherlands lies in the Lower Rhine plain. Only in the extreme south-east, in southern Limburg, are there outliers of the Rhenish Uplands. The country is thus divided into two main landscape forms, the lowlands and the uplands, with the boundary between the two, at around 3m/10ft above sea level, running from Bergen op Zoom in the south-west to Winschoten in the north-east by way of Amersfoort, Harderwijk, Zwolle and Groningen. To the west of this line only the dunes, part of Texel, the Gaasterland region in southern Friesland and the former islands of Wieringen and Urk rise to any extent above the plain.

Lowlands

The lowland region (Laag-Nederland) is basically an area of fenland. The annual inundations of the rivers led to the deposition of riverine clays, the intrusions of the North Sea to the sedimentation of marine clays. As a result numerous islands were formed: an inner ring with old dunes (broad beaches with low dunes) and an outer ring with younger dunes. Behind the dunes an area of mud-flats with old marine clays came into being. As the tides ebbed and flowed water passed through the gaps between the dunes, and this led to the deposit of younger marine clays in the opening, blocking them either wholly or partly.

Uplands

The upland region (Hoog-Nederland) consists of Pleistocene sands. To the north of the great rivers, between the Rhine and the Overijsselse Vecht, is

Regions and Waterways in the Netherlands

an area of morainic ridges of river sand and gravel, which at some points are still covered by rocks of the glacial epoch. The lower-lying parts of this region and the river plains are covered with sand. To the north of the Vecht, in Drenthe, is an area of ground moraines, and in the adjoining lower-lying areas the layer of sand has been covered by fenland.

South of Sittard, at heights of over 30m/130ft, is an area of loess. Here, over many centuries, has been formed an undulating region of hill ridges and plains, for the most part under 200m/650ft. Except in the higher parts the loess overlies older strata dating from the Tertiary and Cretaceous periods. In the higher areas, dissected by rivers, is a landscape of riverine clays. This can be seen most clearly along the Lower Rhine (Lek), Waal and Maas, but the IJssel and Oude IJssel valleys in the east and the old river beds in the west also consist largely of riverine clays.

Topography

An idyllic Zeeland landscape

Natural regions

The Netherlands show a clear division into natural regions, ranging from the coastal areas into the interior: the coastal dunes (*duinen),* which in the Frisian island region are separated from the inner coastline by the *wadden* (shallows, mud-flats); the marine and riverine fenlands (polderland); the sandy heathlands (*zande*) with their expanses of sand and areas of high and low moorland (*hoogveen, laagveen);* tracts of loess soil; and the hills of southern Limburg.

Dunes

The conformation of the dunes is subject to rapid change. Between 's-Gravenzande and Haarlem, running at an acute angle to the coastline, is a band of older dunes, the *geestgronden,* consisting of weathered brownish sand. In this area, between Leiden and Haarlem, are the famous fields of tulips. The expanses of younger dunes with their snow-white sand are up to 5.5km/3½ miles across and reach heights of over 50m/165ft (Schoorl). They form a natural protection for the low-lying land behind them, and accordingly are themselves statutorily protected against destruction.

In the area of the dunes are the former fishing villages which have developed into popular seaside resorts (Zandvoort, Noordwijk, Scheveningen). On the inner side of the belt of dunes have developed larger towns including The Hague, a hunting lodge of the Counts of Holland which became a royal residence.
The dunes are also of importance for their ground-water deposits, formed from rainwater which has seeped through the sand. This water supply was formerly of great importance to the inhabitants of the fenland, a region otherwise short of water. The dunes are now fed with water from the rivers, with the sand serving as a filter.

Fenlands

The fenlands consist of silts deposited at the turn of the tide (sea-fen, *zeeklei*) or along the estuary of a river, reaching far inland (river-fen, *rivierklei*). The dense clayey mass is tempered and made fertile by the siliceous and calcareous skeletons of countless small crustaceans which have died in the brackish water. The fenland of the young polders makes particularly productive arable land; the older fens are largely covered by low moorland (*laagveen*) and are used for grazing.

Origin of the fens and dunes

The fens and dunes along the North Sea coast are the country's youngest geological features. Their development began less than 10,000 years ago, after the end of the last ice age, and is still continuing. After the ice age the steady rise in sea level and the simultaneous subsidence of the land caused the sea to advance slowly but inexorably southward from the Dogger Bank, which was originally attached to the mainland, and the opening up of the Strait of Dover increased the strength of the tides. Off the coast, on the flat

Landscape near Kinderdijk

sea bottom, sand barriers were formed, and from the projecting cliffs of
Cap Blanc-Nez, near Calais, extended a spit of land, along which detritus
and sand were driven north-eastward by the current. The dry sand – as can
still be seen on warm summer days at low tide – is blown up from the beach
to form dunes. Within this barrier, in the shallows and in inlets and river
estuaries, fine silt is deposited, forming the soil of the fenlands.

In origin the older and higher land known as the sandy heathlands (Dutch
zande); the Low German term is (*geest*) is a large Ice Age alluvial fan
formed by the Rhine and the Maas, with its tip around the area where these
rivers emerge from the hills at Bonn and Maastricht, which extends in the
shape of a funnel between the Eems (Ems) estuary to the north-east and the
Schelde (Scheldt) estuary to the south-west. Originally reaching far out into
the North Sea to the Dogger Bank, it now extends at no point to the coast
but ends in a low shelf, a former coastline, with the fenland which has
extended in more recent times towards the sea.
The sandy heathlands consist of gravels and sands. During the ice age their
northern and eastern parts were overlaid by the Scandinavian ice sheet, so
that there are now two types, glacial and riverine.

Sandy heathlands

The soil deposited by the rivers was reshaped by the glaciers and when the
movement of the ice ceased was formed into curving chains of hills, the
most westerly of which extends from Krefeld to Xanten, from Elten by way
of Kleve to Nijmegen, and from Rhenen to the old Zuiderzee coast at
Huizen. In the north the former islands of Urk and Wieringen and the island
of Texel still have glacial cores. The rear echelons of these hills, running in a
north–south direction, extend through the Veluwe from Arnhem to Zwolle
at heights of over 100m/330ft, and east from Deventer through Overijssel
province. In the glaciated area the gravel and sand were overlaid by ground
moraines of clay and sand.

Glaciated
heathlands

Sandy heathland country in the Veluwe area

Limburger uplands

In the Hondsrug in eastern Drenthe the morainic table falls steeply down to the old low-lying moorland in the Eems valley and the fenlands. Melt-water from the ice deposited sand, and the wind blew this into irregularly shaped fields of dunes, which – like the rest of the country – were then overgrown by woodland and fenland.

In the wide channels in which ground-water accumulated great expanses of high moorland were formed, creating landscapes in the Veluwe, Drenthe and Overijssel which resemble certain areas in northern Germany (the Emsland region, Lüneburg Heath).

In the southern Netherlands the riverine heathlands of the Rhine and Maas country in Limburg and Noord-Brabant, untouched by the ice, are even flatter and more featureless than the glaciated heathlands but are otherwise of the same general character. Here heath-covered tracts of sandy soil and inland dunes alternate with swathes of low-lying moorland.

Riverine heathlands

The Struggle with the Sea

The two great dangers to the low-lying fenland are the sea and the great rivers flowing down from the inland regions. At an average level the Rhine has a flow of some 2400 cu.m/528,000 gallons per second, rising to 12,000 cu.m/2,600,000 gallons at high water; the much smaller Maas has an average flow of only 150 cu.m/33,000 gallons per second, rising to twenty times that amount at high water. The protective chain of dunes has not remained unbroken, for the waters of the Rhine, Maas and Schelde, combined with the tides, have torn great gaps in it, exposing the fenlands to the twin dangers of flooding by the rivers and by the sea. Hence the succession of funnel-shaped estuaries, from the Schelde to the Rhine, which have

The sea: an ever-present hazard

15

broken up the provinces of Zeeland and Zuid-Holland into numbers of islands.
From Hoek van Holland (Hook of Holland) to Den Helder the fringe of dunes was originally continuous, but gaps which opened up later had to be closed by dykes.

The river estuaries themselves show a remarkable tendency to change: the openings to the south-west become deeper and thus increase in importance, while those to the north-east gradually silt up. The reason for this is that with the north-eastward movements of the tide from the Channel the ebb currents which scour out the river beds affect the southern arm of a river first. Thus in the course of time the Westereems and Westerschelde have become more important than the Oostereems and Oosterschelde.
The Rhine and Maas estuaries have steadily moved southward in stages. Thus the Roman mouth of the Rhine at Leiden, the Oude Rijn (Old Rhine), has long been silted up. The arms of the river at Rotterdam, through which the bulk of the Rhine's water now reaches the sea as the Waal and the Lek, have retained their older name of Maas (Nieuwe Maas), since the main arm of the river once flowed into the sea here, while it now reaches the sea farther south through the Haringvliet and the Krammer, just north of the Schelde.

Dykes

Human settlement was not possible in a land constantly threatened by flooding. Only when men learned to build up artificial mounds did the first permanent settlements appear in the fenlands, which had much more fertile soil, either for pastoral or for arable farming, than the sandy heathlands. On these artificial mounds (*terpen; singular terp),* were built farm steadings, then villages and finally towns such as Leeuwarden, capital of Friesland.

Security for human settlement, however, became possible only in the early medieval period, when the technique of building dykes was developed. The situation was particularly difficult in the Netherlands, where it was necessary not only to fight off the sea and drain the fenland: danger came also from the Rhine and the Maas, the numerous arms of which ranged over the country, constantly changing their course.

The endangered territory begins below Emmerich, near the Dutch–German frontier, where the rivers divide. From here the Gelderse IJssel, carrying around a ninth of the Rhine's water, flows north through a wide glaciated valley into the IJsselmeer. Beyond this point the Rhine divides into the Nederrijn (Lower Rhine) and the Waal, the principal arm of the Rhine, carrying two-thirds of its water. Lower down there are many different arms, most of which still exist and have names of their own. Among them are the few estuaries which are still open, under various names (Lek, Merwede, Noord, etc.), and many others, including the Kromme Rijn and Oude Rijn; originally also the Eem in the glaciated Gelderse Vallei (Gelderland plain) and numerous other rivers, like the Linge, the Vecht and the Amstel. In addition there are a number of independent rivers such as the Linge and the Hollandse IJssel.
All these arms are "dyke rivers": that is, they deposit sediments carried down from the inland regions and thus raise both the bed and the bank of the river, so as to form a kind of dyke. At times of spate they flood the lower-lying land on both sides of the river. This danger could be countered only by the construction of dykes, and the communal effort involved in the building of dykes and the creation of polders was carried out over many centuries.

Polders

The construction of dykes along the coasts and the banks of rivers, however, dealt only with part of the problem. Since the country lay at such a low level the usual principle of drainage – to allow excess ground-water and rainwater to escape through sluices at low tide – could be applied only to a

limited extent. The country could therefore support additional population
only when windmills became available to raise water continually from the
low-lying polders (fenland enclosed by dykes) – a technology which was
evolved only in the later medieval period. Thereafter water levels throughout the country were very closely controlled. Only in the main branches of
the Rhine, the Lek, the Waal and the Maas and in the estuaries of Zeeland
and Zuid-Holland were the rivers originally allowed to flow freely. All the
other watercourses were canals, and the basic technical device was the
sluice. Only a few streams, such as the Amstel in Amsterdam, show by their
meandering course that they were once free-flowing rivers. These watercourses, flowing at different levels, form a complicated network, a carefully
planned system of waterways. They transport the milk of the cows grazing
in the polders to the farms and dairies and from there to all parts of the
country; similarly fruit, vegetables and other produce are transported from
the fields and orchards to the markets and auctions in the towns. The canals
which traverse the country, once busy with sailing ships with brown or
light-coloured sails, are an abiding memory for visitors to the Netherlands.
The windmills which feature in so many paintings by Dutch old masters
have for the most part disappeared and have been replaced by modern
electrically driven pumps. Only here and there have they been preserved as
romantic relics of the past.

Nowadays the islands off the south coast of the Netherlands with their
ancient and picturesque little towns, formerly rather off the beaten track,
have been brought within easy reach by the construction of new bridges
and causeways. The consequence has been a rapid increase in tourist
traffic. Many new hotels, holiday apartments, bungalow villages, camping
sites and boating marinas have been built in recent years, and the islands
are linked with the mainland by motorways and expressways.

There is still a latent threat to the dunes lining the coast – exposed, particularly in winter, to the destructive effect of the surf which attacks them from
the south and south-west and is gradually driving them back. One of the
most alarming examples is the church at Scheveningen, once a fishing
village and now a fashionable seaside resort. Originally it lay well inland,
but within a mere century and a half, as the coastline receded, the sea
caught up with it. The concrete sea-walls built not so many years ago in the
coastal resorts and already beginning to project into the sea beyond other
stretches of coast which have not been similarly protected.

Land Reclamation

In earlier times great stretches of water covering land which might be as
much as 5m/16ft below sea level had to be left as they were. Then with the
aid of windmills it became possible in the 17th and 18th centuries to drain
four large lakes in Noord-Holland (Schermer, Beemster, Purmer and
Wormer); but it was only when steam power became available that the
Haarlemmermeer (area 183 sq.km/71 sq. miles) and the wide expanses of
the IJ at Amsterdam could be drained.

The method of drainage (*droogmakerij*) was simple. A dyke was built round
the area to be drained, with a ring canal (sometimes equipped with mov-
able shutter weirs) to carry off the water pumped out. The bottom of these
lagoons is very fertile, since the *zeeklei* (marine clay) surfaces here, and the
drained areas therefore provide excellent arable land, equalled only by the
most recent polders on the fringes of the Frisian *wadden*. The boggier parts
of the fenland can be used only as pasture.

The biggest land reclamation venture, made possible only by 20th century
technology, was the draining of the Zuiderzee, which as a result of large-
scale intrusions of the sea in medieval times had grown into a huge
saltwater bay. In 1924 the narrow channel between Noord-Holland and the

Poldering of
the Zuiderzee

island of Wieringen was closed, and in 1932 the 30km/19 mile long dam from Wieringen to Friesland was completed. Technically it was a tremendous undertaking, for the movement of the tides meant that several cubic kilometres of water surged into and out of the Zuiderzee twice every day, and as the construction of the dam advanced simultaneously from the north-eastern and south-western ends the force of the tides through the narrowing gap grew steadily stronger.

With the completion of the barrier dam, the Afsluitdijk, the Zuiderzee ceased to exist and gave place to the IJsselmeer, which is now a freshwater lagoon. Once the sea had been shut out it was a relatively simple matter to create polders by draining areas within the lagoon, though it involved a very considerable deployment of resources. First the area between Noord-Holland and the island of Wieringen (20,000 hectares/50,000 acres) was poldered. Then in 1942 the first actual Zuiderzee polder, the Noordoost-polder (North-East Polder; 47,600 hectares/119,000 acres) adjoining the provinces of Friesland and Overijssel, was completed. The western part of the fishermen's island of Urk was incorporated in the dyke. Since then the two Flevoland polders, Oostflevoland (54,000 hectares/135,000 acres) and

Land reclamation in Flevoland.

Zuidflevoland (43,000 hectares/107,500 acres), have been drained. A channel has been left between the Flevoland polder and the mainland in order to give old seaport towns like Elburg and Harderwijk access to the sea and to avoid lowering the water table of the higher land on the adjoining mainland.

The last polder planned is Markerwaard (40,000 hectares/100,000 acres), adjoining Noord-Holland. It was originally due to be completed by 1980, but various environmental protection groups objected to the project and the government withdrew it for further consideration.

The remaining part of the IJsselmeer, to the north, will still have an area of 110,000 hectares/275,000 acres.

The draining of the Zuiderzee was the largest coastal reclamation project anywhere in the world; but in 1957 another huge enterprise was approved – the Delta Plan for damming the estuaries of the Rhine, the Maas and the Schelde and enclosing the island world of Zuid-Holland and Zeeland.

The Delta Works (Deltawerken)

From time immemorial the people of the Netherlands have had to fight against the flooding of their country. During the Middle Ages there were extensive floods every few years, engulfing large areas of land and many towns and villages. With advances in dyke-building techniques such catastrophes became less frequent, but the threat could never be entirely discounted. Then in the night of January 31st–February 1st 1953 a hurricane blew up over the Dutch North Sea coast and, combined with the spring tide, whipped the waves up to unprecedented heights. The dykes were breached in hundreds of places; 250,000 hectares/625,000 acres of land were flooded, 1835 people and more than 200,000 animals were drowned, and almost 75,000 buildings were destroyed or damaged. Rebuilding began at once, and all the breaches in the dykes were closed within a year.

Flooding

The Struggle with the Sea

Delta Plan

But it was not enough merely to repair the dykes: steps had to be taken to ensure that such a disaster could not happen again. It was decided to shorten the much indented coastline of the delta area in the south-west of the country by 700km/435 miles so as to reduce the surface exposed to attack by the sea and decrease the danger of flooding. The estuaries of the Rhine, the Maas and the Schelde, reaching far inland, were closed off by barrier dykes, leaving only access for shipping to Rotterdam (the Nieuwe Waterweg) and to the Belgian towns of Ghent and Antwerp (the Westerschelde).

The Delta Plan also provided for increasing the height of the dykes along the North Sea coast from Belgium to Germany. Construction work lasted over thirty years and cost some 10 billion guilders. Since the completion of the project a flood on the scale of the 1953 disaster is, statistically, to be expected only every 4000 years.

Storm-surge barrier

The first part of the scheme to be undertaken was the construction of storm-surge barriers – the largest and most costly hydraulic engineering project in the world. The first such barrier was built in 1958 on the Hollandse IJssel at Krimpen, with a bridge 560m/610yds long. The gates, weighing 670 tons, are closed only in the event of a storm or a high water level, in order to protect the lowest-lying area in the Netherlands (6m/20ft below sea level) and its population of over 2 million.

Zaandkreekdam
Veerse Gat Dam

The 830m/910yd long Zaandkreekdam between North and South Beveland, with a lock providing access to the Oosterschelde, was completed in 1960. The same year saw the damming of the Veerse Gat, north of Veere, by a 2.8km/1¾ mile long dyke between North Beveland and Walcheren.

Hydraulic technology

The Delta Plan showed the difficulty of solving problems of hydraulic engineering by existing methods. The established types of structure were no longer adequate, and it was necessary to develop and test new techniques. The first dam had used closed caissons round the construction sites, but these are unsuitable for structures of considerable length. Some 70 million cu.m/15 billion gallons of water passed through the Veerse Gat with the ebb and flow of the tides, so that here it was necessary to use open caissons measuring 45×2×20m (150×6½×65ft), which were first set in place and consolidated and were closed only at low tide. Open caissons can be more accurately sited and can cope with the strong tidal movement.

Cableway

For longer dams there is a still further refined solution: the use of a cableway. This transports concrete blocks for the construction of a small dam, which is later enlarged. Where brushwood had formerly been used in the building of such a dam, asphalt, concrete and man-made materials were now employed. In the construction of locks and piers small artificial islands are established, from which the foundations are driven into the sea bottom. After completion of the work the sea is admitted again.

Grevelingendam

The next stage in the Delta Plan was the construction in 1965 of the 6km/3¾ mile long Grevelingendam between Duiveland and Overflakkee, in the building of which 170,000 tons of concrete were used. The final gap, some 1200m/1300yds wide, was closed with the help of the cableway.

Zeelandbrug

The Zeelandbrug (Zealand Bridge), which had not originally formed part of the Delta Plan, was completed in the same year. 50m/165ft high, with 50 arches, the bridge, which links North Beveland with Duiveland, is one of the longest in Europe (5022m/5492yds). Since the government did not consider that this bridge was necessary the high construction costs were borne by the provincial authorities.

Volkerak

The Volkerak, between Overflakkee and Noord-Brabant, was dammed in 1969. This involved the construction of an artificial island, known as Hellegatsplein, in the Volkerak. Here the A 29 motorway runs from Noord-

The Zealand Bridge, one of the longest in Europe

Brabant into Noord-Holland, with a branch road crossing to Zeeland on a 1200m/1300yd long bridge. The lock complex here consists of three large locks (320×24m/1050×80ft) and a smaller one (145×16m/475×52ft).

The Haringvlietdam between Goeree and Voorne, completed in 1970, reduces the inflow of seawater and will gradually eliminate salt water from the river as far up as the Biesbosch. The dam, 1km/¾ mile long, with a lock for the passage of ships, is borne on 21,800 piles.

Haringvlietdam

The complete damming of the Brouwershavense Gat took no less than ten years, and involved the building up of sand islands and the use of open caissons. The opening in the dyke was closed with the help of a cableway. Salt water continued to be admitted through a sluice.

Brouwershavense Gat

The various building projects were undertaken in order of increasing difficulty. On this basis the complete damming of the Oosterschelde (Easter Scheldt) was left to the last.

Oosterschelde Dam

In 1967 three artificial islands were established; two of them were linked by a dam, and a bridge provided communication with the mainland. Almost at once there were violent protests. Environmental protection groups, fishermen and mussel-farmers feared that the conversion of these tidal waters into a freshwater lagoon would endanger the habitat of numerous marine plants and animals. Only by retaining open access to the North Sea, they claimed, could the rich mussel and oyster beds, the seventy species of fish and twenty-five species of birds be preserved. Faced with this strong public opposition, the government decided in 1974 to built not a solid dam but a storm-surge barrier which would be closed during flood tides but would remain open in normal circumstances. Since experience of such a major project was lacking, construction work was postponed while numerous experiments with models were carried out.

The Struggle with the Sea

Work on the project was resumed with the building up of a dyke round the Oosterschelde. This was followed by the construction of the storm-surge barrier, consisting of strong steel plates between concrete piers. Altogether 65 piers, each 40m/130ft long, were used on the old artificial islands. After the sea bed had been levelled a foundation of gravel and sand was built up, and the piers, weighing 18,000 tons, were embedded with extreme precision in their exact place in this foundation. The barriers, computer-controlled, are closed only when danger threatens.

The Oosterschelde Dam was formally opened in presence of Queen Beatrix in 1986. To the Dutch it ranks as one of the modern wonders of the world.

Markieezaatsdam
Oesterdam
Philipsdam

Following the construction of the Oosterschelde barrier other dykes were built in order to ensure that the tidal movement should be preserved but should not extend as far as the Schelde–Rhine Canal, and that the salt water should be kept separate from the fresh water. This was achieved by the construction of the Markieezaatsdam at Bergen op Zoom, the Oesterdam (1990) to the west of this and the Philipsdam between the Grevelingendam and St Philipsland (1988), with two locks measuring 280×24m/920×80ft and one measuring 75×9m/245×30ft.

After a construction period of thirty-five years the Dutch can look back on an outstanding technological achievement. The south-western coast of the Netherlands is now many times more secure against flooding, and the Delta Works are expected to challenge the might of the sea for the next 200 years.

Delta Expo

On the artificial island of Neeltje Jans, reached on the new expressway along the Oosterschelde storm-surge barrier, is Delta Expo, a permanent exhibition illustrating the 2000-year history of Dutch hydraulic engineering, the culmination of which is the Delta scheme. It includes an information centre, a shop, a café and a film theatre.

The Oosterschelde storm-surge barrier, closed only in the event of danger

With the help of a variety of displays, videos, models and film shows visitors can follow the development of techniques from the simpler methods of the past – after the catastrophe of 1953 sandbags were still used to close the breaches in the dykes – to the elaborate equipment and technology now available.
The exhibition is open throughout the year. A visit can be combined with a boat trip along the barrier.

Cultural Landscapes

Sandy Heathlands

The sandy heathlands of the Netherlands have been occupied by man since a very early period. Although they offer only poor arable soil and dry pastureland they lie relatively high and provide safe sites for building. The megalithic tombs of prehistoric times (the *hunebedden*, "giants' beds", of Drenthe) give evidence of early occupation. Here too are old villages with their poor arable fields and their expanses of common land – heathland and bog grazed by flocks of sheep. Old roads run through the sandy heathland region to the interior of the country, with little towns (e.g. in Overijssel and Noord-Brabant) established as staging-points along the way. The old traditional crafts of these regions have survived, such as the wool-working which gave rise to the local textile industry. The modern agricultural and industrial development of the sandy heathland regions, however, is to be attributed to the influence of the country's heartland, the fen regions.

Some 5000 years ago the inhabitants of the north-eastern Netherlands were building megalithic chamber tombs of the TRB (Trichterbecher, "funnel beaker") culture. These *hunebedden* (see above) are constructed of large vertical stone slabs supporting flat roof-slabs and forming an elongated chamber. The entrance, closed by a stone door-slab, leads either directly into the tomb chamber or into an antechamber preceding it. The tomb chamber, paved with stone slabs, lies below ground level and is entered by steps. The tomb is surrounded by a circle of smaller stones, originally marking the outer limit of a sand mound over the tomb which over the millennia has been dispersed by the wind. *Hunebedden*

Particularly impressive are the huge roof-slabs, weighing up to 25 tons, which must have been transported and erected with the most primitive techniques – timber rollers, levers and inclined planes.

Altogether there are some 50 *hunebedden* in the Netherlands, most of them in Drenthe. The largest is between Borger and Bronneger; perhaps the best known is the Papeloze Kerk (restored), between Sleen and Schoonoord.

Veen means peat-bog or moorland. Peat was used from an early period as fuel, and in later times was worked on an industrial basis. *Veen* settlements began to be established in the Netherlands, particularly in the moorland regions of Groningen and Drenthe, in the early 17th century. *Veen* settlements

The bogs were drained by means of drainage channels (*wieken*), which flowed into a larger navigable channel. In course of time a network of subsidiary or branch canals (*inwieken*) was developed, followed in a later stage of settlement by smaller *achterwieken*.

The *veen* settlements were established along these channels, which in early times were the only means of communication and transport and frequently extended for miles. Attached to the individual farmsteads were

A hunebed *(megalithic tomb), Borger*

A veen *settlement, on drained moorland*

long strips of land (*hoefen*) between 50m/55yds and 130m/140yds wide, which extended at right angles to the main channels into the drained moorland.

A special technique was used for bringing the land into cultivation. First the upper layer of peat, down to about 50cm/20in, was cut; then the rest of the peat was removed, transported by way of the drainage channels to the towns and sold there, mainly as fuel; and finally the mineral-rich subsoil was mixed with the peat from the upper layer.

The rest of the peat, sometimes covering large areas, was set on fire, with unfortunate effects on neighbouring areas (eye troubles, breathing difficulties) – effects which were sometimes felt as far afield as Scandinavia and France.

In spite of all attempts to improve the soil the *veen* farmers had a hard and thankless task, for the oats, rye, potatoes, sugar-beet, wheat and barley which they grew were more suited to clay soils than to the acid peat soil. To supplement agriculture a certain amount of processing industry developed in the *veen* regions.

The sandy heathland country shows clear evidence of the economic power and cultural patterns of the fenlands. The inhabitants of the heathlands originally depended for their subsistence on modest arable farming and sheep-farming. The only places of some consequence were towns built at bridges and river crossings, such as the old sister towns of Arnhem and Nijmegen (originally Roman foundations) on the Lower Rhine and the Waal and the towns of Venlo, Roermond and Maastricht in the uplands. A characteristic economic activity in some parts of the heathland country was cloth-making, for example around Enschede and Almelo in Twente and around Tilburg and Eindhoven in Brabant.

Influence of
the fenlands

On the whole, however, the outer heathland provinces remained more or less passive until the 19th century. The influence of the fenlands made itself felt first in the most inaccessible heathland areas, that is in the high moorlands, which were increasingly brought into cultivation from the early 17th century onwards and have now, with the exception of some remnants in the Peel area of Brabant, been fully developed. The method of cultivation practised by the *veen* settlements has already been described (examples: *veen* villages in Groningen, Stadskanaal). The use of this technique was encouraged by the demand for fuel from the numerous fenland towns.

During the 20th century the development of the sandy heathland regions has been promoted by agricultural resettlement associations, with the massive use of artificial fertilisers. Processing industries of all kinds and the electrical industry have found it advantageous to settle in the heathland towns with their lower site costs, less expensive types of building and availability of labour. Thus Tilburg, Eindhoven and Helmond have grown into towns of considerable size and the towns in Twente (Overijssel) have become major centres of the textile industry. The industrial development of the Eems region was given a boost by the discovery of oil. The fertile agricultural region around Heerlen, at the southern tip of Limburg, also had large coalfields, connected with the coalfields around Aachen in Germany and in the Kempen area in Belgium. After the closure of the last pit in 1975, however, industry in this area underwent a complete restructuring.

The way of life and the cultural landscape of the heathland towns and villages have increasingly been influenced by the fenland regions. Canals have been driven into the higher heathland regions, thus bringing the whole country into the central canal network. Originally there was a sharp contrast between the fenlands with their prosperous farmsteads of Frisian type and the poor heathland villages with their Saxon-type houses. Nowadays a general Dutch style, influenced by the country's heartland in the fen

Cultural unity

regions, can be recognised, particularly in the structure and architecture of the towns. From Walcheren to Groningen, from Den Helder to Maastricht, the modern Netherlands show a clear cultural unity.

Fenlands

Thanks to its geographical situation and the advantages which this brings from the point of view of communications, and to its possession of soil of greater fertility than in other parts of the country, the Dutch fenland belt has become the economic and political heartland of the country. As a result its cities have developed into major commercial centres. In its early days this amphibious country was totally unequipped for the development of any advanced culture. It had the advantage, on the other hand, of being impregnable at least to mainland enemies. Thus the fight for independence by the "Sea Beggars" (Watergeuzen) was favoured by natural conditions. The Spaniards were able to take Haarlem, lying on the edge of the dunes, but could never reach Amsterdam; and similarly Louis XIV of France was unable to cross the estuaries of the Rhine and the Maas.

Fenland towns

From the point of view of communications two important fenland towns were Leiden, the Roman Lugdunum, founded on the estuary of the Rhine, and Utrecht, established at a river crossing (trajectum), in higher country, which inherited from antiquity its status as an episcopal city. In later times two groups of fenland towns can be distinguished – those looking towards the Rhine and Maas estuaries and the towns on the Zuiderzee. At the upper end of the tidal areas of the rivers there grew up the early medieval trading towns of Wijk bij Duurstede on the Lek, Tiel on the Waal and later Dordrecht, an entrepot between the Rhine and the Thames, situated at the head of the delta. Round the Zuiderzee, the huge bay reaching far inland which in earlier times was of great importance as the estuary of the Rhine, there developed the towns of Deventer and Kampen on the IJssel, Hoorn and Enkhuizen in Noord-Holland and finally the largest of all the Zuiderzee towns, Amsterdam, lying on the estuary of the IJ. Its counterpart on the Rhine estuary, Rotterdam, developed at a much later stage. Common to both these cities is the purely fenland character of their siting within the protection of a dam, as their names indicate, and their situation at the mouth of small river arms, the Amstel and the Rotte. Almost all their streets are canals (grachten), that is, waterways embanked by dykes. An exception is Kalverstraat in Amsterdam, a narrow street which was originally a cattle track running alongside plots of land between two grachten.

Amsterdam

Building on marshy ground is difficult. It is necessary to drive an elaborate and expensive network of piles deep into the ground to reach a firm subsoil of ice-age date. Characteristic features of the fenland towns are the grachten, the narrow building plots occupied by gable-fronted houses and the close-packed layout, even towards the fringes of the town. Nowhere can this be seen more clearly than in Amsterdam, the national capital. In the medieval period, when the various Zuiderzee towns were trading with North Sea and Baltic ports, Amsterdam was a small and unimportant place. It began to develop only in the age of discovery, when it became the headquarters of the Dutch East India Company and the greatest commercial city in the Netherlands, and indeed in the whole of continental Europe. The construction of the new rings of grachten round the medieval core of the town in the 17th century bears witness to this expansion. For centuries the access to the port of Amsterdam was through the Zuiderzee: it was only with the advent of steam navigation that the North Holland Canal to Den Helder was constructed and the North Sea Canal (several times enlarged) was cut through the dunes to IJmuiden. On the landward side the Merwede Canal was enlarged and developed into the great Amsterdam–Rhine ship canal to Tiel on the Waal.

Rotterdam

The real commercial centre of the Rhine estuary, however, is Rotterdam, which took over from Dordrecht and is now the country's leading port, with the largest turnover in the world, accessible from the interior by the Lower Rhine, the Lek, the Waal and the Merwede. But even Rotterdam had its problems in the 19th century when the passage of shipping was threatened by the silting up of the arms of the Brielse Maas and it became necessary to construct a channel reaching the sea at Hoek van Holland (Hook of Holland), the Nieuwe Waterweg.

Trade in the fenland towns was followed by the processing of imported colonial products. Characteristic of this development are the Zaanstreek (Zaanstad) in the vicinity of Amsterdam and the Langstraat at Waalwijk in the area of the Rhine estuary.

Types of Farmstead

Travelling through the Netherlands, visitors will be struck by differences in the types of farm, particularly the older farms, in different parts of the country. Some ten different types, which can be classified in four groups, can be distinguished.

The best known kind of farmstead is the Frisian type, which is found not only in the province of Friesland itself but also in the former Frisian regions of Groningen and the northern part of Noord-Holland.
The basic form is the *stolpboerderij* ("bell farm"), a square thatched building which brings together under one roof the farmhouse, the barn and the animals' quarters. In a later period the living quarters were faced with brick and – as a sign of prosperity – given a proper façade, and the lower part of the roof was tiled (the higher the tiled section, the wealthier the farmer).

Frisian type

This basic type was much imitated, frequently in altered form. Thus a similar type, the *stelpboerderij*, which is rectangular rather than square, can still be seen in southern Friesland.

Farmhouse in the Open-Air Museum, Arnhem

Later it became usual to separate the farmhouse from the steading. There now developed the *kop-romp-boerderij* ("head and rump farm"), with most of the living accommodation in the tiled "head" and the farm buildings and some living accommodation in the thatched "rump". In the *kop-hals-romp-boerderij* ("head, neck and rump farm") the farm buildings and living quarters are completely separate, with a wing between them.

Also reminiscent of the *stolpboerderij* is the Oldambt type of farm. The living quarters and farm buildings are under one roof, but the living quarters, with a tiled roof, are clearly distinguished from the farm buildings.

Hallehuizen

In the eastern Netherlands the *hallehuis* (hall-house) type of farm is commonly found. Like a hall-church, the *hallehuis* is divided by two rows of posts into a wide middle section and two narrower "aisles". The living quarters and farm buildings were not separated from one another, and straw for the livestock was stored on a crossbeam under the roof. This type of farm originated in Twente but was also common in the north (Drenthe) and west (Overijssel, Gelderland, Utrecht, Zuid-Holland) of the country.

The Twente and Drenthe farmhouses are very similar. Sometimes they have the entrance on one side of the building.

T-shaped farmhouse

In the T-shaped farmhouse the living quarters are in the form of a T, with the farm steading to the rear; the wider the T-shaped part, the more prosperous the farmer. The living quarters could be extended at either end by the addition of "show" rooms or parlours which were used only on Sundays or other special occasions.

Dwarshuis

In Limburg and Brabant there was the *dwarshuis* ("cross house" or "transverse house"), in which the farm buildings were set at right angles to the ends of the living quarters. In Limburg there was a variation of this type in which the fourth side of the square thus formed was closed by a wall. The farmhouse could then be entered only by the front door – reflecting an increased need for security. In Brabant the main part of the building extends along the road, with the barns to the rear.

Zeeuwse schuurgroep

In the *Zeeuwse schuurgroep* ("Zealand barn group") all the different parts of the farm – the farmhouse and the various farm buildings – are separate.

Many examples of these different types of farm can be seen in the Netherlands Open-Air Museum in Arnhem (see entry).

Windmills

The windmills of the Netherlands are surely the best known features of the landscape. Once numbering some 10,000, they were used as flour mills, oil mills and sawmills, but predominantly for the drainage of the polders lying below sea level.

Drainage of the polders

When the polders were enclosed by dykes from the 11th century onwards, it became necessary to lower the water-table in order to make the land habitable and suitable for cultivation. At first the water was raised and fed into drainage channels by scoop wheels worked by human or horse power. By the 17th century, however, there were already considerable numbers of pumping stations driven by wind power in the country to the north of Amsterdam. Another method, still to be seen in use today, is the *tjasker* mill, a simple transportable windmill used solely for raising water, in which the sails drive an Archimedean screw.

Post mill

A number of different types of windmill are distinguished according to their structure. The oldest is the post mill (*standaardmolen*), which is found from

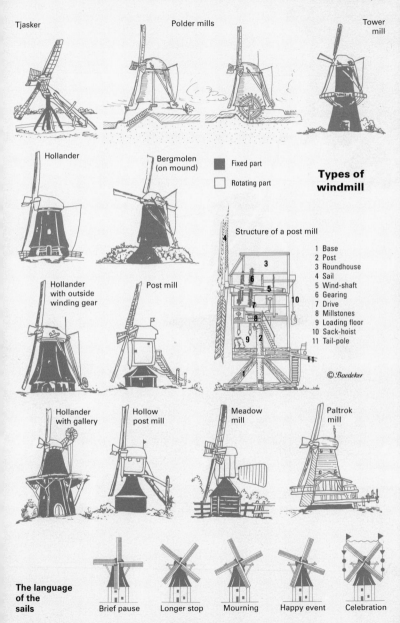

Tjasker

Polder mills

Tower mill

Hollander

Bergmolen (on mound)

■ Fixed part

☐ Rotating part

Types of windmill

Hollander with outside winding gear

Post mill

Structure of a post mill

1 Base
2 Post
3 Roundhouse
4 Sail
5 Wind-shaft
6 Gearing
7 Drive
8 Millstones
9 Loading floor
10 Sack-hoist
11 Tail-pole

© Baedeker

Hollander with gallery

Hollow post mill

Meadow mill

Paltrok mill

The language of the sails

Brief pause

Longer stop

Mourning

Happy event

Celebration

the 13th century onwards. This is a square structure, with the sails on the front and the *staart* on the rear, a tail-pole with the help of which the whole body of the mill is turned on a vertical axis to catch the wind. Windmills of this type, used mainly for milling grain but also for the hulling of rice and pepper, as an oil-press or a sawmill, are found in the central Netherlands. The windmills of Zuid-Holland are based on the same principle but are octagonal rather than square.

A development of the post mill is the hollow post mill (*wipmolen* or *kokermolen*), in which only the upper part of the mill-house turns in the wind. In the smock mill or tower mill (*bovenkruier*), also known in eastern Friesland as the Hollander after its area of origin, only the cap, bearing the sails, revolves.

Hollow post mill, smock mill

In the inland regions windmills are often sited on a mound or, in a town, on the old town walls in order to make the most of the wind. When the mill is not working messages can be conveyed by the position of the sails, as in the telegraph stations which operated around 1800. The Dutch are said to have used this method of signalling during the Second World War in order to convey information to the pilots of Allied aircraft.

There are now only some 1000 windmills left in the Netherlands, some of them still working or capable of working. Mostly dating from the 18th and 19th centuries, they have been carefully restored and conserved. On National Windmill Day (the second Saturday in May) the mills are set in motion.

The best known group of windmills is at Kinderdijk, to the east of Rotterdam. There are nineteen mills, which work every Saturday during the summer. There are a number of windmills of different types in the Netherlands Open-Air Museum at Arnhem and others at Zaandam (north of Amsterdam), and there are windmills on the old town walls of Schiedam (west of Rotterdam).

Climate

The climate of the Netherlands is under strong maritime influence, for no part of the country is more than 150km/95 miles from the sea. As a result there are only relatively slight annual and daily temperature variations, and rain falls throughout the year.

Although the climatic pattern is generally very uniform there are a number of regions which show characteristic patterns of their own: the coastal strip, to north and south; the lowlands of the interior, to north and south; and southern Limburg.

Climatic regions

The climatic characteristics of different parts of the Netherlands are shown in the climatic diagrams on page 32, which give the monthly average temperatures and rainfall at five typical weather stations. The blue columns show the rainfall in millimetres, in accordance with the scale in the right-hand margin, while the orange band shows the temperature in °C, the upper edge giving the average maximum day temperature and the lower edge the average minimum night temperature, in accordance with the red scale in the margin.

Climatic diagrams

On the basis of these diagrams it is possible to estimate climatic conditions between the various weather stations by applying the following rules:
(a) Oceanic influence becomes steadily weaker from the coast inland. Temperature variations between day and night and between summer and

◀ *De Valk windmill (Windmill Museum), Leiden*

Five typical weather stations in the Netherlands

Explanations
in text

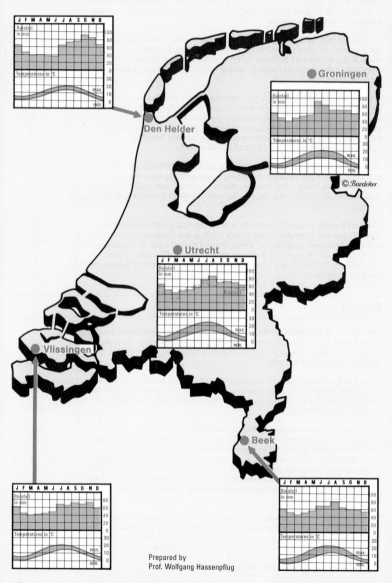

Prepared by
Prof. Wolfgang Hassenpflug

winter increase, and the duration of sunshine, degree of cloud cover, rainfall and other climatic features vary accordingly: see below.
(b) Going from north to south, there are slight tendencies towards an increase in duration of sunshine and in temperature and towards a decrease in rainfall.

Coastal Strip

The coastal strip, together with its girdle of dunes and the West Frisian islands, enjoys a climate which is distinctly better than that of its hinterland. Particularly in the early summer there is more sunshine and less cloud cover than only a few miles inland. This is because when air masses coming from the North Sea charged with moisture are blown over the land by the prevailing west winds they are slowed down over the relatively rugged land surface and rise higher, leading to condensation and the formation of clouds. In the hinterland, into which the clouds are now driven by the wind, the sky becomes heavily overcast and rain may fall, while on the beaches it is still sunny or only slightly overcast.

Den Helder and Vlissingen weather stations

In the immediate coastal region there are over 1600 hours of sunshine in the year (1665 hours at Den Helder, with a maximum of 283 hours in June). The strong sunlight, however – all the stronger because of the purity of the air – does not seem unpleasantly warm, since the fresh breezes which are always blowing, mainly from the west, temper the heat and stimulate the skin and the whole human organism. The healing influence of the maritime climate is still further enhanced – most strongly on the very edge of the sea – by the sea salt which is atomised, as in an aerosol, by the surf.

The wind blows all the time along the coast (at Den Helder with an average speed over the year of 6.8m/22ft 4in per second). The highest wind speeds occur in winter: these are the hurricanes which when combined with storm tides constitute such a threat to the very existence of the Netherlands. In January the velocity of the wind at Den Helder averages 7.7m/25ft 4in per second.

Between June and July the monthly rainfall and the number of days with rain increase considerably. The rain becomes more abundant, often falling in the form of violent showers or cloudbursts. From September to November there is more rain on the coast than farther inland: thus in October the coast has 80mm/3in of rain, while inland, on the frontier with Germany, the figure is barely 60mm/2½in.

Water temperatures near the coast in February, thanks to the Gulf Stream, are around 3–4°C/37–39°F in the north and 5–6°C/41–43°F in the south. In August temperatures are around 16°C/61°F in the north and around 17°C/63°F in the south; near the beach and in the Waddenzee they are still higher.

As a result of the moderating influence of the sea summer temperatures are not unduly high and low temperatures are rare in winter. A frost-free period of some 240 days begins in mid April and continues until the beginning of December, and there are on average 40 days of frost during the winter. In the oceanic climate maximum and minimum temperatures are reached up to two months after the sun has reached its highest and lowest points, in August and in February.

Clouds – formed by the cooling of air heavily charged with water vapour – occur with particular frequency in late autumn and winter and in the area of the Rhine. Over the country as a whole there are between 30 and 50 days with clouds (with visibility under 1000m/1100yds).

There are slight climatic changes along the coast from north to south. Wind strengths, cloud cover and rainfall decrease from north to south, while the annual duration of sunshine and winter temperatures increase – the result of increasing distance from the paths of the depressions to the north of the Netherlands.

Lowlands of the Interior

Utrecht and
Groningen
weather stations

There are marked climatic differences between the coastal strip and the lowlands of the interior but only slight variations within the lowlands themselves. The climatic diagrams are thus valid also for the surrounding area.

Daily and annual variations in temperature are higher than on the coast, as can be seen by comparing the temperature bands for Utrecht and Groningen, with their greater thickness and more marked curve, with those for Den Helder and Vlissingen. It is also distinctly warmer during the day than on the coast.

The length of the annual frost-free period decreases steadily from the coast to the inland regions, falling in the eastern Netherlands to 160 days. Conversely, the number of days with frost rises to 80 in the Bourtange moorlands in the north-east of the country; in this area there is a danger of frost as late as May.
The north of the country (Groningen weather station) is somewhat colder than the Utrecht area (annual average temperature at Groningen 8.6°C/47.5°F, at Utrecht 9.3°C/48.7°F). As a result cattle can stay out in the fields longer in the south of the country and can be driven out again after the winter two weeks earlier than in the north-east.

The annual duration of sunshine in some inland areas falls by more than a hundred hours as compared with the coast (1549 hours at Amsterdam, 1490 at Utrecht and 1337 at Winterswijk, 110km/68 miles east of Utrecht). Conversely, the amount of cloud increases from the coast towards the inland regions: on the coast there are between 140 and 160 days with 80% cloud cover, in the east of the country 170 to 180 days. Cloud cover in the inland regions is, however, particularly low in September.

Annual rainfall ranges between 700mm/47½in and 800mm/48½in. There are frequently local increases in rainfall as a result of slight differences in altitude, such as the rise in the ground from the fenlands to the heathlands: there, as on the coast, the air masses rise, leading to condensation and cloud formation. The highest numbers of days with rain are found in the immediate hinterland of the coast (Groningen 212, Utrecht 213).

On the 27% of the country's area lying below sea level 300mm/12in of excess rainfall must be pumped out annually.

Wind strengths fall markedly from the coast towards the interior (annual average velocity at Utrecht 3.3m/10ft 10in per second, at Den Helder 6.8m/22ft 4in per second). Nevertheless the wind leaves its mark on many parts of the country – driving clouds across the sky, providing the motive force for windmills, distorting trees near the coast.

As a result of the greater differences in air pressure wind speeds in winter are between 1 and 1.5m (3 and 5ft) per second higher in winter than in summer. West winds predominate; north and east winds occur more frequently in spring, particularly in the north of the country.

Southern Limburg

Beek
weather station

Southern Limburg is a small area on the Maas at the southern tip of the Netherlands. The highest part of the country and the farthest from the coast, it has the most markedly continental climate, very different from other regions. Minimum night temperatures in winter are below freezing point (January average 0.8°C/33.4°F) and maximum day temperatures in summer rise above 20°C/68°F). Rainfall is more evenly distributed over the year than on the coast, and the number of days with rain (189) is the lowest in the whole of the Netherlands.

Flora and Fauna

Flora

The Netherlands belong to the Euro-Siberian floral region of the Holarctic province. Within this region a number of sub-regions can be distinguished, among them the Atlantic/European area (characterised, for example, by holly, ivy, broom, foxgloves and bell heather) and the Central European area. The boundary between these two sub-regions, a transitional zone between 20km/12½ miles and 40km/25 miles wide, runs through the whole of the Netherlands parallel to the coast, reflecting the less maritime character of the climate with greater distance from the coast.

Floral regions

The pattern of the flora is, of course, influenced by regional differences in soils and land forms as well as by the climate.

The flora of the Netherlands was also enriched by influences from neighbouring areas. From the south-east elements of the flora of the Pontic region reached as far as the Maas/Rhine valley: typical examples are the pasqueflower and sea holly, which has spread as far as the polder country. From the boreal region of Scandinavia numbers of moorland plants have penetrated as far as Kempen.

Influence of neighbouring areas

The natural vegetation of the Netherlands survives only in occasional remnants, since so much of the country has been brought into cultivation. The sandy soils of the heathlands in the Atlantic region were originally covered with mixed forests of birch and oak, which in course of time degenerated as a result of the progress of cultivation into great expanses of Atlantic heathland and in recent times have been replanted with conifers.

Heathlands

Particularly interesting plant communities are found in the mud-flats, dunes and polders along the North Sea coast and in the few surviving areas of bogland.
Typical beach plants are the halophytes, which need salt to live and therefore prosper only on saline soil. The best known representatives of this genus are the sea aster and the glasswort, the latter a plant pioneer which colonises not only newly reclaimed polders but even strips of coastal land which are flooded by the sea.
In the dunes, which have been planted with marram grass, sea couch grass and dwarf pines to prevent erosion, a characteristic plant, in addition to the halophytes, is the sand violet (*Viola rupestris*). As the salinity of the soil is reduced the halophytes give place to pastureland; and in the final stage the former marshland is occupied by arable land and lush meadows.

Mud-flats, dunes and polders

A very distinctive landscape form is high moorland or raised bog, though this has now largely been drained and brought into cultivation except in parts of the Peel region.

High moorland

An area of high moorland is formed, independently of the ground-water level, by the steady expansion of bog mosses, which with their sponge-like consistency absorb rainwater and raise the level of the ground. The lower layers of the moss die and in course of time turn into peat.

The characteristic plants of this biotope are cotton grass and sedge, crowberry and Labrador tea. At a later stage these are supplemented by heaths and finally various species of trees, in particular alder, pine and birch.

Seabirds on Texel

Unlike high moorland, low moorland (found in south-western Friesland and north-western Overijssel) depends on ground-water. It is, therefore, richer in plant nutrients, and the vegetation cover differs accordingly. Characteristic plants are reeds, reed-mace, rushes, sedge, shrubs and mosses. When dried out the low moorland areas turn into marshy meadowland, marsh woodland and meadow woodland.

Low moorland

Fauna

The original fauna of the Netherlands, which was never distinguished by a great variety of species, has been much reduced by the activity of man, who has brought the remotest corners of the country into cultivation. The natural flora has been preserved only in a few areas which are too small to support large species of animals. As beasts of prey disappeared, however, roedeer, red deer and wild pigs lost their natural enemies and but for human intervention would have risen to unacceptable numbers.

The roedeer, the commonest of the larger mammals, prefers sparse woodland with dense undergrowth, from the shelter of which it ventures out into open country and the vicinity of human settlements. It is thus found only in the sandy heathland regions, never in the open fenlands of Zeeland, Holland and Friesland.

Roedeer

A predator rarely seen in the inland regions is the seal. During the day seal packs can be seen on flat sandy stretches along the coast; at night they go hunting.

Seals

The Waddenzee, between the Dutch mainland and the West Frisian islands, is a paradise for water birds almost unique in Europe.

Birds of the Waddenzee

◀ *River landscape, Delden (Overijssel)*

Population

Gulls

The characteristic birds of mud-flats like the Waddenzee are various species of gulls. The commonest is the herring gull, with a yellow bill, white breast and grey upper parts. Also very common is the great black-backed gull, a daring predator whose favourite prey is eiderduck chicks but which also hunts other seabirds. It can be recognised by its white breast and black upper parts.

Sandwich tern, spoonbill

The West Frisian islands are the largest breeding grounds in Europe of the Sandwich tern. When hunting it flies with bent head over the water, diving suddenly down when it spots its prey. Texel is the breeding ground of large numbers of spoonbills – large waders which are not otherwise found in continental Europe except in Austria and Hungary. A spoonbill in flight can be distinguished from a heron, which is also common, by its extended neck and bill.

Oystercatchers, geese and ducks

Among the most conspicuous of the shore birds is the oystercatcher, which may be up to 43cm/17in high. It can crack mussel-shells with its razor-sharp yellow beak. Also frequently seen on the islands are various species of geese (pink-footed goose, barnacle goose, brent goose) and ducks (shelduck, eider, long-tailed duck), the yellow-legged ringed plover and the smaller Kentish plover.

Dunlin

Another very common shore bird is the dunlin, large flocks of which are to be seen in the Waddenzee. In winter it has streaked brownish-grey upper parts and white under parts with a grey breast; in summer it has chestnut plumage with streaked black upper parts.

Fish

The fish population in inland waters has been much reduced by increasing pollution of the water. The salmon, once a delicacy from the Rhine and the Maas, has now almost died out. Still common, however, are crayfish. In the Waddenzee, in addition to eels and mussels, there are numerous species of crustaceans which are found only in salt water.

Population

The Netherlands have a total population of some 15 million. In addition to the Dutch there are around 200,000 Frisians. A minority of recent origin is constituted by immigrants from the country's former overseas territories – some 176,000 from Surinam and the Netherlands Antilles and 9600 Ambonese from Indonesia.

The number of foreigners living in the Netherlands increased by 25% between 1980 and 1988 to about 600,000. The largest group consists of Turks (28%), followed by Moroccans (22.3%), with smaller numbers from the United Kingdom (6.8%), Germany (6.7%) and Belgium (3.9%).

Within the territory of the Netherlands there was an intermingling of a number of Germanic tribes between the 2nd millennium B.C. and the 5th century A.D. – Frisians in the north, Saxons in the east and Franks in the south. Of these only the Frisians have preserved a separate identity, and their language is now officially recognised alongside Dutch. After the former Dutch colonies became independent, from about 1949, there was a wave of immigrants from Indonesia and the Netherlands Antilles, but these amount in total to only about 2% of the population.

From 1945 onwards the annual rate of population increase was around 1.1% – the result of a high birth rate (19 per 1000) and a death rate which, owing to the favourable age structure of the population, was relatively low (8 per 1000). Towards the end of the 1960s, with the popularity of the "Pill", the birth rate fell sharply for a time, but it is still around 15 per 1000, a relatively high figure for Europe. The death rate has remained unchanged. The present annual rate of growth is thus around 0.8% (including the effect of a net immigration of 20,000).

Population density is about 412 to the sq.km (1067 to the sq. mile) – the highest in the world with the exception of Monaco. Even within the relatively small area of the Netherlands, however, there are considerable regional differences. The highest densities (over 1000 to the sq.km, or 2590 to the sq. mile) are reached in the area in the west of the country known as Randstad Holland, which includes the most important cities and towns in the Netherlands (Amsterdam, Haarlem, Leiden, The Hague, Delft, Rotterdam, Dordrecht and Utrecht). This is the largest concentration of population in the country, with over 40% of its total population in only 10% of its area.

Other concentrations of population are in Brabant (Bergen op Zoom, Roosendaal, Breda, Tilburg, 's-Hertogenbosch and Eindhoven), Twente (Almelo, Borne, Hengelo and Enschede) and southern and central Limburg. Between these are expanses of mainly agricultural land, much less densely populated, with a number of larger towns (Nijmegen, Arnhem, Apeldoorn, Groningen).

The high degree of urbanisation in the Netherlands is indicated by the fact that only some 20% of the population live in rural areas. It is reflected also in the occupational structure of the population. Agriculture, forestry and fishing now account for only 7% of the working population, while the industrial sector provides employment for 36% and the services sector takes by far the largest share, with 57%. This kind of ratio between the secondary and tertiary sectors of the economy is matched only by very few of the industrial nations of the world. It is a sign of the extraordinarily high degree of development of the Dutch economy, which must surely leave little room for further expansion.

Urbanisation

In 1986 some 63% of the population of the Netherlands professed the Christian faith. The population of the southern provinces of Limburg and Noord-Brabant is predominantly Roman Catholic (36% of the total population), while in the rest of the country Protestant churches predominate (26%). The largest Protestant denomination is the Nederlandse Hervormde Kerk (18.5%), followed by the Gereformeerde Kerk. Of the older groups there are still some Arminians and Mennonites. 32.6% of the population profess no religion, most of them in the towns of Randstad Holland. There are also 4.5% of Muslims, Hindus, Buddhists and Jews.

Religion

Education

The origins of the Dutch educational system go back to the foundation of the Batavian Republic in 1789. The first education act was passed in 1801.

Since 1848 local authorities, rather than the state, have been responsible for the provision of schools, with financial assistance from the state. Private schools associated with particular religious denominations are not subsidised.

Only since 1917 have public and private education been on an equal footing, freedom of education being now enshrined in the constitution. Nowadays a quarter of all schools are publicly run, three-quarters by Protestant or Catholic bodies.

School attendance for all children became compulsory in 1900, and in 1985 the starting age was reduced from 6 to 5½. After completing ten years of education 16-year-olds who are not staying on at school are required for a further year to attend part-time classes twice a week.

Compulsory attendance

Over 3.5 million children are in full-time education. During the compulsory ten years education is free; thereafter fees are payable. Schoolchildren and students from poorer families may receive assistance from the government or their church. Some 17% of total government expenditure (almost 39 billion guilders) is accounted for by education.

Fees

Education

<table>
<tr><td>Types of school</td><td>After a period of pre-school education, usually two years, children spend six years in a primary school, followed by between four and six years in a secondary school. Parents are free to choose the type of school for their children. On the basis of a national examination teachers recommend pupils for the various types of secondary school – general, pre-academic, vocational. Only the first year of secondary education is common to all types of school.</td></tr>
<tr><td>Vocational higher education</td><td>In each type of secondary school pupils sit a national examination in their final year for a certificate which qualifies them for higher education. Vocational higher education provides training in commerce and administration, industry, domestic economy, agriculture, social work, health care, art and teaching. The courses last four years.</td></tr>
<tr><td>Universities</td><td>For admission to a university a qualifying certificate is required, usually obtained after six years at a pre-academic secondary school.</td></tr>
</table>

There are 21 universities and other higher educational establishments in the Netherlands, the oldest and most famous of which is Leiden University, founded by William of Orange in 1575. The greatest scholars of the day taught at Leiden, among them Herman Boerhaave, Christiaan Huygens, Hugo Grotius and the French philosopher Descartes.
Other important universities are Utrecht (founded 1614), Rotterdam, Amsterdam, Nijmegen and Maastricht. There are colleges of technology at Delft, Eindhoven and Enschede, a business school at Tilburg, a theological college at Apeldoorn and a college of agriculture at Wageningen.

There are two stages of university study. The first degree is obtained after four years' or a maximum of six years' study and the *doctoraal examen*, which entitles the student to the title *doctorandus* (abbreviated Drs). Thereafter the graduate can specialise or work for a higher degree.

Leiden University

In addition to the general schools and vocational schools there are also special schools, both primary and secondary, for physically or mentally handicapped, maladjusted and disturbed children.

Special schools

Adult education is provided in "open schools", and there are also "open universities" in many towns.

Adult education

Government and Administration

The Kingdom of the Netherlands (Koninkrijk der Nederlanden) consists of five regions, with twelve provinces, and a number of Caribbean islands (the Netherlands Antilles – Bonaire, Curaçao, Saba, Sint Eustatius and Sint Maarten – and the island of Aruba) as overseas territories.

The national capital is Amsterdam, though the seat of government is The Hague, which is also the seat of the International Court of Justice.
The official language is Dutch, together with Frisian in Friesland.

The Netherlands are a member of the Benelux economic and customs union, a member of the United Nations and a founding member of NATO and the European Community, and belong to the Council of Europe and the European Parliament.
The form of government is a constitutional monarchy.

The coat of arms of the Kingdom of the Netherlands shows a crowned golden lion on a blue ground. The red, white and blue flag dates from the 17th century; the colours are derived from the arms of the Princes of Orange.

Coat of arms and flag

The Dutch national anthem, "Wilhelmus", which has fifteen eight-line verses, was written in 1568 by the poet and diplomat Filips van Marnix, Heer van St-Aldegonde. Each verse begins with the name of William of Nassau. The tune was originally a popular French air with frequent alternations between 2/4, 3/4 and 4/4 time.

National anthem

The Kingdom and the Royal House

The connection between the Netherlands and the princely house of Orange-Nassau dates back to the year 1403, when Count Engelbert of Nassau married Johanna of Polanen, Breda and the Lek, who brought him great possessions in the Low Countries (Netherlands). These estates were part of the principality of Burgundy, a collateral branch of the French royal house.

The House of Orange-Nassau

The Counts of Nassau were originally Counts of Laurenburg, with their residence on the river Lahn (a right-bank tributary of the Rhine, in Germany). In 1101 they built a new castle at the town of Nassau and from the mid 12th century called themselves Counts of Nassau.

The first Count of Nassau was Walram von Laurenburg (1146–98). His son Henry II, known as the Rich, inherited all the Nassau possessions and built the castle of Dillenburg. In 1255, however, Henry's sons divided the territory between them, establishing the Walramian and the Ottonian lines.

Government and Administration

From the Walramian line sprang the princely house of Luxembourg, from the Ottonian the house of Orange-Nassau.

The wealth acquired by Engelbert of Nassau and increased by later marriages brought Engelbert and his heirs great influence at court. When Charles V of Habsburg, who was already king of Spain as well as Emperor, acquired Burgundy around 1500 the Count of Nassau became a high dignitary at the imperial court. Engelbert's last direct descendant was René de Chalon, who in addition to his possessions in the Netherlands also held the principality of Orange in France. When he died in 1544 his 11-year-old nephew William of Nassau inherited all his lands. He was brought up at Charles V's court in Brussels, where he held a position of high honour.

Stadholders

In 1559 Charles VI's successor as king of Spain, Philip II, appointed William of Orange-Nassau (William the Silent) Stadholder (Dutch *Stadhouder*) – that is, his governor or representative – of Holland, Zeeland and Utrecht. Although in the absence of the monarch his sovereign rights rested with the States General (which represented the towns and the nobility) these rights were in fact exercised by the Stadholder, who as the first servant of the States General held the real power. In that capacity he also commanded the troops of the Dutch provinces.

When, during the reign of Philip II, the liberties granted to the people of the Netherlands by Charles V were restricted by a tax reform which required them to meet the cost of the Spanish occupation forces the provinces rebelled. William of Orange, as representative of the States General, now became one of the principal spokesmen for the nobility and the townspeople, and when Spanish troops were deployed to suppress the rebellion he became leader of the fight for independence. After his death in 1584 two of his sons carried on his work and won independence for the Netherlands.

The Princes of Orange continued to use the title of Stadholder which had been held by William; but the municipal and provincial authorities regarded the post as unnecessary in peacetime and were afraid that it might lead to the loss of the provinces' autonomy. Accordingly when William II died in 1650 no new Stadholder was appointed. Only in Friesland did the house of Nassau retain the post of Stadholder.

When France attacked the Netherlands in 1672, however, a Prince of Orange, William III, was again appointed Stadholder. When he died childless in 1702 his grand-nephew Johan Willem Friso, Count of Nassau and Stadholder of Groningen and Friesland, succeeded him but was unable to gain the title of Stadholder of the other five provinces. The Stadholdership was not held by a prince of the house of Nassau until 1747, when the country was again at war.

Constitutional monarchs

After the period of French occupation (1795–1813) the son of the last Stadholder (William IV) was called back to the Netherlands. Ruling first as sovereign prince and from 1815 as a constitutional monarch, he was the first king of the United Netherlands. The present queen, Beatrix Wilhelmina Armgard, who came to the throne in 1980, was the eldest daughter of Queen Juliana and Prince Bernhard and is the fifth monarch of the house of Orange. In 1966 she married Claus von Amberg, a German diplomat, who was created Prince of the Netherlands and Jonkheer van Amberg. The royal couple have three sons, the eldest of whom, Willem Alexander, is heir to the throne with the title of Prince of the Netherlands.

Formal documents signed by the queen begin with the formula "We, Beatrix, by the grace of God Queen of the Netherlands, Princess of Orange-Nassau, etc., etc., etc.". The triple "etc." covers the title of Princess of Lippe-Biesterfeld and an impressive string of titles borne by earlier princes of the house of Orange and first employed by King William I in a proclama-

The Queen's golden coach: a symbol of the monarchy

tion of November 1813: Duke of Limburg, Marquis of Veere, Hereditary Prince of Vlissingen, Count of Katzenelnbogen, Vianden, Diez, Spiegelberg, Buren, Leerdam and Culemborg, Burgrave of Antwerp, Baron of Breda, Diest, Beilstein, Grave, Cuyk, IJsselstein, Cranendonck, Eindhoven, Liesveld, Herstel, Warneton, Arlay and Nozeroy, Hereditary Lord and Baron of Ameland, Lord of Borculo, Bredevoort, Lichtenvoorde, Loo, Geertruidenberg, Clundert, Zevenbergen, Hooge and Lage Zwaluwe, Naaldwijk, Polanen, Sint Maartensdijk, Soest, Baarn, Ter Eem, Willemstad, Steenbergen, Montfoort, Sint Vith, Butgenbach, Daasburg, Niervaart, Turnhout and Besançon.

Under the constitution the crown can descend in either the male or the female line. It passes to the eldest son or (if there are no sons) the eldest daughter of the monarch and his or her descendants. If the monarch has no children the next in line are his or her brothers and sisters and their children. Succession in the collateral line can extend to the third degree of relationship. If, on the death of the monarch, there are no heirs a successor is appointed by Parliament.

Succession to the throne

This order of succession was introduced in the interests of the state and is binding on the ruling house. In accordance with this principle, the heir is not permitted to alter the order of succession by renouncing the throne, but succeeds automatically on the death (or abdication) of the monarch.

Form of Government

Under the 1815 constitution executive power is vested in the Crown, to which ministers are responsible. King William I was an enlightened despot who ruled by royal decree. Since the constitutional reform of 1848 the monarch has been inviolable, while ministers are responsible to the

State opening of Parliament in the Knights' Hall

elected national assembly. Since then the Netherlands have been a constitutional monarchy with a system of parliamentary government. The monarch and ministers together form the Crown. All draft laws (bills) are first discussed by the Council of State and then examined by Parliament. Laws come into force only after signature by the monarch and the minister responsible.

Ministers are appointed by the Queen. Governments are formed with the help of a *formateur,* who usually becomes prime minister of the new government. The ministers, who come from the government party, form the Council of Ministers. There are also secretaries of state, who together with the ministers form the Cabinet. Secretaries of state may attend meetings of the Council of Ministers, but only in an advisory capacity.

Council of State

The highest consultative organ of the Crown in matters of legislation is the Council of State (Raad van State), the members of which are appointed by the Queen, who is President of the Council but is usually represented by a Vice-President (sometimes jokingly referred to as the Viceroy). The Queen's consort and the heir to the throne (when of the age of 18 or over) are entitled to sit and to vote in the Council.

Parliament

The Parliament of the Netherlands, the Staten-Generaal (States General), consists of two chambers. The First Chamber (Eerste Kamer), which is the less important of the two, has 75 members elected by the provincial States for a six-year term. The 150 members of the Second Chamber (Tweede Kamer) are elected every four years by direct popular election. The two chambers have different powers: thus the First Chamber cannot take the initiative in legislation but can merely agree or disagree.

While the Queen and her ministers together form the executive, the ministers and Parliament form the legislature.

Netherlands

Koninkrijk der Nederlanden
Kingdom of the Netherlands

(NL)

—— Boundaries of provinces

Province	Land area in sq. km. (sq. miles)	Population	Chief town
1 Groningen	2342 (904)	555,000	Groningen
2 Friesland	3366 (1300)	599,000	Leeuwarden
3 Drenthe	2660 (1027)	439,000	Assen
4 Overijssel	3338 (1289)	1,015,000	Zwolle
5 Gelderland	5013 (1936)	1,794,000	Arnhem
6 Utrecht	1331 (514)	976,000	Utrecht
7 Noord-Holland	2667 (1030)	2,365,000	Haarlem
8 Zuid-Holland	2906 (1122)	3,229,000	The Hague
9 Zeeland	1787 (690)	356,000	Middelburg
10 Noord-Brabant	4949 (1911)	2,172,00	's-Hertogenbosch
11 Limburg	2169 (837)	1,099,000	Maastricht
12 Flevoland	1411 (545)	194,000	Lelystad
Kingdom of Netherlands	41,864 (16,164)[1]	14,897,000	The Hague/Amsterdam

[1] Total area including water

45

Nowadays the members of the royal house generally restrict their participation in the business of government to formal and state occasions.

Judiciary

The principle of the separation of powers (the legislature, the executive and the judiciary) guarantees the independence of judges, who are bound only by law and equity. All judges are appointed for life.

There are four tiers of courts. The first level consists of the 62 district courts. The next level is formed by 19 *arrondissementsrechtbanken,* one in each of the 19 *arrondissements.* Above these are five appeal courts. The final court of appeal and supreme court is the Hoge Raad (Supreme Council), which can overturn the decisions of lower courts, basing its judgments on the findings in fact of the lower court.
The overriding principle, however, is to secure uniformity in the administration of justice.

Administration

Provincial
administration

The Netherlands are divided into twelve provinces, each of them with its own parliament, the Provincial States (Provinciale Staten), the members of which are elected every four years. From the membership of the States are elected the members of the executive organ of the province, the Deputiertenstaaten. The President of both the States and the Deputiertenstaaten is the Commissaris der Koningin (Queen's Commissioner), who is appointed by the Crown. The number of members of both bodies depends on the population of the province.

Local
administration

Local government is in the hands of town or district councils, which are elected by the local population every four years. The council in turn elects an executive committee to run its business. The chairman of the council and of the executive committee is the burgomaster, appointed by the Crown for a six-year term (which may be extended). The number of members of both the council and the executive committee again depends on the population of the area.

The country's 850 communes (towns and districts), which are grouped in 129 "economic and geographical areas", enjoy a considerable measure of independence. Other recently introduced units are the 80 "nodal areas" (*nodale gebieden),* defined on the basis of social structure, and the 40 regions established by the Commission for the Coordination of Regional Investigation Programmes (COROP).

There are also a number of water authorities (Hoogheemraadschappen and Waterschappen) responsible for the protection of water supplies in particular areas.

Seventeen towns in the Netherlands have a populations of over 100,000, ranging from Dordrecht with 108,000 inhabitants to Amsterdam with 693,000. The smallest commune in the country is Katwoude (Noord-Holland) with a population of 241.

Economy

The Netherlands are now a modern industrial country with a very high proportion of the working population employed in the tertiary sector of the economy. The number of people working in that sector began to exceed those employed in industry after the Second World War. This is a phenomenon characteristic of highly developed economies. Although the development of industry in this once predominantly agricultural country, which also enjoyed world fame as a commercial and seafaring nation, began to take off dramatically only after the Second World War, it now accounts for the largest share of the net domestic product (45%). Agriculture, occupying some 60% of the country's area, contributes only 7% of the net domestic product.

Industry

Dutch industry is almost entirely dependent on imports for the supply of raw materials, for the Netherlands have practically no minerals. Even the coalmines in southern Limburg have recently been closed down, since they could not compete with the great fields of natural gas now being worked in the provinces of Groningen, Friesland and Drenthe and on the North Sea shelf. In comparison with natural gas the extraction of oil plays only a minor role. In the past shortage of raw materials prevented the development of heavy industry as the basis of the economy, as happened in Belgium, Germany and other typical industrial countries. There developed instead export-oriented, labour-intensive processing industries producing semi-finished goods and high-value finished products. A significant metallurgical industry has been built up only within the last few decades at IJmuiden on the North Sea Canal, in an area well situated from the point of view of transport and communications. Ore and coal carriers from overseas can now be discharged directly at the foundries. The same applies to the aluminium works at Delfzijl on the Eems estuary.

The country's traditional shipbuilding industry still flourishes at Rotterdam, Schiedam and Amsterdam, but many shipyards have closed during the last fifteen years. Other branches of the metalworking industry are engineering, car manufacture (DAF/Volvo) and the manufacture of agricultural machinery, office equipment, tools, metal furniture and household equipment.

Shipbuilding and Metalworking

Rotterdam: one of the world's leading container ports

47

Economy

Foodstuffs industries

The most important sector of the economy, however, is still foodstuffs and associated industries. Innumerable small and medium-sized firms process local and imported agricultural products, tobacco, spirits and beer. The brewing giant Heineken is active in both these latter fields.

Chemical industry

The most significant growth sector is the relatively young chemical industry, the capacity of which has multiplied many times in the last fifteen years. A leading place is occupied by the oil refineries and large petrochemical plants around Rotterdam and Amsterdam, followed by fertiliser, salt, dye and detergent factories (Unilever and AKZO). The Netherlands are also one of the world's leading producers of synthetic materials (DSM).

Electrical industry

Another important branch is the electrical industry, closely associated with the name of Philips, a firm of international reputation with its headquarters in Eindhoven.

Concentrations of population in the Netherlands

48

The main centres of the traditional textile industry, still of great importance, are Twente and Amsterdam.

Textiles

The largest industrial agglomeration in the Netherlands is Randstad Holland, the name given to the great concentration of industry and population in the west of the country which occupies 10% of its total area. Here are concentrated some two-thirds of the economic potential and almost half the population of the Netherlands. The principal towns in this area are Amsterdam, Haarlem, Leiden, The Hague, Delft, Rotterdam, Dordrecht and Utrecht. The advantages of situation enjoyed by Randstad Holland lead to an ever greater concentration of industry and density of population and create major problems for the rest of the country, where the economic and social potential is thus being steadily eroded. The country's planners have been trying for more than twenty years to arrest or reduce this regional imbalance, and some success has been achieved in promoting development in disadvantaged areas such as Noord-Brabant, Limburg, Nijmegen, Arnhem, Terneuzen and Vlissingen.

Randstad Holland

Agriculture

The agriculture of the Netherlands has reached a degree of intensiveness achieved by no other European country, and is, therefore, very much export-oriented. It is still necessary, however, to import certain staple foodstuffs such as wheat, since domestic production is insufficient to meet the needs of the population.

The most labour- and capital-intensive branch of agriculture, producing the highest surpluses for export, is commercial horticulture, which occupies some 5% of the country's agricultural land. Around 7% of the area devoted to horticulture is under glass, mainly south of The Hague and north of

Horticulture

The world-famed tulips of the Netherlands

Rotterdam. The crops grown under glass include cucumbers and tomatoes as well as grapes and flowers.

Flower-growing

The main crops grown in the open are vegetables, fruit, bulbs and flowers. The principal growing areas are the Betuwe, southern Limburg and South Beveland. The great bulb-growing areas (tulips, daffodils, hyacinths) are between Haarlem and Leiden and between Alkmaar, Enkhuizen and Den Helder.

In addition to the land behind the dunes new areas in the polders are constantly being brought into cultivation, including the last polder planned in the IJsselmeer, destined to be a major bulb-growing area.

Land in the fenland regions – in the Westland (between the Nieuwe Waterweg and The Hague), Amstelland and the Streek (between Hoorn and Enkhuizen) – is also intensively developed for horticulture. The clayey soil of the fenlands is mixed with dune sand (a combination provided by nature in the tulip country south of Haarlem, where the fenland is covered with a thin layer of drift sand) to improve its quality, and advantage is taken of the mild maritime climate to grow early vegetables under glass, so that these areas can not only meet the large local demand but also supply London and the Ruhr area. The Betuwe, a tract of riverine fenland between the Waal and the Lower Rhine, is famed for its fruit.

Stock-farming

Stock-farming also plays an important part, almost two-thirds of the country's agricultural land being occupied by pastureland. The main products are butter and cheese. Stock-farming is concentrated mainly in the provinces of Friesland and Noord-Holland. Apart from cattle, poultry farming is also of importance.

Mixed farming – i.e. arable as well as pastoral – is the general rule, with corn as the predominant crop. Many farms also grow crops for seed, pulses, oil-producing plants, sugar-beet and potatoes.

Attempts have been made in recent years to stem the rapid growth of agriculture by commercial afforestation.

Transport

Shipping

The most important elements in the system of transport and communications in the Netherlands are the inland waterways and seaports, for the availability of low-cost transport, particularly of bulk goods, is the basis of the whole economy. Rotterdam is the largest seaport and inland port not only in Europe but in the world. Considerably smaller, but still of great importance in European trade, is the port of Amsterdam. The network of inland waterways which provides links between the seaports and the European hinterland now has a total length of 4350km/2703 miles. There are some 20,000 boats plying on the waterways, now threatened with competition from the recently completed pipelines for the transport of bulk goods such as oil and natural gas.

The Netherlands have a first-rate network of roads, which also play an important part in the transport of goods. There are some 1400km/870 miles of motorway. Rail traffic is of relatively minor importance, having suffered both from the increased use of road transport and from the numerous pipelines for the transport of oil and natural gas. Although the railways carry 230 million passengers a year there are still more than 5400 traffic jams and tailbacks on the roads.

Bascule bridge, Middelburg

Tourism

Since the end of the Second World War the Netherlands have developed into a major tourist country. Favourite holiday areas are the West Frisian islands and the seaside resorts on the North Sea coast such as Scheveningen, Noordwijk and Bergen. The towns and villages on the IJsselmeer also draw many visitors. Volendam, near Edam, is famed for the traditional costumes still worn there. The improvement in road connections as a result of the Delta Plan has brought large numbers of visitors to the islands of Zeeland. Old cities and towns like Amsterdam, Leiden, Delft, Gouda, Haarlem and Middelburg, with their treasures of art and architecture, are also powerful tourist attractions, as are the bulb fields when the flowers are in bloom. The Hoge Veluwe National Park to the north of Arnhem and the open-air museums at Arnhem, Enkhuizen and Zaandam also attract large numbers of visitors.

Most foreign visitors come from Germany, followed by the United States, Britain and France.

History

<table>
<tr><td>Prehistory and
early historical
period</td><td>The earliest traces of human settlement, dating back some 30,000 years, are in the east of the country.

During the Neolithic period (around 4000 B.C.) the loess areas in the south and the heathlands in the north are settled by Celts. Evidence of their presence is provided by numerous megalithic tombs (*hunebedden*, "giants' beds") in the province of Drenthe.

The fenlands, less attractive to human settlement, are occupied only around 1500 B.C. by Germanic tribes, who build their settlements on artificial earth mounds (*terpen*) which provide protection from floods.</td></tr>
<tr><td>1st c. B.C.</td><td>The northern coastal areas are occupied by Frisians, the Rhine delta by a Germanic people, the Batavians, and the eastern territories by Saxons.</td></tr>
<tr><td>58 B.C. to
A.D. 400</td><td>The territory of the Netherlands is under Roman rule.
Between 58 and 51 B.C. Julius Caesar conquers Gaul, the northern part of which is occupied by a Celtic people, the Belgae. Between 12 B.C. and A.D. 9 the Romans try, without success, to occupy Germanic territory on the right bank of the Rhine. In A.D. 69–71 there is a great rising of the Batavians, led by Civilis.</td></tr>
<tr><td>4th and 5th c.</td><td>The Salian Franks occupy the territory between the Maas (Meuse), the Schelde (Scheldt) and the Lower Rhine. In 382 the episcopal see is moved from the Belgian town of Tongeren (Tongres) to Maastricht. Around 440 Chlodio, ancestor of the Merovingian dynasty, makes Tournai in southern Belgium his capital.</td></tr>
<tr><td>c. 481–843</td><td>The Netherlands are incorporated in the Frankish kingdom.</td></tr>
<tr><td>6th–8th c.</td><td>Spread of Christianity. Utrecht becomes the see of a bishop. St Willibrord, a missionary from Northumbria, travels throughout the country; he is murdered at Dokkum in 754.</td></tr>
<tr><td>843</td><td>Under the treaty of Verdun the Carolingian empire is divided: the area west of the Schelde goes to France (Charles the Bald), the lands to the east to Lothair (Lotharingia, the present-day Netherlands).</td></tr>
<tr><td>870</td><td>Under the treaty of Mersen (Meerssen, near Maastricht) Lotharingia is divided between France and Germany.</td></tr>
<tr><td>10th–14th c.</td><td>Establishment of counties, duchies and towns. After the disintegration of the Carolingian empire numerous independent feudal domains are formed, which seek by frequently changing amalgamations and alliances to weaken the suzerainty claimed by the larger neighbouring states. In the 11th century the name Low Countries or Netherlands begins to be applied to these territories as a whole; until the end of the 18th century the term also includes Belgium.</td></tr>
</table>

Brabant:
In 1006 this territory, under Count Lambert van Leuven, becomes a duchy (originally called Lower Lotharingia). In 1288 Brabant is united with Limburg, in 1355 with Luxembourg and in 1430 with Burgundy. The Golden Bull issued by the Emperor Charles IV in 1349 grants it freedom from all foreign jurisdictions. In the 15th century Brabant is a great centre of industry, trade and culture. In 1648 it is divided into North and South Brabant.

Breda:
In 1404 the town and lordship pass by marriage into the hands of the Counts of Nassau-Dillenburg, who in 1530 acquire, again by marriage, the principality of Orange in southern France.

Friesland:
The part of Friesland lying between the Zuiderzee and the Eems (Ems) is conquered by the Counts of Holland in the 13th and 14th centuries after a long period of conflict.

Gelderland:
The County of Gelderland, established during the 11th century, is incorporated in the early 13th century into the County of Zutphen and the Veluwe. In 1339 Gelderland becomes a duchy, and from 1379 is ruled alternately by Jülich, the Counts of Egmond, Kleve and Burgundy.

Holland:
The County of Holland is established in the mid 11th century within the Duchy of Lower Lotharingia. At the end of the century it acquires Zeeland (part of the County of Flanders) and part of the diocese of Utrecht. Between 1247 and 1256 Count William II is king of Germany, in opposition to the Emperor Frederick II. At the end of the 13th century Count Floris V conquers western Friesland (now part of Noord-Holland). In 1299 Holland is united with Hainault.

Limburg:
The County of Limburg, established around 1060, becomes a duchy within Lower Lotharingia at the beginning of the 12th century. Between 1221 and 1226 it is united with Luxembourg and from 1288 with Brabant. It is divided in 1648.

Utrecht:
The bishopric of Utrecht, established in 696, acquires considerable territorial possessions in the 10th and 11th centuries; Bishop Balderik (918–76) is for many years the principal representative of imperial power in the Low Countries. In 1528 the Emperor Charles V gains secular authority over the area by treaty. In 1577 the Princes of Orange introduce the Reformed faith. In 1579 the Union of Utrecht is concluded in the town.

From the unification of the Low Countries to domination by Spain 15th–16th c.
The separation of the Low Countries from the Holy Roman Empire is initiated by Duke Philip the Good of Burgundy, who gains possession of several counties. Soon afterwards the Low Countries fall into the hands of the Austrian Habsburgs, who add other territories to them. Spain gains control of them by inheritance.

The Dukes of Burgundy unite almost the whole of the Low Countries under 1384–1473
their rule. Philip II, the Bold, is involved in conflict with the duchies of Brabant and Limburg.

Duke Philip III, the Good, conquers Holland and Zeeland. During his reign 1419–67
the Netherlands enjoy a first period of economic development, wealth and luxury. This is also the first great period of Dutch painting (Jan van Eyck is Philip's court painter).

Duke Charles the Bold, the wealthiest and most ambitious prince of his 1467–77
time, keeps the nobility and the towns in subjection. He acquires Gelderland, so that the whole of the Netherlands except Friesland now belongs to Burgundy. In 1477 Charles is killed at Nancy.

Maria, daughter and heiress of Charles the Bold, marries Maximilian of 1477
Austria, the future Emperor Maximilian I. The Burgundian Low Countries

thus become a Habsburg possession. Their son Philip I, the Fair, rules Burgundy from 1494.

1519–56

The Emperor Charles V (born in Ghent in 1500) brings Friesland (1523), Utrecht (1527), Overijssel (1528), Groningen (1536), Drenthe (1536) and Gelderland (1543) under Habsburg control. In 1548 he unites the seventeen Low Countries in an independent Burgundian League. His object is to form these territories into a single strong state and to reduce the ancient liberties which restrict the power of the Crown.

From 1520 Luther's teachings begin to penetrate into the Low Countries, but from 1550 onwards Calvinism becomes the dominant creed in the northern provinces. Charles V seeks to repress the new faith (inquisition established 1522) because it endangers the internal unity of the state.

1556

The Low Countries fall to Spain when Charles V's world empire disintegrates after his abdication. He is succeeded by Philip II.

1533–84

In 1533 William I (the Silent), son of William the Rich of Nassau-Dillenburg and Juliana von Stolberg, inherits from his cousin René de Chalon various territories in France (including the principality of Orange) and the Netherlands. In 1559 Philip II appoints him Stadholder of Holland, Zeeland and Utrecht. In 1566 William the Silent, along with Counts Egmond and Hoorn, becomes leader of the fight for independence. In 1567 he flees to Germany, but returns in the following year with an army. In 1584 he is murdered in Delft by a fanatical Catholic, acting at the behest of Philip II.

1586–1648

The Struggle for Independence and the Making of the State
Seven Protestant provinces in the north of the country (the Union of Utrecht) rise against Spanish rule, under the leadership of William the Silent. At the end of the Thirty Years' War they gain their independence.

1556–98

Philip II of Spain (Charles V's son), the dominant figure of the Counter-Reformation, seeks to impose his absolute authority on the freedom-loving Netherlands. He sends in Spanish troops, rides roughshod over the rights of the States General and the nobility and tries with fanatical intolerance to eradicate the Protestant faith.

1559–67

Under Stadholder-General Margaret of Parma, Charles V's daughter, unrest and resistance grow. Cardinal Granvelle, adviser to the Crown, is recalled by the king in 1564 on the insistence of the Prince of Orange.

1566

The Dutch nobles submit a petition to Margaret of Parma calling for the revocation of the edict establishing the Inquisition and the withdrawal of Spanish troops. The name of "Beggars" (Geuzen) applied to the rebels is said to have arisen on this occasion, when Margaret was asked by one of her courtiers: "Comment, Madame, avez-vous peur de ces gueux?" ("Why, Madam, are you afraid of these beggars?"). The name was then adopted by the rebels as a title of honour. Those who attacked by sea were known as the Sea Beggars (Watergeuzen).

The leaders of the rising are William of Orange and Counts Egmond and Hoorn. Catholic churches are devastated by rioters (the "iconoclastic fury").

1567–73

During the governorship of the Duke of Alba Philip II sends more troops to suppress the revolt. Thousands of people are executed. William of Orange flees to Germany. Egmond and Hoorn are beheaded in Brussels in 1568.

1568

Beginning of armed resistance. William assembles troops, thrusts into the Netherlands and puts himself at the head of the rebels. He encourages and assists the Sea Beggars, who capture a number of coastal towns with their fleet. The Spaniards are compelled to raise the year-long siege of Leiden when William orders the dykes to be opened in 1574.

Leiden University is founded in 1575.

The seven northern Protestant provinces of Friesland, Gelderland, Groningen, Holland, Overijssel, Utrecht and Zeeland join in a defensive alliance, the Union of Utrecht; the agreements between them form the constitution of the Dutch Republic until 1795. The Catholic provinces in the south, in the Walloon country and Flanders, form the Union of Arras, which swears allegiance to Spain. The separation between the two parts of the country is now complete – foreshadowing the later frontier between present-day Belgium and the Netherlands. 1579

The northern provinces declare their independence in the "Act of Disobedience" (Akte van Ongehoorzaamheid). 1581

1585–1625

Prince Maurice (Maurits) of Orange, son of William the Silent and now Stadholder, takes many towns and drives the Spaniards completely out of the northern provinces by his victory at Nieuwpoort on the Belgian coast in 1600. In 1604, after a three-year siege, the Spaniards capture the stronghold of Oostende (Ostend), the last Dutch base in the southern provinces. This marks the final division of the Low Countries into a northern and a southern part, with the exception of a brief interlude in 1792–1830. In 1607 Admiral Jacob van Heemskerk defeats a Spanish fleet off Gibraltar.

The economy and maritime trade of the Netherlands now flourish as never before, and Amsterdam becomes the most important commercial city in Europe.

The "fearful flood" of 1634: a 17th century print

In 1596 Cornelis de Houtman lands on Java and Willem Barentsz discovers Spitzbergen. In 1602 the United East India Company (Verenigde Oostindische Compagnie) is established for the purpose of sailing and trading to the east of the Cape of Good Hope. In 1609 the British navigator Henry Hudson, sailing in the service of the East India Company, discovers the bay in North America which bears his name. In 1613 the first settlement in Surinam is established. In 1616 Willem Schouten rounds Cape Horn. In 1619 Batavia (now Djakarta) is founded.
In 1621 the Dutch West India Company is founded for the purpose of trading with America and Africa. The two companies acquire territory in the Malay Archipelago and in South America.

Conflicts between the province of Holland and the other provinces, and between supporters of the States General on the one hand and adherents 1609–19

The petition of the Dutch nobility (1566)

of the house of Orange and the Stadholder on the other, lead to domestic discord. The dispute between the Gomarists (strict Calvinists) and the moderate Arminians, who are supported by the Grand Pensionary (highest dignitary) of Holland, Johan van Oldenbarnevelt, endanger public order. The Synod of Dordrecht in 1618 condemns the Arminians, and Maurice of Nassau has the 72-year-old Oldenbarnevelt executed in 1619.

1621–48

In 1628, during the Thirty Years' War, Admiral Piet Hein captures the Spanish silver fleet on its way home from the Spanish possessions in South America. Dutch troops conquer northern Brabant.

1648–1792

Greatness and Decline
Under the treaty of Westphalia in 1648 the independence of the Dutch Republic is recognised, as are its conquests in northern Brabant and Limburg and its acquisitions of colonial territories. It becomes a leading commercial nation and one of the strongest sea powers in the world.

Dutch painting reaches its apogee (Frans Hals, Rembrandt, Jan Steen, Vermeer). Leiden University has a European reputation. The philosopher Baruch Spinoza (1632–77) lives in The Hague from 1670.

In the 18th century domestic conflicts arise between opponents of the house of Orange and the Stadholders, and these, combined with the loss of much of the fleet, lead to the country's decline.

1648

Independence of the Netherlands recognised by Spain.

1624–58

The north-east of Brazil is occupied between 1624 and 1654.
Dutch settlement on Manhattan (1625). Foundation of Nieuw Amsterdam (later to be renamed New York) in 1626. Conquest of Curaçao (1634). Conquest of Malacca (1641). In 1645 Abel Tasman discovers Tasmania and

New Zealand. The first Dutch colony at the Cape of Good Hope is founded in 1652. Ceylon is conquered in 1658.
Many of these territories are lost to Britain during the period of French occupation. The others are granted independence after the Second World War.

Grand Pensionary Jan de Witt, an opponent of the house of Orange, guides the destinies of the state with a firm hand. | 1653–72

The Dutch fight two naval wars with Britain. In the first war they win several naval victories under Admirals Michiel de Ruyter and Maarten Tromp but in the second (during which Admiral de Ruyter blockades the Thames) they are finally defeated. | 1652–54, 1664–67

De Witt enters into a triple alliance with Britain and Sweden and compels Louis XIV to make peace. | 1668

There is a popular rising when the French invade the Republic; de Witt is murdered. | 1672

War between France and the Netherlands. The French conquer Gelderland and Utrecht, but their advance is halted when the Dutch breach the dykes. De Ruyter is victorious in a number of naval battles with Britain, which is now allied with France. Brandenburg and Austria support the Netherlands. In the treaty of Nijmegen the Dutch lose no territory and gain Maastricht. | 1672–78

William III of Orange, Stadholder of the Netherlands, becomes king of Britain in 1689. Since he has no heirs the title of Prince of Orange passes to Johan Willem Friso, Stadholder of Friesland. | 1672–1702

The 18th century is a period of decline from the prosperity and cultural flowering of the 17th. European conflicts frequently impinge on the Netherlands. The "Patriots" (opponents of the house of Orange) run the country until 1747 without a Stadholder, and in 1786 drive out Stadholder William V, who is brought back in the following year by Prussian troops. | 1702–92

War with Britain during the War of American Independence. Much of the Dutch fleet is lost, leading to the country's final decline. | 1780–84

In the First Coalition War the Netherlands and Belgium are occupied by France. | 1792–94

The Netherlands under French control | 1792–1813
The Netherlands and Belgium are conquered by the Revolutionary armies and are finally incorporated in the French Empire.

The Netherlands and Belgium are united in the Batavian Republic, a state organised on the French model. | 1795–1808
The Dutch colonies are occupied by Britain in 1802.

Napoleon establishes the Kingdom of Holland. | 1806–10

The kingdom of Holland is incorporated in the French Empire. | 1810–13

Kingdom of the Netherlands | from 1813
The French are driven out (1813) and Prince William, son of the last Stadholder, takes over the government.
Britain returns the Dutch colonies (1814).

Unsuccessful attempt to unite the Netherlands and Belgium in a single state (1815). Belgium declares its independence (1830), which is not recognised by King William I of the Netherlands until 1839.

History

1815	The Kingdom of the Netherlands, with William I of Orange as king, is recognised by the Congress of Vienna. William also becomes Grand Duke of Luxembourg in a personal union. Britain gives up the Dutch East Indies but retains its other colonies. Western New Guinea is occupied in 1828.
1830	Rising in Belgium, which declares its independence.
1831–39	In 1831 Prince Leopold of Coburg is elected king of Belgium. The western part of the Grand Duchy of Luxembourg is assigned to Belgium (1839). The provinces of Brabant and Limburg are divided between the Netherlands and Belgium.
1839	Opening of the first railway line in the Netherlands, between Amsterdam and Haarlem.
1840–90	During the reigns of William II (d. 1849) and William III conflicts between Conservatives and Liberals and between Catholics and Calvinists destabilise the domestic political situation.
1840–53	183 sq.km/71 sq. miles of land are reclaimed from the sea by the poldering of the Haarlemmermeer.
1890	On the death of William III in 1890 the personal union with Luxembourg comes to an end and the crown passes to the Walramian branch of the house of Nassau-Weilburg. The law is changed to permit a woman to succeed to the throne.
1890–1948	During the reign of Queen Wilhelmina, daughter of William III, much social legislation is introduced.
1914–18	The Netherlands maintain strict neutrality during the First World War. Over a million Belgians flee north.
1917	Introduction of universal suffrage for men.
1918	Unsuccessful attempt at revolution by the Social Democratic Workers' Party led by Jelle Troelstra.
1919	Introduction of universal suffrage for women.
1920	The draining of the Zuiderzee (IJsselmeer) begins.
1929–36	Economic crisis; over 400,000 unemployed.
1939–45	Second World War. German troops occupy the Netherlands, and the royal family and government escape to Britain. Strikes in February 1941 and May 1943 against the deportation of Jews. Strike by railwaymen in 1944. The war costs some 205,000 lives, plus over 30,000 victims of the war in Indonesia. War damage is estimated at 25 billion guilders.
1944	Belgium, the Netherlands and Luxembourg establish the Benelux customs union, which is brought into effect in stages between 1944 and 1948.
1948	Coronation of Queen Juliana (b. 1909).
1949	The former colonial territory of the Dutch East Indies (Java, Sumatra, Borneo, Celebes and the Moluccas) becomes the independent Republic of Indonesia, with Djakarta (formerly Batavia) as its capital. In 1963, after a brief war, Indonesia annexes western New Guinea (West Irian).
1953	Great floods in the west of the country cost some 1870 lives. A law is passed authorising the closure of the arms of the sea in the Delta.

The Netherlands join NATO. 1954
Surinam and the Netherlands Antilles are granted self-government but remain part of the Kingdom of the Netherlands.

Constitutional reform designed to limit government expenditure. 1956

Establishment of the European Economic Community. 1957

A customs and economic union of the Benelux states is established. The 1958 economic union comes into force on January 1st 1960.
Introduction of new social insurance provisions, including a state pension.

Educational reform: simplification of the school system. 1962

Crown Princess Beatrix (b. 1938) marries a German aristocrat, Claus von 1966 Amberg.

Birth of an heir to the throne, Prince Willem Alexander. 1967
The largest field of natural gas in the world is discovered in the province of Groningen.

New income law: regulation of wage settlements. 1970

Netherlands Guiana becomes independent as the Republic of Surinam. 1975
The "Ambonese" (Moluccans) stage terrorist attacks and take hostages in Amsterdam and at Wijster (Drenthe).

Prince Bernhard, Queen Juliana's husband, having been implicated in the 1976 "Lockheed affair", resigns all his public offices but remains a member of the Council of State.
Another hostage-taking by Moluccans at a school in Bovensmilde leads to strained relations between coloured minorities and the people of the Netherlands.

Another hostage-taking by Moluccans: a train hijack near Assen which is 1978 brought to an end by the army.

Economic stagnation. Cuts in state expenditure. "Plan 81", designed to 1979 reduce unemployment, fails to produce the desired effect.

Queen Juliana abdicates on age grounds and is succeeded by her eldest 1980 daughter, Beatrix.

A Parliamentary election results in the emergence of a new political force. 1981
The left-wing Liberal Democrats '66 gain a great electoral success and join the government.

A further election leads to the formation of a Grand Coalition. Rudolphus 1982 (Ruud) Lubbers becomes head of government.

The island of Aruba in the Caribbean is granted partial independence 1986 within the Kingdom of the Netherlands (January 1st).
Foreigners who have lived in the Netherlands for not less than five years are given the vote in local government elections.
The Oosterschelde storm-surge barrier, the most costly hydraulic engineering project in the world, comes into operation, completing the Delta Plan.

The first conference on the environment involving ministers from Euro- 1987 pean Community and EFTA countries is held in Noordwijk. The subjects discussed include prevention of air pollution, climatic change, protection of the soil, prevention of nuclear accidents and pollution of the sea.

History

<table>
<tr><td>1988</td><td>The speed limit on motorways is raised from 100km p.h./62 m.p.h. to 120km p.h./75 m.p.h.</td></tr>
<tr><td>1989</td><td>The government coalition breaks up because of disagreements over the financing of environmental protection (May).</td></tr>
</table>

1988   The speed limit on motorways is raised from 100km p.h./62 m.p.h. to 120km p.h./75 m.p.h.

1989   The government coalition breaks up because of disagreements over the financing of environmental protection (May).

On September 14th the Christian Democratic prime minister, Rudolphus Lubbers, is entrusted by the Queen with the task of forming another coalition. The Social Democratic Workers' Party returns to Parliament after eight years' absence.
The programme of the new coalition government provides for further decentralisation (i.e. an extension of the powers of local and provincial authorities as opposed to the central government), measures to reduce unemployment, European unification and the protection of the environment.

1990   Parliament passes a law extending the permitted opening times of shops. As from 1991 shops can stay open for half an hour longer on weekdays and an hour longer on Saturdays.

1991   In December the Heads of the twelve countries of the European Community meet in Maastricht and sign an agreement in principle on political, economic and monetary union.

Famous People

Karel Appel, a native of Amsterdam, is one of the best known and most controversial Dutch painters of the period since the Second World War. He received his first important commission in 1949, when he painted a mural, "Vragende Kinderen" ("Questioning Children"), for the Amsterdam Town Hall – a picture which provoked such a storm that it had to be covered over for a time.

In 1950 Appel settled in Paris and became associated with the international experimental school. He was one of the founders of the COBRA group (named after the initial letters of its members' home towns – Copenhagen, Brussels and Amsterdam), to which such artists, now internationally known, as Corneille, Constant, Alechinsky, Asger Jorn and Lucebert belonged.

In the 1950s Appel's work featured in many important exhibitions and he received international distinctions and prizes, including the UNESCO Prize at the Venice Biennale in 1954 and the Guggenheim Prize in 1960.

His painting technique with its thick layers of paint in brilliant primary colours is reminiscent of naïve painting and the expressionistic art of the modern Primitives. There are many of his works in the Stedelijk Museum, Amsterdam.

Karel Appel
Dutch painter
(b. 1921)

Hendrik Petrus Berlage is one of the best known of modern Dutch architects. Born in Amsterdam, he studied in Zurich, worked for a time in Frankfurt am Main and travelled to Italy. Practising as an independent architect, he developed an individual style – a severe style which concealed nothing – which had great influence both in the Netherlands and beyond. Among his most celebrated works are the Amsterdam Commercial Exchange (1898–1903), the bridge over the Amstel which bears his name and the Gemeentemuseum in The Hague. He also designed chairs and other furniture.

Hendrik Petrus
Berlage
Dutch architect
(1856–1934)

Comenius (Jan Amos Komensky), a Slovak from Moravia, was an early reformer in the field of education. His object was to make it possible for all to get a general education, and his ideas were expounded in his writings, which form an encyclopedic survey of the knowledge of his time.

His most famous work, "Orbis sensualium pictus", the earliest known edition of which was published in Nürnberg in 1654, was the first European schoolbook based on the modern principle of visual instruction. On each page is a woodcut, with an explanation in simple language (in Latin and Dutch) below it.

Comenius died in Amsterdam in 1670 and is buried in the Noorderkerk.

Johannes Amos
Comenius
Slovak
educationalist
(1592–1670)

Desiderius Erasmus, known as Erasmus of Rotterdam, was born in Rotterdam, the second child of an illegitimate union between a priest from Gouda named Rutger Gerard and the daughter of a doctor. Losing his parents at the age of 14, Erasmus studied in Deventer and 's-Hertogenbosch and in 1487 entered Steyn monastery. After being ordained as a priest in 1492 he became secretary to the bishop of Cambrai. In 1499–1500 he studied in Paris, where he learned Greek and came into contact for the first time with the ideas of humanism. His first visit to England alienated him from scholasticism. Then followed an unsettled period, during which he stayed briefly in Louvain (Belgium), Italy, England and Basle. Returning to Louvain, he came into conflict with the professors of theology. After the Reformation Erasmus fled in 1529 to Freiburg (south-western Germany), but returned in 1535 to Basle.

Opinions on Erasmus differ widely. Some see him as a strict Catholic, since in his youth he belonged to the Catholic reform movement known as

Desiderius
Erasmus
Dutch scholar
and writer
(1469–1536)

Famous People

Comenius

Erasmus

Van Gogh

Devotio Moderna, which preached a practical Christianity of loving service. For others he is a great humanist, in virtue of his satirical attacks on the church and the theology of the day. His dispute with Luther marked a break between the Reformation and humanism.

Erasmus was not only a critic of the church and of contemporary life but a considerable writer. His first work, "Antibarbari" (1492), reflected humanist ideas. From his time in Paris date "Adagia" (a collection of maxims and proverbs) and "Colloquia" ("Conversations"). In 1511 appeared his best known work, "Laus stultitiae" ("The Praise of Folly"). Other works include his "Novum Instrumentum" (1516; a Greek translation of the New Testament) and "De libero arbitrio" (1524; "On Free Will").

The Praemium Erasmianum (Erasmus Prize), founded in 1958 under the patronage of Prince Bernhard, is awarded to persons or institutions which have contributed to strengthening the European consciousness or enriching European culture. Recipients of the prize, which amounts to 100,000 fl, have included politicians, artists and scholars.

Anne Frank
(1929–45)

Anne Frank, a Jewish girl of German origin, became internationally known with the publication of her "Diary", which has been translated into many languages and made the subject of a film.

The Frank family fled from Frankfurt to Amsterdam in 1933 to escape Nazi persecution, and throughout the German occupation during the Second World War lived in hiding in a house in the city. During this period (June 12th 1942 to August 1st 1944) Anne kept a diary, which ended when the whole family were discovered and sent to the Belsen concentration camp. Anne and her sister died in Belsen, their mother in Auschwitz; only their father survived. After the liberation of Amsterdam Anne's diary was found in the family's hiding-place and published.

Vincent van Gogh
Dutch painter
(1853–90)

Vincent van Gogh, the son of a pastor, was born in Zundert, near Breda. After working for an art dealer in The Hague he became a lay preacher in the mining district of Borinage in southern Belgium. In 1883, having been dismissed from his mission, he turned to painting, depicting the peasants and workers of his home district in heavy forms and dark colours. To this first period (his "Brabant period") belongs "The Potato-Eaters". Van Gogh deliberately depicts peasant life in all its coarseness, using his choice of colours to reinforce the effect. In 1886 he went to Paris, where his brother Théo was a successful art dealer, and came into contact with many artists, including Gauguin. He now adopted the painting techniques of Impressionism, also leaning briefly towards Pointillisme. The colours of his still lifes and portraits now became brighter and the forms less heavy, with sharp highlights. Then, after moving in 1886 to Arles and later to Auvers-

Mata Hari

Alfred Heineken

Rembrandt

sur-Oise, he evolved his own completely new style, painting landscapes and townscapes, still lifes (particularly sunflowers) and portraits in brilliant expressive colours, applied with coarse brush-strokes. After suffering several intermittent attacks of mental trouble he was finally admitted to a mental home at St-Rémy, where he continued to work at high pressure, with the courage of despair, until his death by his own hand at the age of 37. During his lifetime Van Gogh made little impression on the public and was dependent on financial help from his brother. It was only some decades after his death that he was recognised as an artist who had gone beyond Impressionism and inspired the new school of Expressionism. His pictures, notably "Sunflowers" and "Bridge at Arles", now command astronomic prices at auction.

The Frisian dancer and alleged spy Mata Hari was born Margaretha Geer-truida Zelle in Leeuwarden (Grote Kerkstraat 28). The daughter of a well-to-do citizen who was reduced to poverty, she sought from an early age to escape from the cramping circumstances of life in her small home town. She went to The Hague and after some time married an officer of good family, with whom she spent several years in Dutch overseas territories. Returning to Europe, she made her debut in Paris as a "free dancer", concealing her identity under the exotic pseudonym of Mata Hari. In 1914 she appeared in the Theatre Royal in The Hague.

Mata Hari
Dutch dancer
(1876–1917)

Even during her lifetime legends gathered round her career. Her love affairs with both French and German officers during the First World War led to her being suspected of espionage, and in February 1917 she was arrested by the French counter-espionage service. Although her guilt could not be conclusively proved, she was guillotined in October of that year.

"Freddy" Heineken was born in 1924 to a family with a brewing tradition going back to 1873 which determined his own career. He began work in the family firm in 1942, and in 1946 went to the United States to establish a branch of the firm and promote exports. In 1964 he became a member of the board, in 1969 vice-chairman and in 1971 chairman. In 1983 he became a knight in the Order of the Netherlands Lion and in the following year he was appointed *chevalier* in the French Legion of Honour.

Alfred Henry
Heineken
Dutch brewer
(b. 1924)

The Heineken brewery has a market share of two-thirds of Dutch beer consumption and a worldwide export market (sometimes under different names) in over 170 countries. This success is largely due to Freddy Heineken. In 1967 he entered into a co-operative agreement with one of the largest French brewing firms, and in 1968 Heineken bought the Amstel brewery.

The firm has a variety of other interests – the production of fruit juices, mineral waters, spirits and malt, the import and export of wine and other alcoholic drinks, the Horeca chain of hotels, restaurants and cafés. Its annual turnover is more than 2 billion guilders.

Joris Ivens
Film director
(1898–1969)

Joris Ivens, nicknamed the "Flying Dutchman", was born in Nijmegen, the son of a photographer. After studying in Rotterdam and Berlin, where he made the acquaintance of Wassily Kandinsky and Bertold Brecht, he became technical director of the family firm, Capi, in 1926. He was one of the founders of the avant-garde Amsterdam Film League. His first short film, "The Bridge" (1927), and the later "Surf" and "Rain" contain typically Dutch themes to which he constantly recurred in his later work – rain, wind, stormy seas and man's struggle with nature. His film "New Earth" (1943), on the draining of the Zuiderzee, continued the series.

Although Ivens ranks as a classic of the documentary film, his subjective presentation of his subject also leaves room for poetry and imagination. Essentially a cosmopolitan, he shot most of his films outside the Netherlands, and by the 1960s had already become a legend. There was scarcely a theatre of war in modern times where he was not to be found. He was also concerned to document social, political and economic problems, as in his "Borinage" (1934), on a Belgian miners' strike. After his film "Indonesia Calls" he was branded as a traitor because he did not represent the interests of the colonial power. He was completely rehabilitated only in 1985, when he was awarded the Grand Culture Prize by the Netherlands government.

From 1968 Ivens lived mainly in Paris. He shot his last film, "A Story of the Wind" (shown at the Venice Film Festival in 1988), at the age of 89 in China, accompanied by his lifelong companion Marceline Loridan. He died in Paris after seventy years of film-making.

Joseph Marie
Antoine Hubert
Luns
Dutch politician
(b. 1911)

Joseph Luns, born in Rotterdam, studied law in Leiden and Amsterdam and economics in London. A member of the Catholic People's Party, he was involved in diplomacy from 1938 to 1952, promoting European integration – in the Foreign Ministry and as a diplomat in Berne, Lisbon and at the United Nations. In 1952 he became a minister without portfolio, assisting the foreign minister, and from 1956 to 1971 was himself foreign minister. The climax of his political career was his appointment as Secretary General of NATO in 1971. He retired from that post in 1985 and since then has lived in Brussels.

Gerard Leonard
Frederik Philips
Engineer and
businessman
(1858–1942)

Gerard L. P. Philips, a mechanical engineer, was born in Eindhoven and began his career as a representative of German electric power companies. In 1891, together with his brother Anton Frederik, he founded the firm known from 1912 as the Philips Gloeilampenfabrieken which originally manufactured light bulbs. In 1922 he retired and handed over the chairmanship of the firm to his brother.

The Philips works are now one of Europe's largest electrical concerns, operating in more than 72 countries throughout the world. Their production has been extended from lighting products to television sets, electronic components, consumer electronics and domestic equipment.

Rembrandt
Harmensz
van Rijn
Dutch painter
(1606–69)

The most celebrated Dutch painter, Rembrandt van Rijn, was born in Leiden and after a productive period of creative activity there moved in 1632 to Amsterdam. In 1634 he married Saskia van Uylenburgh, a wealthy woman of good family. In 1639 he bought a house (the Rembrandthuis) in Jodenbreestraat.

During his first ten years in Amsterdam Rembrandt became the most popular portrait-painter of the day, and almost two-thirds of his commissioned portraits date from this period. He was able to satisfy his sitters' desire for prestige portraits without sacrificing the delineation of character. In addition to his impressive portraits (e.g. of Burgomaster Six), group portraits ("The Anatomy Lesson of Dr Tulp") and self-portraits (double portrait with Saskia; the painter as the prodigal son) he produced pictures of equal quality on Biblical themes and later also landscapes.

Spinoza   *Joost van den Vondel*   *William I*

When Rembrandt increasingly refused to subordinate his artistic intentions to his sitters' desire for a grand portrait, commissions began to fall off, and his "Night Watch" was turned down by those who had commissioned it.

After the death of his wife in 1642 Rembrandt became involved in personal and financial difficulties, and in 1656 his house and possessions were sold by auction. His son Titus and Hendrickje Stoffels, with whom he now lived, acted from 1660 as art dealers for the sale of his works, but for the rest of his life he was burdened with debt and living in increasing artistic and social isolation: his wall painting for the new Town Hall of Amsterdam, "The Conspiracy of the Batavians", was rejected by the municipality.

When Rembrandt died he was buried outside the Westerkerk, and only later were his remains moved to a tomb inside the church.

Rembrandt left 562 paintings, 300 etchings and 1600 drawings. His best known works are the "Night Watch" (1642), the "Anatomy Lesson of Dr Tulp" (1632), "The Syndics of the Drapers' Guild" (1661–62) and the "Jewish Bride" (1665), all in the Rijksmuseum in Amsterdam; his best known self-portrait is in the Mauritshuis (The Hague); and almost all his etchings and many of his drawings are to be seen in the Rembrandthuis in Amsterdam.

The works of Baruch de Spinoza, a native of Amsterdam, had a great influence on western philosophy, including Fichte and Hegel. Spinoza was a rationalist whose metaphysical views were arrived at by mathematical reasoning from definitions and axioms. This ran counter to his Biblical and Talmudic training in the Jewish community of Amsterdam, which in 1656 excommunicated him. In 1673 he turned down the offer of a chair at Heidelberg University.

His best known work, "Ethics, presented by Geometric Methods", was written about 1662 but not published until 1677.

Spinoza's house in The Hague, where he died in 1677, has been occupied since 1927 by the Spinoza Institute.

Baruch
(Benedictus)
de Spinoza
Dutch philosopher
(1632–77)

Joost van den Vondel, the greatest Dutch poet of the Renaissance, was born in Cologne. His work covers a wide range, including satirical, historical, patriotic and religious poems and 32 plays, the best known of which are "Gijsbreght van Aemstel" (1637) and "Lucifer" (1654). He also translated the Psalms, Ovid and Virgil into Dutch.

Vondel, who took an active part in the political and ecclesiastical controversies of his day and in 1641 became a convert to Catholicism, died in Amsterdam at the age of 91. The city's largest park is named after him.

Famous People

**William I
of Orange
Stadholder
(1533–84)**

Prince William I of Orange, known as William the Silent, was born in Dillenburg (Hesse, Germany), the eldest son of Count William I of Nassau-Dillenburg and his wife Juliana von Stolberg-Wernigerode. Although a Protestant, he received a Catholic education at the court of Charles V's sister Maria, Stadholder-General of the Netherlands, in Brussels. He became the ruling Prince of Orange in 1544. He was married several times – to Anna van Buren in 1551, Anne of Saxony in 1561 (divorced 1571), Charlotte de Bourbon in 1575 and Louise de Coligny in 1583.

In 1561 William, together with Counts Egmond and Hoorn, led Dutch opposition to Philip II's introduction of the Inquisition, and during the first half of the war of independence played the leading role. It was he who initiated the petition of the Dutch nobility to the Spanish government. After some early failures, including the unsuccessful attempt to take Brabant, his efforts to achieve independence and freedom of religious belief for the Netherlands were rewarded by the union of all the Dutch provinces in 1576. Soon after being declared an outlaw by Philip II William was assassinated in the Prinsenhof in Delft by a Catholic named Balthasar Gérard.

**William of Holland
German king
(1227–56)**

William of Holland was the son of Count Floris IV of Holland and his wife Elizabeth of Brunswick-Lüneburg. After the deposition of the Emperor Frederick II by Pope Innocent IV for sacrilege and oath-breaking the Pope appointed William of Holland in 1247 as successor to the anti-king Heinrich Raspe and he was crowned at Aachen in 1248. When the Rhenish League of Cities was established in 1254 to maintain peace and order in the absence of an Emperor William became its head. Before setting out for Rome to be crowned as Emperor he undertook a winter campaign against the West Frisians, during which he was killed.
Perhaps his most important legacy to the people of the Netherlands was the building of the Knights' Hall in the Binnenhof in The Hague.

**William III
of Orange
Stadholder of
the Netherlands
and king of
England
and Scotland
(1650–1702)**

Prince William III of Orange was born in The Hague and brought up for a time by the Grand Pensionary, Jan de Witt. In 1674 he became hereditary Stadholder of the Netherlands and in that capacity successfully resisted the attempt by Louis XIV (Dutch War, 1672–79) to establish French predominance in Europe.
In 1677 he married the Stuart princess Mary, whose father, a Catholic, became king of England and Scotland as James II in 1685. In 1688 William landed in England and drove out James II, whereupon Parliament recognised William and Mary as joint monarchs. When William died childless in 1702 the title of Prince of Orange passed to his grand-nephew Johan Willem Friso, Count of Nassau and Stadholder of Friesland.

Art and Culture

In this section the term Netherlands applies to the present-day country of that name; the term Low Countries is used in the old sense, covering present-day Belgium as well as the Netherlands.

Art

Prehistory and Early Historical Period

The territory of the present-day Netherlands has been inhabited since prehistoric times. The earliest finds date back 6000 years (Bandkeramik ware from Limburg). The *hunebedden* ("giants' beds"; megalithic tombs) of the TRB (Funnel-Beaker) culture date from the 3rd and 2nd millennia B.C. From the Bronze Age onwards (900 B.C.) the dead were buried in burial mounds. The Iron Age (750–500 B.C.) is represented by material of the Hallstatt culture. Between 500 and 250 B.C. Germanic tribes (mainly Batavians) began to penetrate ever farther into the territories on the left bank of the Rhine, where they encountered a Celtic people, the Belgae. In 58 B.C. the region was conquered by Julius Caesar (see his account in the "Gallic War") and came under Roman rule, though there are few remains of this period.

Among the many fine collections of prehistoric and Roman antiquities are the Provincial Museum in 's-Hertogenbosch, the National Museum of Archaeology in Leiden and the Bonnefanten Museum in Maastricht.

Museums

After the fall of the West Roman Empire the country was occupied by Salian Franks. Around A.D. 480 the Netherlands became part of the Frankish kingdom. The region was Christianised at least as early as the 6th century, and Utrecht became the see of a bishop in 696.

Carolingian art

Under the Carolingians the Frankish kingdom was consolidated, as is shown by the royal strongholds and the monasteries built during this period. In Nijmegen there still survive the palatine chapel of St Nicholas in the Valkhof, modelled on Charlemagne's chapel in Aachen, which was consecrated by Pope Leo III in 799, and an apse probably dating from 1155.

Romanesque

Under the Carolingians German influence was at first predominant, and in the Maas valley in particular influences from the Rhineland are readily detectable. Here widely famed goldsmiths and brass founders were at work, producing works of art which found their way all over the Christian West. A notable example of their work is the reliquary of St Servatius (12th c.) in St Servaaskerk in Maastricht.

Art in the Maas region

The finest example of monumental Romanesque church architecture is St Servaaskerk in Maastricht, probably the oldest church in the Netherlands (begun in the 6th century; nave and eastern crypt much altered around 1000), with a west porch which is believed to date from Carolingian times. The transept and choir date from the early 11th century; the south doorway and north cloister are Gothic.

Churches

The Church of Our Lady in Maastricht, built in the 11th century on a Roman substructure, still shows influence from the Rhineland in its massive west

work, originally designed for defence, with its fortress-like façade and almost total absence of openings (no windows or doorways). Another example is the church of St Amelberga in Susteren.

In the 12th century the massive architecture of early Romanesque loosens up a little. Examples of this are the church of Rolduc Abbey (Kerkrade) and the Church of Our Lady in Roermond. Notable Romanesque churches in the northern provinces are St Pieterskerk in Utrecht, St Lebuinuskerk in Deventer and the St Plechelmus Basiliek in Oldenzaal. Romanesque churches are also found in Groningen and Friesland from the mid 12th century onwards: brick-built, decorated internally with frescoes.

Bust of St Servatius Museum

The Catharijneconvent Museum in Utrecht displays numerous examples of Christian art in the Romanesque period.

Gothic

Early Gothic in the Netherlands shows a fairly limited range of forms, and it is only later, in the 13th century, that it achieves a degree of luxuriance, in what is known as Brabantine Gothic. The finest example of this is St Janskathedraal in 's-Hertogenbosch, which was built between 1280 and 1412 on Romanesque foundations and altered in Late Gothic style in the 15th and 16th centuries. Its most notable features are the flying buttresses on the outside of the choir, a belfry with a carillon of 48 bells and choir-stalls of 1480. Another fine Late Gothic church is the aisled Grote Kerk of Breda (15th–16th c.), which has a 97m/318ft high belfry with a carillon of 49 bells.

Churches

In the north there are only a few churches with stone vaulting. For the most part they have flat timber roofs or timber vaulting over the nave. An exception is the Grote Kerk in Dordrecht. Only part of Utrecht Cathedral, built in 1254 on the site of an earlier (10th c.) Romanesque church, has survived; the nave, which was flanked by double aisles, was destroyed in a storm in 1674. The 112m/367ft high tower (1321–82; carillon of 46 bells), free-standing since the catastrophe, was built by Jan van Henegouwen and has a characteristic two-stage form which was frequently imitated. The massive Bovenkerk in Kampen (1369–1693) was designed by Rutger of Cologne. St Pieterskerk in Leiden, begun in 1338, has a rather old-fashioned air. Other examples are St Laurenskerk in Alkmaar, St Pancraskerk in Leiden, St Bavokerk in Haarlem, St Janskerk in Gouda and the Nieuw Kerk in Amsterdam. Also to be mentioned in this connection is the former Dominican church (consecrated 1294) in Maastricht, now used as a concert hall.

There are also numerous examples of secular buildings in Gothic style – town gates, cloth halls, belfries, guild-houses, town halls and burghers' houses. The best known are the town halls of Gouda, Middelburg and Haarlem. Also notable are Huis Oudaen and the Paushuize in Utrecht, Middelburg Abbey (now provincial government offices) and the town gates of Amersfoort, Kampen and Delft.

Secular buildings

Apart from the fine work produced by the brass founders of the Maas valley very few works of sculpture have survived from the medieval period. Notable examples of architectural sculpture are to be seen in the Church of Our Lady and St Servaaskerk in Maastricht (tympana and capitals c. 1170, west front first half of 14th c.). The Rijksmuseum in Amsterdam also has a number of interesting pieces of sculpture. Only a few altarpieces of the Romanesque and Gothic period survived the destruction of images by the Reformers. Also of interest in this connection are St Janskathedraal in 's-Hertogenbosch and the Church of Our Lady in Roermond. There are also some fine carved wooden choir-stalls dating from this period.

Sculpture

◀ The tower of Utrecht Cathedral, the highest in the Netherlands

The Romanesque church of St Servatius, Maastricht

Painting
Hieronymus Bosch

The greatest painter of the 15th century in the Netherlands was Hieronymus Bosch (1450–1516), who made a radical break with tradition and cannot be assigned, either in technique or in style, to any previously known school. He developed a very distinctive style of his own in allegorical pictures of almost limitless fantasy, swarming with figures and painted with extreme exactitude, combining sharp realism with fascinating and often perverse grotesquerie and malicious satire. His pictures, usually religious in content, are almost impossible to interpret. They have a dreamlike and indeed nightmarish quality, though the details are often appealingly playful. Among his leading works are the triptych known as "The Garden of Earthly Delights", the "Last Judgment" and the "Hay-Wain". Another painter of the period is Geertgen tot Sint Jans of Leiden.

Renaissance

Architecture

The Renaissance could make its way only gradually in the Netherlands in face of the rich traditions of the earlier period. At the end of the 15th century churches were still being built in Gothic style, such as the Grote Kerk (St Bavokerk) in Haarlem. At first (beginning of 16th c.) only decorative forms were taken over from the new style.

Lieven de Key (*c.* 1560–1627) built the Stadhuis in Leiden and the Vleeshal in Haarlem, one of the finest examples of Dutch Renaissance architecture (originally 1603; partly restored after a fire in 1929). Hendrick de Keyser (1565–1621) built the Zuiderkerk (1603–11) in Amsterdam and the Town Hall (1618) of Delft.

Other examples of Renaissance architecture are the Town Hall of The Hague, the Weigh-House in Hoorn and the Westerkerk in Amsterdam. There are also a number of notable buildings of this period in Friesland, including the town halls of Bolsward and Franeker, the Kanselarij (Courthouse) in Leeuwarden and the town gate of Sneek.

The art of faience came to the Netherlands from Italy in the late 16th century, gradually becoming established and reaching its peak in the 17th century. Particularly famous is Delft ware, with a strong white tin glaze and painted decoration (commonly in cobalt blue), with motifs frequently taken from Japanese and Chinese models (*chinoiserie*), but also with genre scenes of Dutch life. The main products were vases, wall and floor tiles and decorative plates.

In the field of painting the influence of the Renaissance increased in the 16th century. Painters of the school known as the Romanists were under strong Italian influence, though they still retained something of the restlessness of Late Gothic with its sense of new beginnings. The Mannerists, naturally also indebted to the late Renaissance painting of Florence, gave expression to the spiritual turmoil and tension of the Counter-Reformation. A leading Romanist was Jan van Scorel (1495–1562), who became curator of the Papal collection of antiquities in the Belvedere and then returned to Utrecht and Haarlem (paintings of biblical history, portraits).
The finest work of Lucas van Leyden (1494–1533) is represented by his etchings ("Ecce Homo"); he shows less originality as a painter, strongly influenced by Dürer.
Among leading Mannerists were Carel van Mander (1548–1606), who was also an art historian ("Het Schilder-Boeck"), Hendrik Goltzius (1558–1617) and Cornelis Cornelisz, whose "Massacre of the Innocents" was a landmark in the development of group painting.

Baroque

The old-established differences between the northern and southern parts of the Low Countries, which had been increasing since the Renaissance, were exacerbated by the religious and political separation between them in the late 16th century. From about 1600 Flemish and Dutch art began to follow separate paths. This period coincided with the achievement of independence by the northern provinces and the great flowering of the Dutch economy known as the Golden Age.

The Baroque architecture of the Netherlands reflected the influence of Palladio and was much more severely classical than the architecture of Flanders. It was stamped by the personality of Jacob van Campen (1595–1657), who built the old Town Hall (1648; now the Royal Palace) in Amsterdam, the Nieuwe Kerk in Haarlem and the Mauritshuis in The Hague.
Pieter Post (1608–69) built Huis ten Bosch in The Hague, now the residence of the royal family, and the Town Hall in Maastricht. Other notable architects were Philip Vinckeboons (1607–87) and the Husly family. Many houses on the Amsterdam *grachten*, such as the Trippenhuis on the Kloveniersburgwal, also date from this period. Daniël Marot and Jacob Roman built the hunting lodge (later a royal palace) of Het Loo at Apeldoorn for Prince William III.
This architectural tradition continued into the 18th century, though the French classical influence became increasingly permeated by Baroque.

Sculpture was also under strong Italian influence. Hendrick de Keyser, noted as an architect for his boldly conceived towers, was also a sculptor; notable among his work in this field was his impressive monument to William the Silent in Delft (1608–19) and the tomb of Engelbert II of Nassau in the Grote Kerk in Breda. The tradition of showy marble tombs continued into the 18th century.
During this period many churches were equipped with carved wooden pulpits, choir screens (Enkhuizen) and choir-stalls (Dordrecht).
Among other important sculptors who worked in the Netherlands were two Belgians, Artus Quellinus (Royal Palace, Amsterdam) and Rombout Verhulst (tomb monuments).

Art

Painting

During the 17th century the painting of the Low Countries held the leading position among the countries north of the Alps, as it had in the 15th century. Its two leading representatives, Rubens in the Catholic south and Rembrandt in the Protestant north, incarnate the different characters of Flemish and Dutch art, now following separate courses. These two small countries produced an extraordinary abundance of outstanding painters whose influence often continued to be felt into the 19th century.

Frans Hals

Around the turn of the 16th and 17th centuries numerous painters were at work in the Netherlands, the most notable of whom, after Rembrandt, was Frans Hals (1580–1666), a pupil of Carel van Manders, who painted scenes from everyday middle-class life, genre scenes, portraits and group portraits of town guards. He developed the group portrait to achieve a variety of presentation and an accurate delineation of character previously unknown (Frans Hals Museum, Haarlem). He captures the reality of the passing moment and achieves almost impressionistic effects with his seemingly hasty brush-strokes.

Rembrandt

The towering artistic personality of Dutch Baroque painting was Rembrandt Harmensz van Rijn (1609–69), who worked first in Leiden and later in Amsterdam. His life was full of conflicts and vicissitudes, but as the most powerful and most versatile genius of the Baroque period he was the undisputed leader of his time, both as a painter and as a graphic artist. His etchings of landscapes follow in the footsteps of Hercules Seghers (1589–1645).

The subjects of Rembrandt's paintings cover the whole range of his period, but particularly portraits and Biblical scenes. Interiors are dramatised by contrasts between light and shade: Rembrandt carries chiaroscuro, indirectly derived from Caravaggio, to the peak of perfection. Facial expressions reflect inner conflict. Stark naturalism and extreme spiritualisation

Meat Hall, Haarlem

Rembrandt's "Night Watch"

Frans Hals's "Regentesses of the Old Men's Almshouses"

alternate with phases of mild serenity. All his life Rembrandt was concerned with self-portraiture to an extent matched by no other artist. Many of his drawings, often with a heavy wash, and well over 300 etchings are known to us.

Rembrandt carried to its highest peak the group portrait – that typical expression of Dutch civic pride, which had been developed with such mastery by Bartholomeus van der Helst (1613–70) and Frans Hals.

His famous "Night Watch", depicting a company of the town guard, encountered a hostile reception from the public for its treatment of light; and in his later years he was so far out of line with contemporary taste that he was thought little of in the later 17th century and subsequent periods. His true greatness was not fully appreciated until the late 19th century, since when there has been a steady development of research and study of his work.

The third great Dutch master of the 17th century was Jan van der Meer, known as Vermeer of Delft (1632–75), who, compared with Rembrandt, left only a small body of work (some 40 paintings). His special genius was expressed in the realistic depiction of interiors – clean and comfortable burghers' houses, with only a few figures, usually engaged in undemanding domestic activities, such as the "Young Woman Reading a Letter", the "Lace-Maker" and the "Kitchen Maid". Vermeer was an outstanding master of technique, and his paintings, which are mostly of small size, are of great charm in their use of colour (a delicate light blue, lemon-yellow). Also famous are his only two landscapes, the "View of Delft" and "Street in Delft".

Vermeer

A sensation was caused after the Second World War by the revelation that numbers of false Vermeers had been painted by the highly skilled forger

Hans van Meegeren, whose work had deceived leading art experts. The "Christ at Emmaus" in the Boymans–Van Beunigen Museum in Rotterdam was unmasked in 1945 as a fake painted by Van Meegeren in 1936.

Other painters

Among other major painters of the period were Pieter de Hooch (1629–84); Jan Steen (1626–79), a master of genre painting with an unerring eye for the human comedy; Adriaen van Ostade (1610–85), another master of genre painting, with strong chiaroscuro effects, and of etching; Gerard ter Borch or Terborch (1617–81), also a genre painter, who set his scenes mainly in elegant burghers' houses; and Jacob van Ruisdael (1630–81), who painted vast open landscapes with heavy clouds and a feeling of sombre solitude.

The stream of talent began to dry up towards the end of the 17th century. The great traditions of the past were carried on during the 18th century by competent craftsmen including Jan van Huysum (1682–1749) with his richly coloured flower paintings, without any power of their own to achieve further development or renewal.

18th and 19th centuries

18th century Dutch art reflects the decline which set in after the great flowering of the 17th century.

Architecture

Until the middle of the 18th century the archaeological styles of the 17th century and French influences continued to prevail. The second half of the century showed signs of the decline which continued well into the following century.
In the 19th century, as in other European countries, Historicism (the simultaneous imitation of different historical styles) predominated in the Netherlands, influencing the style even of dwelling-houses in the larger towns. A leading architect of the period was P. J. H. Cuypers (1827–1921), who stood at the turning-point from Historicism to modern architecture. Among his most notable buildings were the Central Station and the Rijksmuseum in Amsterdam.

Sculpture

Historicism found a fertile field in sculpture. Among sculptors of the period were J. Mendes da Costa (1863–1939), L. Zijl (1866–1947) and P. Pander.

Painting

Considerable artistic personalities began to appear only at the turn of the century – artists such as Jozef Israëls (1824–1911), who had affinities with the French Barbizon school; the Impressionist Johan Barthold Jongkind (1819–91); the members of the Hague School, who combined representations of nature and genre scenes with neo-classical reminiscences of the 17th century; and such well known painters as G. H. Breitner (1857–1923). F. Vester and Jan Toorop (1858–1928).

19th and 20th centuries

Architecture
H. P. Berlage

The work of Hendrik Petrus Berlage (1856–1934) marks the beginning of modern architecture. Notable examples of his style are the Commercial Exchange (Koopmansbeurs, 1898–1903; unfinished) in Amsterdam and the St Hubertus hunting lodge (with complete interior furnishings) in the Hoge Veluwe, near Arnhem.

Amsterdam
School

Berlage founded the Amsterdam School, which broke completely away from the eclecticism of the 19th century (Scheapvaarthuis in Amsterdam, 1914;. W. Kromhout, Th. Sluyterman and L. A. H. Wolf worked in the Art Nouveau style. Berlage's work was carried on by M. de Klerk, as well as P. L. Kramer and M. van der Mey (who distanced himself from Berlage and tended towards Expressionism).

Piet Blom's "cube houses"

Zadkine's "Destroyed City"

Sculpture Park, Kröller-Müller Museum

Art

De Stijl

The foundation of the group known as De Stijl attracted architects with a leaning towards Cubism. These include J. J. P. Oud (1890–1963), R. van 't Hoff, J. Wils and G. T. Rietveld (1888–1964), who collaborated with T. van Doesburg and played a major part in the foundation of CIAM (the Congrès Internationaux d'Architecture Moderne). Doesburg's ideas were carried on by the Abstraction – Création group in Paris.

Functionalism

In addition to J. J. P. Oud many leading Dutch architects subscribed to the ideas of western European functionalism, increasing the international impact of modern Dutch architecture. The romantic tendencies of the Amsterdam school were now left behind.

One very individual personality was W. M. Dudok (1884–1974), who designed brick buildings of massive bulk (Hilversum Town Hall) and was influenced by the American architect Frank Lloyd Wright. The Delft School (Enschede Town Hall, 1933), founded by C. M. Granpré Molière, played a major part in reconstruction after the Second World War.

After its destruction during the war Rotterdam became a centre of building and planning activity, thanks to the work of such men as J. S. Bakema (first pedestrian precinct in Europe) and J. H. van den Broek, who developed a new functionalism. The ideas of CIAM took on a fresh lease of life. The views of the Delft School continued to prevail in the building of Catholic churches. The large numbers of modern buildings erected, however, soon led to the development of a kind of routine style, with few architects of outstanding quality. Team X, Aldo van Eijk and the Forum group tried to find new patterns of urban development. Herman Hertzberger designed the new Music Centre in Utrecht and the offices of the Centraal Beheer insurance company in Apeldoorn.

Sculpture

The sculpture of the first half of the 20th century was less impressive than the architecture. After the Second World War, however, it received a fresh stimulus from numerous public commissions. Sculptors of this period included J. Raedecker, H. Krop, C. van Pallandt, M. Andriessen (the "Dock Worker"), W. Couzijn, V. P. Esser, G. Romijn and S. Tajiri, a Japanese American working in the Netherlands. The striking monument in Rotterdam to the "Destroyed City" was the work of the Russian/French sculptor Ossip Zadkine (1954).

Painting
Van Gogh

Around the turn of the century the break with tradition was finally consummated, most notably in the work of Vincent van Gogh (1853–90), who became one of the earliest exponents of Expressionism and also influenced the Fauves. With his troubled personal life, van Gogh gave expression to his inner anxieties in his seemingly flickering brush-strokes. His sharp, harsh colours, thickly applied, betray deep emotion and a passionate obsession (landscapes, particularly of Provence; portraits, still lifes). Once again Dutch painting had won a leading role; but the variety and international character of modern trends militated against the evolution of unified national styles.

Jan Sluijters (1881–1957) was another painter of the period who inclined towards Expressionism.

Piet Mondriaan

One of the pace-setters in modern painting was Piet Mondriaan (1872–1944), who became acquainted with Cubism in Paris and paved the way for

Types of gable on *gracht* houses

Stepped gable   Beak gable   Neck gable

the development of abstract painting in the Netherlands by his creation of Neo-Plasticism. He was co-founder in 1917, with Theo van Doesburg, of the journal "De Stijl". He worked mainly with primary colours, and his aesthetic principles influenced painting, architecture, sculpture and design in equal measure. In 1940 he emigrated to New York, where he found a wide response and exerted a powerful influence on the development of North American painting after the Second World War.

Willem de Kooning (b. 1904), who went to the United States in 1926, is a typical representative of Abstract Expressionism and Action Painting.

Other artists and schools

The graphic artist and painter Hendrik Werkmann (1882–1945), whose importance in the field of artistic typography has only now been recognised, was shot by the Gestapo shortly before the end of the Second World War. Another interesting graphic artist was M. C. Escher (1898–1972), whose Mannerist-seeming work combined abstract sculpture, illusionistic effects and an anticipation of Pop Art.

C. Willink (1900–83) propagated the new Realism (Neue Sachlichkeit). Two Dutch artists, Karel Appel (b. 1921) and Constant (C. A. Nieuwenhuys, b. 1920), founded an international group of artists called COBRA (from the places of origin of its members – Copenhagen, Brussels and Amsterdam) in Paris in 1948; the other members of the group were a Belgian, Pierre Alechinsky (b. 1927), Corneille (Cornelis van Beverloo, b. 1922), who worked in Paris and Amsterdam, and a Dane, Asger Jorn (A. Jorgensen, 1914–73).

Op Art developed after the Second World War out of abstract Constructivist trends; like Tachisme (Informel), it drew many of its ideas from Suprematism, De Stijl and Piet Mondriaan. The painter Edgar Ferhout (b. 1912) ranged from pure Realism to Tachisme. The COBRA group combined the restless and informal painting techniques of the postwar period with features derived from folk art, primitive art and Art Brut.

All the widely varying trends of the contemporary art scene, with their ever greater mingling of categories, the increasingly strong impact of the artist's personality, "actions", "happenings", the Fluxus movement, Process Art, etc., are represented in the Netherlands by numerous exponents.

Gracht Houses

Characteristic features of many Dutch towns are the *grachten* (canals lined by streets), which have earned Amsterdam, for example, the name of "Venice of the north". Originally designed as defensive moats, the *grachten* soon acquired importance as waterways for the transport of goods to and from the merchants' houses along their banks. In addition the *grachten*, only 2m/6½ft deep, served, and still serve, as a drainage system.

The buildings lining the *grachten* are closely packed together, for land was at a premium on the soil of the fenlands. The houses are tall and narrow, but also deep, so as to give each of them direct access to the *gracht*. With their façades in tones of brown and red, contrasting with the window-frames, which are often white, the *gracht* houses give variety and colour to the townscape.

Types of gable on *gracht* houses

Bell gable

Neo-classical gable

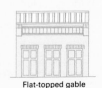
Flat-topped gable

Gable types

The gables, often elaborately shaped and decorated, contribute to this variety, giving each house a different aspect. Although there are only six basic types there are infinite variations and imaginative forms of ornament. The plainest type of gable, the "beak" gable, was mainly used on ordinary warehouses. The stepped gable predominated in the late 16th and early 17th centuries. The "neck" gable (sometimes called the "bottle" gable) formed a transition to the "bell" gable, which became the most popular form in the mid 17th century. Neo-classical types of gable came into favour around 1770. The central part of the gable might be richly ornamented; or sometimes a flat-topped gable was preferred.

Most of the gables and façades lean slightly forward. It was a requirement that the houses should be built in this way so as to facilitate the hoisting of furniture and other articles into the house. The steep and narrow staircases inside the house were quite unsuitable for carrying up heavy articles, which were hoisted up with the help of a pulley on the attic storey.

Literature

Origins

The boundary between the French-speaking and Dutch-speaking areas in the Low Countries runs across the middle of Belgium, and along this line a bilingual literature developed from the medieval period onwards, the Belgian literature written in Dutch being described as Flemish literature. In the Middle Ages Latin was used as the written language. Unlike the origins of the Flemish and French literature which developed in the 12th and 13th centuries in the territory that is now Belgium, the origins of Dutch literature cannot be clearly established because of a lack of manuscripts. The oldest known sentence in Dutch was written around 1100 by a Flemish copyist: "Hebban olla uogala nestas beginnan hinase hic enda thu" ("All the birds, except thee and me have begun to build nests"). Among the first books in the Dutch language are "Elckerlyc", "Mariken van Nieumeghen" and "Van den Vos Reinaerde".

Geuzenliederen

Pamphlet
literature

The Reformation led to a sharp division between Dutch and Flemish literature. The *geuzenliederen* of this period, which celebrated the revolt of the northern provinces against the Spaniards, gave rise to the Dutch national anthem "Wilhelmus", written by Philips van Marnix, Lord of Sint Aldegonde (1540–98). The controversies of the Reformation were reflected in a considerable pamphlet literature, the most notable product of which was a satire by Philips van Marnix directed against the Catholic church.

Renaissance
literature

After the capture of Amsterdam by the Spaniards in 1585 most of the prosperous burghers fled to the northern provinces, particularly to Amsterdam. During this period, when Flemish literature had lost its previous importance, the literature of the Renaissance began to develop in the Netherlands, reaching its finest flowering in the 17th century. The leading writers of this period were Pieter Corneliszoon Hooft (1581–1647), author of "Nederlandsche Historiën" and "Emblemata Amatoria" (sonnets, 1611); Gerhard Adriaensz Bredero (1585–1616); and Joost van den Vondel (1587–1679), the Dutch master of the Baroque drama.

The poet and statesman Jacob Cats (1577–1660) is famed for his numerous poems written in a popular and edifying vein. His works still occupy a privileged place in the library of a Dutch household.

Classical
literature

In the second half of the 17th century the influence of French classical literature penetrated into the Netherlands. The leading representatives of this trend were the dramatist L. Rotgans (1633–1710), Daniël Heinsius (1580–1655), who wrote the first Dutch novel of adventure, Belle van Zuylen, the lyric poet H. K. Poot (1689–1733) and P. Langendijk. Around 1720 a number of weekly journals (*spectatoriale geschriften*) began to diffuse the ideas of the Enlightenment. The outstanding literary figure of the period was Jan van Effen (1684–1735), whose principal work was "De Hollandsche Spectator".

From around 1770, under the influence of German, French and English models, Romantic literature began to develop in the Netherlands. Its leading representatives were R. Feith and W. Bilderdijk. The poet A. Staring countered the exuberance of the Romantic school with his cool sobriety. A less highflown brand of Romanticism is found in the works of E. J. Potgieter (1808–75), who was the leading literary critic of his day.

Romantic literature

The leading Dutch literary figure of the 19th century was Eduard Douwes-Dekker (1820–87), who wrote under the pseudonym Multatuli. He was not committed to any particular literary trend, and his works can thus be compared with those of the roughly contemporary Belgian lyric poet Guido Gezelle.

Multatuli

Around 1880 there came to the fore a group of young writers who called themselves the Beweging van Tachtig (the "Eighties Movement") and, inspired by French Naturalism and Impressionism on the one hand and English Romantic literature on the other, sought to give Dutch literature international significance. The chief representatives of the movement were W. J. T. Kloos (1859–1938), H. Gorter (1864–1927), A. Verwey (1865–1937) and J. van Eeden (1860–1932).

Beweging van Tachtig

In the first half of the 20th century many new trends emerged. The first of these was New Romanticism. The New Romantic poets – P. N. van Eyck (1887–1954), J. C. Bloem (1887–1966), M. Nijhoff (1894–1953) and G. Achterberg (1905–62) – used new stylistic features. The novelist A. van Schendel (1874–1946) also belonged to this school.

New Romanticism

Other writers of the period were M. ter Braak (1902–40) and E. du Perron (1899–1940), who was born in India. The works of A. de Vries were set in Drenthe, those of A. Coolen (1897–1961) and A. M. de Jong (1888–1943) in Brabant, those of H. de Man in the river country of Holland.

Expressionism reached the Netherlands about 1914. Outstanding writers of this school were F. Bordewijk (novels), S. Vestdijk (1897–1971) and H. Marsman (1899–1940). Simon Carmiggelt (1913–87) wrote humorous short stories, Hella S. Haasse (b. 1918) psychological novels and tales.

Expressionism

No Dutch book since the end of the Second World War has had such a worldwide readership as "Het Achterhuis" (1946), published in English as "The Diary of Anne Frank", the record of her life in the Amsterdam hideout where she was concealed from 1942 to 1944.

Anne Frank

In the 1950s a new generation of writers came to the fore, rejecting all formal principles in poetry and calling themselves the "Atonal" school. The best-known exponents of this trend are L. J. Swaanswijk and H. M. J. Claus. Details intended to shock are a characteristic feature of their prose and dramatic works, which veer towards Neo-Naturalism. Other writers of this school are W. F. Hermans (b. 1921), G. K. van het Reve (b. 1923), H. Mulisch (b. 1927) and Jan Wolkers (b. 1925).

"Atonal" literature

The leading representative of the Zeventigers ("Seventies") group is Heere Heeresma (b. 1932). Others on the younger literary scene are the novelists A. Burnier (b. 1931; women's problems) and Jaap Harten (b. 1930) and the lyric poet J. Bernief (b. 1937). Three other writers who should be mentioned are the essayists M. 't Hart and J. M. A. Biesheuvel and the literary critic K. Fens.

Zeventigers

A special position in the literary life of the Netherlands is occupied by Frisian literature. The first writer in the Frisian language was Gysbert Japicx (1603–66).

Frisian literature

Customs and Traditions

The folk traditions of the Netherlands find expression not so much in colourful parades and great popular festivals as in a variety of features forming a distinctive pattern of local colour, ranging from traditional costumes, picturesque old towns, windmills, carillons, mechanical organs and fields of flowers to traditional but unspectacular ways of life and customs.

One striking characteristic of the Dutch way of life is that people do not usually have curtains on the windows of their homes, so that passers-by can look right into the house.

Costumes

Dutch people's consciousness of tradition tends to be expressed in small everyday matters. There are still parts of the country, particularly in rural areas, where the wearing of traditional costumes is quite natural and common. Dutch traditional costumes for everyday wear are, of course, simple and practical, not to be compared with the elaborate costumes for special occasions found in Yugoslavia, Italy or France. Typical of many Dutch local costumes – most of which go back to the 18th and 19th centuries – are long baggy trousers for men, peaked or winged caps for women and the world-famed clogs. In the more prosperous areas the women may also wear valuable jewellery of gold, silver or red coral.

Country people wearing traditional costume can be seen particularly in Zeeland (South Beveland, Walcheren, Axel), Noord-Holland (Volendam, Marken, Huizen) and Friesland (Hindeloopen); but they may also be encountered in the provinces of Overijssel (Twente, Staphorst/Rouveen, Salland, Kampen), Flevoland (Urk), Gelderland, Utrecht (Bunschoten, Spakenburg), Zuid-Holland (Scheveningen, Katwijk) and Noord-Brabant (round Breda and 's-Hertogenbosch) and in northern Limburg.

Marken: folk dances on the ice

Carnival is an important event in only a few places, mostly along the frontier with Germany, where the influence of the Rhineland is felt (Venlo, Maastricht).

Carnival

Flower festivals and flower parades are popular events in the Netherlands.

Flower festivals

In the warmer months folk traditions and traditional costumes can be seen at the Alkmaar cheese market and in various little fishing towns.

One great ceremonial occasion in The Hague is the state opening of Parliament on Prinsjesdag, when the Queen drives to Parliament in a state coach with a royal escort.

Quotations

Baedeker's
"Belgium and
Holland:
Handbook for
Travellers"
(13th German ed.,
1875)

The kermises are the Dutchman's Carnival: they give him, particularly in the lower classes, a welcome opportunity to drink and enjoy himself. It is said that maidservants taking up employment sometimes make it a condition that they shall have a few days and nights free at kermis time. They spend these days with their sweethearts, and indeed sweethearts can be hired for the occasion; it is even said that two girls often share a sweetheart if the cost is too much for one. Swarms of persons of both sexes, inflamed by brandy, parade through the streets of the large towns in full daylight, with wild shouting and singing. In this respect the kermises are the darker side of Dutch life. – Booths selling waffles and *broedertjes* or *poffertjeskramen* drive a roaring trade during the kermis. The waffles are made in one part of the booth, and the other part is divided into small cells in which they are eaten. At the entrance to the booth a woman, usually of some presence, sits in front of a large pan with numerous round depressions, into which she adroitly throws the dough; this is soon baked, and the *broedertjes* (small round cakes) are taken out and laid out for sale.

Mention must also be made of the interesting national costumes, which except in the large towns have been preserved in Holland more than in any other country. They are particularly curious on the islands of Urk and Marken.

In some Dutch towns the custom prevails of affixing bulletins to the doors of houses in which persons are ill, in order that their friends may be apprised of the state of their health without knocking or ringing. A similar notice is usually displayed on houses belonging to the better classes after the birth of a child; it gives new information on the condition of the mother and child every morning for a period of nine days, for example *"De kraamvrouw en het kind zijn naar omstandigheden welvarende"* or *"De kraamvrouw en het kind hebben deze nacht redelyk wel doorgebragt"*, signifying that the mother and child are well or have had a good night. On visits to the mother and child (*kraamvisiten*) *kandeel* (a kind of mulled wine) is served to the visitors, with *kaneelkoekjes* (cinnamon cakes) and *muisjes* (sugared caraway seeds).

At Haarlem and Enkhuizen the birth of a child is announced by means of a *klopper*, a small placard adorned with red silk and lace. A small piece of white paper inserted into it signifies that the child is a girl. In the case of twins there are two *kloppers*.

Betrothals are concluded in the following manner. The young man asks the girl's parents for permission to enter the house (*acces vragen*), and then the young people are regarded as *geëngageerd;* that is, they live as bride and groom. As such an "engagement" is often lightly entered into, so it is not seldom dissolved. After the first proclamation there is held the *felicitatie*, when the families and friends of the bridal couple wish them joy in the bride's house. The invitation to this occasion takes the form of *bruidsuiker* (sweet cakes of all kinds) and *bruidstranen* ("bride's tears": a kind of spiced wine) sent to the guests beautifully wrapped up with decorated labels.

Funerals are announced by *aansprekers* (undertaker's men), dressed in black and wearing tall hats draped with crape, who go first to members of the family and friends and then round all the houses in the neighbourhood, with the words *"Wordt bekent gemaakt dat overleden is de Wel Edele Heer N. N. op de Prinsengracht"*, etc.

Scouring and scrubbing (*schoonmaken*) are a true passion with Dutch housewives. This happens once a week, usually on Saturdays. All the furniture and furnishings and the whole of the house itself, internally and externally, are swept and polished with woollen dusters, brushes, brooms and water – rooms and passages, doors and windows, even the street in front of the house. In the cleaning of the windows the maids use a hand-spray, which they operate very skilfully. On the upper floors they come out on to the windowsills and pour great quantities of water over the windows and the house. Spiders are regarded with particular aversion, and vermin are fortunately as rare as cobwebs.

Holland may be considered in many respects as the most wonderful country, perhaps, under the sun: it is certainly unlike every other. What elsewhere would be considered as impossible has here been carried into effect, and incongruities have been rendered consistent. "The house built upon the sand" may here be seen *standing;* neither Amsterdam nor Rotterdam has any better foundation than sand, into which piles are driven through many feet of superincumbent bog earth; and to form a correct idea of these and other wonderful cities and towns standing on the morass, one must not forget the millions of solid beams hidden under ground which support them. We speak contemptuously of anything which is held together by straws, yet a long line of coast of several provinces is consolidated by no other means than a few reeds intermixed with straw wisps, or woven into mats. Without this frail but effectual support, the fickle dunes, or sand-hills, would be driven about into the interior, and would overwhelm whole districts of cultivated land. In Holland the laws of nature seem to be reversed; the sea is higher than the land; the lowest ground in the country is 24 feet below high-water mark, and, when the tide is driven high by the wind, 30 feet! In no other country do the keels of the ships float above the chimneys of the houses, and nowhere else does the frog, croaking from among the bullrushes, look down upon the swallow on the house-top. Where rivers take their course, it is not in beds of their own choosing; they are compelled to pass through canals, and are confined within fixed bounds by the stupendous mounds imposed on them by *human art,* which has also succeeded in overcoming the everywhere else resistless impetuosity of the ocean: here, and nowhere else, does the sea appear to have half obeyed the command, "Thus far shalt thou go, and no farther".

The Dutchman may be said to have made even the wind his slave. It might be supposed that the universal flatness, and the absence of those elevations which afford shelter to other countries, would leave this at the mercy of every blast that blows, to sweep everything before it. So far is this from being the case, that not a breath of air is allowed to pass without paying toll, as it were, by turning a windmill. These machines are so numerous, that they may be said to be never out of sight in a Dutch landscape. In the suburbs of great cities they are congregated like armies of giants spreading out their broad arms, as if to protect the streets and houses which they overlook. With us they are rarely used except to grind corn: in Holland they are employed almost as variously as the steam-engine; they saw timber, crush rape-seeds for oil, grind snuff, beat hemp, etc.; but the principal service which they perform is in draining the land; and here the Dutch have most ingeniously set the wind to counteract the water. At least one half of the windmills have water-wheels attached to them, which act as pumps, and, by constantly raising the water into the canals, alone keep the low land dry and fit for cultivation and the habitation of man. As, however, experience has shown that a first-rate mill is advantageously applied to raise water only 1 ell (= 3ft 3in) at once, 3 or 4 are often planted in a row on stages one above the other, each pumping up the water to the stage above it. They are constructed of much larger dimensions than with us: a single sail is often 120 feet long, and the usual length is 80 feet. There are said to be 9000 windmills in Holland, and the annual cost of them is valued at 3,600,000 dollars.

Murray's
"Handbook for
Travellers on
the Continent"
(16th ed., 1867)

Quotations

Jan Campert
Dutch writer
(1902–43)

There is no land
so lovingly embraced by water
as, between the Westerschelde and Sloe,
the beach of Walcheren.

Albert Camus
French writer
(1913–60)
"The Fall"

This land inspires me. I love the people who throng the pavements, crushed between the houses and the water, hemmed in by veils of fog, by cold land and a sea steaming like a wash-boiler.

Simon Carmiggelt
Dutch journalist
(1913–87)

Here we live, twelve million men and women. All quiet people, no orators, no singers, no dancers. Our political passions are allowed to flare up every four years, but they don't. And yet we are the people who, more than any other, are scattered all over the globe. So long as we have our own educational system and our own broadcasting companies, everything is all right. We are twelve million individualists, and in spite of that we are tolerant. In our restricted living space we need to be. We live side by side with one another, and yet each of us likes to be alone.

Erasmus of
Rotterdam
Dutch scholar
(1469–1536)

If we consider manners and customs in everyday life, there is no people that leans more to humanity and kindness or is less given to intemperance or cruel behaviour. They are upright in character, without baseness or falsity, not open to dubious vices – perhaps only to a certain liking for enjoyment, in particular for festivities. The reason for this, I believe, lies in the wonderful provision of all that conduces to enjoyment; on the one hand the ease with which goods can be imported and on the other the natural fertility of the country, traversed by navigable rivers full of fish and rich in lush pastureland.

It is said that no other land has so many towns in such a narrow space. If there are not many truly learned scholars in this people, particularly in the classics, this may be due to the luxurious life they lead or to the fact that they are more interested in moral than in scholarly excellence.

Georg Forster
German scientist
(1754–94)
"Letters from the
Low Countries"

We walked up to the area where the famous Haarlem flower gardens lie ... It was a warm morning; the sun shone from a clear sky, and in its light we admired the colours of nature, whose magnificence and splendour are so far beyond all imitation and all power of expression. We looked over the whole area of a great flower garden in which tulips in different colours alternated with one another in long beds, forming strips of fiery colours, lemon-yellow, snow-white, carmine and many other shades.

Whereas in the past this branch of horticulture was overvalued, it is now unduly underrated. For surely it is no small matter that man can modify nature without deforming it.

We spent a pleasant day or two seeing the sights of Leiden and the surrounding area and meeting the scholars of the town. If a man full of the prejudices against the Dutch which are all too prevalent, particularly in Germany, were suddenly transferred here he might well wonder whether he was really on Dutch soil – so much is solid learning united here with genuine urbanity and polite manners, but above all with modesty and attentive respect for strangers, based on a sense of the scholars' own worth and never descending to the petty vanity of the pedant. The good manners of the professors here are a natural consequence of this self-esteem, combined with a ready recognition of the merits of others.

The boatmen on the canals, like the rest of their countrymen, show a politeness which is quite unusual in Germany, without the slightest affectation or pretence. They greet passers-by with great heartiness and friendliness, take off their hat to everyone, great or small, answer questions readily and obligingly, help travellers on their way – showing in their behaviour, as in their dress and in all other respects, the straightforwardness characteristic only of prosperous nations. Politics are their favourite topic of conversation, the newspapers their only reading, the tobacco-pipe their recreation, a glass of gin their refreshment.

Father, Mother and Margot still cannot get used to the bells of the Westerkerk, which ring every quarter of an hour. I do like them, and there is something soothing about them, particularly at night . . . The back part of our house is really an ideal hiding-place. Even though it is damp and rather crooked and lopsided, it would be difficult to find anything so comfortable in Amsterdam, perhaps in the whole of Holland.

Anne Frank
(1929–45)
"Diary"

. . . Where for countless years
the Old Rhine has flowed through Leiden
and an eternally young band
pursue the quest for learning.

Queen Juliana
of the
Netherlands
(b. 1909)

The Dutch may ascribe their present grandeur to the virtue and frugality of their ancestors as they please; but what made that contemptible spot of ground so considerable among the principal powers of Europe has been their political wisdom in postponing everything to merchandise and population, the unlimited liberty of conscience that is enjoyed among them and the unwearied application with which they have always made use of the most effectual means to encourage and increase trade in general . . .

Bernard de
Mandeville
English physician
and philosopher
(1670–1733)
"Fable of the
Bees"

In pictures and marble they are profuse; in their buildings and gardens they are extravagant to folly. In other countries you may meet with stately courts and palaces of great extent that belong to princes, which nobody can expect in a commonwealth where so much equality is observed as there is in this; but in all Europe you shall find no private buildings so sumptuously magnificent as a great many of the merchants' and other gentlemen's houses are in Amsterdam and some other great cities of that small province; and the generality of those that build there lay out a greater proportion of their estates on the houses they dwell in than any people upon the earth.

Hendrik Marsman
Dutch writer
(1899–1940)

Thinking of Holland,
I see broad rivers
flowing lazily
through endless lowlands;
rows of unbelievably
slender poplars
like tall feathers
standing at the end;
and sunk in the
massive space below
are the farmhouses
scattered about the land,
clumps of trees, villages,
truncated towers,
churches and elm-trees
in magnificent combination.
The air lies low down
and the sun is slowly
bathed in grey and
many-coloured vapours,
and in all the provinces
the voice of the water
with its eternal
threat of disaster is heard.

Lady Mary
Wortley Montague
(1689–1762)
Letter, 1716

(Rotterdam)
All the streets are paved with broad stones, and before the meanest artificer's doors, seats of various coloured marbles, and so neatly kept that I'll assure you I walked almost all over the town yesterday, incognito, in my slippers without receiving one spot of dirt, and you may see the Dutch maids washing the pavement of the street with more application than ours do our bedchambers. The town seems full of people with such busy faces, all in motion, that I can hardly fancy that it is not some celebrated fair, but I see 'tis every day the same. 'Tis certain no town can be more advantageously situated for commerce. Here there are 7 large canals on which the merchant ships come up to the very doors of their houses. The shops and warehouses are of a surprising neatness and magnificence, filled with an incredible quantity of fine merchandise, and so much cheaper than what we see in England, I have much ado to persuade myself I am still so near it.

Here is neither dirt nor beggary to be seen. One is not shocked with those loathsome cripples so common in London, nor teased with the importunities of idle fellows and wenches that choose to be nasty and lazy. The common servants and little shopwomen here are more nicely clean than most of our ladies, and the great variety of neat dresses (every woman dressing her head after her own fashion) is an additional pleasure in seeing the town.

Multatuli
(Eduard
Douwes-Dekker)
Dutch writer
(1820–87)

The Dutchman thinks a lot of his river dykes and of the floods they cause. For centuries he has been raising the bed of his rivers – soon he will have them flowing on piles above his head – and he neglects the opportunity offered to him of raising his land because he prefers to block the openings from the sea with the material so kindly provided by nature. The consequences are wet land and dry harbours.

Jan Prins
(Chr. L. Schepp)
Dutch writer
(1876–1948)

(On the statue of Erasmus in Rotterdam)
Erasmus has still not reached
the last line on his page.
He is at ease under his elm-trees;
he feels at home in the centre of the city.

Simon Schama
Historian
(b. 1945)
"The
Embarrassment
of Riches"

To its first generation of patriotic eulogists, Dutchness was often equated with the transformation, under divine guidance, of catastrophe into good fortune, infirmity into strength, water into dry land, mud into gold. This arrogation of a special destiny, marked by suffering and redemption, was not so particular to the Dutch as they imagined. But the uncanny way in which geography reinforced moral analogy gave their collective self-recognition great immediacy. Those who had come through flood and had survived could hardly miss the differentiating significance of *beproeving*, or ordeal. So the trial of faith by adversity was a formative element of the national culture . . .

The tidal deluges of the late medieval period occupied the same place in the collective folk memory of south Hollanders and Zeelanders as the visitations of the Black Death in Flanders and Italy. Over two centuries later Romeyne de Hooghe still pictured the St Elizabeth's Day flood as the primal catastrophe of the Netherlandish nation. The calamities seemed to portend an apocalyptic end to a sinful world, a winnowing of souls, or – an image that meant a great deal to the Dutch – a wiping clean of the slate of iniquity . . .

It was an axiom of Dutch culture that what the flood gave, the flood could take away. So their fear of drowning in destitution and terror was exactly counterbalanced by their fear of drowning in luxury and sin. To defend their nation's hard-won freedom, even with God's help, demanded the physical resources of strength and power that the waters had provided. But should they begin to wallow in complacency and affluence, they would provoke nemesis, either from the brute elements, or from the covetousness of overbearing neighbours . . .

Diderot wittily combined the Dutch predilection for both fire and spirits by calling them "living alembics, distilling, in effect, themselves". And the standard caricature Dutchman in English prints is barrel-shaped in girth, sozzled with gin and often seen lighting the next pipe with the smoldering embers of the last.

The Dutch reputation for hard drinking went back at least to the early sixteenth century, when Lodovico Guicciardini noted it as "abnormal". Like many later commentators he attributed it to the need to ward off the chilly vapors that rose from the bogs and ditches among which the Dutch dwelled . . .

No visitor to Holland, from Fynes Moryson to Henry James, failed to notice the pains that the Dutch took to keep their streets, their houses and themselves (though there was less unanimity about this) brilliantly clean. The spick-and-span towns shone from hours of tireless sweeping, scrubbing, scraping, burnishing, mopping, rubbing and washing. They made an embarrassing contrast to the porridge of filth and ordure that slopped over the cobbles of most other European cities in the seventeenth century.

What excitement when you look at the map: the Afsluitdijk like an elastic band keeping the two parts of the country the right distance apart.

Karel Soudijn
Dutch
psychologist
(b. 1940)

Doorn will never forget the German Emperor, for he was very popular, not only because he paid tradesmen generously. In every citizen of Doorn – myself included – there is a feudal spirit which gives us no peace until a noble lord looks down benevolently on us.

Simon Vestdijk
Dutch writer
(1898–1971)

In the same year we stayed for the first time in Huis ten Bosch while in The Hague for the opening of the States General. It was more like camping than living in a house! The old building had stood empty since the death in 1877 of Queen Sophie, my father's first wife. In what a lamentable state we found it, what hopeless dilapidation! And what a stormy time had left its mark on this beautiful house!

Queen Wilhelmina
of the Netherlands
(1880–1962)

Suggested Routes

The routes suggested in this section are designed to help visitors travelling by car to plan their trip in the Netherlands, leaving them free to vary the routes according to their particular interests and the time available.

The routes can be followed on the map at the end of this book, which will facilitate detailed planning of the trip.

The suggested routes take in the main places of interest described in this guide, though some of them involve a detour off the main route. In addition there are many suggestions for excursions and round trips in the entries for particular places in the A to Z section of the guide.

In the description of the routes, places for which there is a separate entry in the A to Z section are shown in **bold** type.

All the towns, villages, regions, rivers, etc., mentioned in the main section of the guide, whether the subject of a separate entry or not, are listed in the Index at the end of the volume, making it easy to find the description of a particular place.

The distances shown in brackets at the head of each route will help motorists to estimate the time required for each trip; they relate to the main route, excluding any detours.

1: Nijmegen via Utrecht to Amsterdam (c. 130km/80 miles)

Main route

From the old town of **Nijmegen**, picturesquely situated above the Waal, the main arm of the Lower Rhine (which divides into two just above the town), the A 52 motorway runs along the fringes of the fertile fenlands of **Betuwe** to the capital of Gelderland province, **Arnhem**. Not to be missed here are the Netherlands Open-Air Museum and the Hoge Veluwe National Park, with the Kröller-Müller Museum.

From here the fast A 12 motorway, which offers no particular features of interest, continues to the university town of **Utrecht**, with a cathedral which is one of the finest churches in the Netherlands.

The A 2 motorway runs north-west from Utrecht to **Amsterdam**, capital of the Netherlands, with its many attractions. The sightseeing programme should include a trip through the canals and harbours of this "Venice of the North".

Alternative routes

For a more varied route from Arnhem to Amsterdam, take the road which runs along the right bank of the Rhine, skirting the south side of of the **Veluwe**, an area of woodland and heath which extends north to the IJssel-meer, and passing through Wageningen, **Amerongen** and **Doorn**. Another possibility is the road which runs via Ede, **Amersfoort** and the Gooi, passing the royal residence of Soestdijk.

2: Maastricht via 's-Hertogenbosch to Rotterdam (c. 210km/130 miles)

Main route

This route starts from the southern tip of **Limburg**, the most southerly and the hilliest of the Dutch provinces, which is traversed throughout its entire length by the Maas valley and contains extensive coalfields. From the provincial capital, **Maastricht** (old churches), with the beautifully situated town of **Valkenburg** lying a little to the east, the A 2 motorway runs north, following the Maas for much of the way and passing close to the frontier towns of Sittard and **Roermond**. It cuts through the province of Noord-Brabant with its varied landscapes and through the "heart of Brabant", the beautiful region of heath and woodland between **'s-Hertogenbosch** and *Tilburg*, with its lakes and tracts of dune-like country. The town of 's-Hertogenbosch, on the road from the modern industrial town of **Eindhoven** to **Utrecht**, has the finest Gothic cathedral in the Netherlands. From a motorway junction to the north of 's-Hertogenbosch the A 15 motorway runs west to **Gorinchem**, on the Waal, and **Dordrecht**, a typical old Dutch town with a handsome Grote Kerk. From here it is a short distance to **Rotterdam**, the great port city rebuilt after its destruction in the Second World War. A cruise round the harbour is a recommended.

A rewarding detour from Sittard is to the abbey of Rolduc at **Kerkrade**, close to the German frontier, which has one of the finest Romanesque churches in the Netherlands. The road runs through the not particularly attractive mining country of southern Limburg. — Detour

From 's-Hertogenbosch there is an alternative route via the industrial town of **Tilburg** to the important road junction point of **Breda**, and then through a region of pastureland watered by the river Mark to the large bridge over the Hollands Diep, an arm of the sea reaching deep inland which is joined a little way upstream by the Nieuwe Merwede and a subsidiary arm of the Maas. At Dordrecht the road crosses the Oude Maas and then, just before Rotterdam, the Nieuwe Maas (with an alternative route through the Maas Tunnel under the river). — Alternative routes
From Breda it is also possible to take a road which runs through the area round the estuary of the Maas and the Waal, near the Biesbosch, a dyked island complex traversed by the Nieuwe Merwede canal, which, together with the Hollands Diep was created by the great flood on St Elizabeth's day in 1421.

Between 's-Hertogenbosch and Tilburg an attractive detour can be made into the heathland of Noord-Brabant, for example to the beautiful lake (bathing facilities) of De IJzern Man ("Iron Man") and Oisterwijk with its large nature park, or to the leisure park of De Efteling at Kaatsheuvel (**Tilburg**). — Detour

3: Breda through Zeeland to Rotterdam (*c.* 260km/160 miles)

From **Breda** the A 58 motorway runs west through a mainly agricultural region with some beautiful wooded areas. Beyond **Bergen op Zoom** it enters the province of **Zeeland** and continues through an area of dyked fenland between the Ooster- and Westerschelde to the former island of Zuid-Beveland, a fertile area with prosperous villages (traditional costumes) which is particularly beautiful when the trees are in blossom. The road then continues over the Sloepolder to the former island of Walcheren, which was flooded by the Allies in October 1944 by the bombing of four dykes in order to disrupt the German defence of the Schelde estuary and open up the road to Antwerp. The island has now been brought back into cultivation and once again justifies its name of the "garden of Holland"; traditional costumes are frequently to be seen here. From **Middelburg**, capital of the province of Zeeland, the route continues along the Walcheren Canal to the former naval port of **Vlissingen**, where the Schelde flows into the North Sea. — Main route

From Middelburg there is an attractive trip (*c.* 50km/30 miles) round the island of Walcheren, passing through the pretty little town of **Veere**, the seaside resort of Domburg and the village of Westkapelle. — Round trip

Suggested Routes

Main route   The route continues over the Oosterschelde Dam, a storm-surge barrier completed in 1986. On the artificial island of Neeltje Jans there is an interesting exhibition, Delta Expo, on the 2000-year history of Dutch hydraulic engineering and on the Delta Plan. The dam links Walcheren with the island of Schouwen-Duiveland, the chief place on which, to the east, is **Zierikzee**, once a fortified town.

From here N 59 leads on to the island of Overflakkee and over the Haringvliet Bridge to join A 29, which runs north to Rotterdam.

4: From Rotterdam along the coast to Amsterdam and back via Utrecht (*c.* 190km/120 miles)

Main route   From **Rotterdam** the A 13 motorway runs north-west through polder land, passing close to the picturesque town of **Delft**, internationally famed for its tin-glazed earthenware, to **The Hague**, the seat of government and one of the principal tourist centres in the Netherlands with its numerous museums (including the Mauritshuis gallery), its historic Binnenhof and its beautiful surroundings. A little way north of The Hague is the old university town of **Leiden**, with its fine Renaissance architecture. The road then passes through the bulb-fields (particularly beautiful in the spring, when the flowers are in bloom) to **Haarlem**, capital of the province of Noord-Holland, which is famed not only as a flower-growing centre but also for its Frans Hals Museum and the Müller organ in St Bavokerk. From here the A 5 motorway runs east to **Amsterdam**, from which the return is on A 2 to **Utrecht** and from there A 12 to Rotterdam.

Detours   No visit to The Hague is complete without a trip to the fashionable seaside resort of **Scheveningen**, which lies within the city limits. The resorts of **Katwijk** and **Noordwijk** are best reached on the road which branches off just before the bridge over the Rhine at Leiden, returning either direct to the motorway or to the Haarlem road at Sassenheim.

A special attraction between Leiden and Haarlem is the display of flowers at Keukenhof.

From Haarlem a detour can be made to **Zandvoort**, the largest seaside resort in the Netherlands after Scheveningen, continuing by way of Bloemendaal, another popular resort, and then through magnificent dune scenery back to Haarlem.

Another attractive possibility is a diversion from the motorway north of Rotterdam to **Gouda**.

5: From Amsterdam across the IJsselmeer to Leeuwarden and Groningen (*c.* 210km/130 miles)

Main route   This route, on an excellent, quite fast, road (A 7 to Friesland, A 31 to Leeuwarden, N 355 to Groningen) runs through the provinces of **Noord-Holland**, **Friesland** and **Groningen**, passing through typically Dutch scenery, with great expanses of pasture and arable land, numerous windmills, thatched farmhouses and old Dutch villages.

From **Amsterdam** the route goes through a number of industrial towns on the river Zaan, in a well-watered polder area, and then continues close to the chain of dunes along the North Sea coast, with a series of holiday and seaside resorts.

After passing through **Alkmaar**, famed for its cheese market, the road follows the North Holland Canal to the Waddenzee and then continues on a dyke along the Amstelmeer to the former island of Wieringen.

At Den Oever the road reaches the coast of the IJsselmeer (formerly the Zuiderzee), crosses the **Afsluitdijk** to the coast of Friesland and continues to the port of **Harlingen**.

Beyond this there is a fairly featureless road through flat pasture and arable land, with trim farmhouses, by way of the little town of **Franeker**, a former university town which is well worth a visit, and **Leeuwarden**, capital of Friesland, to the provincial capital of **Groningen**, the largest and liveliest town in the northern Netherlands.

Egmond and **Bergen aan Zee** are among the most attractive resorts on the North Sea coast of the Netherlands, with beautiful broad sandy beaches. Egmond is most easily reached from Heiloo, just south of Alkmaar; Bergen is reached from Alkmaar on a road which passes through the summer resort of Bergen-Binnen, beautifully situated amid wooded dunes, a favourite resort of painters.

Detours

Even visitors who are pressed for time should make a detour to the naval port of **Den Helder**. From here there is a ferry to the beautiful island of **Texel**, famed for its sheep-farming, its magnificent beaches and its nature reserves with their abundance of seabirds.

The islands of **Vlieland** and **Terschelling** are reached from the Frisian port of **Harlingen**.

Visitors with an interest in the history of Friesland will find it worth while to branch off from the Leeuwarden–Groningen road to the ancient little town of **Dokkum**, where St Boniface was martyred.

The quickest route from Amsterdam to Den Oever is the road which runs via **Edam**. Detours can be made from this road to the fishing villages of **Volendam** and **Marken**, which are famed for their beautiful traditional costumes.

For a shorter and faster route to Friesland and Groningen, leave Amsterdam on the A 1 motorway, going south-east, and then turn into A 6, which crosses the Gooimeer into the South Flevoland (Zuidelijk Flevoland) polder, which was drained in 1968, with the town of Almere (**Flevoland**), founded in 1975 to take overspill population from Randstad Holland. This gives an opportunity of seeing the large nature reserves planned in this area and tracts of relatively young polder at different stages of cultivation. The road then comes to Lelystad, the chief place in Flevoland, which is of interest for its planning, with separate streets and paths for different forms of traffic. From here the route continues over the Ketelbrug to the **Noordoostpolder** (North-East Polder) and the Frisian lake district, an area of rather melancholy beauty with numerous windmills used for pumping water, which has excellent facilities for water sports and attracts many visitors during the summer months. After passing through **Sneek** and Leeuwarden the road comes to Groningen.

Alternative route

It is worth making a detour to the little fishing port of **Urk**, on a former island in the IJsselmeer, which still preserves an old-world character, with picturesque traditional costumes.

Detour

6: Groningen via Zwolle to Nijmegen (*c.* 200km/125 miles)

This route, on excellent roads (A 28 to Zwolle, A 50 to Arnhem, A 52 to Nijmegen) runs from north to south through the eastern Netherlands. It passes through the province of **Drenthe**, a region of woodland, heath and bog with many of the megalithic tombs known as *hunebedden* or "giants' beds" (for a rewarding detour through the Hondsrug see below), and then through **Overijssel** province. From here it is possible either to continue up the flat IJssel valley or to take the road which traverses the **Veluwe**, with its beautiful expanses of forest and its hills rising to 110m/360ft, to **Arnhem** on the Lower Rhine, capital of the province of **Gelderland**. From there the A 52 motorway continues south, skirting the fertile Veluwe, to the river Waal and **Nijmegen**.

Main route

For visitors interested in the prehistory of the Netherlands there is plenty to see in the province of Drenthe. Those who cannot spare the time to follow

Detours

the route through the Hondsrug (described below), where most of the "giants' beds" in Drenthe are to be found, should at least make a detour from Vries (between Groningen and Assen) to Tinaarloo station, where there is a well preserved example, or turn off at Havelte into the Frederiksoord road, along which (3km/2 miles) are several *hunebedden*.

From Dieverbrug, between **Assen** and Meppel, a detour can be made to the beautifully situated summer resort of Dwingeloo, at the entrance to the Dwingeloosche Heide Nature Reserve.

For water sports enthusiasts there is an excursion from Meppel to the Blauwe Hand, a hamlet on a narrow strip of land between the Beulaker and the Belter Wijde, in a polder region with numerous lakes. From here, if time permits, it is possible to continue to the charming "water village" of **Giethoorn**.

From **Zwolle**, capital of the province of Overijssel, it is well worth making a detour to the old Hanseatic town of **Kampen**, with its massive town gates and beautiful St Nicolaaskerk, situated on the IJssel just above its outflow into the IJsselmeer.

The attractive town of **Apeldoorn** should be visited for the sake of the royal palace of Het Loo.

Between Apeldoorn and Arnhem a trip can be made to the village of Hoenderloo, at the entrance to the Hoge Veluwe National Park, which can also be reached on a country road from Apeldoorn to Arnhem skirting the National Park.

Only 1km/¾ mile from Arnhem is the Netherlands Open-Air Museum, which it is worth visiting – perhaps particularly at the end of a visit to the Netherlands – to get a general survey of the life and culture of the country.

Alternative routes

A rewarding detour of 32km/20 miles, passing many *hunebedden,* leads from Groningen through the Hondsrug, a range of sandy hills, to **Emmen** and then via **Coevorden** to the Schoonebeek oilfield, continuing by way of the straggling moorland villages in the Balkburg area to **Zwolle**.

Visitors who already know Apeldoorn and the Veluwe should continue up the IJssel valley from Zwolle to **Deventer** and **Zutphen**, and then via the summer resorts of Dieren, Steeg and Velp, under the south-east side of the Veluwe, to Arnhem (additional distance 10km/6 miles). It is also possible to combine both routes, using the link roads between Deventer or Zutphen and Apeldoorn. Perhaps the most rewarding route is the detour (28km/17 miles) from Zwolle via Deventer, Zutphen and Apeldoorn to Arnhem.

A picturesque water-gate in Sneek (Friesland) ▶

The Netherlands from A to Z

Aalsmeer

D 6

Province: Noord-Holland
Population: 22,000

Situation and characteristics

The town of Aalsmeer lies on the ring canal of the Haarlemmermeer polder, south-west of Amsterdam. A third of its area is occupied by water, the so-called Westeinderplassen: hence the town's name ("Eel Sea"). Aalsmeer has an international reputation for its flower auctions, the largest in Europe.

During the Middle Ages the town owed its importance to fishing, stock-farming, the peat trade and, from 1450, horticulture, which became increasingly important as the nearby town of Amsterdam grew in size and population. This development was promoted by the draining of the Haarlemmermeer in the 19th century. The town's horticultural activity began with the cultivation of lilac, but later switched to pot plants and cut flowers. There are now well over 600 flower nurseries in Aalsmeer, the greenhouses cover an area of some 600 hectares/1500 acres, and the annual turnover of the flower auctions is more than £100 million.

*Flower auctions

Just outside the town is the huge auction complex, established in 1928, in which more than 2 billion cut flowers (some 50% roses and 10% carnations) and over 150 million plants are sold annually. Some 80% are exported, over half of them to Germany. The Aalsmeer auctions, together with the other Dutch flower auctions, determine the international price levels of flowers and plants, since 60% of all exports come from the Netherlands. The average annual value of these exports is over £1.5 billion.

The Aalsmeer auctions are held Monday to Friday, starting at 6.30am Visitors are welcome to watch between 7.30 and 11am; since the auction attracts large numbers of people, it is advisable to be there early. Activity, however, continues round the clock.

Church

Also of interest is the four-aisled Dutch Reformed church (16th c.) in the centre of the town.

Achterhoek

G/J 6/7

Province: Gelderland

Situation and characteristics

The Achterhoek ("rear corner"), also known as the Gelderse Achterhoek, lies to the south of Overijssel province in eastern Gelderland, bounded by the river IJssel and the Oude (Old) IJssel. It is a sandy plain between 10m/35ft and 50m/165ft above sea level; with its wide river valleys and prominent morainic ridges it was formed during the second-last ice age (the Saale/Riss glaciation), when the glaciers advancing from the north extended over this part of the Netherlands.

Southern Achterhoek

The southern part of the Achterhoek was formerly an expanse of marshland and heath which was brought into cultivation and is now covered by arable land, pasture and forest, with outcrops of ancient rock here and there. Numerous small streams flow through this idyllic region. In a nature reserve at Winterswijk some patches of bogland, with rare species of orchids, have been preserved.

Neighbourly help and co-operation plays a great part in the life of this region. The importance of the community is demonstrated, for example, in the large-scale celebrations of weddings, attended by hundreds of guests. Other great communal occasions are the patronal festivals of the churches and numerous other village celebrations, which give the local craftsmen (particularly clog-makers and basket-workers) an opportunity of showing their skill.

The northern part of the Achterhoek is known as the Graafschap ("County"). In this area with its extensive deciduous forests and thickets of rhododendrons there are many old castles and country houses, some of them still lived in, others used for a variety of purposes, such as offices or town halls. Between Vorden and Ruurlo there are no fewer than eight old houses of this kind.

Graafschap

The population's main source of income is agriculture, particularly from butter-making and poultry farming. This is a region of small villages, with small isolated farmsteads scattered about between them. Industry has been established mainly along the banks of the IJssel and the Oude IJssel, in the form of brickworks and iron foundries; there are also a number of hosiery factories and cotton-processing and woodworking plants.

Economy

Afsluitdijk

E 2

The Afsluitdijk (Enclosing Dyke) which closes off the IJsselmeer, 30km/18½ miles long by 90m/100yds across, links the provinces of Noord-Holland and Friesland. Built between 1927 and 1932, it converted the Zuiderzee into an inland lake, now known as the IJsselmeer. The Zuiderzee itself was an inland lake until Roman times; but during the early Middle Ages the level of the North Sea rose and gigantic storm tides broke through the land and made the Zuiderzee an inlet of the sea. Thereafter the government and people of the Netherlands wrestled with the problem of recovering the land drowned by the sea; but it was not until the 19th century that the technological resources for carrying through such a project became available. After severe food shortages in the Netherlands during the First World War and further heavy damage caused by a storm tide in 1916 the government approved a plan devised by a water engineer named Cornelis Lely, the object of which was twofold – to reclaim land for agriculture and to prevent further penetration by the sea. The construction of the Afsluitdijk had the effect of reducing the length of dykes in the IJsselmeer area by some 300km/185 miles.

Situation and *Characteristics

At the near (south-western) end of the Afsluitdijk is a group of sluices, the Stevinsluizen, which control the water level in the IJsselmeer. On the seaward side of the dyke are a number of harbour basins enclosed by stone walls.

An excellent motorway (A 7) runs north-west from Den Oever in Noord-Holland on the inland side of the dyke, below the crown. To the right there are extensive views of the IJsselmeer; the view of the Waddenzee to the left is blocked off by the grass-covered crown of the dyke. In 6.5km/4 miles, on right, is a monument marking the point where the dyke was finally closed

Driving over the Afsluitdijk

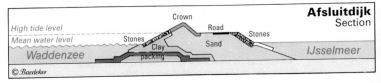

Afsluitdijk
Section

High tide level
Mean water level
Waddenzee
Crown
Road
Stones
Stones
Clay packing
Sand
IJsselmeer
© Baedeker

The Afsluitdijk linking Noord-Holland and Friesland

on May 28th 1932. Here there are a car park, an outlook tower with a small restaurant and a footbridge over the motorway; from the viewing platform there is a far-ranging prospect over the sea. Beyond this point is Breezandijk, an artificial island with a small harbour which was the starting-point for the construction of the dyke. 11km/7 miles farther on is another large group of sluices, the Lorenzsluizen; to the right is a car park, and beyond this, on the left, a restaurant. From here it is 4km/2½ miles to the end of the dyke (petrol station), on the west coast of the province of Friesland.

Alkmaar

D 4

Province: Noord-Holland
Population: 88,000

Situation and townscape

Alkmaar lies on the North Holland Canal, 8km/5 miles from the coast of the North Sea. The charming old town centre, with many fine architectural monuments and old guild-houses and burghers' houses of the 16th to 18th centuries, has been preserved unspoiled. With its famous cheese market, it is one of the best-known tourist attractions in the Netherlands.

Characteristics

Alkmaar is the main centre of an extensive rural area, with schools and shops which are patronised by many inhabitants of the province. Its economy depends principally on the varied range of industry established to the north-east of the town, attracted by its excellent transport facilities. The main types of industry are engineering, papermaking, textiles and foodstuffs (canning plants, chocolate manufacture), together with organ-building.

History

Alkmaar was founded in the 10th century and first appears in the records in 939. It received its municipal charter in 1254. Its heyday, however, came

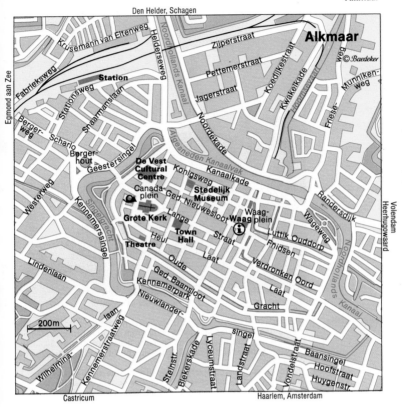

only after the Dutch wars of liberation from Spanish rule, in which Alkmaar played a special role, being the first town to beat off an attack by Frederick of Toledo, the Duke of Alba's son, in 1573 by opening the sluices and flooding the surrounding countryside: a victory which initiated the final defeat of the Spanish forces.

Sights

From the Grote Kerk the town's main street, the Langestraat, runs east to the Mient (Fish Hall). On the right (No. 46) is the Town Hall and in Doelenstraat, on the left, is the Municipal Museum. From the end of the Langestraat a street on the left leads through the Mient area to the Waagplein, in which the cheese market is held. In the picturesque old part of the town around the Mient, on the *grachten* of Luttik Oudorp and Verdronkenoord and in the adjoining streets there are many old gabled houses of the early 16th century. At the end of the Verdronkenoord, in Bierkade, on the North Holland Canal, is the elegant Accijnstoren (Excise Tower), which dates from 1622. From here Bierkade leads to the Victoriepark, in which stands a monument commemorating the defence of the town against the Spaniards in 1573.

Tour of the town

Alkmaar: picturesque old houses and the Mint Tower

* Cheese market

Alkmaar's chief tourist attraction is its cheese market, which is held, strictly in accordance with tradition, every Friday from mid April to mid September between 10am and noon (also on Thursday between 6.30 and 7.30pm and on Saturday between 12 noon and 1pm) in front of the Weigh-House in the Waagplein.

The square is almost completely covered with large round cheeses (over 23 tons of Edam and Gouda cheese). The cheese-porters, dressed in white and wearing hats in the colours of their guild, carry the cheese (sometimes as many as 80 Edam cheeses at a time) on cradle-like racks to be weighed in the weigh-house and loaded into trucks. All the different kinds of cheese are sampled and checked for quality; but this is only for show, the real cheese market being held in the Stock Exchange.

Cheese described as *jong* (young) must be at least four weeks old; *jong belegen* must be at least two months old, *belegen kaas* four months old and *extra belegen* seven months old; and "old" cheese must be over ten months old.

The old town of Alkmaar is of great interest. Among the buildings of historical and artistic importance are the following:

Grote Kerk

At the west end of the old town, which is surrounded by beautiful gardens laid out on the line of the old fortifications, is the Grote Kerk or St Laurentiuskerk (Reformed), a fine Late Gothic church built between 1470 and 1520, with a carillon. It occupies the site of an earlier church which was destroyed in 1468 by the collapse of its unfinished tower. Notable features of this cruciform basilica – a fine example of Brabantine Gothic – are the pulpit (1665), the Baroque stalls, the monument of Count Floris V of Holland (d. 1296) in the choir, a Late Gothic organ (1511) in the north ambulatory and a 16th century brass in the south transept. There is also a large organ of 1645 (recitals in July and August at 11.15am and 12.15pm on Fridays).

The municipal Weigh-House (Waag), at Waagplein 2, was originally the chapel of a religious house dedicated to the Holy Ghost (1341); it was converted into a weigh-house in 1582. In the tower (1595–99) is a carillon of 1688.

Weigh-House

The Weigh-House now contains the Cheese Museum (Kaasmuseum; open: from the beginning of April to the end of October, Mon.–Sat. 10am–4pm, Fri. 9am–4pm).

Cheese Museum

The eastern section of the Late Gothic Town Hall (Stadhuis) dates from the early 16th century, the western part from 1694. Of particular interest are the Council Chamber, the hall containing a cupboard in the traditional style of the Schermer area, the Polder Room and the Renaissance magistrates' room. The Nierop Room, with a wooden ceiling and period furniture, dates from 1634. Open: Mon.–Fri. 9am–12 noon and 2–4pm.

Town Hall

The Municipal Museum (Stedelijk Museum), at Doelenstraat 5, was formerly, from the 17th century, the headquarters of St Sebastiaans Schutterij (Marksmen's Guild), which from the 14th century to the beginning of the 19th acted as the town guard. The museum displays paintings of the 16th and 17th centuries and of the Bergen school, a collection of coins and material on the history of the town. Open: March to December Tue.–Fri. 10am–5pm, Sun. 1–5pm.

Municipal Museum

The Hofje van Splinter (1646), at Ritzevoort 2, is an old people's home for eight ladies, notable for its fine paving and its barrel-vaulted timber roof borne on five Tuscan columns.

Other sights

The Wildemans Hofje in the Oude Gracht, originally a barn, was converted into a temporary church in 1658.

St Johanneskerk was founded in the mid 15th century by the Knights of St John and was rebuilt after a fire in 1760. It has an 18th century hanging pulpit and an organ by Christian Müller.

The Mient (Fish Hall) was built in 1591 and restored in 1644. The pump dates from 1785. A market is held here every Friday morning between 7am and 12 noon.

The Molen van Piet, an old flour mill (1769) on the line of the former town walls, at the end of Ritzevoort, is still in use.

In Nieuwesloot, on a site occupied from medieval times to 1500 by the convent of Mary Magdalene, are the Hof van Sonoy (1576; fine 17th century tympanum over the doorway), which was occupied for a time by William I's representative, and the Huis van Achten, notable for its Regents' Room and its fine woodcarving.

The Hans Brinker Museum, at Voordam 6, has a collection of sledges and skates (open: April to September, Tue.–Fri. and Sun. 1–5pm; October to March, Sun. 1–5pm). At Houttil 1 is the De Boom National Beer Museum (open: November to March, Tue.–Sat. 1–4pm, Sun. 1–5pm; April to October, Tue.–Sat. 10am–4pm, Sun. 1–5pm).

Surroundings of Alkmaar

South-east of the town lies the Schermer polder, with the Prinses cheese farm at Ursem. In Schermerhorn, at Noordervaart 2, is a windmill dating from 1634, now a museum (open: May to September, Tue.–Sun. 10am–5pm, October to April, Sun. 10.30am–4.30pm).

Schermer

The little town of De Rijp is best known as the birthplace of the 17th century water engineer Jan Leeghwater. In the 17th century it had a fishing fleet which was later used for whaling.

Graft–De Rijp

The Late Gothic cruciform church (1529; Reformed) has oak barrel vaulting and 24 magnificent stained glass windows.
The Town Hall, built in 1630 on the initiative of Jan Leeghwater, has three tall gables and an imposing flight of steps leading up to the entrance.

In 1970 the two towns of Graft and De Rijp were amalgamated. The local museum (In 't Houten Huis, Jan Boonplein 2) illustrates the history of the two communities. Open: Easter to June and September–October, Sat. and Sun. 11am–5pm; July and August, Tue.–Sun. 11am–5pm.

Also within easy reach of Alkmaar are Egmond aan Zee (see entry), Den Oever (see Afsluitdijk) and Broek op Langendijk (see entry).

Almelo   H 5

Province: Overijssel
Population: 62,000

Situation and characteristics
Almelo, lying close to the German frontier, was formerly the chief textile centre in the Twente area in the eastern Netherlands. From about 1830 woollen and cotton goods were produced in factories and exported; in earlier days flax had been processed in home workshops. Merchants from Vriezenveen (north of Almelo) had a trading post as far afield as St Petersburg.

The metalworking industry also made an important contribution to the town's economy. At the peak of its development industry provided employment for 80% of the working population.

Huis Almelo
The moated castle of Almelo was originally built in the 13th century. It was extensively renovated in the mid 17th century and again in the 19th century. The 14th century chapel was rebuilt in the 18th century as a church, when the tower was given a timber spire. In the choir, built in sandstone at the end of the 15th century, can be seen the tomb of Count van Rechteren (1722).

Museum
The local museum (Museum voor Heemkunde) at Korte Prinsenstraat 1 occupies the former Latin School (1783) and rector's house. It contains collections on the history of the town, the old textile and tobacco industries and peat production, as well as old floor and wall tiles. Recent additions are a baker's shop and the baker's house. Open: Tue.–Sat. 12.30–5pm.

Almere

See Flevoland

Alphen aan den Rijn

Province: Zuid-Holland
Population: 58,000

Situation and characteristics
The industrial town of Alphen aan den Rijn, which now incorporates the former villages of Aarlanderveen, Zwammerdam and Oudshoorn, lies in the centre of the province of Zuid-Holland on the busy Oude Rijn. The most important establishment in this industrial region is the country's second largest publishing house, Samsom-Kluwer.

Avifauna bird park
2km/1¼ miles west of the town centre is the Avifauna bird park (open: all year round), in which many species of rare birds from all over the world live

in conditions as close as possible to their natural habitat. Nearby rises an 85m/280ft high telecommunications tower (1963).

Surroundings of Alphen aan den Rijn

To the north of Alphen aan den Rijn are a number of lakes of some size which are much frequented by sailing enthusiasts. From the Avifauna bird park there are boat trips to the Braassemer Meer.

Braassemer Meer

9km/6 miles south of Alphen is Bodegraven, well known for the production of farm cheese (cheese market on Tuesdays).

Bodegraven

Ameland

F/G 1

Province: Friesland
Population: 3200

Ameland is one of the West Frisian islands (see entry). Most of the island, which has an area of 6000 hectares/15,000 acres, is now a nature reserve. Ameland can be reached by car (advance reservation on ferry necessary), but since the greatest distance to be covered is only 20km/12½ miles the most convenient form of transport is a bicycle.
Ameland's main source of income is the tourist trade, to which agriculture comes second. There are only four villages on the island – Hollum, Ballum, Nes and Buren.

Situation and characteristics

In the 14th century Ameland belonged to Bavaria, although its neutrality was recognised from 1396 onwards. It was granted full independence and neutrality by the Spaniards in 1598. In 1801 it became part of Friesland, with which it was connected by a causeway until 1883.

History

The chief place on the island is Nes, where the ferry from Holwerd puts in. The days when Ameland was a whaling centre are recalled by the 18th century *commandeurshuizen* – the homes of the captains of the whaling fleet – to be seen in Nes and the other villages.
The most prominent feature of the village is the church tower (1664) with its characteristically Frisian saddle roof. The church itself dates from the 13th century.

Nes

The Ameland Natural History Museum on the seafront promenade illustrates the varied natural pattern of the island. Open: November to March, Sat. 1–5pm; April to June and September to October, Mon.–Fri. 10am–12 noon and 1–5pm, Sat. 1–5pm; July and August, Mon.-Fri. 10am–5pm and 7–9pm.

Natural History Museum

A tower standing by itself at Ballum is thought to have belonged to the chapel of a castle which once stood here.

Ballum

Hollum is the most westerly village on the island. When the island was taken by the Sea Beggars the church was destroyed, but it was rebuilt in 1678. In the churchyard are the graves of captains of the island's whaling fleet and British airmen shot down during the Second World War.

Hollum

The Amelandse Oudheidkamer (Museum of Antiquities), at Herenweg 1, is housed in one of the old *kommandeurshuizen*, 't Sorgdragershûske (1751), with its original furnishings and displays of traditional costumes and other items illustrating life and work on the island. Open: April to October, Mon.–Fri. 9.30am–12.30pm and 2–4.30pm, Sat. and Sun. 2–4.30pm; November to March, Wed. and Fri. 2.30–4.30pm.

Amelandse Oudheidkamer

Coastal scenery, Ameland

Lifeboat

Another feature of local interest is the Hollum lifeboat, which is pulled into the sea by ten horses. Eight horses were drowned when it was being launched in 1979; they are buried nearby.

Amerongen   F 7

Province: Utrecht
Population: 6600

Situation

Amerongen lies on the south side of the Utrechtse Heuvelrug, a range of hills which here reaches its highest point (69m/226ft).

Andreaskerk

The Andreaskerk (St Andrew's Church) dates from the second half of the 15th century; the nave was altered in 1660.

Kasteel Amerongen

The medieval castle of Amerongen, set in a large park, was destroyed by the French in 1673, and only part of the keep survives. A new castle was built between 1676 and 1681, and the interior was remodelled in the late 19th century by P. J. H. Cuypers. Of particular interest are his ceiling paintings in the Upper Gallery, the Dining Room and the Tapestry Room. The castle was occupied from 1918 to 1920 by the ex-German Emperor Wilhelm II. Open: April to October, Tue.–Fri. 10am–5pm, Sat. and Sun. 1–5pm.

Historical Museum

An old tobacco store at J. H. v.d. Boschstraat 46 is now occupied by the Amerongen Historical Museum, which illustrates 300 years of tobacco growing in the south-east of Utrecht province. Open: April, Tue.–Sat. 1.30–5pm, Sun. 1–5pm; May to October, Tue.–Sat. 10am–5pm, Sun. 1–5pm.

Koppelpoort, Amerongen

Surroundings of Amerongen

From Amerongen a road runs up the Lower Rhine valley to Rhenen (pop. 17,000), a little town dominated by the Cuneratoren (1492–1531), one of the finest Late Gothic towers in the country, reminiscent of the tower of Utrecht Cathedral. Pilgrims used to come here to revere the relics of St Cunera, which are still preserved in the St Cunerakerk.

Rhenen

To the east of Rhenen is the Grebbeberg, which was a defensive position of the Dutch army in May 1940. Those who fell in the Second World War are commemorated by a monument and a military cemetery.
On the hill is a zoo, the Ouwehands Dierenpark.

Grebbeberg

Amersfoort

E 6

Province: Utrecht
Population: 94,000

The lively and attractive town of Amersfoort lies amid expanses of forest and heathland at the confluence of several small streams which here join to form the river Eem. The well preserved old part of the town with its historic buildings is surrounded by a double ring of canals.

Situation and
*townscape

Amersfoort is the economic and cultural centre of the Eem valley and the region known as the Gelderse Vallei (Gelderland plain), with a number of higher educational establishments, large markets and important industrial plants (electrical engineering, car assembly, engineering, chemicals). There are also food-processing factories which handle most of the agricultural produce of the surrounding area.

Economy

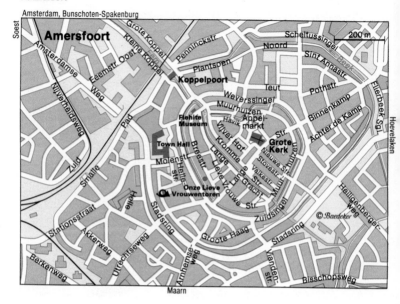

Many of the town's inhabitants commute to work in the nearby provincial capital, Utrecht, or in Amsterdam, 50km/30 miles away.

History

Amersfoort first appears in the documents in 1028, and received its municipal charter in 1259. Thanks to its textile factories and its well-known breweries it developed into a flourishing and prosperous trading town and became a member of the Hanseatic League.

By the first half of the 15th century the town had already expanded beyond its circuit of walls, and a new and larger ring of walls was built between 1450 and 1561. Within the circuit of canals of the original moat lies the well preserved medieval town, with only a few later gabled houses dating from the Renaissance.

The Town

Grote Kerk
(St Joriskerk)

In the Hof, the main square of the old town, stands the Gothic Grote Kerk or St Joriskerk (St George's Church), a hall-church begun in 1243 and completed in 1534. Notable features of the interior are the beautiful Gothic rood screen (15th c.), an organ by Naber with 39 stops and the tomb of the famous Dutch architect Jacob van Campen.

Onze Lieve
Vrouwentoren

South-west of the church rises St Mary's Tower (Onze Lieve Vrouwentoren), almost 100m/330ft high. This imposing Late Gothic tower, with a carillon of 47 bells by the famous François Hemony, is one of the finest of its kind in the Netherlands. It originally belonged to St Mary's Church, which was destroyed by a gunpowder explosion in 1787.

Koppelpoort

From O. L. Vrouwekerkhof (St Mary's churchyard) the outer ring canal runs north to the 15th century Koppelpoort, a water and land gate spanning the Eem in the outer ring of fortifications. The water gate (restored) could be closed with the aid of a windmill.

Flehite Museum, Amersfoort

In the Westsingel, a street along the far side of the outer canal, is the Flehite Museum (No. 50), which contains a historical collection, including mementoes of the Amersfoort-born statesman Johan van Oldenbarnevelt (1547–1619), and a collection of applied and decorative art. Open: Tue.–Fri. 10am–5pm, Sun. 2–5pm.

Flehite Museum

The Westsingel continues round the outer canal and after crossing Utrechtsestraat joins the Zuidsingel. In this street, on the right, is the Mariënhof (1480), a former monastery which is now occupied by the National Archaeological Service.

Mariënhof

Beyond this a bridge crosses the canal, on the far side which on the right, is the Monnikendam, a 15th century water gate.

Monnikendam

On the north side of the old town are the Muurhuizen, a row of picturesque old houses built on the line of the old town walls after they were superseded by the outer circuit of walls, and, to the east of these, the Kamperbinnenpoort, the oldest of Amersfoort's town gates (13th c.).

Muurhuizen, Kamper-binnenpoort

A notable modern building is the Exhibition Hall in the Zonnehof (by G. Rietveld, 1959).

Exhibition Hall

Surroundings of Amersfoort

South-west of the town, on the Amerfoortse Berg (49m/160ft: fine panoramic views), stands the Belgian Monument, commemorating the Belgian refugees who came to Amersfoort during the First World War. South of Laan 1914 is the site of a Nazi concentration camp established in 1941 in which some 35,000 Dutch people were imprisoned. A monument commemorates the many inmates of the camp who died here.

Belgian Monument

Muurhuizen: houses on the old town walls

To Hilversum
via Soestdijk

The road to Hilversum (see entry) runs north-west by way of Soest to Soestdijk (see Baarn, Surroundings). 4km/2½ miles beyond Soestdijk, in the southern outskirts of Baarn, the road forks. The road to the left passes through a wooded area and comes in 1.5km/1 mile to the Kasteel de Hooge Vuursche, which is now a hotel. 6km/4 miles beyond this is Hilversum.

Amsterdam   D 5

Province: Noord-Holland
Population: 692,000

N.B.

The description of Amsterdam in this guide is deliberately abridged, since there is a separate Baedeker guide to the city.

**Amsterdam, Capital of the Netherlands

Situation

Amsterdam lies in the province of Noord-Holland at the junction of the Amstel with the IJ, an arm of the IJsselmeer. Including its ten outer suburbs, Amsterdam has a population of over a million, forming the largest conurbation in what is known as "Randstad Holland".

Importance

Amsterdam is capital of the Kingdom of the Netherlands, but is neither the permanent royal residence nor the seat of government, both of which are in The Hague. With its City University, its Free University (a Reformed Church foundation), the Royal Dutch Academy of Sciences and numerous other research institutes and academies of music, over forty museums and the

The northern Venice: a gracht in Amsterdam ▶

world-famous Concertgebouw Orchestra, Amsterdam is the country's leading cultural centre.

Townscape

The houses of the old town, which is laid out in a pattern of concentric segments in the shape of a fan, are built on piles driven through an upper layer of mud and bogland into the firm sandy bottom up to 18m/60ft below the surface. Within an area of some 800 hectares/2000 acres are crowded some 6750 buildings dating from the 16th–18th centuries. In the 160 canals (*grachten*), which are about 2m/6½ft deep, are more than 2400 houseboats. The 1281 bridges linking the 90 islands give the town an attractive and often very picturesque aspect. Eight of the bridges are wooden bascule bridges; the most famous of these is the Magere Brug.

Around the oldest part of the town are a series of 16th and 17th century extensions, reaching out to the Singelgracht. The most influential architects of this period were Hendrick de Keyser, Jacob van Campen and Philip Vingboons. From 1870 onwards new districts began to develop beyond the Singelgracht, many of them designed by P. J. H. Cuypers. Throughout the 20th century the city has continued to expand, a major influence during the early part of the century being H. P. Berlage, founder of the Amsterdam school of architecture.

Among Amsterdam's other attractions are five windmills, nine carillons and 42 historic organs.

Economy

Commerce; the port

Amsterdam is the focal point and cornerstone of the Dutch economy, thanks mainly to its importance as a commercial centre and the country's second largest port. The Dutch capital market (including the Bank of the Netherlands and other financial institutions) and the main Dutch shipping lines are based in the city; and although the port, with an annual turnover of 25 million tons, falls far behind Rotterdam (240 million tons), it is still an important transhipment and storage point for oil, mineral ores and grain, and to a lesser extent for coal, general cargo, oil-seed and animal feed.

Industry

Apart from the services sector of the economy, industry also plays an important role, for Amsterdam lies in the centre of a huge industrial zone which extends from IJmuiden, at the outflow of the North Sea Canal into the sea, and Hilversum, south-east of Amsterdam. Of particular importance is the industry which has developed in the area of the port since the Second World War, stimulated by a gigantic petrochemical and chemical complex which is supplied with much of its oil by a pipeline from the oil port of Rotterdam. Other important branches of industry are shipbuilding, steelworks, engineering, car manufacture, aircraft construction and textiles. The world-famed Heineken and Amstel breweries, however, have been closed down and transferred to Zoeterwoude, near Leiden, leaving only offices and a visitor centre.
Finally there is the city's very specialised industry of diamond-cutting, which came to Amsterdam after the occupation of Antwerp by the Spaniards in 1576.

Tourism

Amsterdam has developed into a major tourist centre only since the 1950s. It is now visited by almost 1.5 million foreign tourists annually, with a total of 3 million overnight stays. In addition some 7 million visitors come on day trips. Accommodation for visitors is provided by some 270 hotels, with 20,000 beds, and six camping sites, and their varying interests and needs are catered for by 42 museums, 52 theatres, 40 cinemas and 36 discos, as well as by more than 1400 bars and cafés, 574 coffee-shops and 755 restaurants.

History

Amsterdam was originally a fishing village at the outflow of the Amstel into the IJ, an inlet on the Zuiderzee, which was then open to the sea. A dyke was built here in 1270; then in 1275 the village received customs privileges from Count Floris V which granted the inhabitants the right of free passage and free trade in their own goods within the County of Holland. It received its municipal charter in 1300. In 1317 Count William III took over control of the town from the Bishop of Utrecht. During the Middle Ages it enjoyed a period of prosperity, especially after it became the customs post for beer imported from Hamburg. This led to busy trading activity, which developed still further when the town became a member of the Hanseatic League in 1368. Following the so-called "miracle of the Host" the town also became a place of pilgrimage; and when the future Emperor Maximilian I was cured of illness during a pilgrimage in 1489 he granted the town the right to include his crown in its coat of arms.

Amsterdam was almost completely destroyed by fire in 1421, but it was rapidly rebuilt. in 1481 it was surrounded by new stone walls. By 1538 the population had risen to over 30,000.

The town's real heyday began with the struggle for independence. In 1566 its churches and religious houses were stormed by supporters of the Reformation, but the Protestants suffered bloody persecution when the Duke of Alba's forces occupied the town in the following year. At the beginning of the rebellion by the northern provinces Amsterdam was pro-Spanish, but after surrendering to William of Orange it joined in the fight for independence from Spain, in which it played a successful part. As a result of the devastation of Ghent and the decline of Antwerp many merchants, manufacturers and artists moved north from the Spanish Netherlands. Amsterdam now developed into one of the world's leading commercial towns, a centre of learning and culture and a city with flourishing industries and a cosmopolitan population. The "Satisfactie van Amsterdam" laid down that no one should be persecuted for his faith, and thereafter victims of persecution from all over Europe flocked to the city – people from the Spanish-occupied southern Netherlands, craftsmen from Germany driven out by the Thirty Years' War, Jews expelled from Spain and Portugal, Huguenots from France, Protestant refugees from England. Within a period of ten years or so the population doubled in size.

After a fleet mainly chartered by Amsterdam merchants discovered the sea route to India round Africa in 1597 the United East India Company (Verenigde Oost-Indische Compagnie), in which Amsterdam merchants were the leading shareholders, was established in 1602. In 1611 the Commodity Exchange and Stock Exchange were founded. In 1613, during the fourth extension of the city, the triple ring of canals (Herengracht, Keizersgracht, Prinsengracht) was constructed, and the working-class district of Jordaan grew up to the west. By 1620 the population had risen to 100,000, and Amsterdam had become Europe's leading commercial city. In the mid 17th century Rembrandt, Bol, Flinck and Ruisdael were active in Amsterdam. The city attached importance to its ability to defend itself, and all male citizens between the ages of 18 and 60 were under an obligation to take part in the defence of the city if necessary and were enlisted in the town guard. One unit of the guard, commanded by Captain Frans Banning Cocq, had themselves painted by Rembrandt in 1642 in the famous "Night Watch".

Between 1780 and 1784, as a result of Dutch participation in the War of American Independence, Amsterdam lost much of its fleet, and thus also lost its maritime predominance; and as a result of its union with France (1795) and the continental blockade (1806–13) during the Napoleonic period its trade was completely destroyed.

After the French period the city sought to recover its former commercial importance. The construction of the North Holland Canal (1819–25), which

Middle Ages

The struggle
for independence

17th century

18th and 19th
centuries

was intended to obviate the difficult approach to the city through the Zuiderzee, did not have the expected effect. Amsterdam began to recover its prosperity only after the building of the North Sea Canal in 1875 and the Merwede Canal linking the two arms of the Rhine, the Waal and the Lek, in 1892. The first railway line in the Netherlands, between Amsterdam and Haarlem, was opened in 1839. In a local government election in 1913 the Social Democrats won a majority on the city council, and since then Amsterdam has continued to be a centre of democratic socialism.

Second
World War

Amsterdam was occupied by German forces in May 1940, and soon afterwards the first anti-Jewish measures were introduced. On February 25th 1941, in the "February Strike", workers protested against the deportation of Jews from the city. Although resistance to the German occupation was particularly strong in Amsterdam (underground press, concealment of Jews and other victims of persecution, direct action against the occupying forces), almost the entire Jewish population of the city had been deported by the end of the war. In spite of the armistice agreed om May 5th 1945 there was further bloody fighting on May 7th, ended on the following day by the intervention of Canadian forces. The conduct of the city's population during the war led Queen Wilhelmina in 1984 to add the words "heldhaftig, vastberaden, barmhartig" ("heroic, resolute, compassionate") to its coat of arms.

Post-war period

After the war a period of reconstruction began. In 1952, with the opening of the Amsterdam–Rhine Canal, the link with the river Waal was improved and Amsterdam was able to assert its position as the country's second largest seaport and inland port.

The marriage of Princess Beatrix with a German, Claus von Amberg, on March 10th 1966 was the occasion of violent demonstrations in the city, which resulted in the dismissal of the burgomaster and the chief of police. The celebration of the city's 700th anniversary in 1875 led to further clashes in the Nieuwmarkt district between the police and demonstrators protesting against the demolition of houses during the construction of the city's Metro (underground) system.

In 1979 more than 60,000 people were registered as wanting accommodation in Amsterdam, and empty houses were occupied by squatters (*krakers*). On April 30th in that year Queen Juliana abdicated and the new queen, Beatrix, took the oath to uphold the constitution in the Nieuwe Kerk. Outside the well protected security zone round the palace and the church there was violent rioting, directed not so much against the queen as against the city's acute housing shortage. A year later a law was passed requiring all empty houses to be registered. Squatting was prohibited, but nevertheless continued.

The 1980s

In 1986 Amsterdam launched an application to host the Summer Olympics in 1992 but was defeated by Barcelona. In September 1986 the city's new opera house, the Muziektheater, in the Waterlooplein was opened. The Town Hall (Stadhuis) was rehoused in the same building in 1988, and the citizens of Amsterdam now refer to it as the Stopera (Stadhuis/Opera).

Diamonds

For many people Amsterdam is not only a gem of a city but the city of gems, in which diamonds have been cut and traded for many centuries.

History

The city's diamond industry came into being in the 16th century. The exact date of its establishment is taken to be 1586, so that Amsterdam was able some years ago to celebrate its 400th anniversary as the city of diamonds. The development of the industry was promoted by refugees, including many diamond-cutters, from what is now Belgium who left home to escape

Amsterdam's luxury industry: diamond-cutting

religious persecution and settled in the Netherlands. Later periods brought both prosperity and setbacks. Around 1750 there were only some 600 craftsmen employed in the trade, but the discovery of diamonds in South America, particularly in Brazil, led to a great upsurge of activity, and when diamonds were found in South Africa in 1867, and thereafter were mostly cut in Amsterdam, the city developed into one of the world's leading centres of the diamond trade. Appropriately, therefore, the first diamond exhibition in the world was held in Amsterdam in 1936.

During the Second World War the city's diamond industry declined. Tens of thousands of Amsterdam Jews, including 2000 diamond-cutters, were deported and died in concentration camps. Amsterdam now has about a dozen of diamond-cutting establishments and more than 60 firms engaged in the diamond trade. Now as in the past the description "cut in Amsterdam" is a guarantee of high quality and craftsmanship.

One of the world's nineteen diamond exchanges (four of which are in Antwerp) is in Amsterdam.

The diamond (from Greek *adamas*, "unconquerable") is one of the world's most valuable precious stones, notable for its extreme hardness. It consists of pure carbon in crystallised form (usually octahedral or dodecahedral, more rarely cube-shaped).

The diamond

Diamonds are found in kimberlite, an eruptive rock forming pipe-like intrusions (worked to a depth of 2000m/6500ft) and in alluvial deposits and river gravels. The most productive sites are in Africa (Zaire, South Africa, Ghana, Sierra Leone, Namibia, Botswana, Tanzania, Liberia, Central Africa, Ivory Coast, Angola), Australia (third place among diamond-producing countries in 1989), the Soviet Union (Urals), South America (Venezuela, Brazil, Guyana), Indonesia and the East Indies.

More than three-quarters of all diamonds produced are used for industrial purposes (in earth drills, stone saws and glass cutters; for drilling, grinding

Uses of
diamonds

111

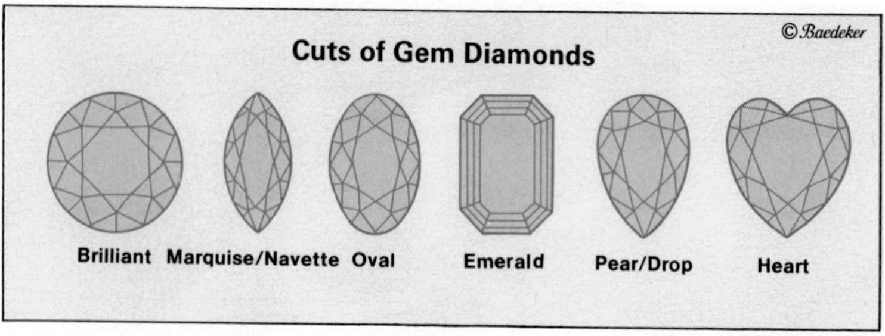

Cuts of Gem Diamonds © *Baedeker*

Brilliant   Marquise/Navette   Oval   Emerald   Pear/Drop   Heart

and polishing metals and synthetics; as sensors in precision engineering equipment, phonographic styluses, hardness testers, wire-drawing dies, etc.). Since 1955 it has been possible to produce synthetic industrial diamonds under extremely high pressures and at very high temperatures.

Value

The value of a gem diamond depends not only on its cutting but also on its colour, its degree of clarity (purity) and its weight. These four criteria – cut, colour, clarity and carat weight – are known as the "four Cs".

Types of cut

Of the types of cut illustrated above the most popular is the brilliant cut. As a result cut diamonds are commonly referred to as brilliants, though strictly speaking this term should be applied only to diamonds which have the full brilliant cut with 58 facets. The marquise (navette), oval, emerald, pear-shaped and heart-shaped cuts also have 58 facets. Other types of cut are the baguette (24 facets), the octahedron (16 facets) and the carré (a square cut).

The facets are the surfaces created by cutting, which must be at certain angles to one another in order to obtain the maximum refraction of light ("sparkle" or "fire"). The largest (horizontal) facet is called the "table".

Shades of colour

The following shades of colour are distinguished:
River: pure white ("blue-white")
Top Wesselton: fine white
Wesselton: white
Top crystal: slightly tinted white
Crystal: tinted white
Top Cape: distinctly tinted white, slightly yellowish
Cape (light yellow): yellowish

Most highly valued are "fancy" diamonds in pure strong colours such as yellow, brandy-brown, pink, green and blue.

Degrees of purity

Internally flawless (under magnification), with no inclusions (impurities)
VVSI (very very small inclusions)
VSI (very small inclusions)
SI (small inclusions)
I Piqué (distinct inclusions)
II Piqué (larger inclusions)
III Piqué (coarse inclusions)

Weight

The weight of a diamond is measured in carats (1 ct = 0.2 gram). The word carat originally came from Arabic and meant the dried carob seed formerly used in weighing diamonds in India and gold in Africa. The word was taken into international use through Dutch as a measure of the weight of diamonds (and also of the purity of gold).

Famous diamonds

The largest brilliant is the Cullinan I diamond (530 carats) in the British crown; it was part of the largest rough diamond ever found (the Cullinan,

3106 carats), which was divided into 105 parts. The second largest brilliant is the Centenary diamond (rough 599 carats, cut 350 carats), found in a mine near Pretoria in 1986. Other well-known large diamonds are the Excelsior (rough 955 carats, divided into 22 brilliants), the Jonker (rough 726 carats, divided into 12 brilliants), the Nizam of Hyderabad (cut 340 carats), the Great Mogul (cut 280 carats), the Jubilee (rough 651 carats, cut 245 carats), the Star of Yakutia (232 carats), the Orloff (cut 200 carats), the Victoria (rough 469 carats, cut 184 carats), the Koh-i-Noor ("Mountain of Light"; rough 191 carats, cut 186 carats), the Regent (rough 410 carats, cut 140 carats) and the Florentine (137 carats).

A visit to a diamond-cutting establishment is an interesting and instructive experience. After a conducted tour (usually free of charge) visitors have an opportunity of looking round the showroom and, if they wish, making a purchase.

Diamond-cutting establishments

The following establishments welcome visitors between the hours stated (which may be reduced in winter). An appointment for a visit should be made by telephone.

Amsterdam Diamond Center, Rokin 1–5, tel. 24 57 87 (open: Mon.–Wed., Fri. and Sat. 10am–5.30pm, Thur. 10am–8.30pm, Sun. 10.30am–5.30pm).
Bonebakker & Zoon, Rokin 86–90, tel. 23 22 94 (open: Mon.–Fri. 9.30am–5.30pm, Sat. and Sun. 10.30am–5pm).
Coster Diamonds, Paulus Potterstraat 2–4, tel. 76 22 22 (open: Mon.–Sat. 9am–5pm, Sun. 10am–5pm).
Diamonds Bab Hendriksen, Weteringschans 89, tel. 26 27 98 (open: Mon.–Sat. 9am–6pm, Sun. 10am–6pm).
Gassan Diamond House, Nieuwe Achtergracht 17–23, tel. 22 53 33 (open: Mon.–Sun. 9am–5pm).
Holshuysen-Stoeltje, Wagenstraat 13–17, tel. 23 76 01 (open: Mon.–Sun. 9am–5pm).
River Diamonds Center, Weteringschans 79A, tel. 27 52 55 (open: Mon.–Sun. 9am–5pm).

Warning

While in Amsterdam you should keep a particularly careful eye on your property.
In recent years, partly as a result of the drug scene, there has been an alarming increase in crime in the city, directed not only against the local people but against the less wary visitors. Thefts and robberies are common occurrences – in the street, in the airport, in hotels, restaurants and trams – and cars are frequently broken into.
You should, therefore, carry anything of value on your person, and should leave absolutely nothing of consequence in a parked car. The glove-box should be left unlocked, and the car radio should preferably be removed. Unless you take these precautions you may well find, after a short walk round the town or a sightseeing tour, that the contents of your car have disappeared.

Shopping in Amsterdam

In Amsterdam's principal shopping streets can be found both exclusive shops and department stores of international standing. Favourite shopping areas are pedestrian zones like Kalverstraat (many shoe shops; Vroom & Dreesmann's department store), Nieuwendijk (Hema department store, with low-priced goods), Heiligeweg, Winkelcentrum Amsterdam-Noord and Amsterdam-Poort.
Amsterdam's oldest department store, the Bijenkorf ("Beehive"), at Damrak 90, sells a wide range of goods of excellent quality.

Map of Amsterdam showing the following labeled locations:

Jacob Catskade, Kattensloot, Willemsstraat, Haarlemmerstraat, Hav gebo, van Hallstraat, Lindengracht, Noorderkerk, Craft Centre, Frederik Hendrik-plantsoen, Westerstraat, Anjeliersstraat, Nassaukade, Marnixstraat, Egelandtiersstraat, Keizers gracht, Heren gracht, Singel, Spuistraat, burgwal, Nieuwe, Hugo de Grootstraat, Hendrikstraat, Frederik, Anne Frank House, Wester-kerk, Raadhuisstraat, Nieuwe Kerk, Dam, Kostverloren, Rozengracht, Money-Box Museum, Royal Palace, Dam, Clercqstraat, Rozenstraat, Laurierstraat, Prinsen gracht, Keizers, Heren gracht, Singel, Voor-, Kalverstraat, Rokin, Nes, Driega hui, de Bilderdijk, Da Costa, Nassaukade, Marnixstraat, Singel, Phonogr. Museum, Histor. Museum, Begijn-hof, N.Z., Bellamyplein, gracht, Kinkerstraat, Bible Museum, Univ. Library, Madame Tussaud, Spui, Alla Piei Mus, Kinkerstraat, van Lennepstraat, Prinsen gracht, Leidse gracht, Heren gracht, Munt-toren, Jacob, Constantijn, straat, Bellevue Theatre, Stadsschouwburg, Leidseplein, Leidsestraat, Kerkstraat, Nieuwe Spiegelstraat, Vizelstraat, Rembra, gracht, Fod Mus, Wilhelmina Gasthuis, 1e Helmers-, Overtoom, straat, Leidseplein, Keizers-, Kerkstraat, gracht, Overtoom, Vondel-, Hugensstraat, Vossiusstraat, Hooftstraat, Spiegelgr, Prinsen-, gracht, Nieuwe, Vizelgr, Looiersst, Den Haag, Vondelpark, Pieter, Cornelisz, Jan Luykenstraat, Rijks-museum, Eeghenstraat, Van Gogh-Museum, Overholland Museum, Hobbemakade, Stadhouderskade, straat, Eeghenstraat, Willemsparkweg, Stedelijk Museum, Museumstraat, Quellijnstraat, Gerard Do, van, Concert-gebouw, Bol

Haarlem

Den Haag

World Trade Center · RAI Congress Centre

Amsterdam

300 m

Afgesloten IJ

IJ-Tunnel

IJ-Haven

Ruyterkade

Central Station

...tionsplein

Front

...kade

St Nicolaas

Schreierstoren

Amstelkring Museum

Oude Kerk

Oosterdokskade

Oosterdok

Prins Hendrikkade

Oostelijke Handelskade

Piet Heinkade

Dijksgracht

Katenburgerstraat

Wittenburgerstraat

Waag

Nieuwmarkt

Montelbaanstoren

Zeedijk

Waals

Eilandsgr

Oude Schans

Maritime Museum

Grote ...

Trippenhuis

Zuiderkerk

...brouw

...ersity

Rembrandthuis

Waterlooplein

Valkenburgerstraat

Rapenburgerstr

Hoogte

Nieuwe Vaart

Kadijk

Stadhuis/Muziektheater

Mr. Visserplein

Portuguese Synagogue

Plantage

Entrepotdok

Doklaan

Sarphatistraat

Jewish Historical Museum

Botanic Garden

Plantage Middenlaan

Zoo ("Artis")

Mauritskade

Willet-Holthuysen Museum

Heren...

Nieuwe

Keizers...gracht

Plantage Muidergracht

Aquarium

Six ...ection

Amstel

Nieuwe

Weesperstraat

Kerkstraat

Plantage

Muidergracht

Magere Brug

Nieuwe

Prinsengracht

...straat

Tropical Museum

Carré Theatre

Sarphati...

Mauritskade

Linnaeusstraat

Frederiksplein

Rijnspoorplein

Oosterpark

Oosterparkstraat

Ajax-Stadion

...trachtsestraat

Stadhouderskade

Amstel

Ruyschstraat

Blasiusstraat

Oosterparkstraat

Vrolikstraat

Govert Flinckstraat

Jan Steenstraat

© Baedeker

Between the Amsterdam *grachten* (canals) there are a variety of small shops and boutiques selling an extraordinary range of goods. They include a number of highly specialised shops – one selling nothing but cookery books, another offering 200 different kinds of beer, still another which stocks kites of all kinds, either in kit form or ready to fly.

Amsterdam has more than a dozen markets (see Practical Information, Markets), including the flea market in Waterlooplein and the floating flower market in the Singel.

Other shopping facilities are offered by the city's second-hand bookshops, shops for collectors and shops selling craft articles of various kinds.

Sightseeing in Amsterdam

Sightseeing walks

In the following pages the sights of Amsterdam are described in a series of walks – first in the central area within the inner ring of *grachten* (Prinsengracht and Nieuwe Prinsengracht); then a walk from the city centre to the southern districts of the city, with the Rijksmuseum, the Van Gogh Museum and the Stedelijk Museum; and finally the rest of the city.

These walks are followed by some suggestions for excursions in the immediate surroundings of the city.

* Sightseeing by coach

There are numerous sightseeing tours round the city, its *grachten* and its port, many of them starting from two city centre streets, the Damrak and Rokin. There are also after-dark tours; one trip with an atmosphere all its own is a "candlelight tour" by boat.

During the summer there are sighteeing tours every hour or more often, in winter less frequently.

Central Area

Dam

The traffic hub of the inner city is the Dam, a large square on the western edge of the oldest part of Amsterdam. Although it is neither the geographical nor the administrative centre of Amsterdam, it is still the real heart of the city. It gave the city its name; for the Dam, which came into being around 1270, separates the river Amstel from the IJ (an arm of the Zuiderzee), and it was here that the first settlement on the site of Amsterdam was established, a village whose inhabitants gained their subsistence from fishing and stock-farming.

National Monument

In the centre of the square stands the National Monument, which was unveiled on May 4th 1956, the national day of mourning. This obelisk of light-coloured stone, 22m/72ft high, designed by J. J. P. Oud and J. W. Rädeler, is a memorial for those who died in the Second World War and a monument to the Dutch Resistance, to the country's liberation and to peace. Enclosed within the obelisk are eleven urns containing earth from the seven provinces of the Netherlands. Every year on May 4th the Queen and Prince Consort lay wreaths at the foot of the monument, and at 8pm on that day there are two minutes of silence throughout the country in memory of those who died.

** Royal Palace

On the west side of the square is the Royal Palace (originally the Town Hall), in which the Queen resides when in Amsterdam.

The building, which is borne on 13,659 piles, was begun in 1649 by Jacob van Campen. The exterior is in severely classical style; the interior is sumptuously appointed. The Town Hall was completed in 1665, under the

The heart of Amsterdam: the Dam and the Royal Palace

direction of Daniël Stalpaert, with the erection of the 51m/167ft high tower (which contains a carillon).

This imposing building, a masterpiece of 17th century Dutch classical architecture, was for some two centuries the political centre of the city and the Republic. In 1808, however, Louis Bonaparte, the new king of Holland, took over the Town Hall as his residence; and the Empire furniture with which he equipped it is still one of the finest collections of the kind in the world.

After the fall of Napoleon the palace was returned to the city, which could not afford to restore it to its former function and therefore ceded it to King William I as a temporary residence. Then in 1935 the city bought it back and had it thoroughly restored for use on official and ceremonial occasions; it finally came into use for these purposes in 1968.

The most magnificent of the royal apartments, which are richly decorated with marble sculpture, is the Burgerzaal (Burghers' Hall), one of the finest ceremonial halls in Europe. In this room was held the ball on the occasion of the marriage of Princess Beatrix to Claus von Amberg in 1966. The Throne Room contains a fine painting by Ferdinand Bol. The Vierschaar (Court-Room) has four magnificent caryatids by A. Quellinus the Elder.

The Palace is open daily in June, July and August from 12.30 to 4pm; from September to May there is a conducted tour every Wednesday at 2pm.

Adjoining the Palace is the Nieuwe Kerk (New Church) or St Catharinakerk, in which kings and queens of the Netherlands have been crowned since 1814. Queen Beatrix was crowned in the church (which had just undergone a 22-year period of restoration and renovation) on April 30th 1980.   *Nieuwe Kerk

The church is no longer used for worship, and now provides accommodation for art exhibitions, antiques fairs, etc. There are regular organ recitals.

117

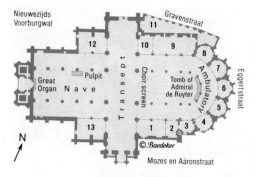

Nieuwe Kerk
St Catharina

1 Marksmen's Chapel
2 Eggert Chapel
3 Chapel of Our Lady of the
  Seven Sorrows (Sills Chapel)
4 Verbergen Chapel
5 Meeus Chapel
6 Masons' Chapel
7 Boelens Chapel
8 Clothworkers' Chapel
9 Chapel of Holy Cross
10 Lady Chapel
11 Deaconry
12 Old Choir of Holy Cross
13 Headmaster's house

This imposing Late Gothic cruciform basilica was founded in the early 15th century and dates in its present form from around 1490. It was almost completely destroyed by fire in 1645 but was soon rebuilt, though the tower remained unfinished because of shortage of money.

The interior is sumptuously furnished. The brass choir screen, on a marble base, was the work of Jacob Lutma; the carved Baroque pulpit is by Albert Vinckenbrinck, the organ case by Jacob van Campen.
There are a number of important tombs, notably the Baroque tomb, by Rombout Verhulst, of Admiral Michiel A. de Ruyter (d. 1676) in the choir. Also buried in the church are the writers Joost van den Vondel (d. 1679; tablet on wall) and Pieter Corneliszoon Hooft and the bell-founders François and Pierre Hemony.

The church is open Mon.–Sat. 11am–4pm, Sun. 12 noon–5pm.

Commercial Exchange

From the Dam the broad Damrak, one of the main traffic arteries of the city centre, runs north-east to the Central Station, passing on the right the Commercial Exchange (Koopmansbeurs), an imposing brick building by H. P. Berlage (1899–1903) which set the pattern for modern Dutch architecture.

Central Station

At the north end of the Damrak a wide bridge crosses the open Havenfront to the Stationsplein, in which is the Central Station (Centraal Spoorweg Station), built by P. J. H. Cuypers on three artificial islands in the IJ and borne on 8678 piles. Opened in 1899, the station has a very fine first-class waiting room in Art Nouveau style. The façade shows the influence of neo-classical palace architecture. When the Japanese, around 1900, were looking for a model for a new railway station in Tokyo they chose Amsterdam.

Schreierstoren

Prins Hendrikkade (formerly known as the Buitenkant) runs south-east along the south side of the open Havenfront and the Oosterdok, passing on the right St Nicolaaskerk (1885–86; R.C.). At the intersection of Prins Henrikkade and Geldersekade, just beyond the church, is the Schreierstoren ("Weepers' Tower"; 1487), a semicircular brick-built tower which is a relic of the first town walls. The name seems to have arisen from a stone built into the wall of the tower carved with the figure of a weeping woman: hence the legend that the fishermen's wives used to gather here and weep at the departure of their menfolk.

Farther east, at the corner of the Binnenkant, is the Scheepvaarthuis (Shipping House; 1913), an interesting example of Dutch Art Nouveau architecture, with the headquarters of various shipping companies. Beyond this, at Prins Hendrikkade 137, is a house once occupied by Admiral de Ruyter.

The Commercial Exchange: a precursor of modern architecture

Amsterdam's Central Station: classical and palatial

Amsterdam

Zeedijk

From the Schreierstoren a narrow street, Oudezijds Kolk, leads south-west into the Zeedijk, one of Amsterdam's oldest streets, with many houses leaning at an angle from the vertical. At No. 1 is a 15th century house which is thought to be the oldest surviving building in the city.

Walletjes

In the oldest part of Amsterdam, between the Oudezijds Voorburgwal and Achterburgwal (in the triangular area between the Central Station, the Dam and the Nieuwmarkt), are the *walletjes,* the city's red light district (*rose buurt*). The "oldest profession" has been officially tolerated here since the 14th century.

Amstelkring Museum

In an old merchant's house at Oudezijds Voorburgwal 40 is the Amstelkring Museum, with the "hidden" Roman Catholic church (17th c.) of Ons Lieve Heer op Zolder (Our Lord in the Garret) in the attic storey. In addition to the church itself (with altar and organ) there are a number of 17th and 18th century rooms which now display a collection of ecclesiastical antiquities, furniture, pictures and prints. Open: Mon.–Sat. 10am–5pm, Sun. 1–5pm.

*Oude Kerk

Farther south, in the Oudekerkplein, stands the Oude Kerk (Old Church; Reformed), Amsterdam's oldest church. Originally a small cruciform church, it was built in 1306 on the site of a slightly earlier wooden church; part of the tower dates from that period. It was the first hall-church (a church with aisles of the same height as the nave) in Noord-Holland and the model for other churches in the region. It was dedicated by the bishop of Utrecht to St Nicholas, protector of fishermen and seamen and Amsterdam's patron saint.

Soon after the building of the church there were plans for its enlargement. In 1370 the choir was extended by the addition of two chapels and an ambulatory, and around 1500 side chapels were built on to the aisles. During the 16th century the hall-church began to be converted into a basilica. The nave was heightened (1536), and in 1558 a low tower was added. On the south side were built a new doorway and the "Iron Chapel", at the west end a baptistery chapel, on the north side a Late Gothic doorway and at the east end, adjoining the choir, the Lady Chapel (Lieve Vrouwe-kapel; 1553).
From the tall west tower (1565) there are fine views of Amsterdam.

*Stained glass

From the pre-Reformation period date three magnificent stained glass windows of the Dutch High Renaissance (1555; scenes from the life of the Virgin) and the beautifully carved choir-stalls.

Oudekerksplein

Oude Kerk
St Nicolaas

1 South doorway (entrance)
2 Iron Chapel
3 Smiths' Chapel
4 St Sebastian's Chapel
5 Seamen's Chapel
6 Remains of Chapel of Holy Sepulchre
7 Chamber of the Guild of Our Lady
8 Old Women's Choir
9 New Women's Choir (stained glass)
10 Tomb of St Joris
11 Holy Sepulchre
12 Chapel of the Buckwheat Merchants
13 Old north doorway (c. 1520)
14 Bargeman's Chapel
15 Hamburg Chapel
16 Old Baptistery (c. 1462)
17 Lijsbeth Gaven Chapel
18 Chapel of the Poor

Oude Kerk   Zuiderkerk

Many famous citizens of Amsterdam are buried in the church, including
Rembrandt's wife Saskia and a number of distinguished admirals.

From here Oude Kennisstraat and Molensteeg lead to the Nieuwmarkt   Weigh-House
(New Market Square), in which is the municipal Weigh-House (Waagge-
bouw). Originally the St Antoniepoort, a relic of the 15th century town
walls, it was converted into a weigh-house in 1617, after the town had
expanded beyond the old walls.

On the upper floor is the Guild House, in which each guild (painters, smiths,
surgeons, etc.) had its own entrance. In the 17th century the surgeons gave
anatomical lectures here – frequently attended by Rembrandt.

From 1819 the Weigh-House served at different times as a barracks for
firemen, a municipal record office and a museum. For a time it also housed
the Jewish Historical Museum, which moved into larger premises in 1987.
It is now a Centre for Information and Communication.

From the Nieuwmarkt Kloveniersburgwal runs south-west. Off its western   Wijnkopers-
side opens Koestraat, at Nos. 10–12 of which is the Wijnkopersgildehuis   gildehuis
(Wine Dealers' Guild-House), now housing the Dutch Wine Museum. Three
houses built in 1551 were combined into one in 1611 and then rebuilt
between 1633 and 1655. The gable and doorway were built by Pieter de
Keyser (1633). The main feature of the interior is the Guild Hall.

In the picturesque canal-side street, at Kloveniersburgwal 29, is the Trip-   Trippenhuis
penhuis, an elegant patrician house built by Justus Vingboons for the Trip
brothers, wealthy cannon-founders, which has been occupied since 1808
by the Dutch Academy of Sciences.
The chimneys, in the form of mortars, point to the source of the brothers'
wealth.

121

The Weigh-House, originally one of the town gates

Opposite the Trippenhuis, at No. 26, is the Kleine Trippenhuis, a smaller house built in the same style and the same materials. It is traditionally believed to have been built after a servant in the Trippenhuis exclaimed, "If only I had a house as wide as its doorway, how happy I should be!".

Oostindisch Huis

At the corner of Kloveniersburgwal and Oude Hoogstraat stands the Oostindisch Huis, the oldest part of which was built by Hendrick de Keyser in 1606. It is laid out round a courtyard with very handsome façades. The façade of the north wing dates from 1633, that of the east wing from the late 19th century.

Stadhuis

Oude Hoogstraat leads back to the Oudezijds Achterburgwal and over a bridge to the old Stadhuis (Town Hall). Originally a convent of St Cecilia, the building was converted after the Reformation into the residence of the Stadholder, the Prinsenhof, and was later occupied by the Admiralty. It became the Town Hall when King Louis Napoleon took over the original Town Hall as his palace.

The building is laid out round an inner courtyard. The main feature surviving from the original complex is a pilastered façade of 1661. The front facing on to the *gracht* was built in 1925 in the style of the Amsterdam school.

In 1988 the municipal administration moved to the new Stopera building in Waterlooplein.

On the opposite side of the *gracht,* at No. 185, is the old Spinhuis (Spinning House) of 1645.

Agnietenkapel

South of the Stadhuis, along Oudezijds Voorburgwal (No. 231), is the Agnietenkapel, originally belonging to a convent of 1470, which in 1632 became the home of the Atheneum Illustre, later Amsterdam University. It now houses the University's historical collections.

Oostindisch Huis

Between Kloveniersburgwal and Grimburgwal is Oudemanhuispoort, an arched passage containing a number of second-hand bookshops. As its name indicates ("Old Men's Gate"), it was formerly the entrance to an old people's home founded in 1754. The site is now occupied by one of the main buildings of the City University, which now has more than 17,000 students.

University

Founded in 1877, it was the first university in the Netherlands to establish, after the Second World War, a faculty of social and political science. The University has the reputation of being progressive, and played a prominent part during the student unrest of the years 1964–66 (the "Provo" period).

Diagonally opposite the University, at the point where Oudezijds Voorburgwal, Oudezijds Achterburgwal and Grimburgwal meet, can be seen the famous Driegrachtenhuis (House on Three Canals).

Driegrachtenhuis

Near the University, in Zandstraat, is the Zuiderkerk (South Church; 1603–11), the first church built after the Reformation as a Protestant place of worship. It was designed by the famous architect Hendrick de Keyser, who is buried in the church.

Zuiderkerk

The South Church has not been used for worship since 1929. During the Second World War it served as a mortuary for the many victims of the "hungry winter" of 1944–45; from 1950 it was used as an exhibition hall (particularly by the municipal planning department); and more recently it has housed various social and cultural activities.

The 80m/260ft high tower (1614) is one of the finest in Amsterdam. The carillon in the octagonal spire came from the workshops of the Hemony brothers.

123

Amsterdam

Jewish quarter

The former Jewish quarter of Amsterdam lay between Houtkoopersburgwal in the north and Binnen-Amstel in the south. The first Jewish refugees from Portugal, Germany and Poland came to Amsterdam towards the end of the 16th century and settled in the area around Waterlooplein. The particular charm of this quarter lay in its numerous little shops selling second-hand goods, drapery and greengroceries. During the Second World War more than 70% of the city's Jewish population were deported, and little is now left of the former atmosphere of the quarter.

Stopera

New life, however, has come to this area. In Waterlooplein is Amsterdam's Opera House, the Muziektheater, which along with the Town Hall occupies a modern multi-purpose building, now known as the Stopera (Stadhuis/Opera).The Opera House was opened in 1986, the new Town Hall in 1988.

A reminder of the former Jewish presence is provided by the Jewish Historical Museum (see page 125).

Normaal Amsterdams Peil

In the passage between the Town Hall and the Opera House, set against the backdrop of a 25m/80ft long cross-section of the Netherlands, is a replica of the Normaal Amsterdams Peil (standard water-mark), which showed the mean water level of the North Sea. The original mark is under the paving in front of the Royal Palace.

Vlooienmarkt (Flea Market)

After an absence of almost ten years the famous Amsterdam flea market has returned to Waterlooplein, where it was held from 1886. It offers a varied and colourful assortment of wares ranging from useful and usable items to the merest junk.

Rembrandthuis

In the main street of the Jewish quarter, Jodenbreestraat (No. 4), is the Rembrandthuis (built 1606), in which Rembrandt spent the happiest and most successful years of his life (1639–60) with Saskia.

Stopera: modern and functional

The house was bought in 1906 by the Stichting Rembrandthuis (Rembrandt House Foundation) and opened as a museum. It contains an almost complete collection of Rembrandt's graphic work (some 250 etchings and drawings) and paintings by his teachers and pupils. Open: Mon.–Sat. 10am–5pm, Sun. 1–5pm.

Jodenbreestraat runs south-east into Mr Visserplein, named after L. R. Visser (1871–1942), who became chairman of the Hoge Raad (Supreme Council) in 1939 but was dismissed by the German occupation authorities in November 1940 and then joined the Dutch Resistance.

Mr Visserplein

Just south of Visserplein is J. D. Meijerplein, named after Jonas Daniël Meijer (1780–1834), a leader of the High German Jewish community in Amsterdam (see below). In the centre of the square can be seen a statue, De Dokwerker ("The Dock Worker"), commemorating the strike by the workers of Amsterdam in February 1941 in protest at the anti-Jewish measures of the German occupation forces.

J. D. Meijerplein

On the north side of J. D. Meijerplein, approached through a forecourt surrounded by low houses, is the Portuguese Synagogue (1671–75), the largest of the three synagogues in the square. Designed by Daniël Stalpaert and Elias Bouman on the model of Solomon's temple, it is oriented to the south-east, the direction of Jerusalem. The interior is divided into three aisles by four Ionic columns.
The synagogue (restored 1953–59), the finest in the Netherlands, contains an Ark of the Law in fine wood from Brazil and magnificent candelabra.

Portuguese Synagogue

On the south side of J. D. Meijerplein (No. 2–4) is the Jewish Historical Museum (Joods Historisch Museum), which was opened in 1987. It occupies the High German Synagogue complex, named after the High German Jewish community, formed of refugees from Germany and Poland, which

*Jewish Historical Museum

Jewish Historical Museum

grew up here from 1635 onwards. The first of the four synagogues, the Grote Synagoge (Great Synagogue), was built in 1670 but soon proved to be too small. A second, smaller, synagogue, the Obbene Sjoel, was built adjoining the Grote Synagoge, and this was followed in 1700 by the Driet Sjoel and in 1752 by the Nieuwe Synagoge or Neie Sjoel (New Synagogue). In 1955 the Jewish community sold the synagogue complex to the city of Amsterdam, which in the mid seventies resolved to convert it to a new use. The buildings were restored and linked with one another by a structure of glass and steel, producing a very attractive building of transparent effect which now houses the most important Jewish museum outside Israel.

The tour of the museum complex begins in the New Synagogue, where visitors are introduced to "Aspects of Jewish Identity", the five main themes in which are religious belief, Zionism, persecution and survival during the Nazi period, culture and the influence of Dutch life and culture.

In the Great Synagogue is displayed the museum's collection of ritual objects – silver Torah pointers, Torah mantles and crowns, curtains and canopies. On the east side of the synagogue, directed towards Jerusalem, is the Ark of the Law, of white marble. Open: daily 10am–5pm.

From Visserplein Muiderstraat leads into the eastern districts of the city.

Magere Brug

Of all Amsterdam's bridges, numbering over a thousand, the Magere Brug, near Weesperstraat, is the most frequently photographed. This plain timber bascule bridge was originally built in 1671 as a footbridge. After being several times rebuilt it was demolished in 1929 and was originally to be rebuilt as a modern electrically operated bridge. It was finally decided, however, to reconstruct the bridge in its original form; the work was directed by an architect named Mager, whose name it bears.
To the south of the bridge are the Amstel Sluizen, a train of locks.

The Magere Brug, the most photographed of Amsterdam's bridges

Near the east end of the tree-lined *gracht,* at Amstel 218, is the Six Collec-*Six Collection tion (Collectie Six), one of the finest private collections of 17th century Dutch masters (including Rembrandt). The gallery can be visited only with a card of introduction from the Rijksmuseum, obtainable on production of passport.

South and west of the city centre is the Herengracht, which dates from the *Herengracht year 1612, when a plan was drawn up for the construction of a ring of canals (the Heren-, Keizers- and Prinsengracht).
In Amsterdam's golden age (second half of 17th century) the Herengracht was the town's best residential area. It was so much sought after that the town council was compelled to restrict the width of the patrician houses to 8m/26ft – though there were some exceptions, as the "House for a Prince" (No. 54) shows. Behind the houses with their magnificent façades (no fewer than 400 of them protected as national monuments) are beautiful gardens, each exactly 51.5m/169ft long. For a city built on piles they represent an extraordinary luxury. Building in the gardens was prohibited by law, except for garden houses and coachmen's houses.

On the Herengracht are the Theatre Museum (Nederlands Theaterinstituut) Willet Holthuysen Museum and the Willet Holthuysen Museum (No. 605), in a patrician house of 1687 which was bequeathed to the city of Amsterdam by Mrs Willet Holthuysen in 1889 and opened as a museum in 1896. It has fine furniture of the 16th–18th centuries, rich collections of porcelain and glass and a good library. The garden is laid out in 18th century style. Open: daily 11am–5pm.

Just south of the Amstel lies Rembrandtsplein, once the site of the butter Rembrandtsplein market. It received its present name when a statue of Rembrandt was erected in the gardens in 1852. Since the mid 19th century this square has ranked together with Leidseplein as one of the city's leading centres of entertainment, with numerous cafés, bars and night spots.

Patrician houses on the Herengracht

The Mint Tower, part of the old fortifications

Begijnhof: an oasis of peace in the city centre

Munttoren	From Rembrandtsplein Reguliersbreestraat runs north-east to Muntplein, in which stands the Munttoren (Mint Tower). The name dates from 1627, when for a brief period of two years Amsterdam enjoyed the right to mint coins – Utrecht, where the coinage was normally minted, being then in the hands of the French. The tower was part of the town's medieval defences, which were almost completely destroyed in a great fire in 1620, when only the lower part of the tower survived. On the stone stump Hendrick de Keyser, the municipal architect, erected a timber superstructure, with a carillon by Hemony.
Allard Pierson Museum	From the Muntplein there is a good view of the Amstel and the Allard Pierson Museum (Oude Turfmarkt 127), which has a fine collection of antiquities from Egypt, Cyprus, the Near East, Mesopotamia, Iran, Greece and Rome. Open: Tue.–Fri. 10am–5pm, Sat. and Sun. 1–5pm.
University Library	To the west of the Munttoren, in the Singel, is the University Library (No. 423), one of the largest libraries in the Netherlands (over 2 million volumes), distributed among a number of institutes.
	No. 425 houses valuable manuscripts and incunabula, as well as the Bibliotheca Rosenthalia (Jewish literature) and the Museum of the Press (Nederlands Persmuseum). Here too are the J. A. Dortmond Museum of Writing, which traces the history of writing from around 3000 B.C. to the present day, the Frederik van Eeden Museum, devoted to the Dutch writer and social reformer of that name, and the Vondel Collection (relating to the 17th century poet and dramatist Joost van den Vondel).
Begijnhof	Between the Spui and Kalverstraat, in the Gedempte Begijnensloot, is the Begijnhof, an idyllic little spot in the centre of the city, a quiet courtyard of old houses which provide low-rent accommodation for old ladies and young girl students.

128

The Begijnhof was founded in 1346, when it lay outside the town, to house pious Catholic women (*begijnen*), who lived in a religious community and devoted themselves to the care of the sick and the poor. They were not required to take any vows, they could come and go freely and they were allowed to have personal property. When Amsterdam became Protestant in the 16th century the Begijnhof became a hospice and the church was given over to a Scottish Presbyterian congregation, the *begijnen* retaining only the right to be buried in their old church. The last *begijn* living here died in 1971.

The Kalverstraat is the meeting-place of half the city's population. With its chic and fashionable shops, boutiques and perfumeries it is Amsterdam's most celebrated shopping street – though the "best" address is now P. C. Hooftstraat. First mentioned in the records in 1393, the Kalverstraat owes its name to the old calf market. The first tradesmen to establish themselves here were, accordingly, butchers, followed by other craftsmen including shoemakers and basketmakers. By the mid 18th century there were more than 200 shops of all kinds in the street, as well as coffee-houses and lodging houses. It is now a pedestrian precinct, frequented every day by more than 100,000 shoppers and window-shoppers.

Kalverstraat

The only Madame Tussaud's outside London was opened at Kalverstraat 156 in 1970 and has now moved to Dam 20. In addition to contemporary figures such as Queen Beatrix there are also historical characters including Napoleon and Peter the Great. A whole room is devoted to Rembrandt. The "Garden of Earthly Delights" recreates the fantastic world of Hieronymus Bosch. Visitors can also see the workshops in which the wax figures are produced. Open: daily 10am–6pm, in July and August until 7pm.

Madame Tussaud's Panopticon

The Historical Museum of Amsterdam has been housed since 1975, the year in which the city celebrated its 700th anniversary, in the old Municipal Orphanage (1578–1860) in St Luciensteeg. The name of the street recalls the convent of St Lucia, founded in 1414, which once stood on the site.
The museum has a large and interesting collection of material on the history of the city. Open: daily 11am–5pm.
Adjoining the museum, in St Luciensteeg, now roofed over, are group portraits of the old town guard.

Historical Museum

In Raadhuisstraat, to the west of the Dam, is the Money-Box Museum (Spaarpottenmuseum), with a collection of some 12,000 money-boxes from all over the world. Open: Mon.–Fri. 1–4pm.

Money-Box Museum

On Prinsengracht is Amsterdam's most popular church, the Westerkerk, in which Queen Beatrix married Claus von Amberg in 1966. The tower, familiarly known as "Langer Jan" (Long John), is the tallest in the city (85m/280ft) and one of Amsterdam's best known landmarks.
The building of the church was begun by Hendrick de Keyser in 1620, after Amsterdam had adopted the Protestant faith. Although in Renaissance style, it still contains many Gothic features, both externally and internally. After Keyser's death the work was completed by Jacob van Kampen (1630) and the tower added. The tower, topped by the imperial crown of Maximilian I of Austria, contains a carillon of 48 bells which can be heard on the hour. Notable features of the interior are the organ (1622), with allegorical paintings by G. de Lairesse, and the marble column set up in 1906 in commemoration of Rembrandt.

*Westerkerk

Rembrandt, who died in poverty, was originally buried outside the church and later moved into the interior. His tomb (probably empty) is on the north side of the church.

At Prinsengracht 263 is the house in which the Frank family, who had fled from Frankfurt in 1933 to escape Nazi persecution, hid from 1942 to 1944 during the German occupation. Here Anne Frank wrote the world-famed "Diary" which has been translated into 51 languages. On August 4th 1944

Anne Frank House

Rijksmuseum

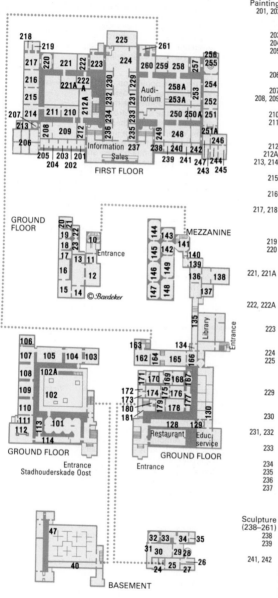

FIRST FLOOR
Paintings (201–236)

201, 202	15th c. Dutch painters: Geertgen tot Sint Jans, Jan Mostaert
203	J. C. van Oostsanen
204	Lucas van Leyden
205	Jan Cornelisz Vermeyen, Maerten van Heemskerck
206	Pieter Aertsz Joachim Bueckelaer
207	Jan Brueghel the Elder
208, 209	Werner van den Valckert, Frans Hals
210	Hendrik Overcamp
211	Rembrandt, "Jeremiah lamenting the Fall of Jerusalem", etc.
212	Passage
212A	Special exhibitions
213, 214	In course of reorganisation
215	Bartholomeus van der Helst
216	Paulus Potter, Jan Steen
217, 218	Jacob van Ruisdael, Adriaen van Ostade, Adriaen and Esaias van de Velde
219	Jan Steen
220	Willem van de Velde the Younger, Jan van de Capelle
221, 221A	Dutch painting on Italian themes: Asselijn, Berchem, Both, Dujardin
222, 222A	Emanuel de Witte, Jan Vermeer, Pieter de Hooch
223	The history of Rembrandt's "Night Watch"
224	"Night Watch"
225	Non-Dutch masters: Fra Angelico, Tiepolo, Goya, Murillo, Rubens, Van Dyck
229	Rembrandt, "Self-Portrait as the Apostle Paul"
230	Rembrandt, "Syndics of the Drapers' Guild"
231, 232	Ferdinand Bol, Nicolaes Maes
233	In course of reorganisation
234	Aelbert Cuyp
235	Melchior d'Hondecoeter
236	Dujardin
237	Sale of reproductions and catalogues

Sculpture and applied art (238–261)

238	Limoges enamel
239	Bronze statuettes from a tomb
241, 242	15th and 16th c. sculpture (Adriaen van Wezel, etc.); tapestry, "The Orange Harvest" (c. 1500)

the family was arrested and sent to concentration camps. Only Anne's father, Otto Frank, survived; Anne herself died in Belsen two months before the end of the war.

The house was restored in 1957 by the Anne Frank Foundation. In the front part of the house is an exhibition of documents on the persecution of Jews in the Third Reich. The rear part, in which was the Frank family's hiding-place, has been left largely as it was. Open: July and August, Mon.–Sat. 9am–7pm, Sun. 10am–7pm; September to June, Mon.–Sat. 9am–5pm, Sun. 10am–5pm.

Noorderkerk

Farther north stands the Noorderkerk (1620–23), with a ground-plan in the form of a Greek cross.

South of the Central Area

Fodor Museum

From the Muntplein Vijzelstraat runs south to Keizersgracht. At No. 609 is the Fodor Museum, which since 1863 has housed the collection assembled by a wealthy coal merchant, C. J. Fodor. The museum puts on temporary exhibitions of works by contemporary Amsterdam artists. Open: daily 11am–5pm.

Van Loon Museum

On the opposite side of Keizersgracht (No. 672) is the Van Loon Museum, in a house built by A. Dortsman in 1672. Now decorated and furnished in mid-18th-century style, it gives an excellent impression of the living conditions of wealthy Amsterdam citizens of that period. Open: Mon. only 10am–5pm.

Heineken Brewery

At the corner of Stadhouderskade and Ferdinand Bolsstraat are the former premises of the Heineken Brewery, one of the largest brewing firms in the Netherlands. The building now houses only offices and a visitor centre.
The firm received its licence to brew beer in the mid 19th century and took over the old-established Hooiberg brewery, which dated from medieval times, when beer was the staple drink of the population.

**Rijksmuseum

The world-famed Rijksmuseum occupies a neo-classical brick building at Stadhouderskade 42 designed by P. J. H. Cuypers (1877–85). Apart from its magnificent collection of old masters it offers a comprehensive survey of the art and culture of the Netherlands. It is particularly rich in early Dutch applied art, medieval Dutch sculpture and modern Dutch painting.

Dutch history

In the eastern half of the ground floor is the department of Dutch history, with an abundance of material on naval, military and colonial history. Particularly notable are the 17th century Dutch marine paintings.

*Print Cabinet

In the western half of the ground floor is the National Print Cabinet (Prentenkabinet), with over a million prints and drawings and a fine library. Adjoining is a section containing sculpture of the 12th–16th centuries, stained glass, textiles, domestic implements and utensils and period furniture.

**Dutch painting

On the first floor can be found one of the great collections of Dutch painting as well as sculpture and applied art (including faience).
Only the most important of the great range of works on show can be referred to here. Among the most notable are Rembrandt's "Night Watch" (restored after being slashed with a knife in 1975), one of the largest and most celebrated of his works (1642) and his "Anatomy Lesson of Dr Deyman", "Syndics of the Drapers' Guild" and "Jewish Bride"; several expressive portraits by Frans Hals, including the "Merry Drinker", and his group portrait of the town guard (completed by Pieter Codde); several of Jan Steen's fine humorous works, but also his religious paintings "Christ at

Emmaus" and "Adoration of the Shepherds"; and works by Gerard Terborch, Gabriel Metsu and Pieter de Hooch, who is represented by some of
his finest works.

Among the museum's greatest treasures are the works by Vermeer, including his "Street Scene". Notable among the landscapes is Jacob van
Ruisdael's "Mill at Wijk bij Duurstede".

The Flemish painters of the 17th century are represented by Rubens (sketch
for the "Crucifixion") and Antonie van Dyck. Among Italian painters are
Crivelli, Bellini and Mantegna, Veronese, Tintoretto and Bassano; among
Spanish artists Velázquez ("Still Life"), Murillo ("Annunciation", "Virgin
and Child"), Cano and Cerezo.

The south-west wing of the museum contains its collection of modern
Dutch paintings, which together with the pictures in the Stedelijk Museum
presents a comprehensive survey of Dutch painting in the 19th century.
Also in this wing is the department of Asiatic art.

The Rijksmuseum is open Tue.–Sat. 10am–5pm, Sun. 1–5pm.

In Van Baerlestraat is the imposing Concertgebouw (Concert Hall), opened   Concertgebouw
in 1888.
The original Concertgebouw Orchestra, 65 strong, was directed by Willem
Kes, who established the reputation of both the orchestra and the concert
hall. Famous conductors, including Willem Mengelberg (1895–1945) and
Bernard Haitink (1961–88), have carried on the tradition. Reger, Debussy,
Hindemith, Milhaud and Stravinsky all conducted performances of their
works in the Concertgebouw. The present musical director (since 1988) is
Ricardo Chailly.
The building was completely renovated between 1985 and 1988, when a
new glass-fronted foyer was added. The concert hall itself, which is acousti-
cally one of the finest in the world, was left unchanged.

The Rijksmuseum, one of the world's great art galleries

Amsterdam

*Stedelijk
Museum

The Stedelijk Museum (Municipal Museum) at Paulus Potterstraat 13, founded in 1890, was built between 1893 and 1895 to the design of A. W. Weissman, the city architect. It ranks as one of the leading European collections of modern art (including painting, sculpture, assemblages, environments, etc.). The emphasis of the collection lies mainly on Dutch and French painting of the 19th and 20th centuries.

The museum owes its existence to the appreciation of art and the generosity of leading citizens of Amsterdam. Its nucleus was the collection bequeathed to the city by Sophia Suasso de Bruin, later supplemented by Chr. P. van Eeghen's collection of contemporary art and other collections (not confined to contemporary works).

Only part of the collection can be shown at any one time, and the displays are periodically changed.

SECOND FLOOR

**Stedelijk
Museum**

SECOND FLOOR
201 Sale of
       reproductions

FIRST FLOOR

GROUND FLOOR

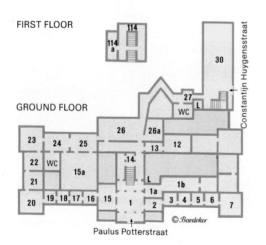

FIRST FLOOR
114 Print Room
       (graphic art)
114a Study Room
       (graphic art)

GROUND
FLOOR
1   Entrance
     lobby
1b   Cloakroom
15   Information
15a Lecture room
26   Restaurant
26a Library and
     reading room

L   Lift

The following is merely a selection of the schools and artists represented:

De Stijl: Theo van Doesburg, Piet Mondriaan, Gerrit Rietveld.
COBRA: Karel Appel, Corneille, Asger Jorn.
Colourfield painting: Kelly, Louis, Newman.
Pop Art: Roy Lichtenstein, Robert Rauschenberg, Rosenquist, Andy
   Warhol.
Nouveau Réalisme: Armand, Spoerri, Tinguely.
Barbizon school: Camille Corot, Charles Daubigny.
Other painters: Paul Cézanne, Claude Monet, Georges Braque, Wassily
   Kandinsky, Marc Chagall, Jean Dubuffet, Ernst Ludwig Kirchner, Oskar
   Kokoschka, Max Ernst, Willem de Kooning, Pablo Picasso, Kasimir Male-
   witsch, Henri Matisse, Paul Gauguin.

The museum's Sculpture Garden contains numerous works by Rodin,
Henry Moore, Renoir, Laurens, Visser and other sculptors.

The museum has a large library and a restaurant for visitors. Open: daily
11am–5pm.

The world's largest collection of works by Van Gogh, originally in the ✱✱**Van Gogh**
Stedelijk Museum, has been housed since 1972 in the new Rijksmuseum **Museum**
Vincent van Gogh at Paulus Potterstraat 7, designed by Gerrit Rietveld. The
collection contains 200 paintings, 500 drawings and 700 letters, as well as
works by Van Gogh's contemporaries Gauguin, Toulouse-Lautrec and
Monticelli.
The museum offers a unique survey of the various phases in the artist's
development, from the early realistic works painted in dark tones ("The
Potato-Eaters", 1885) to the glowing colours and broad brush-strokes of his
Impressionist phase in Arles ("Sunflowers", "The Sower").

Van Gogh Museum, with the world's largest collection of Van Gogh's works

The museum has a library of literature on Van Gogh and his times. Open: Tue.–Sat. 10am–5pm, Sun. 1–5pm.

Film Museum

A short way west is Vondelpark. At No. 3, a pavilion (1880) in the park, is the Netherlands Film Museum, with a collection of film cameras and projectors, a documentation centre, a library (7500 volumes) and film and photographic archives. The films themselves are kept in a special store at Overveen. Open: Tue.–Fri. 10am–5pm.

Leidseplein

From the Vondelpark we cross Stadhouderskade and come to the Leidseplein, Amsterdam's second great centre (along with the Rembrandtplein) of amusement and entertainment. The Stadsschouwburg (Municipal Theatre), the famous Hôtel Américain (by J. Springer, 1892–94) and the numerous pavement cafés (including the Café Reynders, a favourite haunt of artists), together with the large numbers of visitors, both from home and abroad, give the square its cosmopolitan aspect.

Planning Exhibition

From here Leidsestraat leads north-east, crossing the Prinsengracht and the Leidsegracht, to the Keizersgracht, at No. 440 of which is the exhibition hall of the Municipal Planning Department, with a display of plans, drawings, photographs and models illustrating the development of the modern city and residential districts. Open: Tue.–Fri. 12.30–4.30pm.

Bible Museum

At Herengracht 366, in two *gracht* houses dating from 1662, is the Bible Museum (Bijbels Museum). The reception room has fine ceiling paintings by Jacob de Wit (1717).
The museum offers a variety of background information about the Bible and displays finds from Egypt and Palestine, valuable old editions of the Bible and Jewish cult objects. Open: Tue.–Sat. 10am–5pm, Sun. 1–5pm.

From the end of the Leidsegracht the Herengracht and Vijzelstraat lead back to the Muntplein.

Eastern Districts

Hortus Botanicus

In the Plantage district, to the east of Mr Visserplein, beyond the Nieuwe Herengracht, lies the Hortus Botanicus (entrance at Plantage Middenlaan 2).
The Hortus Botanicus, the botanic garden of the City University, has a collection of exotic flowers, trees and plants from all over the world, ranging from the primeval forest of the tropics to the desert and to Japanese gardens. Its history goes back to the old monastic herb gardens. In 1554, when a herbal describing plants both for their own sake and for their medicinal qualities was published, the Vlooienburg Botanic Garden was established, with some 2000 native Dutch trees, plants, herbs and shrubs. After several changes of site and extensions the gardens passed into the hands of the University in 1877. Open: Mon.–Fri. 9am–4pm, Sat. and Sun. 1–4pm.

Artis Zoo

East of the Hortus Botanicus, at Plantage Kerklaan 38–40, is the Artis Zoo (the name is short for Natura Artis Magistra, "Nature the Teacher of Art"). Most of the more than 6000 animals live in open enclosures modelled so far as possible on their natural habitat.
Notable features of the Zoo are the Aquarium, with some 700 species of fish the second largest in the world (after Berlin), and the Nocturnal Animals House. There is also a Children's Farm.

The Zoological Museum associated with the Zoo has collections of insects, birds, amphibians, reptiles, etc. Open: daily 9am–5pm.

Muiderpoort

From the east end of Plantage Middenlaan the Muidergracht leads to the Muiderpoort, a town gate in neo-classical style built by C. Rauws in 1770 after the collapse of the earlier gate of 1663.

In Singelgracht (entrance at Linnaeusstraat 2A) is the Tropical Museum of the Royal Tropical Institute, with an exhibition of arts and artifacts from tropical and subtropical countries. The Tropical Institute developed out of the old Colonial Institute, whose original function was to disseminate information about the Dutch colonies. Interest is now concentrated on the problems of the Third World. Attached to the main museum is a children's museum, TM Junior. Open: Mon.–Fri. 10am–5pm, Sat. and Sun. 12 noon–5pm.

Tropical Museum

At the north end of the Nieuwe Herengracht is the Kadijkplein. At Hoogte Kadijk 147 lies the Kromhout Shipyard (Werft 't Kromhout), one of the oldest shipyards in Amsterdam, which saw the transition from wood to iron in shipbuilding. The yard was reopened in 1973 to work on the restoration of historic old vessels. Open: Mon.–Fri. 10am–4pm.

Kromhout Shipyard

To the north of Kadijkplein, at Kattenburgerplein 1, is the Netherlands Maritime Museum (Nederlands Scheepvaartmuseum). The nucleus of the museum was the collection assembled by the Historic Shipping Society from 1916 onwards. Between 1973 and 1981 an old warehouse, the Lands Zeemagazijn, was renovated to house the present museum, which illustrates the history of seafaring from Roman times to the present day with a collection of ship models, globes, navigational instruments, 5000 pictures and 30,000 drawings. There is a library of more than 50,000 volumes. Open: Tue.–Sat. 10am–5pm, Sunday 1–5pm.

Netherlands Maritime Museum

From the Museum the Kattenburgergracht leads to the Winnenburgergracht and Oostenburger Gracht, on which are two old ropewalks of about 1650, the Lijnbanen, belonging to the Admiralty and the East India Company. On the gable is the emblem of the East India Company, the letters VOC.

Lijnbanen

From the Zoo the Plantage Kerklaan leads by way of Roeterstraat to the Nieuwe Prinsengracht; at No. 130 is the Geological Museum of the University, with a large collection of minerals and fossils. The central feature is the Timor Collection of material of the Permian and Triassic periods.

Geological Museum

Southern Districts

In the south-eastern district of Nieuw Zuid (Apollolaan, Churchilllaan, Beethovenstraat and Stadionweg), are some fine examples of Dutch Art Nouveau architecture. In Europaplein, to the south of Churchilllaan, is the RAI Congress and Exhibition Centre (1959–65), which has an area of over 45,000 sq.m/54,000 sq.yds.

Nieuw Zuid

At Tolstraat 7 the NINT (Nederlands Instituut voor Nijverheid en Techniek) Museum of Technology illustrates modern technological developments in a variety of fields (energy, photography, telecommunications, etc.). Open: Mon.–Fri. 10am–4pm, Sat. and Sun. 1–5pm.

NINT Museum of Technology

Going along the Europaboulevard, turn right into De Boelelaan. At the corner of Drentestraat (No. 21) are the offices of the Turmac Tobacco Company, with the Peter Stuyvesant Collection (begun in 1960), which contains 700 pictures and 100 works of sculpture by modern artists like Appel, Constant and Corneille. Open: Mon.–Fri. 9am–12 noon and 1–4pm.

Peter Stuyvesant Collection

At the west end of Stadionweg can be found the Olympic Stadium (1928), which has seating for 60,000 spectators. There are plans to demolish it and build a new stadium in its place.

Olympic Stadium

To the north along Amstelveenseweg is the old Haarlemmermeer Station (No. 264), which now houses the Tramway (Tramlijn) Museum. Trips in old

Tramway Museum

Amsterdam

Free University

Farther south lies the Buitenveldert district, in which is the Free University (Vrije Universiteit), with Christian affiliations, which was founded in 1880. A botanic garden in the University grounds displays the native Dutch flora. In the main building, at De Boelalaan 1105, is a collection of material on the history of the botanic garden (established 1967).

Here too is the Bilderdijk Museum, devoted to the poet Willem Bilderdijk (1756–1831); it can be seen by appointment.

Amsterdamse Bos

To the west of the Free University extends the great expanse of the Amsterdamse Bos, a wooded area laid out in 1934, during the world economic crisis, as a means of providing work for the unemployed. The Bosmuseum, on Koenenkade, illustrates the varied vegetation in the park, which in addition to native trees and shrubs includes some 150 species of trees from all over the world. Open: daily 10am–5pm.

The *Port of Amsterdam

Situation and Importance

On the north side of the Central Station, in De Ruyterkade, are a series of jetties (*steigers*) used by numerous motor launches and ferries. The port installations were developed from 1872 onwards, following the construction of the North Sea Canal, in an attempt to recover for Amsterdam, then being overshadowed by Rotterdam, something of its former importance.

The port of Amsterdam lies 18.5km/11½ miles from the open sea and, thanks to the great sea locks at IJmuiden, is not affected by the movement of the tides. Several thousand vessels put in here every year, giving the port an annual turnover of some 14 million tons. It also handles some 37,000 passengers a year.

Port Area

The whole of the port installations are on land reclaimed from the IJ. The shipping channel was deepened and quays were constructed on artificial

The port of Amsterdam

islands. On the south side of the IJ are the main docks, including the Westerdok (on the outer side of which is the quay used by the Holland-America Line, Stenenhoofd), the Oosterdok and the IJhaven.

To the west of the Westerdok are the Houthaven (Timber Harbour), the Minervahaven, the Coenhaven and the impressive Petroleumhaven, at the end of the North Sea Canal.

Still farther west is the Westhaven (still in course of development), with loading installations for coal, oil, minerals and grain, oil storage tanks, oil refineries and chemical plants.

On the north side of the IJ are numerous smaller docks and the locks on the North Holland Canal. A short way west of the Central Station, on the harbour front, stands the 13-storey, 60m/200ft high Havengebouw (Harbour Building), built by Dudok van Heel in 1958–60, with a restaurant from which there are panoramic views. On the Oosterdok is the Netherlands Maritime Museum (see above).

Harbour Building

For container traffic there is a new Container Terminal. With modern roll-on-roll-off vessels lorries can drive straight into the ship. A much improved link with the European hinterland was provided with the opening in 1952 of the Amsterdam–Rhine Canal, which is of particular importance for the transport of mineral ore to the blast-furnaces of the Ruhr.

Transfer of goods

Surroundings of Amsterdam

In summer there are excursions in motor launches (departing from Stationsplein or De Ruyterkade) to Monnickendam, Volendam and Marken (see entries). Another interesting trip is to Zaanstad (see entry), with the Zaanse Schans (houses and windmills, timber-built in traditional style, and narrow canals).

Excursions in motor launches

Between Amsterdam and Haarlem is Halfweg, with an old steam pumping station. Farther west lies the Spaarnwoude recreation park (see Haarlem, Surroundings).

Halfweg

Another popular trip, starting from Stadhouderskade, is up the Amstel, past the Kalfje inn, to the village of Ouderkerk. Adjoining the church is a Jewish cemetery with numerous handsome tombstones of Portuguese Jews.

Ouderkerk

Schiphol Airport (see Practical Information, Airports) lies 10km/6 miles south-west of Amsterdam on the Haarlemmermeer polder, some 4m/13ft below sea level. The airport is used by more than 80 airlines, linking it with 185 cities in 90 different countries. With some 15 million passengers a year Schiphol takes fifth place among European airports. On the roof of the main building is a restaurant with views of the runways.

Schiphol Airport

The Aviodome at Schiphol, a museum of air and space travel, is well worth a visit. Its main attractions are twenty vintage aircraft, a replica of Lilienthal's "hang-glider" and old Fokker aircraft, including a Fokker F 7A, which in its day was the world's leading commercial aircraft. Open: May to September, daily 10am–5pm; October to April, Tue.–Fri. 10am–5pm, Sat. and Sun. 12 noon–5pm.

Aviodome

Apeldoorn

G 6

Province: Gelderland
Population: 146,000

Apeldoorn

Het Loo Palace

Situation and characteristics

The town of Apeldoorn, which first appears in the records in 793, lies on the eastern edge of the Veluwe (see entry), an expanse of sandy woodland and heath rising to a height of 110m/360ft between the Rhine, the IJssel and the Eem.

Apeldoorn is now a select residential town with beautiful parks. It has a theological college, a Roman Catholic seminary and colleges of engineering and automobile technology. It is also the commercial centre of the surrounding area, with a varied range of industry (metallurgy, paper-making, textiles, chemicals; manufacture of fishing nets and computers).

Berg en Bos
Apenheul

Apeldoorn's most beautiful park, Berg en Bos, an area of natural woodland, lies on the Wilslaan. In summer there are magnificent illuminations here. In the park is the Apenheul, an enclosed area of 300 hectares/750 acres in which monkeys live in freedom among the visitors, in conditions designed to resemble their natural habitat. Open: April to June, daily 9.30am–5pm; July and August, daily 9.30am–6pm, September and October, daily 10am–5pm.

Other fine parks are the Oranjepark, the oldest of Apeldoorn's parks, and the Wilhelminapark.

*Paleis Het Loo

2km/1¼ miles north of the town is the royal palace of Het Loo (1685–92), built by Jacob Roman and Daniël Marot as a country residence for King William III. At the beginning of the 19th century the palace was extended by King Louis Bonaparte and the gardens were laid out in the French style. Het Loo was the favourite residence of William I and III, and after her abdication in 1948 Queen Wilhelmina lived here until her death in 1962. In the early eighties the palace was renovated in its original style.

Part of the palace is now an interesting museum, and the collection of pictures, furniture and coins belonging to the house of Orange-Nassau attracts visitors from all over the world.

The palace also houses the Museum of the Chancery of the Netherlands Orders of Knighthood, with displays of orders and medals. In the park is the castle (14th–15th c.) of Oude Loo. The royal stables contain a collection of old cars and coaches belonging to the royal family. Open: Tue.–Sun. 10am–5pm.

Surroundings of Apeldoorn

South-east of Apeldoorn lies the village of Loenen. Here, set in beautiful gardens, is the Huis ter Horst, a brick-built Renaissance mansion (16th c.). In 1791 the façade was rebuilt in stone, with a classical pediment.
To the west of the village is a cemetery with the graves of 2761 victims of the Second World War (soldiers, resistance fighters, forced labour deportees).

Loenen

Visitors can take a trip in an old steam train from Apeldoorn station along the Veluwe to Dieren on the IJsel, a distance of 22km/14 miles.

Steam railway

See Veluwe

De Hoge Veluwe National Park

See Veluwe

Kröller-Müller Museum

Appingedam

J 2

Province: Groningen
Population: 13,000

The little medieval town of Appingedam, 30km/19 miles north-east of Groningen, was until the 14th century a port on the Waddenzee and the only walled town in the province apart from Groningen. The walls were pulled down after the conquest of the town by Charles V in 1536.

Situation and characteristics

The Nicolaikerk, built in the first half of the 13th century, was originally aisleless; the transepts and the choir were added in the second half of the century, the apse in the 14th century. Further extensions gave it its present form as a hall-church, with aisles of the same height as the nave. During restoration work in 1950 it was decorated with attractive wall and ceiling paintings. The pulpit dates from 1665, the organ from 1744.

Nicolaikerk

The Town Hall (1637), originally a courthouse, has a fine Renaissance façade.

Town Hall

On the Damsterdiep are a number of interesting old houses with kitchens built out over the water.

Damsterdiep

Arnhem

G 7

Province: Gelderland
Population: 128,000

Arnhem, capital of the province of Gelderland, lies for the most part on the right bank of the Lower Rhine, a few kilometres below the point where the IJssel branches off the Rhine. Part of the town is situated in the hills fringing the Veluwe, an extensive area of woodland and heath.
Arnhem is of more than merely regional importance, with law courts and the offices of several government agencies and the provincial government of Gelderland, as well as several higher educational establishments, including a school of drama, a college of music and a forestry school.

Situation and characteristics

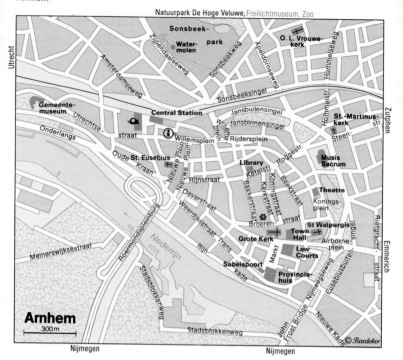

Natuurpark De Hoge Veluwe, Freilichtmuseum, Zoo

Industry also plays a major part in the economy of the town. Of particular importance is a tin-smelting plant established in 1929 which processes ore from Surinam and produces approximately a fifth of the total world output of tin. Apart from this there are several chemical and metalworking plants and various other factories.

History

Arnhem first appears in the records in 893, but it is believed to occupy the site of the Roman settlement of Arenacum mentioned by Tacitus. It received its municipal charter, however, only in 1233, from Count Otto III of Gelderland. Thanks to its advantageous position on the Rhine its trade prospered in the Middle Ages, and from the 15th to the 17th century it was a member of the Hanseatic League. The Emperor Charles V made it the chief place in Gelderland. Arnhem twice fell into the hands of the French, in 1672–74 and again from 1795 to 1813, when it was taken by Prussian forces. During the Second World War Arnhem suffered heavy damage, particularly during the fighting between the German occupying forces and the British paratroops dropped in September 1944 and later when the town was taken by the Allies in April 1945, when only 150 houses were left in a habitable condition. After the war the town was quickly rebuilt.

The Town

Town centre

The traffic hub of Arnhem is the Willemsplein, near the Central Station. Just to the south of this square is the Nieuwe Plein, from the south end of which

142

The Grote Kerk with its commanding tower

the town's narrow main shopping street (successively named Rijn-, Vijzel-, Ketel- and Roggestraat) extends east to the Velperplein. From this street various side streets run south to the oldest part of the town, in which, near the Rhine, is the spacious Markt (market square).

At the north end of the square stands the Grote Kerk (15th c.; Reformed), which was badly damaged during the Second World War but later rebuilt. From the tower (which contains a carillon) there are fine views. In the choir is the imposing marble monument of the last Duke of Gelderland, Charles of Egmond (d. 1538), an opponent of Charles V. Immediately east of the Grote Kerk is the Old Town Hall, known as the Duivelshuis (Devils' House) after the three figures of devils at the entrance. The Town Hall was built about 1540 for Maarten van Rossem, Duke Charles's general.

Grote Kerk

Old Town Hall

North-east of the Town Hall are the Law Courts (1958–63) and the Archives of Gelderland (Rijksarchief Gelderland; 1880). At the south end of the square is the Provinciehuis (1954), the seat of the provincial government, with a beautiful courtyard and council chamber (Statenzaal). Immediately west of it stands the Sabelpoort (14th c.; side facing the square 1642), all that remains of the old town walls.

Law Courts
Provinciehuis

Sabelpoort

Farther south the bridge over the Rhine ("a bridge too far") was held by British paratroops for four days against overwhelming odds during the airborne operation in 1944; it is now called the John Frost Bridge in honour of the commander of the paratroops, who are also commemorated by a monument at the north end of the bridge.

"A bridge too far"

From the bridge a ring of gardens runs north on the line of the former town walls along the east side of the old town, passing on the left the St Walpurgisbasiliek (R.C.), the town's oldest church (consecrated 1422; fine pulpit) and the Stadsschouwburg (Municipal Theatre). On Velperplein can be found the Musis Sacrum Concert Hall (with exhibition rooms).

143

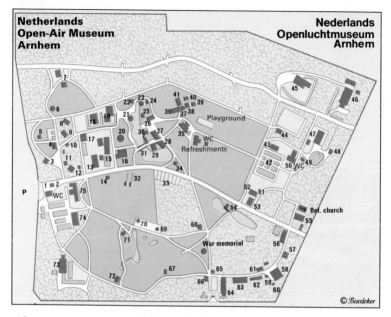

Netherlands Open-Air Museum Arnhem

Nederlands Openluchtmuseum Arnhem

1 Entrance
2 Information
3 Horse-driven oil mill (Zieuwent, Gelderland)
4 Veluwe farmhouse (Vierhouten)
5 Fowler's hut (Aerdenhout, Noord-Holland)
6 Beekeeping exhibition
7 Betuwe farmhouse (Varik)
8 Sheep-pen (Ederveen, Gelderland)
9 Day labourer's cottage (Nuspeet, Gelderland)
10 Pebble floor (Geesteren, Gelderland)
11 Achterhoek wheelwright's shop (Woold, Gelderland)
12 Achterhoek farmhouse (Harreveld, Gelderland)
13 Vollenhoven farmhouse (Kadoelen, Overijssel)
14 Dovecote (Hamersveld, Utrecht)
15 Farmhouse (Staphorst, Overijssel)
16 Farmhouse (Zuid-Scharwoude, Noord-Holland)
17 Achterhoek farmhouse (Beltrum, Gelderland)
18 Farmhouse (Giethoorn, Overijssel)
19 Large farmhouse (Oud-Beijerland, Zuid-Holland)
20 Drainage mill (Gouda, Zuid-Holland)
21 Sawmill (Numansdorp, Zuid-Holland)
22 Volendam fisherman's hut
23 Drainage mill (Gouda, Zuid-Holland)
24 Sheep-pen, Texel
25 Fisherman's cottage (Marken, Noord-Holland)
26 Boatyard (Marken, Noord-Holland)
27 Exhibition
28 Middle-class house, Zaandam (souvenir shop)

29 Merchant's house (Koog a/d Zaan)
30 Cart-shed with house attached (Zaan area)
31 Double bascule bridge (Oudekerk a/d Amstel, Noord-Holland)
32 Shooting range
33 Plots with old-fashioned crops
34 Windmill (flour mill; Huizen, Noord-Holland)
35 Laundry (Overveen, Noord-Holland)
36 Burgher's house (Bedum, Groningen)
37 Barn (Woold, Gelderland)
38 Farrier's shed (Scherpenzeel, Gelderland)
39 Two workmen's cottages (Zandeweer, Groningen, and Beemster, Noord-Holland)
40 Clog-maker's workshop
41 Row of workmen's cottages (Tilburg, Noord-Brabant)
42 Herb garden
43 Herb exhibition
44 Sheep-pen (Daarle, Overijssel)
45 West Frisian farmhouse (Midlum)
46 Farmhouse (Beertra, Groningen)
47 Farmhouse (Zeijen, Drenthe)
48 Day labourer's cottage (Onstwedde, Groningen)
49 Village school (Lhee, Drenthe)
50 De Hanekamp inn (Zwolle, Overijssel)
51 Horse-mill for crushing grain (Wormerveer, Noord-Holland)
52 Parlour (Hindeloopen, Friesland)
53 Farmhouse (Arnhem, Gelderland)

54 Watermill of papermaking factory (Veluwe)
55 Farmhouse Etten en Leur, Noord-Brabant)
56 Kempen farmhouse (Budel, Noord-Brabant)
57 Brewery and bakehouse (Ulvenhout, Noord-Brabant)
58 Small South Limburg farmhouse (Krawinkel)
59 Roadside chapel (Margraten, Limburg)
60 Boundary post (Roosteren-Susteren, Limburg)
61 South Limburg barn (Terstraeten)
62 Archery butts (Roermond, Limburg)
63 Exhibition
64 Lecture room and exhibition
65 Summer-house (Meppel, Drenthe)
66 Toll-collector's house (Zuidlaren, Drenthe)
67 Boundary post of a hunting preserve (Arnhem, Gelderland)
68 Windmill (flour mill; Gouda, Zuid-Holland)
69 Small drainage mill (Wouterswoude, Friesland)
70 Small drainage mill (Gorredijk, Friesland)
71 Twente bakehouse (Denekamp, Overijssel)
72 Small Twente bakehouse (Beuningen, Overijssel)
73 Exhibition of traditional costumes
74 Woodshed (Haarlem, Noord-Holland)
75 De Oude Bijenkorf restaurant

In the Netherlands Open-Air Museum

To the west of the Central Station, at Utrechtseweg 87, is the Municipal Museum (Gemeentemuseum), set in gardens on the Reeberg (fine views of the Rhine countryside). It occupies an old mansion which was converted to house the museum in 1918. Its collections include archaeological material giving evidence of early settlement in Gelderland, valuable medieval coins, glass (including some examples of Roman glass), silver (seven "guild cups", used at guild festivities in the 17th century), paintings of the 17th–19th centuries (including views of the town) and works by artists belonging to the school of "Magical Realism" (Pyke Koch, Dick Ket), Chinese and Japanese porcelain of the 17th and 18th centuries and Delft ware. Open: Tue.–Sat. 10am–5pm, Sun. 11am–5pm.

Municipal
Museum

On the western outskirts of the town, at Heijenoordseweg 150, lies Het Dorp, a model settlement for the physically handicapped. The money for its construction was collected within 24 hours by contributions from viewers of a television programme.

Het Dorp

To the north of the station extends the wooded municipal park of Sonsbeek (500 hectares/1250 acres), with the Belvedere, from which there are far-ranging views over the Betuwe, and the Witte Molen, a 15th century drainage mill (exhibition of objects relating to the miller's craft).

Sonsbeek

North of the town (leave on Zijpendaalseweg and turn right into Schelmseweg, or on Apeldoornseweg and then left into Schelmseweg: distance 4km/2½ miles), set in beautiful wooded country, is the Netherlands Open-Air Museum (Nederlands Openluchtmuseum; area 33 hectares/82 acres). The museum was founded in 1912 on the initiative of ordinary citizens concerned to ensure that the way of life and folk art of the different parts of the country should not be destroyed by the development of industry.

**Netherlands
Open-Air Museum

Although the museum originally concentrated on the living and working conditions of the rural population (farmers, craftsmen, shepherds and

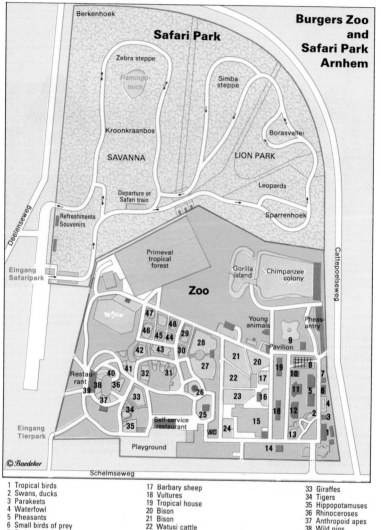

Burgers Zoo and Safari Park Arnhem

1 Tropical birds	17 Barbary sheep	33 Giraffes
2 Swans, ducks	18 Vultures	34 Tigers
3 Parakeets	19 Tropical house	35 Hippopotamuses
4 Waterfowl	20 Bison	36 Rhinoceroses
5 Pheasants	21 Bison	37 Anthropoid apes
6 Small birds of prey	22 Watusi cattle	38 Wild pigs
7 Owls	23 Yaks	39 Nocturnal animals
8 Small birds of prey	24 Reindeer	40 Pigmy hippopotamuses
9 Flamingoes	25 Panthers	41 Small mammals
10 Large birds of prey	26 Hamadryas baboons	42 Polar bears
11 Cranes	27 Camels	43 Lions
12 Pheasants	28 Asian wild horses	44 Peccaries
13 Pelicans, ducks	29 Emus	45 Hyenas
14 Birds of prey	30 Dwarf zebus	46 Sealions
15 Cinema	31 Predators	47 Waterfowl
16 Bears	32 Elephants	48 Pigs

fishermen) down to 1900, it now also takes in the urban and industrial setting. Thus in addition to numerous typical farmers' and fishermen's houses, windmills of all kinds and a variety of craftsmen's workshops visitors can also see a steam sawmill from Groenlo, a steam-driven dairy from Veenwouden and an entire group of houses from the Zaan area. All the various buildings were brought here from their original sites, complete with their furniture and equipment, and are now arranged in provinces. In the main exhibition building there are periodical displays of traditional costume. A cart-shed houses various types of cart and coach. Open: April to October, Mon.–Fri. 9am–5pm, Sat. and Sun. 10am–5pm.

Some 500m/550yds west of the Open-Air Museum is Burger's Zoo, with over 2000 animals. Chimpanzees and gorillas can be watched from an observation post. Other attractions are the rich collection of birds, the wolves' forest, the small tropical house and the magnificent rock enclosures. Associated with the Zoo is the Safari Park, which visitors can tour either in the "safari train" or in their own car, passing through an African-style savanna and observing lions, giraffes, rhinoceroses and cheetahs roaming around freely in an approximation to their natural habitat. Open: daily in summer 9am to 8pm, in winter 9am to sunset.

*Burger's Zoo

Some 2km/1¼ miles east of the town centre, on the south side of IJssellaan, is the recently opened Presikhaaf shopping centre, which is patronised by German shoppers from the Ruhr area as well as by local people.

Presikhaaf

In the suburb of Bronbeek, between Arnhem and Velp (Velperweg 147), is a former old soldiers' home, once occupied by army veterans and invalids from the Dutch East Indies. The souvenirs and mementoes they brought back with them formed the basis of the Bronbeek Museum (Museum van het Koninklijk Tehuis voor Oud-Militairen). Open: daily 9am–12 noon and 12.30–5pm.

Bronbeek Museum

Surroundings of Arnhem

In the residential suburb of Oosterbeek are the Airborne Monument and the Airborne Museum, housed in the former Hartenstein Hotel, which was the British commander's headquarters during the Arnhem operation. Open: Sat. 11am–5pm, Sun. 12 noon–5pm.

Oosterbeek

The medieval moated castle of Doorwerth is entered over a drawbridge. Originally built in the 13th century, the castle was enlarged in the 15th and 16th centuries, almost completely destroyed during the heavy fighting of 1944 and carefully restored between 1945 and 1982. Open: April to October, Tue.–Fri. 10am–5pm, Sat. and Sun. 1–5pm.

Doorwerth

The castle houses the Netherlands Hunting Museum (Nederlands Jachtmuseum). Open: April to October, Tue.–Fri. 10am–5pm, Sat. and Sun. 1–5; November to March, Sat., Sun. and public holidays 1–5pm.

South-east of Arnhem, in the angle between the Rhine and the Waal, is the castle of Doornenburg, which was reduced to rubble during the Second World War. Now restored, it ranks with Muiderslot (Muiden) and Loevenstein (see Gorinchem) as one of the finest medieval castles in the Netherlands. Conducted tours April to September, Sun. at 2.30 and 4pm; July and August also Tue.–Thur. at 11am and 1.30 and 3pm, Fri. and Sat. at 1.30 and 3pm.

Doornenburg

See Veluwe

De Hoge Veluwe National Park

See Veluwe

Kröller-Müller Museum

147

Provincial Museum, Assen

Assen

Province: Drenthe
Population: 49,000

Situation and characteristics

Assen, capital of the province of Drenthe, lies in beautiful wooded country at the junction of two inland waterways, the Drenthse Hoofdvaart and the Noord-Willemskanaal. It became an independent commune only in 1807 and received its municipal charter from King Louis Bonaparte in 1809. Thereafter it rapidly developed into the principal town in Drenthe and an important junction for inland shipping. The population rose from only 600 in 1809 to over 13,000 at the beginning of the 20th century, and since then has more than tripled.

Unlike other provincial capitals in the Netherlands, Assen has no historic buildings, having been an insignificant village until the 19th century, with no great past to look back on.

Provincial Museum

Assen has, however, one sight that should not be missed, the Provincial Museum at Brink 1 and 5, housed in the former Provinciehuis and the Ontvangershuis. Attached to the Provinciehuis are the Drostehuis (1774–78) and the abbey church (1662; enlarged 1817). The intermediate block was built by P. J. H. Cuypers in 1885. The museum has an outstanding collection of weapons, implements, pottery and other objects of the Stone and Bronze Ages, including human bodies preserved in bogs. All these objects were found in the immediate surroundings of the town. Open: daily 11am–5pm.

Gouvernement

Adjoining the museum is the neo-Gothic Gouvernement, on the site of a convent of Cistercian nuns dissolved at the Reformation, of which there remain only the church (now part of the Town Hall) and part of the 13th century cloister.

The superb rooms of the Ontvangershuis (Tax-Collector's House), which have been preserved in their original style, give a good impression of the way of life of a provincial official in the 17th and 18th centuries.

Ontvangershuis

Surroundings of Assen

A rewarding excursion from Assen is to the Hondsrug, a low ridge of hills to the east and south-east of the town. In this area more than 50 megalithic tombs (*hunebedden*) of the Stone and Bronze Ages, belonging to the TRB culture (see History), have been found. The Papeloze Kerk tomb, between the villages of Sleen and Schoonoord, is particularly worth visiting; it has largely been restored to its original condition and has been made accessible for visitors. The largest *hunebed* in Drenthe, which has been known since 1685, lies between Bronneger and Borger.

Hondsrug:
megalithic tombs

South of Assen, at Hooghalen, is Kamp Westerbork, originally established in 1938 as a reception camp for Jewish refugees from Germany and Austria and used by the German occupying forces as a transit camp for the deportation of Jews. This dark chapter in history is commemorated by a memorial, some twisted railway lines and the buffers at the end of the line.
In the immediate vicinity is a radio telescope. There is another at Dwingeloo.

Westerbork

Farther west is the village of Orvelte, which has been rebuilt as it was in 1830, so that much of the village is now a lived-in open-air museum. Here visitors can see farmhouses of traditional Saxon type ("hall-houses": see Facts and Figures, Cultural Landscapes), which are entered through the Tolhuis (toll-booth), a large village shop, a miller's house and various workshops. In some of the workshops local craft products (pottery, hand-carved domestic implements and utensils) are on sale. There are also a number of painters' studios.

Orvelte

To the north of Assen flows the Drenthse Aa, a system of several small streams which meander over a wide area.

Drenthse Aa

Baarn

E 6

Province: Utrecht
Population: 25,000

The picturesque little town of Baarn, which received its municipal charter in 1350, lies in wooded country north of Utrecht. This is a popular recreation area for the inhabitants of the surrounding towns, with good walking country extending in the west to Hilversum and in the south to Bilthoven.

Situation and
characteristics

The church goes back to the 14th century, and the brick-built tower (heightened in the 16th century) and nave date from that period; the choir and aisles were probably added in the 15th century.

Church

To the north of Baarn is Kasteel Groenendaal, which now houses the Nationaal Centrum voor Bos, Natuur en Landschap, an organisation dedicated to the protection of the state forests. Open: Tue.–Fri. 10am–5pm, Sat. and Sun. 12 noon–5pm.

Kasteel
Groenendaal

In wooded country to the west of Baarn is Kasteel Lage Vuursche, now a hotel.

Kasteel
Lage Vuursche

The Cantonpark botanic garden is of interest for its East Asian flora.

Cantonpark

Surroundings of Baarn

South-east of Baarn is the village of Soestdijk, at the far end of which stands Soestdijk Palace, the residence of Queen Juliana the Queen Mother and

Soestdijk

Barger-Compascuum

Kasteel Groenendaal, Baarn

Prince Bernhard. Nearby is Kasteel Drakensteyn, which is occupied by Queen Beatrix. Beyond this is Baarnse Bos, a beautiful wooded area.

Barger-Compascuum

See Emmen, Surroundings

Barneveld   F 6

Province: Gelderland
Population: 41,000

Situation and characteristics

Between Amersfoort and Apeldoorn lies the little town of Barneveld, with an important college of agriculture. The town's fame as a centre of poultry farming and egg production rests on the brown Barneveld hen, one of the best known Dutch breeds.

An unusual tourist attraction is the Poultry Museum, which is unique of its kind in Europe. Here visitors can see "historic" incubators, incubator lamps and egg-sorting machines and get a general impression of Dutch poultry farming from the cocks and hens of many breeds which range freely around.

Monument to Jan van Schaffelaer

In front of the Gothic hall-church (15h c.; Reformed) is a monument to Jan van Schaffelaer, who about the year 1482 threw himself down from the church tower in order to save the village from hardship.

The Kasteel Jan van Schaffelaer (1854) stands in a park (open to the public) east of the village. In July and August this is the scene of the Oud Veluwe Markten (Old Veluwe Market Days), when old handicraft firms display their products.

Kasteel
Jan van
Schaffelaer

The Nairac Museum has a collection of local archaeological material, traditional costumes and other items characteristic of the region. Open: Tue.–Fri. 10am–12.30pm and 1.30–5pm, Sat. 12 noon–5pm.

Nairac Museum

Bergen   D 4

Province: Noord-Holland
Population: 14,000

From Alkmaar an excellent road runs north-west through flat pastureland to Bergen, also called Bergen-Binnen or Bergen in het Bosch. This popular summer resort, much favoured by artists, has numbers of holiday houses charmingly situated in wooded country and numerous hotels and attractive restaurants.

Situation
Bergen-Binnen

In the town are the ruins of a church which was burned down in 1574 and a monument to the Russian soldiers who fell here in 1799 (see Den Helder).

5km/3 miles beyond this is Bergen aan Zee, a quiet seaside resort with a beautiful broad beach. There is an aquarium with 50 tanks containing marine animals of all kinds, and also a seal pool. Open: April to October, daily 10am–6pm; November to March, Sat., Sun. and daily during the holidays 11am–5pm.

Bergen aan Zee

Surroundings of Bergen

The coast road runs north from Bergen-Binnen, passing through stretches of wooded dunes and skirting the Boswachterij Schoorl, a tract of land 5km/3 miles wide which is now a nature reserve. This is one of the broadest swathes of dunes in the Netherlands.

Boswachterij
Schoorl

5km/3 miles north-west of Schoorl, between Camperduin and Petten (Nuclear Research Centre and European School), are the great dykes of the Hondsbosse Zeewering (sea-wall).

Hondsbosse
Zeewering

Bergen op Zoom   C 8/9

Province: Noord-Brabant
Population: 47,000

The former fortress town of Bergen op Zoom ("Bergen on the Edge"), in the west of the province of Noord-Brabant, is now, since the construction of the Schelde–Rhine Canal, linked with the Oosterschelde (see Facts and Figures, The Struggle with the Sea) by a train of locks, bringing it within easy reach of Antwerp and Rotterdam by sea.

Situation and
characteristics

Although over the centuries the town was frequently besieged it managed to maintain active trading relations with Britain. Major contributions to its economy are made by oyster and lobster culture, fishing for anchovies, the growing of asparagus and strawberries and a variety of industries (metalworking, woodworking, textiles, foodstuffs, etc.).

An important trading town in the Middle Ages, Bergen op Zoom received its municipal charter in the 13th century and was granted exemption from

History

Grote Kerk, Bergen op Zoom

customs duties in the 14th. During the Dutch fight for freedom the town was surrounded with massive fortifications by the Duke of Alba. In spite of this the Spanish forces were compelled to evacuate the town in 1577 and thereafter, until 1605, tried unsuccessfully to retake it. A further attempt by the Marquis of Spinola to take the town in 1622 was equally unsuccessful. It was finally recaptured by French troops under Count Loevendal in 1747.

Town Hall

In the Grote Markt is the 15th century Town Hall (Stadhuis); the façade dates from 1611. The entrance lobby is decorated with the coats of arms of prosperous burghers. A particularly notable feature is the magnificent Late Gothic chimneypiece (1521) from the Markiezenhof (see below).

Grote Kerk

The Gothic Grote Kerk or St Geertruidskerk (13th c.) contains numerous monuments of the 16th–18th centuries. From the tower (carillon) there are fine views, extending in clear weather as far as Antwerp.

Markiezenhof

In Steenbergsestraat is the Markiezenhof (Margrave's Palace; 1475), with a beautiful façade, which now houses the Municipal Museum (Gemeente-museum). Open: June to August, Tue.–Sun. 11am–5pm; September to May, Tue.–Sun. 2–5pm.

Gevangenpoort

At the west end of Lieve Vrouwenstraat is the Gevangenpoort (15th c.), a relic of the old fortifications.

Surroundings of Bergen op Zoom

Tholen

North-west of Bergen op Zoom is the Tholen peninsula, with the town of Tholen (pop. 19,000). It owes its name to the tolls once levied on shipping here.

After a great fire in 1452 which left only the lower part of the church tower still standing the Grote Kerk (or Onze Lieve Vrouwenkerk) was rebuilt in Late Gothic style but remained unfinished. Beautiful stained glass (lily patterns) in the transept.

The Town Hall (Stadhuis), with its stone front and hexagonal turret, was also rebuilt after the great fire. The Rococo staircase leading up to the large council chamber dates from 1758.

Betuwe   D/E 7

Province: Gelderland

The Betuwe, in the eastern Netherlands, is an alluvial plain formed after the last ice age and bounded on the north by the Lower Rhine and its continuation the Lek, on the south by the Waal and on the west by the Linge, a small river in the Rhine delta. With some 100 inhabitants to the sq.km (260 to the sq. mile), the Betuwe is one of the most thinly populated areas in the Netherlands. In the past it was always an inaccessible region, like the neighbouring plains of Bommelerwaard, Land van Maas en Waal and Rijk van Nijmegen. It helped the northern Netherlands in their struggle to break away from Spanish rule in the 16th and 17th centuries, since it constituted a formidable barrier to movement between north and south.

Situation and characteristics

The main element in the economy of this flat plain, protected by dykes from flooding by the rivers, is agriculture. The low-lying river meadows are used for grazing, the higher river terraces for arable farming. Near the German frontier intensive fruit-growing predominates.

Economy

Biesbosch   D 7/8

Province: Noord-Brabant

The Biesbosch (from *bies,* "rushes", and *bosch,* "woodland") is an area south-west of Dordrecht formed when the dyke on the Maas burst and the St Elizabeth's Day floods on November 19th 1421 engulfed great tracts of land in the south-western Netherlands and altered the geography of the whole area, inundating over 40,000 hectares/100,000 acres of land. Since the 18th century more than four-fifths of the flooded land has been reclaimed. An area of 6000 hectares/15,000 acres was left as it was, and now forms the Biesbosch nature reserve and bird sanctuary.

Until the end of the 1960s the Biesbosch was directly connected with the sea and subject to changing tide levels. As a result it developed a flora which tolerated brackish water and was the home of numerous waterfowl. Since the damming of the Haringvliet there is no variation in water level, and both flora and fauna have adapted to the new environment.

Situation and characteristics

The Biesbosch is criss-crossed by a network of footpaths and cycleways and by countless rivers and streams which offer excellent facilities for water sports (sailing, surfing). In spite of the large numbers of visitors the natural environment has remained largely unspoiled.

Sport

The Biesbosch nature reserve can be reached by car only from the east (preferably via Werkendam). The south-west part of the area, with its three large reservoirs of drinking water, is closed to road traffic. The Biesbosch can also be reached by boat from Drimmelen, Geertruidenberg or Lage Zwaluwe.

Access

Bollenstreek

Provinces: Noord- and Zuid-Holland

Situation
* Bulb-fields

Bollenstreek:
bulb-fields

The Bollenstreek (from *bol*, "bulb") is the 13km/8 mile long stretch of land between Haarlem and Sassenheim (north of Leiden) with its great expanses of bulb-fields (over 2600 hectares/6500 acres). The show of flowers begins with the first crocuses in mid March, followed by daffodils, hyacinths and tulips.

History of tulip-growing

In the second half of the 16th century the Austrian ambassador in Turkey, Ogier Ghislain de Busbecq, brought back a quantity of tulip bulbs and presented some of them to Charles de l'Ecluse (Carolus Clusius), who took the bulbs to Leiden in 1593 and grew tulips on the sandy heathland on the inland side of the dunes. He was so successful that during the first half of the 17th century a real "tulip mania" developed, and fortunes were spent on buying new varieties. The States-General put an end to this speculation by ordinances issued around 1636.

Nowadays over 14,000 hectares/35,000 acres of land are still devoted to bulb-growing.

Tour of the bulb-fields

A good view of the bulb-fields can be had from the train which runs through the middle of them between Leiden and Haarlem. For a closer view a round trip by car is recommended, starting from Haarlem (68km/42 miles, with detours 78km/48 miles).

Heemstede

Leave Haarlem on the Hoofddorp road (N 201), which in 4km/2½ miles comes to Heemstede (pop. 26,000; Museum of Land Reclamation), on the edge of the Haarlemmermeer polder. Here, where N 201 bears left, keep straight ahead, passing on the left the Flora flower show grounds. 3.5km/2 miles farther on is Bennebroek, with the Linnaeushof Recreation Park (summer flower show and children's flower parade).

Flora
Linnaeushof

Vogelenzang
via Katwijk
to Lisse

3km/2 miles beyond this is Vogelenzang, with the Frans Roozen nurseries. From here N 206 continues through bulb-fields which are continuously in bloom from April to mid May to Noordwijk-Binnen (14km/8½ miles), from which a detour can be made to the popular seaside resort of Noordwijk aan Zee, 2km/1¼ miles west. From Noordwijk-Binnen the road continues to Katwijk aan den Rijn, 3km/2 miles west of which is Katwijk aan Zee (see Katwijk). Here we leave the main road and take the road which runs via Valkenburg to Leiden, turning north-west from there to Oegstgeest and then west via Warmond to Sassenheim, and from there on N 208 to Lisse.

** Keukenhof

1km/¾ mile north-west of Lisse is Keukenhof. During the Middle Ages this 28 hectare/70 acre park was the "kitchen garden" of an estate belonging to Countess Jacobaea of Bavaria. Since 1949 it has been a popular tourist attraction, with restaurants and sunny terraces, exhibitions and presentations of various kinds.

Keukenhof: a paradise of flowers

The Keukenhof is the world's largest open-air flower show. Every year more than 700 varieties of tulips can be seen in bloom here. The charm of Keukenhof lies in its endless variety of colour; and even before the flowers bloom in the open thousands of tulips, hyacinths, crocuses and daffodils can be seen flowering in the 5000 sq.m/6000 sq.yds of hothouses. The park itself is also very beautiful, with its lakes and watercourses and old trees. Open: from the end of March to the end of May, 8am–8pm (no admission after 6.30pm).

Bolsward

F 3

Province: Friesland
Population: 10,000

Bolsward, near Sneek in north-western Friesland, is one of the eleven Frisian towns. It was once a prosperous port and Hanseatic town on the Middelzee, but since the Middelzee was drained this has been mainly an agricultural area. Bolsward has two vocational colleges (dairying industry). There are a number of popular festivals during the summer.

Situation and characteristics

The history of the town can be traced back to 715. In the 9th century a tower house was built on the higher ground here which provided security from flooding. The town became a member of the Hanseatic League in 1412 and received its municipal charter in 1455.

History

The red brick Town Hall, built by local craftsmen in 1614–16, is the finest Renaissance building in Friesland. In the 18th century the original façade was replaced by a handsome Baroque gable and a Rococo external staircase. The tower has a carillon. Notable features of the interior are the magnificent Council Chamber, the period furniture, pictures and silver.

*Town Hall

Bolsward Town Hall: exterior . . .   *. . . and the entrance stairway*

Grote Kerk

The Gothic Grote Kerk or Martinikerk (15th c.) is one of the largest churches in Friesland (nave 60m/200ft long), with a high saddleback roof. The aisles are separated from the nave by massive columns. The choir-stalls (15th c.) and pulpit (1662) are decorated with carvings of Biblical scenes. Other notable features are the magnificent grave-slabs from the little Broerekerk (1281) and the organ by the Groningen organ-builder A. A. Hinsz (1775–81). There are frequent organ recitals in the church, which has excellent acoustics.

Surroundings of Bolsward

Witmarsum

10km/6 miles north-west of Bolsward is Witmarsum, birthplace of Menno Simonsz (1496–1561), founder of the Mennonite sect. The little village church (Reformed) was built in his memory in 1633.

Exmorra

3km/2 miles west of Bolsward is Exmorra, where the old grocer's shop and the village school (1885) can be visited.

Aldfaers Erfroute

In the triangular area between Bolsward, Workum and Makkum visitors can follow the Aldfaers Erfroute, which takes in the villages of Exmorra, Allingawier, Ferwoude and Piaan and several small museums. It is well worth while continuing to Makkum (see entry), Workum, Hindeloopen (see entry) or Stavoren.

Borger

H 3

Province: Drenthe
Population: 13,000

Borger, south-east of Assen, is famed for its megalithic tombs (*hunebed-den*, "giants' beds") and for its traditional Drenthe weddings in local costume (*wasschups*). On the road to Bronneger, at No. 27, is the largest *hunebed* in the Netherlands, the Onbesuisde Steenhoop (the "reckless heap of stones"), 22m/72ft long. There are 47 surviving stones.

Situation and characteristics

In a former orphanage, 't Flint 'nhoes, at Bronnegerstraat 12, is a museum and information centre on the megalithic tombs of Friesland and the TRB culture (see History). Open: Fri. 6.30–8.30pm.

Museum

Bourtange

J 3

Province: Groningen
Commune: Vlagtwedde (pop. 16,000)

Bourtange lies in the extreme south-east of Groningen province, on the German frontier (closed to all but local cars). The village grew up on a sandy ridge (*tange*) amid boggy moorland, which was brought into cultivation by peasant farmers (*boeren*): hence its name.

Situation and characteristics

The sandy ridge was fortified by Prince William of Orange in 1580; then in 1605 it was strengthened by Prince Maurice, against the wishes of the bishop of Münster; and, now with five bastions, it proved impregnable until the end of the 17th century. During the 18th century its defences were still further strengthened.
Since the restoration of the old core of the village in 1967 this star-shaped stronghold has been protected as a national monument. Open: April to October, Tue.–Fri. 10am–12.30pm and 1–5pm, Sat.–Mon. 1–5pm.

Bourtange Castle

Breda

D 8

Province: Noord-Brabant
Population: 120,000

Breda lies near the Belgian frontier in western Noord-Brabant, at the junction of the rivers Mark and Aa. A cultural centre, with numerous research and educational institutions, and the see of a Roman Catholic bishop, it is mainly famed as one of the country's leading industrial towns, with engineering firms, factories producing synthetic fibres, matches and foodstuffs and a brewery. It is also an important tourist centre.

Situation and *importance

Breda grew up in the 12th century under the protection of a castle, received its municipal charter in the mid 13th century and from the late Middle Ages onwards played an important role in the history of the Netherlands. Fortified in 1534 by Count Henry of Nassau, the town withstood numerous sieges. The Compromise of Breda in February 1566 marked the beginning of the revolt of the Netherlands against Spanish rule. In March 1590 Prince Maurice of Nassau took the Spaniards by surprise, bringing seventy men secretly into the town in Adriaan van Bergen's peat boat. The Peace of Breda in 1667 ended the second naval war with Britain and recognised Dutch ownership of the East Indies. The town's fortifications again played an important part during the wars with the French in 1793–95 and 1813. When the navigable river Mark gradually silted up during the 18th century Breda's importance as a trading town declined, but with the coming of the railway its rise into a major industrial centre began.

History

The Town

In the centre of the old town, which is surrounded by a ring of canals (*singels*), is the Grote Markt. On the north side of the square are the Grote

Grote Markt

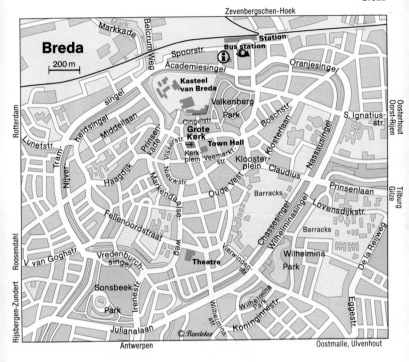

Breda

200 m

Kerk or Onze Lieve Vrouwekerk and the 18th century Town Hall (Stadhuis).
On the south side stands the old Vleeshal (Meat Hall).

The Grote Kerk (Reformed) was begun in 1290 in Gothic style; but the choir,
in addition to rich Late Gothic features, also shows Renaissance influences.
The magnificent tower, 97m/318ft high, was built between 1468 and 1509;
the top section was added after a fire in 1694. The tower was completely
restored between 1944 and 1969. In the Prince's Chapel to the left of the
choir, behind a richly carved grille, is the imposing Renaissance tomb (16th
c.) of Count Engelbrecht II of Nassau (Stadholder-General of the Netherlands in the reign of the Emperor Maximilian I; d. 1504) and his wife
Cimburga of Baden (d. 1510) – an alabaster masterpiece which was the
work of either Tommaso Vincitore of Bologna (architect of Breda Castle) or
Pietro Torrigiani, a Florentine. There are a number of tombs in the ambulatory, including (on the same side as Engelbrecht II), the monument, behind
a fine iron grille, of Count Engelbrecht I (d. 1443) and his son John of
Nassau (d. 1475), together with their wives. Other notable features are the
Late Gothic choir-stalls (carved with scenes satirising the clergy) and the
pulpit (c. 1600); in the baptistery a copper font made in Mechelen in 1540 by
Joos de Backer of Antwerp; on the left, by the organ, a large painting (c.
1500) of St Christopher; and, in the north transept, a wall painting of the
Annunciation (c. 1450).

Grote Kerk

*Renaissance
tomb

The oldest part of the Town Hall (Stadhuis) is the Great Hall, with the

Town Hall

◀ *Grote Kerk, Breda: evening*

Breda Castle

adjoining "Cleyn Raedthuys" (Little Town Hall). In 1767 the court architect, P. W. Schonck, combined three adjoining houses, giving them a unified façade. In 1898 an extension was built on to the right-hand side of the Town Hall, and in 1925 there were further additions, including the council chamber (with stained glass by J. Nicolas). In the Great Hall is a copy of Veláz-quez's famous painting of the "Surrender of Breda" (original in the Prado, Madrid). A small doorway leads into the garden, with an old coach-shed, now used as a conference room. From here there is a good view of the rear façade of the Town Hall.

Meat Hall

Municipal
Museum
Diocesan Museum

On the south side of the Grote Markt (No. 19) is the old Meat Hall (Vleeshal), with a handsome 17th century sandstone doorway and a gable of 1733. Together with the building once occupied by the Marksmen's Guild of St George it now houses the Municipal Museum (Stedelijk Museum voor Geschiedenis en Oudheidkunde) and the Diocesan Museum (Bisschoppe-lijk Museum). Open: Tue. and Sun. 1–5pm, Wed.–Sat. 1.30–5pm.

Kasteelplein

North-east of the Grote Kerk is the Kasteelplein, with a number of old buildings and an equestrian statue of William III of Orange (1921). On the west side of the square is the Museum of Ethnology. The building known as De Prins Cardinaal takes its name from Don Ferdinand, who from 1634 to 1637 was Stadholder of the southern Low Countries, representing his brother Philip IV of Spain. The building later became a restaurant and hotel.

*Breda Castle

At the north end of the Kasteelplein is Breda Castle (Kasteel van Breda), which first appears in the records in the 12th century. In the 14th century Jan I of Polanen built a new castle, with four corner towers, and a chapel, both of which were several times pulled down and rebuilt. The present castle, the ancestral home of the Counts of Orange-Nassau, was built in 1530 by Count Henry III, tutor and counsellor to the Emperor Charles V, and later extended by King (and Stadholder) William III. Henry commissioned

Tommaso Vincitore of Bologna to convert the old fortified castle into a handsome modern palace, and while the palace was under construction he lived in an old water-mill which then stood on the site. One of Prince William I's sons was the first member of the family to live in the palace. Later, when the palace became the Royal Military Academy, an additional storey was added (1826–28).

Also dating from the time of Count Henry III are the two towers of the Spanjaardsgat (see below) and the Blockhuis, the official residence of the commandant of the Military Academy, which was occupied for a time by Prince William I.

The grounds of the palace are entered by the Stadhouderspoort. The coat of arms of Stadholder William V is a later addition.

At Kasteelplein 25 is the Museum of Ethnology (Volkenkundig Museum Justinus van Nassau). The original building was altered by Justinus, the illegitimate son of Prince William I; then in 1680 it passed into state ownership and became the official residence of the governor of Breda. Here in 1810 Napoleon expressed his displeasure at his unwelcoming reception in the town. From 1828 to 1923 the house was the official residence of the commandant of the Military Academy.

Museum of Ethnology

The Museum displays the ethnographic collection of the Military Academy, with material from all over the world but particularly from the Netherlands Indies. There is a library of over 6000 volumes. Open: Tue.–Sat. 10am–5pm, Sun. 1–5pm.

In Cingelstraat is the Spanjaardsgat, a water-gate flanked by two towers (to the left the Granaattoren, to the right the Duiventoren) and a length of wall. Here, according to the legend, Adriaan van Bergen and seventy men slipped into the town in a peat boat and took it by surprise. Since the Spanjaardsgat was not built until 1610, however, the actual point of entry must have been on the north side of the castle.

Spanjaardsgat

Kasteel Bouvigne, Ginneken

Kasteel Nijenrode, Breukelen

Port quarter	There are a number of handsome old buildings in the port quarter of Breda, and many reminiscences of the time when ships could still sail up the river and discharge their cargoes here. In the 1960s, however, the construction of an underground car park led to the partial silting up of the old harbour.
Gasthuispoort	In the Stadkantoor restaurant in the Vlaszak, to the east of the town centre, can be seen remains of the old Gasthuispoort, one of the three main medieval town gates, which was discovered during building work in 1976.
Begijnhof	In Catharinastraat is the Begijnhof, which is still occupied by Beguines. In the 13th century the Beguines lived near the castle, but were later driven out by the extensions to the castle. When their former church, the St Wendelinskapel, was handed over to Protestant Walloons in 1648 they remained without a church until the new church at the end of the Begijnhof was built in 1836. The two churches and the 29 little houses survived the Second World War unscathed. Attached to the Begijnhof is a herb garden with hundreds of different species of plants.
Valkenbergpark	To the rear of the Begijnhof lies the Valkenbergpark, at the north gate of which is the Nassau Barony Monument (1905), set up to mark the 500th anniversary of the union of the lordship of Breda with the house of Nassau (1404). The monument, designed by the well known architect P. J. H. Cuypers, shows the coats of arms of twenty communes in the surrounding area and the lion of Nassau with a royal crown, sword and heraldic shield.

Surroundings of Breda

Ginneken	3km/2 miles south of Breda is Ginneken, a large village which is now incorporated in the town, with the handsome moated castle of Bouvigne (17th c.), which formed part of the defences of Breda.
	In 1614 the castle was purchased by William I's son Prince Frederick Henry, who made it his headquarters during the siege of Breda in 1637.
	In 1930 there was a plan to demolish the castle and build bungalows on the site, but the plan was frustrated when the municipality bought the castle and restored it. Since 1977 it has been occupied by the Hoogheemraadschap (Water Cooperative) of Western Brabant.
	South-west of the castle extends the Mastbos, a beautiful wooded park of over 500 hectares/1250 acres.
Chaam	7km/4½ miles south-east of Breda is the village of Chaam, famed for the Acht van Chaam, a cycle race which takes place shortly after the Tour de France. The village's main sources of income are agriculture and tourism.
Baarle-Nassau	9km/6 miles beyond Chaam is Baarle-Nassau, with its sister village of Baarle-Hertog or Baerle-Duc (pop. 1500), a Belgian enclave in Dutch territory which has been separated from Baarle-Nassau since the 15th century.
	Altogether there are twenty-one Belgian enclaves in the Netherlands and eight Dutch enclaves in Belgium. In some cases the boundary runs through the middle of a house, and the national affiliation of the house is then determined by the position of the front door.

Breukelen
E 6

Province: Utrecht
Population: 10,000

The village of Breukelen, north-west of Utrecht, is famed for its medieval castles – Nijenrode (1270), which was rebuilt in the 19th century and is now occupied by Utrecht University; Gunterstein (17th c.), with its tall chimneys; and Oudaen (16th c.). North of the river Vecht are many houses built in the 16th and 17th centuries by wealthy Amsterdam merchants.

The town has also the distinction of having given its name to Brooklyn, New York.

Brielle   C 7

Province: Zuid-Holland
Population: 15,000

Brielle (or Den Briel; traditionally called Brill in English), is the chief place on the island of Voorne, which lies to the south of the Europoort. In the 16th century it was an important stronghold on the estuary of the Maas. On April 1st 1572 the Sea Beggars, having been expelled from England, captured the town and thus sparked off the northern provinces' fight for independence.

Situation and characteristics

The Grote Kerk or St Catharijnekerk (unfinished) was built in the 15th century in Brabantine Late Gothic style, with a massive stone tower containing a carillon of 48 bells by François Hemony (1660).

Grote Kerk

The Town Hall (Stadhuis; 14th c.), in the market square, has a façade of 1793 in Louis XIV style. On the gable are the words "Libertatis Primitiae" ("The First Fruits of Liberty").

Town Hall

The Tromp Museum, housed in a building (1623) which was formerly a state prison and weigh-house, is devoted to the history of the town and the celebrated Admiral Tromp, a native of Brielle.

Tromp Museum

To the north of the town is the Brielse Meer, once the estuary of the Maas and now an area much favoured by water sports enthusiasts.

Brielse Meer

Broek op Langendijk   D 4

Province: Noord-Holland
Population: 15,300

A road runs north from Alkmaar to Broek op Langendijk through a vegetable-growing area traversed by numerous canals. From 1903 until quite recent times the vegetables (mainly cabbages) were shipped in flat-bottomed boats to the auction hall in Broek; but as a result of the redistribution of agricultural land in the area the transport of vegetables by boat became increasingly difficult, and finally the auction hall was closed. Now, after renovation, It houses a museum devoted to the landscape of the region and the life and work of the inhabitants. There are still, however, daily auctions at which visitors can buy vegetables, fruit and flowers. Open: beginning of May to end of September, Mon.–Fri. 10am–5pm.

Coevorden   H 4

Province: Drenthe
Population: 14,000

Coevorden, situated on a strategically important site in south-eastern Drenthe, became a fortified town in the 16th century, and part of the town walls and the fortified castle (the only one in Drenthe; now occupied by the Town Hall) have been preserved. Around 1700 the circuit of walls was extended. An annual goose market is held in the town, at which the "goose-girl of the year" is chosen – the one who brings the first ten geese to market on the morning of market day. The old Arsenal now houses the Municipal Museum, with material illustrating the history of the region; open: Mon.–Fri. 10am–12.30pm and 1.30–5pm. The Reformed church is on a Greek cross plan with a dome over the crossing.

Culemborg

See Wijk bij Duurstede

Delft

C 7

Province: Zuid-Holland
Population: 88,000

Situation, townscape and characteristics

Delft lies on the river Schie between Rotterdam and The Hague. The picturesque old part of the town is ringed by canals.
Delft has a University of Technology and a number of research institutes. It also has a variety of industry (engineering, car manufacture, electrical engineering, building materials, paper and packaging). The manufacture of Delft ware, which was world-famed from the 17th to the mid 18th century, has recently been revived. Delft was the birthplace of the scholar and statesman Hugo de Groot (Grotius, 1583–1645), the painter Jan Vermeer, whose "View of Delft" is in the Mauritshuis in The Hague, and the scientist Antoni van Leeuwenhoek (1632–1723).

History

The town is believed to have developed in the Middle Ages around a feudal estate. It received its municipal charter in the 13th century, and thereafter carpet-making, brewing

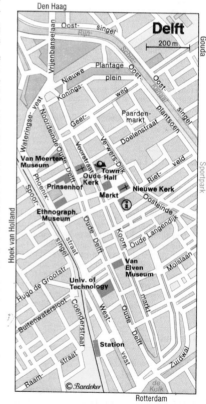

Delft Town Hall

Oude Kerk

and trade flourished. In order to compete with the rival towns of Dordrecht, Schiedam and Rotterdam Delft established an outer harbour at Delfshaven on the Maas in the early 15th century.

The town reached its peak of prosperity in the 17th century, when the manufacture of Delft ware began to develop. This was the period when most of the magnificent buildings which have been preserved in the old town were erected.

The Town

In the centre of the town, which is traversed by numerous canals, is the spacious Markt. In the centre of the square can be seen a bronze statue of Hugo Grotius (by F. Stracké, 1886). On the east side of the square stands the Nieuwe Kerk (formerly St Ursulakerk; organ recitals in summer), a Gothic church built between 1396 and 1496. The 108m/354ft high tower is in Brabantine Gothic style, with a carillon of 1663; there are fine views from the top.

*Nieuwe Kerk

In the choir is the magnificent tomb of William I of Orange (William the Silent), one of the great masterpieces of Dutch Baroque sculpture (by Hendrick de Keyser, 1614–21). It is richly decorated with symbols glorifying the dead man. Under a white canopy borne on black marble columns is a white figure of William the Silent, surrounded by bronze allegorical figures including Justice (with scales), Freedom (with sceptre and hat), Valour (clad in a lion's skin) and Faith (with a book and a model of a church). In a vault below the tomb are buried 41 princes and princesses of the house of Orange (including Queen Wilhelmina, who died in 1948). In the ambulatory, to the right, is the monument of King William I (d. 1843 in Berlin), and

*Tomb of William I

on the wall above this is a memorial relief (by Antonio Canova, 1806) of Prince Frederick William of Orange (d. 1799), brought here from Padua, where he was originally buried. On the north wall of the choir is the marble monument of Hugo Grotius, and to the right of this, in the floor, can be seen the place where he is buried.

Town Hall

On the west side of the Markt, standing alone, is the Town Hall (Stadhuis), in Renaissance style (façade restored 1966), which contains a number of fine paintings of the 16th–18th centuries. The original Town Hall was built in the early 13th century; then in the 15th century a stone tower, known as Het Steen, was built on the brick substructure of the original tower. In 1618 the Town Hall was destroyed by fire, leaving only the tower still standing, and was then rebuilt in its present form by Hendrick de Keyser. The façade is richly articulated by pilasters and sculpture. On the small gable is a figure of Justice. In the interior are a number of handsome rooms, including the Orange Gallery and the Council Chamber.

Weigh-House

Behind the Town Hall is the old municipal Weigh-House (Waag), now the Municipal Theatre. Adjoining it is the Meat Hall (Vleeshal), identified by two ox-heads.

Oude Kerk

North-west of the Town Hall, reached by way of the Hippolytusbuurt, stands the Oude Kerk (Heilige Geestkerkhof; Reformed), built around 1250, with a slightly leaning tower and fine timber vaulting of 1574. The tower, originally 14th century, was rebuilt in 1450 in a style very characteristic of "Coastal Gothic", with four corner turrets round the pyramidal roof. The church contains a number of important works of art – a carved pulpit of 1548; in the choir the marble tomb of Admiral Piet Hein (d. 1629), who captured the Spanish silver fleet in 1628; in the chapel to the left of the choir the tomb of Admiral Maarten Tromp (d. 1653), who commanded the Dutch navy in thirty-two naval battles; and on the wall of the porch the monument

Lambert van Meerten Museum

Delft tiles: a favourite souvenir

of the scientist Antoni van Leeuwenhoek. The painter Jan Vermeer is also buried in the church.

To the west of the Oude Kerk is the Oude Delft, a canal traversing the town from north to south on which there are a number of picturesque old houses. Other interesting old houses are to be seen in the immediate vicinity of the church, in Voorstraat, Hippolytusbuurt, the Wijnhaven and the Koornmarkt.

Oude Delft

Opposite the Oude Kerk, at Agathaplein 1, is a picturesque group of buildings, the Prinsenhof. Built around 1400 as the nunnery of St Agatha, it was secularised after the Reformation and from 1575 was the residence of the Princes of Orange until Prince Maurice of Orange moved the seat of government to The Hague.

*Prinsenhof

The Prinsenhof has tragic associations in the history of the Netherlands, for it was here that William the Silent was assassinated in 1584. The mark of the bullet which killed him can still be seen on the staircase leading to the dining room.

Housed in the Prinsenhof is an interesting museum, mainly devoted to the eighty years of war with Spain (1568–1648). There are also numerous items of local interest, portraits of members of the house of Orange and displays illustrating the history of Delft ware. In the oldest part of the convent (c. 1430) is a two-storey cloister which is unique in the Netherlands. Open: Tue.–Sat. 10am–5pm, Sun. 1–5pm; June to August also Mon. 1–5pm.

To the south of the Prinsenhof, at Agathaplein 4, is the small Nusantara Ethnographic Museum, with exhibits illustrating the cultures of Indonesia. Open: Tue.–Sat. 10am–5pm, Sun. 1–5pm; June to August also Mon. 1–5pm.

Ethnographic Museum

North of the Prinsenhof, on the Oude Delft, is the Lambert van Meerten Museum, an important collection of applied art, with period furniture and paintings and an extensive display of Delft ware, all well displayed and presented on the museum's two floors. Open: Tue.–Sat. 10am–5pm, Sun. 1–5pm; June to August also Mon. 1–5pm.

*Lambert van Meerten Museum

At Oude Delft 167 stands the Gemeenlandshuis (Dyke Office) of the old County of Delfland (from 1644). In the early 16th century this was the residence of Jan de Sluyter, Dyke-Master of Delfland and Burgomaster of Delft. The stone gable is decorated with handsome coats of arms.
At Oude Delft is the Begijnhof, with a Late Gothic tower and a Baroque "hidden church" (built by Daniël Marot in 1743) in which Catholics worshipped in secret during the persecutions.

Gemeenlandshuis

In the southern part of the Oude Delft is the 17th century Armamentarium (entrance at Korte Geer 1), the old Arsenal of the States of Holland (restored and extended in 1696). Since 1913 it has housed the Netherlands Military Museum. Until recently the museum was confined to the postwar period, but it now also includes the collections of pre-1945 material previously to be seen in Leiden. Open: Tue.–Sat. 10am–5pm, Sun. 1–5pm.

Armamentarium

To the south of the Town Hall, at Koornmarkt 67, the Paul Tétar van Elven Museum contains the collection assembled by the painter of that name (1823–96). With its old furniture and Delft tiles, the artist's studio is redolent of the atmosphere of its period. Van Elven was teacher of drawing at the Delft Polytechnic (now the University of Technology). Open: May to September, Tue.–Sat. 1–5pm.

Van Elven Museum

Going south-east from the choir of the Nieuwe Kerk along the Oosteinde canal, we come to the picturesque Oostpoort, situated at the junction of a

Oostpoort

Delfzijl

number of canals at the south-east corner of the old town. The twin towers of this old town gate, built about 1400, were heightened in the 16th century by the addition of octagonal upper storeys and pointed roofs. From here there are fine views of the town.

University of Technology

On the south side of the old town are the administrative offices of the University of Technology, originally founded in 1863, which now has some 10,000 students. The modern university buildings lie in the south-east of the town, beyond the Rhine–Schie Canal.

De Porceleyne Fles

At Rotterdamseweg 196, on the south side of the town, is the Porceleyne Fles, the porcelain manufactory in which the Delft ware ("Delft Blue") which has been famed since the 17th century is still produced (showroom).

Delfzijl   J 2

Province: Groningen
Population: 24,000

Situation and characteristics

The industrial town and port of Delfzijl, founded in the 13th century, lies in the Groningen marshland area which extends along the coast of the Waddenzee from Friesland to the estuary of the Eems. The inhabitants' main source of income is agriculture. The principal crops on the fertile soil of this area are wheat, sugar-beet, barley and rape. Characteristic features of the landscape are the handsome farmhouses of the old *terp* villages with their unusually large barns. Much of the agricultural produce of the region is exported, mostly by water.

Delfzijl is linked with Groningen by the Eems Canal (navigable by vessels of 2000 tons), along the banks of which numerous fields of natural gas are now being worked.

Sights

Features of interest in the town are a number of old houses, the Adam mill (1795) and the Maigret Monument, commemorating George Simenon, who conceived the figure of Inspector Maigret in a sailing ship off Delfzijl.

Surroundings of Delfzijl

Winschoten

South of Delfzijl is Winschoten (pop. 20,000), where large deposits of salt were formerly worked. The Reformed church has preserved 13th century Romanesque work in the walls and the façade of the choir.

At Oostereinde 4 is an old steam pump working a double Archimedean screw, one of the last of its kind in existence. Open: May to mid September, Tue.–Sat. 2–6pm; mid September to April, on the last Sunday in the month 11am–5pm.

North-west of the town are three old flour mills, De Volharding (1783), De Berg (1854) and Dijkstra (1862), which are set working twice a month, usually on Saturday.

Den Bosch

See 's-Hertogenbosch

Den Burg

See Texel

Den Haag

See The Hague

Den Hoorn

See Texel

Deventer

G 6

Province: Overijssel
Population: 66,000

The old Hanseatic town of Deventer lies on the right bank of the IJssel. Although it has preserved a number of beautiful old houses in the town

Situation and characteristics

View of Deventer with St Lebuinuskerk

169

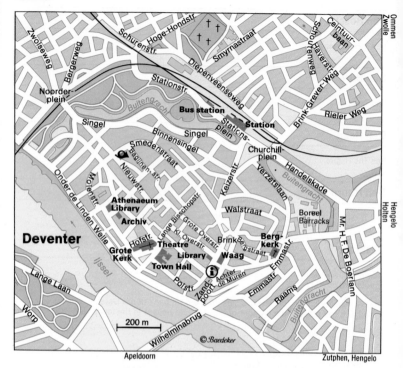

centre it is predominantly a town of modern aspect with active industries, the most important of which are carpet-making and the manufacture of bicycles. It is also famed for its honey cakes (*kruidkoeken*).

History

The origins of the town go back to the Carolingian period (809), though there is evidence that the site was occupied 3000 years ago. By the 9th century Deventer had developed into an important trading town, and during the medieval period it became a member of the Hanseatic League. It received its municipal charter in the 13th century. It was the birthplace of the theologian Geert Groote (1340–84), founder in 1376 of the monastic community of Brothers of the Common Life. Among members of the brotherhood were Erasmus (who lived in Deventer in 1475–76), Thomas à Kempis, Pope Hadrian VI and Descartes. The painter Hendrick Terbruggen was born in Deventer in 1588; his painting of the four Evangelists can be seen in the Town Hall.

The Town

°Grote Kerk
(Lebuinuskerk)

According to legend the town's first church was built in 765 by St Lebuinus. This was devastated in 800, and in 1040 Bishop Bernoldus, who had fled from Utrecht to escape the Normans, founded a new church. Of this Romanesque basilica there survive only the crypt, the groined vaulting, two rows of columns with cube capitals and parts of the choir and the east transept. In the 15th century a massive Gothic basilica was built (west aisle, tower, ambulatory, Raadskapel and north aisle). The tower (1612) has a Baroque spire by Hendrick de Keyser and a carillon by François Hemony (1655).

At the north-west corner of the Grote Kerk can be seen the remains of the former parish church, the 15th century Mariakerk. After being partly demolished in the 17th century it was used for many years as a weapon store.

On the south-east side of the Grote Kerk is the Town Hall (Landhuis), which consists of two medieval buildings, the Landhuis (the original Town Hall) on the Kerkhof and the Wanthuis in Polstraat.

In the 17th century the Landhuis was given a gabled front in Renaissance style and the Wanthuis a pilastered side façade (by Philip Vingboons). The imposing stone façade on the Grote Kerkhof was built in 1693 by Jacob Roman.

The Town Hall contains a fine group portrait of the burgomasters and councillors of Deventer (1667) by Gerard Terborch, who was himself a town councillor towards the end of his life. Open: Mon.–Thur. 8am–4pm, Fri. to 2pm.

A little way north-west of the Grote Kerk, in Noordenbergstraat/Klooster (No. 12), is the Athenaeum Library, founded in 1560, which contains 120,000 volumes, together with 500 manuscripts and incunabula (some of them from the old monastery which stood here). From 1630 to 1879 the library belonged to the Athenaeum College of Deventer.
Across the street from the Library, at Klooster 3, are the Municipal Archives.

From here Papenstraat leads to the Brink, Deventer's spacious main square, which has a number of old houses with handsome façades.

The most striking building on the Brink is the Late Gothic Weigh-House (Waag, 1528–31), with a handsome external staircase. The Weigh-House, together with the adjoining House of the Three Herrings (De Drie Haringen, 1575), has been occupied since 1915 by the Municipal Museum of Antiquities, with a variety of exhibits illustrating the history of the town and surrounding area. On the outside wall hangs a copper cauldron in which counterfeiters used to be executed by being boiled in oil or water. Open: Tue.–Sat. 10am–5pm, Sun. 2–5pm.

On the west side of the square (No. 89) is the Penninckshuis (1588), originally a Mennonite church. The Renaissance-style façade is decorated with symbolic figures of the Christian virtues. In front of the house is a statue of Albert Schweitzer.

The Toy and Tinware Museum (Speelgoed en Blikmuseum), at Brink 47, occupies the former Kronenburg and Vogelensang warehouses. The collection of toys was originally assembled by the painter Jan Stekelenburg; the tinware was presented by the manufacturers, Thomassen & Drijver. Open: Tue.–Sat. 10am–5pm, Sun. 2–5pm.

To the east of the Brink, reached by way of Bergstraat, is the Bergkwartier, an old quarter of the town near the banks of the IJssel with a distinct and rather melancholy character of its own. The name is thought to be derived from the local fishermen who sailed to Bergen in Norway. Many old houses with handsome façades have been restored by the firm of Bergkwartier with government subsidies.

The Bergkwartier is dominated by the 12th century Bergkerk or St Nicolaaskerk, situated on higher ground. This was originally a cruciform Romanesque basilica with two towers. In the early 15th century a new choir, a nave flanked by broad aisles and a transept were added, the towers were heightened by the addition of spires and finally the church was given a vaulted roof and decorated with wall paintings. Of the original church there remains only the Romanesque transept, with round-headed niches.

Mariakerk

Town Hall

Athenaeum Library

Brink

Weigh-House

Museum of Antiquities

Penninckshuis

Toy Museum

Bergkwartier

Bergkerk

Achter de Muren	On the south-west side of the town the streets known as Achter de Muren ("Behind the Walls") lead through the double town walls to the banks of the IJssel, from which there is a fine view of the town.
Surroundings	20km/12½ miles east of Deventer on E 8 is the little town of Markelo, noted for its festivals and exhibitions.

Diepenheim

See Goor

Doesburg

G 7

Province: Gelderland
Population: 11,000

Situation and characteristics	The old Hanseatic town of Doesburg, at the junction of the Gelderse and the Oude IJssel, received its municipal charter in 1287. The town walls were built by Menno van Coehoorn in the 17th century.
Sights	The town has a number of handsome brick buildings in the style of the Lower Rhine. Among them are the Grote Kerk or St Martinikerk (15th–16th c.); the Weigh-House (Waag), now a restaurant; and the Old Town Hall, which now houses the Regional Museum (De Roode Toren; Roggestraat 9–13). The Museum is open Tue.–Fri. 10am–12 noon and 1.30–4.30pm, Sat. 1.30–4.30pm; May to August, also Sun. 1.30–4.30pm.
	In the Gildenhof are a number of shops and workshops (potter's, pewterer's, cheese dairy, mustard and vinegar factory) and a small museum. Open: Mon.–Fri. 10am–5pm, Sat. 11am–4pm.

Doetinchem

G 7

Province: Gelderland
Population: 41,000

Situation and characteristics	Doetinchem, east of Arnhem, was during the Middle Ages the only Hanseatic town on the Oude IJssel. Rebuilt after its destruction during the Second World War, it has taken on a fresh lease of life as the industrial centre of the Achterhoek area.
Sights	The town's main features of interest are the Grote Kerk or St Catharinakerk, a Gothic hall-church of the 14th–16th centuries, and the wall windmill on the IJsselkai, now occupied by the tourist information office (VVV).

Surroundings of Doetinchem

Huiz Slangenburg	Near the town, in beautiful wooded country, is Huiz Slangenburg, a 17th century country house on the site of a medieval castle (not open to the public; information centre open June to September, Wed.–Sun. 1–5.30pm).

Dokkum

G 2

Province: Friesland
Commune: Dongeradeel
Population: 25,000

Dokkum, the most northerly town in the Netherlands, has long been a place of pilgrimage as the scene of the martyrdom in 754 of St Boniface, an English Benedictine monk and missionary.

On the town walls (restored) are two flour mills, De Hoop ("Hope") and Zeldenrust ("Seldom at Rest").
The 15th century Grote Kerk or St Martinuskerk has a fine pulpit of 1751 and organ-case of 1688.
The Town Hall (1608) has a handsome Rococo council chamber.

The Renaissance-style Admiraliteitshuis at Diepswal 27, built in 1618 as headquarters of the Admiralty of Groningen and Friesland, has been occupied since 1963 by the Streekmuseum, a regional museum displaying finds from the early *terp* settlements, objects from an old monastery, Frisian costumes, antiques, jewellery, etc. Open: April to September, Mon.–Sat. 10am–5pm; October to March, Mon.–Sat. 2–5pm.

Doorn

Province: Utrecht
Population: 10,000

The little town of Doorn, where the ex-Kaiser of Germany, Wilhelm II, spent his last years, lies south-east of Utrecht.

The ex-Kaiser bought Huis Doorn in 1920 and lived there until his death in 1941. Originally a medieval castle, the house was rebuilt in classical style in the 18th century. The gatehouse was altered by the ex-Kaiser in Dutch Renaissance style.

Huis Doorn: home of the ex-Kaiser

The house is set in a large and beautiful park.

The house is now open to the public as a museum. It preserves the original furniture and furnishings, with many of the ex-Kaiser's personal possessions, including a collection of snuff-boxes belonging to Frederick the Great, military orders and uniforms, family photographs and pictures. Open: mid March to October, Mon.–Sat. 9.30am–5pm, Sun. 1–5pm.

Surroundings of Doorn

Langbroeker Wetering

The Langbroeker Wetering ("Langbroek Waterway") is a stretch of territory along the Kromme Rijn, in which are a number of castles dating from the 13th and 14th centuries and rebuilt in the 18th and 19th centuries. The castles (not open to the public) are reminiscent of the châteaux of the Loire and have earned this area the popular name of the "Loire of the Netherlands". Among them are Beverweerd, Sterkenburg, Moersbergen, Hardenbroek, Sandburg, Zuylenburg and Broekhuizen (built 1810 in Empire style).

Kasteel Maarsbergen

North of Doorn, at the village of Maarsbergen, is Kasteel Maarsbergen (restored), which dates from the 17th century.

Van Gimborn Arboretum

To the west of the village lies the Van Gimborn Arboretum (established 1924), an area of 23 hectares/57 acres planted with conifers and deciduous trees, heath plants, dwarf shrubs and a Tsuga forest. Open: Mon.–Fri. 8am–4.30pm, Sat. and Sun. 10am–4.30pm.

Dordrecht   D 7

Province: Zuid-Holland
Population: 108,000

Situation and
*importance

The ancient town of Dordrecht (Dordt for short) lies just south-east of Rotterdam, picturesquely situated between the Oude Maas (here navigable for large ocean-going ships) and the Noord and Dordtse Kil, two branches of the Rhine. It has shipyards and shipping offices and is also an important water sports centre. In the past, thanks to its favourable situation, it was the wealthiest trading town and port in the Netherlands, but was overtaken in the 18th century by Antwerp and Rotterdam. Dordrecht is now both a seaport and a river port, handling some four million tons of goods annually, mostly goods in transit. In addition to its metalworking, shipbuilding and chemical industries it has extensive service industries.

History

According to the Ghent Chronicles Dordrecht was destroyed by the Norsemen in 937. It first appears in the records, however, only in 1138, under the name of Thuredri(c)ht. When it received its municipal charter in 1220 it was already an important commercial town, trading with England, the Rhineland and Flanders. The St Elizabeth's Day flood in 1421 left the area south of Dordrecht under water and hampered the economic development of the town, since its communications by land were now largely severed. In 1457 much of the town was destroyed in a great fire.

In the 16th century Dordrecht took on a fresh lease of life, and in the latter part of the century it became an important centre of the fight for liberation. After the capture of Brielle in 1572 the town came out in support of Prince William, and it was in Dordrecht that the twelve towns which had declared their independence met and appointed William I Stadholder of Holland. Their meeting marked the establishment of the United Provinces.
In 1618–19 the Dordrecht Synod met here to settle the conflict between Calvinists and Lutherans.

A number of important painters were born in Dordrecht during the 17th century, including Ferdinand Bol, Aelbert Cuyp and Nicolaas Maes; some of them were pupils of Rembrandt. Also born in Dordrecht were the two great statesmen Johan (1625–72) and Cornelis (1623–72) de Witt. Johan became Grand Pensionary of Holland (in effect prime minister and foreign minister) in 1653 and Cornelis became burgomaster of Dordrecht in 1666. As opponents of the Prince of Orange, the brothers were murdered in 1672 in The Hague (in the Gevangenpoort of the Binnenhof).

In the early 18th century Dordrecht was overtaken as a port first by Amsterdam and then by Rotterdam. It began to recover some importance only towards the end of the 19th century.

The Town

The attractive Voorstraats Haven is the town's principal canal, whose winding course is followed through the centre of the town by its main shopping street, the Voorstraat, lined with handsome houses (e.g. No. 178).

At the west end of the Voorstraat, in the Grote Kerkbuurt, is the Grote Kerk or Onze Lieve Vrouwekerk (Church of Our Lady). Legend has it that a chapel was built here about 1300 by St Sura, a saint much loved by the townspeople who was killed by the builders of the chapel out of greed for money but rose from the dead. A new church was built in the 14th century, and after

Voorstraat

*Grote Kerk

175

Grote Kerk, Dordrecht: Brabantine Gothic

the great fire of 1457 was given its present form, in Brabantine Gothic style, between 1460 and 1502. As a result of a fault in construction the tower began to sink, and was completed only to a height of 70m/230ft. Later it was topped by four Baroque clock faces. A carillon of 49 bells was installed in 1949.

The Grote Kerk is the only church in Holland with stone vaulting and one of the largest churches in the country, with a length of 108m/354ft and a height of 24m/79ft. The beautiful interior has 56 columns with cabbage-leaf capitals.

*Choir-stalls

In the high choir, which is closed by a Baroque brass choir-screen presented to the church by one Diodati in 1744, are magnificent oak choir-stalls, carved in Renaissance style by a Flemish craftsman, Jan Terwen, in 1538–41, which are the finest of their kind in the Netherlands.
The carvings on the north side depict secular triumphal processions, including that of the Emperor Charles V, king of Spain and ruler of the Low Countries. On the south side the risen Christ is represented in a triumphal car drawn by the four Evangelists, preceded by Old Testament figures (including Adam and Eve, Noah and Moses) and followed by Death and Sin, in fetters, and martyrs, monks and Fathers of the Church. The procession ends with the triumphal chariot of the Church, drawn by Faith, Love and Hope.

Round the choir are twelve chapels. In the Jerusalem Chapel at the east end are three stained glass windows depicting important events in the history of the town: on left the St Elizabeth's Day flood of 1421, in the centre the great fire of 1457 and on right the surprise attack by English troops led by Jan van Egmond in 1480.
The windows in the south transept also have beautiful stained glass on historical themes, reflecting the important role played by Dordrecht in the

Arend Maertenshofje

history of the Netherlands. The figures of two Sea Beggars recall the
liberation of the town from Spanish rule in 1572, and there are also representatives of the Dordrecht Synod.

The chapels on the south side of the nave were built at the expense of the
town's guilds (the cloth-dealers, the merchants, the bakers, the fur-dealers,
the dyers).

Also of note is the large organ, built in 1671 by Nicolaas Hagen of Antwerp.
The organ-case is decorated with the coats of arms of Dordrecht and of
former burgomasters. On the magnificent pulpit (1765) are scenes from the
life of Christ.

The former Town Hall (Stadhuis) was built in 1544, but the classical-style   Town Hall
pedimented doorway with the town's coat of arms in the pediment and four
Ionic columns dates only from 1835–42. Over the entrance is a square
bell-tower. The new Town Hall (Stadkantoor) is on the Spuihaven.

On the Visbrug (Fish Bridge), which leads to the Groenmarkt, can be seen a   Visbrug
monument (1922) in honour of Johan and Cornelis de Witt. The house
named De Gulden Os at Groenmarkt 53 has a very fine gable.

Farther north is Scheffersplein, with a statue of the painter and sculptor Ary   Scheffersplein
Scheffer, who was born in Dordrecht. Near here, in Voorstraat, is the
entrance to Het Hof, the old law courts. This was the meeting-place in 1572   Het Hof
of the States of Holland, which led to the independence of the northern
provinces. At No. 188 is the Muntpoort (1555).

From Scheffersplein it is a short distance by way of Steegoversloot to   Dordrecht
Museumstraat, in which (No. 40) is Dordrecht Museum, housed in the   Museum
former municipal lunatic asylum.

The museum has sections devoted to the Hague and Amsterdam Schools,
the Dutch Romantics, Ary Scheffer, 20th century art and the Dordrecht

Groothoofdspoort

Simon van Gijn Museum

Impressionists. On the wall of the staircase leading to the upper floor is a panoramic picture of Dordrecht, 7m/23ft wide. In addition to paintings by Dordrecht artists of the 17th–19th centuries (Ferdinand Bol, Aelbert Cuyp, Ary Scheffer, Nicolaas Maes) the museum also possesses works by leading modern painters such as Jan and Charley Toorop, Jan Sluyters and Wim Schumacher. Open: Tue.–Sat. 10am–5pm, Sun. 1–5pm.

Arend Maertenshofje

At Museumstraat 38 is the entrance to the Arend Maartenshofje, a group of almshouses founded in 1625 for the widows of soldiers. In the beautiful gardens is a fine wrought-iron fountain.

Wijnstraat

To the east of the Groenmarkt is Wijnstraat. No. 79 was built in 1650 to the design of Pieter Post. At No. 81 is Huis Beverenburg, with stone window-framing of 1556.

Farther east we come to the Groothoofdspoort (rebuilt in Gothic style in 1618), once the principal town gate and now the only relic of the old town walls. Its handsome domed tower is a prominent landmark. On the river front can be seen a fine stone relief of the Virgin of Dordrecht, surrounded by the coats of arms of Dutch towns. From the north side there is a charming view of the junction of three rivers, the Oude Maas, the Noord and the Beneden Merwede. On the opposite side is Papendrecht.

Groothoofdspoort

Van Gijn Museum

From here Kuipershaven leads into Nieuwe Haven, a quarter dating from the 17th century. Originally occupied mainly by warehouses, it began to develop into a select residential district in the early 18th century. The handsome burgher's house at No. 29 was built in 1729 by Johan van Neurenberg, later burgomaster of Dordrecht; then in 1864 it was sold to the banker and art collector Simon van Gijn, who bequeathed it in 1922 to the Old Dordrecht Society, which opened it in 1925 as a museum. It was acquired by the town of Dordrecht in 1949.

This imposing mansion, still with decoration and furnishings in the original style, gives a good impression of a patrician house of the 18th and 19th centuries. The ground floor corridor has rich stucco decoration. The Tapestry Room is hung with tapestries from a Brussels workshop founded in the 16th century, with scenes in Louis XIV style from the Italian pastoral "The Faithful Shepherd". Particularly fine is the Renaissance Room, which has an oak chimneypiece (c. 1550) with figures of "wild men", originally made by the gifted wood-carver Jan Terwen (who also carved the choir-stalls in the Grote Kerk) for the Marksmen's Guild of Dordrecht. Other rooms of great interest are the kitchen, fully equipped, with a blue-tiled chimney; the dining room with its glassed-in veranda and its beautiful ceiling painting by Willy Martens (1856–1927); and the study, with oak panelling and leather wall-covering (a rarity in the 19th century). There are displays of silver, china and glass, and, in the summerhouse in the garden, a large collection of toys. Open: Tue.–Sat. 10am–5pm, Sun. 1–5pm.

At the end of Nieuwe Haven is the Blauwpoort or Catharijnepoort (1652), where a number of old warehouses have been preserved. From here there is a fine view of the broad river and the busy movement of shipping, with the dykes on the other bank around Zwijndrecht. Farther west is a four-lane tunnel carrying traffic under the Oude Maas.

Blauwpoort (Catharijnepoort)

Drenthe

G–J 2–4

Provincial capital: Assen
Area: 268,057 hectares/662,101 acres
  (land area 265,568 hectares/655,953 acres)
Population: 437,000

Heathland lake, Drenthe

Dronten

Situation and characteristics	The province of Drenthe is a region of mainly flat land lying between 10 and 20m (35 and 70ft) above sea level in the extreme north-east of the Netherlands' great expanses of sandy heathland.
	The most conspicuous heights in Drenthe are the moraines, rising to 32m/105ft, of the Hondsrug, a range of hills formed during the second-last ice age (the Saale/Riss glacial) which extends for 50km/30 miles from Emmen in the south-east to Groningen in the north-west. From here the land slopes almost imperceptibly down towards the west. It consists of marls laid down during the Saale/Riss glacial with deep overlying layers of sand deposited in later phases of the ice age.
Veen settlements	During the ice ages large expanses of low moorland were formed over the layers of sand at the lowest points in Drenthe. In depressions in the higher parts of the region there came into being extensive tracts of high moorland, which have now been completely drained and brought into cultivation as *veen* settlements (see Facts and Figures, Cultural Landscapes; A to Z, Emmen). This applies particularly to the Groningen *veen* settlements. Most of the moorland settlements in Drenthe are situated around Beilen and Hoogeveen, in the south of the province.
Agriculture	There were formerly great expanses of heath between the traditional farming villages of Drenthe outside the moorland area, but over the last 80 years these have been replaced partly by plantations of pines but mainly by fields of rye, oats and potatoes. Most of the holdings are of less than 20 hectares/50 acres, but in the high moorland areas holdings of 50 hectares/125 acres are by no means rare.
Industry	In Drenthe industry takes second place to agriculture. Only in the south-east of the province is there any significant amount of industry, for after the cutting of peat was abandoned in this area a large labour force became available for employment. In addition the extraction of oil round Schoonebeek and Meppel has become of increasing importance in recent years.
Towns	The principal town in this very thinly populated region, which has only 100 inhabitants to the sq. kilometre (250 to the sq. mile), is the provincial capital, Assen (see entry). After it comes Emmen (see entry), near the German frontier.
Megalithic tombs	A special feature of Drenthe is the large number of the prehistoric megalithic tombs known as *hunebedden* ("giants' beds": see Facts and Figures, Cultural Landscapes; A to Z, Emmen). These are constructed of huge slabs of stone carried from Scandinavia by glaciers during the Saale/Riss glacial and deposited here, particularly in the Hondsrug area. The best known *hunebedden* are to be found north of the village of Havelte, close to the road to Frederiksoord.

Dronten   F 5

Province: Flevoland
Population: 24,000

Dronten, on the Oostflevoland (East Flevoland) polder, is the central shopping and market centre for the polder, now developed for agriculture. The most notable feature of the town is De Meerpaal, an interesting modern building (called, on the Greek model, an Agora) which is used for a variety of purposes (the weekly market, exhibitions, sporting events, etc.).

Surroundings of Dronten

Ketelhaven	5km/3 miles north of Dronten, on the shores of the Ketelmeer, is the Ketelhaven Museum of Marine Archaeology (Museum voor Scheepsar-

cheologie), with remains from the Roman site of Castellum Nigrum Pullum and from ships wrecked in the Zuiderzee. Also at Ketelhaven is one of the sluices used in the draining of the Oostflevoland polder.

South of Dronten, near the village of Biddinghuizen, is the Flevohof (Spijk-weg 30), a combination of an agricultural exhibition and a recreation centre, with periodical exhibitions on all aspects of farming life, model farmhouses, farmsteads and houses for growing early fruit and vegetables, an auction hall and a collection of 5500 cactuses and succulents. Farther south, on the shores of the Veluwemeer, is a large recreation area, with boating harbours, bathing beaches, water sports facilities and camping sites.

Flevohof

Duits–Nederlandse Natuurpark (German–Dutch Nature Park)   G 9/10

Between the towns of Venlo and Roermond (see entries), south-east of the Maas, extends the German–Dutch Nature Park, established in 1976. This low-lying area on the Lower Rhine, with its river meadows, its bogs and its tracts of farming land, is a popular recreation area for the inhabitants of neighbouring cities such as Eindhoven in the Netherlands and Krefeld-Duisburg in Germany. Some of the footpaths and trails in the park cross the Dutch–German frontier (no frontier controls).

Edam   E 5

Province: Noord-Holland
Population: 24,000

Edam Town Hall

Egmond

Situation and importance

The historic old town of Edam, in the polder area on the IJsselmeer, is world-famed for its round red and yellow Edam cheeses. The inhabitants live by industry, agriculture, stock-farming and fishing.

Edam cheese

Edam grew up round a dam on the Ee, which linked the little river Purmer with the Zuiderzee. When the damming of the rivers flowing into the Zuiderzee began in 1230 (see Facts and Figures, The Struggle with the Sea) a settlement was established for the transhipment of goods, and when tolls began to be levied it developed into a trading town.

Edam received its municipal charter in 1357. Its heyday was in the 16th century, when shipbuilding, herring-fishing and the cheese trade brought the town prosperity. The warships with which Admiral de Ruyter defeated the British fleet were built in the Edam shipyards, In 1573 William of Orange granted the town the right to have a weigh-house in recognition of its valour and the part it played during the siege of Alkmaar.

Edam has a number of features of interest:

Grote Kerk

The Grote Kerk or St Nicolaaskerk in Grote Kerkstraat is a Late Gothic hall-church with a 15th century tower and beautiful 17th century stained glass. The furnishings of the church also date mainly from the 17th century.

Town Hall

The Town Hall (Stadhuis), on Damplein, with its domed timber tower, was built in 1737. The floor of the registry office is still strewn with sand, as in the Middle Ages. There is a small collection of pictures in the very fine Council Chamber.

Damsluis

Opposite the Town Hall is the Damsluis. The bridge over the sluice has fine Late Gothic iron railings.

Speeltoren

The 15th century tower of the old Church of Our Lady (destroyed) has the oldest carillon in the Netherlands (1560).

Municipal Museum

The Municipal Museum (Stedelijk Museum) at Damplein 8 occupies a house dating from 1540, with a beautiful façade of 1737. It has a curious floating cellar in the form of a boat. The most striking items in the museum are the paintings of three local characters – the "Fat Man" (who is said to have weighed 445 pounds), the "Man with a Beard" and the "Big Girl" (depicted life-size, 2.5m/8ft 2½in tall). Open: Mon.–Sat. 10am–4pm, Sun. 2–4pm.

Weigh-House

In the Weigh-House (Waag) in the Kaasmarkt the original weights can still be seen.

The water between the two bridges in Spuistraat is known as the *boerenverdriet* ("farmers' sorrow") because the farmers' boats often get stuck here. In July and August there are boat trips in the IJsselmeer.

Surroundings

The fishing village of Volendam (see entry) lies within the commune of Edam.

Egmond

D 4

Province: Noord-Holland
Population: 11,000

To the west of Alkmaar, across the former Egmonder Meer, which was drained in 1556, is Egmond an den Hoef, the ancestral seat of the Counts of Egmond, who later established themselves in the southern Netherlands. The remains of their castle, destroyed by the Spaniards in 1573, can still be seen.

3km/2 miles south, on the road to Castricum, is Egmond-Binnen, once famed for its Benedictine abbey, which was destroyed in 1573 (rebuilt 1935). The abbey church was the last resting-place of many Counts of Holland.

2km/1¼ miles west of Egmond aan den Hoef is Egmond aan Zee, a popular seaside resort with a good beach.

Eindhoven

F 9

Province: Noord-Brabant
Population: 191,000

The modern industrial town of Eindhoven, on the river Dommel, was until the second half of the 19th century a small town of no particular note or importance. Its rapid growth began after the establishment of the Philips works in 1891, and by 1918 the town had a population of 64,000. In recent decades it has developed into the largest town in the southern Netherlands and the fifth largest in the country. The production of light bulbs earned it the name of the "Lichtstad" ("City of Light"). The most important industrial establishment after the Philips works is the DAF car manufacturing plant. Other industries include the manufacture of glassware, plastics, paper, textiles and tobacco goods.

Situation and characteristics

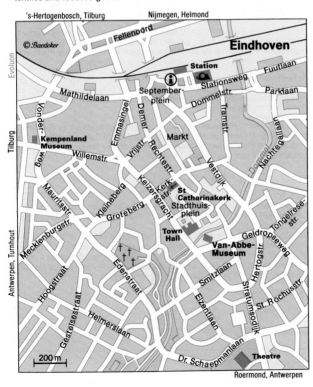

183

Eindhoven, with a commuter belt extending into Belgium, is of importance not only as an industrial town but as the chief centre of a large surrounding area. It has a University of Technology (founded 1956), two colleges of social science, a school of industrial design, several scholarly libraries and a chamber of commerce.

The Town

Philips Monument
Near the station is a monument to A. F. Philips (d. 1951), son of the founder of the firm, Gerard L. F. Philips (see Famous People).

Carillon
In Jacob-Oppenheim-Straat is a 45m/148ft high metal structure housing the largest carillon in the Netherlands (61 bells), presented to the town in 1956 by the Philips staff.

St Catharinakerk
The neo-Gothic St Catharinakerk (1867) was designed by the well known 19th century architect P. J. H. Cuypers.

Van Abbe Museum
The Van Abbe Museum at Bilderdijklaan 10 is one of the most important galleries of modern art in the Netherlands. The collection was bequeathed to the city of Eindhoven by the cigar manufacturer Henri van Abbe in 1936, but it was not possible to open the museum until after the end of the Second World War.
The museum was enlarged in 1978. The collection now consists mainly of works by modern painters, in particular Marc Chagall and the De Stijl and COBRA groups. Open: Tue.–Sun. 11am–5pm.

Evoluon
Until 1989 the Evoluon (Noord-Brabantlaan 1A), an interesting modern building rather like a flying saucer, housed a museum of science and technology established by the Philips concern in 1966 to mark the firm's 75th anniversary. It is now occupied by a high-class restaurant.

Animali
At Roostenlaan 303, near the Rondweg (ring road), is the Animali Park, an area of 4 hectares/10 acres with huge aviaries containing thousands of European and exotic birds, as well as packs of monkeys. Open: April to October, daily 9am–6pm.

Kempenland Museum
The Kempenland Museum, housed in the old Steentjeskerk as St Anthoniusstraat 5–7, illustrates the history and culture of the Kempenland, the area around Eindhoven; for example 19th century farming life and the cottage textile industry. Open: Tue.–Sun. 1–5pm.

Surroundings of Eindhoven

Nuenen
North-west of Eindhoven is Nuenen (pop. 21,000). Van Gogh lived from 1883 to 1885 in the pastor's house, which has been restored to its original style.
Van Gogh is also commemorated by a monument erected in 1932 and by the Van Gogh Documentation Centre at Papenvoort 15, with an exhibition of photographs and documents on his stay in Nuenen, including a map showing the location of scenes and subjects painted by him in and around the town. Open: Mon.–Fri. 9am–12 noon and 2–4pm.

Peel
See Noord-Brabant

Oisterwijk
See Tilburg

Elburg
F 5

Province: Gelderland
Population: 20,000

Vispoort, Elburg

The old Hanseatic town of Elburg, in northern Gelderland, received its municipal charter in 1396. To escape the threat of flooding the site of the town was continually moved farther inland. The old part of Elburg has preserved its character as a fortified town, with its streets laid out on a regular grid.

Situation and characteristics

The Gothic Grote Kerk or St Nicolaaskerk (1392–1465) has wall paintings, a large organ of 1825 and a smaller organ in the choir. The tower can be climbed only during July and August.

Grote Kerk

In Jufferenstraat (No. 8) is the former St Agnietenklooster (Convent of St Agnes), founded in 1418. The double chapel (1463–80) formerly served as the Town Hall. The convent is now occupied by the Municipal Museum (Gemeentemuseum), with collections of material illustrating the history of the town, and the National Organ Museum. Open: Mon. 2–5pm, Tue.–Fri. 9.30am–12 noon and 2–5pm.

Agnietenklooster

Municipal Museum

The Vispoort, one of the old town gates, was built in 1397 and rebuilt in 1592. It now houses the Fisheries Museum (Visserijmuseum), which documents the story of fishing in the Zuiderzee.

Fisheries Museum

Other features of interest are the town walls, with their bastions and casemates (access at Vispoort); the old rope-walk on the former Binnengracht, the last of its kind; the synagogue (1855), now occupied by the tourist information office; and the Groene Kruidhof, a herb garden attached to an old inn at Ellestraat 52 (open: May to October, daily 10am–8pm).

Other sights

Surroundings of Elburg

Drontermeer	West of Elburg, on the Drontermeer, are the old fish auction hall (1916) and a garden called De Vier Jaargetijden (The Four Seasons) in which a believer in natural healing carries out experiments with homeopathic remedies.
Doornspijk	South of Elburg is the village of Doornspijk, with the ruins of the church of St Ludger, built about 1300 and several times enlarged. Ludger (742–809) was the first Dutch preacher of the Gospel.

Emmen   J 4

	Province: Drenthe Population: 92,000
Situation and characteristics	Emmen lies in western Drenthe, near the German frontier. Together with the surrounding moorland villages it is a developing town.
Noorder Dierenpark	The Noorder Dierenpark (Animal Park) has a varied collection of animals, with a savanna in which African animals roam freely and a butterfly garden (1000 butterflies of 25 species). It is the only zoo in the Netherlands which is entitled to call itself a museum.
Oudheidkamer De Hondsrug	The Hondsrug Museum of Antiquities, in an old farmhouse of 1865 at Marktplein 17, has a collection of material on the history of the town, ranging from prehistoric finds to folk art.

Surroundings of Emmen

Megalithic tombs	In the surrounding area (e.g. at Odoorn and Schoonoord) there are altogether eleven of the megalithic tombs known as *hunebedden* (see Facts and Figures, Cultural Landscapes; A to Z, Drenthe). One tomb which is particularly worth seeing is De Papeloze Kerk between Sleen and Schoonoord, to the west of Emmen, which has largely been preserved in its original state and is easily accessible.
Neolithic bridge	South-east of Emmen, at Nieuw-Dordrecht, is a Neolithic bridge built of tree-trunks: an indication of the difficulties experienced by Stone Age man in making roads through the peat-bogs.
Barger-Compascuum Open-Air Museum	10km/6 miles east of Emmen, at Barger-Compascuum, is the Oale Compas Open-Air Museum, a faithful reconstruction of an old moorland village. Visitors can tour the site either on the peat railway or in a boat. Open: mid March to October daily 8am–6pm.
Schoonoord	The Zeven Marken open-air museum in Schoonoord (Tramstraat 73) gives a picture of life in south-eastern Drenthe in the 19th century (workshops, barns, an old school, etc.). Open: Easter to October, daily 9am–6pm.

Enkhuizen   E 4

	Province: Noord-Holland Population: 16,000
Situation, *townscape and characteristics	Enkhuizen, situated on the IJsselmeer and traversed by numerous canals, ranks as one of the prettiest towns in the Netherlands. Its trade with the Baltic countries, and later its herring fisheries, enabled it to develop into a

flourishing and prosperous port town with a population of some 40,000; but decline set in when most of the merchants moved to Amsterdam, and the final blow came with the destruction of its herring-fishing fleet of 400 vessels in 1625 and the silting up of its harbour. Nowadays the economy of the town depends mainly on tourism, papermaking, metal-processing, fishing and bulb-growing.
Enkhuizen was the birthplace of the painter Paulus Potter (1625–54), whose life-size "Bull" can be seen in the Mauritshuis in The Hague.

Enkhuizen was the administrative centre of Friesland until 1289, when western Friesland became part of the County of Holland. Count Floris V granted the town its municipal charter in 1355, and thereafter it began to flourish. The town walls were built around 1550 and strengthened in the early 17th century. Enkhuizen was one of the first towns to revolt against Spanish rule in 1572. Its ships, along with those of Hoorn, Edam and Monnickendam, took part in the naval battle in October 1573 in which a Spanish fleet commanded by Admiral Bossu was defeated.

History

The population fell sharply after an outbreak of plague in 1636. With the construction of the Afsluitdijk (see entry) Enkhuizen's importance as a port was reduced, and as a result the town's economy has increasingly come to depend on agriculture and horticulture.

The Town

From the station there is a good view of the harbour (Spoor- or Buyshaven and Buitenhaven), with its innumerable boats and yachts. From the harbour there are boats to Medemblik (see entry), Stavoren and Urk (see entry) and a ferry to the Zuiderzee Museum.

Harbour

The landward side of the harbour is dominated by the Dromedaris Tower, a relic of the town's fortifications (1540). The tower, which was heightened in 1649, has a carillon by the Hemony brothers which ranks among the finest in the Netherlands. From the tower (round, with the addition of a gatehouse) there is a fine view of the harbour quarter. It served at one time as a prison, and some of the cells can still be seen.

Dromedaris Tower

On the façade of a house at Zuiderspui 1 can be seen the coats of arms of Medemblik, Enkhuizen, West Friesland, Orange and Hoorn.

Old houses on Oude Haven

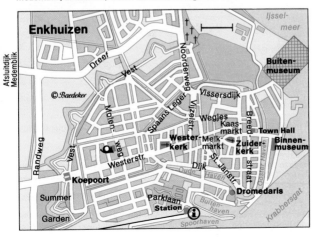

Enkhuizen
Zuidersee Museum

 1 Limekiln
 2 Lifeboats
 3 House
 4 House
 5 Bait-nets
 6 House
 7 Brush-making workshop
 8 Mill
 9 House
10 House
11 Dyke store
12 Steam laundry
13 House
14 Farmhouse
15 Slipway
16 House
17 Farmhouse
18 House
19 Flax-oven
20 Timber-store

21 Painter's store
22 House and post office
23 Chapel
24 Turner's workshop
25 Shop selling decorations
26 Farmhouse
27 Grocer's shop
28 Farmhouse
29 Ropewalk
30 Slipway
31 Shop
32 House
33 Shed
34 Smoke-house
35 Tannery store
36 "De Vier Gebroeders" (a
   hektjalk)
37 "De Hoop" (a
   broeierspraam)

A house at Dijk 32, dating from 1625, displays the motto "Contentement passe rychesse" ("Contentment is worth more than wealth").

Westerstraat

The street called the Dijk which runs along the north side of the Oude Haven leads to Venedie and the Melkmarkt, from which Westerstraat goes off on the left. Two interesting houses in this street are No. 76 (Late Gothic façade, 16th c.) and No. 158 (Renaissance façade).
At the end of the street is the Koepoort, an old town gate (1649; roof 1730).

Westerkerk

The Westerkerk or St Gomaruskerk (15th–16th c.) is a Gothic hall-church with timber vaulting. Between the church and the bell-tower is the verger's

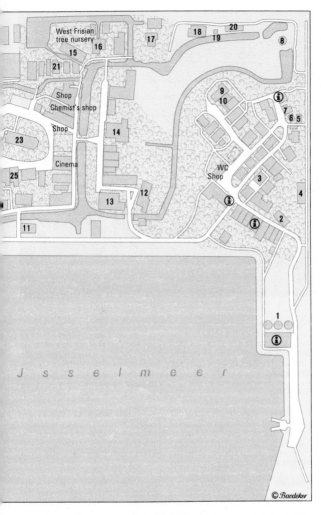

house, with a fine stepped gable of 1600. The bell-tower, originally built in 1519, was renovated in neo-classical style in the 19th century, with a wooden facing.

The most striking features of the interior are the wooden choir screen (1542), one of the finest in the northern Netherlands, and the pulpit (1567), a copy of the pulpit of the Grote Kerk in The Hague. There is a fine 17th century library with hundreds of theological works, some of them of great value.

Choir screen

Facing the church is the imposing gabled façade of the old Mint (16th c.).

Dromedaris Tower

Zuiderkerk

Near the east end of Westerstraat stands the Zuiderkerk or St Pancraskerk, which dates from the early 15th century. The tower was built in 1450 and heightened between 1518 and 1526 by the addition of an octagonal upper section and an onion dome (total height 75m/245ft). It has a carillon by the Hemony brothers (originally 35 bells, later increased to 45). The paintings on the timber ceiling (1484) were covered with whitewash at the Reformation but were exposed in the early 20th century by the removal of the whitewash.

Waagmuseum

In the Kaasmarkt (No. 8) is the old Weigh-House (Waag) of 1559, its colourful façade decorated with several coats of arms; it is now a museum. Notable features are the old scales for weighing butter and cheese; the Chirurgijnskamer (surgeons' room) on the first floor, the meeting-place of the town's doctors from 1639; the delivery room (18th c.); a sick-room (1910); and a dental surgery (1920).

Town Hall

From the Kaasmarkt Nieuwstraat leads into Zwaanstraat, in which is the Town Hall (Stadhuis), a magnificent example of Dutch architecture of the Golden Age, built at the end of the 17th century and little altered since then. The handsome sandstone façade is excellently preserved, as is the richly decorated and furnished interior (particularly the Burghers' Hall and the burgomaster's room), with pictures, ceiling and wall paintings and valuable tapestries. The walls of the fine Council Chamber (1705) are clad with Utrecht velvet. On the second floor is a small museum of antiquities.

Behind the Town Hall is the old Prison (1612).

*Zuiderzee Museum

Near the Town Hall, at Wierdijk 18, is the Binnenmuseum, the indoor part of the Zuiderzee Museum, the outdoor section of which can be reached only by boat. The Binnenmuseum is housed in the Peperhuis, a 17th century warehouse of the East India Company. It illustrates the history of shipping

In the Zuiderzee Open-Air Museum

and fishing in the old Zuiderzee with displays of implements and equipment, house interiors, everyday objects, regional costumes, ship models and old fishing boats (in the main hall).

500m/550yds north is the Buitenmuseum (Outdoor Museum), an open-air museum consisting of 135 buildings with gardens, canals and streets dating from 1880–1932 from the area around the former Zuiderzee. Open: daily April–Oct. 10am–5pm.

On Breedstraat, which runs south from the Town Hall, are a number of interesting old buildings with Late Gothic or Renaissance façades (Nos. 14, 41, 59, 60 and 61). There are also a number of houses of the 16th–18th centuries in Westerstraat and the Dijk. | Old houses

Near the Koepoort is the Summer Garden, an experimental garden (open: only in summer) with various species of flowers grown in the Streek, the flower-growing area between Enkhuizen and Hoorn. | Summer Garden

On the north side of the town is the Wilhelminapark, with an interesting "dwarfs' village" (open: daily in summer, at weekends in autumn). | Sprookjes Wonderland

Surroundings of Enkhuizen

South of Enkhuizen lies Grootebroek, where a flower show, the West Frisian Flora, is held annually in February. The show, at which the latest developments in bulb-growing are displayed, attracts large numbers of flower-lovers as well as bulb-growers. | **Grootebroek** West Frisian Flora

See also Hoorn, Surroundings

Enschede

Province: Overijssel
Population: 145,000

Situation and characteristics

The town of Enschede, situated on the Twente Canal near the German frontier, is the centre of the Dutch cotton industry and also an important cultural centre in the eastern Netherlands. It is the largest town in Overijssel, with a Textile College, a University of Technology founded in 1961, an Academy of Art and three celebrated museums.

Industry began to develop in Enschede around 1830, and there was a rapid increase in the population of the town, which previously had been a place of no particular importance.
Associated with the town's traditional cotton and woollen industries are spinning and weaving mills and bleacheries, as well as artificial fibre and clothing factories. Textile machinery and other equipment are also produced in the town.
In recent years other branches of industry (chemicals, electrical products) have been established in Enschede in order to avoid the over-dependence on a single industry which would leave the local economy vulnerable in an economic crisis.

History

Enschede received its municipal charter in 1325. Much of the town was destroyed in a great fire in 1862. It suffered heavy damage in 1944 but was rapidly rebuilt and is now a modern industrial town with wide new streets.

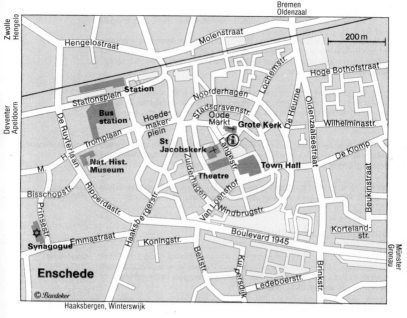

Synagogue in Oriental style

The Town

The Grote Kerk (Reformed), originally Romanesque (1200), was enlarged in 1480. In 1842 it was rebuilt as an aisleless church. After the 1862 fire it was reconstructed in its original form.

Grote Kerk

St Jacobskerk (R.C.), built in 1933, incorporates both Romanesque and Gothic features and contains very fine Stations of the Cross.

St Jacobskerk

The Town Hall (Stadhuis; 1930–31), modelled on Stockholm Town Hall, was designed by G. Friedhoff.

Town Hall

The best known of Enschede's three museums is the Twente Museum (Rijksmuseum Twente), situated at Lasondersingel 129–131, in the north of the town. It has a fine collection of antiquities and pictures, together with old manuscripts, woodcarving, Delft ware and valuable tapestries.
The pictures and the museum building itself were gifted by the Van Heek cotton-manufacturing firm. All the main periods of art in Flanders and the Netherlands from the 15th century to the present day are represented in the gallery. Open: Tue.–Fri. 10am–5pm, Sat. and Sun. 1–5pm.

Twente Museum

At De Ruyterlaan 2, west of the town centre, is the Natural History Museum (Natuurmuseum), with a collection of rare birds, insects, reptiles, mammals, minerals and fossils from the Enschede area. Open: Tue.–Sat. 10am–5pm, Sun. 1–5pm.

Natural History Museum

Near the Museum, at Prinsestraat 126, stands the Synagogue (1928), a building of rather Oriental aspect with a copper dome. After thorough restoration it ranks as one of the finest synagogues in Europe.

Synagogue

In the south-west of the town, at the corner of Hacksbergerstraat and Industriestraat, is the Museum of the Textile Industry (Textielindustriemuseum), which illustrates the history of the textile industry from its cottage origins to the present day.

Textile Museum

From the town centre Langestraat runs east to the street known as De Klomp, at No. 35 of which is the Elderinkshuis (1783), the only major building in the town to have survived the great fire of 1862.

Elderinkshuis

In the Volkspark, to the west of the town, is a war memorial by Mari Andriessen (1953), an impressive work of sculpture depicting a Jewish woman, concentration camp inmates, a dead child, a soldier and a resistance fighter.

War Memorial

At Bentstraat 43 is the National Museum of Goods Vehicles (Nationaal Vrachtwagen Museum), with veteran vans and lorries made by the Kromhout (1935) and DAF (from 1950) firms and DAF cars from 1959 onwards.

National Museum of Goods Vehicles

Near Twente military airport is the Aviation Museum (Luchtvaartmuseum).

Aviation Museum

Also worth a visit is the Horstlanden Pinetum, on the campus of the University of Technology in Drienerloo, with coniferous trees from Europe, America and Asia.

De Horstlanden Pinetum

Flevoland

E–G 3–6

Provincial capital: Lelystad
Area: 211,816 hectares/523,186 acres
(land area 141,175 hectares/348,702 acres)
Population: 194,000

The province of Flevoland, at the south end of the IJsselmeer, came into being only in 1986, when the Oostelijk and Zuidelijk (East and South) Flevoland polders, previously under direct government administration, were combined with the Noordoostpolder (North-East Polder), then part of the province of Overijssel, to form a new administrative unit. East and South Flevoland are separated from the mainland by a wide channel known as the Veluwemeer – a necessary feature, since without it the water table in the higher coastal areas would have fallen to an unacceptably low level.

Situation and characteristics

The polder, an expanse of clay soil lying 4–5m/13–16ft below sea level, has been turned over to agricultural use and is very thinly populated. Apart from scattered farms there are only six settlements on the whole area of the polder.

East Flevoland, the older part of the polder (drained between 1950 and 1957), has an area of some 54,000 hectares/135,000 acres, two-thirds of it belonging to the commune of Dronten (see entry) and the remaining third to Lelystad (below). The land was brought into cultivation in the mid sixties, when some 2000 farming units were established. At the outset they grew mainly rape, oats and barley; they now also produce wheat, sugar-beet, fruit and vegetables. The east coast, along the Veluwemeer, was planted with trees and is now an attractive recreational area, with parks and boating harbours.

East Flevoland

Lelystad, capital of the province, lies on the IJsselmeer. Although it was founded only in 1967, it already has a population of almost 60,000. The layout – which is not without its critics – has been designed in accordance with modern town planning principles (e.g. separation of traffic routes according to type of use, service facilities in town centre). The Nieuwe Land ("New Land") Museum, which gave an interesting account of the drainage and development of the polder, was unfortunately burned down in 1986 and has not been rebuilt. To the north of the town are the 143m/470ft high chimneys of a power station fuelled by natural gas. In the Expositiegebouw in the harbour area is the information centre of the two state agencies

Lelystad

◀ Locks in Lelystad

responsible for the Zuiderzeewerken and the IJsselmeerpolder. Nearby, at the Houtribsluizen (locks), is the end of the Lelystad–Enkhuizen dyke, built to close off the Markerwaard polder in the south-west corner of the IJsselmeer.

Round Lelystad are a number of biological institutes and a fish hatchery.

South Flevoland

To the south of East Flevoland is the younger South Flevoland polder, finally won back from the sea in 1968, with an area of 43,000 hectares/107,500 acres. Cultivation of the reclaimed land began only in 1978 and is not yet complete. On this polder the various stages of development can be seen, from the pre-cultivation measures carried out by the state by way of barley growing to the final phase in which wheat is grown.

Oostvaarders-
plassen

A quarter of the area of the Flevoland polder has been left in its natural state, as in the extensive Oostvaardersplassen nature reserve, an area of lakes with large numbers of migrant birds, including spoonbills and cormorants. The birds can be watched from an observation post on the Knardijk.

Almere

At the south-eastern tip of the polder is the town of Almere (pop. 57,000), one of the youngest communes in the Netherlands, founded only in 1975. The town consists of three parts – Almere-Stad, Almere-Haven and Almere-Buiten. Almere lies within the commuting area of Amsterdam, where most of its population work, but industry is also developing in the town.

Noordoostpolder

See entry

**"Polder
blindness"**

As Flevoland was an entirely new creation, its development was systematically planned from the outset, the towns and other settlements, industrial areas, nature reserves, roads and canals being laid out on the drawing-board in accordance with strictly functional principles. As a result motorists unfamiliar with the area have difficulty in judging distances on the dead straight roads: hence the expression polder blindness.

Franeker

F 2

Province: Friesland
Commune: Franekeradeel
Population: 21,000

Situation and
*townscape

Franeker, one of the eleven towns of Friesland, lies to the west of Leeuwarden. It first appears in the records in 1085; in the 12th century it was surrounded by walls and a moat; and it received a municipal charter in 1417. It is a charming little town with its ring of canals and its fine old buildings.

History

A university – the second in the Netherlands, after Leiden – was founded in Franeker in 1585, making it the cultural centre of the north of the country. The most celebrated student of the Frisian Academy was the French philosopher Descartes. The university was dissolved by Napoleon in 1811 and was replaced in 1815 by an Athenaeum, which continued in existence until 1843.

The Town

St Martinikerk

The central feature of the town is St Martinikerk, an aisled pseudo-basilica (consecrated 1421), with the aisles continued by an ambulatory round the choir. The barrel-vaulted timber roof is borne on 30 columns. Notable features are the tombstones of university professors and the Gothic choir-stalls.

The richly decorated façade of Franeker Town Hall

The Renaissance Town Hall (Stadhuis) in Raadhuisplein, built in 1591, has a
richly decorated façade, with coats of arms, and a handsome external
staircase. The roof has three stepped gables and is topped by an elegant
octagonal tower. Some rooms in the building are open to visitors; particularly fine is the Council Chamber, its walls faced with gilded leather.

Town Hall

Two old professors' houses, the Coopmanshûs (1746) and the Valcknier-
shûs (1662), at Voorstraat 49, are now occupied by the Coopmanshûs
Museum, with a collection of material on the history of the town and the
university. There are also mementoes of Anna Maria van Schuurman
(1607–78), a well known poet in her day, who corresponded with Descartes
and in addition to writing verses was also a painter and silhouette artist.
The Senate Room, with portraits of professors, has been preserved. Open:
Tue.–Sat. 10am–5pm; May to September also Sun. 1–5pm.
In the same building is the Kaatsmuseum. *Kaatsen* is a Frisian ball game
which is particularly popular in Franeker. Adjoining the Bogt van Guné, the
oldest students' drinking-place in the Netherlands, is an old *kaatsen* pitch
which is still in use.

Coopmanshûs
Museum

Opposite the Town Hall, at Eise Eisingstraat 3, is an unpretentious house
containing a feature which in its day was famed far beyond the bounds of
Friesland. This was a planetarium constructed in 1774–81 by Eise Eisinga, a
wool-comber and amateur astronomer, on his living-room ceiling. Some of
his fellow-citizens had been led by a local newspaper to believe that, as a
result of the unusual position of certain planets, the end of the world was
near; and to dispel their superstitious fears he devised this planetarium
showing the movements of the planets. His ingenious system of gears,
which also shows the date and time of day, is still in perfect working order.
Open: Tue.–Sat. 10am–12.30pm and 1.30–5pm; May to August also Mon.
10am–12.30pm and 1.30–5pm, Sun. 1–5pm.

*Planetarium

Friesland

Korendragers-huisje

At Eise Eisingastraat 28 is the Korendragershuisje (1634), the guild-house of the corn-porters.

Martinahuis

In Voorstraat, apart from a number of elegant old professors' houses, there are two buildings of particular interest: the Martinahuis (No. 35) of 1498, the only surviving tower house in the town, which until 1983 contained the offices of the commune of Franekeradeel, and the 16th century Camming-hahûs (No. 12A), now occupied by the Frisian Numismatic Museum (Fries Munten en Penningkabinet). The museum has a collection of coins minted in Friesland between the 7th and 18th centuries. Open: May to September, Mon.–Fri. 1–5pm.

Numismatic Museum

Friesland

E–G 1–3

Provincial capital: Leeuwarden
Area: 534,000 hectares/1,460,000 acres
(land area 336,000 hectares/840,000 acres)
Population: 599,000

Situation and characteristics

The province of Friesland in the north-eastern Netherlands is ringed on the west and north by the Waddeneilanden or West Frisian Islands (see entry), which are continued to the east by the (German) East Frisian Islands. On the south-west, west and north-west Friesland extends to the IJsselmeer and the Waddenzee, and on the south and south-east it is bounded by the Wouden, an area of sandy ridges which forms a transition to the ground moraines of the Drenthe plateau. In the east it merges into the marshland of Groningen.

History

The old Greater Frisian kingdom, Frisia Magna, extended at the beginning of the Christian era from the Belgian coast at Bruges to the river Weser, but

Sloten harbour, Friesland

thereafter was taken over by powerful neighbours. The south-western part of its territory as far as the Rhine estuary at Katwijk was conquered by the Romans. In the 7th century the Franks occupied Greater Friesland and Christianised it. The Benedictine monk St Boniface, who was probably martyred at Dokkum (see entry), was one of the first missionaries. Around 785 Friesland was conquered by Charlemagne. Western Friesland was incorporated in the province of Noord-Holland at an early stage. In the early medieval period the seven independent Frisian territories between Alkmaar and the river Weser formed an alliance against the Norsemen – still commemorated in the Frisian coat of arms and flag (seven diagonal bands in cobalt-blue and white with seven red waterlily leaves).

Friesland is the only part of the Netherlands with a second official language. In much of the province Frisian is spoken as well as Dutch. This is an independent West Germanic language, with three variant forms – East Frisian, spoken in the Saterland area in the German province of Lower Saxony; North Frisian, spoken on the Schleswig-Holstein coast and on some of the German North Sea islands; and West Frisian, still spoken by some 400,000 people in Friesland and on the West Frisian islands. West Frisian died out almost completely as a written language from the 16th century onwards, and until the 20th century remained alive only in country areas. Then the Frisian Academy, founded in 1938, revived the movement to secure official recognition for the language which had first emerged during the Romantic period in the 19th century. Thereafter the Frisian language was increasingly taught in schools and at the universities of Groningen and Amsterdam, and a translation of the Bible into Frisian was published. Even street signs are now bilingual; and with its own language the province also has its own literature and culture.

Language

Friesland consists of two different natural regions. In the west there are great expanses of fenland, partly (along the North Sea coast) reclaimed from the sea and partly (farther inland) in areas once occupied by freshwater lakes. In the Frisian lake district, a popular recreation and holiday area for water sports enthusiasts near the town of Sneek, there are still many remnants of these lakes.

In eastern Friesland there are great expanses of moorland, most of which have now been brought into cultivation. Between these areas are lakes formed in areas of poor drainage as a result of the peat-cutting which has brought the surface below sea level.

Natural regions

Originally the characteristic form of settlement in this region was the *terp* village, in which the houses, with their typical pyramidal roofs, were tightly packed together on a mound (*terp*), usually man-made, which gave them protection against flooding in the event of a storm tide or a breach in the dykes. Few of these *terp* villages are to be seen today: they have mostly given place to scattered settlements which have the advantage that the farmhouses are nearer their fields.

Terp villages

The Friese Terpen Route in north-eastern Friesland, linking the towns of Harlingen, Leeuwarden and Dokkum (see entries), is a good way of seeing the *terp* country. Perhaps the most typical of the *terpen* to be seen on this route is the Hogebeintoren, which rises to a height of almost 8m/26ft above the surrounding ground level.

Between the 5th and 12th centuries some 600 *terpen* were formed in Friesland. There are some 400 in Groningen province, where they are known as *wierden*.

Friese Terpen Route

Agriculture is the predominant element in the economy of Friesland. With the exception of a narrow strip of very fertile arable land parallel to the coast of the Waddenzee in which sugar-beet, corn, flax and seed potatoes are grown the whole of the province is occupied by pastureland, since the heavy clay soil does not lend itself to intensive cultivation. The farms,

Agriculture

usually of between 20 and 50 hectares (50 and 125 acres), specialise in the rearing of Frisian cattle and the production of butter.

Industry
Milk produced on the farms is made into butter and cheese in numerous local dairies. There are also a number of food-processing plants, as well as some small shipyards building the boats, mostly under 50 tons, which ply on Friesland's dense network of canals.

Towns
The principal Frisian towns, in addition to the provincial capital Leeuwarden, are Sneek, Harlingen, Dokkum and Bolsward (see entries).

Gaasterland
On the south coast of Friesland lies the Gaasterland area, built up on a core of old sandy soil. From the steeply scarped coast at Mirns and Oudemirdum there are fine views of the IJsselmeer.

Geertruidenberg
D 8

Province: Noord-Brabant
Population: 6600

Situation and characteristics
Geertruidenberg, lying north of Breda on the edge of the Biesbosch nature reserve (see entry), is one of the oldest towns in the Netherlands, with a municipal charter granted in 1213. In 1421 the town was cut off from Dordrecht by the St Elizabeth's Day flood, and during the eighty years of the fight for independence there was bitter fighting in this area between Dutch and Spanish forces. There are still some remains of a fortress taken from the Spaniards by Maurice of Nassau in 1593.

St Geertruidkerk
The St Geertruidkerk in the Markt was built in the early 14th century and enlarged in the 15th.

Town Hall
Adjoining the church is the Town Hall (Stadhuis). Originally dating from the Middle Ages, it was rebuilt in 1768 with a handsome façade in Louis XV style.

Museum
The municipal museum, the Oudheidkamer De Roos (Markt 46), has a collection of material on the history of the town. Open: daily during the holidays, 10am–12 noon and 1–4pm.

Gelderland
E–J 5–8

Provincial capital: Arnhem
Area: 514,400 hectares/1,286,000 acres
(land area 501,000 hectares/1,252,500 acres)
Population: 1,784,000

Situation and characteristics
Gelderland, the largest of the twelve provinces of the Netherlands, is bounded on the north-east by Overijssel, on the north-west by the Flevoland polder in the IJsselmeer, on the west by the provinces of Utrecht and Zuid-Holland, on the south by Noord-Brabant and Limburg and on the east by Germany.
An opinion poll has shown that this province with its very varied topography is regarded by more than half the population of the Netherlands as the area they would most like to live in.

According to legend this hilly region in a country which is otherwise flat was created by giants walking through the area who got sand in their clogs and emptied it out here. The scientific explanation is different. During the second-last ice age (the Saale/Riss glacial) ice from the North Pole travelled into northern Gelderland and thrust the land surface up into a range of hills up to 100m/330ft high. To the south of the hills the broad forest-covered valley of the Rhine and the Maas came into being.

In prehistoric times Gelderland was inhabited by Celts, and later, like the rest of the country, by a Germanic people, the Batavians, who were then driven north by the Romans at the beginning of the Christian era.

After a period of Frankish rule (11th c.) the area passed into the hands of the Counts (from 1339 Dukes) of Gelderland. Their ancestral castle was in the town of Geldern (now in Germany), which gave its name to the duchy of Gelre and the province of Gelderland. The lion which was the heraldic animal of the Dukes of Gelderland still features in the coat of arms of the province.

During the Middle Ages several towns in Gelderland belonging to the Hanseatic League (Elburg, Harderwijk, Kampen, Zutphen, Arnhem and Nijmegen) enjoyed a considerable measure of prosperity, carrying on trade with the Baltic countries (fish), Belgium (cloth), Germany (wine) and England (wool). When trade declined in the 15th century Gelderland became involved in a struggle with Burgundy to maintain its independence, but after bitter fighting during the reign of Duke Charles it fell to Burgundy (the last of the Dutch provinces to do so) and was incorporated in the empire of Charles V.

Gelderland is divided by three great rivers into three regions. The Rhine separates the Veluwe (see entry) from the Gelderland river country, which is bounded on the south by the Maas. The IJssel, a tributary of the Rhine, forms the boundary between the Veluwe to the north-west and the Achterhoek (see entry) to the east. During the Middle Ages the IJssel was an important commercial waterway; nowadays, with its subsidiary arms and inlets, it offers magnificent facilities for water sports.

The Gelderland river country lies between the Rhine and the Maas and is traversed by the Waal, a broad subsidiary arm of the Rhine, and the Linge. It is very different from the rest of the province, its pattern of development having been determined by the rivers. In earlier times the rivers followed meandering and changing courses through the region, regularly flooding the surrounding countryside and leaving deposits of silt. Over the centuries many miles of dykes were built to control them, and the Waal became an important waterway carrying traffic to the great ports on the North Sea (particularly Rotterdam), the Ruhr, Switzerland, Belgium and France, while the Rhine and the Maas steadily increased in importance as waterways linking the various parts of the country with each other and with foreign lands.

In spite of this the people of the river country remained relatively isolated, since until the Second World War the rivers could for the most part be crossed only by ferry. Since then north–south communications have been improved by the construction of railway bridges and motorways.

The fertile silt deposited by the rivers has fostered the development of horticulture, stock-farming and fruit-growing. In spring the country is gay with the blossom of many thousand apple, pear, cherry and plum trees.

Agriculture makes a major contribution to the economy of Gelderland. In addition to the fruit-growing and stock-farming of the river country there is much horticulture (vegetables, pot plants, cut flowers, mushrooms) in the rest of the province, and stock-farming is also of importance – calves, pigs, poultry (see Barneveld). There is an important college of agriculture at Wageningen.

Since the beginning of the 20th century, however, the province's main source of income has been industry. Although no tobacco is now grown in Gelderland, as it was in the 18th century, it has retained its tobacco-processing industry. The iron formerly worked in the Achterhoek provided the raw material for the development of metallurgical industry.

Gelderland landscape, with a modern windmill

More recently new branches of industry have been established around Arnhem, Nijmegen and the smaller town of Ede, including the multinational AKZO chemical corporation, which began in 1911 as a small firm producing artificial silk, and the large newsprint plant at Renkum.

The province's third largest town, Apeldoorn, has developed in a different direction, as an administrative centre and a residential town favoured by retired people.

Tourist attractions

Gelderland has much to offer visitors and holidaymakers. At Arnhem there are the Hoge Veluwe nature reserve, with the Kröller-Müller Museum (see Veluwe), the Netherlands Open-Air Museum and Burger's Zoo and safari park. Apeldoorn has the palace of Het Loo, built by Prince William III in the 17th century on the model of Versailles, which is now a museum of the house of Orange-Nassau. The old imperial city of Nijmegen has preserved evidence of its glorious past, such as the remains of Charlemagne's stronghold and the ruins of a chapel built by Frederick Barbarossa.

Geleen

See Limburg

German–Dutch Nature Park

See Duits–Nederlandse Natuurpark

Giethoorn

G 4

Province: Overijssel. Commune: Brederwiede
Population: 12,000

Punt traffic in Giethoorn

The picturesque village of Giethoorn lies in an extensive area of former peat-bog to the east of the Noordoostpolder (see entry). Traversed by a network of canals, it has hardly any streets, the main means of transport being small boats which are punted along the canals. Accordingly it is popularly known as the "Venice of the North".

Situation and characteristics

At Binnenpad 43 is De Oude Aarde, a museum with an interesting collection of minerals and semi-precious stones. Open: March to October, daily 10am–6pm; November to February, Sat. and Sun. 10am–6pm; in school holidays, daily 10am–6pm.

Museum

"Histomobil", at Cornelisgracht 42, has a collection of coaches, carts and other simple forms of transport. Open: May to October, daily 10am–6pm.

Histomobil

At Binnenpad 123 is the Speelman Museum, with a collection of barrel-organs and other instruments played by street musicians. Open: April to October, daily 10am–6pm.

Speelman Museum

An old farmhouse at Binnenpad 52, 't Olde Maat Uus, is now open to the public as a museum. Open: May to October, Mon.–Sat. 11am–5pm, Sun. 12 noon–5pm; November to April, Sat. 11am–5pm, Sun. 12 noon–5pm.

't Olde Maat Uus

Goes

B 8/9

Province: Zeeland
Population: 32,000

The town of Goes, once the residence of Jacobaea of Bavaria, Countess of Holland (1401–36), is now the economic centre of the former island of

Situation and characteristics

Goor

Zuid-Beveland. In earlier times the town's trade was mainly in salt and fish; nowadays horticultural produce is increasingly predominant.

Grote Kerk

The Grote Kerke or Maria Magdalenakerk, a cruciform basilica without a tower in Brabantine Late Gothic style, was built in the mid 15th century, destroyed by fire in 1618 and rebuilt in 1621. It has a fine organ of 1641–43 with a beautifully painted organ-case.

Town Hall

The 15th century Gothic Town Hall (Raadhuis) was remodelled in Rococo style in 1775. It has a fine Rococo council chamber with a stucco ceiling and panelled walls.

Weigh-House, Meat Hall

Immediately adjoining the Town Hall are the Weigh-House (Waag) and Meat Hall (Vleeshal).

Old houses

There are a number of old houses in the Markt and Turfkade, including the Gothic House, one of the finest houses in Zeeland.

Goor

Province: Overijssel
Population: 12,000

Situation;
Kasteel Weldam

To the west of Enschede is the little town of Goor, with the moated castle of Weldam (not open to visitors), near the Twente Canal. Originally built in 1389, it was converted into a country mansion in 1568. In the 19th century two new doorways were added on the rear front. The castle is set in a beautiful French-style garden laid out in 1886.

Surroundings of Goor

Diepenheim

South of Goor, in the Salland area, is the village of Diepenheim (pop. 2700), near which are a number of fine castles: Huis te Diepenheim (1330; rebuilt 1645), with a very handsome doorway; Nijenhuis (1457, rebuilt 1650; tower 19th–20th c.); Huize Westerflier (1046; rebuilt in 18th c.) and Huize Warmelo (17th c.), which at one time was the home of Princess Armgard, Prince Bernhard's mother.

Also of interest is De Haller, a watermill which is still used to grind grain when the water level is high enough (restricted access).

Gorinchem

Province: Zuid-Holland
Population: 28,000

Situation and
characteristics

The busy town of Gorinchem or Gorkum, lying on the borders of three provinces (Zuid-Holland, Utrecht and Noord-Brabant), was once an important stronghold. It was one of the first places captured from the Spaniards by the Sea Beggars (1572).
In the Lingehaven the Linge, which flows through the Betuwe between the Rhine and the Waal, joins the Merwede. From here there are fine views of Woudrichem and Kasteel Loevestein (see below).

Town walls

Much of the town's circuit of walls and bastions has been preserved; the only surviving town gate is the Dalempoort (16th c.).

Church

Of the old 15th century parish church there remains only the 60m/200ft high St Janstoren (1517). The present church was built in 1845.

In the Bethlehemshuis at Gasthuisstraat 25 is a small local museum, "Dit is in Bethlehem" (open: Wed.–Sun. 2–5pm).

Museum

Surroundings of Gorinchem

South-east of Gorinchem, on the Maas estuary, stands Kasteel Loevestein. Built in 1357 as the stronghold of a robber baron, the castle served as a state prison in the 17th century. Its most celebrated inmate was the great legal scholar Hugo de Groot (Grotius), who was confined here in 1619 but escaped in 1621, with his wife's help, hidden in a chest of books. There is a small museum. Restored in 1986, Loevestein ranks as one of the finest fortified castles in the Netherlands.

Kasteel Loevestein

Farther south is the pretty little town of Woudrichem, situated in a strategically important position at the junction of the Maas and the Waal. Of the old fortifications there survive only a few stretches of ruined walls and the 16th century Waterpoort.
The Hervormde Kerk, a cruciform church dating from the 15th century, was rebuilt in 1573 after a fire. The 17th century organ-case, originally in the Kloosterkerk in The Hague, was presented to the church by Prince William III. The tower, built of brick and stone, was damaged in a storm in 1717; it was not restored to its original height but was topped by a balustrade.
Other features of interest are the former Town Hall (1592) and a 15th century house, once the residence of Jacobaea of Bavaria, which is now occupied by a convent of Franciscan nuns.

Woudrichem

Gouda

D 7

Province: Zuid-Holland
Population: 62,000

The old market town of Gouda lies in a fertile polder area between Utrecht, Rotterdam and The Hague, at the point where the Gouwe flows into the Hollandse IJssel. It is a very typical Dutch town with its picturesue *grachten* and many historic buildings in the old part of the town.

*Situation and *townscape*

Gouda is famed for its cheese (*Goudse kaas*), which is made either in factories or on farms (*boerenkaas*, "farm cheese"). The large round cheeses weigh between 5 and 10kg (11 and 22lb). Gouda cheese is sold in different levels of fat content (*volvet*, full fat, with over 48% of fat, or *mager*, lean, with over 20% of fat) and different ages (young, "middle-aged" and old).
Other local products are stoneware, candles, clay pipes and syrup waffles.

Gouda cheese

After receiving its municipal charter from Count Floris V of Holland in 1272 Gouda rapidly developed into an important trading town.
The town was taken in 1572 by the Sea Beggars and thereafter played a prominent part in the States of Holland. In the 17th century, however, it declined. Later, after the traditional cloth-making industry had given place to the manufacture of pipes and the production of cheese, and particularly after the beginnings of industrialisation, Gouda again developed into an important economic centre.

History

Gouda was the birthplace of Cornelis Houtman (1565–99), one of the first seamen to sail to the East Indies, who was murdered on Sumatra during his second voyage.

The Town

In the spacious triangular Markt is the imposing Town Hall (Stadhuis), a Late Gothic building (by Jan Keldermans, 1449–59) which was originally

*Markt; *Town Hall*

Gouda

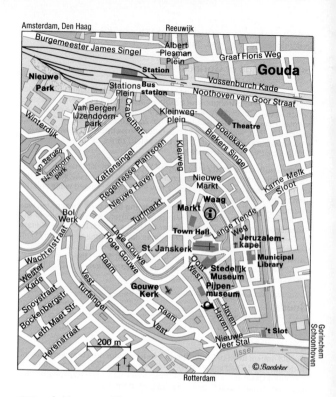

surrounded by a moat. The handsome external staircase in Renaissance style was added in 1603. After undergoing a series of alterations the Town Hall was returned to its original aspect during restoration work carried out between 1947 and 1952. On the east wall is a carillon which rings every half hour, with moving figures representing the granting of the town's charter by Count Floris V in 1272.

Visitors can see round the interior (admission charge). In the Trouwzaal (Marriage Hall) is a 17th century tapestry by David Rufelaer made in Gouda.

Every year in mid December Kaarsjesavond (Candle Evening) is celebrated in the Markt, when the ordinary electric lighting gives place to innumerable candles (2500 on the Town Hall alone).

Weigh-House

On the north-east side of the square is the handsome Weigh-House (Waag), a typical example of Dutch Renaissance architecture (by Pieter Post, 1668). Over the entrance can be seen an interesting stone relief depicting the weighing of cheeses.

**Grote Kerk

A little way south of the Markt stands the Grote Kerk or St Janskerk (Reformed), which dates from the 15th and 16th centuries. 123m/404ft long by 45m/148ft wide, it is the largest church in the Netherlands. The first church on the site was built in the early 13th century, badly damaged in a great fire in the town in 1361 and rebuilt in the form of a hall-church (i.e.

Stained glass in St Janskerk, Gouda ▶

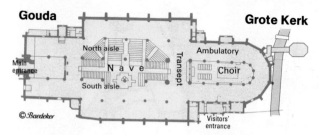

Gouda   Grote Kerk

© Baedeker

with aisles of the same height as the nave). After two further fires in 1438 and 1552 only the choir remained unscathed. Later the present cruciform basilica with a belfry was built (restored 1964–80).

**Stained glass

The church has a superb series of vividly coloured stained glass windows, the *Goudse glazen*, on both Biblical and historical themes, which show the transition from the ecclesiastical to the heraldic and allegorical style of glass painting. The destruction of images in 1566 left 40 windows undamaged, and these were supplemented by 30 others, presented by princes and prelates and later by allied Dutch towns. The finest of the stained glass was the work of Wouter and Dirck Crabeth between 1555 and 1577 (Nos. 5–8, 12, 14–16, 18, 22–24 and 30). The most recent window, "War and Liberation" (1947), was designed by Charles Eyck.

Other notable features of the interior are the timber vaulting of the nave and aisles, which are separated from one another by short round columns, the fine organ of 1736 (supplemented in 1974 by an organ in the choir) and the burial chapels. Open: Mon.–Sat. 9am–5pm.

Catharina Gasthuis Municipal Museum

Behind the Grote Kerk, at Oosthaven 10 and Achter de Kerk 14, stands the former Catharina Gasthuis (from the 14th century until 1910 the municipal hospital), which has been occupied since 1939 by the Municipal Museum. The building, much altered over the centuries and renovated in 1965, contains an old pharmacy, a hospital kitchen, a torture chamber and an 18th century school.
The museum also has collections of pictures (including group portraits of the town guard and the regents of the hospital), coins, drawings, old toys and surgical instruments. Open: Mon.–Sat. 10am–5pm, Sun. 12 noon–5pm.

Pipe Museum

Farther south, on the other side of the *gracht* (Westhaven 29), is the De Moriaan Pipe Museum, in a 17th century merchant's house. In addition to tobacco the merchant dealt in pepper, tea and sugar refined on the premises. ("De Moriaan" means the "Moor" or "black man", the 18th century symbol of smoking). In the old tobacco and herb shop is displayed an interesting collection of Gouda clay pipes – in the early 17th century Gouda was the main centre of the Dutch pipe-making industry – pottery and tiles of the 16th and 17th centuries. Open: Mon.–Fri. 10am–5pm, Sun. 12 noon–5pm.

Other sights

To the east of the Grote Kerk, in Jeruzalemsstraat, is the Jeruzalemkapel (15th c.).
Two interesting buildings in Spieringstraat are the former Orphanage (Weeshuis) of 1642, now the Municipal Library, with a fine carved coat of arms over the entrance, and, at the south end of the street, a flour mill, 't Slot (1832), on the site of the old castle (Slot) which was demolished in 1577.

Gouda's Late Gothic Town Hall, with a Renaissance staircase

Surroundings of Gouda

North of Gouda lie the Reeuwijk Lakes (Reeuwijkse Plassen), formed as a result of peat-cutting, which are now a popular water sports area with several hotels and restaurants.

Reeuwijk Lakes

North-west of Gouda on the old road to Leiden is the little town of Boskoop, on the river Gouwe. It is situated in an important agricultural and fruit-growing area – Boskoop is the name of a variety of hard-skinned apple which keeps exceptionally well – where roses, rhododendrons, azaleas, clematis and shrubs of the yew family are grown in large nurseries. The best time to visit the area is when the flowers are in full bloom.

Boskoop

See entry

Oudewater

See entry

Schoonhoven

Graafschap

See Achterhoek

's-Gravenhage

See The Hague

Groningen

H 2

Province: Groningen
Population: 168,000

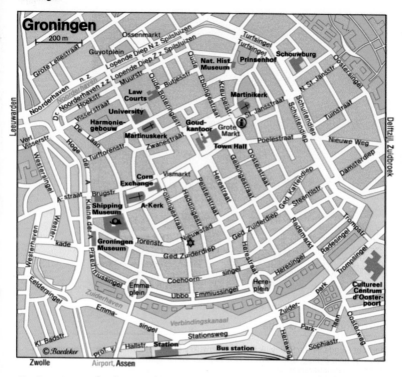

Groningen

200 m

Leeuwarden

Zwolle   Airport, **Assen**

© Baedeker

Delfzijl, Zuidbroek

Situation and importance	Groningen, capital of the province of that name, lies at the junction of the Drenthse Aa (here called the Hoornse Diep) with the Winschoter Diep. Its harbour is accessible for small coastal shipping by way of the Reitdiep, which flows into the North Sea 20km/12½ miles north-west, or the Damsterdiep and the Eems Canal. To the south of the town is Eelde Airport.

Groningen, the seat of a University founded in 1614 and other research institutes and the see of a Roman Catholic bishop, is the most important town in the northern Netherlands. As the main centre for Groningen province and parts of the neighbouring provinces of Drenthe and Friesland it has one of the largest livestock, fruit, vegetable and flower markets in the country. Its corn exchange was for many years the only one in the Netherlands, and is now one of the largest in Europe. Seagoing vessels of up to 2000 tons can reach Groningen from its outer port, Delfzijl, on the Eems Canal. When Groningen still had an open link with the sea the effect of the tides was felt as far up as the town. The main industries are shipbuilding, chemicals, electrical apparatus and appliances, furniture and papermaking; and both agricultural and industrial products are exported by water as well as by rail or road. In Groningen are the offices of the Netherlands Gas Union, a number of government agencies and the Post Office.

History

Although there was a settlement on the site in ancient times, Groningen first appears in the records in 1040, when the Emperor Henry III granted the bishop of Utrecht a fief in the town, together with the right to coin money. The town received its municipal charter later in the 11th century. In the mid

13th century it broke away from its subordination to Utrecht, and in 1284, already a prosperous trading town, it became a member of the Hanseatic League and developed into one of the leading commercial centres in northern Europe. In 1515 it was incorporated in the duchy of Gelre, and in 1536 it was conquered by the Emperor Charles V.

Around 1579 Groningen joined the Union of Utrecht, but a year later it was occupied by the Spaniards, who were finally driven out by Maurice of Nassau in 1594.

Between 1608 and 1616 the town was surrounded by a 7km/4½ mile long circuit of walls, with seventeen towers. After a further siege in 1672, which the town successfully withstood, its fortifications were strengthened in 1698 by the celebrated Dutch military engineer Menno van Coehoorn. In 1874 the old walls gave place to a ring of promenades and canals. During the Second World War Groningen, and particularly the town centre with its gabled houses of the 16th–18th centuries, suffered severe damage, but this was quickly made good after the war.

Groningen was the birthplace of the painters Jozef Israëls (1824–1911) and W. H. Mesdag (1831–1915), both members of the Hague School.

The Town

Groningen's principal shopping street is Herestraat, at the north end of which is the Grote Markt, the central feature of the town. From this square the Vismarkt (Fishmarket) runs south-west to the A-Kerkhof.

Grote Markt

On the west side of the Grote Markt stands the neo-classical Town Hall (Stadhuis; 1777–1810). Behind it is a modern extension (1962) which fits in well with the older building.

Town Hall

The Renaissance Goudkantoor (Gold Office; 1635) was originally the provincial tax office and later the gold assay office. Its magnificent façade is unfortunately concealed by the extension to the Town Hall.

Goudkantoor

St Martinikerk *Provinciehuis*

Groningen

St Martinikerk

At the north-east corner of the Grote Markt is the St Martinikerk (Reformed), a brick Romanesque/Gothic basilica (13th c.). In the 15th century the church was rebuilt in Late Gothic style: the old choir was replaced by a new one with tall Gothic vaulting and an ambulatory, and a chapel and sacristy were built on to the north side. During restoration work in 1924 16th century wall paintings were brought to light in the choir. The old organ was built in 1480 by the humanist and musician Rudolf Agricola (1442–85), who came from the Groningen area.

The tower (1464–82; several times burned down and rebuilt; carillon) is the second highest in the Netherlands (96m/315ft) and Groningen's most prominent landmark.

Provinciehuis

To the east of the church, in St Jansstraat, is the neo-Renaissance Provinciehuis, the seat of the provincial government. In the mid 16th century it was the headquarters of the marksmen's guild. It was restored in 1917 in the style of the 17th century. Notable features of the interior are the Hall of the States (Statenzaal), with portraits of members of the Orange family (17th c.), and the wood panelling and timber vaulting of 1697.

Huis Cardinaal

Beside the Provinciehuis is the Huis Cardinaal, with a Renaissance façade (1559) and a tower between its two wings. The medallions of Alexander the Great, King David and Charlemagne on the gable give the building its other name, "House of the Three Kings".

Prinsenhof

The Prinsenhof was originally a monastery (15th c.), in which Princes Maurice and Willem Lodewijk stayed in 1594. Later it successively became the residence of the Stadholder of Friesland, a school and a military hospital. It is now the offices of the regional broadcasting corporation, Omroep Noord.
Behind the Prinsenhof (entrance from Kattenhage or Turfsingel) is the Prinsenhoftuin, a 17th century rose and herb garden.
On the Zonnewijzerpoort on Turfsingel is a sundial of 1731 with a Latin motto and the letters W and A, referring to Stadholder William Frederick and his wife Albertina Agnes.

Natural History Museum

Adjoining the Prinsenhof, at St Alburgstraat 9, is the Natural History Museum, founded in 1929 by the Royal Dutch Natural History Association. It is notable particularly for its collection of native Dutch animals, displayed in their natural surroundings. Open: Tue.–Fri. 10am–5pm, Sat. and Sun. 2–5pm.

Oude Boteringestraat

In Oude Boteringestraat, north-west of the Grote Markt, are a number of interesting old houses:
No. 17: in neo-Renaissance style.
No. 19: a replica (1913) of a medieval winehouse which stood in the Grote Markt until 1775 and at one time had been a tax office. Over the entrance is a fish with a coin in its mouth, symbolising the extravagant spending of the municipal authorities.
No. 24: one of the oldest stone-built houses in the town, dating from the Middle Ages.
No. 23: a mid 18th century house with thirteen temples on the gable.
Nos. 36–38: a courthouse of 1755, restored in the early 20th century.
No. 44: the former residence of the Queen's Commissioner. The house, in Louis XVI style, was built in 1791 by a doctor named J. v.d. Stege who had made his money in the Dutch East Indies.

Kortegaard

At the end of Oude Boteringestraat is the old Guard-House (1634): the name of the street is a corruption of Corps de Garde. The officers' quarters were on the heated second floor of the building, while the other ranks had the draughty arcaded gallery.

Spilsluizen

To the right is the Spilsluizen *gracht*, at the end of the town's open link with the sea. The quay is therefore on two levels, one for high tide and the other for low tide.

The Prinsenhof, Groningen: residence of the Stadholder of Friesland

From Oude Boteringestraat Broerstraat leads to Academieplein, with the Academiegebouw, the administrative offices of Groningen University. Founded in 1614, the University now has over 10,000 students. The present building, in neo-Renaissance style, was erected in 1907–09 after a fire in 1906 which destroyed the old University building. On the façade are various allegorical figures.
Opposite the Academiegebouw is the new University Library (1985) and to the south the neo-Gothic Martinuskerk (R.C.), by P. J. H. Cuypers. Farther south, at Poststraat 6, is the Biologico-Archaeological Institute, with a collection of prehistoric material (open: Wed. 2–4.30pm). Still farther south, at Zwanestraat 33, is the University Museum (open: Tue.–Fri. 10am–4pm, Sat. and Sun. 1–4pm).

University

Near the Academiegebouw, at the corner of Oude Kijk in 't Jatstraat and Uurwerkersgang, can be seen a building called Harmonie, originally a club (1840), which served for many years as the Municipal Theatre. The name Kijk in 't Jat ("Look into your Hand") is explained by reference to the numerous drinking-houses in the area: a drinker homeward bound after an evening's carousing would look to see whether he had enough money left for a final drink.

Harmonie

To the west of the Grote Markt is the Vismarkt (Fishmarket), now a flower market. On the west side is the Corn Exchange (Korenbeurs) of 1865, in which corn is still sold every Tuesday. On the façade are figures of Ceres (the earth goddess), Mercury (god of traders and thieves) and Neptune (god of the sea and seafaring).

Vismarkt
Corn Exchange

Beyond the Corn Exchange is the A-Kerk, formerly called the Dra-Kerk. Originally a Romanesque church (1247) dedicated to the Virgin and All Saints, it was rebuilt in Gothic style in the 15th century, with a very beautiful interior. A tower was added in the 18th century but twice collapsed. The church was restored from 1975 onwards.

A-Kerk

Groningen

Shipping Museum

At Brugstraat 24–26, to the west of the A-Kerkhof, is the Northern Shipping Museum (Noordelijk Scheepvaartmuseum), housed in two medieval buildings, the Gotisch Huis and Canterhuis (the latter with a 19th century extension). The collection illustrates the history of inland and coastal shipping and fishing since Roman times, with ship models, pictures, parts of ships and navigational instruments; there is also a new section devoted to motor-powered boats. Open: Tue.–Sat. 10am–5pm, Sun. 1–5pm.

Tobacco Museum

In the same building is the Tobacco Museum (Tabacologisch Museum) of the Niemeyer company, with a unique collection of material on the history of tobacco-smoking ranging from 3000-year-old American Indian pipes to the present day, illustrating the manufacture of pipes and displaying pipes, snuff-boxes, spittoons and tobacco jars of porcelain, silver, meerschaum, crystal and ivory.

Groningen Museum

At Praediniussingel 59 (reached by turning left at the far end of Brugstraat) can be found the Groningen Museum (Groninger Museum voor Stad en Land), a museum of antiquities and applied art. The collection includes examples of Chinese and Japanese porcelain and pictures, including works by the Groningen-born painters Jozef Israëls (1824–1911) and Hendrik Willem Mesdag (1831–1915). Open: Tue.–Sat. 10am–5pm, Sun. 1–5pm.

Film Museum

The Film Museum at Gedempte Zuiderdiep 139 illustrates the development of films from the early shadow plays of Java and China to the present day. There is a collection of film projectors, and a small cinema for the showing of films. Open: Sat. 1–5pm.

Synagogue

Farther east along the Gedempte Zuiderdiep is the Synagogue (1906), in neo-Oriental style. The building was restored in 1981–82 and is used for concerts and exhibitions as well as for Jewish worship.

North of the old town

On the north side of the Spilsluizen is the Ossenmarkt, with two attractive old gabled houses, one dating from 1624 and the other built in the 18th century by a merchant named J. A. Sichterman. A cattle market was held in the square until 1892.
Farther east is the Guyotplein, named after Pastor H. D. Guyot, who in 1790 founded the first institution for the deaf and dumb in the Netherlands (in this square).
To the north of Guyotplein is the Nieuwe Kerk or Noorderkerk (1660–65), which was modelled on the church of the same name in Amsterdam.

In this area too, at Nieuwe Kijk in 't Jatstraat 104, is the Gerardus van der Leeuw Museum of Ethnology, with a collection of extra-European artefacts. Open: Tue.–Fri. 10am–4pm, Sat. and Sun. 1–5pm.

In north-western Groningen lies a beautiful park, the Noorderplantsoen, laid out on the site of the town's former fortifications.

South of the old town

In the south of the town is the Sterrebos, a small wooded park with a garden restaurant. To the south-west is the large Stadspark (restaurant), with a race track, various sports facilities and a large camping site.

Surroundings of Groningen

Haren

At Haren, 5km/3 miles south of Groningen, is the new (De Wolf) Botanic Garden of Groningen University, established in 1917. Now extending to 20 hectares/50 acres, it has various hothouses, a herb garden and a wild garden in which large numbers of Dutch plants grow in their natural setting (heath, meadowland, woodland).

Tynaarlo

10km/6 miles south of Groningen on A 28, at Tynaarlo station, can be seen a well preserved *hunebed* (megalithic tomb).

15km/9 miles west of Groningen on the Heerenveen road (A 7) is the village of Midwolde. In the little 13th century church is a fine marble tomb by Rombout Verhulst (1646).

Midwolde; *marble tomb

Just south of Midwolde at the village of Leek is Huis Nienoord, with an interesting coach museum. In the park is a beautiful shell grotto. Open: April–Sept. Mon.–Sat. 9am–5pm, Sun. 1–5pm.

Leek

See entry

Uithuizen

Groningen (province)   G–J 1–3

Provincial capital: Groningen
Area: 297,000 hectares/742,500 acres
(land area 235,000 hectares/587,500 acres)
Population: 557,000

The province of Groningen, the "Top of Holland", lies in the extreme north-east of the Netherlands, bounded on the north by the Waddenzee, on the east by Germany, on the south by the province of Drenthe and on the west by Friesland. Largely untouched by tourism, it has sandy soil to the west and east, peat soil in the south-east and clay soil in the north.

Situation and characteristics

Peat-cutting began in the 16th century and led to the establishment of the characteristic *veen* or peat-bog settlements (see Facts and Figures, Cultural Landscapes). In the eastern part of the province, where peat-cutting was for centuries the most important element in the economy, there are many place-names ending in *-veen, -kanaal, -wijk* (district in a town) and *-mond* (river mouth).

Peat-working

One of the oldest *veen* settlements in Groningen province is the long straggling town (25km/15 miles from end to end) of Stadskanaal (pop. 33,000), which is crisscrossed by a network of canals set at right angles to one another. The areas cleared of peat are now fertile arable and pastureland.

Stadskanaal

Archaeological finds have shown that the province of Groningen was already occupied by man in prehistoric times. Some place-names still hark back to Carolingian times. In the Middle Ages monks taught the peasants to build their houses on artificial mounds (*terpen*) which would provide protection from flooding (see Friesland). A number of monasteries were founded in the 12th century, the most important being the Cistercian house of Aduard.
During the 15th century the town of Groningen began to extend its authority far beyond its own boundaries and came into conflict with the inhabitants of the surrounding territories (Ommelanden). During the struggle for independence the Ommelanden were on the side of the States General, while the town was occupied by the Spaniards. The conflict was settled only in 1718, when William IV became Stadholder.
During the period of French rule, from about 1800, the provinces of Groningen and Drenthe together with the German territory of East Friesland were combined to form a *département*. The present provincial boundaries were fixed in 1814.

History

From time immemorial Groningen province was a predominantly agricultural region. Nowadays, however, as a result of the mechanisation of agriculture and increasing industrialisation, only some 10% of the population work on the land; a quarter are employed in industry and half in the services sector.

Economy

As a result of agricultural development, associated particularly with the clearance of peat, two-thirds of the area of the province consists of arable land. The main crops are corn, vegetables and potatoes.

Agriculture

Stadskanaal, a straggling moorland village

Industry	The growing of potatoes led to the production of starch, used in the manufacture of noodles, custard powder and plastics (e.g. for telephones and radio sets). The packaging industry, formerly flourishing, has declined. Also in decline is the shipbuilding industry, since the larger ships now being built cannot negotiate the canals.

The discovery of fields of natural gas – the fourth largest in the world – have given a great boost to the gas industry. Other minerals found in the province are salt, magnesium and potassium, which are profitably worked on an industrial scale.

Haarlem

Province: Noord-Holland
Population: 149,000

Situation and
**townscape

Haarlem, capital of the province of Noord-Holland, lies between Amsterdam and the North Sea, 7km/4½ miles from the coast, on the little river Spaarne (which gives the town its popular name of "Spaarnestad"). This very typical Dutch town, part of "Randstad Holland", now forms a continuous built-up area with the adjoining towns of Heemstede, Bloemendaal and Zandvoort.

Haarlem is the cultural centre of southern Kennemerland, with several research institutes, educational establishments and libraries, and is the see of a Roman Catholic bishop. It is also a considerable industrial town, with shipyards, railway workshops, printing works, engineering and coach-building plants and foodstuffs industries.

*Bulb-growing

Haarlem is famed as a great bulb-growing centre, producing tulips, hyacinths, crocuses and daffodils which are despatched all over the world. The

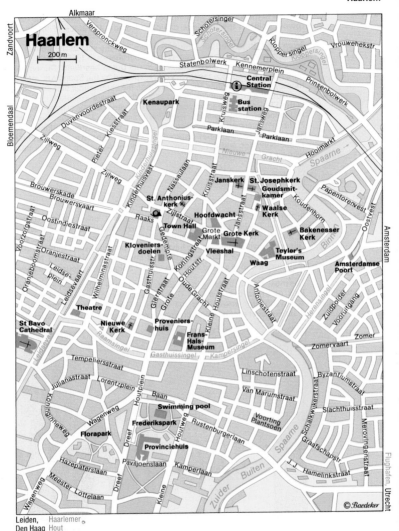

Haarlem

Alkmaar

200 m

Zandvoort

Bloemendaal

Versprockweg
Schotersingel
Kloppersingel
Vrouwehekstr

Statenbolwerk   Kennemerplein

Central
Station

Kenaupark

Bus
station

Prinsenbolwerk

Duvenvoordestraat
Kruisweg
Parklaan   Parklaan
Hooimarkt

Zijlweg
Pieter   Kiesstraat
Brouwerskade
Brouwersvaart
Zijlweg

Nieuwe   Gracht
Spaarne

Nassaulaan
Kinderhuisvest
Kruisstraat

Janskerk   St. Josephkerk
Goudsmit-
kamer

St. Anthonius-
kerk
Hoofdwacht
Waalse
Kerk
Papentorenvest

Raaks   Zijlstraat
Town Hall
Grote
Markt   Grote Kerk
Bakenesser
Kerk

Voorzorgstraat
Oostindiestraat
Oranjestraat
Leidse-
plein

Wilhelminastraat
Gasthuisstraat
Gedempte
Koningstraat
Vleeshal
Teyler's
Museum

Kloveniers-
doelen
Waag   Amsterdamse
Poort

Glasstraat
Grote
Oude Gracht
Kleine Houtstraat
Antoniestraat
Heronsingel
Zuidpolder
Vooruitgang

Theatre

Leidsevaart
Haarlemsingel

Nieuwe
Kerk

St Bavo
Cathedral

Proveniers-
huis

Frans-
Hals-
Museum
Gasthuissingel   Kampersingel

Zomer
Zomervaart

Tempeliersstraat

Linschotenstraat
Byzantiumstraat

Julianastraat   Lorentzplein
Houtplein
Baan

Van Marumstraat
Slachthuisstraat
Merovingenstraat

Koninginneweg
Wagenweg

Swimming pool

Frederikspark
Houtvel
Rustenburgerlaan

Voorting
Plantsoen

Spaarne
Schalkwijkerstraat
Graafschapstr

Florapark

Provinciehuis

Dreef

Wagenweg
Hazepaterslaan
Meester Lottelaan

Paviljoenslaan
Kamperlaan

Kleine   Zuider   Buiten
J.J. Hamelinkstraat

© Baedeker

Leiden,
Den Haag   Haarlemer
Hout

Amsterdam

Flughafen Utrecht

tulip came to the Netherlands from Asia Minor by way of Austria at the end
of the 15th century, and in the following century gave rise to a "tulip mania"
during which extraordinary prices were paid for choice bulbs. A century
later there was a similar craze for hyacinths.

The town has a long history. It first appears in the records in the 10th
century under the name of Harulahem (i.e. a homestead on a narrow

History

217

channel in the sand). Its situation between bogland and rivers at the narrowest point in the province of Holland made it a place of strategic importance.

From the 11th to the 13th century Haarlem was the seat of the Counts of Holland, from whom it received its municipal charter in 1245: it is thus the second oldest town (after Dordrecht) in the Dutch heartland. During the fight for independence the town was recaptured by the Spaniards, after a heroic resistance, in July 1573, whereupon the commander and the entire garrison, the Protestant clergy and 2000 citizens were executed.

In the 17th century Haarlem was the scene of great artistic activity and the residence of many painters, including Frans Hals, Jacob van Ruisdael, Philips Wouverman and Adriaen van Ostade. The city architect Lieven de Key (c. 1560–1627) founded a school of building in the town, and Haarlem's public buildings and the numerous gabled houses in the old town bear witness to its achievements.

The Town
Town Centre

Grote Markt

In the centre of the old town is the Grote Markt, on which ten streets converge. The busy shopping streets are now closed to traffic. In the centre of the square can be seen a statue of Laurens Coster, a contemporary of Gutenberg who is believed to have been the real discoverer of printing.

Around the Grote Markt are the most important of Haarlem's historic buildings. It is thus a good starting-point for a sightseeing tour of the town.

*Grote Kerk
(St Bavokerk)

The most striking building in the Grote Markt is the 140m/460ft long Grote Kerk or St Bavokerk, a Late Gothic cruciform basilica with a slender 40m/130ft high tower over the crossing. The building of the church extended over a long period, beginning with the erection of the choir in the

Grote Kerk (St Bavokerk), Haarlem

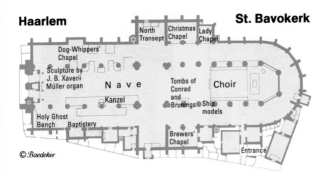

Haarlem

St. Bavokerk

14th century. In the mid 15th century the transepts were added by Spoorwater, a master builder from Antwerp. Around 1475 the old nave was replaced by a new one, 125m/410ft long, flanked by two low, narrow aisles. The tower (now equipped with a carillon by the Hemony brothers which rings every evening) was built about 1520, and the timber vaulting of the choir and nave was completed in 1536. The cedarwood ceiling of the nave – finely constructed as only a nation of shipbuilders could contrive – is borne on 28 round piers. The baptistery on the south side of the church (1593) and the consistory room (1658) were added after the Reformation.

Most of the interior furnishings of the church date from before the Reformation, including the choir and its lectern (1499), the beautifully carved choir-stalls (1512) and the brass choir screen (1509–17). In front of the former chapel of the seamen's guild hang three old models of Dutch warships, a 17th century frigate and pinnace and a 16th century armed merchant ship.

The piers under the tower and in the choir are covered with 15th–16th century paintings depicting symbols of the Apostles, the guilds and church doctrine. In the choir are buried Frans Hals (d. 1666) and Lieven de Key. After the Reformation a small organ was installed in the choir in 1600, followed in 1679 by a pulpit carved by Abraham Snellaert. The pulpit is borne on eagles' wings (the eagle being the symbol of St John the Evangelist), and its brass rails are decorated with snakes, symbolising Satan's flight before the Word of God.

Müller organ

The Grote Kerk has one of the great organs of the world, built by Christian Müller in 1735–38, with a monumental organ-case by the woodcarver and sculptor Jan van Logteren. Over the years the bellows, the mechanics and the keys of the organ have been frequently overhauled and adapted to the musical taste of the time. It has three manuals, 68 stops and 5000 pipes, the largest of which is 10m/33ft long, with a diameter of 40cm/16in. Both for its acoustic qualities and its rich decoration it ranks among the world's finest organs. Among those who have played the organ are Handel and Mozart and, in more recent times, Albert Schweitzer. In July of alternate years an international organ competition is held in the town.
There are regular organ recitals in the church (mid May to mid October, Tue. 8.15–9.15pm; July and August, also Thur. 3–4pm); admission free.

Below the organ is a monumental piece of sculpture (by Jan Baptist Xaverij, 1738), carved from a single block of white marble, with allegorical representations of Poetry, Music and Eternity.

Town Hall

On the opposite side of the Grote Markt stands the Town Hall (Stadhuis), the oldest parts of which go back to a hunting lodge built by Count William

219

Grote Kerk: interior . . .

. . . and Müller organ

Haarlem Town Hall

II of Holland, king of Germany, in 1250. At the end of the 13th century, with the permission of Count Floris V, Dominican monks built a monastery behind the castle, with a chapterhouse, cloisters and a church. After two serious fires in the town Count William V enlarged the castle by the addition of the Gravenzaal (Count's Hall), which soon afterwards was acquired by the municipality of Haarlem. In 1455 a court-house, the Vierschaar, was built, complete with a timber scaffold, which was replaced by a stone one in 1633. After the last execution in 1829 the scaffold remained in place until 1855.

The tower, Haarlem's great landmark and emblem, was built in 1460, but was pulled down in the 18th century when in danger of collapse. In 1913 it was re-erected on the basis of old drawings. The old bell was installed in the new tower, and still rings at the beginning of every town council meeting.

The Pandpoort (1490) was the entrance to the monastery.

The Town Hall and the monastery, with its church, suffered heavy damage during the fight for independence and the wars of religion. In 1579 both buildings were acquired by the town; then in 1590 part of the monastery was converted into the Prinsenhof, a residence for the Stadholder and other distinguished visitors. In 1845 the Gravenzaal was again rebuilt.

In 1597 Lieven de Key, a refugee from Flanders who had become the town's architect and master of works, built the external staircase at the entrance to the Gravenzaal, and in 1620–22 the north wing on Zijlstraat. Some years later (1630–33) the façade was rebuilt in neo-classical style.

Around 1860 an additional storey was added to the cloisters. This was originally an old people's home, and later housed the town's rich art collection, which included such famous works as Frans Hals's eleven group portraits of the town guard. In 1913 the collection was transferred to the present Frans Hals Museum. The Prinsenhof housed the municipal archives until 1936. Later a new wing was built along Koningstraat and Jacobijnenstraat.

The interior of the Town Hall is of great interest, with pictures, wall paintings, historical relics and mementoes, and fine woodcarving. Unfortunately much of the building is occupied by offices and is not open to the public. There are periodic conducted tours of the building (enquire of the door-keeper).

On the north-east side of the Town Hall is the Brinkmann-Passage, with shops, the Brinkmann Brasserie and a restaurant with a terrace facing the Grote Markt. — Brinkmann-Passage

To the right of this is the Hoofdwacht (Guard-House), one of the oldest buildings in the town, with a gable of 1650. This was the site of the old municipal police headquarters and probably of Haarlem's first town hall. — Hoofdwacht

On the south side of the Grote Markt stands the Vleeshal (Meat Hall), built in 1602–03 by Lieven de Key to house both the municipal slaughterhouse and the butchers' guild, which ranks as the finest work of the whole Northern Renaissance. It is now an annexe of the Frans Hals Museum. — *Vleeshal (Meat Hall)

Near the Grote Kerk is the Vishal (Fish Hall), also built by Lieven de Key, which is now occupied by the department of modern art of the Frans Hals Museum. The red and white façade is topped by a stepped gable and beautiful ornamental gables on the roof. — Vishal (Fish Hall)

In Jansstraat, which runs north from the Grote Kerk, is the 14th century Janskerk (on left), originally a monastic church, which now houses the municipal archives. Its most notable features are the wooden tower (1595) and the beautiful inner courtyard (which can be entered only on weekdays). — Janskerk

On the other side of the street is the Mariakapel (Chapel of Our Lady), adjoining which is St Josephkerk, a former episcopal church in neo- — St Josephkerk

221

classical style. It has a figure of the Virgin which was originally in the Bakenesserkerk.

Goudsmitkamer

From the Grote Kerk Lange Begijnestraat leads north past the Begijnhof to Goudsmitspleinje, in which is the Goudsmitkamer. A stone on the façade records that this was the guild-house of the Haarlem silversmiths and goldsmiths in the 17th and 18th centuries.

Waalse Kerk

In the Begijnhof is the 14th century Waalse Kerk, originally the church of the Beguines, with a 16th century sacristy. Since the Reformation it has been a Walloon church.

From here the Groene Buurt leads to the Bakenesser Gracht, along which on the right is the Hofje van Bakenes (1395).

Amsterdamse Poort

At the end of the Bakenesser Gracht is the river Binnen Spaarne, which is crossed on a picturesque drawbridge. To the east can be seen the Amsterdamse Poort (*c.* 1400), Haarlem's only surviving town gate. Flanking the main structure are two octagonal towers, and on the outer side, facing the *gracht*, are two round towers. At the foot of the outer side can be seen some remnants of the old town walls.

*Teyler's Museum

At the end of the Bakenesser Gracht, to the right (Spaarne 16), is Teyler's Museum, the oldest museum in the Netherlands, founded in 1778. Pieter Teyler van der Hulst (1702–78) was a wealthy cloth and silk dealer interested in the arts and sciences who bequeathed his whole fortune for the building of this museum, which is designed to illustrate the development of art and science.

The museum, only the fourth of its kind in Europe (after Oxford, London and Paris), assembled within a relatively brief space of time not only an

Teyler's Museum

Frans Hals Museum

extensive art collection, with numerous drawings and pictures by early Dutch masters as well as by Michelangelo and Raphael, but also an outstanding collection of scientific instruments, minerals and fossils. Open: Tue.–Sat. 10am–5pm, Sun. 1–5pm.

Adjoining the museum is the municipal Weigh-House (Waag), a building of dressed stone erected by Lieven de Key in 1597–98. It was in use until 1915 for the weighing of goods brought in on the river Spaarne.

Weigh-House

Going south along the Spaarne, we see on the other bank (Spaarne 17) the headquarters of the Scientific Society of Holland, in a patrician house of 1794.
At No. 43 is the Oprechte Haarlemmer Olie factory, with a 17th century gable.

Spaarne

To the left of the Oude Gracht is Groot Heiligland. In this street are the Gasthuisjes, a series of hospital buildings with similar crow-stepped gables (1610), formerly belonging to the Sint Elisabeth Gasthuis (St Elizabeth's Hospice).

The Frans Hals Museum was established in a former old people's home – the fourth important building by Lieven de Key in Haarlem (1608) – at Groot Heiligland 62 in 1913, when the municipal art collection was transferred here from the Town Hall. It now occupies a leading position among the art galleries of the Netherlands, giving a predominant place to the work of Haarlem artists.

**Frans Hals Museum

The flourishing economy of Haarlem and the religious tolerance which prevailed after the withdrawal of Spanish troops in 1576 attracted many refugees, particularly from what is now Belgium, and fostered a great

The "Haarlem Academy"

Frans Hals, "Farewell Banquet of the Marksmen's Guild of St Adrian" (1627)

Haarlem Frans Hals Museum

1 Modern art
2 15th/16th c.: Mostaert, etc
3 16th c.: Jan van Scorel, M. van Heemskerck
4 16th c.: Cornelisz van Haarlem, etc.
5 Academy Hall: Goltzius, M. van Heemskerck
6 17th c.: Vroom, Claesz, van Dyck
7 17th c.: Dirk Hals, Molenaer, Verspronck
8 17th c.: van Goyen, van Ostade, Verspronck
9 18th c.: Regents' Room
10 18th c.: Regents' Room
11 Chapel: 17th c. Haarlem silver
12 Portraits of marksmen's guilds by Frans Hals and others
13 Renaissance Room (former refectory)
14 Gilded Leather Room, with dolls' house
15 Portraits of regents by Frans Hals and Verspronck
16 Verspronck, Heda, Ruisdael, etc.
17 De Bray, Jan Steen, etc.
18 Portraits of regents by Frans Hals
19 18th century
20 18th century
21 Miniatures
22 Old pharmacy
23 Glass Cabinet

cultural flowering. In 1583 Carel van Mander, a Flemish painter, came to Haarlem and, influenced by his study of Italian Renaissance art, developed the practice of painting large pictures on Biblical and historical themes, based on a profound knowledge of anatomy. With Hendrick Goltzius and Cornelis Cornelisz he founded the "Haarlem Academy", which marks the high point of Dutch Mannerism. Of particular significance in this respect were the allegorical and mythological figures in rather contrived postures painted by Cornelisz, particularly in erotic scenes. His group portraits of marksmen's guilds prepared the way for Frans Hals, the liveliest and most expressive of all Dutch painters, whose group portraits of marksmen and regents rank as the principal treasures of the museum.

Group portraits

The first groups to commission portraits of this kind seem to have been the marksmen's guilds – companies of volunteers, elected every three years from among the more prosperous citizens to form a kind of civic militia or town guard. The first group portraits (*doelenstukken*), painted in Amsterdam in the early 16th century, were merely an assemblage of individual portraits. Frans Hals contrived to combine the individual members of the group in a dynamic scene of action with something of the effect of a snapshot, as in his pictures of the farewell banquets of the marksmen's guilds of St George (1616) and St Adrian (1627).

Portraits of regents

Frans Hals also painted group portraits of regents (the governors of merchants' guilds and charitable institutions), such as his portraits of the regents and regentesses of the old men's home (both painted in 1664).

The collection also includes many 17th century portraits, still lifes, genre scenes and landscapes (Adriaen van Ostade, Jacob van Ruisdael, Johannes Verspronck, Jan de Bray, Pieter Claesz, Willem Heda, etc.), as well as Haarlem silver, an old doll's house and a reconstruction of a pharmacy with jars of Delft ware.

Modern art

The museum's collection of modern and contemporary art includes pictures, sculpture, textiles, ceramics and graphic art by artists from Haarlem and the surrounding area including Isaac Israël, Jan Sluyters, Karel Appel, Reinier Lucassen and Herman Kruyder.

The museum is open Mon.–Sat. 11am–5pm, Sun. 1–5pm, and sometimes also in the evening (candle-light, music).

From the end of Groot Heiligland it is a short distance by way of the Gasthuisvest to Klein Heiligland, with the Vrouwe- and Antonie Gasthuis (No. 64), a group of 17th century almshouses.

In Grote Houtstraat, Haarlem's principal shopping street, is the Proveniers-huis (No. 144), built in 1591, with a richly decorated gable and an imposing doorway. In 1700 almshouses for old men and women were built round the inner courtyard. Since the marksmen's guild of St Joris has its head-quarters here the almshouses are also known as the St Jorisdoelen.

Proveniershuis

From the end of Grote Houtstraat the Raamvest runs west to the Municipal Theatre (Stadsschouwburg), built in 1918 at the expense of an anonymous citizen of Haarlem.

In Korte Annastraat, which opens off the Raamvest, stands the Nieuwe Kerk, a square brick building. After the destruction of the original church by fire a new church in the same style was built by Jacob van Campen (1645–49), incorporating the graceful Renaissance tower by Lieven de Key (1613). A notable feature of the interior is the magnificent Baroque marble tomb of William of Orange (by Hendrick and Pieter de Keyser, 1614). In the churchyard adjoining the church are the graves of the painters Jacob van Ruisdael and Philips Wouwerman.

Nieuwe Kerk

Farther along the street (Lange Annastraat 41) is the Hofje van Guurtje de Waal (1616, renovated 1783). Beyond this is Tuichthuisstraat, with the Brouwershofje (1586). In the next street on the left, Barrevoetstraat, are the Wijnbergshofje (1662) and the Gasthuishofje or Hofje van Loo (No. 7), a picturesque group of almshouses built in 1489. Unfortunately the widening of the street in 1885 involved the demolition of the houses on the street side, depriving these *hofjes* of their air of seclusion.

Hofjes
(almshouses)

Tuchthuisstraat leads into Gasthuisstraat. A 16th century house at No. 32, the Kloveniersdoelen, which was originally the headquarters of the town guard, now houses the Municipal Library. On weekdays it is possible to enter the inner courtyard by a vaulted passage from the street (1612).

Kloveniersdoelen

From here the street called Raaks leads back to the Gedempte Oude Gracht. On the left is the Head Post Office (by J. Crouwel, 1923), a fine example of the work of the Amsterdam School, with sculpture by Hildo Krop.

Returning to the Grote Markt along Zijlstraat, we pass close to Witte Heren-straat, in which (No. 24) is the Frans Loenen Hofje of 1607, with a handsome doorway. Here too is the Lutherse Kerk, with Luthers Hofje and an open-air pulpit reached from inside the church.

Loenen Hofje,
Luthers Hofje

From the Grote Markt Jansstraat runs north, crossing the Nieuwe Gracht and Parklaan, along which extends Kenaupark, laid out in 1868, to the main railway station (1908), in Art Nouveau style, with fine tile decoration.

Station

Returning to the town centre on Jansweg and crossing the Nieuwe Gracht (at No. 2 of which is the Hofje van Noblet of 1761), we continue along the Spaarne on the Koudenhorn. In this street is the former old men's home and orphanage of the Diakonie (1768), now the police headquarters. At No. 64 is Teylers Hofje, a group of almshouses built in 1785–87 with money bequeathed by Pieter Teyler van der Hulst, with a handsome neo-classical façade and a doorway flanked by Doric columns.

Teylers Hofje

Valkenstraat leads into Bakenesserstraat, with the late 15th century Bake-nesser Kerk (Reformed), notable for the handsome sandstone upper stage of its tower.

Bakenesser Kerk

From the end of the Bakenesser Gracht, turning right along the Spaarne and passing Teyler's Museum and the Weigh-House, we come to Dam-straat, with the Johan Enschedé & Zonen printing works, in which Dutch banknotes and stamps are printed; and so back to the starting-point of the tour in the Grote Markt.

Haarlem

Southern Districts

Provinciehuis

From the southern ring of canals (Raamsingel and Gasthuissingel) Houtplein and its continuation the Dreef run south to the Haarlemmer Hout. On the left of the Dreef lies the beautiful Frederikspark. Beyond this is the Provinciehuis (provincial government offices), formerly known as the Paviljoen, a country house built in 1788 which was occupied from 1806 to 1810 by King Louis Bonaparte and from 1817 to 1820 by the widow of Prince William V of Orange.

Florapark

To the right of the Dreef is Florapark, with a statue of Frans Hals.

*Haarlemmer Hout

To the south of the Provinciehuis extends the Haarlemmer Hout, a remnant of the expanse of forest which once covered much of the Kennemerland, with some ancient trees. The Hildebrand Fountain is decorated with figures representing characters from the well known book "Camera Obscura" by the 19th century writer Hildebrand (the pseudonym of Nicolaas Beets). On the east side of the park, at Kleine Houtweg 135, is the Hofje van Heythuizen (1650).

Western Districts

*St Bavo-kathedraal

At Leidsevaart 146 stands the Roman Catholic Cathedral of St Bavo, a three-aisled cruciform basilica (by J. Cuypers, 1895–1906). 100m/328ft long, 42m/138ft wide and 60m/187ft high, it is a good example of the transition to modern architecture, curiously combined with neo-Gothic and even Arab elements. The tower was added in 1927–30. The cathedral treasury contains valuable silver liturgical utensils and a reliquary with the remains of St Bavo, who is also commemorated by a statue at the east end of the church. Other notable features of the cathedral are the fine stained glass and the sculpture and pictures by well known Dutch artists such as

St Bavo's Cathedral: a mingling of Byzantine and Late Gothic

Toorop, Derkindern and Andriessen. The Willibrord Organ, built in 1923 by the Adema firm, has four manuals and 75 stops; there are periodic organ recitals from Easter to the end of September. Open: April to September, Mon. 10am–12 noon, Tue.–Fri. 2–4.30pm, Sat. 10.30am–12 noon.

Surroundings of Haarlem

5km/3 miles north of Haarlem is Bloemendaal aan Zee, a popular seaside resort.   Bloemendaal
From here the road runs east through the dune country of Kennemerland (nature reserve, with a number of lakes; camping sites) to a cemetery containing the graves of almost 400 people shot here during the German occupation in the Second World War. Then, passing Overveen station, back to Haarlem (7km/4½ miles).

North-east of Haarlem, around Spaarndam, is the Spaarnwoude recreation   Spaarnwoude
area.

Farther east is Halfweg, where a pumping station on the dam between the   Halfweg
Haarlemmermeer and the river IJ was originally used to drain the lake and is still in operation. Open: April to September, Mon. and Thur. 1–4pm, Sat. 10am–4pm.

South of Haarlem is the residential suburb of Heemstede, with a number of   Heemstede
18th century country houses including Bosbeek, Hartekamp and Huis te Manpad.

South-east of Heemstede, at Cruquiusdijk 27–32 (in the direction of Hoofd-   De Cruquius
dorp), is the De Cruquius Museum, housed in one of the three 19th century   Museum
pumping stations used to drain the Haarlemmermeer. When the other two pumping stations were enlarged it was no longer needed, and now houses a museum devoted to the Dutch struggle against water. Open: April to September, Mon.–Sat. 10am–5pm, Sun. 12 noon–5pm; October and November, until 4pm.

At Lisse is the Keukenhof flower park (see Bollenstreek).   Keukenhof

The Hague ('s-Gravenhage/Den Haag)   C 6/7

Province: Zuid-Holland
Population: 444,000

The Hague, officially called 's-Gravenhage, is the third largest city in the   Situation and
Netherlands and part of "Randstad Holland", capital of the province of   **importance
Zuid-Holland, the seat of the Dutch government and the residence of the royal family. It lies close to the North Sea, and the seaside resort of Scheveningen (see entry) is within the city limits.

The Hague, a place of residence much favoured by retired people, in-cluding many from the former Dutch colonies (hence its nickname, the "widow of India"), bears the mark of its function as a political, adminis-trative and cultural centre, with its ministries and embassies, the head-quarters of several international organisations, the International Court of Justice and the Permanent Court of Arbitration. In addition there are nu-merous research institutes, learned societies, academies and higher edu-cational establishments, as well as the headquarters of many banks and commercial and industrial firms.

The Hague is also a city of the arts. Many Dutch painters live here and it is an important centre of the international art trade. The applied arts (furniture, china, gold and silverware) are also well established.

The Hague ('s-Gravenhage/Den Haag)

Street scene with equestrian statue

Economy

According to a popular saying in Rotterdam they make money, in Amsterdam they spend it and in The Hague they talk about it. Industry plays a subordinate role, providing employment for only some 30% of the working population. Although limited in scale the range of the city's industry is wide – textiles, electrical apparatus and appliances, metalworking, furniture, printing, rubber goods, pharmaceuticals, foodstuffs. Most of the industry is in Scheveningen, the largest seaside resort in the Netherlands, and in the harbour area with its convenient transport facilities. Scheveningen is also an important fishing port. The Hague is linked by rail with Amsterdam–Schiphol Airport.

History

The Hague was originally a hunting lodge of the Counts of Holland – hence the first name of the town, 's-Gravenhage, the "Count's preserve" – and from the mid 13th century it was their permanent residence. Around the Binnenhof, the Count's palace, there grew up at an early stage a village of peasant farmers, craftsmen and traders which became known as Den Haag. To this day the city retains something of the character of a village. From the outset the neutrality of The Hague made it well suited to be the seat of government. From 1593 the States General held their meetings here, and in the 17th and early 18th centuries The Hague was the scene of important diplomatic negotiations and a place of luxury and pleasure, with much building activity. The jealousy of the other towns which sent representatives to the States General excluded The Hague from membership, and it remained the "largest village in Europe" until King Louis Bonaparte granted it a municipal charter – though he also reduced its importance by transferring the meeting-place of the States General to Amsterdam. It was only in the middle of the 19th century, when the population passed the 100,000 mark, that The Hague began to come into its own. Today, with its wide streets, spacious squares and promenades and fine residential suburbs, it is a very elegant and attractive town.

The City
Central Area

In this section the main sights of The Hague are described in the form of a tour, starting from the Binnenhof.

In the centre of the old town is the Binnenhof, an irregular group of buildings, some old and some more recent, built around a central courtyard. About 1250 Count William II of Holland began the building of a castle which was completed by his son Floris V, who in 1291 made this his principal residence. From the time of Prince Maurice of Orange-Nassau the Binnenhof was the residence of the Stadholders. It now houses both chambers of the Dutch Parliament as well as a number of government departments. The rectangular complex of buildings has entrances at each end; there is a third doorway, the Grenadierspoort, half way along one side.

*Binnenhof

At the east end of the central courtyard is the Knights' Hall (Ridderzaal), which dates from the time of Floris V. The hall is used for receptions and

*Knights' Hall

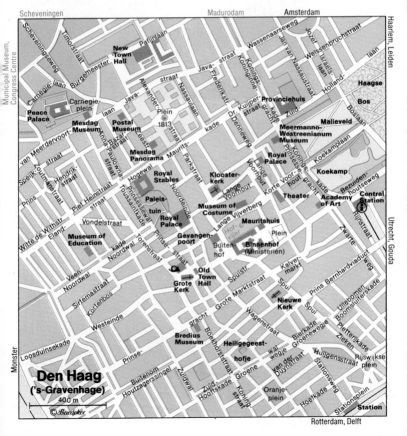

229

The Binnenhof and Hofvijver

Knights' Hall

congresses and also for the state opening of Parliament on the third Tuesday in September (Prinsjesdag), when the Queen drives to Parliament in her golden coach and delivers the speech from the throne. This large Gothic hall (40m/130ft by 20m/65ft) has magnificent stained glass depicting the coats of arms of Dutch towns; particularly fine is the rose window with the arms of the principal noble families of the Netherlands. The heavy timber roof structure with its 18m/60ft long beams has the appearance of an upturned ship. Wooden heads symbolising eavesdroppers from the higher powers are supposed to deter members of the assembly from lying. The hall was built by Gerard van Leiden in the 13th century as a banqueting hall, and in later centuries served a variety of purposes – as a market hall, a promenade, a drill hall, a children's playground, a public record office, a hospital ward, even the offices of the state lottery. It was restored between 1898 and 1904 to serve its present purposes.

Adjoining the Knights' Hall on the east is the oldest group of buildings in the complex, which have been occupied since the time of Philip the Good by law courts.

In the north wing of the Binnenhof are the chamber in which the States General used to meet, the official residence of the prime minister, the government information office, the Rolzaal (1511), in which justice was administered, and the Lairessezaal, with seven paintings by Gerard de Lairesse (1688).

The old meeting-place of the States of Holland (by Pieter Post, 1652), at the west end of the north wing, now houses the First Chamber of the Dutch Parliament. In small niches along the walls are painted medallions depicting notable statesmen. Behind the seat occupied by the President hangs a portrait of King William II under the coat of arms of the Netherlands.

First Chamber

The First Chamber, which has 75 members, sits every Tuesday. Its function is to examine legislation passed by the Second Chamber.

The former ballroom (1790) in the south wing has been since 1815 (when the bicameral system was introduced at the Congress of Vienna) the meeting-place of the Second Chamber of Parliament. The interior furnishings have a rather old-world air. The velvet-covered stools date from the time when the chamber was used as a ballroom. The curious old-fashioned mechanism, by which questions and answers are passed in small metal containers between ministers on the floor of the house and their advisers in the gallery, by means of a kind of lift operated by attendants, has not been replaced by more modern methods of communication.

Second Chamber

Facing the high chair of the President is the table at which ministers sit, and in between are the official reporters, with three microphones to catch interruptions. There is a gallery for the public, another for invited guests and a third (along the side) for diplomats.

The Second Chamber is the legislative authority and watches over the activity of the government.

A new parliamentary building for the various parties is at present under construction. When it comes into use the Second Chamber will be brought into line with modern requirements.

There is an information centre at Binnenhof 8A. Open: Mon.–Sat. 10am–4pm; in July and August also Sun. 10am–4pm. Conducted tours of the Knights' Hall and Parliament can be arranged; they should be booked in advance by telephone.

In the entrance lobby below the Knights' Hall is an exhibition illustrating the history of the Dutch Parliament over more than 500 years, the functions of the two chambers and the role of the monarchy and the head of state with displays of historical documents and objects (admission free).

Exhibition

At the west end of the Binnenhof is the Buitenhof, with an equestrian statue of King William II (d. 1849).

231

The Hague ('s-Gravenhage/Den Haag)

Gevangenpoort

On the north side of the square (Buitenhof 33) stands the Gevangenpoort (Prison Gate), with a collection of medieval instruments of torture. Built in 1296 as the gatehouse of the Binnenhof, it was converted into a prison in the 15th century. Here the brothers Cornelis and Johan de Witt, accused of an attempt on the life of Prince William III, were murdered in 1672. In the square to the north is a monument to Jan de Witt. The old prison and torture chambers have been open to the public as a museum since the beginning of the 20th century, with a collection of pictures, prints and relics illustrating the administration of justice in the 17th century and the imprisonment of Cornelis de Witt. Open: April to September, Mon.–Fri. 10am–5pm, Sat. and Sun. 1–5pm; October to March, Mon.–Fri. 10am–5pm.

William V's
Picture Gallery

Beside the Gevangenpoort, at Buitenhof 35, is Prince William V's Picture Gallery (Schilderijenzaal), with an interesting collection of pictures which, in the manner of the time, are hung close together from floor to ceiling. Built by Prince William V in 1773 as a reception room, it was open to the public on certain days, and is thus the oldest museum in the Netherlands. It displays Dutch paintings of the 17th and 18th centuries which belonged to the Stadholder. Open: Tue.–Sun. 11am–4pm.

At the west end of the Buitenhof lies Gravenstraat. On the left is a shopping arcade built in 1885 on the model of the famous Galleria Emanuele II in Milan. On the right is an elegant shop, La Bonneterie, with a beautiful glass dome.

Oude Stadhuis

Gravenstraat joins the Dagelijkse Groenmarkt, in which stands the Old Town Hall, one of the earliest Renaissance buildings of any size in the northern provinces, built in 1564 on the model of Antwerp Town Hall. The newer part, in Louis XIV style, was built in 1734. The building was further extended in 1883; but thereafter it was decided that a new Town Hall was needed.

* Grote Kerk

To the west of the Town Hall, in Kerkplein, is the Grote Kerk or St Jacobskerk. The oldest part of this Gothic hall-church (14th c.) was badly damaged by fire in 1539. The 100m/330ft high tower, originally built in 1420, is unique in the Netherlands in its hexagonal form. Originally used for military purposes as a lookout tower, it was rebuilt in Renaissance style after a fire. A neo-Gothic spire was added in 1861, but this, popularly known to the people of The Hague as the "nightcap", was removed during restoration work in 1951. The carillon disappeared in 1941 during the German occupation. Since the largest bell, known as "Jhezus", was too big to fit into the tower it was kept in the church, where it can still be seen. In 1959 a new carillon – one of the largest in the Netherlands, with 51 bells – was installed. There are magnificent views from the top of the tower.

In the beautifully vaulted interior of the church, with its high, light choir, are a number of interesting monuments and grave-slabs, including those of the poet and statesman Constantijn Huygens (d. 1687) and his son, the physicist and astronomer Christiaan Huygens (d. 1695) on the rear wall of the choir. Other notable features are the carved wooden pulpit (1550), the coats of arms of Knights of the Golden Fleece, the large organ (1881) and the stained glass in the choir and north transept.

Most royal weddings and baptisms were held in the Grote Kerk. After complete renovation the church was reopened in 1987, and it is now, like so many other churches in the Netherlands, used for secular purposes – exhibitions, trade fairs and other functions. Open: Mon.–Sat. 10am–4pm.

Boterwaag

From the Grote Kerk Schoolstraat runs south to the Grote Markt. At the corner of Prinsegracht can be seen the Boterwaag (Butter Weigh-House, 1681), long a centre of Holland's prosperous butter and cheese trade. After many years of neglect the old building was restored in 1983 and now houses a charming little restaurant and a variety of cultural events (concerts, exhibitions, etc.). Open: daily 10am–4pm.

Farther south, at Paviljoensgracht 72–74, stands the Spinoza House, now a museum, in which the philosopher Baruch Spinoza (1632–77) lived from 1671 until his death and where he completed his "Ethics"; to see the house, make an appointment by telephone. Opposite is an attractive group of almshouses, the Heilige Geesthofje (1616). At the south end of Paviljoensgracht is a statue of Spinoza (1880).

Spinoza House

To the north of the Grote Kerk, at Molenstraat 38, is a "hidden church" – one of the Roman Catholic churches, with inconspicuous exteriors but richly furnished interiors, built during the period when Catholic worship was banned. Conducted visits Wed. at 1.30, 2.30 and 3.30pm.

"Hidden church"

Prinsestraat leads north to Prinsessewal and the Paleistuin (Palace Garden), the gardens, now open to the public, of the Noordeinde Palace. At the far end of Prinsessewal is Hogewal, in which are the Royal Stables (Koninklijke Stallen). In addition to the stables visitors can see numbers of horses and coaches (including a golden coach). Most of the building, however, is now occupied by a garage and workshops.

Paleistuin, Royal Stables

From this point the tour can be shortened by turning right along Noordeinde in the direction of the Buitenhof.

Anna Paulownastraat runs north into the Laan van Meerdervoort, at No. 7F of which is the Mesdag Museum (Rijksmuseum H. W. Mesdag), with a fine collection of paintings presented to the nation in 1903 by the painter Hendrik Willem Mesdag (1831–1915), consisting mainly of works of the French Barbizon School (Corot, Théodore Rousseau, Millet, Daubigny, Delacroix) – the most important collection of this school in the Netherlands – and the Hague School (Jacobus Maris, G. H. Breitner, Jozef Israëls). There is also a collection of porcelain from the Oud Rozenburg factory in The Hague. Open: Tue.–Sat. 10am–5pm, Sun. 1–5pm.

Mesdag Museum

Just north of the Mesdag Museum, in Carnegieplein, is the Peace Palace (Vredespaleis), an imposing brick building (1907–13), for the construction of which Andrew Carnegie, then the richest man in the world, donated 1½ million dollars. The style of the building is a mingling of Gothic and neoclassical. Flanking the long arcaded façade with its steeply pitched roof is an 80m/260ft high tower. Housed in the building are the International Court of Justice, the Permanent Court of Arbitration, the Academy of International Law and a library of international law which until 1955 was the best in the world. Countries from all over the world contributed to the rich decoration of the interior. The marble for the lobbies and the grand staircase came from Italy, the wood for the panelling from Brazil and the United States, the ornamental iron railings surrounding the grounds from Germany. The windows on the ground floor are of Delft lead glass and the walls are clad with Delft tiles. The accumulation of all these various elements, fine though they are in themselves, sometimes produces a rather eclectic effect, as in the monumental entrance, almost Byzantine in style, with its large gold chandeliers, marble floor in rosette patterns and white marble staircase. Open: Mon.–Fri. 10am–12 noon and 2–4pm.

*Peace Palace

Along the Laan van Meerdervoort to the east, on the right, is Zeestraat. At No. 82 of this street can be found the Postal Museum, which provides a comprehensive survey of the development of postal services and telecommunications in the Netherlands from the earliest letters to modern satellite communications. Among the exhibits are an old post office of 1928 with its sorting and bundling machines, a hand-operated telephone exchange of 1912, early telephones and modern subscriber-dialling and fax equipment. There are also a complete collection of the stamps of the

Postal Museum

The Hague ('s-Gravenhage/Den Haag)

The Peace Palace, seat of the International Court of Justice

Netherlands and the former Dutch colonies and a large and representative collection of stamps from other countries. Open: Mon.–Sat. 10am–5pm, Sun. 1–5pm.

Plein 1813

Near here is Plein 1813, in the centre of which stands a monument (by W. C. van Waaijen-Pietersen and Koelman, 1869) commemorating the recovery of Dutch independence in November 1813.

*Mesdag Panorama

At Zeestraat 65B is the Mesdag Panorama, the largest of its kind in the world. Housed in a rotunda, this gigantic picture, 120m/130yds long by 14m/45ft high, was painted by H. W. Mesdag and his wife Sientje Mesdag-Van Houten, together with G. H. Breitner, B. J. Blommers and Th. de Bock. It depicts Scheveningen as it was around 1880, with charming views of the sea, the beach and the dunes.

Panoramas, the "cinema of the 19th century", were the first optical medium designed to create an illusion of three-dimensional effect. The circular painting is indirectly lit from above, the light source remaining out of sight. Between the picture and the spectator is an intervening area – in this case dune sand – with real objects or mock-ups of real buildings to heighten the illusion, leaving the spectator with no point of reference in reality.

The production of panoramas was a costly business. The artists, directed by a team leader, copied on to canvas fixed to scaffolding the sketches which they had made in the field. The painting then travelled from town to town like a circus, often suffering damage in the process. The coming of photography, the cinema and illustrated magazines ended the era of the panorama, which had been a means of informing the public about great events such as battles and about distant lands. Only some twenty panoramas throughout the world have survived to the present day.

This panorama, one of the last survivors from the 19th century, is famed for its three-dimensional effect and is an outstanding example of the work of the Hague School. The building also contains a collection of pictures belonging to Mesdag and his wife and a historical survey of 19th century panoramas. Open: Mon.–Sat. 10am–5pm, Sun. 12 noon–5pm.

At Zeestraat 71 is the Royal Coin Cabinet, with a large collection of coins, medals and cameos.

Coin Cabinet

The line of Zeestraat is continued beyond the Hoge Wal by Noordeinde, which runs past the royal palace of Noordeinde (the Oude Hof). Originally built in 1533, the palace was rebuilt by Pieter Post and Jacob van Campen in 1640 and further altered by King William I in 1814. In 1948 much of the building was devastated by fire, and thereafter it was occupied for some years by an international institute. After thorough restoration in the seventies it is now the Queen's official residence, used for state receptions. In front of the palace are an equestrian statue of William the Silent (1845) and, a little apart, a statue of Queen Wilhelmina.
Opposite the palace is the rear front of the Council of State (Raad van State) building.

Noordeinde Palace

Beyond Noordeinde Palace Heulstraat (on left) leads into Kneuterdijk. In this street is the former royal palace of Kneuterdijk, which dates in its present form from the 18th century. Here Johan van Oldenbarnevelt, Grand Pensionary, spent the last years of his life.

Kneuterdijk Palace

Kneuterdijk continues south into the Lange Vijverberg, at No. 14 of which is the Costume Museum, displayed in rooms furnished in period style. From here there is a charming view of the Hofvijver, the picturesque old palace lake, with the long range of buildings of the Binnenhof reflected in its water.

Museum of Costume, *Hofvijver

At the east end of the lake (Vijverberg 7) is the Historical Museum of The Hague (Haags Historisch Museum), in the premises (completely restored)

Historical Museum

Noordeinde Palace

235

of the old marksmen's guild of St Sebastian, St Sebastiaansdoelen. The museum illustrates the history of the city from early times to the present day with a large collection of material, including old views, archaeological finds, group portraits of marksmen's guilds, coins and video shows. There are periodic special exhibitions on current topics concerning the city. The documentation and information centre is run by the municipal archives department. Open: Tue.–Sun. 12 noon–4pm.

**Mauritshuis

The Korte Vijverberg leads to the Mauritshuis, a handsome mansion standing to the east of the Binnenhof, between the Hofvijver and the Plein. In 1631 the cabbage-garden and oakwood adjoining the Binnenhof were sold to Johan Maurits van Nassau, former governor of Brazil, and Constantijn Huygens. Huygens, together with Jacob van Campen, then designed for Johan Maurits, following treatises by Italian architects, a monumental and elegant residence in strict classical style. The interior of the house, which was built between 1633 and 1634, was the work of Pieter Post, but it was completely destroyed by fire in 1704. Johan Maurits, an amateur of the arts who had brought back scholars and artists from Brazil, furnished his house with pictures and other objects relating to Brazil.

During the 18th century the Mauritshuis was used for a time as an embassy and then as a military school, its cellars for the storage of wine and as a prison for traitors. Later the royal library was moved to the Mauritshuis, and in 1822 the royal picture gallery. The idea of the old term "cabinet of art", a small room containing valuable objects, curios and pictures, is still reflected in the Koninklijk Kabinet van Schilderijen, the Royal Cabinet of Pictures, in the Mauritshuis: the collection is small, but of the highest quality.

During the French occupation 200 pictures were carried off to France, and only 120 of them were recovered in 1815. During the reign of William I, a great patron of art, the finest works purchased by the state came to The

Mauritshuis

Mauritshuis
The Hague

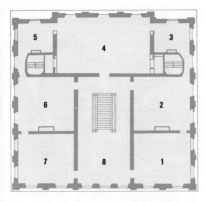

FIRST FLOOR
1 Vermeer Room
2 Steen Room
3 Early 17th century
4 Potter Room
5 Late 17th century
6 Rembrandt Room I
7 Rembrandt Room II
8 Staircase hall

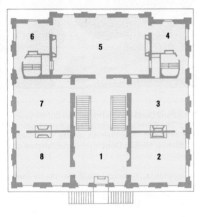

GROUND FLOOR
1 Entrance lobby
2 Van der Weyden
  Room
3 Bosschaert Room
4 Troost Room
5 Golden Hall
6 Holbein Room
7 Flemish Room I
8 Flemish Room II

© Baedeker

Hague – including Rembrandt's "Anatomy Lesson", Vermeer's "View of Delft", Jacob van Ruisdael's "View of Haarlem" and Rogier van der Weyden's "Lamentation", a masterpiece of medieval painting.

The Mauritshuis and many of its pictures underwent extensive restoration between 1982 and 1987, and its floor space was increased by 700 sq.m/7500 sq.ft by an underground extension, not visible from outside, containing a library, a study room and a store. During this period the gallery made numerous new acquisitions, including works by Art de Gelder, Jan Brueghel, Pieter Lastman, Cornelis van Poelenburgh, Salomon van Ruysdael and Jan Sanders van Hemessen. A striking feature of the Mauritshuis is the way in which a renowned collection of pictures is integrated into a historic palace and old and new works are brought into confrontation with one another: thus in the staircase hall the dynamic new ceiling painting by Ger Lataster, "Icarus Atlanticus", contrasts with the historical portraits, and a portrait of Queen Beatrix by Andy Warhol hangs opposite a bust of Prince Johan Maurits van Nassau.

This relatively small collection (to which there is an excellent illustrated guide) surpasses other galleries in the Netherlands by the high average

Rogier van der Weyden, "Lamentation"

level of its pictures. Among the early Dutch works Rogier van der Weyden's "Lamentation" is outstanding. The German school is represented, among other pictures, by three fine Holbeins. The Flemish artists represented include Rubens ("Portrait of Bishop Michiel Ophovius") and Antonie van Dyck.

The chief treasures of the Mauritshuis, however, are the works by Dutch 17th century masters. Frans Hals is represented by a number of brilliant portraits, Rembrandt by fifteen pictures, including the "Anatomy Lesson", "Simeon in the Temple", "Homer", "Saul and David" and three self-portraits, notably the "Self-Portrait in a Feather Hat" – a portrait of the type known as a *tronie* (i.e. depicting a particular human type).

"The Earthly Paradise" is an example of the collaboration between two painters which was common in the 17th century: the figure of Adam was painted by Rubens, while the idyllic setting, with the animals, was the work of Jan Brueghel the Elder.

Other important works are Karel Fabritius's "Goldfinch", three major paintings by Vermeer (the famous "View of Delft", the "Girl with a Pearl" and "Diana"), thirteen of Jan Steen's lively pictures, Paulus Potter's life-size "Bull" and smaller works by Gerard Dou, Gerard Terborch and Gabriel Metsu.

The Mauritshuis is open Tue.–Sat. 10am–5pm, Sun. 11am–5pm.

Plein

In the centre of the Plein, the square to the east of the Binnenhof, is a bronze statue of William the Silent. Until a few years ago the Ministry of the Interior, the Supreme Court (Hoge Raad) and the Ministry of Justice were on the west side of the square, the Ministry of Defence on the south side and the Foreign Ministry on the east side, but most of these have now moved to new premises. The buildings on the west side are being converted for use by members of Parliament.

From the north-east corner of the square Lange Voorhoutstraat leads north into Tournooiveld (on the right, at the near end of the Korte Voorhout, the Koninklijke Schouwburg or Theatre Royal) and the Lange Voorhout, which, with the Kneuterdijk, the Vijverberg and Willemspark, is the most fashionable part of the city.

Lange Voorhout

On the east side of the Lange Voorhout is a palace once occupied by Queen Emma the Queen Mother and now used by ex-Queen Juliana as an official residence for such functions as receiving foreign diplomats.

Royal Palace

Farther west, at No. 34, is the building now occupied by the Supreme Court (Hoge Raad). Built by Daniël Marot in 1734–36, it was occupied by King William I in 1813–14 while waiting for the completion of the Noordeinde Palace, and then until 1819 by his son. From 1819 it housed the Royal Library, which moved in 1982 to a modern building near the Central Station. The statues which stood on the steps of the old building can now be seen in its inner courtyard.

Hoge Raad

At No. 32A is the narrowest house in The Hague, only 1.5m/5ft wide. The 16th century Pagenhuis (Pages' House) at No. 6, originally the home of an armourer, was used from 1748 for the accommodation of Prince William IV's pages.

At the corner of Parkstraat stands the Kloosterkerk. Built about 1400, it is the city's oldest church. It originally belonged to a Dominican house which was demolished in 1583. Thereafter the church was the home for many years of the armourer from No. 6. Open: April to October, Mon.–Fri. 12 noon–2pm.

Kloosterkerk

Going north between the Royal Palace and the Hotel des Indes into Dennenweg and then turning right into Hooistraat and its continuation, Houtweg, we come to the Prinsessegracht. In Koningskade (Nos. 1–2), which runs parallel to Prinsessegracht on the east, is the modern Provinciehuis, the seat of the provincial government of Zuid-Holland.

Provinciehuis

To the north of the Provinciehuis Nassau-Dillenburgstraat 8 houses the Puppet Museum (Museum voor het Poppenspeel), with a collection of some 1000 dolls and puppets up to 200 years old. Since 1980 the museum has belonged to the Dutch Theatrical Institute in Amsterdam. Open: Sun. 12 noon–2pm. From October to June there are puppet shows on Sat. and Sun. at 2pm for children and Fri. at 8.30pm for adults.

Puppet Museum

Farther south, at Prinsessegracht 30, can be found the Rijksmuseum Meermanno-Westreenianum, housing a collection bequeathed to the state by Baron W. H. J. van Westreenen van Tiellandt (d. 1848). This is essentially a museum of the book, with 340 illuminated manuscripts and numbers of early printed books (e.g. Blaeu's Atlas), but the collection also includes ancient vases and sculpture and rarities from China and Japan – illustrating the range of interest of an early 19th century collector. There is also a section (established 1960) devoted to modern printing. Open: Mon.–Sat. 1–5pm.

Meermanno-Westreenianum Museum

Farther along Prinsessegracht in the direction of the Central Station are the Portuguese Jewish Synagogue, the Ministry of Finance and the Academy of Art (Academie van Beeldende Kunsten).

Near the station is the Royal Library, a massive modern building (completed 1982) housing one of the largest libraries in the Netherlands, with around 1½ million books and manuscripts.

Royal Library

Close by stands the National Literary Museum and Archive (Nederlands Letterkundig Museum), with a display of the works of 188 Dutch authors

Literary Museum

from 1750 to the present day, including Betje Wolff, Jan Wolkers, Herman Gorter, Willem Kloos, Menno ter Braak and Simon Vestdijk. In the museum archives articles, etc., about these authors can be consulted. Open: Tue.– Sat. 10am–5pm, Sun. 1–5pm.

Farther east is the new Foreign Ministry.

Commercial district

From the Academy of Art the Herengracht and Korte Poten run west to the Plein. Continuing west from the south-west corner of the square are the Lange Poten and Spuistraat, which with Grote Marktstraat to the south constitute the city's main commercial and shopping quarter.

Nieuwe Kerk

From the end of Lange Poten the Spui leads south to the Nieuwe Kerk (17th c.), in which the De Witt brothers and Spinoza are buried. Open: Wed. 1.30–3pm.

*Nederlands Dans Theater

Facing the Nieuwe Kerk, at the corner of Spui and Grote Marktstraat, is an unpretentious long, low building faced with white plaster slabs and black corrugated iron. The only eye-catching feature of this plain and functional building (by Rem Koolhaas, 1987) is the gold-coloured restaurant in the shape of an inverted cone. Together with the adjoining Dr Anton Philipszaal it provides a home – a need much felt for many years – for the Residence Orchestra (Residentie Orkest) and the Dance Theatre. Since both institutions are largely self-financing the building had to be as cheap as possible and strictly functional.
The foyer, however, is a delight to the eye, with its curving ramps and galleries suspended in the air on three levels against the dark red and golden colouring of the hall.

From the street intersection to the right Hofweg leads back to the Buitenhof.

Dance Theatre, with conical restaurant

Northern Districts

To the north of the Peace Palace is the modern residential district of Duinoord, a kind of garden city with houses built in a style influenced by the old Dutch almshouses (*hofjes*). On the edge of Zorgvliet Park, at Stadhouderslaan 41, is the Municipal Museum (Gemeentemuseum), designed by H. P. Berlage (1935). The museum displays a great range of material relating to the history of the town, 19th and 20th century art, applied and decorative art (ceramics, silver, furniture) and an outstanding collection of musical instruments both traditional and electronic.

*Municipal Museum

Of particular quality is the section of modern art (formed originally from two private collections), with numerous works by Piet Mondriaan and Paul Klee. Open: Tue.–Fri. 10am–5pm, Sat. and Sun. 12 noon–5pm.

A new wing of the same building contains the Museon, which illustrates in popular form the origins of the earth, the development of human life and culture and the achievements of science and technology, using accurate reproductions and models and audio-visual techniques. Visitors can also try their hand at operating computers and other technological apparatus. Many of the exhibits came from the old Museum of Education (Museum voor het Onderwijs). Open: Tue.–Fri. 10am–5pm, Sat., Sun. and public holidays 12 noon–5pm.

Museon

Behind the Museon is the Omniversum, a cinema with a huge screen (40 sq.m/430 sq.ft) in the dome which produces a realistic three-dimensional effect. Open: Tue.–Thur. 11am–4pm, Fri.–Sun. 11am–9pm.

Omniversum

On the other side of Johan de Wittlaan is Catshuis, the official residence of the prime minister, and north of this the Nederlands Congresgebouw (Congress Centre, 1969).

Catshuis, Congresgebouw

At Haringkade 175 can be found Madurodam. Opened in 1952, this miniature town was built at the expense of Mr and Mrs L. M. L. Maduro of Curaçao in memory of their son, who died in Dachau in 1945. Within an area no bigger than a football pitch is laid out a miniature Dutch landscape on a scale of 1:25 – the heart of an old medieval town with canals and gabled houses, churches, historic buildings, castles and palaces, a modern district, Schiphol Airport, factories, roads and a polder complete with windmills and cows (illustrated guide; café-restaurant).

Madurodam

After dark Madurodam is a fairytale-like spectacle (the *Lichtstad),* with its myriad lights in the buildings and streets. There is a *son et lumière* show, the "Madurodam Moonlight Miracle", with magical light effects and stories about life in Madurodam. Open: April and May 9am–10pm; June to August 9am–10.30pm; September 9am–9pm; October to March 9am–6pm. *Lichtstad:* May until 10.30pm; June–August until 11pm; September until 9.30pm.

*Haagse Bos

From the Korte Voorhout Leidsestraatweg goes east between the Malieveld and the Koekamp deer park to the Haagse Bos (Het Bos), a 2km/1¼ mile long expanse of wooded parkland, with beautiful avenues.

At the east end of the park, surrounded by a moat, is the Huis ten Bosch, built by Pieter Post in 1644–46 as a country residence for Amalia van Solms, wife of Stadholder Frederick Henry. The façade was rebuilt by Daniël Marot in 1734–37, and two wings were added in 1748. The first international peace conference met here in 1899. The house is now the residence of Queen Beatrix and her family.

Huis ten Bosch

A notable feature is the octagonal Orange Hall, the 15m/50ft high walls of which were entirely covered by the widowed Amalia van Solms between 1648 and 1653 with pictures in memory of her husband.

Madurodam: the Netherlands in miniature

Surroundings of The Hague

Voorschooten, *Kasteel Duivenvoorde	North-east of The Hague by way of Voorburg and Leidschendam we come to Voorschooten, a few kilometres beyond which a road (3km/2 miles) goes off to Kasteel Duivenvoorde, a medieval castle which was restored in 1631 by Johan van Wassenaer. The original decoration and furnishings have been preserved (family portraits, Delft ware, Chinese and European porcelain, silver). The English-style park is open throughout the year. Conducted visits May to September, Tue.–Sat. at 2 and 3.30pm.
Wassenaar	Beyond this lies Den Deijl, a suburb of Wassenaar (1km/¾ mile off the road to the left). This is an old-established residential district in modern Dutch style, surrounded by parks and woodland, with a Fire Service Museum (open once a week) and the popular leisure park and camping site of Duinrell.
Kijkduin	West of The Hague, on the North Sea coast, extends the new seaside resort of Kijkduin, with excellent bathing facilities.
Voorburg: Huygens Museum	In Voorburg (Westeinde 2) the Huygens Museum is housed in the home of the poet and statesman Constantijn Huygens (1596–1687). The house was built in 1639 to the design of Jacob van Campen, Pieter Post and Huygens himself. The museum contains mementoes and other material on the life and work of Huygens and his son Christiaan, the scientist and inventor of the pendulum clock. Open: Wed., Thur., Sat. and Sun. 2–5pm.
Scheveningen	See entry

Harderwijk

F 5

Province: Gelderland
Population: 34,000

The historic little fishing town of Harderwijk, on the Veluwemeer (IJssel-meer), received its municipal charter from Count Otto of Gelderland in 1231. Although frequently subject to flooding, it was a prosperous port on the Zuiderzee and a member of the Hanseatic League.

The town had a university founded in 1645 (dissolved by Napoleon in 1811), among whose students were the celebrated Dutch physician Herman Boerhaave (1668–1738) and the Swedish biologist Linnaeus (1707–78), who is commemorated by the Linnaeus Tower in the former university botanic garden.

During the 19th century Harderwijk was the port of embarkation for the Dutch Indian army, and officers and other ranks, adventurers and criminals from all over Europe flocked to Harderwijk to enlist. As a result the town became known as the "gutter of Europe".

The oldest part of the Grote Kerk (Reformed) is the 14th century choir. The original tower, 70m/230ft high, collapsed in 1797 and was replaced by a tower over the crossing, with a carillon. During the most recent restoration work fine wall paintings were brought to light.

Grote Kerk

The St Catharinakerk originally belonged to the convent of St Catherine, which after the Reformation housed the university. The church is now used for various cultural events.

St Catharinakerk

Harderwijk has preserved two of its 14th century town gates, the Vispoort (Fish Gate) and Smeeport (Smith's Gate). The town's business quarter later grew up around the Vispoort.

Town gates

The Town Hall (1727) has a handsome council chamber with leather-faced walls.

Town Hall

Vispoort, Harderwijk

Veluws Museum	The Veluws Museum at Donkerstraat 4 displays material on the history of the town and the Veluwe. Open: Mon.–Fri. 9am–5pm; May to September also Sat. 1–4pm.
Dolphinarium	On the Strandboulevard is a dolphinarium which has regular dolphin, sealion and killer whale shows. Open: from the beginning of March to the end of October.

Harlingen

E 2

Province: Friesland
Population: 34,000

Situation and characteristics	Harlingen (Frisian Harns), on the coast of the Wadden-zee opposite the West Frisian islands of Vlieland and Terschelling, was founded in 1243 near the site of the town of Greyn, which was engulfed by the sea in 1134. The harbour of Harlingen, which was formerly a considerable trading town, still exports Frisian products and imports coal, timber and other industrial raw materials. In the harbour area are shipyards, fish-processing plants, woodworking factories and works producing building materials. There are ferries to the islands of Vlieland and Terschelling. The harbour is linked with Leeuwarden by the Van Harinxma Canal.

Lion with town's coat of arms

Grote Kerk	The Grote or Nieuwe Kerk (Reformed) of 1775 occupies the highest point on the *terp* on which the town grew up. It is the successor to a 12th century church, of which there remains only the tower (heightened in the 15th century). Notable features of the interior are the magnificent organ (1776) and the pulpit.
Town Hall	The Town Hall (Raadhuis) at Noorderhaven 86 was built in 1736 by Hendrik Norel. The Council Chamber is particularly fine. The tower, with a figure of the Archangel Michael, the town's patron saint, is a reminder of Harlingen's former importance as a port. The Town Hall was completely restored in 1956.
Hannemahuis Museum	Hannemahuis Museum (Voorstraat 56), in one of Harlingen's many gabled houses, has a collection of valuable old silver and porcelain, pictures, tiles, old town plans and interesting ship models. Open: Tue.–Sat. 10am–5pm, before and after the main season 2–5pm.
Old houses	Around the Town Hall are other handsome patrician houses of the Late Gothic period, the Renaissance and the 17th–19th centuries, bearing witness to the town's one-time prosperity.
English Park	North-east of the town can be found the English Park, with remains of the town's old fortifications.
"Steenen Man"	On the Westerzeedijk, to the south of the town centre, is the "Steenen Man" (Stone Man), a monument erected in 1774 in honour of the Spanish stadholder Caspar de Robles, who had the dykes rebuilt after a violent storm tide in 1570.

Hasselt

G 4

Province: Overijssel
Population: 6800

The Hanseatic town of Hasselt, north of Zwolle, received its municipal charter in 1252. It was mainly of importance as a port for the shipment of Bentheim stone. — Situation and characteristics

The Vispoort (Fish Gate), of Bentheim stone, gives access to the quay. — Vispoort

The Grote Kerk or St Stephanuskerk, a Late Gothic hall-church, was built between 1380 and 1466. The spire was added in 1725. — Grote Kerk

The Late Gothic Town Hall (Stadhuis), with red and white dormer windows and a stepped gable, was built in 1500. The handsome Council Chamber has a collection of pictures and weapons. Open: Mon.–Fri. 10am–4pm. — Town Hall

Hattem   G 5

Province: Gelderland
Population: 12,000

The little town of Hattem, south of Zwolle, was fortified about 1400. One of the town gates, the Dijkpoort, has survived. The Fortuin windmill (1852) now houses a farming museum. — Situation and characteristics

The Town Hall (Raadhuis), in Renaissance style, was built in 1619 and has been several times restored. — Town Hall

The Dijkpoort, one of the old town gates, now houses a bakery museum. There is another bakery museum, Het Warme Land, at Kerkhofstraat 13. Open: May to September, Tue.–Sat. 9.30am–4pm; October to April, Wed. and Sat. 9.30am–4pm. — Dijkpoort

The Streekmuseum in Voermanhuis (Achterstraat 46–48) displays historical material from the surrounding area, together with drawings and paintings by Jan Voerman (landscapes) and Anton Pieck (an illustrator of fairytales and Christmas stories). Open: Tue.–Sat. 10am–4.30pm. — Streekmuseum

's-Heerenberg   G 7

Province: Gelderland
Population of Bergh commune: 17,500

The little town of 's-Heerenberg lies 30km/20 miles south-east of Arnhem, close to the German frontier. A trading settlement grew up here around the castle of the Counts van den Bergh. The town received its municipal charter in 1379. — Situation and characteristics

A round keep built here in the 12th century developed in the 15th century into a tower house, which was enlarged in the 17th century to become the family seat of the Counts van den Bergh. The house has suffered some damage over the centuries. Conducted tours: July to October, Mon.–Sun. at 2 and 3pm; March–June, November and December, Sat. and Sun. at 2 and 3pm. — Huis Bergh

Prominent landmarks in the town centre are the Late Gothic Town Hall (Stadhuis) with its octagonal tower (1580) and the restored Old Mint (Oude Grafelijke Munt), which dates from the 15th century. — Town Hall, Mint

The Gouden Handen leisure park at Emmerikseweg 13 is housed in the grounds of a former monastery. Open: April to October. — Gouden Handen

There is an interesting museum of spare-time art, evolution and extrasensory perception.

Huis Bergh, 's-Heerenberg

Bergher Bos

North of 's-Heerenberg in the hilly Montferland area, which rises to 93m/305ft, is the Bergher Bos, an expanse of mixed woodland which was originally a coniferous forest.

Heerlen

G 11

Province: Limburg
Population: 94,000

Situation and characteristics

Heerlen lies east of Maastricht, close to the German frontier. In the time of Augustus the site was occupied by a Roman trading station called Coriovallum, situated at the intersection of two military roads. The European edition of the "Wall Street Journal" is published here, as well as a number of Dutch periodicals.

Baths Museum

The Museum Thermen (Baths Museum) at Coriovallumstraat 9 displays the remains of Roman baths dating from the 1st century A.D. Open: Tue.–Fri. 10am–5pm, Sat. and Sun. 2–5pm.

St Pancratiuskerk

St Pancratiuskerk, a Romanesque pillared basilica, shows both 12th and 14th century work. Over the choir is the square Rogues' Tower (12th c.), a relic of the old stronghold of Herle.

Geological Museum

The Geological Museum at Voskuilenweg 131, run by the National Geological Service, has a large collection of fossils found in the mines of southern Limburg. Open: Mon.–Fri. 9am–12 noon and 2–4pm.

Castles in surrounding area

To the west of Heerlen is Voerendaal, around which were formerly numerous castles and country houses. Particularly notable is the 15th century Kasteel Cortenbach, which is still surrounded by its medieval moat.

Den Helder

Province: Noord-Holland
Population: 62,000

The port of Den Helder lies at the northern tip of Western Friesland, between the Waddenzee and the open North Sea, opposite the island of Texel. It is linked with Amsterdam by the North Holland Canal.

Situation and characteristics

Den Helder is noted both as the largest naval port in the Netherlands and as an important centre of the bulb trade. The town's principal sources of income are fishing and the textile industry.

Den Helder came into being about 1500, and until the end of the 18th century was no more than a fishing village. Then in 1811 it was strongly fortified by Napoleon, who saw it as the "Gibraltar of the North", and after his fall the Dutch government retained it as a fortress. After the construction of the North Sea Canal it lost much of its importance as an outer port for the Dutch capital to IJmuiden.

History

In 1673 Admiral de Ruyter defeated a combined British and French fleet off Den Helder. In 1799 a force of 10,000 British troops and 13,000 Russians commanded by the Duke of York landed just south of the town. The Russians were sent to take the French in the rear but lost their way in the dunes, and most of them were taken prisoner in the battle of Bergen. The British troops were defeated by General Brune in a skirmish at Castricum and forced to sail home.

The Town

A little way east of the town, beyond the North Holland Canal, is the harbour of Nieuwe Diep, which together with the naval arsenal, the dockyards and the Royal Naval College is known as Willemsoord. In the gardens of the Naval Institute are the mast of a gunboat blown up by Lieutenant van Speyk during the Belgian revolution (picture in Naval Museum) and four cannon from Admiral de Ruyter's flagship "Zeven Provinciën".

Harbour; Willemsoord

In Hoofdgracht is the Torentje Naval Museum, in a former explosives store of 1827. The museum, opened in 1966, documents the history of the Dutch navy from 1813 to the present day. Open: mid January to November, Tue.–Fri. 10am–5pm, Sat. and Sun. 1–4.30pm; June to August also Mon. 1–5pm.

Naval Museum

In Havenplein (Harbour Square; landing-stage for ferries to Texel) is a war memorial commemorating Dutch sailors who fell in the two world wars. Farther west stands a memorial to Dutch lifeboatmen lost at sea.

Memorials

At Keizerstraat 1A is the Reddingsmuseum Dorus Rijkers, a museum of the lifeboat service dedicated to a lifeboatman of that name. Open: Mon.–Sat. 10am–5pm, Sun. 1–5pm.

Reddingsmuseum

From the harbour a dyke entirely built of blocks of Norwegian granite and rising over 60m/200ft from the sea bottom runs out to the village of Huisduinen, with a 69m/226ft high lighthouse (Vuurtoren De Lange Jaap). The dyke, also known as the Zeepromenade because of its magnificent view of the Marsdiep and the island of Texel, shelters a 10km/6 mile long stretch of coast which is constantly threatened by storm tides.

Dyke; Huisduinen

From Huisduinen a bathing beach extends south along the North Sea coast. Inland is the Donkere Duinen nature park. To the south of Den Helder are the residential districts of Nieuw Den Helder and De Schooten.

Yacht harbour, Den Helder

Hellevoetsluis

C 7

	Province: Zuid-Holland Population: 33,000
Situation and characteristics	The old fortified town of Hellevoetsluis lies at the point where the Voornse-kanaal flows into the Haringvliet. Until the construction of the Nieuwe Waterweg the canal was Rotterdam's main link with the North Sea. Here the sailing ships of earlier days waited for a favourable wind which would allow them to put to sea. The harbour is now a water sports centre.
Town Hall	The present Town Hall (Raadhuis), was built by Pieter Post in the 17th century as the headquarters of the Admiralty.
Gesigt van 't Dok Museum	In the Gesigt van 't Dok Museum at Oostzanddijk 30 is an interesting model of Hellevoetsluis in the 19th century. Open: Tue.–Sun. 1–4pm.
Fire Service Museum	The National Fire Service Museum (Nationaal Brandweermuseum) at Industriehaven 8 has a collection of fire service equipment and vehicles since 1600, including the first fire pump, invented by Jan van der Heyden in 1675. Open: March to October, Mon.–Sat. 10am–4pm, Sun. 11am–4pm.
Rijdend Tramway Museum	The Rijdend Tramway Museum possesses an old tram which ran between Hellevoetsluis and Rotterdam until the 1960s.

Helmond

F 8/9

	Province: Noord-Brabant Population: 65,000

The industrial town of Helmond, to the east of Eindhoven, is the chief place in the moorland region known as the Peel (see Kempen). It first appears in the records in the 12th century.

Kasteel Helmond, at Kasteelplein 1, was built in the 15th century. Since being restored in 1923 it has housed the Town Hall and the Municipal Museum (Gemeentemuseum), which is devoted to the history of the town and the Peel region (archaeological finds). Open: Tue.–Fri. 10am–5pm, Sat. and Sun. 2–5pm.

Kasteel Helmond Municipal Museum

The Jan Visser Agricultural Museum at Keizerin Marialaan 5 contains a collection of old agricultural implements. An audio-visual show illustrates the life and work of the peasant farmers of the moorland regions. Open: April to September, Tue.–Fri. 10am–12 noon and 1–5pm, Sun. 1–5pm.

Agricultural Museum

The Communications Centre is an extraordinary structure built up from eighteen cubes, designed by Piet Blom, the architect responsible for the "cube houses" of Rotterdam (see entry).

Communications Centre

Hengelo

H/J 5/6

Province: Overijssel
Population: 77,000

The industrial town of Hengelo (electrical engineering, textiles) lies in the centre of the Twente region, near the German frontier. It originally became known for its linen-weaving, which was introduced by Wolter ten Cate, a native of Danzig.
During the Second World War the town centre suffered heavy damage, and now has many modern buildings.

Situation and characteristics

The architecture of the Town Hall (Stadhuis) is reminiscent of the Palazzo Vecchio in Florence. The 75m/245ft high tower has one of the largest carillons in the Netherlands (46 bells).

Town Hall

The old watermill, De Olde Moele, at Oele, to the south of Hengelo, dates from 1334 but was restored in 1690 after a fire.

Watermill

's-Hertogenbosch

E 8

Province: Noord-Brabant
Population: 90,000

The provincial capital of 's-Hertogenbosch (Den Bosch for short; in French Bois-le-Duc) lies at the confluence of the Dommel and the Aa and on the Zuid Willemsvaart in an area of flat pastureland, much of which is flooded every winter. It is a busy commercial town (important livestock markets), with a varied range of industry (cigar manufacture, foodstuffs, hardware, brewing, etc.).

Situation and *importance

's-Hertogenbosch takes its name from Duke (Hertog) Henry I of Brabant, who gave the town its municipal charter in 1185 in order to secure the northern borders of his duchy against Gelderland and Holland. Excellently situated from the point of view of transport, the fortified town soon developed into a busy trading centre. The situation changed, however, when the town was taken by the Spaniards in 1520. In 1559 's-Hertogenbosch became the see of a bishop. In 1629 the town was recovered by Frederick Henry, and thus became cut off from Brabant. In 1794 it was occupied by the French, but was liberated by the Prussians in 1814. The town's fortifications were razed to the ground in 1856.
's-Hertogenbosch was the birthplace of the celebrated painter Hieronymus (Jeroen) Bosch (1450–1516) and of Theodor van Thulden (1606–69), a friend and pupil of Rubens.

History

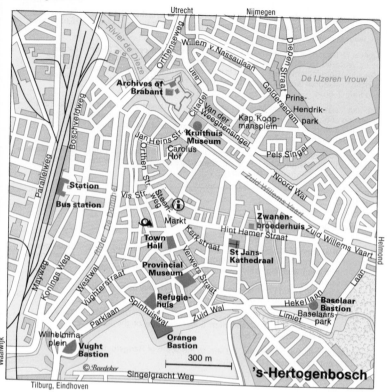

Utrecht   Nijmegen

's-Hertogenbosch

The Town

Markt

The central feature of the town centre, a triangular area between the Dommel and the Zuid Willemsvaart, is the Markt, which is also triangular. From this central point the town's three main streets (Hinthamerstraat, Vughterstraat and Hoge Steenweg) lead to the three angles of the triangle. The town's first circuit of walls enclosed this central area. The markets held twice weekly, on Wednesdays and Saturdays, recall the days when 's-Hertogenbosch was an important market centre for the agricultural region surrounding the town.

In front of the Town Hall is a bronze statue of the town's most famous citizen, Hieronymus Bosch.

De Moriaan

The oldest brick-built house in the town, De Moriaan (Markt 77), a fortress-like structure dating from the 13th century, was probably part of the town wall enclosing the market square. Restored between 1962 and 1966, it now houses the tourist information office (VVV). On the first floor is an exhibition of photographic reproductions of the works of Hieronymus Bosch: there are no originals of his paintings in his native town.

Town Hall

On the south side of the square (No. 1) stands the Town Hall (Stadhuis), originally Gothic but remodelled in Baroque style, with neo-classical features, in 1671. On the front gable is a handsome clock, incorporating mechanical figures representing a tournament between mounted knights which operate every half-hour. The tower (1650) has a carillon of 35 bells which rings every Wednesday between 10 and 11am. Notable features of the interior are the entrance hall, with wall paintings by the *fin de siècle* artist Antoon Derkinderen (1892 and 1897); tapestries by Max van den Gucht (17th c.) in the Council Chamber; and the Gothic vaulting in the cellar (1529; café-restaurant).

From the east side of the Markt either Hinthamerstraat or Kerkstraat will bring you to St Janskathedraal (R.C.), the finest medieval church in the Netherlands. Originally Romanesque (1280–1312), the church was given its present Gothic form between 1380 and 1530. It is 115m/377ft long by 62m/203ft wide, making it the largest church in the Netherlands. The choir was built in the early 15th century, the transept about 1450. The Romanesque tower has a Gothic spire. Work on the church was interrupted by the iconoclastic movement, so that its building was spread over a century and a half. Owing to shortage of money, however, it was left unfinished: some of the buttresses near the west doorway, for example, are not properly finished. In 1529 a wooden tower 85m/280ft high was built over the crossing, but this was destroyed by lightning in 1584 and was not rebuilt; it was replaced instead by a raised dome, on top of which is a large painted eye, a symbol of the Trinity. The outside of the choir is richly articulated by flying buttresses topped by small medieval figures: no other church in the Netherlands is so richly ornamented. Above the windows, all round the church, are reliefs of scenes from the early life of Christ. One of the builders left his own monument on the north side of the church – the "pease soup man", depicted overturning the pot of pease soup brought by his wife for his dinner. Other builders are known only from the masons' marks on columns. A curious feature, perhaps by another mason demonstrating his skill, is the twisted canopy at the east end of the nave, the tip of which is nevertheless directly over the saint's head.

St Janskathedraal

In the busy main square of 's-Hertogenbosch

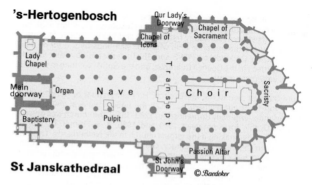

Round the choir is a ring of seven chapels (1480–96). Both the exterior and the interior of the church were richly decorated with medieval sculpture and stained glass. In spite of the destruction of images during the Reformation some remains of this work have been preserved, like the image (probably 13th century) of Zoete Lieve Vrouwe van Den Bosch (Our Sweet Lady of Den Bosch) in the Lady Chapel (1268).

On the columns in the nave and choir are numerous figures of saints. On the south doorway (St John's Doorway) are reliefs of scenes from the life of John the Baptist, and on the south side of the nave and aisles are figures of male saints; while on the north doorway (Doorway of Our Lady) are figures of Mary and the wise and foolish virgins, with figures of female saints on the north side of the nave and aisles.

*Pulpit

*Font

Among the treasures in the spacious interior of the Cathedral are the carved Renaissance pulpit by C. Bloemaert (1566–70) and the large organ (1617–35). Beside the organ is the baptistery, with a fine copper font by Aert van Tricht (1492). The font basin is decorated with figures of cripples waiting to receive the water of life.

By the baptistery is an image by Abraham Bloemaert of Christ and the Virgin interceding for mankind. At the top of the oak organ-case is a clock which displays a series of scenes from a roll of pictures, changing every minute.

*Choir-stalls

The choir has stalls of 1480 which rank as the finest of their kind in the Netherlands and a rear choir screen with carved wooden reliefs in High Renaissance style.

In the choir can be seen the tomb of Sir James Ferguson (d. 1705), commander of the Scottish Brigade under Marlborough.

In the ambulatory (on right) is a wall painting of 1444 and in the first chapel on the left is a 15th century winged altar.

The tower houses a carillon of 50 bells, which rings every Wednesday between 12 noon and 1pm. In summer the tower can be climbed.

The restoration of the Cathedral, which had been going on for some 125 years, was completed in 1985. During this work a number of new features were added, including the liturgical centre under the dome and concrete (rather than lead) settings for the stained glass windows on the south side.

On the south side of the Cathedral is the spacious Parade, with the Bishop's Palace. Behind the palace, in Korte Putstraat, is an old vinegar factory.

Zwanenbroeder-huis

To the north-east of the Cathedral, at Hinthamerstraat 94, is the Zwanenbroederhuis, a white building which is the headquarters of the Illustre Lieve

St Jan's Cathedral . . .

. . . with a richly decorated exterior

Font

Zwanenbroederhuis

Vrouwe Broederschap or Zwanenbroederschap (Illustrious Confraternity of Our Lady or Confraternity of Swans), said to have been founded in 1318. Although it was originally a Roman Catholic society, it began to admit Protestants (among them William I) after the Reformation.

The name Confraternity of Swans comes from the practice, dating back to the 14th century, of serving swans at an annual ceremonial banquet on the fourth Thursday in October. Since 1629 the confraternity has consisted of 36 members, 18 Catholics and 18 Protestants. The membership of this select club now includes five members of the royal family. Open: Fri. 11am–3pm.

Hinthamerstraat

In Hinthamerstraat (and in other streets in the town) are a number of old houses with fine gables. At Nos. 203–205 is the oldest psychiatric clinic in the Netherlands, founded in 1442. At the end of the street is a house with a handsome Gothic gable.

Provincial Museum

Since 1987 the Museum of North Brabant (Central Noordbrabants Museum) has been housed in the former Gouvernementshuis at Verwersstraat 41. This 18th century building in Louis XVI style was from 1820 the official residence of the governor of the town and from 1983 the residence of the Queen's Commissioner for the province. The original palace was extended by the addition of two wings. The Museum has collections of Roman, Germanic, Frankish and later antiquities, manuscripts, pictures, drawings, maps and coins of 's-Hertogenbosch and the province of Noord-Brabant. There is also a large library. Open: Tue.–Fri. 10am–5pm, Sat. 11am–5pm, Sun. 1–5pm.

Fortifications

There are some remains of the town's fortifications, like the Citadel (1639), with cannon pointing towards the town to assert the authority of the state over the citizens. Four of the original five bastions also survive.

The Citadel, restored between 1982 and 1985, now houses the provincial archives.

On the south side of the town is the Oranje (Orange) Bastion, with a cannon of 1511 known as Bose Griet, almost 6.5m/21ft long, with a bore of 17cm/6⅝in. The cannon was cast in Cologne and bears the legend "I protect 's-Hertogenbosch"; it proved, however, to be unfit for use.
Farther east is the Baselaar Bastion.

The Kruithuis (Powder Magazine) at Citadellaan 7 was built in 1618–21 for the storage of ammunition outside the town walls, but only a few years later, in 1629, was taken by Prince Frederick Henry because the defenders were short of ammunition. Its stout walls (1m/40in thick) now protect a museum of modern art. The inner courtyard has a handsome gabled façade. Open: Tue.–Sat. 11am–5pm, Sun. 1–5pm.

Kruithuis Museum

The Refugiehuis on the Spinhuiswal was built by the abbey of St Geertruid at Louvain in the early 16th century to provide a refuge for its monks within the town walls in the event of a siege.

Refugiehuis

In the south-east of the town, on the shores of the Zuiderplas, is the Provinciehuis, a tower block over 100m/330ft high which houses the offices of the provincial government. It contains a collection of modern art (tapestries, sculpture).

Provinciehuis

Surroundings of 's-Hertogenbosch

At Rosmalen, east of 's-Hertogenbosch, is the Autotron Automobile Museum, with some 250 veteran and vintage cars (Mercedes, Spijker, DAF, Bugatti and Peugeot). The museum is set in an amusement park where the attractions include a "traffic park" for children and the "House of the Future", which introduces visitors to possible developments in domestic amenities (e.g. a swimming pool with a glass roof which can be opened by a verbal command). Open: daily April to September 10am–5pm, in July and August to 6pm.

Rosmalen:
Autotron

North-west of 's-Hertogenbosch is the old fortified town of Heusden (pop. 5800), which with its ring of walls and canals was an important element in the defence of Holland between 1580 and 1620. Thereafter the town declined, and in 1913 the harbour was closed down. After restoration work in the 1960s, however, the old harbour is once again operational as a yacht harbour.
Features of interest are the three windmills on the town walls; the Italian-style Grote Kerk or St Catharijnekerk (13th c.); and the Gouverneurshuis at Putterstraat 4, now occupied by the Regional Museum, with a model of the town on the scale of 1:200, pictures and objects belonging to the old guilds, etc. (open: April to September 2–5pm).

Heusden

Hilversum

E 6

Province: Noord-Holland
Population: 85,000

Hilversum, situated in the beautiful Gooiland area in the extreme south-east of Noord-Holland and perhaps best known for its radio and television transmitter, is one of the attractive residential and satellite towns around Amsterdam, with many fine villas belonging to wealthy citizens of the capital, numerous modern buildings designed by famous architects and extensive parks and gardens. Industry (textiles, leather goods, electrical engineering, pharmaceuticals) plays a relatively minor role.
Hilversum, originally a poor Gooiland village, began to develop only after the construction of the Amsterdam–Amersfoort railway line in 1874.

Situation and
characteristics

The new Town Hall (Gemeentehuis) with its tall square tower, built in 1928–30 by the celebrated architect W. M. Dudok, is one of the finest

Town Hall

Town Hall, Hilversum

modern buildings in the Netherlands. The tower contains a carillon installed in 1958. There are a number of other buildings in the town (schools, etc.) in a similar style.

Broadcasting Museum

The Broadcasting Museum (Omroepmuseum) at Melkpad 34 displays a large collection of broadcasting equipment from the earliest days of radio in the 1920s and of television in the fifties to the present day. Open: Wed. 9.30am–5.30pm and on the last Sunday in the month from April to September 10am–5pm, October to March 12 noon–5pm.

Other sights

Other features of interest are the premises of the radio and television companies; the Gooiland Hotel; St Vituskerk (by P. J. H. Cuypers), with its 98m/322ft high tower; and the Noorderkerk. The old Town Hall on the Kerkbrink now houses the Gooiland Museum.

Surroundings of Hilversum

Round trip

For an attractive trip through the Gooiland area, the "garden of Amsterdam", take the road to Laren (5km/3 miles) and continue via Blaricum (7km/4½ miles), Huizen, on the Gooimeer (10km/6 miles) and Naarden (16km/10 miles: see entry) to Bussum (19km/12 miles), from which it is 27km/17 miles back to Hilversum.

Laren

Interesting features of Laren (pop. 12,000) are the artists' colony and the Singer Museum (Oude Drift 1), with a collection which includes modern pictures and sculpture and East Asian art (open: Tue.–Sat. 11am–5pm, Sun. 12 noon–5pm).

Loosdrecht

On the edge of the Gooiland area are the Loosdrechtse Plassen (Loosdrecht Lakes), with excellent facilities for water sports. In Nieuw Loosdrecht

(6km/4 miles south-west of Hilversum) rises Kasteel Sijpestein, rebuilt in the style of the 16th century, with a beautiful garden and a fine art collection. 7km/4½ miles west of Hilversum is Oud Loosdrecht.

There are a number of attractive villages along the river Vecht and the Amsterdam–Rhine Canal: Loenersloot, with a medieval castle which was rebuilt in the 19th century; Vreeland, with its historic old bascule bridge over the Vecht; and the pretty village of Loenen. There are many houses in this area built in the 17th century by wealthy Amsterdam merchants.

Loenersloot,
Vreeland,
Loenen

5km/3 miles north-west of Hilversum is the village of 's-Gravenland, which has a number of handsome buildings, including the 17th century house of Trompenburg.

's-Gravenland

Hindeloopen

E 3

Province: Friesland
Commune: Nyefurd
Population: 11,000

The little town of Hindeloopen on the IJsselmeer, originally a small settlement established in the 8th century, developed in the 14th century into an important trading town and fishing port which enjoyed a period of great prosperity in the 17th and 18th centuries. As a result of its international connections, which extended as far afield as Spitzbergen and the Dutch colonies, Hindeloopen began to differ from the rest of Friesland in its way of life and its language. Characteristic features of the town are its *commandeurshuizen* (sea-captains' houses) and wooden footbridges. It is famed for its painted furniture and its traditional costumes.

Situation and
characteristics

The church (Reformed) is a 17th century rebuilding of an earlier church which was again renovated in the 19th century. The square medieval tower was heightened in 1724 by the addition of a three-stage timber superstructure.

Church

Hindeloopen's *likhuzen* are the small houses in which seamen's wives spent the summer when their husbands were away at sea.

Likhuzen

The Sluishuis (Lock-House) of 1619 has a wooden tower with a 19th century bell. Behind the house is the Leugenbank ("Liars' Bench", 1785), on which the seamen used to sit and tell their tales.

Sluishuis

The Hidde Nijland Museum at Dijkweg 1–3 displays a collection of material of local interest – furniture, costumes, everyday objects, etc. Open: March to October, Mon.–Sat. 10am–5pm, Sun. 1.30–5pm.

Hidde Nijland
Museum

The Frisian Skate Museum (Fries Schaatsmuseum) at Kleine Weide 1 has a collection of skates and other items connected with the Eleven Cities Race (see Practical Information, Sport), which was last run in 1963. Open: March to October and in the Christmas holidays, Mon.–Sat. 10am–6pm, Sun. 1–5pm.

Skate Museum

Hoensbroek

G 11

Province: Limburg
Commune: Brunssum
Population: 30,000

The town of Hoensbroek lies north-east of Maastricht, close to the German frontier.

Situation

Holland

Kasteel Hoensbroek

Kasteel Hoensbroek was built around 1360, but of the original castle, which was destroyed by fire, there remains only a single round tower. The castle was reconstructed in its present form in 1643. It is built on three islands which are surrounded by canals and linked with one another by bridges.

Schutterij Museum

Archaeological Museum

In the castle (at Klinkertstraat 118) are two museums: the Schutterij Museum (Marksmen's Museum), with uniforms, flags, weapons and musical instruments belonging to the marksmen's guilds of the southern Netherlands, and the Archaeological Museum (prehistoric artefacts, including hand-axes). Open: May to September, daily 10am–5.30pm; October to April, daily 10am–12 noon and 1.30–5.30pm.

Holland

B–E 3–8

Situation and characteristics

The fenland region of Holland, in the north-west of the Netherlands, consists of the two provinces of Noord-Holland and Zuid-Holland (see entries). It is bounded on the south by the Haringvliet, the Hollands Diep and the river Merwede, on the west by the North Sea, on the north by the Waddenzee and on the east by the IJsselmeer and a line from Hilversum by way of Utrecht to Gorinchem. Holland, with dyked fenlands all lying below sea level, is sheltered from the North Sea by an almost uninterrupted belt of dunes.

Geology

The subsoil of Holland consists of layers of clay deposited by the North Sea as it slowly advanced from the Dogger Bank after the melting of the Ice Age glaciers, behind mighty coastal barriers of jetsam, rock detritus and sand thrown up by the tides. Later the clay strata were overlaid by great expanses of bogland and thick layers of peat were formed. These have been preserved, however, only in central Holland, since later advances by

Dutch landscape

the North Sea after the beginning of the Christian era covered the bogland in the far north and south of the region with a further layer of clay.

The lakes of central Holland came into being as a result of peat-cutting, which lowered the ground level, forming depressions which were quickly filled with water. Most of the lakes have since been drained and brought into cultivation.

The history of human settlement in Holland is closely bound up with the technique of dyke-building, which by the 12th and 13th centuries was sufficiently developed to convert the fens lying within the tidal area into habitable and fertile polders.

Draining of the fens

The draining of the fenlands which had sunk below sea level as a result of peat-cutting was a no less difficult task than the protection of the land from flooding. The lowering of the ground level was a gradual process over a long period of time, and at first all incoming water drained away at low tide. As the ground level continued to fall, however, it became necessary to pump the water out, with power provided by windmills.

In view of the scale of the work involved the larger lakes were drained only at a very late stage – the Beemster in 1612 and the Haarlemmermeer not until 1852. These areas are known as *droogmakerijen* ("drainage areas").

There is a striking difference in the pattern of settlement between the older fenlands and the more recent *droogmakerijen*. On the older polders the villages consist of a string of farmsteads flanking canals and watercourses, with their small fields extending at right angles to them, while the *droogmakerijen* are characterised by a scattered pattern of settlement, with isolated farmsteads rather than villages.

Types of settlement

The agricultural pattern is determined by the very different quality of the soil, depending on its age and origin. On the sandy soils within the coastal belt of dunes the main crops are vegetables, with bulb-growing in some areas. The old polders are mainly pastureland, with smaller areas devoted to market gardening and the growing of flowers and ornamental plants. Arable land predominates in the young polders (corn, potatoes, pulses and industrial plants), with a certain amount of pastoral farming.

Agriculture

Holland is the economic and cultural heartland of the Netherlands. This has brought about a tremendous concentration of industries of all kinds, combined with one of the highest population densities in the world. The larger towns such as Amsterdam, Rotterdam, Haarlem, Leiden, The Hague, Delft, Gouda, Utrecht and Hilversum combine with others to form a concentration of industry and population which is known as "Randstad Holland" (see Facts and Figures, Population and Economy).

Concentration of industry and population

Although, strictly speaking, the name of Holland should be applied only to the fenland regions described above, it is commonly applied to the whole of the Netherlands; and even the Netherlands Bureau of Tourism uses the emblem shown here, with two symbolic tulips.

Hoorn

E 4

Province: Noord-Holland
Population: 55,000

Hoorn lies in a bay on the IJsselmeer. Formerly the chief town of West Friesland, it is now an important market for livestock and cheese and the

Situation and characteristics

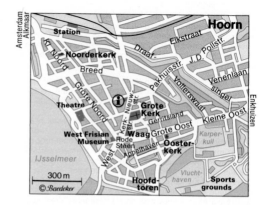

main centre of an extensive farming region. It has foodstuffs, metal-processing and woodworking industries; but tourism is now also making a significant contribution to the town's economy, for Hoorn has two yacht harbours and with its fine 17th century gabled houses it is a very attractive town.

*Townscape

History

Hoorn was founded in the 14th century as a trading settlement and received its municipal charter in 1356. Its heyday was in the 16th century, when it was the leading port in the Zuiderzee. In 1573 a naval battle took place off the coast here between a Spanish fleet and the combined fleets of Enkhuizen, Edam, Monnickendam and Hoorn, in which the Spanish admiral was taken prisoner. In the 17th century the town began to decline, and many merchants moved to Amsterdam. The construction of the Afsluitdijk (see entry) cut its harbour off from the open sea.

Hoorn was the birthplace of the navigator Willem Schouten (1580–1625), who in 1616 rounded the southern tip of America and gave the name of his home town to Cape Horn. Other natives of the town were Jan Pieterszoon Coen (1587–1629), who established Dutch colonial authority in the East Indies, and Abel Tasman (1603–59), discoverer of New Zealand and Tasmania.

The Town

Town Hall

The Town Hall (Stadhuis), in Nieuwstraat, was built in 1402 and originally housed the convent of St Cecilia. In the Council Chamber (1787), once the chapel of the convent, is a painting (by Blanderhoff, 1633) of the naval battle of 1573. In 1613 the façade of the convent was given a new gable and a double staircase. It became the Town Hall in 1796.

Grote Kerk,
St Jansgasthuis

At the end of Nieuwstraat, in Kerkplein, are the Grote Kerk (1883) and the former St Jansgasthuis (1563), with a façade in the style of the early Renaissance.

Rode Steen

From here Kerkstraat leads to the Rode Steen, a square in the centre of which is a statue of Jan Coen.

Weigh-House

In the Rode Steen is the old Weigh-House (Waag), built by Hendrick de Keyser in 1609. During restoration work in 1912 the original blue stonework was replaced by grey stone.

West Frisian
Museum

Opposite the Weigh-House is the Proostenhuis (1632), once the meeting-place of the Council of West Friesland, which is now occupied by the West

Hoofdtoren

Weigh-House

Frisian Museum (Westfries Museum). The Council (Gecommiteerde Raden van het Noorderkwartier) consisted of representatives (*kommitierten*) of the west Frisian towns of Alkmaar, Edam, Enkhuizen, Hoorn, Medemblik, Monnickendam and Purmerend.

The Proostenhuis has a richly decorated stone façade (rebuilt 1908–11) with the arms of the seven west Frisian towns, West Friesland and Orange. The museum displays a collection of material (16th–18th c.) on the history of the town and surrounding area, with numerous group portraits of marksmen's guilds. Open: Mon.–Fri. 11am–5pm, Sat. and Sun. 2–5pm.

Noorderkerk	North-west of the Rode Steen stands the Late Gothic Noorderkerk (1426–1519), which has an oak spiral staircase (1497), a fine choir screen (1642) and Renaissance choir-stalls.
Oosterkerk	In Grote Oost is the Oosterkerk, also Late Gothic (begun 1450), which is no longer used for worship. The choir and transept were built in 1519, and in 1615 the original two-aisled nave was replaced by a new aisleless nave with a fine Renaissance façade. From that period too date the wooden tower over the crossing and the stained glass (1620), depicting the naval battle of Gibraltar (1607) surmounted by the arms of West Friesland. There is a fine Bätz organ (1764). The church, recently restored, is now used for various cultural events.
Oosterpoort	Grote Oost leads into Kleine Oost, at the far end of which, off to the left, is the Oosterpoort, a relic of the old town walls.
Harbour	On the south side of the town lies the picturesque harbour, with the Hoofdtoren, a 16th–17th century tower, and the dyke (fine view of the IJsselmeer).
Other sights	There are numerous old house fronts of the 16th and 17th centuries, particularly in Grote Noord, Bierkade and Grote Oost. In Achterstraat are the St-Sebastiaans-Doelen (1615), the headquarters of the marksmen's guild of St Sebastian, and the Oude Vrouwenhuis (1610), which was an old ladies' home.

Near the Oosterpoort are the Bossuhuizen, painted with scenes depicting the naval battle of 1573 – of which the occupants of the houses no doubt had an excellent view.

Surroundings of Hoorn

To Enkhuizen	A trip to Enkhuizen (see entry) will take the visitor through the most prosperous part of Noord-Holland, where the farmhouses are like trim villas, usually surrounded by water-filled ditches and connected with the road by bridges.

There are three possible routes to Enkhuizen. The main road (18km/11 miles) goes through few places of any interest; there is an alternative road, of about the same length, which passes through the Streek villages of Westblokker, Oostblokker, Westwoud, Hoogkarspel, Grootebroek and Bovenkarspel; but the most rewarding route is the road along the dyke fronting the IJsselmeer.

To Medemblik	There are two routes to Medemblik – either the A 7 motorway, running in long straight stretches through fertile arable and pastureland, and a side road on the right (23km/14 miles), or via Enkhuizen and the coast road from there, which runs through the Andijk polder, a first experimental polder established at the beginning of the operation to drain the Zuiderzee.

Hulst

B 9

Province: Zeeland
Population: 19,000

The old fortified town of Hulst lies in Zeeuws-Vlaanderen (Zealand Flanders) to the south of the Westerschelde. Its medieval walls, which were strengthened in the 17th century, have a total circuit of 3.5km/2¼ miles. Three old town gates – the Gentse Poort (1780), the Dubbele Poort (1771) and the Bollewerckpoort (1506) – still give access to the town centre.

Situation and characteristics

The building of St Willibrorduskerk, a Late Gothic cruciform basilica, began in 1400. The choir was completed in 1460; the nave, which was damaged by fire in 1469, was completely restored only in 1562. In 1645 the church went over to the Reformed faith. Between 1806 and 1929 it was divided into two by a wall, the nave being occupied by the Protestants and the chancel by the Catholics. The wall was pulled down in 1929, and the whole church is now Roman Catholic. The tower was damaged in the Second World War and was restored with a concrete spire.

St Willibrorduskerk

The Town Hall (Stadhuis), with a façade of white dressed stone, was built by Keldermans in 1528–34.

Town Hall

At the Gentse Poort is a monument with scenes from the popular medieval tale "Reinaert de Vos" ("Reynard the Fox"), which is set partly in Hulst and the surrounding area.

Reinaert de Vos Monument

Surroundings of Hulst

North-east of Hulst lies the Verdronken Land van Saeftinge, the "Drowned Land of Saeftinge", an area engulfed by the sea 400 years ago which is now a nature reserve. It may be visited only on a conducted tour.

Verdronken Land van Saeftinge

Kampen

G 4/5

Province: Overijssel
Population: 33,000

The old Hanseatic town of Kampen is picturesquely situated on the left bank of the IJssel, 4km/2½ miles above its outflow into the IJsselmeer. It is the principal town and market centre of the surrounding agricultural area. It has an old-established theological college and a college of agriculture.

Situation and characteristics

The town's main source of income is industry – foodstuffs, shipbuilding, the manufacture of agricultural machinery and building materials, woodworking and the manufacture of cigars, as well as a few smaller industries. Tourism now also makes a contribution to the economy.

Kampen's main tourist attraction, apart from its yacht harbour, is the picturesque old part of the town.

Townscape

Kampen was founded in the second half of the 12th century and first appears in the records in 1227. It received its municipal charter in 1240, and became the most important commercial town in the eastern Netherlands, trading with the Baltic area, France and England. When the town acquired the fertile delta area at the mouth of the IJssel in 1363 it became so wealthy that right into the 20th century the inhabitants paid no local taxes. Its admission to the Hanseatic League in 1441 and its elevation to the status of free imperial city in 1495 gave a further boost to its economy, which suffered a setback in the 16th century when it came under Spanish rule (1578). Only the towns of Kampen, Zwolle and Deventer were represented in the provincial States.

History

The Town

Three of Kampen's 15th century town gates still survive: the rectangular Koornmarktspoort on the banks of the IJssel; the Broederpoort (1465;

Town gates

263

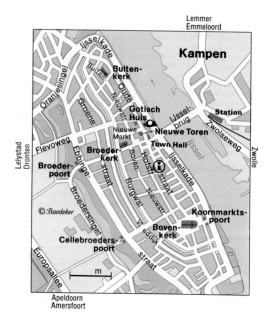

rebuilt in Renaissance style 1615), with four corner towers, on the west side of the old town; and the Cellebroederpoort (1465; rebuilt 1617) to the south, a rectangular structure with two round towers.
Farther south lies the municipal park.

*Town Hall

In Oude Straat is Kampen's finest building, the Town Hall (Stadhuis), with a richly decorated façade. Originally 14th century, it was rebuilt in 1543 after a fire. The badly weathered Late Gothic statues on the façade were replaced in 1933–38 by copies.
The most notable feature of the interior is the Schepenzaal (Magistrates' Hall), with heavy oak panelling, a Renaissance chimneypiece of 1545 and the carved oak stalls of the magistrates. The Town Hall also contains a number of pictures and a complete collection of portraits of the Princes of Orange, beginning with William I. The iron gate at the entrance to the tower was a trophy brought back to Kampen after the capture of Voorst Castle, near Zwolle, in 1362. Visitors are shown the Magistrates' Hall and the Orange Gallery. Open: Tue.–Thur. 11am–12 noon and 2–4pm; May to September also Sat. 1–5pm.

Nieuwe Toren

Immediately west of the Town Hall is the Nieuwe Toren or Heiligengeesttoren (New Tower, Tower of the Holy Ghost; 1649–64), built by Philip Vingboons, with a fine carillon by the Hemony brothers. In summer the tower can be climbed.

Broederkerk

From here Broederstraat runs west to the Broederkerk (1473–90), which originally belonged to a Minorite house, the Minderbroedersklooster. Between the two choirs is an attractive crow-stepped tower. The two aisles of this Gothic hall-church are separated by columns with beautiful leaf capitals.

Bovenkerk

On Muntplein, near the south end of the old town, stands the Bovenkerk (Upper Church or St Nicolaaskerk, a massive structure (14th–16th c.) with a spacious interior.

Nieuwe Toren, Kampen

Broederpoort

This Gothic cruciform basilica, with double aisles flanking the nave and a ring of chapels round the ambulatory, was begun about 1325, but building continued for over 200 years; the north and south doorways were completed in 1500, but the spire on the tower was not added until 1808.
Notable features of the interior are the magnificent Gothic choir, the choir screen (early Renaissance), the Late Gothic stone pulpit, the wall paintings and the Baroque organ (1670–76).

Buitenkerk	At the north end of the old town is the Buitenkerk or Onze Lieve Vrouwekerk (Outer Church, Church of Our Lady; R.C.). The original cruciform church (14th c.) was converted around 1450 into a hall-church (with aisles of the same height as the nave). Particularly impressive are the round columns with Brabantine leaf capitals and the octagonal sacristy – a feature unique in the Netherlands.
Tobacco Museum	The Tobacco Museum at Boterstraat 3 offers an informative survey of the history of tobacco and cigar manufacture. A particular attraction is the longest cigar in the world, manufactured in 1983, which features in the "Guinness Book of Records".
Walkate Archives	The Frans Walkate Archief (with library) at Burgwal 41, originally a private collection assembled by a banker named Frans Walkate, illustrates the history of the town and the province, with old maps, atlases and 19th and 20th century views of the town.

Katwijk   C 6

Province: Zuid-Holland
Population: 39,000

Situation and characteristics	North-east of Leiden, on the North Sea coast, is Katwijk aan Zee, a former fishing village and now a developing seaside resort, which has now joined up with Katwijk aan de Rijn, a little way inland. North of the town is a triple lock which is closed at high tide to prevent salt water from the North Sea entering the Oude Rijn.
Sights	In the Reformed church in Katwijk aan den Rijn can be seen the sumptuous marble tomb (on the north side of the choir) of Willem van Lyere (d. 1654) and Maria van Reygersberg (d. 1673), one of Rombout Verhulst's finest works.

The Reformed church in Katwijk aan Zee has an aisled nave of 1461 which was burned down during a Spanish attack and rebuilt in 1572 on a smaller scale (enlarged 1709).

From the lighthouse in Katwijk aan Zee there are magnificent views of the surrounding country.

Kaatsheuvel

See Tilburg

Kempen   E–G 9/10

Province: Noord-Brabant

Situation and characteristics	The historical region of Kempen occupies the southern part of the province of Noord-Brabant and extends south of Eindhoven far into northern Belgium. To the east it reaches as far as the Maas valley.

The surface topography of Kempen is very uniform. Most of it lies between 5m/15ft and 35m/115ft above sea level. The basement rocks are Cretaceous and Tertiary sediments, which are overlaid by Ice Age gravels and sands carried here by rivers of melt-water from the retreating glaciers. It is a typical area of sandy heathland (see Facts and Figures, Topography; A to Z, Noord-Brabant).

The infertile soil is suitable only for undemanding crops such as rye, oats, potatoes and fodder plants and thus limits the profitability of agriculture. | Agriculture

Until a few decades ago Kempen was a region of heathland and sand drifts with a sparse growth of pines, a few scattered villages subsisting on the poor soil and some small towns; and this is still the pattern in much of the region.

In recent years, however, the rapid advance of industry has brought about profound changes in this agricultural region. | Industrialisation
The origins of this industrial development go back 70 or 100 years. The main concentrations of industry are along the southern frontier of the Netherlands, e.g. at Eindhoven (Philips), Valkenswaard (tobacco industry, cigar manufacture) and Tilburg (textiles).

Kerkrade   G 11

Province: Limburg
Population: 53,000

The industrial town of Kerkrade lies near the German frontier, a few miles from Aachen. The coalmines which were originally opened up by the monks of Rolduc Abbey in 1742 were closed down in the 1960s. | Situation and characteristics

To the east of the town is the Augustinian abbey of Rolduc, founded in 1104, which is now the largest monastery in the Netherlands. Since the mid 19th century it has been occupied by a Roman Catholic seminary for the training of priests. Nothing remains of the medieval monastic buildings, but the 12th century church, a magnificent example of Romanesque architecture, has been preserved. | Rolduc Abbey

The oldest part of this aisled cruciform basilica is the trilobate (clover-shaped) crypt. The interior of the church, which had suffered much damage over the centuries, was restored by P. J. H. Cuypers from 1853 onwards. In the nave is the grave-slab of Duke Walram III of Limburg (d. 1226), who fought in the Third Crusade under Richard Coeur de Lion (1183) and was one of the ancestors of the house of Orange.

Part of the abbey is now occupied by the Mining Museum (Mijnmuseum), commemorating the 18th century mine which brought the abbey prosperity. Open: July and August, Tue.–Fri. 9am–5pm, Sat. and Sun. 1–5pm; September to June, Tue.–Fri. 9am–5pm, Sun. 1–5pm. | Mining Museum

Near Kerkrade are the beautifully situated Anstel reservoir and the Baalsburger- or Bolsbreuchermolen, a watermill rebuilt in 1743 following an older model. | Watermill

Kinderdijk   D 7

Province: Zuid-Holland
Commune: Nieuw Lekkerland
Population: 8600

Rolduc Abbey, the largest monastery in the Netherlands

Situation and
characteristics

Between Rotterdam and Dordrecht, on the river Noord, is the village of Kinderdijk ("Children's Dyke"). The name comes from a legend that during the St Elizabeth's Day flood in 1421 a child's cradle was stranded on the dyke.

**Windmills

The nineteen Kinderdijk windmills, ranging in date between 1722 and 1761, are the largest surviving concentration of windmills in the Netherlands.

The windmills, originally used to drain the fenlands, are now protected as national monuments. Their huge sails have a span of up to 28m/92ft. One of the mills is open to the public Monday–Saturday 9.30am–5.30pm from April to September, and in July and August seventeen of the mills are set in motion on Saturdays (*molendagen,* "mill days").

The mills of Kinderdijk

Kollum

Province: Friesland
Commune: Kollumerland
Population: 12,000

The village of Kollum lies in north-eastern Friesland. Its main features of interest are a number of handsome old houses in Oosterburgstraat and on the Westerdiepswal, the Empire-style Town Hall and above all the Gothic St Maartenskerk (15th c.), a brick-built church with a stone tower and spire (17th c.) and fine paintings on the vaulting.

Surroundings of Kollum

South-west of Kollum is the village of Veenklooster, with the country house of Fôgelsangh State (Kloosterweg 1), built in the 17th century on the site of a Premonstratensian monastery and enlarged in the 18th and 19th centuries. It is now an annexe of the Frisian Museum in Leeuwarden. The house, with the original decoration and furnishings, gives an impression of the life of a Frisian noble family in the 18th and 19th centuries. An old family coach is also on display. Open: May to September, Tue.–Sat. 10am–12 noon and 1–5pm; mid June to September also Sun. 1–5pm.

Veenklooster

Leerdam

Province: Zuid-Holland
Population: 19,000

At the eastern tip of the province of Zuid-Holland, on the river Linge, is the little town of Leerdam, the chief place in the Vijfherenlanden river country between the Rhine and the Waal. In the Middle Ages it was a place of some consequence, the residence of the Counts of Leerdam. It preserves remains of its town walls, including three tower houses on the old ramparts. In addition to its woodworking industry it has been known since the 18th century as a glass-making town. Its particular fame, however, rests on Leerdam cheese, which originally was produced only in the town.

Situation and characteristics

The Hofje van Aerden is a group of almshouses built by Mevrouw van Aerden in 1770 on the site of a castle belonging to the Van Arkel family.

Hofje van Aerden

Here women who had fallen into poverty were accommodated in large houses set round a beautiful courtyard. In a tall building with a domed roof opposite the main entrance is the Regents' Room, with old furniture and a number of paintings by Frans Hals, Gerard Terborch and Jacob van Ruisdael. Open: Tue. and Thur. 2–4pm. In the same building are the Council Chamber and Marriage Room of Leerdam.

National
Glass Museum

At Lingedijk 28 is the National Glass Museum, with a collection of glass from Roman times onwards. Many of the exhibits – which include some unique specimens – were made on Leerdam. Of particular interest are items designed by the well known architects De Bazel, Berlage and Frank Lloyd Wright. Open: Tue.–Fri. 10am–1pm and 2–5pm; April to October also Sat. and Sun. 1–5pm. By previous arrangement a conducted tour of the museum can be combined with a visit to the glass factory.

Church

The Late Gothic church (15th c.) has a Romanesque tower and reticulated vaulting in the choir.

Leeuwarden   F 2

Province: Friesland
Population: 85,000

Situation and
* importance

Leeuwarden, the old capital of Friesland, lies in fertile fenland country formed by the dyking of the Middelzee in the 18th century. It is the economic and cultural capital of Friesland, with various institutions and higher educational establishments. Its cattle market is the largest in the northern Netherlands. Its industrial activity centres on the foodstuffs industries, which process agricultural produce from an extensive surrounding area. The tourist trade also makes an important contribution to the economy.

History

Leeuwarden developed out of three *terp* settlements which merged in 1435 and were granted a municipal charter. Thereafter the town grew into an important trading centre. With the silting up of the Middelzee, however, the town lost its harbour and became instead an agricultural market town and the chief centre of the Ostergos region. From 1524 to 1580 the town was the seat of the Habsburg Stadholder, who was succeeded from 1584 to 1747 by Stadholders of the Nassau-Dietz family. In the 16th–18th centuries Leeuwarden was famed for its fine gold and silverware.

The notorious dancer and alleged spy Mata Hari (Margaretha Geertruida Zelle) was born in Leeuwarden in 1876. Suspected of espionage for Germany, she was executed by the French at Vincennes in 1917 (see Famous People).

The Town

Waagplein

In the south of the old town, star-shaped and enclosed by a ring of canals, is the Wirdumerdijk, a busy shopping street. At the north end of the street, to the left, is the Waagplein, a spacious square with a statue of a Frisian horse.

Weigh-House

In the centre of the square stands the Weigh-House (Waag; 1595–98), a handsome building in Renaissance style in which butter and cheese were sold until 1884. It is now occupied by a bank on the ground floor and a restaurant on the upper floor.

Exchange

At the east end of Willemskade is the Exchange (Beurs), built around 1880 by the city architect, T. Romein, as a replacement for the Weigh-House. It now houses the Municipal Library.

Law Courts

To the west of the Wirdumerdijk is Wilhelminaplein, the most prominent building in which is the classical-style Paleis van Justitie (Law Courts;

1846–52), with an imposing doorway flanked by columns. The building houses both the provincial and the cantonal court.

From the Waagplein St Jacobsstraat runs north to the Hofplein. The most striking building in this square is the whitewashed Hof, which from 1587 was the residence of the Stadholder and later of the Queen's Commissioner. When it was no longer required by the Commissioner it was taken over by the municipality.

Het Hof

Facing the Hof, in Raadhuisplein, is the Town Hall (Stadhuis), a Baroque building erected in 1715 on the foundations of an older house. A new wing was built around 1760. The domed bell-turret over the triangular pediment contains a carillon of 39 bells which rings every Friday between 10 and 11am.
Curiously, the town's coat of arms on the façade wrongly shows the lion with its tail turned inward instead of outward.

Town Hall

In front of the Town Hall can be seen a monument to Count Willem Lodewijk of Nassau-Dietz (d. 1620), Stadholder of Friesland.

To the north of the Town Hall, at Beijerstraat 12 (corner of Grote Kerkstraat), is the family home of the notorious Mata Hari, now occupied by the Frisian

Museum of Literature

271

Leeuwarden

Waagplein, with the Weigh-House

Museum of Literature and Documentation Centre (Fries Letterkundig Museum en Documentatiecentrum), open: Mon.–Fri. 9am–12.30pm and 1.30–5pm.

Coulonhûs

From here Grote Kerkstraat runs west into Doelestraat, with the Coulonhûs (No. 8), an early 18th century patrician house now occupied by the Frisian Academy, which is concerned with the study of Frisian culture.

Princessehof: Municipal Museum

A fine classical-style mansion at Grote Kerkstraat 15, the Princessehof (17th–18th c.), houses the Municipal Museum. The house was once occupied by Princess Maria Louise, Landgravine of Hesse-Kassel (1688–1765), widow of Stadholder Johan Willem Friso.

The museum occupies Nos. 9–15 in Grote Kerkstraat, which include a former wine-store and a mansion of the 15th–16th centuries (Papingstins, No. 13), with a restored onion-domed tower.

The nucleus of the museum was a collection assembled by a local lawyer named Nanne Ottema (1874–1944), a connoisseur of Chinese porcelain. It includes a varied range of ceramics in different styles and techniques, including porcelain from East Asia, Korea and Japan, tiles from Japan, China and South-East Asia, Art Nouveau work (Rozenburg eggshell porcelain) and examples by contemporary potters. Open: Mon.–Sat. 10am–5pm, Sun. 2–5pm.

Oldehove Toren

At the west end of Grote Kerkstraat lies the Oldehoofster Kerkhof, on the west side of which is the Oldehove Toren, an unfinished church tower. From the top of this 40m/130ft high brick tower (1595–98), which is slightly off the vertical, there are extensive views. The church to which the tower belonged was left unfinished because of the subsidence of the ground. Open: May 18th to October 1st, Tue.–Sat. 9.30am–12.30pm and 1.30–4.30pm, or by appointment.

Princessehof (Municipal Museum)

On the north side of the square (Boterhoek) is the new Provincial Library, whose books came from the Franeker Academy and the Buma Library. Adjoining is the Friesland Records Office.

Provincial Library

To the north of Beijerstraat, reached by way of Perkstraat, is the Jacobijne-kerkhof; at No. 7 is the Boshuizen Gasthuis (1652), with two doorways.

Boshuizen Gasthuis

Also in Jacobijnekerkhof is the Grote Kerk or Jacobijnekerk (Reformed), which was given its present form in the 15th century.
It was originally the church of a 13th century Dominican monastery. After the Reformation the choir became the burial-place of the Frisian branch of the Nassau family, whose names and coats of arms can be seen on the walls. The choir was damaged during the French occupation and restored only in 1948.
On the south side of the choir is the Oranjepoortje (1663).
In the verger's house are remains of a 15th century groin-vaulted cloister.

Jacobijnekerk

From the Waagplein Peperstraat and Oude Oosterstraat lead east to the Tweebaksmarkt. At No. 52 is the Provinciehuis, the seat of the provincial government, which from the 16th century was the meeting-place of the States of Friesland. The present façade dates from 1784.

Provinciehuis

Near the Provinciehuis, at Turfmarkt 13, is the Kanselarij (Chancellery), one of Leeuwarden's finest buildings. Built in 1566–71, it shows a mingling of Late Gothic and Renaissance. On the gable can be seen a statue of the Emperor Charles V.

Kanselarij

Opposite the Kanselarij, at Turfmarkt 24, is the Frisian Museum (Fries Museum), in an 18th century patrician house. The most important provincial museum in the Netherlands, it is devoted to the history of Frisian

Frisian Museum

Oldehove Tower (unfinished)

culture from prehistoric times to the 19th century. Its rich collections include Frisian silversmiths' work of the 17th and 18th centuries, ceramics
from Hindeloopen and Makkum, Frisian costumes, drawings and the
"Popta silver" from Popta Slot, Marssum (see below).

Outstanding among the pictures is Rembrandt's portrait of Saskia van
Uylenburgh, painted before his marriage in St Annaparochie (see below).
The museum is open: Tue.–Sat. 10am–5pm, Sun. 1–5pm.

St Bonifatiuskerk   North of the Turfmarkt by way of the Tuinen is the Voorstreek, in which is St
Bonifatiuskerk, a neo-Gothic church built by P. J. H. Cuypers in 1882–84.
The spire, destroyed in a storm in 1976, was rebuilt in 1980.

Surroundings of Leeuwarden

Marssum;   5km/3 miles west of Leeuwarden is the beautifully situated village of Mars-
Heringa State   sum, with the manor-house of Heringa State (Slotlaene 1). The house was
built in the first half of the 16th century by the Heringa family, and was
bought in 1687 by a prosperous lawyer named Henricus Popta (d. 1712):
hence its alternative name of Popta Slot.

The "Popta silver" to be seen in the Frisian Museum in Leeuwarden was
commissioned by Popta.

The house, which has been well restored, is set in a beautiful garden on the
banks of a canal and is abundantly equipped with turrets and gables. The
interior, with its original decoration, old furniture and Frisian silver, is open
to the public. Conducted tours: April to September, Mon.–Fri. at 11am and
2 and 3pm.

St Annaparochie   15km/9 miles north-west of Leeuwarden is the village of St Annaparochie,
in the fertile Bildt polder. This was brought into cultivation by Dutch settlers

in the 16th century, and the language of the local people is still Dutch, not Frisian. Rembrandt was married to Saskia van Uylenburgh in the parish church in 1634.

10km/6 miles north-east of Leeuwarden, at Oenkerk, is the manor-house of Stania State, now housing an agricultural museum, an outstation of the Frisian Museum in Leeuwarden.

Oenkerk

From Leeuwarden there are canals (navigable by vessels of up to 1350 tons) to Harlingen on the Waddenzee and Lemmer on the IJsselmeer. The towns of the western Netherlands – important markets for Frisian agricultural produce – are thus easily accessible. Leeuwarden is also linked with Groningen by a canal.

Canals

Leiden

C/D 6

Province: Zuid-Holland
Population: 108,000

The university town of Leiden (English form Leyden), one of the oldest and most picturesque towns in the Netherlands, lies in Zuid-Holland on the Oude Rijn (Old Rhine), which flows quietly through the town like a canal.

Situation and
*importance

Leiden lies in an extensive flower-growing and market gardening area, the produce of which is marketed in the town and surrounding area and to a considerable extent processed in factories in the town.
More important than the foodstuffs industries, however, are metalworking, engineering and Leiden's world-famed printing industry. The town's textile industry, once so important, is now represented only by a few spinning and weaving mills and finishing factories.

Leiden is one of the leading cultural centres in the Netherlands. In addition to the University with its library of over 1½ million volumes there are a number of other research institutions in the town, including the Rijksherbarium with its collections of dried plants, the Dutch Literature Society and the Royal Institute of Linguistics, Regional Studies and Ethnology (Koninklijk Instituut voor Taal-, Land- en Volkenkunde). Here too is published the "Dictionary of the Dutch Language".

**Leiden, a great
cultural centre

There are also a number of important museums in the town, including the National Museum of Antiquities (Rijksmuseum van Oudheiden) and the National Museum of Ethnology (Rijksmuseum van Volkenkunde).

There was a settlement here in ancient times, known to the Romans as Lugdunum Batavorum. In the 11th century the Counts of Holland built a castle (De Burcht) on a mound at the confluence of the Old and the New Rhine, with a church inside the castle precincts. The only relic of this early period is the Gravensteen, a 13th century stronghold which for many years was a state prison.
The medieval settlement of Leythen was granted a municipal charter in 1266 and developed during the 14th and 15th centuries into the principal centre of the Dutch weaving industry. Thereafter, however, the production of cloth declined sharply as a result of frequent floods and epidemics.

History

In the 16th century Leiden became known for the successful defence of the town against a Spanish besieging force (1573–74), when William the Silent ordered the dykes of southern Holland to be breached.
Tradition has it that the citizens of Leiden, offered the choice between four years' exemption from taxation or the foundation of a university as a reward for their sturdy defence of the town, chose the university. However this may be, the University of Leiden was founded in 1575 and soon rose to European reputation.

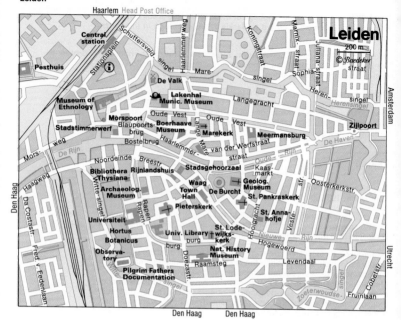

The greatest scholars of their day studied and taught at Leiden University, including the classical scholar Joseph Justus Scaliger (d. 1609), the great international lawyer Hugo Grotius (d. 1645), the mathematician and physicist Christiaan Huygens, the French philosopher René Descartes and the 18th century physician Herman Boerhaave, who established the reputation of Leiden's medical school.

The fame of the University promoted the prosperity of the town, which attracted thousands of refugees, driven out of their own country for their faith, to come to Leiden. As a result the population soon passed the 100,000 mark. During the 17th century, however, outbreaks of plague reduced the population to less than 30,000, and it became necessary to build hospitals and old people's homes. Characteristic features of Leiden are its thirty-five *hofjes,* groups of between ten and thirty almhouses for old people, most of them privately run.
After a long period of decline and poverty the town's economy began to revive in the 19th century with the development of modern industry and commerce, and the population of Leiden has now risen above 100,000 again.

Leiden was the birthplace of many 16th and 17th century painters, including Lucas van Leyden, Rembrandt, Jan Steen, Gerard Dou, Gabriel Metsu, Jan van Goyen, Frans van Mieris and the elder and younger Willem de Velde.

The Town

In addition to its two old churches, its university and its museums Leiden has numerous other features of interest. They are described here in the form of a tour of the town, starting from one of its thirteen museums, the Windmill Museum near the Central Station.

The Windmill Museum lies south-east of the Central Station, with several car parks in the immediate vicinity. It is housed in a seven-storey stone flour-mill of 1743 (De Valk, the "Falcon"), standing on higher ground, which originally formed part of the town's fortifications. In the early 17th century there were nineteen windmills on the town walls (and there are still thirty within the city limits). After restoration in 1964 the mill (including the dwelling-house of the last miller) was opened to the public as a museum. Open: Tue.–Sat. 10am–5pm, Sun. 1–5pm.

Windmill Museum

South of the Windmill Museum by way of the Nieuwe Beestenmarkt and the Turfmarktsbrug (bridge) is the Turfmarkt. To the right is the Blauwspoortsbrug, which until 1610 served as a town gate at the north-west corner of the walls.

Blauwspoortsbrug

At the end of Morsstraat stands the handsome Morspoort (with drawbridge), one of the two surviving fortified town gates of 1669 built by Willem van der Helm. To the left of the gate, on the site of the old Morspoort barracks, is a windmill (De Put), built here in 1987 on the model of an old mill of 1640.

Morspoort

De Put windmill

On the other side of the Rhine (here known as the Galgewater, "Gallows Water"), on the left, is the Stadstimmerwerf, the workshops (1612) of the municipal carpenters. On the right is the Weddesteeg, with a tablet marking the site of Rembrandt's birthplace. At the end of the street is Noordeinde, which leads to the Witte Singel, with a bronze bust of Rembrandt.

Stadstimmerwerf

Here too are the new University Library and the Faculty of Letters. The library is one of the oldest and largest in the Netherlands, with some 1½ million volumes and 20,000 manuscripts.

University Library

View of Leiden, with the Valk windmill

Leiden

Loridanshofje

In the Oude Varkensmarkt, which opens off Noordeinde, is the Pieter Loridanshofje (No. 1), founded in 1655 by a wealthy wool-dyer named Pieter Loridan. Occupied for many years by refugees from Belgium and France, it has been renovated and now provides lodgings for students.

Wagenmakers-museum

Farther along is the Wagenmakersmuseum (Coachbuilders' Museum), housed in the workshops where the last coachbuilder in Leiden was working around 1917. Open: Sun. 1–5pm.

Doelenkaserne

Beyond this is the Groenhazengracht, on the opposite side of which is a doorway (1645) with a figure of St Joris (George) and the dragon. This is the entrance to the old Doelenkaserne (barracks) and Arsenal. The whole complex is now occupied by the University.

Rapenburggracht

At the end of the Groenhazengracht, on the right, is the Rapenburggracht, one of the oldest and largest in the Netherlands, often claimed to be the finest *gracht* in Europe.

Bibliotheca Thysiana

At Rapenburg 8 is the Bibliotheca Thysiana, an important library housed in a handsome building erected by the city architect, Arent van 's Gravenzande, in 1655. The house at No. 31 was occupied by the famous 18th century physician Herman Boerhaave.

*Museum of Antiquities

On the opposite side of the *gracht* (Rapenburg 28) stands the National Museum of Antiquities (Rijksmuseum van Oudheiden), founded in 1818, which has a rich collection of Greek, Etruscan and Roman sculpture, ancient vases and small objects, Egyptian antiquities and prehistoric and Roman material, mainly from the Netherlands.

In the courtyard of the museum is the Nubian temple of Taffah, presented to the Netherlands by President Sadat of Egypt in 1979 in gratitude for Dutch help in saving monuments threatened by the construction of the Aswan High Dam on the Nile.

The museum is open Tue.–Sat. 10am–5pm, Sun. 12 noon–5pm.

Hoogeveenhofje

In Doelensteeg, a side street opening off the Rapenburggracht, is the 17th century Eva van Hoogeveenhofje (No. 7), perhaps the finest of Leiden's *hofjes,* with an attractive façade, patterned brick paving and an old water-pump. Visitors can see the Regents' Room (side entrance on the Doelengracht).

Academiegebouw

On the left bank of the broad Rapenburggracht, a little to the east of St Pieterskerk, is the Academiegebouw, the main building of the University (over 15,000 students). The faculties of medicine and science have been world-famed for centuries. The Rector's Office has been housed since 1581 in the former chapel of a convent of the White Sisters.

The Akademisch Historisch Museum at Rapenburg 73 is devoted to the history of the University. Open: Wed.–Fri. 1–5pm.

*Hortus Botanicus

Beyond the University is the University Botanic Garden, the Academietuin or Hortus Botanicus, which was originally laid out in 1590 and is still a popular resort for the people of Leiden as well as for students. From here Nonnensteeg leads to the Binnenvestgracht, with the Clusiustuin, a reconstruction of the first systematically arranged botanical garden, which originally lay immediately behind the University building. On the other side of the *gracht* can be seen the Hortus Botanicus, with the old Observatory (Sterrenwacht) to the south of it. Open: Mon.–Sat. 9am–5pm, Sun. 10am–5pm; October to March closed Sat.

Pilgrim Fathers Documentation Centre

From here Boisotkade leads to the Municipal Archives and the Pilgrim Fathers Documentation Centre (Documentatie Centrum) at Vliet 45. The "Mayflower" 's voyage to America started from the Vliet. Open: Mon.–Fri. 9.30am–4.30pm.

Archaeological Museum

Farther west, in Doezastraat (entrance in Raamsteeg), can be found the Natural History Museum (Rijksmuseum van Natuurlijke Historie; open only to scholars and students with the permission of the museum authorities). It is particularly rich in the fauna of the former Dutch colonies and is also notable for the fine collection of birds assembled by the leading Dutch ornithologist C. J. Temminck (d. 1858) and a richly stocked department of comparative anatomy.

Natural History Museum

*Bird collection

Behind the Museum lies the small Van der Werf Park, with a monument commemorating Van der Werf, burgomaster of Leiden at the time of the Spanish siege. The park was laid out in an area devastated by the explosion in 1807 of an ammunition ship which, contrary to regulations, had been moored in the centre of the town. On the east side of the park is the Institute of Geology.

Van der Werf Park

On the far side of the Nieuwsteegbrug (bridge) is the Nieuwsteeg, with some of the more modern buildings of the University. Among distinguished scholars who worked here were the physicists Professor H. A. Lorenz (1853–1928; Nobel Prize 1903) and Professor H. Kamerlingh Onnes (1853–1926; Nobel Prize 1913). Lorenz, founder of the theory of electrons, prepared the way for Einstein's theory of relativity. Kamerlingh Onnes succeeded in liquefying helium, producing the lowest temperatures so far recorded, and discovered the superconductivity of metals.

Modern University buildings

From here it is a short distance by way of the Pieterskerkhof to Kloksteeg; at No. 21 is the Jean Pesijnshofje, founded in 1683 by Jean Pesijn. The site had previously been occupied by the Groene Poort or Engelse Poort (Green Gate, English Gate), in which John Robinson, pastor of the Pilgrim Fathers, lived until his death in 1625.

Jean Pesijnshofje

A little way west of the Town Hall is the old St Pieterskerk, in which the liberation of Leiden from Spanish rule is celebrated every year on October

*St Pieterskerk

University Botanic Garden

3rd. The foundations of this Late Gothic cruciform basilica date from 1121, when Leiden's first church was built on this site. At the beginning of the 13th century the building of a new and larger church was begun by Rutger van Kampen. The choir was completed in 1339, the nave with its double aisles later in the 14th century. In 1412 the choir was enlarged by the addition of an ambulatory. At the west end of the nave was a 110m/360ft high tower, which collapsed in 1512 and was not rebuilt. The timber barrel-vaulting extends to the west front, built on to which is a small porch-like structure with a pitched roof.

The church contains the monuments of various university professors; in one of the side chapels is buried John Robinson, who in 1611 founded the first congregation of Independents (Puritans driven out of England) in Leiden; a small monument commemorates Herman Boerhaave; and the painter Jan Steen is also buried in the church. The Late Gothic carved wooden altar dates from the first half of the 16th century. The organ was built about 1640.

As the congregation of the church (Reformed) dwindled and lacked the resources to carry out necessary renovation it was taken over by a private foundation and made available for various public purposes (University and school examinations, trade fairs, exhibitions, etc.). Open: daily 1.30–4pm.

Gravensteen

Diagonally opposite the church is the neo-classical façade of the Gravensteen, a stronghold of the Counts of Holland which in 1463 became a state prison and is now occupied by the University's faculty of law. The oldest part of the building is the two towers, which date from the 13th century, when the Gravenhof, the palace occupied by the Counts of Holland during their visits to Leiden, lay close by. The present façade was built in the 17th century, when the Gravensteen was enlarged. The last execution of a murderer took place in 1853 in the square in front of the building.

Morspoort

St Pieterskerk

At the corner of Lokhorstraat and Schoolstraat is the Latin School (Latijnse School), built in 1599, with a striking stepped gable and red and white window shutters. The school's most celebrated pupil was Rembrandt (between 1614 and 1620).

Latin School

Close by, on the left, is the Pieterskerkgracht; at No. 9 (restored) are the headquarters of Ars Aemula Naturae, a painting and drawing society.

From here Diefsteeg leads to Breestraat, Leiden's principal shopping street, which with its continuations Noordeinde to the west and Hogewoerd to the east traverses the town in a wide S-shaped curve. It is lined with handsome gabled houses in Dutch Renaissance and Baroque style.

Breestraat

At Breestraat 59 is the Rijnlandshuis (Gemeenlandshuis van het Hoogheemraadschap van Rijnland), headquarters of the Rhineland Dyke Administration. The original building of around 1600 was much altered in later centuries. Its most notable feature is the Courtroom by Pieter Post (second half of 17th c.), with painted timber barrel-vaulting.

Rijnlandshuis

On the opposite side of the street are the Municipal Concert Hall (Stadsgehoorzaal) and the Waalse Kerk (Walloon Church; No. 64), which was formerly the chapel of St Catherine's Hospital. Originally Late Gothic, it was enlarged in 1634, and in 1739 was given a new façade with a Baroque tower. To the right can be seen part of the old hospital.

Waalse Kerk

Mandenmakersstraat leads to the Aalmarkt, in which is the municipal Weigh-House (Waag), built by Pieter Post in 1658. The gable is decorated with sculpture by Rombout Verhulst. The Weigh-House is now used for exhibitions.

Weigh-House

From the Visbrug Maarsmansteeg runs south-west to Breestraat. At the intersection with Pieterskerkkoorsteeg and Meermansteeg, set in the paving, is a large hexagonal blue stone, the Blauwe Steen, which in 1321

Blauwe Steen

marked the central point in the town. Here in the Middle Ages criminals condemned to death by the municipal council were executed (those condemned by the Count being executed in front of the Gravensteen), and here too cloth found to be of poor quality was burned.

Town Hall

Near the south end of Breestraat stands the Town Hall (Stadhuis), which has occupied this site since the Middle Ages. In 1597 the old Gothic gable was replaced by a Renaissance façade designed by Lieven de Key. In February 1929 the Town Hall was destroyed by fire, leaving only the façade still standing, though in a badly damaged condition. During the rebuilding the façade and the handsome flight of steps leading up to the entrance were restored. To the left of the steps is the Roepstoel, the town crier's platform, from which Jan Hout, clerk of the municipal council, announced the flight of the Spaniards and the end of the siege on October 3rd 1574. The tower (with carillon) was also rebuilt after the fire.

Behind the Town Hall is the Vismarkt (Fish Market). It has a fountain with square slabs of hard stone on which the fish were cleaned. Beyond this is the Korenbeursbrug; its original name was Korenbrug (Corn Bridge), but since in earlier times corn was bought and sold here the citizens of Leiden call it the Korenbeursbrug (Corn Exchange Bridge). The bridge was roofed in 1825.

De Burcht

From here the Burgsteeg leads to the Burcht (Castle), which is entered through a gateway displaying the figure of a lion with the town's coat of arms. About 1150 a 12m/40ft high mound of sand was built up here, at the confluence of the Old and the New Rhine, to provide a refuge from flooding; and additional protection was provided by a circuit of walls 35m/38yds in diameter, two canals, one at the foot of the hill and one rather farther away (the Hooglandse Kerkgracht, now filled in) and later a sentry-walk round the walls. A keep was planned but was never built.
In the 17th century a tower was built bearing the arms of the burgomasters, who between 1651 and 1764 were also burgraves (governors of the castle). During the most recent restoration work the original gateway of the castle on the opposite side from the present entrance, which had long been walled up, was reopened. From the castle there are fine panoramic views of the surrounding area.

From the Burcht Nieuwstraat runs south-east. In this street is the former Heereslogement (1652; beautiful inner courtyard, garden, gallery on upper floor), now occupied by the Municipal Library.

Hooglandse Kerk
(St Pancraskerk)

Farther south is the beautiful Hooglandse or St Pancraskerk. The first church on the site, timber-built (1315), was replaced in 1377 by a stone church, which between the 14th and the 16th century, when the heyday of Catholicism in the town was over, was several times altered but never completed. There is a story that the building workers found that they could earn more elsewhere and stopped work on the church. As a result the nave is considerably lower than the transept and the choir.
The low tower (1400) at the west end of the nave was left unchanged. The west aisle was built after the Reformation; the timber vaulting of the choir and transepts dates from the 19th century. Under the crossing, in the spacious interior, is the tomb of Burgomaster Van der Werf (d. 1604), defender of the town during the 1574 siege. In the choir can be seen the double tomb of Admiral Justinus van Nassau (d. 1630) and his wife.

St Annahofje

Nieuwstraat runs into the Hooigracht, at No. 9 of which is the St Annahofje or Aalmoeshuis (1492–1507), a beautiful group of almshouses, with a chapel containing the only altar left unscathed during the iconoclastic fury of 1566.

Schachtenhofje

On the other side of the *gracht* (No. 27) is the Schachtenhofje (1671), with a restored gatehouse. In the courtyard is a pump of 1730 which dispenses both rainwater and ground-water.

De Burcht

At Hooglandse Kerkgracht 17 the National Museum of Geology and Mineralogy (Rijl smuseum van Geologie en Mineralogie) has a rich collection of
material, some of it from the former Dutch colonies. The three-gabled
building, with a beautiful inner courtyard, was originally occupied by the
Vrouwengasthuis (Women's Hospice) and from 1583 by the Poorhouse and
Orphanage (Armen-, Wees- en Kinderhuis). Open: Mon.–Fri. 10am–5pm,
Sun. 2–5pm.

Museum of
Geology and
Mineralogy

North of the Museum the Kerkbrug, a 19th century cast-iron bascule bridge,
crosses the Oude Rijn. Just beyond this is Haarlemmerstraat, which runs
east and leads alongside the picturesque harbour to the second of the two
surviving town gates, the Zijlpoort (1667). The other gates were pulled
down in the 19th century.

Zijlpoort

From the Havenplein the Oude Vest, lined with typical Dutch house-fronts,
runs west. As its name indicates (*vest* = "rampart"), this was part of the
town's fortifications between 1355 and 1610. When the town expanded this
stretch of wall was demolished and a new town wall built farther out, on the
line of the Maresingel and Herensingel.

Oude Vest

At Oude Vest 159 is the Meermansburg (1683), Leiden's largest group of
almshouses (30 in number), built by Maarten Ruyckhaver Meerman, a
member of the board of the East India Company. In the handsome Regents'
Room, the office of the manager of the almshouses, are an interesting
collection of old portraits and a clay pipe museum (Pijpenkabinet).

Meermansburg

Farther west, in Lange Mare (a former *gracht*, now filled in), stands the
Marekerk, built between 1638 and 1648 by the city architect, Arent van 's
Gravenzande. This was the first church built for the Reformed faith.
The church, on an octagonal ground-plan, has a narrower upper part
topped by a dome. It has a fine pulpit of 1647 and an organ of 1733 which

Marekerk

283

One of Leiden's many grachten

was originally in St Pieterskerk. The sandstone doorway was the work of Jacob van Campen (1669).

Farther along the Oude Vest is the Municipal Theatre (Schouwburg). Beyond this is Vrouwenkerkstraat, leading into the district known as De Camp, in which there were a number of religious houses in the Middle Ages, as some of the street names still testify.

Boerhaave Zalen

On the right are the Boerhaave Zalen (Boerhaave Rooms), originally a monastery built at the end of the 16th century, which later became a hospital for plague victims and the mentally ill. Since the 18th century physician Boerhaave taught here, it is regarded as Leiden's first university teaching hospital.

St Elisabeths-gasthuis

At the corner of Caeciliastraat and Lijsbethsteeg is the St Elisabeths-gasthuis, a hospice built in 1428 by Jan Dirk Coenen. From 1773 until 1970, when it was restored, it served as an almshouse and later as an old people's home.

Boerhaave Museum

Near here, at Agnietenstraat 10, the Boerhaave Museum on the history of science and medicine was reopened in new premises in 1991; the original museum at Steenstraat 1A had been closed for some years. The collection includes many pieces of apparatus (including microscopes) developed in the University for the purposes of scientific research and used by physicists such as Kamerlingh Onnes, Zeeman, Snellius and van 's-Gravenzande. There are also many exhibits associated with such great names of the past as Christiaan Huygens, Leeuwenhoek and Boerhaave. Open: Tue.–Sat. 10am–5pm, Sun. 1–5pm.

Lakenhal Municipal Museum

On the north side of the Oude Vest, at Oude Singel 32, is the Municipal Museum, housed in the Lakenhal (Cloth Hall) built in 1638–40 and used for its original purpose until 1800, when it was converted into offices. In 1874,

Schouwburg (Municipal Theatre)

after restoration, it was opened as a museum. It has a collection of pictures which includes works by such leading 16th and 17th century artists as Gerard Dou, Jan van Goyen, Lucas van Leyden, Rembrandt and Jan Steen and a collection of applied and decorative art. Open: Tue.–Sat. 10am–5pm, Sun. 1–5pm.

Near the Valk windmill, at Steenstraat 1, is the National Museum of Ethnology (Rijksmuseum voor Volkenkunde), the oldest of its kind in Europe. Founded in 1837, it was housed in a number of separate buildings all over the town until 1937, when it found a new home in the former University Hospital. Its extensive collections come from all over the world, particularly from Indonesia and Japan. The first Japanese items were collected by F. van Siebold, a doctor who lived and worked in Japan from 1823 to 1829. Open: Tue.–Sat. 10am–5pm, Sun. 1–5pm.

Museum of Ethnology

Farther west is the Pesthuis, built in 1658 to house plague victims. Until a few years ago it was occupied by the Army Museum, the collection of which has now been transferred to Delft. It is planned to instal a new natural history museum in the building, which was restored in 1989.

Pesthuis

Surroundings of Leiden

There is an attractive boat trip on the Kager Plassen (Lakes) to Schiphol (daily departures from mid June to end August; there and back in 7½ hours): by way of Leiderdorp and De Zijl to the Kager Plassen (water sports

Kager Plassen

centre), then on the Braassemer Meer and through Aalsmeer to Schiphol, and from there back to Leiden.

In summer there are also boat trips daily between 2 and 6pm to the Kager Plassen and Braassemer Meer.

Rijnsburg

The second most important flower auction in the Netherlands (after the one at Aalsmeer) is held in the village of Rijnsburg, to the west of Leiden. At Laan van Verhof 1 is a nursery which seeks to develop new varieties.

Baruch Spinoza (see Famous People) lived in Rijnsburg from 1861 to 1863, and the Spinozahuis at Spinozalaan 29 has a collection of letters, documents and mementoes of the philosopher. Open: Mon.–Fri. 10am–12 noon and 2–4pm, Sun. 2–4pm.

Zoeterwoude, Koudekerk

Leave Leiden on the road to Alphen aan den Rijn, which runs along the Levendaal and then keeps close to the left bank of the Oude Rijn, along which are long straggling villages with brickworks, old fishermen's houses and windmills. 3km/2 miles from Leiden is Leiderdorp. In another 2km/1¼ miles we reach Zoeterwoude-Rijndijk, with the large Heineken brewery, and 3km/2 miles beyond this the old mill in which Rembrandt's father lived.

Lelystad

See Flevoland

Limburg
E–G 9–11

Provincial capital: Maastricht
Area: 220,851 hectares/545,502 acres
(land area 216,952 hectares/535,871 acres)
Population: 1,100,000

Situation and history

The former County (and later Duchy) of Limburg, to the east of the Maas, was declared by the Congress of Vienna in 1815 to be a province of the kingdom of the United Netherlands, which included the northern provinces of the Netherlands, Belgium and the old diocese of Liège. In 1830, however, economic and linguistic differences between the two parts of the country led to a rising of the southern provinces against the northern ones, from which the southern provinces emerged as the independent state of Belgium; and in 1839 Limburg was divided into a northern and a southern half, belonging respectively to the Netherlands and Belgium. Limburg remained a duchy until 1903, and this is perhaps why the Queen's Commissioner for Limburg is still called Governor and the arms of Limburg province incorporate those of the duchies of Gelderland and Limburg.

South Limburg

Limburg is the most southerly of the Dutch provinces. In South Limburg (Zuid-Limburg), at Vaals, is the Drielandenpunt ("Three Countries Point") where the frontiers of the Netherlands, Belgium and Germany meet.

South Limburg is a plateau ranging in height between 50m/165ft and 300m/1000ft which is built up from Cretaceous limestones, Tertiary sands and massive layers of gravel, overlaid by a fertile layer of loess laid down during the Ice Age. The various tributaries of the Maas dissect the region into a number of different parts. The chalky soil has produced a landscape of great beauty, popularly known as "Little Switzerland".

North Limburg

Farther up the Maas is North Limburg (Noord-Limburg), much of which is flat and featureless, traversed by rivers and canals and dotted with large farms. The Maas, with its characteristic landscape patterned by hedges,

The rolling landscape of Limburg

divides the region into two – to the east a long tract of territory along the German frontier, to the west the Peel country in Noord-Brabant (see entry), with large areas of bogland. In the extreme north-east steep hills – the most southerly hills in the Netherlands, which came into being during the Ice Age – rise out of the Maas valley.

Apart from the towns Limburg is still largely an agricultural province, though since the end of the 19th century industry has come to play a predominant role in the economy. Typical of the region are large scattered villages made up of small and medium-sized farm holdings. Outside the villages there are many larger farms of 50–100 hectares/125–250 acres.

Agriculture

The principal crops are wheat and sugar-beet, with some fruit and dairy farming. North Limburg is an area of arable farming and market gardening (particularly asparagus), as well as mushroom-growing. There are also nurseries growing flowers and vegetables.

The economic structure of the South Limburg industrial region, around the towns of Maastricht, Sittard, Geleen, Heerlen and Kerkrade, was almost exclusively based on coal and lignite mining, but the last of its twelve pits – one of them the largest in Europe – was closed down in 1975. Annual output declined rapidly from some 10 million tons in 1966 to 4.3 million tons in 1970; and now coal must be imported into the region.

Economy

The closing of the pits was accompanied by a planned restructuring of the coal-related industries of the region. One of the best known examples was the establishment of a branch factory of the Dutch car manufacturing firm DAF (now Volvo), which provided employment for much of the work force of the Maurits pit (opened 1924) at Geleen. At Geleen, too, the huge chemical firm DSM became one of the largest employers in South Limburg. Other branches of industry are textiles, papermaking, ceramics, leather goods and glassmaking. Maastricht Airport, near Beek, is now an important centre of air freight traffic.

In spite of the development of industry, however, unemployment has continued to grow.

The main industrial centres in North Limburg are Venlo, Roermond and the smaller towns of Weert and Venray. Venlo has become an important centre of the transport industry, with some thousand transport firms in and around the town. Tegelen, south of Venlo, is a centre of the ceramic industry, with a Pottery Museum.

Tourism

A major tourist and holiday centre is the little town of Valkenburg (see entry), dominated by the ruins of its 13th century castle, which has an underground Mining Museum in a disused pit. There is also a Mining Museum in Rolduc Abbey (founded 1104) at Kerkrade (see entry). At Heerlen (see entry) is the Museum Thermen, with the remains of Roman baths.

River Maas

D–G 7–11

Provinces of Limburg and Noord-Brabant

Course

The Maas (in French Meuse) rises on the Langres plateau in France at a height of 456m/1496ft above sea level and flows through French territory for 450km/280 miles and through Belgium for 192km/119 miles before reaching the Netherlands. For part of its course between Liège and Maastricht it forms the frontier between Belgium and the Netherlands. South of Nijmegen it turns west and flows parallel with the Waal, the southern arm of the Rhine – sometimes linking up with it – for 260km/160 miles before reaching the Biesbosch (see entry) in the delta area and flowing into the Hollands Diep.

Navigability

Plans were developed from an early stage for improving the navigability of the Maas throughout the year. In 1904 it was diverted from Woudrichem (see Gorinchem) to Geertruidenberg (see entry), where the water level at ebb tide was lower. Various bends were straightened and considerable stretches of the river were canalised. The Julianakanaal, a lateral canal between Maastricht and Maasbracht opened in 1935, has been of great benefit to the Limburg industrial region; it lies higher than the surrounding country and gives the impression that ships on the canal are sailing on land.

Maastricht

F 11

Province: Limburg
Population: 116,000

Situation and
**importance

Maastricht, capital of the province of Limburg, lying on both banks of the Maas, has many attractions to offer visitors, especially historic buildings and art treasures. It owes its present importance to its strategic situation in the Dutch-Belgian-German frontier region between the industrial areas of Aachen, Liège, Kempen and Limburg: a factor which has become of increasing importance since the establishment of the European Community.

In addition to its cultural functions, reflected in its numerous educational establishments, Maastricht is a major commercial centre, the chief town in an extensive surrounding area reaching across the Dutch frontier into Belgium. Its wholesale markets, particularly in vegetables and butter, are attracting increasing numbers of foreign buyers. Industry also plays a

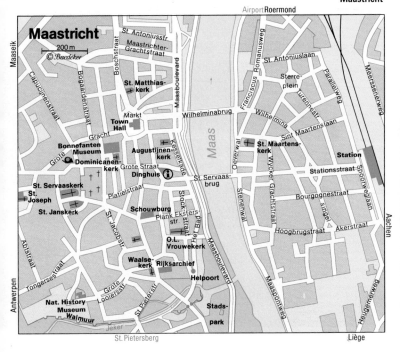

considerable part in the town's economy, the most important branches apart from the giant DSM (Dutch State Mines) chemical works being paper-making, leather-working, brewing, printing, ceramics, cement and glass. The tourist trade also makes a significant contribution to the economy.

The Roman settlement of Traiectum ad Mosam or Traiectum Tungrorum, situated – as the name indicates – at an important crossing-point on the Maas where two military roads met, was founded about 50 B.C., and is thus one of the oldest towns in the Netherlands.

History

The town was fortified in the 3rd century A.D., and in 382 the episcopal see of Tongeren (Tongres) was transferred to Maastricht, which occupied a central situation in the kingdom of the Merovingians and Carolingians. In 722, however, the see was moved from Maastricht to Liège. Around 1202 the town passed into the hands of the Dukes of Brabant, who ruled it, along with the Prince-Bishops of Liège, until the end of the 18th century. In the 14th century the town was surrounded by fortifications, which in later centuries were regularly strengthened.

The bridge over the Maas made Maastricht a place of strategic importance from the earliest times, and over the centuries it withstood more than twenty sieges. From 1621 it was one of the most important fortresses during the Dutch struggle with the Spaniards. The establishment of the kingdom of Belgium in 1830 considerably hampered its economic development, since it was now cut off from much of its hinterland and occupied a peripheral situation in the Netherlands. Around 1867 the fortifications began to be dismantled and demolished.

Maastricht from the St Servaasbrug

The Town

*Viewpoints:
Wilhelminabrug,
St Servaasbrug

On the right bank of the Maas lies the Wijk district of the town, with the railway station and St Maartenskerk (Rechtstraat 2), built by P. J. H. Cuypers in 1854 after the demolition of an earlier church. From here two bridges cross the river to the left bank, on which most of the town lies. The quay wall on the east bank is a relic of the town walls round Wijk.

The Wilhelminabrug (1930–32; fine views of town) leads directly to the spacious Markt. The seven-arched St Servaasbrug was originally built in the 13th century, and also offers a good view of the town. On the bridge can be seen a modern statue of St Servaas (Servatius). Near the bridge a semicircular structure erected in 1984, marks the spot where the Romans built the first bridge over the river.

Vrijthof

At the west end of the St Servaasbrug is Burgstraat, from the far end of which Kleine Staat (to the right) and Grote Staat (to the left) lead to the Vrijthof, shaded by lime-trees. As the name indicates (*vrij* = "free"), this was always an open space. Originally a cemetery, it later became the parade ground of the garrison. Flanking it are the former Guard-House, St Servaaskerk, St Janskerk and a number of cafés.

To the north and south are two other road bridges and a railway bridge.

Town Hall

The old Town Hall (Stadhuis), in the Markt, was built by Pieter Post between 1658 and 1644 as a Cloth Hall. It has a neo-classical façade with pilasters and a handsome doorway approached by an imposing double staircase, designed to enable the two rulers of Maastricht, the Duke of Brabant and the Prince-Bishop of Liège, to enter the Town Hall simultaneously. In the

tower (1684) is a Hemony carillon of 43 bells. Notable features of the interior are the tapestries, the stucco ornament, the ceiling paintings and the fine chimneypieces. Open: Mon.–Fri. 8.30am–12.30pm and 2–5.30pm.

North of the Town Hall, in Boschstraat, stands St Mathiaskerk (14th–16th c.; R.C.), the building of which was largely financed by cloth merchants. It has a beautiful 15th century Pietà.

St Mathiaskerk

South-west of the Markt, at Dominicanerplein No. 5, is Limburg Museum of Art and Antiquities (Limburgs Museum voor Kunst en Oudheiden) or Bonnefanten Museum, installed here in 1987. The name refers to the museum's former home in a convent of Sepulchrine nuns, popularly known as the Bonnefanten because they brought up girls to be good, well-behaved children ("bonnes enfants"). The convent, in Bonnefantenstraat, which had at one time also been a barracks, now houses the University Library. The museum has a good collection of Dutch paintings (including works by Pieter Brueghel the Elder and Younger and Rubens) as well as works by Italian and modern artists. The archaeological section includes prehistoric material (e.g. grave goods from a large tomb at Meerlo), Roman and early medieval grave goods found near St Servaaskerk, a model of the old town and other medieval material. Open: Tue.–Fri. 10am–5pm, Sat. and Sun. 11am–5pm.

Bonnefanten Museum

The stone-built Dominican church in Dominicanerplein dates from the 13th century. There are remains of wall paintings of 1337 and 1619 on the vaulting. Most of the Dominican friary to which the church belonged has been demolished.

Dominicanerkerk

Maastricht

St Servaaskerk (R.C.), a Romanesque cruciform basilica, is the oldest church in the Netherlands, originally built in the 6th century over the grave of St Servatius, first bishop of Maastricht. The oldest part of the present church dates from the year 1000. The aisled nave was built first, followed by the transepts, the choir and new crypts. The porch at the west end is thought to be Carolingian. The west crypt and the transepts date from the early 11th century, the new east crypt under the crossing, the east choir and the towers over the choir from 1171. Around 1087 St Servaaskerk was given the status of an imperial church and became the seat of the imperial chancellery. An imperial throne was set up in the west choir as the emblem of secular power.

On the upper floor of the west choir are the famous Keizerzaal (Imperial Hall; 1165–77) and the Imperial Gallery. During the 13th century work continued at this end of the church but was not completed. The fine south doorway, the Bergportaal, has Biblical statuary of the 13th century. The cloister, with its own doorway on the north side of the church, the chapels flanking the aisles and the vaulting of the nave and transepts date from the 14th and 15th centuries.

In the older crypt is the tomb of Charles of Lorraine. At the west end of the nave is a statue of Charlemagne (1843), with the remains of a 12th century altar of the Virgin on its base. In the south tower hangs one of the largest bells in the Netherlands, known as the Grameer ("Grandmother"), weighing 7 tons.

The church has a rich treasury containing a variety of sacred objects, pictures, statues and above all the Late Romanesque chest reliquary which houses the remains of St Servatius (d. 384). This masterpiece of the metalworker's craft by Godefroid de Claire (12th c.) became known as the Noodkist ("Distress Chest") because in times of danger or difficulty it was carried in procession round the town in order to avert the calamity. Along the sides of the chest are representations of the twelve Apostles, while on the ends are figures of Christ and saints

Other treasures associated with St Servatius are his episcopal crozier, pilgrim's staff, pectoral cross and drinking-cup, a bust of the saint and the famous key to the gates of heaven which Servatius was said to have received from St Paul. There is also a collection of reliquaries (one of them containing an arm-bone of St Thomas), liturgical objects in a variety of styles and ostrich eggs set in gilt metal frames, which – as exotic and unusual objects – were designed to rouse the interest of the masses and attract them to this pilgrimage church. The Treasury is open daily 10am–5pm

During restoration work directed by P. J. H. Cuypers in 1869 the church underwent considerable alteration in accordance with the taste of the time; the Baroque tower over the west choir was remodelled in neo-Gothic style and the crypts were given new columns and a vaulted roof. Further restoration work between 1982 and 1990 reversed these changes, and the old time-blackened walls in the interior of the church are now brilliantly white, with blue, red and gold ornament on the vaulting and leaf capitals. Many unidentified remains dating from the 6th century were found in underground tombs.

South-east of the Vrijthof, set in gardens in the Henric van Veldekeplein, is a statue (by Charles Vos, 1934) of the first Dutch poet, Henric van Veldeke, best known for his translation of the legend of St Servatius.

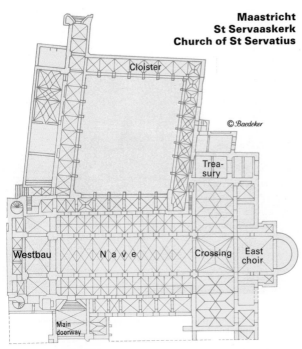

Maastricht
St Servaaskerk
Church of St Servatius

© Baedeker

Cloister

Treasury

Treasury

Westbau Nave Crossing East choir

Main doorway

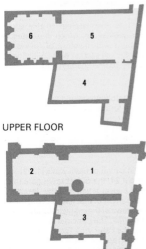

UPPER FLOOR

GROUND FLOOR

UPPER FLOOR
6 Liturgical utensils and relics
  Relic (arm-bone) of St Thomas (11th c.)
  Aquamanile (bronze, 12th c.)
5 Liturgical utensils, sculpture
  and choir-stalls
  Virgin and child with St Anne (wood,
  c. 1660)
4 Textiles
  "Dioscuri Cloth" for remains of
  St Servatius (7th/8th c.)
  Silk fabrics with animal ornament
  (10th c.)
  Old vestments

GROUND FLOOR
3 History
  St Servatius (wood, c. 1155)
  Grave-slabs
  Easter candlestick, ivory seal
2 Relics
  Shrine of St Servatius (c. 1180)
  Reliquaries
  Drinking-horn (15th c.)
1 Items associated with St Servatius
  Portable altar (4th c.)
  Pilgrim's staff (9th c.)
  Crozier (11th c.)
  Bust of St Servatius (c. 1580)

293

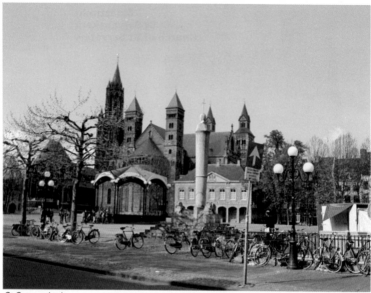

St Servaaskerk

St Janskerk

The Gothic St Janskerk in Henric van Veldekeplein dates from the 14th and 15th centuries and has been a Reformed church since 1632. Its most notable features are its tower, over 70m/230ft high, and its pulpit in Louis XVI style. The church can be seen after service on Sundays.

Natural History Museum

Farther south, by way of Bouillonstraat, is Bosquetplein. In this square (Nos. 6–7) is Maastricht's Natural History Museum, which illustrates the geological development of South Limburg with displays of fossils and different types of rock. There is also a biological section with collections of regional flora and fauna. Open: Mon.–Fri. 10am–12.30pm and 1.30–5pm, Sun. 2–5pm.

Rijksarchief

From the Natural History Museum Grote Looierstraat and Lange Grachtje run east into St Pieterstraat, in which is a former Minorite friary (13th c.). After the Minorites were expelled from the town for treachery in 1638 their church, the Minderbroederskerk, was used as an arsenal and military hospital. Since 1880 it has housed the Rijksarchief, the Archives of Limburg.

Town walls

Farther east are some remains of the first circuit of town walls (1229) – the Helpoort (Hell Gate) at St Bernardusstraat 24, the oldest town gate in the Netherlands, which is now the home of a local artist, and the Jekertoren (tower) and Onze-Lieve-Vrouwewal in the street of that name. From the top of Onze-Lieve-Vrouwewal there are fine views of the municipal park with its five old cannon, the Maas and the Wijk district. The principal remnant of the town's second circuit of walls (c. 1350) is the Pater Vink Toren, named after Pater Vink, unjustly executed by the Spanish authorities in 1579. A little way south, between two 16th century bastions washed by the river Jeker, there is a picturesque view of the Helpoort, the town's principal churches and the municipal park.

Reliquary of St Servatius

Onze Lieve
Vrouwekerk

Maastricht
Onze Lieve
Vrouwekerk

On the east side of Onze-Lieve-Vrouwen-plein stands Onze Lieve Vrouwekerk, the Church of Our Lady. Of the original church built about the year 1000 only the lower part of the west work survives. Around 1150 the building of the west work, the crypts and the transepts began; the east choir was built about 1200, followed by the gallery over the ambulatory and in the 16th century by the north-west doorway.

The fortress-like character of the Romanesque west work with its two stair turrets recalls the church's former function as an element in the town's fortifications; in its monumental simplicity it is unique in the Netherlands. The Late Gothic choir with its large crypt is a particularly notable feature of the interior. The capitals of the black columns in the ambulatory (12th c.) are richly carved.

The side chapel containing the image of Onze Lieve Vrouwe Sterre der Zee (Our Lady Star of the Sea) dates from the 15th century, as does the rebuilding of the north-west doorway.

295

Maastricht

Helpoort

Onze Lieve Vrouwekerk

Meestrechter Geis

The vaulting of the nave, though in 15th century style, dates only from the 18th century. Other features of interest are the west crypt, which belonged to the earlier church, the church treasury, the beautiful 16th century cloister and the west tower. The treasury is open from Easter to mid September, Mon.–Sat. 10.30am–5pm, Sun. 1–4.30pm.

On the east side of Onze Lieve Vrouwekerk is Stockstraat, which, like Meestrechter Smedenstraat at its north end, is lined with smart shops and 17th and 18th century houses with decorative gable-stones in typical Maasland style.

At the end of Stockstraat can be seen a statue (by Mari Andriessen, 1961) of the "Meestrechter Geis", a character from Loe Maas's operetta "Four Maastrichters on their Way to the Moon" (1955) who expresses the cheerful, easygoing way of the hospitable people of Maastricht.

Just to the west of Stockstraat is a small square, Op de Thermen, with coloured lines marking the position of the Roman baths which were excavated here.

Dinghuis

Farther north, at Kleine Staat 1, is the Dinghuis, with half-timbered walls and a handsome stone gable. Originally built in 1470 as a town hall, it was for many years the seat of the High Court: hence the name Dinghuis (Courthouse). In the cellars of the building, now occupied by the tourist information office (VVV), are torture chambers which bear witness to this earlier function.

Casemates

In Tongerseplein, on the west side of the town, are the casemates built between 1575 and 1825 – a maze of vaulted underground passages, powder stores and bomb-proof rooms which can be seen by arrangement

(apply to the tourist information office); the entrance is at the Waldeck
Bastion.

The new Provinciehuis (provincial government headquarters) at Limburg-   Provinciehuis
laan 10 in the Wijk district, opened in 1986, is an example of contemporary
architecture in a very individual style. This irregularly shaped red-brick
building with its numerous angles and turrets stands partly on the right
bank of the Maas and partly on an island in the river. Its picturesque
situation makes a walk there well worth while; the interior can be seen by
arrangement (apply to the reception desk).

Surroundings of Maastricht

To the south of Maastricht are the St Pietersberg Caves, a widely ramified   St Pietersberg
system of tunnels and passages, formed over many centuries by the quar-   Caves
rying of the local marlstone, which provided shelter for the inhabitants
during the town's many sieges. Originally there were some 20,000 passages with a total length of 200km/125 miles. During the Second World War
some of the passages were enlarged, a well was dug and store-rooms, a
bakery and even a chapel were constructed, providing accommodation in
which most of the town's population could take refuge and live for a
considerable period.

Since the rocks were formed on the bottom of an inland sea large numbers
of fossils can be seen in the walls of the caves. The constant low temperature in the caves, shut off as they are from any strong inflow of air,
provides ideal conditions for mushroom-growing. There are regular conducted tours of the caves.

The entrance to the caves is in Fort St Pieter, on the north side of the hill.   Fort St Pieter
The fort, built in 1702 on a pentagonal plan, has bomb-proof rooms and a
circular gallery with embrasures and a number of old cannon. It is open to
visitors.

5km/3 miles west of Maastricht lies Cadier en Keer, with the Africa Centre,   Cadier en Keer
which illustrates the cultures of West Africa with displays of everyday
articles, objects used in ritual ceremonies and other exhibits. Open: Mon.–
Fri. 1–5pm, Sun. 2–5pm.

To the south of the town are a number of old castles, including Kasteel   Castles
Neercanne (now a hotel and restaurant), Kasteel Gronsveld and Kasteel
Mheer.

Makkum   E 3

Province: Friesland
Commune: Wûnseradiel
Population: 12,000

A few miles west of Bolsward, on the IJsselmeer, is the little Frisian town of
Makkum, which has been famed since the 17th century for its *Makkumer
aardewerk* (Makkum earthenware). There are still two manufactories (open
to visitors) in the town. Also of interest are the Weigh-House (Waag; late
17th c.), with the weighmaster's lodging, which is completely faced with
tiles, and the Aardewerk Museum at Pruikmakers Hoek 2 (open: May to mid
September and during Easter and autumn holidays, Mon.–Sat. 10am–5pm,
Sun. 1.30–5pm).

Marken   E 5

Province: Noord-Holland
Population: 2100

Marssum

Situation and
characteristics

Marken is a former island in the IJsselmeer which was separated from the
mainland by a high tide in 1164 and is now linked with the Nes promontory
by a 2km/1¼ mile long dyke built in 1957. The dyke is part of the ring dyke
round the future Markerwaard, the fourth area planned to be reclaimed
from the Zuiderzee (see Facts and Figures, The Struggle with the Sea).
Since the decline of the fisheries following the dyking of the Zuiderzee
Marken's main source of income has been tourism.

In 1232 there was on Marken a daughter house of the Frisian abbey of
Mariengaard, which from 1251 to 1345 owned the whole island. Thereafter
it was purchased by the town of Amsterdam, and as a result was frequently
involved during the Middle Ages in the conflicts between Amsterdam and
the ports on the opposite side of the Zuiderzee (e.g. Kampen). In the 17th
century the shipping trade of Marken flourished. During the French occupation (1811) the island became independent. At the end of the 19th century
there were seventeen villages on Marken; now there are only seven in
addition to the main village of Monnikenwerf.
The principal tourist attractions of Marken are its characteristic old wooden
houses and its traditional costumes.

Houses

Until 1931 all Marken's houses were built on piles. The interiors are as
interesting as the exteriors, with much carved woodwork and beautifully
painted furniture, including a state bed which is never slept in.

Costumes and
customs

Traditional costumes are still frequently worn on Marken. The women wear
a *ryglyf,* a kind of bodice, either dark blue in colour or embroidered, part of
which is allowed to show.
The island is still very Calvinist, and visitors are unlikely to be invited to a
traditional winter wedding. This is preferably celebrated on the frozen
Zuiderzee, with traditional costumes, music and folk dances, including a
round dance by women alone. At Easter there is a lively traditional
procession.

Marken Museum

The Marken Museum at Kerkbuurt 44–47 occupies four old *lookhuisjes,*
which instead of chimneys have only an opening in the roof to let out the
smoke. The museum gives a vivid impression of life on Marken as it was
before the dyking of the Zuiderzee. Open: April to Oct. Mon. to Fri.
10am–5pm, Sun. 12 noon–4pm.

Marssum

See Leeuwarden

Medemblik   E 4

Province: Noord-Holland. Population: 6900

Situation and
characteristics

Medemblik, the oldest town (founded in the 10th century) in what used to
be West Friesland, lies on the IJsselmeer some 20km/12½ miles south of
the Afsluitdijk (see entry). It received its municipal charter in 1289 and
flourished particularly in the 16th and 17th centuries. Until the construction
of the North Holland Canal in the 19th century it was an important port, with
access to the North Sea. It now has only a yacht harbour (cruises on the
IJsselmeer).

Kasteel Radboud

Kasteel Radboud – named after a Frisian king who built a castle here in
early times – was built by Count Floris V of Holland in 1282. During the 14th
and 15th centuries it served as a prison. It lost much of its importance when
the town was enclosed by walls in 1572. At the end of the 19th century the

Kasteel Radboud, Medemblik

castle, by then much dilapidated, was completely restored by P. J. H. Cuypers, though not in its original form. Open: mid May to mid September, Mon.–Sat. 10am–5pm, Sun. 12 noon–5pm; mid September to mid May, Sun. 2–5pm.

An old steam pumping station, De Vier Koggen (1869), houses a collection of steam engines used on ships and in industry, still in working order. Open: May to end October, Wed.–Sat. 10am–5pm, Sun. 12 noon–5pm; July and August also Tue. 10am–5pm.

Steam Engine Museum

Other features of interest are St Bonifaciuskerk, a Late Gothic hall-church (15th c.) with an old tower, which contains the tomb of Lord George Murray, a Jacobite commander at the battle of Culloden (1745) who died in exile in Medemblik; the 17th century Weigh-House (Waag; used for the weighing of cheese); the Town Hall (Stadhuis; 1940); and the former Orphanage (Weeshuis), now housing the Oudheidkamer, a museum of local antiquities.

Other sights

Middelburg

A/B 8/9

Province: Zeeland
Population: 39,150

Middelburg, capital of the province of Zeeland, lies on the Veere–Vlissingen Canal on the former island of Walcheren, surrounded by a star-shaped ring of *grachten* and canals. It is an important market and commercial centre for an extensive agricultural area.
Major contributions are also made to the town's economy by industry (electrical engineering, chemicals, metal-processing) and the tourist trade.

Situation, characteristics and *townscape

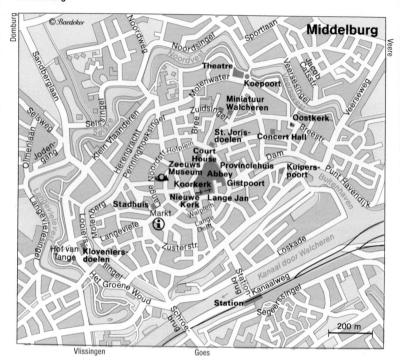

History

Middelburg is one of the oldest towns in the Netherlands, with origins going back to Carolingian times, when it enjoyed a first period of prosperity. Walcheren was able to beat off raids by the Norsemen thanks to its three strongholds – in the dunes to the north the Domburg, to the south the Souburg and in the centre of the island the Middleburg. Later, in 1121, Norbertine monks established themselves here and founded the abbey, around which a settlement of fishermen and merchants grew up.

In 1217 Middelburg was granted a municipal charter, and thereafter it developed into an important trading town, famed for its cloth industry and as an entrepot for French wares. In 1561 it became the see of a bishop. At about the same time, however, its economic decline began, when the silting up of the Arne made it increasingly difficult to use the harbour. In 1574 Middelburg was captured by William the Silent's forces.

During the 17th century many Antwerp merchants settled in Middelburg, and the town entered into competition with Amsterdam. This second period of prosperity was brought to an end by the French occupation, and even the construction of a new harbour in 1817 could not halt the town's decline.

On May 17th 1940 the town suffered heavy damage in a German air attack, but the major buildings and streets (Spanjaardstraat, Bellinkstraat, Herenstraat, etc.) which were destroyed were almost all restored in the original style after the war. In 1975 Middelburg's successful restoration policy earned it the designation of "European Heritage City".

Gracht *houses and houseboats*

The Town

In the centre of Middelburg are two concentric rings of streets, on the line of the old *grachten* constructed to strengthen the town's defences as it grew steadily larger over the centuries. From these inner rings a number of streets lead out to a U-shaped outer circuit of *grachten* with the open end to the north. Farther out again is the line of the old fortifications, bounded on the south side by the Walcheren Canal, which links the town with the open sea.

*Layout

In the Markt stands the Town Hall (Stadhuis), one of the most beautiful Gothic secular buildings in the Netherlands, built between 1452 and 1458 by members of the Keldermans family. Between 1506 and 1520 a Meat Hall (meat market) and a tower were added, and in 1670 and 1780–84 there were further additions in neo-classical style. The Town Hall was almost completely destroyed in the 1940 bombing, but after the war was rebuilt in the original style. On the façade of 1512–13, most of which survived the bombing, are figures of twenty-five Counts and Countesses of Zeeland and Holland, under canopies surmounted by fabulous animals. The windows and doors are closed by red and white shutters – a common practice in the Middle Ages, when windows were not glazed.

*Town Hall

The interior is open to the public. Above the old Meat Hall (now occupied by an exhibition of modern art) is the imposing Burgerzaal (Burghers' Hall), originally the town's first Cloth Hall, which is now used for civic receptions and other great occasions and as a concert hall. Items of particular interest include pictures, Bruges tapestries on mythological themes and a bronze model of Admiral de Ruyter's flagship. Open: March 28th to October 21st, Mon.–Fri.; conducted tours can be arranged through the VVV office.

From the Markt the Langeviele runs south-west to the Achter de Houttuinen *gracht*, on which is the Kloveniersdoelen, built between 1607 and 1611 in

Kloveniersdoelen

Flemish Renaissance style as the headquarters of a marksmen's guild (a *klovenier* was a long musket). Until 1798 the building was occupied by the Van den Bus marksmen's guild, and thereafter it was for many years a military hospital. In 1735 the tower was destroyed when it was struck by lightning; it was rebuilt more than two centuries later, in 1969. The Kloveniersdoelen is now occupied by the Centre for New Music (a college of music and music library).

* Onze Lieve Vrouwe Abdij

On the north-east side of the inner ring stands Onze Lieve Vrouwe Abdij, the Abbey of Our Lady. In 1150 White Canons of the Norbertine order (named after St Norbert of Xanten, who founded the order at Prémontré in France: hence the alternative name Premonstratensian) established themselves in the Carolingian stronghold of Middelburg. In the 16th century the abbey consisted of a picturesque and many-towered complex of buildings laid out round a cloister, including the canons' lodgings, to which were later added a refectory and chapterhouse (now the Provincial Library), a second courtyard, two churches and a tower.

When William the Silent recovered Middelburg from the Spaniards in 1574 the abbey was secularised and became the seat of the provincial administration, the Admiralty and the Mint. Even a cannon foundry was established within the precincts. Only the churches retained their original function, though now for the Reformed faith. Many parts of the complex have two names, reflecting their dual use: the White Tower became the Munttoren (Mint Tower), the Abdijplein the Muntplein, the Refectory the Statenzaal (Hall of the States).

The buildings were almost completely destroyed in the 1940 bombing but were rebuilt after the war in the same style. They now house the Zeeland provincial government, the Roosevelt Study Centre (20th century American history) and the Zeeland Mint. Conducted tours: May to October, Mon.–Sat. 1.30 and 3pm; July and August, also Tue.–Fri. at 11am.

Kloveniersdoelen

Middelburg

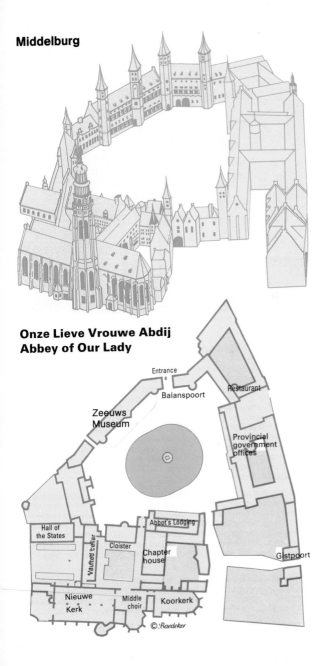

Onze Lieve Vrouwe Abdij
Abbey of Our Lady

Entrance

Balanspoort

Restaurant

Zeeuws Museum

Provincial government offices

Abbot's Lodging

Hall of the States

Vaulted cellar

Cloister

Chapter house

Gistpoort

Nieuwe Kerk

Middle choir

Koorkerk

© Baedeker

Middelburg

Onze Lieve Vrouwe Abdij, the seat of provincial government since the 16th century

Koorkerk, Nieuwe Kerk	The two-aisled Nieuwe Kerk (16th c.), the parish church, and the aisleless Koorkerk (early 14th c.), the abbey church (beautiful reticulated vaulting), were originally joined. Since the parish church had no choir of its own, the west end of the monks' church, known as the middle choir, was used as the choir for the lay congregation. Over this is the tower known as Lange Jan ("Long John"). In this church are the double tomb of the brothers Jan and Cornelis Evertsen, two admirals killed in the English war of 1666, and memorial tablets for Count William of Holland (d. 1256), king of Germany, and his brother Floris (d. 1258). The magnificent marble tomb was the last great work of Rombout Verhulst (1680–82).

After their restoration both churches were provided with organs by the Rijksmuseum in Amsterdam. The organ in the Koorkerk (built in 1481) came from St Nicolaaskerk in Utrecht, that in the Nieuwe Kerk (1892) from a Protestant church in Amsterdam.

Lange Jan	The octagonal tower – a rare feature in the Netherlands – popularly known as Lange Jan, originally dating from the 14th century but several times burned down (most recently in 1940), is the great landmark and emblem of Middelburg. A staircase of 207 steps leads up to the top (91m/299ft), which carries a large imperial crown in honour of Count (King) William II. From the top of the tower there are extensive views over the whole of Walcheren and much of the Deltawerken. Open: May 28th to October 1st, Mon.–Sat. 10am–5pm.
Gistpoort	Not directly connected with the Abbey complex but associated with it is the imposing Gistpoort (1509–12), also known as the Blauwpoort (Blue Gate) from the colour of the stone with which it is faced. On the gable can be seen a statue of Count William II, who extended the abbey in 1255–56.
Zeeland Museum	In the older part of the abbey is the Zeeland Museum (Zeeuws Museum), with collections of antiquities (Egyptian mummies), costumes and natural

history and reconstructions of an old baker's shop and a room from a
farmhouse. Open: Tue.–Fri. 11am–5pm, Sat.–Mon. 1.30–5pm.

Just north of the abbey stands St Jorisdoelen, the guild-house of the
marksmen's guild of St George. The façade (1582), bearing the arms of
Middelburg, Zeeland and the marksmen's guild, was rebuilt in its original
form in 1969–70. On the gable is a figure of St George. The building now
houses the employment exchange.
In front of St Jorisdoelen, in Balansplein, is a fountain which plays in
summer and is illuminated after dark.

St Jorisdoelen

From here St Pieterstraat and Wagenaarstraat lead into Hofplein, in which
are the Law Courts, housed in a mansion of 1765 with wrought-iron window grilles which was once occupied by Van der Perre, governor of
Zeeland.

Law Courts

On the north side of the town, on Molenwater, is Miniatuur Walcheren, a
large model of Walcheren (c. 7000 sq.m/8400 sq.yds; scale 1:20), showing
the town's historic buildings and other features (200 buildings in all) in
appropriate settings. Even the Veerse Meer is represented, with boats
operated by remote control. The model was originally made in 1954 by
hundreds of local people for an exhibition on the reconstruction of the
island. Open: March 31st to October 23rd, daily 9.30am–5pm, in July and
August to 6pm.

Miniatuur
Walcheren

Nearby is the Koepoort (Cow Gate; 1735), the only one of the old town
gates which still survives.

To the south-east stands the Baroque Oostkerk (1647–67; Reformed), the
town's first Baroque building, designed by Pieter Post and Arent van
's-Gravenzande.

Monnickendam

Province: Noord-Holland
Population: 10,000

The little town of Monnickendam, on the shores of the Gouwzee and the
IJsselmeer, is noted mainly for its smoked fish and as a water sports centre.
Until it was overtaken by Amsterdam Monnickendam ranked with Edam,
Hoorn and Enkhuizen as one of the most important ports on the Zuiderzee.

Situation and
characteristics

Monnickendam was founded by monks in the 12th century and received its
municipal charter in 1335. Its situation on the Zuiderzee with its busy
shipping traffic soon brought it prosperity; but when in the 17th century it
came to rely on fishing as its main source of income its circumstances were
much more modest. Its difficulties were aggravated by a succession of
catastrophes: in 1297 it was plundered by the Frisians, in 1494 and 1514 it
was ravaged by great fires and in 1570 it fell into the hands of the Geuzen
(Beggars).

History

The 16th century Speeltoren at Noordeinde 4, the tower of the old town
hall, has a carillon of 18 bells (1596). It now houses a museum of antiquities
from the surrounding area. Open: mid May to mid June, Sat. 10am–4pm,
Sun. 1–4pm; mid June to mid September, Mon.–Sat. 10am–4pm, Fri. also
7–9pm, Sun. 1–4pm; from September 15th, Sat. 10am–4pm, Sun. 1–4pm.

Speeltoren

To the south is the Grote Kerk or St Nicolaaskerk (c. 1400), with a collection
of tiles and majolica.

Grote Kerk

The Town Hall (Stadhuis), at Noordeinde 5, occupies an elegant mansion
built in 1746. The Council Chamber has gold wallpaper and a Rococo

Town Hall

Weigh-House and Speeltoren, Monnickendam

ceiling. On the gable above the main entrance is the figure of a monk (who also features in the town's coat of arms).

An interesting experience in Monnickendam is a visit to an eel-smoking establishment.

From Monnickendam there are boat trips to Marken and Volendam (see entries).

Muiden   E 5

Province: Noord-Holland
Population: 6800

Situation

The little town of Muiden lies south-east of Amsterdam.

*Muiderslot

The town's principal attraction is the Muiderslot, a moated castle built by Count Floris V in 1280 on the estuary of the Vecht in order to assert his authority in the eastern part of his domains. After his death (1296) the Bishop of Utrecht took the castle by storm and reduced it to ruins. In 1370 a new castle was built on the site, and this was the residence until 1795 of a succession of castellans wielding judicial authority. The castle knew quieter times between 1609 and 1674, when it was occupied by the writer Pieter Cornelisz Hooft, who formed a circle of artists and scholars, the "Muiderkring". His best known guests were Joost van den Vondel (see Famous People) and Constantijn Huygens.

Since 1875 the Muiderslot (restored between 1885 and 1909 and again in 1955) has been a national museum. It retains its original 16th and 17th century appointments and contains a collection of mementoes of Pieter Hooft. Also of interest are the herb garden (with 400 culinary herbs) and the plum garden. Open: April to September, Mon.–Fri. 10am–5pm, Sun. 1–5pm; October to March, Mon.–Fri. 10am–4pm, Sun. 1–4pm.

In the vicinity is the Grote Zeesluis, a sea sluice constructed in 1674, when the Zuiderzee was still open to the sea.

Grote Zeesluis

Naarden

E 5/6

Province: Noord-Holland
Population: 16,000

Naarden, chief place in the Gooi area, lies at the south end of the IJsselmeer. It is an attractive little town surrounded by a star-shaped system of fortifications laid out in accordance with the principles of the great French military engineer Vauban (1633–1707).

Situation and characteristics

The harbour of this old fortified town, which first appears in the records in the 10th century, was constructed in 1411, and thereafter it developed into an important fishing port. It suffered a setback when the fortifications were rebuilt and the harbour was closed, but later recovered when its cloth trade prospered. Its main role nowadays is as a commuters' suburb of Amsterdam, 20km/12½ miles away. The tourist trade also makes a contribution to its economy.

The town's principal landmark is the Grote Kerk (St Vituskerk; 14th–15th c.) in Marktstraat, which has a fine choir screen of 1518. In the same street is the handsome Renaissance Town Hall (Stadhuis) of 1602, with a magnificently appointed interior.

St Vituskerk
Town Hall

Near Turfpoortstraat is the Comenius Chapel (Comeniuskapel), with the tomb of the Czech preacher and educationalist Jan Amos Comenius (Komenski; 1592–1670), who spent his last years in exile in Holland.

Comenius Chapel

The Spaanse Huis at Turfpoortstraat 27 houses the Comenius Museum (open: January to mid December, Tue.–Sun. 1–5pm).

Comenius Museum

The Vestingmuseum (Fortress Museum) in the Turfpoort citadel at Westwalstraat 6 has an interesting collection of weapons and uniforms. Open: Easter to October, Mon.–Fri. 10am–4.30pm, Sat. and Sun. 12 noon–5pm.

Vestingmuseum

Within the area of the town, on the shores of the IJsselmeer, is the well known Naardermeer nature reserve and bird sanctuary, the first such reserve established by the Netherlands Association for the Protection of Nature. This expanse of marshland and reedy lakes is a bird-watcher's paradise.

Naardermeer

Nijmegen

F/G 7

Province: Gelderland
Population: 145,800

Nijmegen, the largest town in Gelderland (though not its capital, which is Arnhem), with a Roman Catholic University, lies in the south of the province, only 7km/4½ miles from the German frontier on the left bank of the Waal, the southern branch of the Rhine as it approaches the sea. It is

Situation and
*importance

Bird's eye view of Naarden with its star-shaped fortifications

Naarden's defensive moat

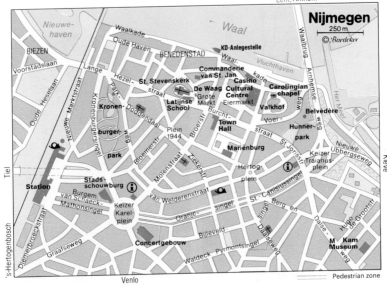

dominated by seven hills, the terraced slopes of which have something of
the air of a gigantic amphitheatre.

Nijmegen ranks with Arnhem as one of the two leading towns in the
province of Gelderland, with the offices of numerous administrative bodies
(including some provincial government departments) and many higher
educational establishments and research institutes as well as a University.
A number of commercial houses and markets for horticultural produce also
make important contributions to the economy.

The decisive factor in the economic life of Nijmegen, however, is industry –
principally metalworking and electrical engineering but also textiles, foodstuffs and chemicals.

Nijmegen's port on the Waal can take ships of up to 6000 tons, making it
one of the most important ports on the inland waterway between Rotterdam and the Ruhr. It is also of regional importance as a transhipment point
serving the province of Gelderland.

Nijmegen was a considerable Roman settlement under the name of Bata-
vodurum and later of Noviomagus. In Carolingian times it was an imperial
residence, and later became a free imperial city and a member of the
Hanseatic League. In 1579 it joined the Union of Utrecht. In 1585 it surren-
dered to the Spaniards, but in 1591 was recaptured by Maurice of Orange.
The 1678 peace treaty between France and the Netherlands was signed in
Nijmegen.

History

Nijmegen's period of economic prosperity began only with the development of industry, after the demolition of its old fortifications between
1877 and 1884. During the Second World War the town suffered heavy
destruction, particularly in the central area, but the damage was rapidly
made good after the war.

Chapel of St Nicholas, Valkhof

Ruins of Frederick Barbarossa's chapel

The Town

Valkhof

On the north side of the town lies the Valkhof, an attractive park on a low hill above the Waal, on the site of an imperial stronghold built by Charlemagne in 768 which under the Saxon, Frankish and Hohenstaufen emperors was frequently the seat of the imperial court. Here the Empress Theophano, wife of Otto II, died in 991, and here in 1165 Henry VI, son of Frederick Barbarossa and Beatrice of Burgundy, was born. The name Valkhof is probably derived from the falcons which Charlemagne's son Louis the Pious kept here for hunting in the nearby imperial forest.

Of the original stronghold there remain only the palatine chapel of St Nicholas (consecrated by Pope Leo III in 799), a building of great architectural interest, and, south-east of this, the ruins of a Romanesque apse (St Maartenskapel) which is thought to date from the time of Frederick Barbarossa (1155). From the chapel there is a fine view over the Waal plain.

Hunnerpark

To the east of the Valkhof, conspicuously situated at the north end of the Hunnerpark, is the Belvedere, an old 16th century watch-tower from which there are far-ranging views (restaurant). From the Hunnerpark the Waalbrug, a massive bridge 700m/765yds long, crosses the Waal to the suburb of Lent, offering the best view of Nijmegen. On the far side of the river is the motorway to Arnhem. On the south side of the Hunnerpark is Keizer Traianusplein, a busy traffic intersection.

St Stevenskerk

The building of the Grote Kerk or St Stevenskerk began around 1260, and the first tower was built in 1307. Little remains from this early period. Around 1400 the nave was rebuilt, and this was followed by the magnificent choir with its ambulatory and ring of chapels, the aisled transepts, the Chapel of the Holy Sepulchre and the south doorway, all complete by around 1560. Beside the church is a square tower (1593) with an octagonal belfry (1604) and an 18th century carillon. The tower and the façade of the

church were rebuilt after suffering severe damage during the Second World War; the interior of the church was restored in 1969.
In the choir is the tomb (1512) of Catherine of Bourbon (d. 1469), wife of Duke Adolf of Gelderland. There are some fragments of wall painting in the burial chapel and ambulatory (16th c.). Other surviving features are part of the choir-stalls (1577), the pulpit (1639) and the organ (1773).

In Stevenskerkhof, only a few yards away from the church, are a number of handsome old houses. imcluding the former canons' lodgings.

On the south side of the church stands the Latin School (Latijnse School), built by the city architect Herman van Herengraves in 1544–45. The striking façade has recessed Gothic trefoil arches and Renaissance friezes. Between the first-floor windows are figures of the twelve Apostles and the text of the Ten Commandments.

Latin School

Between Stevenskerkhof and the Grote Markt is the Kerkboog, a Late Gothic double gateway (1545) with a Flemish Renaissance upper storey of 1606. The gatehouse was once the meeting-place of the doctors' guild.

Kerkboog

The triangular Grote Markt lies in the centre of the old town. In the square is a statue of Mariken van Nieumeghen, the chief character in the 15th century mystery play of that name. According to legend Mariken, having entered into a league with the Devil, was fettered in iron rings but that when her period of penitence was over the rings sprang open of themselves. She is depicted holding the broken rings.

Grote Markt

Adjoining the Kerkbook is the old Weigh-House (Waag) and meat market, a handsome Renaissance building in red brick with black and red dormer windows and two arched doorways.

Weigh-House

The Town Hall (Stadhuis) in Burchtstraat was constructed in 1554–55 by Herman van Herengraves. It was completely destroyed during the Second World War and rebuilt in 1951–53. Only the old tapestries, which had been removed for restoration, escaped destruction. The fine figures of emperors, the heads over the windows and the medallions by Cornelis Sass of Utrecht were replaced by copies.

Town Hall

To the left, at Museum Kamstraat 45, is the Rijksmuseum G. M. Kam, which has an important collection of prehistoric and Roman antiquities, mostly from the Nijmegen area. The original collection was presented to the town in 1920 by Gerhard Marius Kam, an amateur archaeologist. Open: Tue.–Sat. 10am–5pm, Sun. 1–5pm.

Kam Museum

To the north of the Grote Markt, at Franse Plaats 3, is the Commanderie van St Jan. Part of the building (c. 1196) belonged in the Middle Ages to the Knights of St John. Since 1974 it has housed the Municipal Museum (Gemeentemuseum), with a collection covering the art and history of Nijmegen between 1000 and 1900. Open: Mon.–Sat. 10am–5pm, Sun. 1–5pm.

Commanderie van St Jan

The Waalkade has been developed since 1978 as an attractive riverfront promenade designed for recreation and entertainment, with numerous restaurants, cafés and bars. The most prominent feature is the state-run Holland Casino, a long building of white and brown marble.

Waalkade

Nijmegen's Weigh-House

Bridge over the Waal at Nijmegen

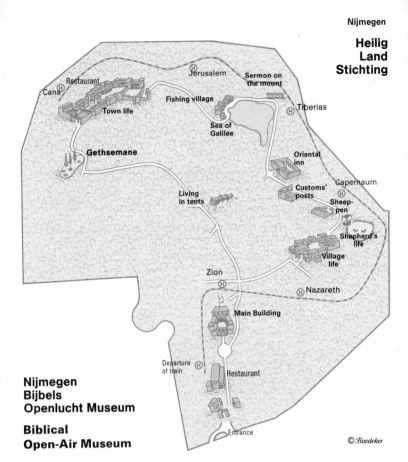

**Heilig
Land
Stichting**

Cana
Restaurant
Jerusalem
Sermon on
the mount
Tiberias
Town life
Fishing village
Sea of
Galilee
Gethsemane
Oriental
inn
Capernaum
Living
in tents
Customs'
posts
Sheep-
pen
Shepherd's
life
Village
life
Zion
Nazareth
Main Building
Departure
of train
Restaurant
Entrance

**Nijmegen
Bijbels
Openlucht Museum**

**Biblical
Open-Air Museum**

© Baedeker

During the construction of the Casino in the late seventies remains of the Roman settlement of Ulpia Noviomagus were discovered. A hypocaust which was excavated here can be seen on the ground floor of the Casino.

*Roman remains

At Waalkade 107 is the Velorama or National Cycle Museum, with some 250 bicycles, from the "hobby-horse" to modern racing machines. Open: Mon.–Sat. 10am–5pm, Sun. 11am–5pm.

Velorama

Surroundings of Nijmegen

To the east of Nijmegen is a tract of beautiful rolling wooded country traversed by a number of roads and many footpaths.
Leave the town on the Groesbeekseweg, which runs south-east from Keizer Karelplein. The road continues along the edge of the woods and comes in 4km/2½ miles to a side road on the left. 300m/330yds along this is the access road to the Biblical Open-Air Museum (Bijbels Openlucht Museum) at Profetenlaan 2, run by the Heilig-Land-Stichting (Holy Land Foundation), with reproductions of the Holy Places of the New Testament (conducted

*Biblical
Open-Air Museum

313

tours; restaurant). When the museum was originally opened in 1911 it was primarily concerned with the religious aspects, but since its remodelling in 1970 the emphasis has moved to the authentic reproduction of everyday life in the late Hellenistic period in which Christ lived. In the conducted tour of the 45 hectare/110 acre site visitors are taken past nomad encampments, an early Palestinian village and the houses of the many different peoples of the period – Jews, Persians, Romans, Greeks, Egyptians, Assyrians. The exhibition room in the main building is devoted to 2000 years of Biblical history.

There is a good general view from Mount Calvary. Visitors can also travel round the site on a miniature railway. Open: Easter to October, daily 9am–5pm.

Berg en Dal

4km/2½ miles east of the Biblical Museum is Berg en Dal, an attractive summer resort situated on the crest of a hill, with extensive views. At Postweg 6 is the Africa Museum, with African masks and sculpture, three African villages and a small zoo. Open: April to October, Mon.–Fri. 10am–5pm, Sat. and Sun. 11am–5pm.

East of Berg en Dal, near the German frontier, rises the Duivelsberg (76m/249ft; café; wide views), above the Wijlermeer.

Noord-Brabant (North Brabant)   C–G 7–10

Provincial capital: 's-Hertogenbosch
Area: 508,346 hectares/1,255,615 acres
(land area 494,416 hectares/1,221,208 acres)

Situation and characteristics

Noord-Brabant, the second largest of the Dutch provinces, takes in the whole of the southern part of the sandy heathland region of the Netherlands with the exception of a narrow strip in the east which belongs to Limburg. It is bounded on the north and east by the Maas, on the west by the Schelde fenlands in Zeeland and on the south by Belgium (see Kempen). As in Limburg, the population is mainly Roman Catholic, with a growth of 30% between 1960 and 1977, compared with a national average of 20%.

Topography

The southern heathland area is a featureless plain lying between 5 and 35m (15 and 115ft) above sea level which continues into the Belgian region of Kempen/Campine. The geological subsoil consists of massive layers of gravel deposited by the Rhine and the Maas in the course of many hundreds of thousands of years which during the last ice age were covered by a layer of sand.

Peel

In the east of the province, near the German frontier, is the Peel area, an expanse of moorland extending from Eindhoven to Venlo, on the border with Limburg. South-east of Asten is a nature reserve (1300 hectares/3250 acres; visitor centre at Ospeldijk) which has escaped destruction by peat cutting. Mostly boggy, it will appeal to nature-lovers with its interesting flora and fauna. Apart from this small area almost the whole of the Peel has been brought into cultivation.

History

At the beginning of the Christian area Brabant, then mostly covered by moorland and forest, offered little scope for settlement by the Romans. In the 8th century it became part of the duchy of Toxandria. With the break-up of that duchy in the 11th century there came into being the duchy of Brabant, which in 1430 was incorporated in Burgundy and later passed to the Habsburg empire. During the northern provinces' struggle for independence the Roman Catholic duchy of Brabant long remained under Spanish control. Under the Peace of Westphalia in 1648 Brabant was divided into two, the northern part being assigned to the States General. In

Woodland scene, Breda

1815 Noord- and Zuid-Brabant were finally separated, and when Belgium achieved independence in 1839 it retained Zuid-Brabant.

Agriculture

The heathlands of northern Brabant have now mostly been brought into cultivation. Some 80% of the area of the province is arable land, and around 12% is planted with coniferous forests. The poor soil, however, is suitable only for undemanding crops including rye, oats, potatoes and simple fodder plants for the feeding of dairy cattle. There is also some pig and poultry farming. The characteristic forms of settlement are hamlets and small villages with trim farm steadings.

Economy

Around 1900 over 40% of the population were employed in agriculture and only 15% in industry. The proportions have now been reversed, with over 50% working in industry, 10% in agriculture and almost 40% in the services sector.

Industry

Industry developed in three phases.
Around 1900 much of the Dutch textile industry moved to Noord-Brabant, which offered the attraction of a large labour force at low wage rates. The main centres were Helmond, Tilburg and Eindhoven. At the same time the cigar industry developed in Kempen and boot and shoe manufacture at Waalwijk. The second phase began around 1920, when the electrical industry (Philips) was established in Eindhoven. Finally after the Second World War the metalworking and electrical industries gave a new stimulus to the economy. After some twenty years of prosperity, however, stagnation set in, particularly in the leatherworking and textile industries. Around 40% of the working population are now employed in metalworking and electrical engineering, 15% in the textile and clothing industries and only 5% in leatherworking. Some new industries have also been established (foodstuffs, tobacco, chemicals).

The heathland towns of Brabant – 's-Hertogenbosch, Rosendaal, Bergen op Zoom, etc. – have three advantages over the fenland regions which have promoted their industrial development: an ample supply of labour, cheap land and lower building costs than in the boggy soil of the fenland regions.

Noord-Holland (North Holland)   D/E 3–6

Provincial capital: Haarlem
Area: 365,640 hectares/903,131 acres
    (land area 266,702 hectares/658,754 acres)
Population: 2,353,000

Situation and
characteristics

The province of Noord-Holland lies in the western Netherlands on the North Sea coast, bounded on the east by the IJsselmeer, on the north by the Waddenzee and on the south by the province of Zuid-Holland. Like Zuid-Holland (see entry), Noord-Holland was a county from the earliest times, later becoming a province.

On topography, the drainage of the fens, types of settlement, agriculture, industry and population, see the entry on Holland.

Medieval
poldering

Until Noord-Holland was dyked and poldered it was under constant threat of flooding, and as a result the Romans could advance no farther north than the line of the present-day North Sea Canal. With the construction of the first dykes of turf and clay around the year 1000 – the earliest was between Bakkum and Limmen, south of Alkmaar – the population of the area began to increase. The largest medieval project was the 126km/78 mile long ring dyke built in the 13th century round what was then West Friesland.

Economic and
political
development

This led to the establishment of numerous small trading towns, particularly on the Zuiderzee, and many of them prospered as members of the Hanseatic League. Noord-Holland played a leading part in the northern provinces' fight for independence, and the Stadholder of Holland soon extended his authority to the other provinces. The North Holland Canal was constructed between 1819 and 1824 to give Amsterdam a link with the North Sea as an alternative to the passage through the Zuiderzee, which was subject to frequent storms. The North Sea Canal, which runs through the IJmuiden dunes to the sea, was constructed in 1865. Locks were built, the IJ – an arm of the IJsselmeer to the east of Amsterdam – was closed by a dam and the area between Haarlem and Amsterdam was poldered.

Along the Zaanstreek and the seaward end of the North Sea Canal a large industrial agglomeration grew up. The first railway line in the Netherlands, between Amsterdam and Haarlem, was opened in 1839. After the First World War the world's first airline was established at the military airfield of Schiphol, and the first regular air service began to operate between Amsterdam and London in 1920.

Noordoostpolder (North-East Polder)   F/G 3/4

Situation and
characteristics

The Noordoostpolder is an area of 47,600 hectares/119,000 acres of fenland reclaimed from the IJsselmeer between 1937 and 1942 (see Facts and Figures, Land Reclamation). Now a peninsula projecting into the IJsselmeer from the east, it has been since 1986 part of the new province of Flevoland.

On the south the polder is separated from the neighbouring Flevopolder and from the mainland by the narrow Ketelmeer; in the north it reaches up to the little town of Lemmer; and on the east it is bounded by a narrow strip of sandy heathland, up to 5m/16ft above sea level, running from north-west to south-east.

This expanse of fertile fenland, lying between 4.5m/15ft and 5.7m/19ft below sea level, is drained by a complicated system of canals, sluices and pumping stations. From Emmeloord, in the centre of the polder, three drainage canals run north to Lemmer, south-west to the former island of Urk (see entry) and south-east to Vollenhove, where the pumping stations and sluices are located.

Drainage of the polder

The new land on the polder is divided into 1600 holdings ranging in size between 12 and 48 hectares (30 and 120 acres). The principal crops are sugar-beet, corn, rape, flax and pulses, with flowers, fruit and vegetables in the south-east.

Agriculture

Leave Kampen (see entry) on the Sneek road, crossing the IJssel and continuing on its right bank (fine views of Kampen to rear) alongside a broad canal. 8km/5 miles from Kampen the road crosses a long bascule bridge over the Ramsdiep, an inlet on the IJsselmeer at the mouth of the Zwarte Water.

Kampen to Lemmer (35km/22 miles)

From here the road continues over the North-East Polder and comes in 3km/2 miles to Ens, a trim polder village, where a road goes off on the left to the new settlement of Schokland (3km/2 miles west), on the site of a former island in the Zuiderzee. The road passes (200m/220yds off on the left) an old church set in a clump of trees, now a museum with an interesting collection of prehistoric material found during the draining of the Zuiderzee. 13km/8 miles farther west, on the shores of the IJsselmeer, is the little fishing port of Urk (see entry), formerly an island, which has preserved its traditional character (picturesque costumes).

9km/6 miles beyond Ens on the Sneek road is a bascule bridge over the Urkervaart, just beyond which is a road junction. To the right is a road to Steenwijk (26km/16 miles), to the left a road to Urk. 1km/¾ mile along this

A gracht *in Lemmer (North-East Polder)*

road is Emmeloord, the new chief town of the polder, with a population of over 20,000.

From the road junction the Sneek road continues north along the Lemstervaart (canal) and then follows a winding course to an inlet of the IJsselmeer. In 15km/9 miles it reaches Lemmer (pop. 8000), a little port on the IJsselmeer which handles a good deal of inland shipping traffic.

Oenkerk

See Leeuwarden

Oirschot   E 8

Province: Noord-Brabant
Population: 11,000

Situation and characteristics	North-west of Eindhoven is Oirschot, which around 1200 was held by the Duke of Brabant. Round the attractive market square are a number of handsome old houses.
St Pieterskerk	St Pieterskerk (R.C.), a Late Gothic cruciform basilica, occupies the site of an earlier church of around 1200. It was burned down in 1944 but was rebuilt in its original form after the war.
Reformed church	The Reformed church, originally the 12th century Mariakapel (Lady Chapel), was used in the 17th century as a weigh-house for butter and is still known as the "Butter Church". It has preserved its 13th century timber roof.
Town Hall	The Town Hall (1463) was rebuilt after a fire in 1513 and much altered in the 18th century.
Hof van Solms	Near the market square is the Hof van Solms, once occupied by Amalia van Solms, wife of Prince Frederick Henry.
Museums: Vier Quartieren	The Vier Quartieren Museum at St Odulphusstraat 11 has a collection of material illustrating everyday life in Brabant. The exhibition in the 16th century Kanunnikenhuis covers the period between 1800 and 1940. Open: Tue.–Sun. 1–5pm.
Hand en Span	The Hand en Span Agricultural Museum occupies a 17th century farmhouse. Open: April to October, daily 10am–5pm.
Oirschotse Heide	To the south of the town lies the Oirschotse Heide, a tract of heathland and wooded country with a number of lakes.

Oisterwijk

See Tilburg

Oldenzaal   J 5

Province: Overijssel
Population: 30,000

Situation and characteristics	Oldenzaal, the oldest town in the beautiful Twente region, lies north of Enschede, close to the German frontier. It was granted the right to hold a market in 1049 and received a municipal charter in 1249.

St Plechelmus, Oldenzaal

St Plechelmuskerk (R.C.), at Gasthuisstraat 10, was built in 945 and dedi- St Plechelmuskerk
cated to Plechelm, a Northumbrian missionary who preached the Gospel in
this area in the 8th century. The oldest part of this cruciform basilica dates
from 1150. The Romanesque tower (with a carillon of 40 bells) was built in
the second half of the 13th century, followed by the choir apse and the
south aisle in the second half of the 15th century.
St Plechelmuskerk is the only well preserved church of its type in the
Netherlands apart from the church of Rolduc Abbey. The treasury contains
the silver-gilt reliquary of St Plechelm (1438). Open: June to August, Tue.–
Thur. 2–4pm.

In Marktstraat are a number of handsome 17th century houses, including Palthe Huis
the Palthe Huis (No. 13), once the home of a textile merchant of that name. It
is now a museum, with an 18th century pharmacy, an old private library
and a number of rooms with their original decoration and furnishing.
Open: Tue.–Fri. 10am–12 noon and 2–5pm, Sat. and Sun. 2–5pm.

Oosterhout

D 8

Province: Noord-Brabant
Population: 48,000

In the Middle Ages Oosterhout, north-east of Breda, was a commandery of Situation and
the Knights of St John, and a number of their granges (*slotjes*) still survive, characteristics
including the 15th century Huize Limburg.

Of the 15th century Gothic St Janskerk there remain only parts of the choir St Janskerk
and the transept. The tower was never completed. Between 1881 and 1883
P. J. H. Cuypers enlarged the church, giving the nave double aisles in place

of the previous single aisles. The most notable feature of the interior is the beautiful stained glass.

St Paulusabdij   St Paulusabdij (St Paul's Abbey) is a Benedictine house, in which the monks occupy themselves with restoring pictures, growing orchids and pottery.

St Catharinadal   The convent of St Catharinadal was founded around 1600, when Norbertine (Premonstratensian) nuns from Breda came to Oosterhout and occupied the house known as the Blauwe Kamer (first half of 16th c.), now the provost's house.

Toy Museum   The Toy Museum displays a collection of toys of between 1600 and 1950 assembled over a period of thirty years by Mr and Mrs Heemskerk. Open: Fri., Sat. and the first and third Sundays in the month 1–5pm.

Surroundings of Oosterhout

Raamsdonksveer   North of Oosterhout is Raamsdonksveer, whose principal attraction is the National Automobile Museum (Nationaal Automobielmuseum) at Steurweg 8, which illustrates the development of the automobile from its beginnings to 1971. The collection ranges from steam cars to electric cars, sports cars and prestigious limousines. Open: Mon.–Sat. 9am–4.45pm, Sun. 11am–4.45pm.

Orvelte

See Assen

Oss   F 7/8

Province: Noord-Brabant
Population: 51,000

Situation and characteristics   The town of Oss, in the Maasland area north-east of 's-Hertogenbosch, was granted a municipal charter in 1399. Its period of prosperity did not begin, however, until the 19th century, when it developed into an important industrial centre. Among firms which have contributed to this development have been the Van den Bergh margarine factory and the Organon pharmaceutical plant (part of the AKZO concern), which processes by-products. Van den Bergh later amalgamated with Jurgens and moved to Rotterdam.

Municipal Museum (Jan Cunencentrum)   The mansion (1898) once occupied by the Van den Bergh family served as the Town Hall from 1921 to 1973. Since 1973 it has housed the Municipal Museum (Gemeentelijk Museum), the Jan Cunencentrum, which has a large collection of pictures of the Hague School (Breitner, Koekkoek, Maris) and the COBRA group (Appel, Corneille, Lucebert) as well as contemporary works. Open: Tue.–Fri. 10am–5pm, Thur. 7–9pm, Sat. and Sun. 2–5pm.

Oudenbosch   D 8

Province: Noord-Brabant
Population: 12,000

Situation   The little town of Oudenbosch lies to the west of Breda. Though small, it has a number of features of interest.

Basilica of SS. Agatha and Barbara

The Basilica of SS. Agatha and Barbara (Basiliek van de HH. Agatha en Barbara) was built by P. J. H. Cuypers between 1865 and 1880 on the model of St Peter's in Rome. The dome of this reduced and simplified copy of the original has a diameter of 68m/223ft. The west front, which dates from the end of the 19th century, is also based on a famous model, the church of St John Lateran in Rome. Some of the interior decoration was the work of the Antwerp sculptor F. de Vriendt.

Basilica of SS. Agatha and Barbara

The chapel of the Instituut Saint-Louis also shows Roman influences in its façade and dome. The Institute, built between 1865 and 1889, housed young Dutchmen ("Zouaves") who volunteered to defend the Pope and the Papal States during the struggle for the unification of Italy in the 19th century.

Instituut Saint-Louis

The Zouave Museum at Markt 31 commemorates the 4000 Dutchmen who belonged to the Zouave Corps for the defence of the Vatican between 1860 and 1870. The museum is housed in the old Town Hall, a neo-classical building of around 1775. Open: May to October, Tue. and Thur. 2–5pm.

Zouave Museum

The Museum of Natural History and Ethnology, at Markt 30A, has a collection of objects brought back from China, Indonesia and Africa by monks of the Oudenbosch monastery. Open: Sun. 2–5pm.

Museum of Natural History and Ethnology

Oudeschild

See Texel

Oudewater

D 7

Province: Utrecht
Population: 7000

Situation and characteristics

East of Gouda on N 207 is the little town of Oudewater, on the IJssel, birthplace of the painter Gerard David (c. 1460–1523). The town has numbers of handsome gabled houses dating from the golden age of Dutch architecture (1600–20), particularly in the Markt, on the harbour and in Leeuwerikstraat and Wijkstraat.

This historic little town with its narrow *grachten* gains its living from agriculture, some small-scale industry and the services sector – though some 60% of the working population work outside the town.

Heksenwaag

The town's best-known sight is the Heksenwaag ("Witches' Weigh-House") at Leeuweringerstraat 2. The scales in this weigh-house (1595) were used for the weighing of women alleged to be witches. In practice most of them were cleared of the allegation, for even in those days few Dutch women weighed less than 50kg/110lb, and if a supposed witch weighed more than that she could not be a witch, since the broomstick would have broken under her weight. Visitors can have themselves weighed, and are then given a certificate of their weight. Open: April to October, Tue.–Sat. 10am–5pm, Sun. 12 noon–5pm.

Grote Kerk

The Grote Kerk (Noorderkerkstraat 20), a 15th century hall-church, has a 14th century tower (carillon), still with its original saddle roof.

Town Hall

The Renaissance-style Town Hall (Stadhuis) of 1588 was destroyed by fire in 1968 but has since been fully restored. It contains a painting of 1575 depicting the atrocities committed by the Spaniards (not open to the public).

Overijssel

F–J 4–6

Provincial capital: Zwolle
Area: 342,000 hectares/844,740 acres
    (land area 333,890 hectares/824,708 acres)
Population: 1,010,000

Situation and characteristics

The province of Overijssel extends across the Netherlands from the IJsselmeer in the north-west to the German frontier in the south-east, bounded on the north by Drenthe and on the south by Gelderland. It offers an attractive variety of landscape – river plains, moorland, ridges of hills, arable land and expanses of sandy soil. In western Overijssel, on the IJsselmeer, are a number of nature reserves and natural watercourses. In the central region of Salland (see entry) are three, and in Twente (see entry) to the east two, morainic ridges formed in the second ice age, rising to heights of up to 90m/300ft.
Overijssel means "over the IJssel" (i.e. beyond the IJssel when seen from the west). In the Middle Ages, when Overijssel belonged to the Bishop of Utrecht, it was known as Oversticht (see below).

History

Overijssel was occupied by man from the earliest times. Around 780 it was conquered by the Franks and incorporated in the Carolingian empire. About the year 1000 it was inherited by the Bishop of Utrecht (Nedersticht), who thus also acquired Obersticht. Owing to the independence of the towns and landowners of Overstichtt, however, he was unable to establish his authority in the region until Burgundian times. In 1522 Overijssel, as it was now called, passed to the Duke of Gelre, and in 1528 to the Emperor

Huis Singraven, Denekamp (Overijssel)

Charles V. During the eighty years' fight for independence, in 1579, Overijssel joined the Union of Utrecht and drove out the Spanish occupying
forces; the Spaniards recovered the territory in the following year, but were
finally expelled from the province by Prince Maurice of Nassau between
1591 and 1597. After the country was liberated from French rule in 1813
Overijssel became a province of the new Kingdom of the Netherlands.

Most of the population is employed in industry and the services sector,
only 10% in agriculture. Some 75% of the area of the province is agricultural land, three-quarters of it pastureland, mostly in small holdings. Stock
farming (cattle and pigs) is predominant. In the north and east of the
province vegetables are grown. As a result of the redistribution of agricultural land and increasingly intensive cultivation productivity has steadily
increased, while at the same time the number employed in agriculture has
fallen since 1947 by almost half.

Agriculture

When Belgium became independent the Netherlands lost the textile industry which had hitherto been a major element in the economy. Steps were
taken from 1840 onwards to re-establish it in the Twente area, but now on
an industrial basis rather than the previous cottage industry. More recently
textiles have been displaced by other branches of industry such as metalworking, leading to unemployment problems in such towns as Almelo,
Hengelo and Enschede. Other industries have also been established – the
extraction of salt (at Boekelo), chemicals, electrical engineering, woodworking, foodstuffs, the extraction of natural gas (Twente) and shipbuilding. The main industrial centres in the province, in addition to the towns in
the east of the province already mentioned, are Deventer, Zwolle and
Kampen.

Industry

The spacious landscapes of Overijssel offer many attractive holiday areas –
in the north-west of the province, along the Vecht, in Salland and north-
western Twente.

Tourism

Peel

See Kempen

Rheden

See Veluwe

Rhenen

See Amerongen

River Rhine (Rijn)   C–G 6/7

Note
In this guide the description of the Rhine valley is confined to the main features of interest: fuller information is given in the AA/Baedeker guide "Rhine".

Course of the
Rhine
The Rhine (Dutch Rijn; Celtic Renos, Latin Rhenus, German Rhein), 1320km/820 miles long from source to sea, is Europe's most important waterway and scenically its most attractive. It originates in the western Swiss canton of Grisons, where the Vorderrhein and Hinterrhein unite to form the Alpine Rhine. It then flows through Lake Constance, goes over the Rhine Falls at Schaffhausen and continues on its way to Basle as the High Rhine. At Basle it turns north and flows through the Upper Rhine plain. Between Mainz and Bingen it follows a westerly course and then bears north-west through the Rhenish Uplands. Within the territory of the Netherlands it divides into a number of separate arms, which finally flow into the North Sea.

Rhine–Maas Delta
The hydrographic pattern of the Rhine and the various arms which convey its water to the sea is highly complex, particularly since it is bound up with the course of the Maas (see entry) and its various ramifications.

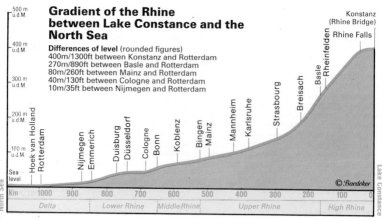

Gradient of the Rhine between Lake Constance and the North Sea

Differences of level (rounded figures)
400m/1300ft between Konstanz and Rotterdam
270m/890ft between Basle and Rotterdam
80m/260ft between Mainz and Rotterdam
40m/130ft between Cologne and Rotterdam
10m/35ft between Nijmegen and Rotterdam

© Baedeker

At the German–Dutch frontier, which for the first 8km/5 miles runs along the middle of the Rhine, the river takes the name of Bovenrijn (Upper Rhine). 2km/1¼ miles farther on it divides into a northern and a southern arm.

Bovenrijn

The northern arm is known as Pannerdens Kanaal as far as Arnhem, where the Gelderse IJssel branches off to flow into the IJsselmeer. From Arnhem to Wijk bij Duurstede (see entry) it is known as the Nederrijn (Lower Rhine).

Pannerdens Kanaal
Nederrijn

Shortly before Wijk bij Duurstede the Kromme Rijn (Winding Rhine) branches off and flows north-west towards Utrecht. Beyond Utrecht the Oude Rijn (Old Rhine) pursues a winding course by way of Alphen aan den Rijn, the old university town of Leiden and Katwijk aan den Rijn to the seaside resort of Katwijk aan Zee, where it flows into the North Sea.

Kromme Rijn
Oude Rijn

Soon after Wijk bij Duurstede the Nederrijn crosses the Amsterdam–Rhine Canal, which provides a link with the Waal; and from this point to its junction with the Noord (linking it with the Merwede) it is known as the Lek.

Lek

Within the city and port area of Rotterdam the river successively bears the names of Nieuwe Maas (New Maas; at IJsselmonde, junction with the Hollandse IJssel), Het Scheur and the Nieuwe Waterweg (New Waterway). Between the oil port of Europoort and the ferry port of Hoek van Holland (Hook of Holland) the Nieuwe Waterweg flows into the North Sea.

Nieuwe Maas
Het Scheur
Nieuwe Waterweg

The southern arm of the Rhine, known as the Waal, flows past Nijmegen and continues broadly parallel to the Maas, a short distance to the south (connected by two canals; the Maas continues as the Bergse Maas and the Amer, and after its junction with the Nieuwe Merwede flows into the Hollands Diep).
At Tiel the Waal is joined by the Amsterdam–Rhine Canal, which provides a connection with the Lek. From the old outflow of the Maas into the Waal near Gorinchem the southern arm of the Rhine is known as the Merwede. At Dordrecht, where the Nieuwe Merwede branches off to flow into the Hollands Diep, the Merwede divides into the Noord (connection with the Lek) and the Oude Maas (Old Maas). The Oude Maas then flows south past Rotterdam and joins the Nieuwe Maas (Het Scheur) opposite Vlaardingen.

Waal

Under the Delta Plan (see Facts and Figures, The Struggle with the Sea), designed to protect 15,000 sq.km/5800 sq. miles of land, the various mouths of the Rhine, the Maas and the Schelde, with the exception of the Nieuwe Waterweg and the Westerschelde, have been closed by dams. The tidal waters of the Oosterschelde are enclosed by a storm-surge barrier which is fully closed only in the event of a storm tide.

Delta Plan

Roermond

G 10

Province: Limburg
Population: 38,000

Roermond, situated at the confluence of the Roer and the Maas, is an important cultural centre as well as the economic centre of the Dutch frontier area sandwiched between Belgium and Germany. It is the see of a bishop (established 1569), with an episcopal seminary. Other cultural institutions include colleges of agriculture and several museums and libraries. There are an important Chamber of Industry and Commerce and a large market for the sale of agricultural produce.
Roermond also has a diversified range of industry. The most important branches are metalworking, electrical engineering and chemicals, followed by textiles, papermaking and foodstuffs (mushroom canning).

Situation and importance

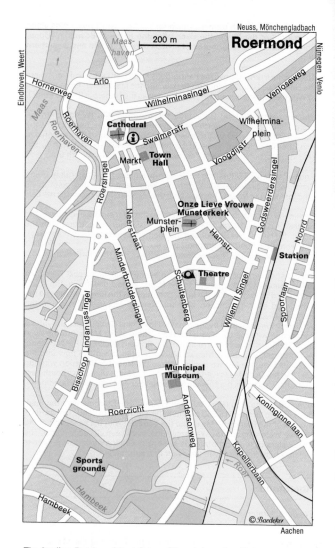

The leading Dutch architect Petrus (Pierre) Josephus Hubertus Cuypers (1827–1921) was born in Roermond; his birthplace now houses the Municipal Museum (see below). Among the buildings he designed were the Central Station and Rijksmuseum in Amsterdam and numerous churches (mostly restorations of medieval churches).

History

The town first appears in the records in the middle of the 12th century under the name of Ruregemunde. It received its municipal charter in 1230, soon afterwards became the chief town of the Overkwartier of Gelderland

and in 1441 joined the Hanseatic League. From 1543 to 1794 it was held by the Habsburgs, and in 1839 became part of the Netherlands.

The Town

Roermond has preserved the aspect of a typical old Limburg town. The Munsterkerk (Onze Lieve Vrouwe Kerk; 1224), originally the church of a convent of Cistercian nuns, shows the transition between Romanesque and Gothic.

*Munsterkerk

Under the crossing is the tomb of the founder, Count Gerard III of Gelre (d. 1229) and his wife Margaretha van Brabant (d. 1231).
The abbey was destroyed by French troops in 1797 but the church was preserved. It was restored between 1864 and 1891 by P. J. H. Cuypers, who replaced the 18th century bell-tower by two towers at the west end, believing that that had been the 13th century builders' intention.

A cruciform basilica with a rib-vaulted roof, the Munsterkerk is one of the finest Late Romanesque churches in the Maas area. The high west end of the church, rising above the nave, is flanked by twin towers. The east end has the trefoil layout characteristic of the Rhineland, with a tower over the crossing crowned by a ribbed dome (17th c.). On the high altar is a Brabantine altarpiece of 1530.

Adjoining the church can be seen a statue of Cuypers by August Falise (1875–1935).

In the Markt stands the Cathedral of St Christoffel (15th c.), destroyed during the Second World War and subsequently rebuilt, when the tower

Cathedral

Roermond Cathedral and Roerhaven

327

with its four little corner turrets (*c.* 1600) was given a modern spire in Baroque style.

The Cathedral has a sacramental altar in Renaissance style (1593), fine 16th century choir-stalls and a pulpit in Louis XIV style by Petrus Vinck (early 18th c.), supported on a figure of St John of Capistrano. Notable among the paintings are Rubens's "Head of the Crucified Christ" and T. W. Bosschaert's "Ascension" (1722). The modern stained glass is by Joep Nicolas.

Municipal Museum

The Municipal Museum (Gemeentemuseum) at Andersonweg 4, once the home of the architect P. J. H. Cuypers, has a good collection of old weapons and pictures. Open: Tue.–Fri. 11am–5pm, Sat. and Sun. 2–5pm.

Pilgrimage chapel

Kallerlaan runs south along the banks of the Roer to the pilgrimage chapel of the Redemptorists (1.5km/1 mile), with a much revered image of Onze Lieve Vrouw in 't Zand.

Surroundings of Roermond

St Odiliënberg

4.5km/3 miles farther up the Roer valley is the village of St Odiliënberg, with a fine Romanesque church (originally the collegiate church of St Peter) containing a beautiful image of the Virgin (1300).

Maasplassen

The Maasplassen are a series of lakes formed in former gravel pits in the Maas valley north and south of Roermond, with a modern water sports centre.

Romanesque church, St Odiliënberg

Rotterdam

Province: Zuid-Holland
Population: 574,000

The port town of Rotterdam, the second largest city in the Netherlands, lies on both banks of the Nieuwe Maas, the southern arm of the Rhine, here joined by the little river Rotte. At this point, and for a good distance upstream, the Maas is still tidal, with a variation in water level between high and low tide of between 1.2 and 2.5m (4 and 8ft).

Since the opening of the Europoort in 1966 Rotterdam has been the largest port in the world in the volume of goods handled, and in consequence has developed into a gigantic commercial and industrial centre whose full growth potential is still very far from being realised. The major imports are oil, mineral ores, grain, timber and fats, the main exports coal and food-stuffs; and Rotterdam is also an important transhipment point for raw tobacco. The city's principal industries are shipbuilding (with the largest shipyard in Europe), engineering, the manufacture of railway rolling stock, electrical engineering, petrochemicals (with the largest plant in Europe), semi-luxury foods and tobacco, clothing manufacture and papermaking. Rotterdam owes its rapid development to its fortunate situation on a navigable waterway with access to the North Sea throughout the year without the intervention of any locks. Its seaport can handle ships of up to 90,000 tons with a draught of up to 12m (39ft), and in addition it has the largest inland port in Europe.

Central Rotterdam was almost completely destroyed by German air attacks in 1940. The energetic rebuilding of the city after the war, re-planned with modern shopping streets and residential districts and with numerous high-rise blocks, has made Rotterdam one of the most modern cities in Europe.

Around the city centre are the districts of Kralingen to the east, Delfshaven to the west and Feijenoord to the south, with an outer ring of suburbs (Overschie, Hillegersberg, IJsselmonde and Pernis) beyond this. Hoek van Holland (Hook of Holland) also lies within the city area; Schiedam, Vlaardingen and Maassluis are independent towns, though closely adjoining Rotterdam on the west. Together with its surrounding satellite towns Rotterdam now forms a highly industrialised conurbation with well over a million inhabitants.

Situation and
**importance

Rotterdam developed out of a settlement founded in early medieval times. A first period of prosperity began in the 13th century, when a dam was built to separate the little river Rotte from the Nieuwe Maas: hence the name Rotterdam. The town received its municipal charter in 1340. Soon afterwards a canal to the Schie linked it with the then important commercial town of Delft, from the prosperity of which it soon began to benefit. This first period of prosperity saw the birth of Rotterdam's most celebrated citizen, the famous humanist Erasmus (born c. 1467, d. 1536 in Basle).
In 1563 most of the town was destroyed by fire. A new phase of development began, however, in 1585, when many thousands of refugees from the Spanish Netherlands settled in Rotterdam. The manufacture of cloth and carpets in particular brought a further period of prosperity. The port was less important in the 17th century, with only about a fifth of the turnover of the rival town of Amsterdam.
The rapid growth of the port began after the split with Belgium, when the Dutch dammed the Schelde (1830–39). The obstacle to the passage of large vessels by the steady silting up of the Maas estuary was removed in 1866 by the construction and constant deepening of the Nieuwe Waterweg, and at the point where it reached the North Sea the new suburb of Hoek van Holland (Hook of Holland) came into being.

History

Airport Den Haag, Amsterdam

Utrecht
Joosterhof, Kralingsee Plas

Waenburgerweg
Stationssingel
Schiekade
Provenierstraat
Hofdijk
Pompenburg
Goudse-
rijweg

Hofplein
Station

Warande

Bljdorp Zoo

Central Station

Stations-
plein

Weena

Hof-
plein

Goudse-
singel

Diamond
Center

straat

Hoek van Holland

Groothandels-
gebouw

Weena

Casino

Stadhuis
plein

Linbaan

Stadhuis

Meent

De
Ontdehoek

Library

Bouwcentrum

De Doelen

Karel

Rodin
sculpture

Schouw-
burg-
plein

Aert van Nesstr

Coolsingel

Beurs
WTC

Grote Kerk

straat

Hoog

Hoog

weg

Groenen-

daal

Westkruiskade

Wester-

Mauritsweg

Olden-

Doormanstr.

barneveltstr.

Beurs-
plein

Nieuwstraat

Het Blaakse
Bos

Stn

Oude
Haven

Tropi-
cana

KD-Anlegestelle (500 m)

Haringvliet

Maasboulevard

van Speyrkstr

Sint-

Maria-

straat

Gouvernestraat

singel

O. Binnenweg

Binnenweg

Historical
Museum

Churchill-
plein

Blaak

Monument

Maritime Museum
"Prins Hendrik"

vest

Westblaak

Wijnhaven

Museumsschiff
"Buffel"

Leuvehaven

Willemsbrug

Willemsbrug

Arnhem, Antwerpen

Mathenesser-

Nieu

Rochussenstraat

laan

Wester-

singel

W. de Withstr.

Eendrachtsstr

Schiedamse

Scheep

Boompjeskade

makershaven

Mariniers-
museum

Maas-

NORDEREILAND

Prins

Hendrik-

kade

Koningshaven

Boymans-
van Beuningen
Museum

Vaste-

land

Schiedamsedijk

Delfshaven

Hoboken
Complex

West-

zee-

dijk

Zalm-
haven

Willems-
plein

Houttaan

Spido
harbour
tours

Stieltjesstraat

Spoorweg

haven

Drooglever-
fortuyn-
plein

Nat. History
Museum

Parklaan

Parklaan

Museum voor
Land- en
Volkenkunde

Willemskade

Veerhaven

Maas

Wilhelmina

Rijnhaven NZ

kade

Parkhaven

Euro-
mast

P a r k

Taxation
Museum

Heuvellaan

Parkkade

Westerkade

Nieuwe

Rijnhaven

Ocean
Paradise

Maastunnel

Rijnhaven ZZ

Katendrecht
Veerlaan

KATENDRECHT

Basaltstraat

Rotterdam

500 m

© Baedeker

Maashaven

Europoort, (Harbour Route) —O— Metro Ahoy' Rotterdam

Two diamond-cutting workshops in Rotterdam are open to visitors:
Diamond Center Rotterdam, Kipstraat 7B, tel. (010) 4 13 45 51
Open: Mon.–Thur. and Sat. 9.30am–5.30pm, Fri. 9.30am–9pm.
SAP, Zuidplein laag 10, tel. (010) 4 10 18 88
Open: Mon.–Sat. 9.30am–5pm.

Diamond-cutting
workshops

The City

Central Area

From the Central Station (1957) take the wide street (Weena) which runs
east to Hofplein; then turn right into the Coolsingel, and continue beyond
Churchillplein into Schiedamsedijk, which passes the Maritime Museum
and leads down to the harbour.
Immediately south of Stationsplein (Station Square) is Kruisplein, and
from the south end of this square the Westersingel continues south, passing the Boymans–van Beuningen Museum. At the end of the Westersingel
turn right into Westzeedijk, which leads to the historic old Delfshaven
quarter, 3km/2 miles west.

Suggested routes

On the west side of Stationsplein is the massive Groothandelsgebouw
(Wholesale Trade Building; 1952–53), which houses a staff of 6000.

Groothandels-
gebouw

Facing the Groothandelsgebouw is the Bouwcentrum (Building Centre;
1947), the headquarters of the Netherlands Architectural Institute (Nederlands Architectuur Instituut), an international information and consultancy
centre which has a library with collections of material on Dutch architecture
and town planning since about 1800 and publishes technical literature and
journals. There are also exhibition rooms in which the Institute puts on
periodic public exhibitions.
New premises for the Architectural Institute on a site near the Boymans–
van Beuningen Museum are due to open in 1992; the architect is Jo Coenen
of Eindhoven, winner of an architectural competition held in 1988.

Architectural
Institute

South of Stationsplein is Schouwburgplein, in which are De Doelen, a
concert hall and congress centre rebuilt in 1966 after its destruction in 1940,
with seating for 2000 and excellent acoustics (exhibition hall), and the
Schouwburg (Municipal Theatre), opened in l988.

De Doelen;
Schouwburg

To the east extends a modern shopping district. The main shopping street,
2km/1¼ miles long, is the Lijnbaan, laid out in 1953 – the first pedestrian
precinct in Europe – with tempting modern shops, covered promenades
and displays of modern art.

Lijnbaan

The main street of the central area on the right bank of the Maas is the
Coolsingel. At the near end of this wide street, on the left, stands the Town
Hall (Stadhuis), built between 1914 and 1920 in Dutch Renaissance style,
with a handsome tower (beautiful carillon) and a richly decorated interior.
In front of it is a statue of the great international lawyer Hugo Grotius, who
was Grand Pensionary of Rotterdam from 1576 to 1586. Opposite the Town
Hall, in Stadhuisplein, is a war memorial designed by Mari Andriessen.
Farther down the Coolsingel, on the left, is the Bijenkorf ("Beehive")
department store (by Marcel Breuer, 1958). In front of it can be seen a
26m/85ft high work of sculpture, "Construction" (1957) – popularly known
in Rotterdam as "the Thing" – by Naum Gabo, a French sculptor of Russian
origin. Opposite the Bijenkorf is the Exchange (Beurs), with the Beursplein
on its south side. In this square is the World Trade Centre, a high-rise
building with a façade of greenish-blue glass.

Coolsingel

To the east of the Coolsingel, at Pannekoekstraat 55, is a special attraction
for children, the Ontdekhoek ("Discovery Corner"), a "hands-on" museum
of technology in which young people between 4 and 14 can gain an
understanding of scientific principles by carrying out simple experiments
for themselves. Open: Tue.–Sat. 10am–5pm.

Ontdekhoek

A short distance away, at Nieuwe Markt 1A, is the National School Museum, which illustrates, in a series of six classrooms, teaching and learning methods from the time of Charlemagne to the present day. Open: Tue.–Sat. 10am–5pm, Sun. 11am–5pm.

National
School Museum

From Beursplein the Hoogstraat runs east and comes to a flight of steps. Here, many centuries ago, a dam was constructed on the Rotte. Crossing the bridge and turning left, we come to one of the oldest parts of the town and one of the areas worst hit by the German bombing. Here, in Grote Kerkplein, is the Grote Kerk or St Laurenskerk, which dates from the 15th century (tower 1449, nave 1460, choir 1490; completed 1515). The church stands on very marshy ground, and even the heavy oak beams set at right angles to one another deep in the subsoil and the 4m/13ft thick foundations have been unable to prevent its 1.5m/5ft thick walls from developing a slight list. Around 1650 the tower began to tilt alarmingly, which led the municipal architect, Persoons, to rebuild its foundations, as can be seen from the extra thickness at the foot of the tower.

*Grote Kerk

The 1940 bombing caused heavy damage, leaving only the side walls and the tower still standing. Rebuilding began in 1952, and the transepts were completed in 1959, the choir in 1962 and the nave in 1968; the 23m/75ft high principal organ was installed in 1973; the modern subsidiary buildings were completed in 1981 and finally the 64m/210ft tower in 1986.

Entering the church by the main doorway under the tower, visitors are struck by the lightness and beauty of the interior. In the reconstruction most of the windows were glazed with brightly coloured glass. The church is a cruciform basilica in the Late Gothic style of the Netherlands, with high, wide aisles and painted wooden barrel vaulting. There are three organs by the Danish organ-builder Marcussen. The principal organ stands on a marble base on the inside wall of the tower. There is another organ in the south transept and a smaller organ on the north side of the choir. In the aisles are the tombs of three naval heroes, E. M. Kortenaer, Witte de With and J. van Brakel. The bronze doors of the main entrance, on the theme of "war and peace", are by the Italian artist Giacomo Manzù. In front of the church is a statue of Rotterdam's most famous son, Erasmus.

Farther east, beyond the railway, is the Nieuwe Markt, in which stands the Municipal Library (the "Pencil"), which has a fine collection of works on Erasmus. Nearby are the "pile dwellings", a modern housing project.

Near the south end of the Coolsingel, to the left, is a white building, the 17th century Schielandshuis (entrance at Korte Hoogstraat 31). Originally the headquarters of the Dykes Administration, it was badly damaged by fire in 1864 but is now restored to its former splendour. Since 1986 it has housed the town's Historical Museum (local history, art and culture). Open: Tue.–Sat. 10am–5pm, Sun. 11am–5pm.

Schielandshuis
Historical Museum

From Churchillplein two wide streets go off – the Blaak on the left and the Westblaak on the right. The Blaak joins the Overblaak, in which is a striking example of modern architecture by Piet Blom, the Kijk-Kubus, a block of houses with cube-shaped upper storeys. Some of the houses, which are fully furnished, can be visited. The scheme is explained and illustrated by photographs, videos and other illustrative material.

*Cube houses

Farther east, beyond the railway, are Geldersestraat and Geldersekade. On Wijnhaven is the Witte Huis (White House), a 46m/150ft high ten-storey office block, the first high-rise building in Europe (1900).

Witte Huis

To the south-east extends the 3km/2 mile long Maasboulevard, which was completed in 1964. From the east end there is a fine view of Rotterdam. To the left is the new Willemsbrug, which crosses the Nieuwe Maas to the southern port installations.

Maasboulevard;
*view

Running south from the Blaak is Leuvehaven, on the site of Rotterdam's first dock, with the gigantic piece of sculpture by the Russian sculptor Ossip

"The Destroyed
City"

◀ *Grote Kerk, with statue of Erasmus*

Schielandshuis (Historical Museum)

Zadkine, "The Destroyed City" (1953). This monumental work, with Cubist and Surrealist features, gives powerful expression to an extraordinary intensity of despair.

*Maritime Museum

At Leuvehaven 1 is the plain windowless concrete structure of the Maritime Museum (Maritiem Museum Prins Hendrik). From the entrance lobby visitors enter the very functional main hall, with gangways leading to the upper floors, which connect with one another without dividing walls. The effect is enhanced by the abundance of glass and steel and the exposed pipes carrying services.

The museum has a large collection of material on the history of shipping and seafaring since the 17th century. In addition to ship models (including a reconstruction of a 2000-year-old vessel), maps and atlases there are numerous pictures vividly depicting scenes from seafaring life, as well as film shows and periodic special exhibitions.

Attached to the main museum is an open-air museum in the Leuvehaven, with more than twenty ships dating from between 1850 and 1950, including two steam tugs, several sailing ships and above all the "Buffel", a rebuilt ironclad of the Dutch Navy (in service from 1868 to 1896), with a completely equipped upper deck, officers' cabins, etc., as well as exhibitions on 19th century seafaring. On the quay are various pieces of equipment, a ropewalk, cranes and naval workshops. Open: Tue.–Sat. 10am–5pm, Sun. 1–5pm.

Willemskade

To the south of the Leuvehaven is Willemsplein, beyond which is Willemskade, starting-point of the fascinating "Spido" harbour cruises. To the east of the Nieuwe Leuvebrug, with the Leuvesluis, is the Boeg, a striking naval war memorial.

Museum of Ethnology

At Willemskade 25A is the Museum of Ethnology (Museum voor Volkenkunde), with geographical and ethnographic collections from Africa, Asia

Modern architecture in Rotterdam: tower block and cube houses

Maritime Museum, with the "Buffel"

and America, ranging from everyday articles and cult objects to modern art. Open: Tue.–Sat. 10am–5pm, Sun. 11am–5pm. There is a speciality restaurant with Caribbean cuisine which is also open in the evening.

Taxation Museum

At the far end of Willemskade is the Veerhaven, with a monument to Pieter Caland, the engineer who constructed the Nieuwe Waterweg. Beyond this, by way of Westplein, is Parklaan; No. 14 is the Taxation Museum (Belastingmuseum), with collections illustrating the taxation system of the Netherlands and the history of smuggling. Open: Tue.–Fri. 9am–5pm, Sat. and Sun. 11am–5pm.

*Park

From the museum Parklaan continues to a park on the south side of Westzeedijk, attractively laid out with clumps of trees, green lawns and a number of small lakes. From the outlook terrace (café) on the hill above Parkkade, on the river front, there are fine views of the Nieuwe Maas with its busy shipping traffic. The International Garden Show (Floriade) was held in the park in 1960.

*Maas Tunnel

At the north-west corner of the park is the access road to the Maas Tunnel, a 1.5km/1 mile long road tunnel (opened 1942) under the Maas, here 800m/880yds wide, which links the city centre with the southern suburbs. There is a parallel tunnel for pedestrians and cyclists. At the north entrance to the tunnel rises the Euromast, erected in 1960 on the occasion of the Floriade. 185m/607ft high, it has two restaurants (views) at a height of 92m/302ft. The top section, the Space Tower, was added in 1970.

*Euromast

Zapata Nordic drilling platform

In the middle of the Maas, opposite the city centre, is the Zapata Nordic drilling platform, claimed to be "the world's first offshore museum on stilts". It can be visited by way of a makeshift bridge or in the course of a Spido harbour cruise. Particularly impressive are the power station, the

Euromast, seen from the Europoort

cement factory, the generators and the storage tanks. From the deck there are fine views of the city and the harbour. Open: daily 10am–5pm.

1km/¾ mile south of the Central Station, a building erected in 1935 (Mathenesserlaan 18) houses the world-famed Boymans–van Beuningen Museum, with a magnificent collection of pictures, sculpture, applied and decorative art (including Persian, Spanish, Italian and Dutch majolica, porcelain, glass, silver, pewter, lace and furniture), drawings and prints. The museum can also be reached from the Westblaak.

**** Boymans–
van Beuningen
Museum**

This is one of the great museums of the Netherlands, with its collections – originally assembled by F. J. O. Boymans (d. 1847) and since then much enlarged – displayed in light modern rooms. The painters of the 14th–16th centuries are particularly well represented, with works by Hubert and Jan van Eyck, Geertgen tot St Jans, the Master of Aix, the Master of the Virgo inter Virgines, Hieronymus Bosch, Hans Memling, Quentin Matsys, Lucas van Leyden, Jan van Scorel and Pieter Brueghel the Elder. The 17th century is represented by Pieter Saenredam, Frans Hals, Rembrandt (including a portrait of his son Titus), Carel Fabritius, Jan Steen and Rubens (26 works); also landscapes by Hercules Seghers, Philips Koninck, Jacob van Ruisdael and Hobbema.

Among Italian painters of the 15th–18th centuries are Vincenzo Foppa, Giambattista Moroni, Titian ("Boy with Dogs"), Tintoretto, Veronese, Guardi and Tiepolo ("Golgotha"). French painters of the 18th century include Watteau, Chardin, Boucher, Nicolas Lancret, J. Pater and Hubert Robert; of the 19th century Daudier, Boudin, Monet, Pissarro, Signac and Gauguin. There are also a number of pictures by Van Gogh.

Among contemporary painters represented are Picasso, Matisse, Chagall, Kandinsky, Franz Marc, Ensor, Tytgat, Permeke, Rik Wouters and Kees van Dongen.

The D. G. van Beuningen collection of 104 pictures and 27 sculptures, acquired in 1958, includes works by Hubert and Jan van Eyck ("The Three

Coolsingel   *Boymans-van Beuningen Museum*

337

Salvador Dalí, "Landscape with Girl Skipping"

Marys at Christ's Tomb") and Pieter Brueghel the Elder ("Tower of Babel").
The museum is open Tue.–Sat. 10am–5pm, Sun. 11am–5pm.

To the south of the Boymans–van Beuningen Museum is the Westzeedijk,
which runs from the Leuvehaven to the Schiehaven. In this area are a
number of smaller docks including the Parkhaven, the St Jacobshaven, the
Schiehaven and the Coolhaven.

*Delfshaven

Here too is the old district of Delfshaven, birthplace of Admiral Piet Hein,
which survived the Second World War unscathed. In the Oude Kerk on the
Voorhaven are a memorial and a bronze tablet commemorating the last
service held here in 1620 by the Pilgrim Fathers before sailing for the New
World.

De Dubbelde
Palmboom
Museum

At Voorhaven 12 is the Dubbelde Palmboom Museum, housed in a 19th
century warehouse with a fine double staircase. It contains a large collection of material on the history of Rotterdam, including archaeological finds
and implements and equipment illustrating the development from the
earliest crafts to the mechanised industry of modern times. Open: Tue.–
Sat. 10am–5pm, Sun. 1–5pm.

Zakkendragers-
huisje

Nearby, at Vorstraat 13–15, is the Zakkendragershuisje (Porters' House), an
old tin-smelting works which is still operating. Visitors can watch objects
being cast in the old moulds. Open: Tue.–Sat. 10am–5pm, Sun.
11am–5pm.

Southern Districts

Noordereiland

The southern districts of Rotterdam on the left bank of the Maas can be
reached either by way of the busy Willemsbrug, parallel to which is a
railway bridge, or through the Maas Tunnel.

The Willemsbrug leads to the Noordereiland, a long island in the middle of
the river. Here, at Maaskade 119, is the Mariniersmuseum, which illustrates

the history of the Corps of Marines from its establishment in 1665 to the present day. Open: Tue.–Sat. 10am–5pm, Sun. 11am–5pm.

On the far side of the Noordereiland is the Koningshaven (1km/¾ mile long), with the oldest port installations on the left bank of the Maas (1873), which is spanned by road and rail bridges. To the south of this is the Feijenoord district, with the Binnenhaven, the Spoorweghaven, the large Maashaven (58 hectares/143 acres), built on the site of the old village of Katendrecht, and the small Charlois (pronounced Sharlóis) Docks.

Harbour

To the west of the Charlois Docks stretches the large Waalhaven (310 hectares/766 acres), one of the largest dock complexes in the world. West of the Waalhaven is the suburb of Pernis, at the junction of the Oude and the Nieuwe Maas, where the Nieuwe Waterweg (Het Scheur) begins. From here the vast Europoort complex (see below) extends westward between the Nieuwe Waterweg and the Brielse Maas (Brielse Meer) to reach the North Sea at Hoek van Holland.

Northern Districts

North-west of the Central Station, at Van Aerssenlaan 49, is Blijdorp Zoo (Diergaarde), established in 1857.
The large Riviera Hall complex contains freshwater and saltwater aquariums, tropical plants and birds. Most of the animals are in open enclosures designed to resemble their natural habitat. The new section called Asia (1990), for example, includes a swamp forest with two large aviaries for exotic birds, a Mongolian steppe, a bat cave, Chinese fauna and a Chinese garden. Open: daily 9am–5pm, in summer to 6pm.

Blijdorp Zoo

In north-eastern Rotterdam, beyond the district of Kralingen, lies a large lake, Kralingse Plas, set in the Kralingse Bos, a wooded area (220 hectares/550 acres) much favoured by the people of Rotterdam at weekends. There are several restaurants and facilities for water sports.

Kralingse Plas

On the south-east side of the Kralingse Plas stands a windmill known as De Ster, a snuff and spice mill of 1740 (restored); closed on Sunday. Farther north are two other windmills, the Prinsenmolen (1648) on the Bergse Voorplas and De Vier Winden (1776) on the banks of the Rotte.

Eastern Districts

To the south of the Kralingse Plas, at Groene Wetering 41, is the Toy Museum, with a collection of rare dolls, dolls' houses and mechanical toys from 1700 to 1940. Open: Sun.–Thur. 11am–4pm; closed July and August.

Toy Museum

Farther south again, at Honingerdijk 64 (near the Maasboulevard), can be found the Trompenburg Arboretum, in the grounds of Trompenburg, an old country house (1820). In addition to beeches, oaks and rhododendrons there are 3000 trees and shrubs from all over the world. Open: Mon.–Sat. 9am–5pm. Admission tickets must be obtained from the VVV office.

Trompenburg
Arboretum

*Europoort

Rotterdam is the largest port in the world, handling over 250 million tons of goods annually and providing employment for many thousands of people, with a hinterland of more than 160 million people living within a radius of 500km/300 miles. The city covers a total area of 247 sq.km/95 sq. miles, half of which is occupied by the port.

Europoort (the "Gateway to Europe") is the name given to the huge western port complex; the term Rijnmond is applied to the whole industrial area between Rotterdam and the coast, taking in a number of other towns.

Rotterdamse Havenroute

Rotterdamer Harbour Route

- - - - ● - - - - Harbour Route, with points of interest   ▨ Port and industrial areas

- **0** **Merwedehaven** (opened 1930, handling general cargo; now transhipment point for fruit, timber, tubes and cement)
- **1** **Europoint complex** (port administration and co-ordination centre)
- **2** **Lekhaven** (opened 1910, handling general cargo; now in course of reconstructing, new terminal for orange juice concentrate on IJsselhaven)
- **3** **Nieuw Delfshaven** (once the site of the great Wilton-Fyenoord shipyards; now filled in and occupied by flats; Jan Backx Harbour and Transport School)
- **4** **Oud Delfshaven** (originally the port for Delft, established in the 14th c.; incorporated in Rotterdam 1886; now protected as a national monument)
- **5** **Parkhaven** (1890–1909; link between the river, the Coolhaven and inland waterways; headquarters of Customs Administration)
- **6** **Maas Tunnel** (constructed 1937–42)
- **7** **Dockhaven** (formerly repair docks and floating docks; filled in 1983 and now occupied by flats)
- **8** **Waalhaven**/East side (1907–30; originally for bulk goods, now mainly timber and timber products, heavy goods, containers and goods for international futures markets; giant 60-ton crane; first oil storage tanks of Royal Dutch Shell on Sluisjedijk, 1888)
- **9** **Waalhaven**/South Side (formerly an airstrip, now a container terminal, with moorings for inland shipping; Professor Rutten Harbour and Transport School)
- **10** **Waalhaven**/West side, Prins Johan Frisohaven (container handling, with overflow terminal; ro-ro terminal; temporary storage for tubes, log timber, cellulose and paper; large power station)
- **11** **Heijplaat** (garden city for shipyard employees; construction of port installations)
- **12** **Heysehaven** (formerly a quarantine station; now supply port for offshore enterprises, for the municipal building organisation and for Third World imports)
- **13** **Prinses Beatrixhaven** (opened 1965, handling general cargo; contained loading gantry, ro-ro ramp, heavy-duty cranes)
- **14** **Prinses Margriethaven** (Europe Container Terminus since 1967; terminal for lighter-carrying ships)
- **15** **Prins Willem Alexanderhaven** (container terminal; transhipment of timber products from northern Europe)
- **16** **Pernis** (a fishing village established in 14th c. on reclaimed land; ship repair yard)
- **17** **Kilometre 1008** (1008km/626 miles from the Rhine Bridge at Konstanz; radar station; on opposite bank the Wilton-Fyenoord shipyard)
- **18** **Benelux Tunnel** (opened 1967)
- **19** **2nd Petroleumhaven** (petrochemical plant)
- **20** **Rotterdamse Ster** ("Rotterdam Star": access to city ring road)
- **21** **Shell Nederland/Texaco** (petrochemical complex; oil pipeline to Germany; reporting office of Environmental Protection Agency for the Rhine delta area)
- **22** **Botlekbrug** (lift bridge, opened 1950, with clearance of 45m/148ft)
- **23** **3rd Petroleumhaven** (Esso refinery, aluminium plant, storage tanks, etc.)
- **24** **Oude Maasweg** (container service, storage tanks, tank-cleaning)
- **25** **Heulhaven** (harbour tugs, fire service and refuse disposal vessels)
- **26** **Botlek** (petrochemicals port; cracking plant, distillation towers)
- **27** **Welplaatweg** (plants producing caustic soda, chlorine and hydrogen; firms trading in chemical products; lamp-black factory)
- **28** **Welplaathaven** (offshore units; storage tanks; raw materials for detergents)
- **29** **Chemiehaven** (storage of raw materials for the chemical, detergent and foodstuffs industries; temporary stage for crude oil; transhipment of grain)

The **Rotterdam Harbour Route** (Rotterdamse Havenroute), marked by this sign, is a sightseeing drive of between 90 and 150km (55 and 95 miles) through Rotterdam's extensive harbour area.

– – – ⋈ – – Metro (with station)

30 **Chemieweg** (view of loading and unloading installations in the Botlek and St Laurenshaven docks)

31 **Agribulk** (grain elevators and stores on the dam closing the Brielse Maas, now the Brielse Meer, completed in 1952)

32 **St Laurenshaven** (minerals)

33 **Chemical plants** (storage tanks for liquid chemicals, production of phenol, transhipment of liquid sulphur, production of sulphuric acid, nitrogen and titanium dioxide)

34 **Verolme Botlek** (Prins Willem Alexander Dock, ship repair yard)

    AVR Chemie (refuse disposal)

    Torontohaven (transhipment of ores, cleaning of tanks)

35 **Rozenburg** (a village known as the "green heart of the Europoort", surrounded by reclaimed industrial sites and dykes)

36 **Rozenburg-Maassluis ferry**

37 **Calandkanaal** (canal for ocean-going ships between the Europoort harbours and the North Sea)

38 **Dam** between Calandkanaal and Nieuwe Waterweg (moorings for offshore construction platforms; factories producing artificial fertilisers and acids)

39 **Harbour mouth** (moorings for Europoort tugs in Scheurhaven; Hoek van Holland ro-ro ferry port on north side of Nieuwe Waterweg)

40 **Calandbrug** (lift bridge with 50m/165ft clearance); Brittanniëhaven (all-round terminal, car terminal)

41 **Europoort Oost**/Merseyweg (plastics factories)

42 **Europoort Oost**/Theemsweg (chemical plants, cement works, container terminal)

43 **Rozenburgsesluis** (lock, 299m/981ft by 23m/75ft, between Hartelkanaal and Calandkanaal)

44 **7th Petroleumhaven** (storage tanks for crude oil and oil products)

45 **De Beer** international seamen's centre

46 **5th Petroleumhaven** (Kuwait Petroleum Corporation)

47 **4th Petroleumhaven** (discharge of crude oil)

48 **Beneluxhaven** Ro-Ro Terminal (North Sea Ferries and P & O Ferries; Eurocentre)

49 **Beneluxhaven** Agribulk (grain elevator, silos, soya-processing factory)

50 **Hartelkanaal** (linking the Maas plain, the Europoort industrial area and the hinterland)

51 **6th Petroleumhaven** (BP refinery)

52 **Brielse Meer** (formerly the Brielse Maas, shut off from the North Sea in 1950 under the Delta Plan; now a recreation area)

53 **Oostvoornse Meer** (formerly the mouth of the Brielse Gat, cut off from the North Sea in 1966; now a lake popular with wind-surfers)

54 **Mississippihaven** (coal terminal, plant for liquefaction of natural gas, transhipment of mineral ores)

55 **Westplaat** (western edge of Maas plain; discharge of sand)

56 **Dredger discharge point**

57 **Europahaven** (Delta Terminal, opened 1984; Europe Container Terminus, with ultra-modern loading and unloading installations)

58 **Maasvlakte** (Maas plain; large coal-fired power station)

59 **Breakwater**

60 **Maasvlakte** (development area; new lighthouse)

61 **Chain of dunes** at mouth of Rhine (Maasmond)

62 **8th Petroleumhaven** (Maasvlakte oil terminal, with rows of storage tanks)

    "Parrot's Beak" (dredger discharge point for heavily contaminated sludge)

Rotterdam

Development

A hundred and fifty years ago Rotterdam's harbour was of no great consequence. Its importance began to increase after the construction of the Nieuwe Waterweg, but the real breakthrough came after the Second World War, when the port, with its open access to the sea, developed an increasing export and import trade. The existing port installations were no longer adequate for the increased traffic; and in addition ships were becoming bigger and the harbour was not deep enough. It was decided, therefore, to extend the port. In 1947 the Botlek area, south of Maassluis, was developed, in 1957 the area south-west of the Nieuwe Waterweg.

The first tanker docked in November 1960. Every inch of land – including a unique nature reserve, was put to use. Warehouses and port installations mushroomed. The existing land area was not enough, and new land was created, extending for some kilometres into the North Sea, such as Maasvlakte, which was built up between the coast and a sandbank, using 170,000,000 cu.m/222,000,000 cu.yds of sand.

Near the Europoort is an area 15km/9 miles long where tankers of up to 200,000 tons, with a draught of up to 23m/250ft (the height of an eight-storey building), can dock.

There are different harbours for different kinds of goods. Rotterdam has the world's largest oil terminal (eight docks), handling over 110 million tons of oil products annually. There are five oil refineries, connected by pipeline with Belgian and German refineries.

There are also terminals for packaged goods and for bulk goods including coal, mineral ores and grain. Rotterdam was one of the first ports in the world to cater for the cost-saving method of container transport, with facilities for the onward transport of containers by road or rail. Foodstuffs such as meat and fruit are stored in refrigerated warehouses. Some 85% of Europe's supplies of citrus fruits, for example, are landed at Rotterdam.

Europoort, the Gateway to Europe

The port has 40km/25 miles of quays, with 1.5 million sq.m/1.8 million sq.yds of warehouses and 90,000 sq.m/108,000 sq.yds of refrigerated stores. The silos have a capacity of some 450,000 tons, and the warehouses for dry bulk goods a capacity of almost 19 million tons. The storage tanks cover an area of over 32 million sq.m/38 million sq.yds.

The Europoort has 18 floating grain elevators, 20 loading gantries, 284 cranes, 18 floating cranes, some 21 quay-mounted grain elevators, 32 container cranes, 46 tugs and 15 landing-stages for roll-on-roll-off transport.

Some 32,000 seagoing ships and 180,000 inland vessels use the port annually. 70% of all goods landed are immediately despatched to ports in other countries; other goods are processed in the Netherlands, but most of them are also exported. Some 500 shipping lines link Rotterdam with over 800 ports round the world. Along the length of the Rhine there are 32 container ports. From Rotterdam trains and lorries carry goods to over 550 destinations every day.

Surroundings of Rotterdam

An attractive trip is to Kinderdijk (see entry) with its nineteen windmills, 22km/14 miles east by way of Rijsoord and Alblasserdam.

Kinderdijk

The little town of Stellendam, south-west of Rotterdam on the Goeree–Overflakkee peninsula, is the scene of the national gladiolus show, Delta Flora, held every year in the Summer Garden (area 1400 sq.m/1675 sq.yds). Hundreds of different varieties of gladioli are on show, together with begonias, freesias, carnations and cornflowers – all set against a backdrop of conifers and birches.
Information:
Stichting Delta Flora
Postbus 2, NL–3240 AA Middelharnis, tel. (01870) 30 02

Delta Flora

Salland

G/H 5/6

Province: Overijssel

The region of Salland, in the province of Overijssel (see entry), lies to the east of the IJssel, surrounded by the sandy heathland areas of Drenthe, Twente and Veluwe.
The great expanses of sandy soil characteristic of Salland were formed in the second-last ice age (the Saale/Riss glacial). Here and there in this featureless plain morainic hills rise to heights of up to 80m/260ft, including the Lemelerberg and the Koningsbelt. North of the Vecht are several areas of peaty moorland.
This almost entirely agricultural region (stock-farming, with a certain amount of arable farming) is dotted with scattered settlements and villages of traditional type. The only towns of any size are Zwolle and Deventer (see entries), in the IJssel plain.

Scheveningen

C 6

Province: Zuid-Holland
A district of The Hague

The fashionable seaside resort of Scheveningen, originally a modest fishing village and now incorporated in The Hague, is famous as the scene of Admiral Michiel de Ruyter's victory over a Franco-British fleet in 1673.

Situation and characteristics

Scheveningen

The **resort

With its broad sandy beach and its seafront promenade, Scheveningen is' an ideal resort for holidaymakers looking for sun and water. Here they can bathe, walk among the dunes, ride, play tennis or go on a fishing trip from the harbour. Other attractions are the swimming pool with artificial waves and the casino.

*Kurhaus

From the fishing harbour in the south-west to the Strandhotel in the north-east the seafront boulevard (Strandweg) runs for 3km/2 miles above the beach along the edge of the dunes, lined by hotels with terraces overlooking the sea. The hub of activity is the imposing Kurhaus in Art Nouveau style (now protected as a national monument), which houses a hotel, a restaurant, the casino, a gallery, promenades and the Kurzaal.

Around the Kurhaus is a residential area and pedestrian precinct laid out on the most modern plan, with gardens, shops, cafés and a fitness centre (sports hall, swimming pool with artificial waves, sauna, solarium, etc.).

Pier

Other attractions (recently renovated) in this part of the town are the Pier with its four island-like extensions (sunbathing terrace, restaurant, "Underwater Wonderland", 45m/148ft high lookout tower) and the Circus Theatre (1750 seats), which is used for concerts and other cultural events.

Pier and bathing station, Scheveningen

Kurhaus, Scheveningen

Scheveningen

Museum of
Marine Biology

At Dr Lelykade 39 is the Museum of Marine Biology (Aquarium), with a wide range of marine flora and fauna from all over the world. There is also a collection of 30,000 sea-shells. Open: Mon.–Sat. 10am–5pm, Sun. 1–5pm.

Monument

1km/¾ mile south-west of the Kurhaus, beyond the old village (in which traditional costumes are still worn), stands the "Monument", an obelisk erected in 1865 to mark the spot where King William I landed in 1813. Every 25 years the landing is re-enacted.

Harbour

Near here is the Vuurtoren (lighthouse), and beyond this is the fishing and boating harbour (fishing trips; ferry service to England). A visit to the fish market and fish auction is an interesting experience for visitors. Numerous speciality restaurants.

Scheveningen
Museum

The Scheveningen Museum (Schevenings Museum) at Neptunusstraat 92 documents the history of the fishing port and resort of Scheveningen, with nautical equipment, ship models, traditional costumes and ornaments and jewellery. Open: Tue.–Sat. 10am–4.30pm; during school holidays also Mon. 10am–4.30pm.

Surroundings of Scheveningen

*Scheveningseweg

From Scheveningen a number of streets, including the Scheveningseweg, laid out in 1666 on a plan by the poet Constantijn Huygens, run south-east into The Hague (4km/2½ miles to the city centre). The Scheveningseweg passes the beautiful Scheveningse Bosjes, in which, near the Wittebrug Hotel, can be found the miniature town of Madurodam (see The Hague).

Westbroekpark
Rosarium

Adjoining the Nieuwe Scheveningse Bosjes on the west is Westbroekpark, with a rose-garden in which thousands of roses are in flower from June to October. Every year rose-growers from all over the world gather here, hoping to win the coveted "Golden Rose of The Hague" for their roses.

Schiedam   C 7

Province: Zuid-Holland
Population: 69,000

Situation and
characteristics

The port of Schiedam, situated at the point where the Schie flows into the Nieuwe Maas, has now joined up with Rotterdam. The town grew up in the 13th century around a castle on the Schie and received its municipal charter in 1275. It was originally inhabited mainly by fishermen and seamen, until around 1700 when *jenever*, a favourite Dutch corn brandy flavoured with juniper, began to be distilled in the town – a tradition which is still maintained. Of the nineteen windmills which once stood on the town walls four survive; one of them is still working.

Sights

There are a number of notable buildings in the old town. The Grote Kerk or St Janskerk (1400) is a hall-church with a 54m/177ft high tower. On the north side of the tower is the Weigh-House (Waag; 1748). Also of interest are the Town Hall (16th c.), the former Corn Exchange (1792), the Provenishuis (almshouse; 1759) and the Zakkendragershuisje (guild-house of the Porters' Guild; 1725).

Municipal
Museum,
Brandy Museum

The 18th century St Jacobsspital at Hoogstraat 112 is now occupied by the Municipal Museum (Stedelijk Museum), which has pictures by the COBRA group (Corneille, Appel, Jorn, etc.), and the National Brandy Museum (Nationaal Gedistilleerd Museum), which initiates visitors into the mysteries of distilling *jenever*. Open: Tue.–Sat. 10am–5pm, Sun. 12.30–5pm.

Schiermonnikoog   G 1

Province: Friesland
Population: 900

Schiermonnikoog (Frisian Skiermuontseach) is the most easterly of the   Situation and
West Frisian islands. Its name comes from the "grey" (*schieren*) monks of   characteristics
Rinsumageest, near Dokkum, to whom the island once belonged. Around
1580 Schiermonnikoog was incorporated in Friesland, in 1638 it was sold
as an independent lordship, and from 1892 to 1945 it belonged to the
German Counts of Bernstorff-Wehningen. It was acquired by the state in
1945.

With a length of 16km/10 miles, a breadth of 4km/2½ miles and a total area
of 4000 hectares/10,000 acres, Schiermonnikoog is the smallest of the
Dutch West Frisian islands. No cars are permitted on the island, large areas
on which – Kobbeduinen (2400 hectares/6000 acres in the east and Kape-
glob in the west) – are nature reserves.

The only village on the island, Schiermonnikoog, was established in 1760   Schiermonnikoog
after an earlier settlement was engulfed by the sea. The church (Reformed)   village
and churchyard date from 1860. The lighthouse, built in 1854, is now a
water-tower. The days when Schiermonnikoog was a whaling centre are
recalled by the whalebone arch set up in honour of the navigator and
discoverer Willem Barentsz.

Schoonhoven   D 7

Province: Zuid-Holland
Population: 11,000

Schoonhoven, half way between Rotterdam and Utrecht, grew up in the   Situation and
13th century at the confluence of the Lek and the Vlist and was granted a   characteristics
municipal charter in 1281. During the Middle Ages the town was frequently
involved in conflict, and in the 15th and 16th centuries it was surrounded by
a circuit of walls, with five gates. It still preserves some remains of its walls,
which were planted with trees in the 17th century, and one of its gates, the
Renaissance-style Veerpoort (1601).
From the 14th century onwards Schoonhoven was famed for its gold and
silverware.

St Bartholomeuskerk was founded in the 13th century. In 1400 it was   St Bartholomeus-
enlarged by the addition of a choir, and in 1450 it was given a new nave and kerk
tower. The tower has long shown a tendency to lean off the vertical, and in
1930 additional supports were inserted in the interior. The stalls are carved
with scenes from the life of Christ.
Other notable features are the 17th century pulpit, with figures of the
twelve Apostles, and the tomb of Olivier van Noort (1558–1627), the first
Dutchman to circumnavigate the globe (*c.* 1600).

The Town Hall (Stadhuis) was built in 1452 in Late Gothic style but was   Town Hall
much altered in later centuries. Restoration in the 1920s left the alterations
as they were but added a doorway, staircase and windows in contemporary style. The domed hexagonal tower contains a carillon of 50 bells.

The Weigh-House (Waag; 1617) stands on a dam above the harbour. In   Weigh-House
summer it operates as a pancake café.

The Gold, Silver and Clock Museum (Nederlands Goud-, Ziver- en Klok-   Gold, Silver
kenmuseum), at Kazerneplein 4, introduces visitors to the crafts of gold-   and Clock
and silversmithing and clock-making. Open: Tue.–Sun. 12 noon–5pm.   Museum

Sloten

Edelambachthuis

The Edelambachtshuis, originally a granary of 1566, displays a large collection of old silver jewellery and other examples of the silversmith's art ranging in date from 1600 to 1900. Open: April to September, Mon. 1–5.30pm, Tue.–Fri. 10am–5.30pm, Sat. 10am–5pm; October to March, Tue.–Sat. 10.30am–5pm.

Sloten

See Sneek

Sneek

Province: Friesland
Population: 29,000

Situation and characteristics

Sneek, the second largest town in Friesland, lies in the Frisian lake district. It is the main centre of an agricultural area, with colleges of agriculture, an agricultural advisory office and a teachers' training college, as well as one of the largest yacht harbours in the country. In summer it is a popular centre for water sports on the Frisian lakes, including the Sneeker Meer (4km/2½ miles from the town). Sneek Week, one of the most important sailing regattas in the Netherlands, begins on the first weekend in August.

Sneek

In addition to the tourist trade, the town's economy depends on a varied range of industry – foodstuffs, textiles, papermaking, chemicals, metalworking. Sneek is also an important market centre for dairy produce.

Town Hall

In Marktstraat the former Town Hall (Stadhuis), a notable 15th century building, has a magnificent Rococo façade (1760) – a rare feature in Friesland. Two fine rooms in the interior are the Rococo Council Chamber, its walls faced with leather, and the Schutterskamer (Marksmen's Room), with mementoes of the old marksmen's guild. Open: Mon.–Fri. 2–4pm.

Grote Kerk

A little way south, in Kerkstraat, is the Gothic Grote Kerk or Martinikerk (15th c.), with a beautiful two-storey sacristy (16th c.; interior remodelled in 18th c.).

The continuation of Kerkstraat, the Oude Koemarkt, runs south to the *gracht* called the Geeuw. Off to the right is the Waterpoort (Water Gate) of 1613, the only remnant of the town's fortifications, which were demolished in the 18th century. This picturesque old gate bridging a canal consists of two octagonal towers joined by a kind of loggia.

Museum of Shipping and Antiquities

The Frisian Museum of Shipping and Antiquities (Fries Scheepvaart Museum en Oudheidkamer) at Kleinzand 14 has a collection of ship models, navigational instruments and pictures of seafaring life. Open: Mon.–Sat. 10am–12 noon and 1.30–5pm.

Sneek: gracht *and Waterpoort*

Surroundings of Sneek

Sloten lies to the south of Sneek in the Gaasterland area, near the Sloter-   Sloten
meer. The smallest of the eleven Frisian towns (pop. 900), it is a picturesque
little place with its *grachten,* its town walls and its handsome old houses,
such as the Town Hall (Stadhuis) of 1759. The fortifications were built by
Menno van Coehoorn in the 17th century. Between the two water gates, the
Sneekerpoort or Woudsenderpoort to the north and the Lemsterpoort to
the south, flows the *gracht* known as Het Diep.

South Holland

See Zuid-Holland

Staphorst   G 4

Province: Overijssel. Population: 13,000

In western Overijssel, amid extensive areas of pastureland, is Staphorst, an   Situation and
old town very conscious of its traditions. Farmsteads along main streets   characteristics
(the Oude Rijksweg and the Gemeenteweg) are painted blue and green.

The manners and customs of Staphorst and the surrounding area differ   Manners and
from those in other parts of the country. The people are strongly Calvinist   Customs
and extremely conservative. Their costumes are different on working days

and on holidays, when the women wear mid-length skirts striped dark blue and black, with blue aprons.

St Odiliënberg   The villagers are not fond of being photographed by tourists, though the children, who also wear traditional costume, do not mind having their photograph taken. In any event permission should always be obtained before taking a photograph.

Nature reserve   South-east of Staphorst lies a nature reserve (woodland, heath, moorland).

Terschelling   E/F 1/2

Province: Friesland
Population: 4600

Situation and characteristics   The island of Terschelling, in the North Sea, can be reached from Harlingen by motor launch or car ferry (advance booking for cars advisable); the crossing takes 2 hours. The island, 28km/17 miles long with a total area of 9500 hectares/23,750 acres, is the second largest of the West Frisian islands. Most of its area is occupied by nature reserves – the sandy Noordwaarder area at the west end and the better known Boschplaat (4400 hectares/11,000 acres), a wooded area to the north-east. Along the north coast are numerous beaches.

West-Terschelling   The chief place on the island is West-Terschelling, where the ferries put in. Here and in the Midsland area to the north-east (handsome gabled houses) are the *commandeurshuizen* (sea-captains' houses) in which the captains of the whaling fleet lived. The Brandaris lighthouse, 54m/177ft high, was built in 1595; its light is visible for up to 40km/25 miles. Until the installation of an electric projector in 1920 the light was provided by a large beacon. Near the lighthouse is the cemetery, with the graves of countless seamen.

Municipal Museum   The Municipal Museum, 't Behouden Huys, is named after the hut in which the navigator and discoverer Willem Barentsz spent the winter of 1596–97. Barentsz was born on Terschelling about 1555. In 1594, while looking for the North-East Passage to India, he discovered the west coast of Novaya Zemlya, a group of islands in the Arctic Ocean, and on his third voyage, in 1596, he discovered Spitzbergen and Bear Island. When his ship was caught in the ice he wintered on Novaya Zemlya in a makeshift hut made from timber from his ship; he survived the winter but died on the way home in the following spring. His journal was discovered in 1871.
The museum is open April to mid June, September–October and during the Christmas and spring holidays, Mon.–Fri. 9am–5pm; mid June to August, Mon.–Sat. 9am–5pm.
In front of the museum are *stoeppalen* (piles supporting a pavement or walkway).

Texel   D 2/3

Province: Noord-Holland
Population: 13,000

Situation and characteristics   The island of Texel can be reached by car ferry from Den Helder (long delays during the main holiday season). With an area of 16,000 hectares/40,000 acres (length 24km/15 miles, breadth 9km/6 miles), it is the largest of the West Frisian islands. The sandy hill in the centre of the island was occupied in Neolithic times.

*Beaches   Texel's beautiful beaches attract large numbers of holidaymakers, both Dutch and foreign, in winter as well as in the main summer holiday season.

The island's principal source of income apart from the tourist trade is agriculture (mainly sheep-farming). Cheese is produced both from ewes' milk and from cows' milk (the well-known Texelaar cheese).

Large areas on the island are designated as nature reserves, as Texel is famous for its bird life. In summer it is the haunt of many thousands of birds, including spoonbills and various species of ducks and sandpipers.

The chief place on Texel is the attractive village of Den Burg in the centre of the island. Six lamb markets are held here during the months of May and June. The village church (Reformed) dates from the 15th century; the upper half of the tower was added in the 16th century, the spire in 1604.
The Museum of Antiquities (Oudheidskamer) illustrates the way of life of the islanders.

In the seaside resort of De Koog is the Ecomare museum of natural history, with a special section devoted to seals. It also surveys the history of the island from the earliest times to the consequences of modern tourism.

De Koog

In the old port of Oudeschild on the south-east coast – now a fishing village – ships used to lie at anchor in the 17th and 18th centuries before setting out on the voyage to the Dutch overseas colonies. Near the harbour is a museum displaying large numbers of objects which have been washed up on the shores of the island.

Oudeschild

At the northern tip of the island, near the village of De Cocksdorp, is a lighthouse, now leaning dangerously off the vertical as a result of the washing away of the dunes by the sea.

De Cocksdorp

The village church (1500; Reformed) of Den Hoorn is the most photographed sight on the island.

Den Hoorn

Landscape on Texel

Tholen

See Bergen op Zoom

Thorn

F 10

Province: Limburg
Population: 2600

Situation and characteristics

Thorn, a charming little town of whitewashed 18th century houses, lies in northern Limburg, close to the Belgian frontier. The centre of the town is closed to cars. The street lighting is still by gas.

Thorn Abbey

The history of Thorn was closely bound up with the Benedictine abbey (for both monks and nuns) founded by Bishop Ansfried of Utrecht about 925. In the 13th century it became a secular house for noble ladies whose abbess had the rank of princess of the Empire. The house was dissolved in 1795, and all that remains is the church (R.C.), a Gothic cruciform basilica of the 14th century. The church was extended in later centuries and was restored by P. J. H. Cuypers between 1860 and 1885, when the tower was heightened in neo-Gothic style.

The interior of the church is whitewashed. Under the crossing is a crypt. In the south transept is the raised "princesses' choir", and at the west end of the church is the "ladies' choir". The high altar (by F. X. Bader, 1769), originally in the Carthusian church in Roermond, was brought here in 1786. The stucco reliefs in the east choir are also by Bader. The most notable of the side altars is a Renaissance altar with a copy of Rubens's "Descent from the Cross".

Thorn abbey church: exterior . . . *. . . and interior*

In the chapterhouse (Kerkberg 2), which contains the archives of the abbey, is a museum, with a model of the town as it was before 1790, various liturgical objects and vestments, and a collection of coins.

Tilburg

Province: Noord-Brabant
Population: 154,000

The industrial town of Tilburg, on the Wilhelminakanaal, is the largest economic and cultural centre of the southern Netherlands after Eindhoven, though it did not receive its municipal charter until 1809. It is the country's principal Roman Catholic centre, with a Catholic University. The town also has colleges of economics, teachers' training, architecture and music.

Situation and *importance

Tilburg's traditional woollen industry still plays a predominant part in the town's economy, producing some 60% of the total output of woollen goods in the Netherlands. In recent years metalworking and other branches of industry have been established in the town to avoid the risks of undue dependence on a single industry.

The Town Hall (Stadhuis) now occupies the white neo-Gothic palace built in 1847–49 for King William II, who died here in 1849.

Town Hall

The Heike Kerk (1828), a handsome building in what is called the Waterstaat style, has a marble high altar (by G. Kerriex, *c.* 1700) from the abbey of St Michiel in Antwerp.

Heike Kerk

Town Hall, Tilburg

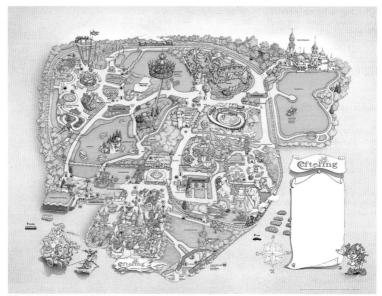

De Efteling: perspective view

Domestic scene in Fairytale Land

Oisterwijk, the "Pearl of Brabant"

The Natural History Museum (Noordbrabants Natuurmuseum) at Spoorlaan 434 has interesting geological, botanical and zoological collections. Open: Tue.–Fri. 10am–5pm, Sat. and Sun. 1–5pm.

The Textile Museum (Textielmuseum) at Goireestraat 96 displays precious fabrics from all over the world and old looms, spinning wheels, etc. Open: Tue.–Fri. 10am–5pm, Sat. and Sun. 12 noon–5pm.

Textile Museum

Surroundings of Tilburg

North of Tilburg, at the village of Kaatsheuvel, is De Efteling Fairytale Park (65 hectares/160 acres; open: Easter to October), with three large lakes (bathing, rowing), Europe's largest haunted castle, a fairytale forest, a fairytale town, a terrace restaurant and a tea-house.

Kaatsheuvel; *De Efteling Fairytale Park

5km/3 miles north-east of Kaatsheuvel is Waalwijk, with the Leather and Shoe Museum (Leder- en Schoenenmuseum), in an old shoe factory at Elzenweg 25. Open: Tue.–Fri. 10am–5pm, Sat. and Sun. 12 noon–4pm.

Waalwijk

South-east of Tilburg on the Hilvarenbeek road can be found the very popular Beekse Bergen amusement and safari park.

Beekse Bergen

East of Bergen on the old road to 's-Hertogenbosch, in dune-like country, is the little town of Oisterwijk, known as the "Pearl of Brabant", with the neo-Gothic St Petruskerk (by P. J. H. Cuypers, 1897), which has a fine wall painting by Charles Eyck, and a railway station of 1865 which is now scheduled as a national monument. South of the town lies the Oisterwijkse Vennen nature reserve (600 hectares/1500 acres), an expanse of heath and wooded country, with several lakes, which is one of the most popular recreation areas in North Brabant.

Oisterwijk; Oisterwijkse Vennen

Twente

Province: Overijssel

Situation and
characteristics

The district of Twente in the eastern Netherlands lies between Salland (see entry) in the west and the German frontier to the east. It is a region of featureless sandy plains, varied only in the east by an area of terminal moraines rising to 85m/280ft, the weathered remains of detritus deposited by the glaciers of the second-last ice age (the Saale/Riss glacial).

Since about 1830 the textile industry of Twente has developed from a traditional cottage industry into the major element in the economy of the region. The spinning and weaving mills and dyeing factories are mostly located in the towns of Enschede, Hengelo, Almelo and Oldenzaal.

Agriculture

Outside these industrial centres Twente is still essentially an agricultural region, dotted with villages of traditional type and isolated farmsteads. Pastoral farming predominates in the north, with extensive areas of grazing and meadowland and only occasional patches of arable land. There is more arable farming south of Enschede, where the soil is better.

Uithuizen

Province: Groningen
Commune: Hefshuizen
Population: 11,000

Situation;
Menkemaborg

Uithuizen lies north of Groningen, near the coast of the Waddenzee. Its most notable feature, in a park on the east side of the town, is the fortified manor-house of Menkemaborg, the finest and best preserved country house in the province of Groningen. It consists of three buildings of the 15th–17th centuries surrounded by a double moat. The interior furnishings (furniture, silver, china) are mostly 18th century, and the gardens with their beautiful rose walks have been restored to their 18th century form. There is a restaurant in the old Schathoes, the servants' or tenant farmer's house in the forecourt. Open: April to October, 10am–12 noon and 1–5pm; October to April, 10am–12 noon and 1–4pm; closed January.

Surroundings of Uithuizen

Usquert

West of Uithuizen, in a dyked area reclaimed from the sea, is the pretty village of Usquert. In the medieval period there was a commandery of the Knights of St John here. Its site is now occupied by two farmhouses, in one of which, Kloosterwytwerd, is a chimneypiece dated 1461 with the arms of the Order of St John.
The Town Hall (1930) was one of the last works of the celebrated architect H. P. Berlage, whose best known building is the Exchange in Amsterdam.

Urk

Province: Flevoland
Population: 12,000

Situation and
characteristics

Since the draining of the Noordoostpolder (see entry) the former island of Urk has been joined to this new part of the mainland. It is the oldest place in Flevoland, first appearing in the records in 966. The first settlement was founded on a low hill which provided security from high tides.

Menkemaborg, the finest manor-house in Groningen province

The construction of the Afsluitdijk (see entry) between the Waddenzee and the IJsselmeer in 1932 reduced the previously busy shipping traffic in the harbour; but the town has nevertheless contrived to preserve its traditional character. Every Friday ships which have been plying in the IJsselmeer and the North Sea return to port; and the superstition that the men must not board their ships again before midnight on Sunday is still observed. The fish auction is also still carried on.

Harbour

The people of Urk are very conscious of their traditions and still wear the local costumes. The women wear a black skirt, a flowered or embroidered shawl and headdress; the men a black jacket and trousers and a striped shirt. The house-fronts are still painted in traditional fashion in green and brown.

Customs

The Old Urk Museum (Museum Oud Urk), in an old farmhouse at Wijk 3, No. 73, displays dolls in traditional local costumes and puts on periodic special exhibitions on the history of the village. Open: June 1st to September 30th, Mon.–Sat. 10am–8pm.

Old Urk Museum

The Hulp en Steun Fisheries Museum (Visserijmuseum) at Wijk 1, No. 44, has models of fishing boats and other exhibits illustrating the local fisheries. Open: May 1st to September 30th, Mon.–Fri. 2–5pm; June 16th to August 31st also Mon.–Sat. 11am–1pm.

Fisheries Museum

Utrecht

E 6

Province: Utrecht
Population: 230,000

Utrecht, capital of the province of that name and the fourth largest city in the Netherlands, lies at the north-east corner of "Randstad Holland" on the

Situation and characteristics

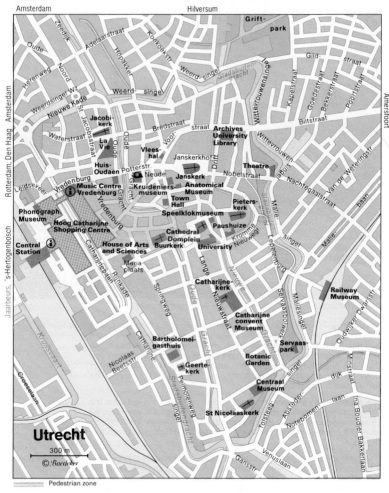

Pedestrian zone

Kromme Rijn, which here divides into the Oude Rijn and the Vecht, and on the Amsterdam–Rhine Canal, exactly on the geographical divide between the fenlands to the west and the sandy heathlands to the east. This position on the natural dividing line between the two territories favoured the development of the town over the centuries, since the heathlands, lying higher, were out of reach of the storm tides of the North Sea and offered ideal conditions for human settlement before the dyking of the fenlands.

Importance

From very early times Utrecht was one of the principal political, economic and cultural centres of the Netherlands. The seat of the provincial administration, with a famous university founded in 1636, it is also an important religious centre, the see of a Roman Catholic and an Old Catholic arch-

Modern architecture, Utrecht

bishop and the seat of the Oecumenical Council, the supreme Roman Catholic authority of the Netherlands. The existence of the University has led to the establishment in Utrecht of other educational and research institutions, including branches of the Royal Netherlands Academy of Science, the Central Institute for Nutritional Research, space research laboratories and the Institute of International Law, to mention only the most important.

But Utrecht is not only an educational, research and ecclesiastical centre: it is also of importance in the services sector, commerce, transport and industry. Industry is concentrated primarily on the west side of the city, where railway lines, roads and canals converge. The most important industrial installations are steelworks and rolling mills, engineering and rolling-stock plants, factories producing electrical apparatus and appliances, petrochemicals and textiles, railway workshops and furniture factories.

Tourism also makes a significant contribution to the economy, for the picturesque old town with its historic buildings, surrounded and intersected by *grachten* and canals, attracts large numbers of visitors, as does the beautiful surrounding country.

Known to the Romans as Traiectum ad Rhenum and later to the Frisians and Franks as Wiltaburg, Utrecht is one of the oldest towns in the Netherlands. The Romans built a *castellum* below (Old Dutch *uut*) a ford (Old Dutch *trecht*) on the Kromme Rijn, and remains of this were found outside the Cathedral; and the situation of the little trading settlement which grew up "below the ford" gave Utrecht its name.

History

The Frankish king Dagobert I (623–638) founded here the first church in the territory of the Frisians, whose first bishop, appointed in 696, was St Willibrord. The bishops (from 1559 archbishops) of Utrecht were powerful and influential prelates, and the town was famed from an early stage for its magnificent churches. It belonged to Lotharingia (Lorraine) and later to the Holy Roman Empire, and was frequently the imperial residence. In 1528 Bishop Henry of Bavaria ceded secular authority over the town to the Emperor Charles V, who built the castle of Vredenburg.

Utrecht was the birthplace in 1459 of Adriaen Florisz, one of the most learned men of his time, tutor to Charles V and later Pope as Hadrian VI.

In 1579 the Union of Utrecht, an alliance between the seven Protestant northern provinces of the Low Countries which paved the way for their separation from the southern provinces, was concluded here under the chairmanship of Count John of Nassau (Jan van Nassau) the Elder, brother of William the Silent. In 1672 the town was sacked by French forces. The treaty of Utrecht in 1713 ended the War of the Spanish Succession.

Alone among the towns of the Netherlands, Utrecht remained within its medieval circuit of walls (built in 1130) until the 19th century, when the town's increasing prosperity led to the development of new residential districts outside the old town.

The City
Central Area

Grachten

The old town is surrounded by the Singel, the old defensive moat, along which extend attractive promenades. On the west side it has been filled in to make way for a new fast road. The central area is traversed by the Oude Gracht and the Nieuwe Gracht or Drift, the water level in which is so low that the vaults in the embankment walls are used as store-rooms; some of them have been converted for use in summer as café-restaurants. In summer too there are attractive motor launch tours of the *grachten*. The Oude Gracht is part of the Kromme Rijn, which divides in the city centre into the Oude or Leidse Rijn (to the west) and the Vecht (to the north).

There are five churches in the old town, situated in the form of a cross, with the Cathedral in the centre, the Boorkerk to the west, St Pieterskerk to the east, St Janskerk to the north and St Nicolaaskerk to the south.

*Cathedral

In the centre of the town lies the Domplein (Cathedral Square), with the Cathedral of St Martin (Reformed), one of the most magnificent churches in the Netherlands, on its east side. Begun in 1254 on the site of an earlier Romanesque church (12th c.) and completed in 1517, the Cathedral now consists only of the choir (completed in 1317), the transepts (1455–79) and two chapels in the outer south aisle, the nave having been destroyed in a thunderstorm in 1674. The ruins were cleared away only in 1826, when the Domplein was laid out on the site. The church was last restored between 1981 and 1988.

The interior of the Cathedral is relatively plain. It contains a number of tombs, some of them badly damaged by the iconoclasts of the 16th century. In a crypt below the choir are preserved the internal organs of the Emperors Conrad II and Henry IV, who died in Utrecht and are buried in Speyer Cathedral in Germany. In the ambulatory are fragments of a Holy Sepulchre, a fine piece of sculpture by Gherit Splintersz (1501). The stained glass was designed by Roland Holst (1926 and 1936). The organ, in an organ-case by Bätz (19th c.), was built up using 17th–19th centuries pipes. The damage wrought by the 16th century iconoclasts is still very evident. The figures of the Apostles formerly on twelve columns are missing, and only one damaged relief remains in place. From 1580 until 1700, the church housed Utrecht University. Open: May to September, daily 10am–5pm; October to April, daily 11am–4pm.

On the south side of the choir is the picturesque cloister (14th–15th c.), which, with the Pandhof, links the Cathedral with the University. Above the windows are scenes from the life of St Martin, patron saint of the church,

Cathedral

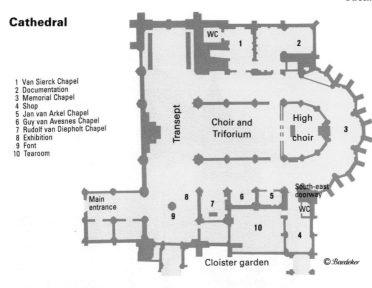

1 Van Sierck Chapel
2 Documentation
3 Memorial Chapel
4 Shop
5 Jan van Arkel Chapel
6 Guy van Avesnes Chapel
7 Rudolf van Diepholt Chapel
8 Exhibition
9 Font
10 Tearoom

Labels within plan: WC · 1 · 2 · Transept · Choir and Triforium · High choir · 3 · South-east doorway · WC · Main entrance · 8 · 7 · 6 · 5 · 9 · 10 · 4 · Cloister garden · © Baedeker

the town and the province of Utrecht. In the centre of the beautiful cloister garden is a fountain with a bronze figure of a monk writing (1913).

In the Domplein the outlines of the nave and other buildings associated with the church are marked by black stones. A bronze plaque on the cathedral wall shows the position of the Roman *castellum* and the churches in the area. To the west of the cloister are a statue (1833) of Count John of Nassau, who played a major part in bringing about the Union of Utrecht (1579), and a reproduction of a Danish runic stone in Jutland (980).

Since the destruction of the nave in 1674 the tower (Domtoren) has been completely detached from the church. Built between 1320 and 1382, it stands 112m/367ft high. Between 1505 and 1509 thirteen bells, weighing altogether 31 tons, were cast by Gerrit van Wou of Kampen from the metal of the previous bells. A carillon of 35 bells was installed in 1664 by the Hemony brothers, who obtained some of the metal they required by melting down the six smallest bells in the tower. The carillon was increased to 50 bells in 1982, when the bells missing from the tower were also replaced.

*Tower of Cathedral

The tower, once the symbol of episcopal authority, is the tallest church tower in the Netherlands, and was frequently imitated (Amerongen, Amersfoort, Groningen, Maastricht). From the platform, 100m/330ft above ground level (a strenuous climb: 465 steps), there are magnificent views (orientation table).
In the tower are two chapels, St Michael's Chapel (the bishop's domestic chapel) and the Egmond Chapel (exhibition on the tower). Open: Sat. and Sun. 12 noon–5pm; April to October also Mon.–Fri. 10am–5pm.

Adjoining the tower is the garden of the old Bishop's Palace (Florahof), with some fine pieces of sculpture originally intended for a cloister.

The administrative offices of the University (founded 1636; 20,000 students) are in buildings which belonged to the chapter of the Cathedral. The chapterhouse itself, in which the Union of Utrecht was signed, is now the

University

Utrecht Cathedral

Aula (Great Hall) of the University. Part of the University is housed in 19th century buildings on the north side of Janskerkhof. The new University quarter, De Uithof, with the Botanic Garden and a hospital, lies to the east of the city.

Museum of Mechanical Musical Instruments

From the Cathedral tower Servetstraat runs west and crosses the Oude Gracht on the Maartensbrug (to right, an attractive view of the Vismarkt) into Zadelstraat. To the right, at Buurkerkhof 10, can be seen the Buurkerk, now housing the National Museum "From the Musical Box to the Barrel-Organ" (Nationaal Museum van Speelklok tot Pierement), with a collection of mechanical musical instruments from the 18th century to the present day, including domestic instruments like musical boxes, street organs, dance organs, fair organs, orchestrions and player pianos.
The popularity of the barrel-organ in the Netherlands is due to the fact that local firms not only hire out organs but guarantee to maintain and service them. Open: Tue.–Sat. 10am–5pm, Sun. 1–5pm.

Buurkerk

The Buurkerk is the oldest parish church in the city (12th c.). It was rebuilt in the 13th century, after a fire, as a cruciform basilica with a massive brick tower. Parts of this older building can still be seen in the present church, which has been twice rebuilt since then. The choir was pulled down in 1586; the site is now occupied by Choorstraat. Open: Tue.–Sat. 10am–5pm, Sun. 1–5pm.

Mariaplaats

Farther along Zadelstraat is Mariaplaats. In this square is the House of Arts and Sciences (Gebouw voor Kunsten en Wetenschappen; 1840), with a music school and halls for theatrical performances and lectures, which was burned down in 1988.. At the south-west corner of the building is the Romanesque cloister of St Maria, all that remains of a church founded by King Henry IV in the 11th century and demolished in the 19th century.

South-west of Mariaplaats, beyond Catharijnebaan, is a large office block occupied by Netherlands Railways (Nederlandse Spoorwegen).

Street-organ in the Museum of Mechanical Musical Instruments

North-west of Mariaplaats, extending to Vredenburg, is Hoog Catharijne, one of the largest under-cover shopping centres in Europe. In this luxurious complex 180 shops with a total floor area of 250,000 sq.m/300,000 sq.yds offer shoppers an immense and varied range of wares. The complex also includes facilities for refreshment (restaurants, cafés, bars) and entertainment (four cinemas).

*Hoog Catharijne
shopping centre

The shopping centre is linked with the new Central Station to the west – the most important junction in the national and international rail network of the Netherlands. South-west of the station are the new Jaarbeurs congress centre, with the Trade Fair grounds, and the new head office of the Rabo-Bank.

In one wing of Hoog Catharijne, at Gildenkwartier 43, is the Phonographic Museum, which illustrates the development of sound-recording from the invention of Edison's phonograph (1877) and E. Berliner's gramophone (1887) to the present day. There is also a model of an early recording studio. Open: Tue.–Sat. 10am–5pm.

Phonographic
Museum

On the left-hand side of the picturesque Oude Gracht (Weerdzijde), at No. 99, stands Huis Oudaen, a fortress-like patrician house of the 14th century with a fine doorway of 1680. The treaty of Utrecht (1713) which ended the War of the Spanish Succession was signed in this house. Restored in 1986, it is now a popular restaurant.
On the opposite side of the *gracht* is Huis Drakenburg, which may be even older than Huis Oudaen.

Huis Oudaen

At the north end of the Oude Gracht is St Jacobikerk (Reformed), founded in 1173 and rebuilt in 1423 as a Gothic hall-church. Between 1476 and 1500 two new choirs and two chapels were built. The tower (1334) was badly damaged by a hurricane in 1674 and restored only in 1953.

St Jacobikerk

**Shopping Centre
Hoog Catharijne**

LEVEL 1

Vredenburg-
kwartier
Clarenburg-
kwartier
Radboud-
kwartier
Jaarbeurs-
kwartier
Godebald-
kwartier
Gilden-
kwartier
Stations-
kwartier

To the left is Vredenburg (Vreeburg), a large and busy square on the site of the castle of Vredenburg, destroyed in 1577.

To the east of the Oude Gracht along Potterstraat lies the Neude. In this square are the imposing Head Post Office (1919–24) and, opposite it to the south, the Neudeflat, a 15-storey tower block (1963) occupied by the municipal administration. In Voorstraat, which branches off the north-east corner of the square, is the Vleeshuis (Meat Hall; 1637).

St Janskerkhof

A narrow street, Kintgenshaven, with numbers of 17th century houses and the Hoogt cultural centre, leads by way of Slachtstraat and Lange Jansstraat to the Janskerkhof (flower market on Saturday morning). To the right, beyond a monument to Franciscus Donders, a celebrated 19th century ophthalmologist, is the Statenkamer (the meeting-place of the States of Utrecht), originally a Minorite friary (Minderbroedersklooster) and now a University institute.

St Janskerk

In the centre of the square is St Janskerk (Reformed), a Romanesque basilica (*c.* 1050) with a choir of 1539 and a façade of 1682. In the 13th century the original columns were reshaped as pillars; in the 17th century they were removed altogether; and during restoration work in 1986 they were rebuilt in their original form. The painted wooden barrel-vaulting dates from the 13th century. After the Reformation, from 1584 to 1817, the church housed the Municipal Library, and from 1636 to 1817 the University Library. Open: Mon.–Fri. 9am–5pm.

To the north-east are the State Archives (entrance in the Drift). Close by, in Wittevrouwenstraat, the University Library contains some 850,000 volumes and 2500 manuscripts, including such famous items as the 11th century Utrecht Psalter.

From the Janskerkhof Nobelstraat runs east to the Lucasbolwerk (bastion), now laid out in gardens, and the Stadsschouwburg (Municipal Theatre), designed by Dudok (1940).

St Pieterskerk

North of the Cathedral, in Pieterskerkhof, stands St Pieterskerk (Walloon). It was the earliest of the five churches in the old town (consecrated 1048). In the Romanesque crypt is the sarcophagus of the founder, Bishop Bernold. Notable features of the church itself are the capitals of the columns in the nave, the wall paintings in the north aisle and the 12th century reliefs in Maasland style. The high choir and transepts are Gothic. The south choir was rebuilt in the 15th century. The west front, flanked by two Romanesque towers, was damaged in the 1674 hurricane.

At the corner of Achter St Pieter and the Kromme Nieuwe Gracht is the Provinciehuis, seat of the provincial government. Part of it occupies the Paushuize ("Pope's House"), built in 1517 for the then provost of St Salvator's, the future Pope Hadrian VI.

Provinciehuis

In the Nieuwe Gracht, which runs south from the Pausdam, can be found the former House of the Teutonic Order (No. 3; entrance Hofpoort).

At Nieuwe Gracht 63, in a former hospice of the Order of St John, is the Catharijneconvent National Museum (Rijksmuseum Het Catharijneconvent), which is concerned with the history of Christianity in the Netherlands. Opened in 1978, it brought together the collections of the Haarlem Episcopal Museum, the Archiepiscopal Museum of Utrecht and the Old Catholic Museum, and is now the country's largest collection of medieval art treasures, with sections devoted to church interiors, religious beliefs, the worship of the saints and medieval monasteries. There is also much 17th and 18th century material. Among notable exhibits are liturgical vestments, valuable Books of Hours and a model of the Cathedral in its original form, with explanations of its architectural history. Open: Tue.–Fri. 10am–5pm, Sat. and Sun. 11am–5pm.

Catharijneconvent National Museum

At the south end of the Nieuwe Gracht, to the right, is the small University Botanic Garden; to the left is Servaas Park, in which is the Observatory.

From the Catharijneconvent Museum a narrow street, Catharijnesteeg, leads west into Lange Nieuwstraat, with St Catharijnekerk (No. 36). The

St Catharijnekerk

Huis Oudaen: a fortress-like patrician house

UPPER FLOOR

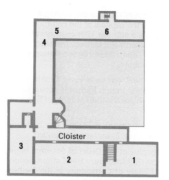

UPPER FLOOR

1 Old Catholic Museum
2 Exhibition room
3 17th century Catholic and Protestant art
4 Catholicism after the Reformation
5 Conflicts within the Calvinist church
6 Consequences of the Reformation

GROUND FLOOR

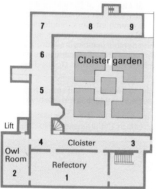

GROUND FLOOR

1 Church buildings and interiors
2 Religious ideas in the Middle Ages
3 Medieval monasteries
4 Worship of the saints
5 The cultural climate of the early 16th century
6 Origins of the Reformation
7 Humanism and art
8 Reaction of the Catholic church

BASEMENT

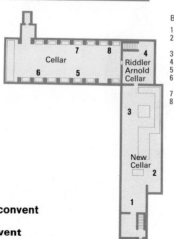

BASEMENT

1 Christianisation of the Netherlands
2 Church and state in the Middle Ages
3 The Christian calendar; vestments
4 Medieval piety; death
5 The Sacraments
6 Books of Hours, devotional literature
7 The sacrifice of the Mass
8 The Bible

**Rijksmuseum
Het Catharijneconvent**

**Catharijneconvent
Museum**

church was begun by the Carmelite order in 1468 and completed by the Knights of St John in 1550. It was a Protestant church from 1635 to 1815, when it was returned to the Catholics. In 1853 it became the cathedral of a Roman Catholic archbishop, and is thus the principal Catholic church in the Netherlands.

At the south end of Lange Nieuwestraat is Agnietenstraat, in which, to the right (No. 1), is the former Agnietenklooster, a convent of Augustinian nuns, of which there remain the chapel (1512–16) and the refectory. Together with the adjoining Artillery Stables these now house the Municipal Museum (Centraal Museum) and the provincial archaeological collections. Utrecht painters from the 15th century onwards are particularly well represented – the "Romanists" influenced by the Italian Renaissance, with their principal representative Jan van Scorel, and the Mannerist painter Abraham Bloemaert, who had an enduring influence on the "Utrecht Caravaggists", also well represented in the collection (H. Terbrugghen, G. Honthorst, Dirck van Baburen, Paulus Bor, etc.). — Municipal Museum

The museum also has a collection of costume from the 18th century to the present day, rooms furnished in period style, sculpture, silver and a collection of material on the history of Utrecht. Notable among the archaeological exhibits is an old ship of around 1200.

Open: Tue.–Sat. 10am–5pm, Sun. 1–5pm.

Associated with the Municipal Museum is the Rietveld–Schröderhuis, the only modern building in the Netherlands listed as a world heritage monument. In the manner of the De Stijl movement, it was built for Mr T. Schröder-Schräder by Gerrit Rietveld in 1924. It can be seen by appointment (made by telephone). — Rietveld–Schröderhuis

In Nicolaaskerkhof, south-west of the Centraal Museum, stands St Nicolaïskerk, a cruciform church with two Romanesque towers (12th c.). In one of the towers is a carillon by the Hemony brothers. — St Nicolaïskerk

In the Catharijneconvent Museum

367

Kasteel de Haar, Haarzuilens

Near the south end of the Oude Gracht, at the corner of Tolsteegzijde and Eligenstraat, can be seen a Frisian sacrificial stone attached to a chain which is associated with the Devil in an old legend.

Geertekerk

Off the Oude Gracht to the west is the 13th century Geertekerk (restored 1956), now occupied by the Remonstrants (a sect also known as the Arminians after their spiritual father Arminius). Close by, at Lange Smeestraat 40, is the Bartholomeigasthuis, founded in 1407 as an old people's home. The Regents' Room has fine tapestries by the Delft tapestry-weaver Maximilian van der Gucht.

Eastern Districts

Maliebaan

To the east of the Binnengracht, which runs along the side of the old town, extends the famous Maliebaan, a 750m/820yd long avenue of lime-trees. In 1672–73 it was spared by the French army on the express orders of Louis XIV.

Railway Museum

In the old Maliebaan Station, at Johan van Oldenbarneveltlaan 6, is the Netherlands Railway Museum (Nederlands Spoorwegmuseum), which offers an excellent survey of public transport, particularly railways and tram systems, with models and old vehicles and rolling-stock. Open: Tue.–Sat. 10am–5pm, Sun. 1–5pm.

At the north-east end of the Maliebaan, on the right, lies the little Hoogelandse Park and south of this, in Koningslaan, in the Wilhelminapark.

Surroundings of Utrecht

Around Utrecht is a beautiful and fertile region traversed by the arms of the Rhine and by canals, with many country houses and parks. The city is linked by good roads with surrounding towns and villages including Haarzuilens (5km/3 miles north-west) with its fine castle (see below), De Bilt (with the headquarters of the Royal Netherlands Meteorological Institute), Bilthoven (8km/5 miles north-east), Zeist (see entry), Driebergen and Doorn (see entry), and with towns in the Gooi such as Hilversum (16km/10 miles north: see entry) and Bussum (22km/14 miles north).

Haarzuilens was once the seat of the Van Zuylen van Nijevelt family. In the mid 19th century P. J. H. Cuypers built the present castellated house, De Haar, on the site of the old 15th century castle. The house (part of which is open to the public) contains magnificent tapestries, Louis XIV and Louis XVI furniture, Persian carpets, Chinese vases and a collection of pictures. The house is set in a very beautiful park and gardens, with trees which were brought on horse-drawn carts from woods 20km/12½ miles away.
Open: from March to mid August and from the beginning of October to mid November, Mon.–Fri. 11am–4pm, Sat. and Sun. 1–4pm.

Haarzuilens

Utrecht (province)

D–F 6/7

Provincial capital: Utrecht
Area: 140,179 hectares/346,242 acres
        (land area 133,109 hectares/328,779 acres)
Population: 965,000

Utrecht, the smallest province in the Netherlands, is centrally situated, between Noord- and Zuid-Holland in the west and Gelderland in the east. The province is traversed diagonally by the Utrechtse Heuvelrug, a ridge of hills which marks the boundary between the upland country (Hoog-Neder-land) and the lowlands (Laag-Nederland: see Facts and Figures, Topography). The west of the province is occupied by drained moorland and expanses of pastureland.

Situation and characteristics

The Utrecht Hills are a morainic ridge formed in the second-last ice age (the Saale/Riss glacial). From the Zeist area in the west the ridge runs south-east, gradually gaining height, to reach its highest point (69m/226ft) at Amerongen, and then comes to an abrupt end in the Grebbeberg to the east of Rhenen, on the edge of the Gelderse Vallei (Gelderland plain). Until just after the Second World War tobacco was grown on the south side of the hills. Mostly covered with forest, they are now a favourite holiday region.

Utrechtse Heuvelrug

In Roman times the course of the Rhine was different from what it is today. There was a good crossing at the point where Utrecht now stands, and accordingly the Romans built a *castellum* there which they called Traiectum ad Rhenum, the nucleus of the later trading town. After the Roman withdrawal Franks and Frisians settled in the region. The town became an archiepiscopal see around 700, and thereafter the archbishop gradually extended his authority over the present province of Utrecht, as well as to Overijssel and Drenthe. In 1456 Burgundy began to compete with the archbishop for predominance in the area. At the beginning of the 16th century the territory was incorporated in the duchy of Gelre, and in 1528 it passed into the hands of Spain.

History

Utrecht was one of the first provinces to break away from Spanish rule, and it was here that the northern provinces formed the Union of Utrecht in 1579. From 1672 to 1674 the area was occupied by the French; thereafter it was governed by a stadholder. After the French withdrawal from the Netherlands in 1813 Utrecht acquired its present status as a province of the Netherlands.

Apart from stock farming, agriculture plays a relatively small part in the economy of the province. Industry enjoyed a period of rapid development

Economy

in the early 20th century and again after the Second World War. The chemical and metalworking industries – including some firms which moved here from Amsterdam – flourished along the Amsterdam–Rhine Canal, to the west of Utrecht. Other industrial concentrations developed at Amersfoort and, increasingly, at Veenendaal in the south-east of the province. Electrical engineering, woodworking, textiles and the foodstuffs industries are also of some importance. The traditional tobacco and textile industries of Veenendaal have almost died out.

Vaals   G 11

Province: Limburg
Population: 11,000

Situation and characteristics

In the extreme south-east of the Netherlands, near the town of Vaals, rises the country's highest hill, the Vaalser Berg (321m/1053ft). Here, at the Drielandenpunt, the "Three Countries Point", where the frontiers of the Netherlands, Belgium and Germany meet, there are fine views of the foothills of the Ardennes, the Eifel hills and the Limburg mining area. Surrounded by free imperial territories, this was in the past a place of refuge for Huguenots, Mennonites and Calvinists.

Sights

Vaals has a brick-built Lutheran church of 1737 which is now a cultural centre, with fine Rococo stalls once occupied by the Clermont family, prosperous cloth merchants in Vaals in the 18th century.
In Clermontplein is the Town Hall (1761), originally a mansion of the Clermont family.
At Raren, to the west of Vaals, is another house belonging to the Clermonts, Vaalsbroek, built in 1761 on the ruins of an older house of 1516.

Viljen

5km/3 miles north-west of Vaals lies the village of Viljen, with St Martinuskerk, a neo-Gothic hall-church of 1864. Situated at an altitude of 195m/640ft, it is the highest church in the Netherlands.

Valkenburg aan de Geul   F 11

Province: Limburg
Population: 18,000

Situation

*Holiday resort

The romantic little town of Valkenburg lies in the picturesque Geul valley, in the Limburg uplands, below the only hilltop castle in the Netherlands. It has long been a very popular holiday resort. A hundred years ago its main tourist attractions were its caves: it now also attracts visitors with its Casino, decorated in the style of the twenties, and its spa facilities in the futuristic Thermae 2000, the largest spa establishment in the Netherlands after Nieuweschans in Groningen. Valkenburg also has the country's oldest functioning railway station (1853).

St Nicolaaskerk

St Nicolaaskerk is a Late Gothic pseudo-basilica (14th c.), with a nave which was enlarged in 1891 and transepts and a choir which were lengthened in 1904. Its most notable feature is a triptych with scenes from the life of St Remigius.

Castle ruins

On the south side of the town rises the Dwingelrots (Castle Rock), which is crowned by the ruined castle of the lords of Valkenburg. The castle was founded in the 12th century; the tower and the fortified communicating passages, some of them hewn from the rock, are later. After several sieges, and several rebuildings, the ruined castle was abandoned in 1672. There was a secret passage from the castle to the caves hewn from the rock below. Open: Easter to mid October, daily 10am–5pm.

Ruins of Valkenburg Castle

Valkenburg has a number of handsome old houses, such as Huis Den Halder (17th c.), Huis Ost (Literary Museum, open: Wed. and Sat. 2–5pm; for special exhibitions also Sun. 2–5pm), Huis Genhoes (15th–16th c.) and the Spaanse Leenhof, now occupied by the tourist information office.

Old houses

Of the old 14th century fortifications there remain two town gates, the Grendelpoort and the Berkelpoort, and some lengths of wall on the west side of the town.

Town walls

The local marlstone was already being used as a building material in Roman times. The underground quarrying of the stone has left a series of caves – the Gemeentegrot (Municipal Cave), which was used as a bomb shelter during the Second World War; the Fluweelen Caves; and the Panorama Cave, with an exhibition illustrating the origins and development of man.

Caves

In the Cave Aquarium (Cauberg) are more than 40 tanks containing both river and sea fish. Open: May to September, daily 10am–5pm.

Cave Aquarium

The Steenkolenmijn, a model coal-mine at Daalhemerweg 31, illustrates the technology of mining in the South Limburg coalfield with a display of authentic mining equipment. Open: daily 9am–5pm.

Steenkolenmijn

In Plenkertstraat is a reproduction of Early Christian catacombs dating from the Roman period.

Catacombs

Veere

Province: Zeeland
Population: 4900

Veere

Situation and °townscape

The picturesque little town of Veere, a favourite haunt of artists, lies on the north-east coast of Walcheren, 7km/4½ miles north of Middelburg.

In the medieval period Veere, which was surrounded by walls in 1358, was an important trading town and fishing port. After the marriage of the lord of Veere, Wolfert van Borssele, with the daughter of King James I of Scotland in 1551 the Scottish staple at Veere became an important outlet for the sale of Scottish wool. The town's prosperity was brought to an end by the French occupation in 1799. In 1958 the fishing harbour was cut off from the sea by the construction of the Veerse Gat dam, and Veere is now only a sailing centre and holiday resort.

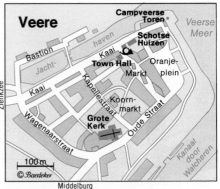

Schotse Huizen

Veere has preserved a number of handsome old burghers' houses. The most interesting of these are the Schotse Huizen (Kaai 25–27), which contain the records of the Scottish wool merchants who lived in Veere as well as a collection of local antiquities.

Town Hall

The Town Hall (Stadhuis; 1470) at Markt 5 is the finest Town Hall in Brabantine Late Gothic style after that of Middelburg. The fine statuettes of members of the Borssele family on the façade are reproductions (1934) of the originals by Michiel Ywijnszoon (16th c.), which are now in the Schotse Huizen. The belfry at the top of the tower is also 16th century. The interior decoration of the Town Hall dates mostly from 1699. There is a small museum in the Vierschaar (courtroom), the most notable exhibit in which is a silver-gilt goblet presented to the town in 1546 by Maximilian of Burgundy.

Onze Lieve Vrouwekerk

The massive Church of Our Lady (15th–16th c.) seems out of proportion with the little town. From the tower there are fine views of the surrounding area. Beside the church is a handsome fountain-house of 1551.

Campveerse Toren

The only surviving part of the town's fortifications of 1550 is the Campveerse Toren (Campveer Tower; restored 1950), long a place of refuge for the population and now a restaurant.

Surroundings of Veere

Round trip

From Veere take the road which runs north-west, crosses the Veerse Gat dam and continues over the Oosterschelde Dam to the Delta Expo museum on the artificial island of Neeltje Jans (see Facts and Figures, The Struggle with the Sea, Deltawerken). The route then continues to the island of Schouwen–Duiveland and via Serooskerke to Zierikzee (see entry), from which the Zeelandbrug (a toll bridge, 5km/3 miles long, borne on 48 double piers; completed 1966) returns to Noord-Beveland, and so back to Veere.

Veere, a sleepy little town on the Veerse Meer

Veluwe   F/G 5/6

Province: Gelderland

The Veluwe lies in the province of Gelderland, to the south of the Veluwe- Situation and
meer, a narrow arm of the IJsselmeer which separates Flevoland from the characteristics
mainland. It is bounded on the east by the river IJssel and on the south by
the Rhine; to the west it merges into the Gelderse Vallei (Gelderland plain)
and the Utrechtse Heuvelrug, the Utrecht Hills.

In recent years almost all the old Veluwe villages have developed into
holiday resorts, for the tourist trade is an important source of income for
the local people, supplementing the meagre revenue from agriculture
(undemanding arable crops, production of butter and eggs).
In the central Veluwe, a thinly populated tract of sandy soil, there are no
towns: these all lie on the outer fringes of this inhospitable area. The
principal towns are the IJsselmeer ports of Harderwijk and Elburg (see
entries), together with Arnhem and Apeldoorn (see entries) and Ede.

Large areas in the Veluwe are designated as nature reserves, notably the Nature reserves
National Parks of Hoge Veluwe and Veluwezoom, which is part of the
Deelerwoud (Deelen Forest).

North of the popular holiday resort of Rheden, with the villages of De Steeg Veluwezoom
and Velp, lies the Veluwezoom, once a hunting reserve of the Princes of
Orange, with tracts of heath and woodland, flocks of sheep and herds of
Scottish highland cattle. In this area is the highest point in Gelderland, the
Posbank (110m/361ft).

**Hoge Veluwe National Park

Situation and characteristics

The Hoge Veluwe National Park, the main attraction in this very popular tourist area (easily reached on the A 12 motorway), lies between Arnhem and Apeldoorn, with entrances at Schaarsbergen on the south, Otterlo (north-west) and Hoenderloo (north-east). With a total area of 5500 hectares/13,750 acres, the National Park is the largest continuous nature reserve in the Netherlands (fully enclosed). In the wooded area to the north are a sculpture park and the Kröller-Müller Museum (see below).

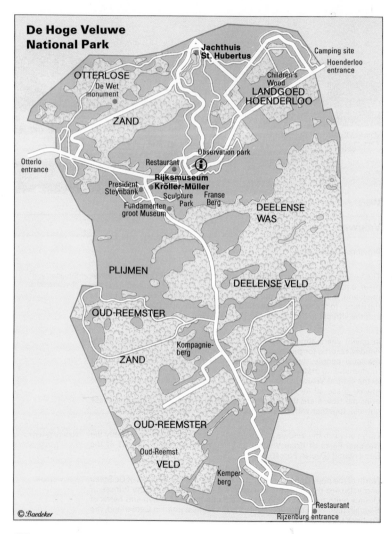

De Hoge Veluwe National Park

Jachthuis St. Hubertus
Camping site
Hoenderloo entrance
OTTERLOSE
De Wet monument
Children's Wood
LANDGOED HOENDERLOO
ZAND
Observation park
Otterlo entrance
Restaurant
Rijksmuseum Kröller-Müller
President Steynbank
Sculpture Park
Franse Berg
Fundamenten groot Museum
DEELENSE WAS
PLIJMEN
DEELENSE VELD
OUD-REEMSTER
ZAND
Kompagnie-berg
OUD-REEMSTER
Oud-Reemst VELD
Kemper-berg
Restaurant
Rijzenburg entrance
© Baedeker

Veluwe

The estate and hunting reserve of Hoge Veluwe were made over by Mr and Mrs Kröller-Müller, both art-lovers and nature-lovers, to the Hoge Veluwe National Park Foundation in 1935. They had previously bought the property to save this almost completely unspoiled area from development for industry.
Anton Kröller was a successful businessman who had made his money in shipping, the North American grain trade and mining in Spain and North Africa. His wife Helene (née Müller) devoted herself to building up one of the largest private art collections in the Netherlands.

History

The Hoge Veluwe, the best preserved part of the Veluwe, is a large area of sandy soil which was given its present form during the Ice Age. Its featureless expanses of dunes, interspersed with heath and woodland, are interrupted in the south and east by moraines between 80 and 100m (260 and 330ft) high formed during the second-last ice age (the Saale/Riss glacial). This was an area of vast forests, patches of which were cleared for cultivation during the Middle Ages. Expanses of heath were left, grazed by large flocks of sheep, and the heath was cut for use in fertilising the soil. The sand was blown off these bare patches, sometimes burying whole villages; dunes were built up from drift sand (e.g. the Franse Berg) and some areas were reduced to wasteland. In the 19th century reafforestation schemes were launched in order to prevent the drifting of sand. Some depressions were filled with rainwater, forming lakes, mostly in the Deelense Veld (e.g. the Deelense Was).

Geography

The Hoge Veluwe is partly wooded and partly heathland. In addition to the plantations of conifers (mainly pines) in the southern and north-eastern parts of the National Park there are red oaks (originally from North America), rhododendrons – particularly in the sculpture park and around St Hubertus lake – and deciduous trees. Particularly striking are the old and bizarrely shaped pine-trees and the juniper bushes which have grown naturally.
The best shows of heather in summer are in the dry Oud-Reemster Veld (along with mosses and pampas grass) and the damp Deelense Veld (along with bell heather).

Flora

From observation points in the centre and north-west of the National Park visitors can watch native animals including red deer, roe deer and wild pigs as well as moufflon (wild sheep from Sardinia and Corsica). In winter a variety of birds can be heard all over the park – marigold finches, titmice, chaffinches, bramblings, woodpeckers, jays, magpies and thrushes.

Fauna

The best plan is to start the tour of the park from De Aanschouw, the visitor centre, where you are offered a wide range of information about the National Park and can hire a bicycle free of charge. It is also possible to hire riding horses, and there are facilities for langlauf skiing in winter.
From mid September to mid October, the rutting season of the red deer and moufflon, access is restricted. It is forbidden to feed the animals.
The removal of plants, the picking of flowers and the breaking of branches are, of course, prohibited.

The National Park is open throughout the year from 8am to sunset.

The distinguished architect H. P. Berlage worked for the Kröller-Müllers for many years. Among other things he designed a museum (never built) and the St Hubertus hunting lodge which was built between 1914 and 1920 on the northern border of the old hunting preserve. Named after the patron saint of hunting, St Hubert, it symbolises the saint's legend: it is laid out in the form of a deer's antlers and the outlook tower is in the shape of a cross. The sequence of rooms, from the dark vestibule through a series of increasingly lighter rooms to the sunny living room, symbolises St Hubert's progress towards faith.

St Hubertus hunting lodge

Moufflons in the Hoge Veluwe National Park

**Kröller-Müller Museum

The museum

The Kröller-Müller Museum (Rijksmuseum Kröller-Müller) was designed by a Belgian architect, Henry van de Velde, in 1937–38. Constructed in light brown brick and originally thought of as a temporary building, it has become the permanent home of the magnificent art collection assembled by Helene Kröller-Müller between 1908 and 1935. The layout of the museum is in line with her idea of bringing art and nature together so that each should enhance the other.

The extension to the building by W. G. Quist in 1975–77 was carefully designed to fit into the landscape. The walls were now entirely built of stone or of glass. Whereas Van de Velde had followed the traditional 19th century pattern of museum-building, with a symmetrical layout and numerous separate sections, Quist was influenced by the modern De Stijl and Neue Sachlichkeit movements. Both parts of the museum, however, share the same consistent simplicity and lack of ornament.

The Sculpture Garden laid out in 1961 also reflects Mrs Kröller-Müller's conception of a symbiosis between art, architecture and nature. The idea has been much imitated in recent years.

The collection

The original private collection, which was transferred to the ownership of a foundation in 1928, is housed in the older part of the museum. Advised by an art expert of the time, H. P. Bremmer, Mrs Kröller-Müller became a very active collector, with the object of assembling a collection which should give a general impression of the development of painting. This involved including works both by the "realists" and by the "idealists", who gave expression to the concrete phenomena of reality in accordance with their own subjective vision. Thus the collection – which by 1933 amounted to some 4000 drawings, 275 works of sculpture and several hundred pictures – was not in any sense intended as a historical survey of art. It ranges from medieval art (Lucas Cranach, Hans Baldung Grien, Gerard David) to Asian,

Marta Pan, "Floating Sculpture" (1961)

Ger van Elk, "No Name"

Auguste Renoir, "The Clown"

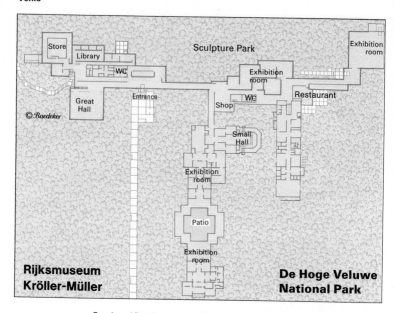

Rijksmuseum Kröller-Müller

© Baedeker

De Hoge Veluwe National Park

Greek and Dutch ceramics. The main emphasis, however, is on work of the late 19th and early 20th centuries, and its fame rests principally on its 280 paintings and drawings by Van Gogh, mainly from his stays in The Hague, Brabant, Paris and Provence ("Bridge at Arles").

The following is merely a selection of the museum's treasures:
Symbolism and Art Nouveau: Odilon Redon, James Ensor, Jan Toorop;
Impressionism and Expressionism: Edouard Manet, Claude Monet, Paul
    Cézanne, Paul Gauguin, Auguste Renoir;
Pointillisme: Georges Seurat, Paul Signac;
Cubism: Pablo Picasso, Georges Braque, Fernand Léger, Juan Gris;
De Stijl: Piet Mondriaan, Bart van der Leck.

The collection also includes works by other artists including Camille Corot, Jean-François Millet, Matthijs Maris, Honoré Daumier and Johan B. Jongkind.

The extension to the museum displays sculpture, reliefs and drawings since 1950 by Joseph Beuys, Marino Marini, Vasarély, Caro, Philip King, Louise Nevelson, Jan Schoonhoven and Jesus R. Soto.

The Sculpture Garden has works by Jean Dubuffet, Claes Oldenburg, Henry Moore, Chaim J. Lipchitz, Mark di Suvero, Auguste Rodin, Lucio Fontana, André Volten, Carel N. Visser, Barbara Hepworth, Evert Strobos, Kenneth Snelson, Fritz Wotruba and Aristide Maillol.

The Museum is open April to October, Tue.–Sat. 10am–5pm, Sun. 11am–5pm; November to March, Tue.–Sat. 10am–5pm, Sun. 1–5pm.

Venlo

G 9

Province: Limburg
Population: 64,000

Venlo, on the Maas, is the cultural, administrative and economic centre of northern Limburg. As an important traffic junction point between Rotterdam and the Ruhr, Venlo has been well placed, particularly since the end of the Second World War, for the development of industry and the establishment of international commercial firms handling the produce of the market gardens in the surrounding area. The main branches of industry are engineering, the production of optical apparatus, wire-drawing, electrical engineering, textiles, building materials and woodworking.

Situation and characteristics

Venlo, originally a little trading town of no particular importance, was granted a municipal charter in 1343. In 1481 it became a member of the Hanseatic League. Lying as it did in a frontier area, it was strongly fortified, but in spite of this it was compelled to surrender on a number of occasions – in 1543 to Charles V's forces, in 1543 to Alexander Farnese, in 1632 to Prince Frederick Henry and in 1702 to Marlborough. In 1713 it was incorporated in the United Netherlands. The development of industry and a rapid increase in population began after the demolition of the old fortifications in 1868. Venlo suffered heavy destruction during the Second World War but was rapidly rebuilt, to become the modern town it is today.

History

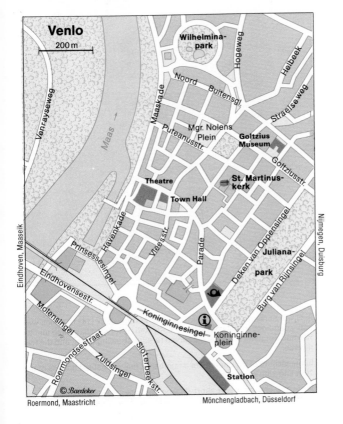

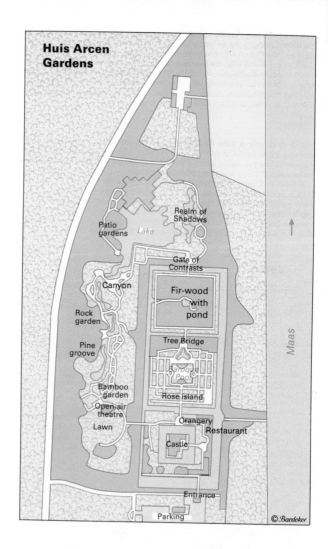

The Town

Hoofdkerk

In Grote Kerkstraat is the Hoofdkerk or St Martinuskerk (1411), which was badly damaged in 1944 but subsequently well restored. It has a fine font by Herman Potgieter (1621) and a carved reredos showing Christ and the two thieves.

Gabled houses

In the vicinity of the church are a number of fine old gabled houses of the 16th and 18th centuries.

Town Hall

From the church it is a short distance by way of Gasthuisstraat to the picturesque Town Hall (Stadhuis), a rebuilding by Willem van Bommel of

Emmerich (1596–1601) of an earlier town hall of 1550. The neo-Renaissance façade and the corner turrets on the rear of the building were added during restoration work in 1888. The Council Chamber, its walls faced with leather, contains a number of good pictures. The market hall on the ground floor now houses the municipal archives.

The Goltzius Museum, at Goltziusstraat 21 (south-east of the Town Hall), displays a collection of material on the history of the town and surrounding area as well as some fine porcelain. Open: Tue.–Fri. 10am–4.30pm, Sat. and Sun. 2–5pm.

Goltzius Museum

Surroundings of Venlo

South-east of Venlo, on the banks of the Maas, lies the little town of Tegelen, with the Jochum Hof botanic garden in the Steyl district. In addition to hothouses with tropical and subtropical plants there are a Regional Garden, which presents a cross-section of the flora of northern Limburg, and the Tiglien Garden, which seeks to reconstruct the prehistoric landscape of the region.

Tegelen;
Jochum Hof

10km/6 miles north of Venlo, farther down the Maas valley, is the beautifully situated village of Arcen, now a popular summer resort, with a moated castle of 1650, Huis Arcen. The gardens have been open to the public since 1988, with a magnificent display of flowers and plants, including a rose garden, a futuristic glasshouse for subtropical plants, the Casa Verde, and Japanese and Chinese gardens. The pavilions in the gardens and the house itself are used for art exhibitions and other cultural events.

Huis Arcen
Gardens

Vlieland
D/E 2

Province: Friesland
Population: 1100

Vlieland, the most westerly and the smallest of the West Frisian islands (12km/7½ miles long, 2km/1¼ miles across), has a beautiful beach. It can be reached by ferry from Harlingen. No cars are allowed on the island.
The Vliehors sand-flats to the west of the island are now a gunnery range.

Situation and
characteristics

Since West-Vlieland was engulfed by the sea in the 18th century Vlieland's only village has been Oost-Vlieland, situated at the eastern tip of the island amid coniferous and deciduous woodland. The village church (1605) contains a fine pulpit, an 18th century organ, a number of tombs and one of the five brass lamps presented to the church by Admiral de Ruyter, who – like Admiral Tromp – had a house on the island.

Oost-Vlieland

Vlissingen
A 9

Province: Zeeland
Population: 44,000

The important port town of Vlissingen (traditionally in English Flushing) lies on the south coast of the former island of Walcheren, where the Schelde, here more than 4km/2½ miles wide, flows into the North Sea. Vlissingen and IJmuiden are the only Dutch ports of any size situated directly on the North Sea. Ferry services to Breskens and to Sheerness in Kent.

Situation and
characteristics

Vlissingen

Statue of Admiral de Ruyter

The outer harbour for seagoing vessels, 12m/40ft deep, is separated by locks from two inland docks, which are linked with Middelburg by the Walcheren Canal. Around the harbour and along the canal a variety of industries have been established, the most important being shipbuilding, engineering, fish-processing and leather-working. More recently chemical and petrochemical plants have also been established. Since the completion of the Delta Plan the Vlissingen industrial zone is due to be increased by some 30,000 hectares/75,000 acres. The necessary energy is provided by a conventional and a nuclear power station.

Vlissingen first appears in the records in 1247. In 1315, already a considerable port, it received its municipal charter. It played an important part during the Dutch rising against Spain: after the capture of Brielle by the Sea Beggars Vlissingen was the first town in the Netherlands to fly the flag of freedom (1572). It was the birthplace of the celebrated Admiral Michiel de Ruyter (1607–76) and the poet Jacobus Bellamy (1557–86).

St Jacobskerk

In the Oude Markt stands the Grote Kerk or St Jacobskerk (14th c.), rebuilt in its original style after a fire in 1911.

**Town Hall
Municipal Museum**

The Town Hall (Stadhuis), in Houtkade, dates from 1733. In Bellamy Park is the Municipal Museum (Stedelijk Museum), with local antiquities and mementoes of Admiral de Ruyter. Open: mid June to mid September, Mon.–Fri. 10am–5pm, Sat. and Sun. 1–5pm; mid September to mid June, Tue.–Fri. 10am–12.30pm and 1.30–5pm, Sat. and Sun. 1–5pm.

In Beursplein is the Oude Beurs (Old Exchange; 1672). Close by is the Rotunda, with a statue of Admiral de Ruyter (by L. Royers), commemorating the naval hero who saved the Netherlands during the third war with Britain. From here there is a fine view of the harbour and the sea. To the south can be seen the coast of Zeeuws-Vlaanderen (Zealand Flanders).

Gevangentoren

Resort area

From the Rotunda the Boulevard de Ruyter, in which can be seen the Gevangentoren (Prison Tower; 1563), and Boulevard Bankert run northeast to the resort area, with a beautiful beach extending to the south of the town.

Volendam

E 5

Province: Noord-Holland
Commune: Edam–Volendam
Population: 24,000

Situation and characteristics

The village of Volendam, part of the commune of Edam, lies on the IJsselmeer. As with other ports on the IJsselmeer, the local fisheries have suffered from the dyking of the Zuiderzee.

Costumes

Volendam – the Roman Catholic counterpart to Marken (see entry) – is famed for its traditional costumes. Not surprisingly, therefore, the tourist trade has become the principal source of income. The older inhabitants are still proud to wear the local costumes – for men baggy woollen trousers, for women a flowered dress, a striped pinafore, a coral necklace and, when appropriate to the weather, a blue and white striped scarf. On Sundays and holidays the women wear the famous winged lace cap, which during the week is often replaced by a simpler cotton cap.
At the harbour visitors can have themselves photographed in local costume.

Sights

Apart from the harbour (boat trips to Marken and Monnickendam) and the picturesque old houses there are a number of other features of interest: the wooden church of 1685 (restored 1985);

Fishermen of Volendam

the collection of over 100 paintings by 19th century artists in the Spaander Hotel, on the harbour;
the Volendam Museum at Kloosterbuurt 5, with displays of traditional costumes and models of fishing boats (open: April to September, daily 10am–5pm);
a house at Oude Draaipad 8, De Gouden Kamer, where the walls are papered with millions of cigar bands, arranged to form pictures (e.g. of New York's Statue of Liberty). Open: during the season, daily 9am–6pm. At Slobbeland visitors can see how the houses used to be built on piles.

Vorden

See Zutphen

Waddeneilanden/West Frisian Islands   D–H 1–3

Provinces of Groningen, Friesland and Noord-Holland

Strung out along the north and north-west coasts of the Netherlands are the West Frisian islands (in Dutch Waddeneilanden) of Texel, Vlieland, Terschelling, Schiermonnikoog and Rottum, lying at varying distances (between 2km/1¼ miles and 15km/15 miles) off the mainland. The West Frisian islands are continued to the east by the East Frisian islands off the coast of Germany. The chain of islands protects the mainland, from which they are separated by the Waddenzee, from the open North Sea.

Situation and characteristics

As recently as 2500 years ago the Waddenzee was a large expanse of moorland which was sheltered from the destructive force of the sea by a

Origins

383

barrier of sand mixed with flotsam and jetsam cast up by the waves. Thereafter the steady rise in sea level resulting from the melting of the glaciers of the last ice age combined with the subsidence of the land led to the flooding of great stretches of the old moorland. The most devastating storm tides occurred during the Middle Ages, when both the Waddenzee and the Zuiderzee (now, since the construction of the Afsluitdijk in 1932, the IJsselmeer) came into being.

The present chain of islands is the remnant of the old coastal barrier, breached in many places by the sea. On the seaward side the West Frisian islands are fringed by young dunes, which tend to be driven steadily eastward by marine currents and westerly winds. This movement has now largely been halted by the planting of marram grass and the construction of groynes.

Economy
*Tourism

In addition to sheep farming, fishing and arable farming in some areas the summer tourist trade is now a major element in the islands' economy. The miles of beaches of light-coloured sand are among the most beautiful in the world, and many visitors are also attracted by the many nature reserves, in which thousands of seabirds nest or spend the winter, for example on the north coast of Texel (Schorren) and on the islands of Vlieland and Terschelling (Boschplaat).

Wijk bij Duurstede   E 7

Province: Utrecht
Population: 15,000

Situation and
characteristics

The little town of Wijk bij Duurstede is situated at the point where the Rhine becomes the Lek and the little Kromme Rijn branches off and flows northwest. In the early medieval period this was the site of an important inland port town, Dorestad, which was devastated by the Norsemen in the 9th century.

Castle ruins

A new settlement later grew up around a castle built here in the 13th century. During the Middle Ages this was a residence of the bishops of Utrecht, the most famous of whom was Bishop David of Burgundy (15th c.), who gathered many of the leading figures of the day around him. In the early 18th century the castle fell into ruin, and there now remain only a few fragments of walls, a square keep and a round corner tower (15th c.) with a diameter of 15m/50ft.

Town walls

In addition to some remains of walls Wijk has preserved one of the town gates, the Rijnmolenpoort, on which is the Rijn en Lek windmill, a flour-mill built in 1659. In spite of appearances, however, this is not the windmill depicted in Jacob van Ruisdael's painting "Windmill at Wijk bij Duurstede" (now in the Rijksmuseum, Amsterdam), which stood some 200m/220yds farther west.

Grote Kerk

The Markt, in the centre of the old town, is dominated by the Grote Kerk (14th c.; unfinished), a cruciform basilica the great size of which no doubt shows the influence of the bishops of Utrecht. The massive tower is richly articulated, with balustrades, buttresses and deep niches.

Town Hall

The Town Hall (Stadhuis), a sober building with a high entrance staircase, was built by Gijsbert van Vianen and Peter van Cooten (1666).

Surroundings of Wijk bij Duurstede

Culemborg

West of Wijk bij Duurstede, on the Lek, lies Culemborg (pop. 21,000). The town, which received its municipal charter in 1318, contains many buildings which are now protected as national monuments, like the Grote Kerk (St Barbarakerk), the Town Hall and St Elisabethsweeshuis (St Elizabeth's Orphanage). Part of the old fortifications was converted into a park in the first half of the 19th century.

Willemstad

C 8

Province: Noord-Brabant
Population: 3300

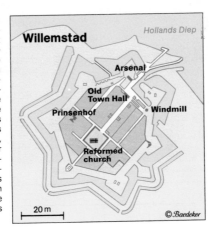

The little fortified town of Willemstad is situated near the point where the Hollands-diep divides into two arms, between which lies the island of Goeree–Overflakkee. William the Silent gave orders in 1583 for the construction of this star-shaped fortress with its seven bastions, two gates and regular street layout; the builder was Adriaen Anthonisz. After William's murder in 1584 his son Maurice named the town Willemstad in his honour.

Situation and characteristics

On the ramparts is a whitewashed windmill, the D'Oranje flour-mill (1734).

D'Oranje mill

Willemstad's octagonal Reformed church was the first church in the Netherlands to be built for a Protestant congregation (1596–1607). The original furnishings had to be replaced when the interior of the church was destroyed by fire in 1950. The pulpit came from a church at Hoogvliet (1659), the choir-stalls (1670) from a church in Graft.

Reformed church

The Prinsenhof or Mauritshuis, built in 1623 as a hunting lodge for Stadholder Maurice (Maurits) of Nassau, is now the Town Hall. Around it is a herb garden, the Kruidentuin.

Prinsenhof (Mauritshuis)

The former Town Hall (1587; rebuilt 1620) at Raadhuisstraat 2 now houses the Ceramic Museum (Ceramisch Museum), with pottery and other wares (17th–20th c.) recovered by excavation.

Old Town Hall

The Arsenal (1793) is in neo-classical style, with two gates on the harbour side.

Arsenal

3km/2 miles west of Willemstad are the Volkenraksluizen, a train of locks which forms part of the Deltawerken (see Facts and Figures, The Struggle with the Sea, Deltawerken).

Locks

On the banks of the Rhine, Wijk bij Duurstede (page 384)

Winschoten

See Delfzijl

Workum

Province: Friesland
Commune: Nijefurd
Population: 11,000

Situation and characteristics

In the early medieval period Workum was situated on the coast of the Zuiderzee, but moved farther inland in the 14th century. In the 15th century it was a considerable port and trading town, and was also famed for its brown and green pottery and its decorated faience.

Grote Kerk

The Grote Kerk (St Geertruidskerk) is the largest medieval cruciform basilica in Friesland, with a free-standing tower. Construction of the church began in 1550 with the choir. The main features in the interior are the choir screen (16th c.), the organ (17th c.) and the carved wooden pulpit (18th c.). Of particular interest, too, are the richly painted biers of the various guilds in the aisles.

Other sights

Among other features of interest in Workum are St Werenfriduskerk, a neo-Gothic pseudo-basilica (1877); the Doopsgezinde Vermaning, a Mennonite church disguised as a barn (1694); the Gothic Town Hall, rebuilt in the 18th century; the red brick Weigh-House (Waag; 1650) in the Markt; the De Hoop shipyard, where historic old vessels are restored; a *tjasker* mill, the only windmill of this type in Friesland which is still working; and old houses with stepped gables along the rivers Súd and Noard.

St Geertruidskerk, Workum

Zaanstad

D 5

Province: Noord-Holland
Commune: Zaanstad
Population: 129,000

The commune of Zaanstad or Zaanstreek, now a highly industrialised and densely populated area 10km/6 miles north of Amsterdam, takes in a number of what were originally separate settlements on or near the river Zaan. The first sawmills were built here in the 16th century and promoted the development of the woodworking and shipbuilding industries.

It was at Zaandam that Tsar Peter the Great of Russia spent four months in 1697 under the name of Peter Mikhailov in order to learn the crafts of carpentry and shipbuilding – a visit which provided the theme for Albert Lortzing's opera "Zar und Zimmermann" ("Tsar and Carpenter"). His stay is commemorated by the Czaar-Peterhuisje (Tsar Peter's House; open: Tue.–Sat. 10am–1pm and 2–5pm) at Krimp 24 and the Tsar Peter Monument in the Damplein.
Other features of interest in the town are the Oud-Katholieke Kerk (Old Catholic Church; 1695) at Papenpad 12; an old sawmill, Held Josua, behind the station; and a watermill of 1650, De Ooievaar, on the south side of the Juliabrug.
Near the locks on the Zaan are the two Accijnshuisjes (early 18th c.), where tolls were levied on ships entering and leaving the port.

Just north of Zaandam is the Zaanse Schans open-air museum, a little corner of "picturebook Holland": a reconstruction of a Zaanland village of around 1700. The museum was established in 1949 by the Stichting Zaanse Schans, a private organisation concerned to preserve old buildings threatened by industrial development. Typical old wooden houses and windmills

Situation and characteristics

Zaandam

*Zaanse Schans

387

Zaanse Schans open-air museum

of the 17th and 18th centuries were taken down, re-erected here and carefully restored.

The reconstructed village gives a very vivid impression of life in earlier centuries, largely because almost all the houses are lived in.

At the beginning of the 18th century there were about 500 windmills in the Zaanstreek area. Half of them ground grain, and also mustard, oil-seeds, cocoa, spices and tobacco; the others were sawmills, for in the 17th century the woodworking industry played a major part in the economy of the area. Few now survive; but at Zaanse Schans there are an oil mill, a paint mill, a mustard mill and a sawmill. Other features include a cheese-making dairy, an old bakery, a grocer's shop, a clog-maker's workshop, a pewterer's workshop and the Zaans Uurwerken Museum (Clock Museum), with a collection of old Dutch clocks.

Visitors can take a very attractive boat trip on the Zaan, with the old houses and windmills as a charming backdrop.

Koog aan de Zaan

The Windmill Museum (Molenmuseum) at Museumlaan 18 in Koog aan de Zaan presents a very informative picture of the windmills of the 17th and 18th centuries with the help of scale models and documents. Open: Tue.– Fri. 10am–12 noon and 1–5pm, Sat. and Sun. 2–5pm.

A visit to Het Pink, an old oil mill of 1610 in Pinkstraat, will complete the picture. It is open and working on the first Saturday in the month.

Westzaan

The main sights of Westzaan are the Grote Kerk in Torenstraat (periodic exhibitions in July and August); the Prinsenhof mill (1722) in Weelsloot; the Schoolmeester mill (1695) in Guisweg, the only papermill in the world which is still working; the Town Hall (Stadhuis) in Kerkbuurt, a former courthouse in Louis XIV style, with a domed tower (1781); and the Zuidervermaning church (1731) at Zuideinde 231, which has a particularly beautiful interior.

Krommenie has a watermill dating from 1640, De Woudaap.	Krommenie
Graft is the oldest village on Schermer island, first mentioned in the records in 1325. It has a handsome Town Hall (Stadhuis) of 1613.	Graft
De Rijp was the birthplace of J. A. Leeghwater (1575–1650), inventor of the diving bell. Features of interest: the museum in the "Wooden House" at Jan Boonplein 2, with a collection which includes tiles, pottery, old charts and whale skeletons (open: from Easter to May and in September and October, Sat. and Sun. 11am–5pm; June to August, Fri.–Wed. 10am–5pm), and the Weigh-House (Waaggebouw; 1690) at Kleine Dam 2, with 24 stained glass windows.	De Rijp
Purmerend has been an important market town since 1484. Its chief attraction for visitors is the cheese market which is held every Tuesday from July to September. Also of interest is the domed church, with a famous Garrels organ.	Purmerend
Broek in Waterland is one of the prettiest villages in Holland, with 18th century wooden houses set round a large pond. It still has two cheese-makers and a clog-maker.	Broek in Waterland

Zaltbommel   E 7

Province: Gelderland
Population: 9500

The little town of Zaltbommel, which was already fortified by the 13th century, lies on the left bank of the Waal, which at this point is tidal. The old part of the town recalls the time when Zaltbommel was a member of the Hanseatic League. Of the old fortifications only one gate, the Waterpoort, survives.	Situation and characteristics
The Grote Kerk or St Maartenskerk was rebuilt in 1304. The oldest part of the building is the choir with its large windows. The nave, flanked by aisles, dates from the 15th century, as does the four-storey tower, the town's principal landmark; the spire was destroyed by fire in 1538. The church has fine wall paintings, including a figure of St Christopher (1540).	Grote Kerk
The Town Hall, with a wooden bell-turret, dates from 1724, the neo--classical Weigh-House (Waag) from 1797. Also of interest are the Gasthuistoren, the tower of a 15th century alms-house chapel; the medieval Waterpoort; and the Huis van Maarten van Rossum at Nonnenstraat 5, birthplace of Maarten van Rossum, a general in the service of the Duke of Gelderland in the 16th century, which now houses the Historical Museum. In the Markt and the side streets opening off it are fine old 16th and 17th century houses.	Other sights

Zandvoort   D 5

Province: Noord-Holland
Population: 15,600

Zandvoort, on the North Sea coast to the west of Haarlem, has an international reputation as one of the leading Dutch seaside resorts, with over 1½ million "visitor nights" a year. It is also famed for its 4.2km/2½ mile long motor and motorcycle racing circuit, opened in 1948, venue of the Zandvoort Grand Prix (Formula 2) at	Situation and characteristics

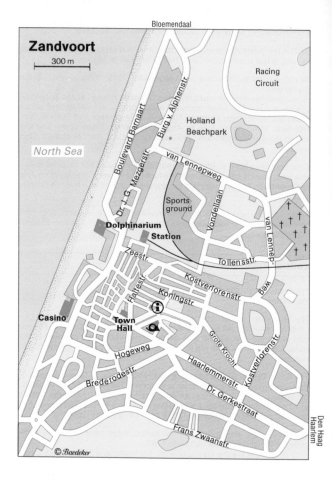

the end of July and the Grand Prix of the Netherlands (Formula 1) at the end of August.

In spite of the multiple activities of a modern resort Zandvoort seeks to preserve its original character; thus in the redevelopment of the northern part of the town efforts are being made to retain the atmosphere of the old fishing village, which until 1828 had a population of no more than 700. At the same time the Folk Union and the Old Zandvoort Society are concerned to preserve traditional customs and the old local costumes.

Sights

Among the attractions of Zandvoort – in addition to the sea and the broad beaches – are the 60m/200ft high outlook tower with its restaurant; the Dolphinarium at Burgemeester van Fenemaplein 2 (dolphin and sealion shows); and the Casino, on the 18th floor of the Hotel Bouwes (Bad-huisplein 7). The Casino, the highest point on the Dutch coast, is open from 2pm to 2 in the morning; visitors can try their luck with a minimum stake of 5 guilders.

Beach, Zandvoort

There is plenty of good walking to be had in the Amsterdamse Duinwater-leiding (Amsterdam Dunes Water Supply) area, an expanse of 3600 hectares/9000 acres of attractive dune country.

Zandvoort also offers facilities for a wide range of sports, including golf, minigolf, riding and tennis.

Zeeland   A–C 8–10

Provincial capital: Middelburg
Area: 303,900 hectares/750,600 acres
     (land area 179,100 hectares/442,400 acres)
Population: 355,500

The Dutch region of Zeeland (in English Zealand), in the delta of the Rhine, the Maas and the Schelde, includes all the islands and peninsulas in the south-western Netherlands (Walcheren, Zuid- and Noord-Beveland, Schouwen–Duiveland, Tholen, St Filipsland and Goeree–Overflakkee), together with Zeeuws-Vlaanderen (Zealand Flanders), a narrow strip of the mainland between the Westerschelde and the Belgian frontier. With the exception of Goeree–Overflakkee (in Zuid-Holland) the Zeeland region coincides exactly with the province of the same name.

Situation and characteristics

Zeeland is one of the world's youngest areas of land, reclaimed from the sea only within the last 1800 years by man-made dykes. Much of the province lies below sea level, for the old peat bogs, flooded by the sea before the dykes were built and then overlaid with silt, gradually subsided over the centuries, forming extensive depressions (*kommen*). The oldest parts of the islands, enclosed by dykes before the 13th century, were

Dykes

On a Zeeland farm

particularly affected. These areas have been repeatedly exposed to devastating floods, most recently in 1953. On this last occasion neither the protective belt of dunes on north-western Walcheren, Schouwen and Goeree nor the dykes were able to withstand the assaults of the waves, and in order to prevent similar catastrophes in future all the major estuaries in Zeeland were closed off from the North Sea by dams under the Delta Plan (see Facts and Figures, The Struggle with the Sea). The only exceptions were the Nieuwe Waterweg, which gives the port of Rotterdam access to the North Sea, and the Westerschelde, the seaway to Antwerp.

Zeeland is predominantly an intensively farmed agricultural region. The villages and their arable land lie on the higher ground less exposed to flooding, while the lower-lying areas are occupied by pastures and meadowland. In the more recently poldered and less densely populated areas the holdings range in size between 20 and 50 hectares (50 and 125 acres); in the older areas on the islands they are considerably smaller. The main crops are grain, sugar-beet and potatoes.

The principal industrial areas are along the canal which runs through Zeeuws-Vlaanderen (Zealand Flanders) from Terneuzen to Ghent (coking plants, metalworking, chemicals, glassware, sugar-refining, textiles), the eastern part of Zeeuws-Vlaanderen (textiles), Vlissingen (shipbuilding) on the island of Walcheren and the provincial capital Middelburg, now a thriving tourist centre.

Zeist

E 6

Province: Utrecht
Population: 60,000

The mansion of Huis te Zeist, set in beautiful gardens, was built by Jacob Roman and Daniël Marot in 1677–86 for Willem Adriaan van Nassau-Odijk on the foundations of an earlier medieval castle. Willem Adriaan was the son of Lodewijk van Nassau-Beverweerd, an illegitimate son of Prince Maurice of Nassau. He spent his early days in Paris, and when he came into the property in 1677 he resolved to build a miniature Versailles at Zeist. In 1745 the house passed into the hands of Cornelis Schellinger, a wealthy Amsterdam ironmaster who belonged to the Moravian Brethren. In Broederplein and Zusterplein are a number of handsome houses built by Schellinger for members of his community; some of them are still occupied by Moravian Brethren, others by the Ancient Monuments Department.

Huis te Zeist

During the 18th and 19th centuries Huis te Zeist was occupied by a variety of tenants. In 1924 the house, then in a dilapidated condition, was bought by the town and, after thorough restoration, is now used for exhibitions, receptions and various cultural events. Conducted tours: Sat. and Sun. 2.30–4pm; July and August, daily 2.30–4pm.

7km/4½ miles east of Zeist, on a hill (62m/203ft) to the left of the road, is the Austerlitz Pyramid, erected by French troops in 1805 to commemorate Napoleon's victory over Austrian and Russian forces at Austerlitz in that year. From the top of the hill there are fine views of the surrounding area.

Austerlitz Pyramid

Zierikzee

B 8

Province: Zeeland
Population: 9900

Zierikzee is the chief place on the island of Schouwen–Duiveland in the Rhine–Maas delta, which consists of six communes with a total population of 26,000.

Situation and characteristics

The island's main tourist attractions are Zierikzee's yacht harbour, its picturesque old town centre and the beautiful sandy beaches fringed by wooded dunes up to 38m/125ft high at the west end of the island.

*Townscape

The main sources of income are the thriving tourist trade and agriculture. The principal crops grown on the island's fertile fenland soil are grain, root crops, flax and vegetables, much of the produce being processed by Zierikzee's foodstuffs industries. The town's real economic development began when communications with the island were improved by the Delta Plan. The opening of the 5km/3 mile long Zeelandbrug (Zealand Bridge) in 1966 brought Schouwen–Duiveland closer to Noord-Beveland and the mainland, and it was also linked with neighbouring islands by the construction of dams.

Economy

The Town

The spire of the 60m/200ft high St Lievenmonstertoren (the tower of a collegiate church destroyed by fire in 1832) is a conspicuous landmark. Begun in 1454 by the celebrated master builder Anthonis Keldermans, it was originally to be 206m/676ft high, but was left unfinished.

St Lieven-monstertoren

The Town Hall (Stadhuis) at Meelstraat 8, with a wooden belfry (carillon), was built by Bloemaert in 1554. In it is the Municipal Museum, with ethnographical and historical exhibits.

Town Hall

On the opposite side of the street is the 15th century Tempeliershuis, and close by, in Havenplein, the old Vismarkt (Fish Market; 1616).

Tempeliershuis

Zierikzee preserves three of its old town gates, relics of its former fortifications. The Noordhavenpoort (by Bloemaert, 1559) has a very handsome

Town gates

façade. The Zuidhavenpoort is a square gate-tower with corner turrets (14th c.), designed to protect the harbour as well as the entrance to the town. On the north side of the town is the oldest of the town's gates, the Nobelpoort, with twin towers topped by tall steeples.

Surroundings of Zierikzee

An attractive tour (c. 55km/35 miles) of the northern part of the island (Schouwen):

Brouwershaven

14km/8½ miles north of Zierikzee is the little town of Brouwershaven, with a beautiful hall-church (13th–15th c.), a Renaissance Town Hall (Stadhuis; 1599) and a statue of the poet Jacob Cats (1577–1660).

Renesse

Burgh-Haamstede

13km/8 miles west of Brouwershaven is Renesse, with Slot Moermond, a castle built in its present form in 1513 (17th c. Renaissance tower). From here a road runs 10km/6 miles south-west by way of Burgh-Haamstede to Westerschouwen, on the south-west coast of the island, from which there are fine views of the sea, Schouwen and the island of Noord-Beveland. 4km/2½ miles east of Westerschouwen is Burghsluis, from which the road, skirting the coast for part of the way, continues to Zierikzee (15km/9 miles).

Zuid-Holland (South Holland)   B–E 6–8

Provincial capital: The Hague
Area: 336,188 hectares/830,384 acres
(land area 290,611 hectares/717,809 acres)

394

Zierikzee Town Hall

The province of Zuid-Holland (South Holland) lies in the west of the Netherlands, bounded on the west by the North Sea, on the north by Noord-Holland (North Holland), on the east by the provinces of Utrecht and Gelderland and on the south by Zeeland. Until they were separated in 1840 North and South Holland formed a single county.

On topography, the draining of the fens, types of settlement and the economy of the province see the entry on Holland.

Situation and
characteristics

The most important branch of agriculture is stock-farming, which accounts for almost half the province's agricultural land. After it come arable farming (30% of agricultural land) and market gardening (two-thirds of it in hothouses).

South of The Hague is a large area given up to fruit and vegetable growing, with large auction halls at Naaldwijk and Bleiswijk. Much land is also occupied by nurseries producing cut flowers, which are auctioned at Bleiswijk, Rijnsburg (near Leiden) and Aalsmeer (see entry). North of Leiden is a bulb-growing area.

Agriculture

The local fisheries, once a major source of income, are becoming increasingly less important. Apart from Scheveningen, Katwijk and the island of Goeree–Overflakkee the principal fishing grounds are now in the Nieuwe Waterweg.

Fisheries

Since the end of the Second World War there has been a steady development of industry. New port and industrial establishments have been established along the Nieuwe Waterweg, the most important being the Europoort (see Rotterdam, Europoort). Rotterdam and Dordrecht have become major centres of electrical engineering, metal-processing and shipbuilding. There are other industrial concentrations along the Nieuwe Maas and the Noord, at Delft, The Hague, Leiden, Alphen and Gouda.

Industry

The service trades are concentrated in The Hague, the seat of government, and the university towns of Leiden, Delft and Rotterdam. Transport and

The Nobelpoort, Zierikzee's oldest town gate

shipping are mainly centred in Rotterdam and Dordrecht. The tourist trade also makes an important contribution to the economy of the North Sea coastal resorts and the historic towns and art centres.

Zutphen
G 6

Province: Gelderland
Population: 31,000

Situation and characteristics

Zutphen (from Zuid Veen, "South Fen"), situated at the confluence of the Berkel with the IJssel and at the west end of the Twente Canal, was once capital of the County of Zutphen, which from 1127 belonged to Gelderland. The town received its municipal charter in 1190 and became a member of the Hanseatic League towards the end of the 14th century. It was taken by the Spaniards in 1572 but recovered by Prince Maurice of Nassau nineteen years later.
The battle of Zutphen (1586), in which Sir Philip Sidney was killed, was fought at Warnsveld, just to the east of the town.

Economy

Zutphen is now the cultural and administrative centre of the Veluwe and Achterhoek. Its major industries are engineering, brickmaking, chemicals and woodworking, together with papermaking and textiles.

The Town

Groenmarkt

In the Groenmarkt, the town's elongated main square, are a number of old gabled houses.

Wijnhuistoren

At the east end of the square stands the Wijnhuistoren (Wine-House Tower), rebuilt in 17th century style after a fire in 1920, with a carillon of 1925.

Grote Kerk (St Walburgskerk), Zutphen

To the north of the Groenmarkt, at Rozengracht 3, is the Broederenklooster, a 14th century Dominican house now occupied by the Municipal Museum (Stedelijk Museum). Open: Tue.–Fri. 11am–5pm, Sat. and Sun. 1.30–5pm.

Broederenklooster
Municipal
Museum

South of the Groenmarkt is the Gravenhof, with the Grote Kerk or St Walburgskerk (Reformed), which dates from the 12th century.
Notable features of the interior are the wall and ceiling paintings of the 15th and 16th centuries, a fine bronze font of 1527 and a 15th century chandelier in the choir.
The chapterhouse (1561–63; curious carved capitals) contains the original chained library, with 400 manuscripts and incunabula, some of them of great value, still fastened to the reading desks. Open: mid June to mid September, Mon.–Sat. 10am–12 noon and 2–4pm. Conducted tours: May to mid June and second half of September, Mon.–Sat. at 11am and 2 and 3pm.

Grote Kerk

*Font

On the north side of the church stands the Town Hall (Stadhuis; 18th c., restored 1956). Behind it is the Gothic Burgerzaal (Burghers' Hall; 15th c.), originally the meat market and later the butter market.

Town Hall

To the north of the church is the Drogenapstoren (1444–46), a handsome old town gate.

Drogenapstoren

Immediately adjoining the Drogenapstoren is the Zaadmarkt (Seed-market), with a number of handsome brick-built houses of the 16th and 17th centuries.

Zaadmarkt

Two other relics of the town's fortifications are the Berkelpoort (1312), a picturesque water-gate, and the Nieuwstadspoort (1536).

Berkelpoort
Nieuwstadspoort

The Berkelpoort, Zutphen's picturesque old water-gate

Surroundings of Zutphen

Bronkhorst	10km/6 miles south of Zutphen in the IJssel valley lies Bronkhorst, a pictur-esque village of old houses and narrow streets. Granted a municipal char-ter in 1482, it is the smallest town in the Netherlands, having failed to grow beyond its original size. Features of interest are the church (1460), the Hooghe Huys, a 17th century farmstead with a tall farmhouse, and the town pump. There are a number of local craftsmen still practising their crafts in the traditional way. The castle of the lords of Bronkhorst stood from 1000 to 1153 on a nearby hill.
Vorden	In and around Vorden, 5km/3 miles south-east of Zutphen, are eight old manor-houses with extensive estates. Notable among them are Huis Vor-den (16th c.), an L-shaped building with a square corner tower which is now the Town Hall; Kasteel Hackfort (14th c.; rebuilt in 18th c.), with two round towers; and Huis Wiersse, set in an English-style park (rhododendrons).

Zwolle   G 5

	Province: Overijssel Population: 100,000
Situation and characteristics	Zwolle, capital of the province of Overijssel, lies on the Zwarte Water (Black Water), a small stream which flows 20km/12½ miles north-west to join the Zwarte Meer, an inlet on the IJsselmeer, a few miles east of the IJssel. It is the economic and cultural centre of an extensive region which takes in parts of Drenthe, the Veluwe and the adjoining North-East Polder. It has many local government and other offices, higher educational establish-ments and important commercial houses. Its cattle market, one of the

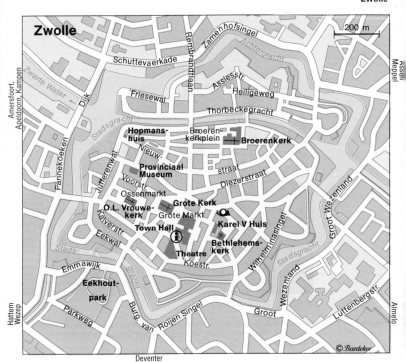

largest in the Netherlands, is of more than regional importance. Zwolle is also a considerable industrial town (vehicle assembly, engineering, food-stuffs, building materials, textiles, woodworking, leatherworking, chemicals).

Zwolle first appears in the records in 1040. It consisted of three neigh-bouring communes, two of which were granted municipal charters in 1230. Zwolle became a member of the Hanseatic League in 1348. In 1572 it was taken by William the Silent, and in 1579 it joined the Union of Utrecht.

History

The Town

In the Grote Markt is the 15th century Grote Kerk or St Michaëlskerk (Reformed). In the fine interior is a richly carved pulpit (1622) by Adam Straes of Weilburg in Hesse, who apparently felt it necessary to add an inscription explaining that in carving the brutal and sensual faces of the characters depicted he had no evil intentions. The organ is a world-famous instrument by Arp Schnitger (early 18th c.) with four manuals and 4000 pipes. Below it is the beautiful Consistory Room (1690), which contains a group portrait of the five pastors and the sexton of the church. In the choir can be seen the tomb of the painter Gerard Terborch (1617–81), who was a native of Zwolle.

Grote Kerk

Built on to the north side of the church is the picturesque Renaissance Hoofdwacht (Guard-House; 1614).

Hoofdwacht

399

St Michaëlskerk, Zwolle

Town Hall

South of the church, at the corner of Sassenstraat, stands the 15th century Town Hall (Stadhuis), with the magnificent Schepenzaal (Magistrates' Hall), now the Marriage Hall.

Bethlehemskerk

To the east of the Town Hall is the little Bethlehemskerk (14th c.), originally the church of an Augustinian house.

Sassenpoort

At the end of Sassenstraat rises the Sassenpoort (Saxon Gate; 1408) with its five spires, from which there is a good view of the Burgemeester van Roijensingel.

Statenzaal

Running east from the Grote Markt is the town's principal shopping street, Diezerstraat, on the right-hand side of which is the neo-Gothic Statenzaal (Hall of the States; 1898).

Onze Lieve
Vrouwekerk

To the west of the Grote Markt lies the Ossemarkt, in which is the 15th century Onze Lieve Vrouwekerk (Church of Our Lady; R.C.), with a 19m/62ft high tower known as the Peperbus ("Pepper-Box"; fine panoramic views).

Provincial
Museum

In a 16th century house at Voorstraat 34 is the Provincial Museum, which has a series of rooms furnished in different styles, from Gothic to Art Nouveau. There is an interesting archaeological collection in the vaulted cellars. Open: Tue.–Sat. 10am–5pm, Sun. 2–5pm.

St Michaëlskerk

On the north-eastern edge of the town, at Middelweg 32, stands the Roman Catholic parish church of St Michael (1964). In the porch is the grave-slab of St Thomas à Kempis (1380–1471), author of "The Imitation of Christ", who lived in a monastery on the Agnietenberg (3km/2 miles north-east of Zwolle; monument) from 1407 until his death.

Parks

In the immediate vicinity of the town are a number of beautiful parks (good walking).

Bridge, Rotterdam ▶

Practical Information from A to Z

Accommodation

See Camping and Caravanning, Hotels, Self-Catering, Youth Hostels

The National Board of Tourism publishes two useful brochures, "Bungalow", listing bungalow parks with accommodation in holiday bungalows (chalets), and "Group Accommodation", listing a wide range of group accommodation, from the basic to the luxurious, for young and old alike.

Airlines

KLM

The Dutch national airline, KLM (Koninklijke Luchtvaartmaatschappij, Royal Dutch Airlines: addresses below), operates mainly on international routes: see Getting to the Netherlands.

KLM offices also supply information on the services of NLM and NetherLines.

NLM

A subsidiary of KLM, the Nederlandse Luchtvaartmaatschappij (NLM; NLM City Hopper), mainly operates domestic services, with some services to other European countries (e.g. to London, Brussels and some German cities). For NLM addresses, see Air Travel. See also Getting to the Netherlands.

NetherLines

NetherLines, another KLM subsidiary, also flies to neighbouring countries (e.g. to Birmingham, Bristol, Cardiff, London and Southampton in the UK and to Luxembourg, Mulhouse and Nuremberg).

Martinair Holland; Transavia

Martinair Holland and Transavia operate international charter flights. Information: Amsterdam–Schiphol Airport.

KLM in the Netherlands

Royal Dutch Airlines

Head office: Amsterdamseweg 55, NL–Amstelveen, tel. (020) 6 49 91 23
Postal address: P.O. Box 7700, NL–1117 ZL Amsterdam Airport Schiphol

Reservations, Amsterdam: G. Metsustraat 2–6, 1071 EA, tel. (020) 6 49 36 33
Reservations and flight information in Departures Hall, Amsterdam–Schiphol Airport, tel. (020) 6 74 77 47

Reservations, Rotterdam: Coolsingel 18, tel. (010) 4 24 13 99
Reservations and flight information: tel. (010) 4 74 77 47

KLM Abroad

United Kingdom

KLM Building, 8 Hanover Street, London W1R 9HF, tel. (071) 750 9200, reservations 750 9000

USA

437 Madison Avenue, New York NY 10022, tel. (1 800) 777 5553

Canada

2 Bloor Street West, Suite 1803, 18th floor, tel. (416) 323 9620, reservations 323 1515

Offices of Foreign Airlines in Amsterdam

Stadhouderskade 4, tel. (020) 6 85 22 11   British Airways

Singel 540, tel. (020) 6 26 22 77   TWA

World Trade Center, Tower A, 8th floor,   Air France
Strawinskylaan 813, tel. (020) 75 48 81

Airports

Amsterdam International Airport, tel. (020) 6 49 91 23   Amsterdam–
Reservations: tel. (020) 6 74 77 47 (24-hour service)   Schiphol

The leading Dutch international airport (*luchthaven*) is Schiphol, 12km/7½
miles south-west of Amsterdam on the E 10 motorway (Amsterdam–The
Hague), where numerous well-known airlines (see Airlines) and car hire
firms (see Car Rental) have desks. There are also a duty-free shopping
centre (see Shopping, Souvenirs), conference rooms, cafeterias, bars and
restaurants, facilities for changing money, a post office and a pharmacy.
Outside the airport building are taxi ranks and bus stops.

There are fast train services every 15 minutes on the Schiphollijn (Schiphol   Schiphollijn
Line) from the airport to the Central Station, the World Trade Center and the
RAI Congress Center in Amsterdam, to the Central Station in The Hague
and to Rotterdam (with onward connections to other destinations in the
Netherlands and elsewhere in Europe).

KLM Wegvervoer runs daily bus services (KLM Hotel Shuttle; Orange Line   Bus services
and Yellow Line) between the airport and various Amsterdam hotels.   to hotels

"Signpost" at Schiphol Airport

Air Travel

Information: KLM Wegvervoer, Postbus 7700, NL–1117 ZL, Luchthaven Schiphol, tel. (020) 6 49 56 51 and 6 49 56 31.

Rotterdam–
Zestienhoven

Rotterdam Airport, tel. (010) 15 54 30 and 47 27 45
Reservations: tel. (010) 4 74 77 77
There are flights to Rotterdam from London (Heathrow), Paris (Charles de Gaulle) and other European airports.
The airport has a small duty-free shopping centre.

Sightseeing flights over Rotterdam can be arranged.

Other airports

Other airports served by NLM (see Airlines) are Eindhoven (tel. 040/51 61 42) and Maastricht (reservations and information tel. 020/74 77 47, flight information tel. 043/66 66 88).

Air Travel

The Dutch domestic airline NLM (Nederlandse Luchtvaart Maatschaapij) flies regular services (city-hopper flights) from Amsterdam–Schiphol to Eindhoven, Maastricht and Rotterdam.

Information:
NLM City Hopper BV
Postbus 7700
NL–1117 ZL Schiphol Oost
tel. (020) 6 49 22 27 and 6 49 56 95

NLM-Reizen, a special department of NLM City Hopper, can arrange tours, either for individuals or for groups, to towns served by NLM.

KLM

KLM also flies between Amsterdam and Eindhoven.
Information:
KLM, Leidseplein 1–3, tel. (020) 6 49 36 33
At Schiphol Airport: tel. (020) 6 74 77 47

Sightseeing
flights

Sightseeing flights over various Dutch towns (e.g. Alkmaar, Edam, Haarlem, Naarden, Volendam, etc.) are operated from Amsterdam–Schiphol by NLM: tel. (020) 6 49 32 52.
For information about sightseeing flights over Rotterdam, the windmills and the Delta, apply to VVV Rotterdam (see Information).

Antiques

The Netherlands are a happy hunting ground for lovers of art and antiques (*antikwiteiten*). In Amsterdam alone there are some 200 antique dealers, many of them offering objects of the highest quality – though prices are no lower than in other European cities.

The range of interest is wide – furniture, glass, porcelain, jewellery, gold and silver, old prints and books, fine examples of Art Nouveau, Persian miniatures, nautical instruments, old dolls and toys.

Visitors interested in antiques will find much to tempt them at the art and antique markets and fairs held in various Dutch towns. Particularly noted for such events are the towns of Delft and Maastricht (see Markets and Events).

Aquariums

See Leisure and Theme Parks

Banks

See Currency

Beaches

Along the 300km/200 miles of coastline from the West Frisian islands in the north to the Schelde estuary in the south are more than fifty seaside resorts.

General

The most fashionable resort is Scheveningen, with its broad seafront boulevard and good shops and boutiques. In addition to a wide range of facilities for active holidays (see Sport) there are numerous resorts offering quiet seaside holidays (for example on the West Frisian islands, all easily accessible by ferry: see Ferries), and suitable for holidays with children (e.g. Katwijk).

See Facts and Figures, Climate; When to Go

Weather

The water of the North Sea, combined with the high iodine content of the air, has a bracing effect.
During the summer the quality of the water along the whole length of the coast is monitored by the Dutch authorities.

Quality of water

In many resorts notices are posted giving the times of high and low tides.

Tides

Most of the sandy beaches are wide and slope gently down to the sea. They are usually cleared and tidied during the night or in the early morning.

Beaches

In 1989 the following seven seaside resorts were granted the "blue flag of Europe" by the Foundation for Environmental Education in Europe (FEEE), which seeks to promote improvement in the quality of water and beaches: Domburg/Oostkapelle, Nieuw-Haamstede, Hoek van Holland, 's-Gravenzande, Noordwijk, Zandvoort, Camperduin/Schoorl.

"Blue flag" beaches

The beaches are equipped with kiosks (sometimes including lavatories), at which beach umbrellas, mattresses, wind-screens, etc., can be hired. Ice-cream stalls cater for the thirsty, and there are also booths selling fish specialities.

Facilities on beaches

The seaside resorts are well equipped with dance halls, discothèques, bars and cafés of various kinds; in the larger places there are cinemas and theatres; and in Scheveningen and Zandvoort, for example, there are night clubs and casinos (see Casinos).

Entertainment after dark

The 1750km/1100 mile long "Green Coast Road" runs along the coast from the Netherlands to Norway, passing through five countries.
The road and its side roads are signposted (e.g. along the coasts of Noord-Holland, Zuid-Holland and Zeeland).

"Green Coast Road"

Certain secluded areas along the Dutch coast are reserved for naturists. Topless bathing is permitted on almost all beaches.

Nude bathing

Information: Dutch Federation of Naturist Clubs (NFN), Postbus 1391, NL–3500 BJ Utrecht.

Bathing Beaches

⊙ Bathing Beaches

Beach Regulations

Sleeping on the beach is prohibited. (Beaches are cleaned during the night and in the early morning.)

Car parking on the beach is prohibited.

Dog-owners must not allow their dogs to run free on the beach between sunrise and sunset.

For the protection of the dunes care must be used in lighting fires.

Rubbish bins on the beach and in the dunes must be used.

Dutch beaches have a fringe of surf, and those who bathe in the surf must be strong swimmers, since there are sometimes unsuspected undertows. Visitors should enquired at the beginning of their holiday about conditions on the local beach and should observe any regulations laid down (e.g. flags indicating whether bathing is safe or not). | Hazards

During the season many beaches, particularly those offering some hazard, have beach wardens (life guards, police). | Beach wardens

Boat Hire

See Sport

Bus Services

See Public Transport

Business Hours

The Netherlands Accommodation Centre (Nederlands Reserverings Centrum, NRC) in Leidschendam is open Monday to Friday 8am to 8pm, Saturday 8am to 2pm. | Accommodation Centre

See Currency | Banks

See entry | Chemists

Cinemas in the larger towns frequently have two evening showings, one at 6.45, the other at 9.30. | Cinemas

Information about the time and place of local markets can be obtained from local tourist information offices (VVV, etc.). See also Markets. | Markets

Most Dutch museums are closed on Mondays on grounds of economy. For information about current opening times, apply to the local tourist information office. | Museums

See Postal, etc., Services | Post offices

Almost all shops are closed on one morning or afternoon in the week, some for a whole day; some department stores are closed on Monday morning. Closing days are posted on individual establishments.
The usual opening hours are: Monday to Friday from 8.30 or 9am to 5.30 or 6pm, Saturday from 8 or 8.30am to 4 or 5pm. Some shops close at lunchtime. | Shops

407

Bakers and butchers often close at 1pm on Saturdays.
In holiday areas many shops remain open longer than usual in the evening and at weekends during the main season.

Late opening (Koopavend)
In many towns there is a late shopping evening (Koopavend) on Thursday or Friday, when shops remain open until 9pm. On these evenings some banks also stay open longer.

VVV offices
The VVV tourist information offices are usually open Monday to Friday from 9am to 5pm, Saturday 10am to 12 noon; during the summer they are also open in the evening and on Sunday afternoon.
VVV offices in Amsterdam, The Hague and Rotterdam: see Information.

Camping and Caravanning

Sites
The Netherlands have about 2000 camping sites. More than 600 selected sites (i.e. those which accept advance bookings), indicating those which have log cabins (see below), and giving detailed information about them, are listed in a booklet, "Holland Camping", which can be obtained from the Netherlands Bureau of Tourism (see Information).

Classification
Many (though not all) camping sites are classified in categories according to the facilities and amenities they offer – minimum-standard, simple, comfortable, very comfortable, first-class or luxury.

Facilities for disabled
Some sites have facilities for the disabled: for details see the booklet mentioned above. It is advisable to check in advance with the particular site.

Information
Further information can be obtained through national camping organisations.

Booking
Advance booking is advisable during the main holiday season, particularly on sites near the coast. The addresses and telephone numbers of sites are given in the booklet mentioned above.

Log cabins
Many camping sites have "trekkershutten" – log cabins (no heating) with an area of around 10 sq.m/110 sq.ft which can accommodate a maximum of four people (who must bring their own sleeping bags, eating equipment, etc.). They are ideal for walkers and cyclists, since they are never more than 25km/15 miles apart. The maximum length of stay is three nights. The trekkershutten are listed in a brochure, "Trekkershutten Nederland", obtainable from VVV offices.
Advance booking is necessary through the Nederlands Reserverings Centrum, Postbus 404, NL–2260 AK Leidschendam, tel. (070) 320 25 00.

"Wild camping"
"Wild camping" (i.e. camping outside official camping sites) is prohibited, as is the parking of trailer or motor caravans elsewhere than on camping sites.

Car Ferries

See Ferries

Car Rental

Car rental firms have offices in all the larger towns in the Netherlands and at Amsterdam-Schiphol Airport.

InterRent/Europcar, now amalgamated, have a particularly extensive network of offices.

Rates vary according to the type of car and length of hire. In addition to the   Tariffs
basic hire charge there is a charge per kilometre. Some firms include the
insurance premium in the hire charge; others charge it separately.

Before hiring you should enquire about the most favourable tariff, since
otherwise possible special offers (e.g. a weekend rate) may not be mentioned. It is advantageous to book in advance.
For a car hired for a week or longer outside the main season the charge will
be much below the usual tariff.

Normally national driving licences are accepted. Some hirers require the   Driving licence
prospective driver to be at least 18 (or sometimes 23) years of age or to
have held a driving licence for at least a year (sometimes two years).

Further information can be obtained from VVV offices.

Postbus 22528   Avis
NL–1100 DA Amsterdam
tel. (020) 5 64 16 11

Desk in Arrivals Hall, Schiphol Airport
tel. (020) 6 04 13 01

Saturnusstraat 25   Hertz
NL–2132 Hoofddorp
tel. (02503) 3 43 34 and 83 16 31 (reservations)

Desk in Schiphol Airport
tel. (020) 6 01 54 16

Hertz also rents minibuses for families.

Kruisweg 605   InterRent/
NL–2132 NA Hoofddorp   Europcar
tel. (02503) 3 44 33

Desk in Arrivals Hall, Schiphol Airport
tel. (020) 6 01 54 39

Kruisweg 823   Sixt/Budget
NL–2132 NG Hoofddorp
tel. (02503) 7 12 00 (head office)
and 1 70 30 (reservations)

Desk in Arrivals Hall, Schiphol Airport
tel. (020) 6 04 13 49

Some firms (e.g. InterRent/Europcar) also have trailer and motor caravans
available for hire.

Bookings can be made before leaving home through local offices of the
international rental firms.

Casinos

Games of chance are becoming increasingly popular in the Netherlands, as
in other countries. The games most commonly played are French and
American roulette, blackjack, punto banco and baccarat.

Formal dress is required. No one under 18 is admitted. A passport or other form of identity document must be presented.

Admission tickets are available on a daily, monthly or annual basis.

Opening times | Casinos are usually open daily from 2pm to 2 in the morning.

Holland Casinos | There are "Holland Casinos" in Amsterdam, Breda, Groningen, Nijmegen, Rotterdam, Scheveningen, Valkenburg and Zandvoort.

Castles and Palaces

Most of the castles and palaces in the Netherlands are mentioned in the A to Z section of this guide in the entry for the appropriate town or province. The following is a selection of castles and palaces in the various provinces. Unless otherwise indicated there is a charge for admission.

Opening times | Since opening times are subject to alteration it is advisable to check that a particular castle will be open by telephoning the number given below or enquiring of the local VVV office.

Friesland

Marssum | Heringa State or Poptaslot (16th c.; furniture, porcelain, silver, etc.)
Slotlaan 1, tel. (05107) 12 31
Open: Apr.–Sept., Mon.–Fri.
Conducted tours by prior arrangement

Gelderland

Ammerzoden | Kasteel Ammersoyen (*c.* 1300; objects found in castle moat)
Kasteellaan 1, tel. (04199) 12 70
Open: Apr.–Oct., Tue.–Sat. 10am–5pm, Sun. 1–5pm (on Easter Monday, Whit Monday and Ascension 10am–5pm

Doornenburg | Kasteel Doornenburg (13th c.)
Kerkstraat 27, tel. (08812) 14 56
Open: Apr.–Sept., Sun. Conducted tours at 2.30 and 4pm; in July and Aug. also at 11am and 1.30 and 3pm Tue.–Thur., and at 1.30 and 3pm Fri. and Sat.

Doorwerth | Kasteel Doorwerth (13th c.; Netherlands Hunting and Wild Life Museum)
Fonteinallee 1, tel. (085) 33 25 32
Open: Apr.–Oct., Tue.–Fri. 10am–5pm, Sat., Sun. and pub. hols. 1–5pm; Nov.–Mar., only Sat., Sun. and pub. hols. 1–5pm (closed Dec. 26th and Jan. 1st)

Hernen | Kasteel Hernen (*c.* 1500)
Dorpsstraat 40, tel. (08873) 19 76
North wing open: Apr.–Oct. Tue., Thur. and Sat., Easter Monday, Whit Monday and Ascension 10am–12 noon and 2–5pm

Hoenderloo | Jachtslot St Hubertus (1914–20; a hunting lodge of the Kröller family, with original furniture and furnishings), in the Hoge Veluwe National Park
Tel. (05768) 14 41
Open: May–Oct., daily 10–11.30am and 2–4.30pm

Kasteel Loevestein (c. 1360; formerly a state prison, in which Hugo Grotius was confined), opposite the town of Woudrichem, at the junction of the Maas and the Waal
Tel. (01832) 13 75
Open: Apr.–Oct., Mon.–Fri. 10am–5pm, Sat. and Sun. 2–5pm
Poederoyen

Kasteel Rozendaal (14th c.; temporary exhibitions on castles)
Park 1, tel. (085) 63 48 53
Open: April to Oct.,Tue.–Sat. 10am–5pm, Sun. 1–5pm
Rozendaal

Huis Bergh (medieval; medieval art)
Hof van Bergh 1, tel. (08346) 6 12 81
Open: Mar. to June, Nov.–Dec. Sat., Sun.; July to Oct. Mon.–Sun. conducted tours 2 and 3pm.
's-Heerenberg

Kasteel de Cannenburgh (14th c.; furniture and furnishings)
Maarten van Rossumplein 4, tel. (05788) 12 92
Open: Apr.–Oct., Tue.–Sat. 10am–5pm, Sun. 1–5pm; Easter, Whitsun and Ascension 10am–5pm
Vaassen

Groningen

Borg Verhildersum (c. 1700; permanent exhibition, "History of the Marshes and the Land", and temporary special exhibitions; garden in French style)
Wierde 40, tel. (05957) 14 30
Open: Good Friday to Oct., Tue.–Sun. and pub. hols. 10.30am–5.30pm
Leens

Fraeylemaborg (c. 1600; furniture, portraits of the House of Orange, porcelain; temporary exhibitions)
Hoofdweg 32, tel. (05982) 15 68
Open: April to Dec. Tue.–Sun. and pub. hols. 10am–12 noon and 1–5pm
Slochteren

Menkemaborg (c. 1400; furniture, portraits, glass, etc.)
Menkemaweg 2, tel. (05953) 19 70
Open: Apr.–Sept., daily 10am–12 noon and 1–5pm; Oct.–Mar., Tue.–Sun. 10am–12 noon and 1–4pm. (Closed Jan.)
Uithuizen

Limburg

Kasteel Hoensbroek (13th/17th c.; Museum of Limburg Militia, Archaeological Museum and collections from Africa and Asia)
Klinkertstraat 118, tel. (045) 21 11 82
Open: daily 10am–5.30pm (closed on Christmas Day, New Year's Day and Carnival)
Hoensbroek

Kasteel Valkenburg (c. 1100; ruined)
Grendelplein, tel. (04406) 1 27 27
Open: Apr.–Oct., daily 10am–5pm
Valkenburg

The Kasteel Den Halder in Valkenburg now houses the Limburg VVV office, tel. (04406) 1 39 93, which produces a brochure on the "Euregio Maas–Rijn" holiday region (the Belgium and Dutch provinces of Limburg, the Belgian province of Liège and the area round Aachen in Germany), with information about recreation and leisure facilities, art, culture and nature.

Noord-Brabant

Kasteel Heeze (17th c.; furniture, pictures, tapestries)
Kapelstraat 25, tel. (04907) 6 14 31
Open: Mar.–Oct., Wed. and Sun. 2 and 3pm, and by appointment
Heeze

411

Castles and Palaces

Helmond
Kasteel Helmond (1402; family portraits, old artifacts and models; temporary exhibitions)
Kasteelplein 1, tel. (04920) 4 74 75
Open: Tue.–Fri. 10am–5pm, Sat., Sun. and pub. hols. 2–5pm (closed New Year and Carnival)

Noord-Holland

Amsterdam
Koninklijk Paleis (Royal Palace, 1648; pictures, sculpture, etc.)
N.Z. Voorburgwal 147, tel. (020) 6 24 86 98
Open: Easter, mid June to Aug. and during autumn holidays, daily 12.30–4.40pm; Sept.–May, conducted tour at 2pm (groups by telephone appointment)

Medemblik
Kasteel Medemblik/Radboud (c. 13th c.; temporary exhibitions in Knights' Hall, collection of West Frisian coats of arms; audio-visual presentation)
Oudevaartsgat 8, tel. (02274) 19 60/31 44
Open: mid May to mid Sept., Mon.–Sat. 10am–5pm, Sun. 2–5pm; mid Sept. to mid May, Sun. 2–5pm

Muiden
Muiderslot (c. 13th c.; 17th c. furnishings; herb garden)
Herengracht 1, tel. (02942) 13 25
Open (conducted visits only): Apr.–Sept., Mon.–Fri. 10am–5pm, Sun. and pub. hols. 1–5pm; Oct.–Mar., Fri. 10am–4pm, Sun. 1–4pm (closed Sat., New Year and Dec. 25th–26th)

Santpoort
Slot Brederode (c. 1300, ruined; collection of excavated material; permanent exhibition, "The Eighteen Burghers of Brederode")
Velserenderlaan 2, tel. (023) 37 87 63
Open: Mar.–Nov., Mon.–Fri. 10am–5pm

Overijssel

Denekamp
Huis Singraven (c. 1415; furniture, pictures, tapestries, pottery)
Molendijk 37, tel. (05413) 19 06 and 20 88
Open: mid Apr. to Oct.; conducted visits Tue.–Fri. at 11am and 2, 3 and 4pm; groups on Sat. by appointment

Wijhe
Kasteel 't Nijenhuis (15th c.; old and modern art, furniture, porcelain, etc.; admission free)
't Nijenhuis 10.
Conducted visits by appointment, tel. (05729) 14 34

Utrecht

Amerongen
Kasteel Amerongen (1286; Chinese porcelain, French furniture)
Drostestraat 20, tel. (03434) 5 42 12
Open: Apr.–Oct., Tue.–Fri. 10am–5pm, Sat., Sun. and pub. hols. 1–5pm

Doorn
Huis Doorn (c. 18th c.; furniture, tapestries, snuff-boxes)
Langbroekerweg 10, tel. (03430) 1 22 44/1 23 42
Open: Mar.–Aug., Mon.–Sat. 9.30am–5pm, Sun. 1–5pm

Haarzuilens
Kasteel de Haar (1890–92; furniture, pictures, tapestries, etc.)
Kasteellaan 1, tel. (03407) 12 75/38 04
Open: Mar. to mid Aug. and mid Oct. to mid Nov., Mon.–Fri. 11am–4pm, Sat., Sun. and pub. hols. 1–4pm

Maarssen
Slot Zuylen (c. 1300; rebuilt in the form of an 18th century country house)
Tournooiveld 1, tel. (030) 44 02 55
Open: mid Mar. to mid May and mid Sept. to mid Nov. Sat. and Sun. 1–4pm; mid May to mid Sept., Tue.–Thur. 10am–4pm
Conducted visits Fri. 10am–12 noon, Sat. 2–4pm, Sun. 1–4pm

Kasteel Sijpestein (medieval; Chinese and Loosdrecht porcelain, furniture, glass, ceramics, etc.)
Loosdrechtsedijk 150, tel. (02158) 3 32 08
Conducted visits: Apr. to mid Sept., Tue.–Sat. at 10.15 and 11.15am and 2, 3 and 4pm, Sun. at 2, 3 and 4pm (groups by appointment)

Nieuw-Loosdrecht

Slot Zeist (1686; period rooms in French style, temporary exhibitions)
Zinzendorflaan 1, tel. (03404) 2 17 04
Conducted visits: Sat. and Sun. at 2.30 and 4pm, June to Aug. also Tue.–Fri. at 2.30pm (closed on pub. hols.)

Zeist

Zuid-Holland

Binnenhof (13th c.; Parliament and government offices)
Information centre at Binnenhof 8A, tel. (070) 3 64 61 44
Open (including Good Friday and Ascension Day): Mon.–Sat. 10am–4pm, in July and Aug. also Sun. 10am–4pm; audio-visual presentation, exhibition and conducted visit to Knights' Hall (closed Sun., pub. hols. and New Year)

The Hague

Kasteel Duivenvoorde (17th c.; family portraits, furniture, porcelain)
Laan van Duivenvoorde 4, tel. (01717) 37 52
Open: May–Sept; conducted visits Tue.–Sat. at 2 and 3.30pm (on Ascension Day at 10.30am and 3.30pm)

Voorschoten

Cheese Factories and Farms

There are two categories of Dutch cheese, "factory cheese" and "farm cheese". Factory cheese is produced in a dairy factory, farm cheese (*boerenkaas*) on a cheese or dairy farm (*kaasboerderij)*, of which there are more than 700 throughout the Netherlands.

Many organised excursions from Amsterdam (for example to Volendam and the Marken peninsula) include a visit to a cheese-making farm, where visitors can buy fresh cheese as well as such items as cheese-boards and cheese-knives.

It is also possible, of course, to visit cheese farms on your own; they are readily identifiable by their advertising signs. It is advisable to make an appointment in advance (for addresses see the telephone directory).

The following is a list of the principal cheese-making establishments.

Clara Maria (sales counter)
Bovenkerkerweg 106, tel. (02974) 2 79
Open: Mon.–Sat. 9am–6pm, Sun. 9–11am (admission free)

Amstelveen

De Jacobs Hoeve (sales counter)
Hogedijk 8, tel. (02995) 15 97
Open: daily 8am–6pm (admission free)

Katwoude

Heileuver (sales counter)
Dalmsholterdijk 17, tel. (05291) 82 32
Visited by telephone appointment

Lemelerveld

'n Ibbink
Arfmansteeg 1, tel. (05735) 17 97
Open: Mon.–Sat. 9am–5pm, Sun. 10am–5pm (groups by appointment)

Ruurlo

J.T. Neeleman (sales counter)
Zwaagsterweg 36, tel. (05979) 16 25
Visited by appointment

Scheemda

A selection of Dutch cheeses

Zaandam	De Catherina Hoeve (farm cheese) De Kwakels 2, tel. (075) 21 58 20 Open: daily 9am–6pm (admission free)
Cheese market (Kaasmarkt)	An essential on every visitor's programme is a visit to a cheese market, for example in Alkmaar, Edam or Gouda (see Markets). Information from local tourist offices.
	See also Food and Drink

Chemists

Opening times	Mon.–Fri., 8 or 9am to 5.30pm Some chemists' shops are open on a rota basis in the evening, during the night and at weekends. Information about this emergency service is posted up in chemists' shops and usually also in VVV offices. When a chemist is closed a notice on the door will indicate the nearest shop that is open.
Pharmacy at Schiphol Airport	There is a pharmacy in the Arrivals Hall at Schiphol Airport.
Prescriptions	Visitors who require regular supplies of medicine should carry with them, and present to the chemist, a prescription with the Latin name of the drug.
Emergency calls	See Emergencies

Cinemas

There are numerous cinemas (*bioscoopen*) in the larger towns. Foreign films are shown in the original version with Dutch subtitles.

Information about cinema programmes can be obtained from the newspapers, posters and the programmes of events obtainable from VVV offices.

Some cinemas have reduced prices on certain days.

See Business Hours

Conferences and Congresses

The Netherlands are well equipped to cater for business travel, and there are numerous congress centres and facilities for holding conferences, seminars and meetings of various kinds. There are frequently large exhibition halls attached to the congress and conference centres.

Nederlands Congres Bureau (NCB)
Amsteldijk 166, NL–1079 LH Amsterdam
tel. (020) 6 46 25 80; fax (020) 4 45 94 35

Dutch Congress
Bureau

VVV offices in Amsterdam and other large towns have special sections (Visitors and Convention Bureaus) which help in the organisation of congresses and conferences.

Visitors and
Convention
Bureaus

Facilities for "floating" conferences are offered by the KD German Rhine Line, which also operates in Dutch waters.
Address:
Köln-Düsseldorfer Deutsche Rheinschiffahrt AG
Frankenwerft 15, D(W)–5000 Köln (Cologne) 1
tel. (0221) 20 88–0

Conferences
aboard ship

There are large congress centres in:
Amsterdam (RAI Congress Center)
Groningen (Martinihal Center)
The Hague (Netherlands Congress Center)
Maastricht (Maastricht Exhibition)
Noordwijkerhout (Leeuwenhorst Congress Center)
Rotterdam (De Doelen Congress and Concert Building and Sportpaleis
  Ahoy)
Utrecht (Jaarbeurs Congress and Convention Center)
Veldhoven (Koningshof Congress Center)

Congress centres

See also Trade Fairs

Consulates

See Diplomatic and Consular Offices

Currency

The unit of currency in the Netherlands is the Dutch guilder (*gulden*) or florin (abbreviated hfl, fl, F or gld), which consists of 100 cents.

There are banknotes for 5, 10, 25, 50, 100, 250 and 1000 guilders, issued by the Dutch central bank, the Nederlandse Bank.

Banknotes

There are coins in denominations of 5, 10 and 25 cents, 1 guilder, 2½ guilders and 5 guilders. The 5 cent coin (the *stuiver*) is bronze; the 10 cent (*dubbeltje*), 25 cent (*kwartje*), 1 guilder and 2½ guilder coins are nickel; and

Coins

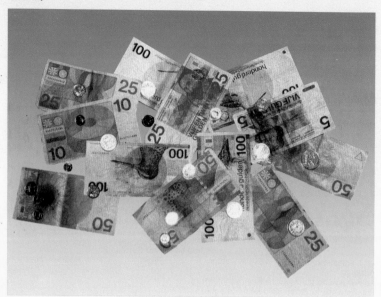

Dutch banknotes

the 5 guilder piece is bronzed nickel (since it is rather similar to the 5 cent coin, care is required when changing money).

The coins are produced by the National Mint in Utrecht. Since 1982 they have borne the effigy of Queen Beatrix; the older coins with the likeness of Queen Juliana are still current.

Exchange rates

These are subject to fluctuation and can be obtained from banks, travel agents and exchange offices. Exchange rates are published daily in most national newspapers.

Import and export of currency

There are no restrictions on the import or export of either Dutch or any other currency.

Traveller's cheques, Eurocheques

It is advisable to take money in the form of traveller's cheques or to use Eurocheques.

Eurocheques can be cashed up to the equivalent of £100 per cheque.

Changing money

Money can be changed in post offices, frontier exchange offices (Grenswisselkantoren, GWK), banks and, in some holiday resorts, VVV offices. Since rates of commission vary, it is advisable to enquire about this before changing money.

Banks are usually open Mon.–Fri. from 9am to 4 or 5pm. On the late shopping evening (see Business Hours) some banks are open until 9pm.

The frontier exchange offices are government agencies in which all kinds of currencies can be exchanged, traveller's cheques and Eurocheques can be cashed, money can be drawn by holders of credit cards and travel insurance can be taken out. There are GWKs at all the major frontier crossings and in 35 railway stations (including the station at Schiphol Airport). They are open Mon.–Sat. from 8am to 8pm, Sun. 10am to 4pm, and sometimes also in the evening.

Offices open 24 hours a day:
GWK in Central Station, Amsterdam
GWK at Oberhausen–Arnhem frontier crossing on the A 3 motorway
GWK at the Antwerp–Breda frontier crossing

Most of the international credit cards (as well as traveller's cheques and **Credit cards**
Eurocheques) are accepted in banks, frontier exchange offices and the
larger hotels, restaurants and shops.
Cash can be obtained at frontier exchange offices with the following credit
cards: Access, AirPlus, American Express, Diner's Club, Eurocard, JCB,
Master Card, Visa.

10-guilder (and in some cases 25-guilder) notes can be used to obtain **Note-operated**
petrol from note-operated petrol pumps. **petrol pumps**

A useful phrase:
"Ik wou graag geld opvragen" ("I should like to draw some money").

Visitors who lose a credit card, traveller's cheques, Eurocheque card or **Loss of credit**
Eurocheques should report the loss at once by telephone (confirmed in **cards, etc.**
writing) to the issuing authority so that illicit payments can be stopped.

Customs Regulations

Personal effects, holiday equipment and sporting gear (including canoes
up to 5.50m/18ft long), and food and fuel for the journey can be taken into
the Netherlands without payment of duty. For sporting guns and ammunition a Dutch shooting licence is required. Owners of cars fitted with CB
radio and car telephones should check on the current regulations with their
motoring organisation.
In addition visitors can take in, duty-free, specified amounts of alcoholic
liquor, tobacco goods and perfume. For goods obtained duty and tax paid
in the European Community the permitted amounts are 1½ litres of spirits
over 22% vol or 3 litres of spirits under 22% vol, fortified or sparkling wine;
5 litres of still wine; 90 cc of perfume; 375 cc of toilet water; and 300
cigarettes or 150 cigarillos or 75 cigars or 400 grams of tobacco. For goods
obtained outside the European Community or from a duty-free shop within
the Community the permitted amounts are 1 litre of spirits over 22% vol or
2 litres of spirits under 22% vol, fortified or sparkling wine; 60 cc of
perfume; 250 cc of toilet water; and 200 cigarettes or 100 cigarillos or 50
cigars or 250 grams of tobacco.

The import into the Netherlands of hand-guns or other firearms and ammu- **Prohibited**
nition, meat and sausages, fruit, flowers, plants and protected (endan- **imports**
gered) species of animals is prohibited.

Cycling

A very helpful brochure, "Cycling in Holland", and a fact sheet listing **Information**
bicycle hire firms can be obtained from the Netherlands Bureau of Tourism.

Cycles by rail: Netherlands Railways (Nederlandse Spoorwegen): for
address see Railways

Loss of, or damage to, cycles carried by rail; write to:
Nederlandse Spoorwegen, Afdeling CZ 22, Postbus 2025,
NL–3500 HA Utrecht, tel. (030) 35 32 27

The Netherlands have an extensive network of cycleways, totalling over **Cycleways**
11,000km/6800 miles. In some areas they may also be used by mopeds.

Bicycles – a popular means of transport in the Netherlands

Since the country is so flat, most of these tracks should present no problems even for inexperienced cyclists. On the West Frisian islands of Schiermonnikog and Vlieland, where there are no cars, the bicycle is the regular means of transport.

Since there are frequently strong southerly or south-westerly winds, it is advisable to plan your itinerary in such a way as to have the wind in your back so far as possible.

There are beautiful cycle tracks through the dunes, well away from motor roads. There is a magnificent through route from Den Helder in Noord-Holland to Hoek van Holland in the province of Zuid-Holland, and the North Sea Route follows the coast from Den Helder to the Belgian–French frontier.

In the larger towns it is advisable to leave your bicycle in a guarded bicycle park; elsewhere you should padlock it and, so far as possible, keep an eye on it.

Signposting

Cycleways are indicated by a circular blue sign with a white bicycle. Cyclists and moped riders are required to use cycleways so marked.
There are also "optional" cycleways, marked by a rectangular black sign with the legend "fietspad" or "rijwielpad", which are recommended for cyclists but are banned to moped riders.
White signs with a legend in red and a red bicycle indicate that the road is less suitable for cars but particularly suitable and interesting for cyclists.

Along the cycleways are the so-called *paddestoelen* ("mushrooms") – low white milestones or direction indicators with the number of the route (as shown on the ANWB maps: see below), distances and names of towns and villages.

The Stichting Fiets (Bicycle Foundation, Europaplein 2, NL–1018 GZ Amsterdam, tel. 020/42 55 50), in association with the ANWB (the Dutch motoring organisation, originally founded as a cycling club), publishes a series of booklets, with maps, describing round trips for cyclists, which foreign motorists can obtain through their own motoring organisation. (The guides and other publications of the ANWB are available only in Dutch).
The Staatsbosbeheer (National Forestry Administration) and the Vereniging tot Behoud van Natuurmonumenten (Association for the Preservation of Natural Monuments) also publish descriptions of long-distance cycle routes through nature reserves and national parks.
For other maps, see the entry Maps.

Maps

Before taking your own bicycle to the Netherlands you should check that it meets the requirements of Dutch regulations in the following respects: steering, brakes and lighting in good order; a clearly audible bell; a white or yellow rear mudguard at least 30cm/12in. long; a reflector on the rear mudguard and one between the spokes; and reflecting pedals.

Taking your own bicycle

It is also easy to hire a bicycle in the Netherlands, either from the cycle parks at railway stations or from a private cycle hire firm (*fietsverkuur*). A passport or other identity document must be produced, the hire charge must be paid in advance and a deposit (which may take the form of a Eurocheque) will be required.
It is advisable to book in advance. The bicycle must be returned to the original hiring point.

Bicycle hire

Bicycles can be carried on trains, with a special bicycle ticket (*fietskaart*). You must see to the loading and unloading of the bicycle yourself. Bicycles cannot be carried during the morning and evening rush hours (Mon.–Fri. 6.30–9am and 4.30–6pm).

Transport of bicycles by rail

A booklet available at all Dutch railway stations, "Fiets en Trein", contains detailed information about the hiring and transport of bicycles, together with a list of stations at which bicycles can be put on to the train.

"Fiets en Trein"

Suggested Routes

The varied landscape of the Netherlands offers scope for a range of attractive cycle trips – along the coast, round the IJsselmeer, through polders, forests, fields of flowers, National Parks and nature reserves, towns and villages. Combined trips by bicycle, boat and rail are also possible.

The Netherlands Railways (Nederlandse Spoorwegen), in co-operation with the Kunstlijn (Art Line) Foundation, has laid out a kind of contemporary open-air museum along the railway line from Zwolle to Emmen, and it is possible to cycle along a section of the route. Works of art are also displayed in and around other stations.

Art along the track

Arrangements can sometimes be made to have your luggage transported from hotel to hotel. Thus the VVV in Assen, Drenthe, provides facilities of this kind for cyclists touring in the province of Drenthe.

Luggage-free cycling

Another possibility is an organised boat trip – for individuals, families or groups – starting from Amsterdam, with bicycles available on the boat for all participants.
Information:
Cycletours
Keizersgracht 181
NL–1016 DR Amsterdam
tel. (020) 6 27 40 98

Cycle/boat holidays

Round trips   Round trips, with accommodation in beautifully situated youth hostels, are run by NJHC–Future Line Travel, Prof. Tulpstraat 2, NL–1018 HA Amsterdam, tel. (020) 6 23 32 72 and 6 22 28 59.

Canoeing and cycling trips in the Biesbosch and cycle and moped trips in the Rhine delta are organised by the Dordrecht VVV.

Cycling events   Between April and October there are numerous cycling events, including the National Cycling Day (Fietsdag) at the beginning of May, the Eleven Cities Tour through the province of Friesland (information from the Friesland VVV in Leeuwarden) and various four-day trips (*fietsmeerdagse*).

Diplomatic and Consular Offices

Netherlands Embassies

United Kingdom   38 Hyde Park Gate
London SW7 5DP
tel. (071) 584 5040

USA   4200 Linnean Avenue NW, Washington DC 20008
tel. (202) 244 5300

Canada   275 Slater Street (3rd floor)
Ottawa, Ontario K1P 5H9
tel. (613) 237 5030

Embassies and Consulates in the Netherlands

United Kingdom   Embassy:
Lange Voorhout 10
NL–2514 ED Den Haag
tel. (070) 3 64 58 00

Consulate General:
Koningslaan 44
NL–1074 AE Amsterdam
tel. (020) 6 76 43 43

USA   Embassy:
Lange Voorhout 102
Den Haag
tel. (070) 3 62 49 11

Consulate General:
Museumplein 19
Amsterdam
tel. (020) 6 64 56 61 and 6 79 03 21

Canada   Embassy:
Sophialaan 7
Den Haag
tel. (070) 3 61 41 11

Distances

The distances (in kilometres) between selected towns in the Netherlands are given in the table on page 422.

Drugs

The trade in, and use of, narcotic drugs in the Netherlands is prohibited by law, though hitherto the sale of marijuana in so-called "coffee shops" has been tolerated – a distinction being made between the use of "hard" and "soft" drugs in order to prevent drug-takers from "going underground". This liberal Dutch policy, however, has been brought to an end by an agreement between the Netherlands, Belgium, Luxembourg, France and Germany, due to come into effect in 1992, for the removal of frontier controls between these countries and for the exchange of information between their police forces about those involved in the drug scene.

The Jongeren Advies Centrum (Young People's Advice Centre) offers advice on drugs and drug use, free of charge and anonymously, as well as legal assistance. The organisation has branches throughout the Netherlands: for addresses see local telephone directories.

Advice for drug-users

Electricity

The Netherlands have adopted the international norm (IEC 38) on standard voltages, and by the year 2003 the whole country will be on a nominal voltage of 230 volts AC. Appliances set to the traditional 220 volts AC, however, can continue to be used without difficulty.

Power sockets are of the normal European type. Visitors from Britain, North America and other countries outside Europe should carry suitable adaptors for razors and other appliances.

Emergencies

The emergency number to call almost anywhere in the Netherlands is 0611 (charge 25 cents).

Telephone kiosks give the telephone numbers of the police, fire service and ambulance service. Immediate aid in case of accident or injury is provided by first-aid posts in hospitals.

All motorways have emergency telephones for summoning help in case of accident or breakdown.

AIDS information line (Mon.–Fri. 2–10pm): (06) 3 21 21 20.

AIDS

The Commission of the European Community plans to introduce a uniform number for calling the police in all Community countries, later followed by uniform numbers for the fire service, emergency medical aid, ambulance and other emergency services.

See under Motoring

Breakdown assistance

Events

The Netherlands Bureau of Tourism publishes annually a brochure listing festivals and other events, including trade fairs and congresses, throughout the Netherlands.

Calendar of events

Leiden Jazz Week
Vakantiebeurs (Tourism and Leisure Trade Fair), Utrecht
International Film Festival, Rotterdam

January

Events

Distances in km	Amsterdam	Almelo	Amersfoort	Apeldoorn	Arnhem	Assen	Breda	Deventer	Dordrecht	Eindhoven	Enschede	Den Haag	Groningen	Haarlem	Heerlen	's-Hertogenbosch	Hoek v. Holland	Leeuwarden	Maastricht	Nijmegen	Rotterdam	Utrecht	Venlo	Vlissingen	Zwolle
Amsterdam	–	143	44	83	99	184	105	101	97	122	154	57	202	19	216	87	78	139	215	122	73	38	183	191	111
Almelo	143	–	103	61	82	95	198	48	185	165	24	188	117	168	229	146	209	136	235	100	184	125	164	296	47
Amersfoort	44	103	–	43	48	144	93	61	81	107	114	84	172	66	201	72	105	151	200	71	80	21	135	194	71
Apeldoorn	83	61	43	–	27	117	140	16	125	107	72	128	145	108	171	88	149	134	177	44	124	65	106	238	44
Arnhem	99	82	48	27	–	140	111	40	103	81	93	116	168	115	147	62	137	157	153	18	118	62	82	212	67
Assen	164	95	144	117	140	–	238	95	226	223	115	229	30	209	288	204	250	66	294	261	225	166	223	339	74
Breda	105	198	93	140	111	238	–	155	31	59	209	72	266	120	149	49	81	235	148	93	51	74	116	100	165
Deventer	101	48	61	16	40	95	155	–	143	123	53	146	123	126	188	104	167	127	194	59	142	83	123	256	38
Dordrecht	97	185	81	125	103	226	31	143	–	91	196	45	254	93	181	64	54	225	180	99	24	62	148	118	153
Eindhoven	122	165	107	107	81	223	59	123	91	–	176	132	251	138	88	32	141	240	87	63	111	88	155	160	150
Enschede	154	24	114	72	93	115	209	59	196	176	–	199	137	179	240	157	220	162	246	111	135	136	175	307	73
Den Haag	57	188	84	128	116	229	72	146	45	132	199	–	253	42	222	104	20	190	221	135	21	61	189	139	156
Groningen	202	117	172	145	168	30	266	123	254	251	137	253	–	203	316	232	274	63	322	187	253	194	251	367	102
Haarlem	19	168	66	108	115	209	120	126	93	138	179	42	203	–	232	103	63	140	231	138	69	54	199	187	136
Heerlen	216	229	201	171	147	288	149	188	181	88	240	222	316	232	–	126	231	305	24	129	201	182	65	250	215
's-Hertogenbosch	87	146	72	88	62	204	49	104	54	32	157	104	232	103	126	–	109	221	125	44	79	53	93	150	131
Hoek v. Holland	78	209	105	149	137	250	81	167	54	141	220	20	274	63	231	109	–	211	230	144	30	82	198	139	177
Leeuwarden	139	136	151	134	157	66	235	127	225	240	162	190	63	140	305	221	211	–	311	176	206	163	240	324	91
Maastricht	215	235	200	177	153	294	148	194	180	87	246	221	322	231	24	125	230	311	–	135	200	181	71	249	221
Nijmegen	122	100	71	44	18	159	93	59	99	63	111	135	187	138	129	44	144	176	135	–	114	85	64	194	86
Rotterdam	73	184	80	124	118	225	51	142	24	111	195	21	253	69	201	79	30	206	200	114	–	57	168	109	152
Utrecht	38	125	21	65	62	166	74	83	62	88	136	61	194	54	182	53	82	163	181	85	57	–	149	175	93
Venlo	183	164	135	106	82	223	116	123	148	64	175	189	251	199	65	93	198	240	71	64	168	149	–	217	150
Vlissingen	191	296	194	238	212	339	100	256	118	160	307	139	367	187	250	150	139	324	249	194	109	175	217	–	266
Zwolle	111	47	71	44	67	74	165	38	153	160	73	156	102	136	215	131	177	91	221	86	152	93	150	266	–

February	Carnival, mainly in the southern provinces
March	Amsterdam BP Holland Rally
	Antiques Fair, Amsterdam
	Blues Festival, Amsterdam
March–May	Tulip Show in the Frans Roozen nursery, Vogelenzang
	Open-Air Flower Show, Keukenhof

International Cello Competition, The Hague
European Fine Art Fair, Maastricht
Antiekbeurs (Antiques Fair), Rotterdam

International Art and Antiques Fair, Breda | April

Flower Parade (from Haarlem via Bennebroek, Hillegom and Lisse to Noordwijk)

Spring Dance (an international festival of modern dance and movement) | April/May

International Rose Show, The Hague | April–October

Vlaggetjesdag (Flag Day; marking the opening of the herring-fishing season), Scheveningen | May
Japanese Garden in Clingendael Park in bloom from May to mid June, Scheveningen
National Cycling Day (throughout the country)

Jazz in the Woods (street parades, open-air concerts), Apeldoorn

International Old-Style Jazz Festival (open-air concerts, street parades, etc.), Breda

KunstRAI (displays of contemporary art by Dutch and Western European galleries), Amsterdam | May/June

Guided (wading) walks on the Waddenzee | May–September

Jazz in Duke Town (international jazz festival), 's-Hertogenbosch | June
Air Show, Scheveningen
Rowing Regatta for the Royal Holland Cup, Amsterdam
Holland Festival (programme of cultural events throughout the month), Amsterdam and The Hague
Flemish Festival, Rotterdam
Cycle tour of eleven Frisian towns, Bolsward
Pinkpop (international open-air pop festival), Landgraaf
Whitsun International Car Race, Zandvoort
Sheep-Shearing Festival (with shearers' banquet), Ede
Paardendag ("Horse Day": two days of equestrian events), The Hague
Summer Festival, The Hague
International Kite Festival, The Hague
National Navy Days, Den Helder
Op Roakeldais (international folk-dancing festival), Warffum
Poetry International, Rotterdam
Catamaran race round the island, De Koog (Texel)

Vondelpark Open-Air Theatre (plays, music), Amsterdam | June–September

TT Race (an international motorcycle road race for the Netherlands Grand Prix), Assen | June–July
Medieval Castle Festival, Noorbeek
International Festival of New (Avantgarde) Music, Middelburg
Parkpop (pop festival), The Hague
International Organ Competition in St Bavokerk, Haarlem

Ballet Festival, Amsterdam | July
International Jazz Festival, Amsterdam
Horse Day (trotting races), Wassenaar
Guitar Weeks, Zwolle
Leidse Lakenfeesten (summer festival for visitors)
North Sea Jazz Festival, The Hague

	Skûtsjesilen (races with old cargo yachts and market boats on the Frisian lakes)
	Kaagweek (international yacht races), Warmond
	KLM Open Golf Championship, Zandvoort
	Swinging Scheveningen (street parades; jazz, Dixie)
	Delta Flora (summer flower show: until beginning of August), Stellendam
July/August	Every Thursday: Zuiderzee Days, Enkhuizen
	Schnitger Concerts (recitals on the Schnitger organ in St Michael's Church), Zwolle
	Kinderdijk Windmill Days (mills in operation; round trips), Nieuw Lekkerland
	Tilting at the Ring (in traditional costume, on horseback and with decorated coaches: July 12th and Aug. 16th), Middelburg
	Summer Show (Frans Roozen nursery, with 500 species of flowers and plants), Vogelenzang
August	International Folk Dancing Festival, Odoorn
	Flower Parade (Rijnsburg–Leiden–Noordwijk), Rijnsburg
	Sneek Week (international yacht races on Sneeker Meer), Sneek
	Sail Amsterdam (with parade of windjammers)
	Flevo Totaal: musical festival in the Flevohof, Biddinghuizen
	Flower Parade, Leersum
	Mussel Day (opening of the mussel season, with fair; trips in fishing boats, etc.), Yerseke
	Windmill Day (windmills in operation and open to visitors), Zaandam
	Zaanse Schans Festival (folk market, traditional crafts), Zaandam
	International Firework Festival, Scheveningen
	National Tattoo, Breda
	Festival of Old Music, Utrecht
	Uit Markt (cultural events), Amsterdam
	Gaudeamus Music Week, Amsterdam
September	Flower Parade from Aalsmeer to Amsterdam
	Pop Park Open-Air Festival, Rotterdam
	Harvest and Fruit Parade, Tiel
	Illuminations of the Kinderdijk windmills (round trips), Nieuw Lekkerland
	Prinsjesdag: state opening of Parliament by Queen Beatrix, The Hague
October	Autumn Flora (flower show), Laren
	Brandaris Bolkoppen Race (tug-of-war between fishing vessels on the IJsselmeer, with various events on land), Enkhuizen
	Art and Antiques Fair, Delft
	Jazz Festival, Maastricht
	Heineken Jazz Festival, Rotterdam
	Zuidlaardermarkt (the largest horse market in Western Europe), Zuidlaren
October/ November	Pictura Antiquairs Nationaal (antiques fair: furniture, pictures, carpets, clocks, gold and silver, dolls, etc.), Amsterdam
November	Stagedoor Festival, Amsterdam
	National Flower Show, Aalsmeer
	Arrival of Sinterklaas (Santa Claus), in various towns
December	Gouda by Candlelight (Christmas illuminations, barrel-organ recitals, choral singing)

Ferries

The most important ferry services within the Netherlands are those to the West Frisian islands and the Zeeland peninsula. There are also ferries at points where rivers and canals cut across the roads.

(The 8km/5 mile long Zealand Bridge linking Schouwen–Duiveland with Noord-Beveland is a toll bridge).

The ferries from Den Helder to the island of Texel, from Harlingen to the island of Terschelling (reservation necessary) and from Holwerd to the island of Ameland (reservation necessary) carry cars; the ferries to the car-free islands of Schiermonnikoog and Vlieland do not.

Car parking facilities at the ferry ports are adequate.

Parking

There are regular bus services between various railway stations and the ferry ports: from Groningen station to Lauwersoog (for the crossing to Schiermonnikoog), from Leeuwarden station to Lauwersoog and Holwerd (for the crossing to Schiermonnikoog or Ameland) and from Den Helder station (for the crossing to the island of Texel).
Harlingen station is some 500m/550yds from the ferries to Vlieland and Terschelling.
From Vlissingen (ferry port at railway station) there is a ferry to Breskens (western Zeeuws-Vlaanderen), and from Kruiningen (bus service from station to ferry port) there is a ferry to Perkpolder (eastern Zeeuws-Vlaanderen).

Bus services
between railway
stations and
ferry ports

There are international ferry services (carrying cars) between the Netherlands and Britain and between the Netherlands and Sweden.

International
ferry services

The Principal Ferry Services within the Netherlands

FERRY SERVICE	FREQUENCY	INFORMATION
To the West Frisian islands		
Lauwerskoog to Schiermonnikoog (passengers, bicycles; no cars)	4 times daily (45 min.)	tel. (01593) 90 50 and 90 79
Harlingen–Vlieland (passengers, bicycles no cars)	3 times daily (90 min.)	tel. (05620) 29 69
Harlingen–Terschelling (passengers, cars, bicycles)	5 times daily (90 min.)	reservations: tel. (05620) 27 70
Holwerd–Ameland (passengers, cars, caravans, bicycles)	6 times daily (45 min.)	reservations: tel. (05191) 61 11
Den Helder–Texel (passengers, cars, bicycles)	half-hourly	tel. (02220) 1 93 93 (no reservations)
To Zeeland		
Breskens–Vlissingen (passengers, cars, bicycles)	half-hourly	tel. (01172) 16 63/33 50, (01184) 6 59 05/7 88 99 (no reservations)

FERRY SERVICE	FREQUENCY	COMPANY
Perkpolder–Kruiningen (passengers, cars, bicycles)	Mon.–Fri. half-hourly; Sat., Sun. hourly	tel. (01148) 12 34/26 92, (01130) 14 66/28 28

Noord-Holland to Friesland
(beginning of May to mid Sept.)

Enkhuizen–Stavoren (passengers, bicycles, mopeds)	several daily (80 min.)	tel. (05277) 34 07
Enkhuizen–Urk (passengers, bicycles, mopeds) cars by arrangement)	twice daily (except Sun. and pub. hols.; 90 min.)	tel. (05277) 34 07 (reservation necessary)

International Car Ferry Services

FERRY SERVICE	FREQUENCY	COMPANY
Britain–Netherlands		
Harwich–Hoek van Holland	daily	Stena Line
Harwich–Hoek van Holland	daily	Sealink
Hull–Rotterdam/ Europoort	daily	North Sea Ferries
rness–Vlissingen	daily	Olau Line
Sweden–Netherlands		
Göteborg–Amsterdam	once or twice weekly	Scandinavian Seaways

Information and Reservations on International Ferry Services

Stena Line	25 Buckingham Gate London SW1E 6LD tel. (071) 630 1819
North Sea Ferries	King George Dock, Hedon Road Hull HU9 5QA tel. (0482) 77177
Olau Line	Sheerness Kent ME12 1SN tel. (0795) 666666
Scandinavian Seaways	DFDS Travel Centre 15 Hanover Street London W1R 9HG tel. (071) 493 6696

Festivals

See Events

Fishing

See Sport

Flowers

The Netherlands are famed as Europe's largest supplier of flowers. Although in the field of horticulture the production of fruit has somewhat declined, the growing of bulbs (crocuses, hyacinths, daffodils, tulips, etc.) and decorative plants, particularly for the cut flower market, is a major element in the country's economy.

Bulbs have been cultivated in the Netherlands since about 1600. They originally came from Asia; the first tulip bulbs were brought from Turkey in 1590.

The international garden show, Floriade 1992, is to be held in The Hague–Zoetermeer.

Great fields of flowers are to be seen particularly between Leiden and Haarlem, between Haarlem and Den Helder and around Enkhuizen.

The National Board of Tourism published a very useful brochure, "Flowers Holland", which contains general information about flower-growing in the Netherlands and gives the dates of flower shows, flower parades, flower markets and auctions, etc.

Information

Detailed information about the flower-growing areas and sightseeing routes can be obtained from local tourist information offices (see Information). The best time to visit the flower fields is during the week: at weekends they tend to be swamped by visitors.

Since the import of bulbs into other countries is permitted only with a certificate of health from the Dutch authorities, visitors will be well advised not to buy bulbs to take home, but to order them from a firm specialising in

Export of bulbs

Bulb-fields south of Haarlem

the export of Dutch bulbs: for example Willemse, Postbus 530, NL–6500 AM Nijmegen.

Events

Millions of visitors come every year to the flower-growing areas of the Netherlands, attracted not only by the fields of flowers themselves but by a variety of special events – flower parades, flower markets (see Markets) and flower auctions such as the celebrated auctions of Aalsmeer (see entry).

Calendar of Blossom

Spring

End of March to mid May: tulips and other bulbs in the west of the country (e.g. between Leiden and Haarlem and between Haarlem and Den Helder). Many gardens display flower mosaics.

Mid April to mid May: fruit-trees in blossom in the Betuwe (between the Rhine and the Maas), in the south of Limburg province and in Zuid-Beveland (Zeeland).

There are various sightseeing routes named after the fruit which the trees will later produce (the Apple Route, the Cherry Route, the Pear Route), signposted by emblems representing the various types of fruit.

Second half of May: fields of rape (*koolzaad*) in bloom, in Flevoland, Friesland, Groningen and the Noordoostpolder. Here too there may be signposted routes.

Summer

Flowers for cutting: carnations, freesias, gerberas and gladioli, but above all roses (e.g. over 20,000 roses in the Westbroekpark in The Hague).

August/September: heather in flower in the east of the country.

Autumn

Chrysanthemums.

Winter

An abundance of flowers grown in greenhouses; the five-day Kerstflora (Christmas Flower Show).

Botanic Gardens

There are something like a hundred botanic (or botanical) gardens, mostly attached to universities, in the Netherlands. The best known are the two botanic gardens of Amsterdam University (at Middenlaan 2 and van der Boechorstraat 8), the Hortus Botanicus of Leiden University (founded 1590: see A to Z, Leiden) and the Botanic Garden of Utrecht.

Flying

See Sport

Food and Drink

Dutch cooking is rich but easily digestible. In addition to typically Dutch dishes (Neerlands Dis: served in restaurants bearing the symbol of a red, white and blue soup tureen) there are also French, Chinese, Turkish, Indonesian and other specialities.

For further information on Neerlands Dis, tourist menus and restaurants belonging to the Alliance Gastronomique Néerlandaise see Restaurants.

Pavement cafés: a familiar sight in summer

Cafés

Cafés in the Netherlands are more akin to bars than cafés in the British sense, and are often run in association with restaurants as café-restaurants. Their decor resembles that of a living room in a house, with thick, almost carpet-like, covers on the tables.

Café-restaurants

The equivalent of the British café is the tearoom or koffiehuis.

Tearoom, koffiehuis

A very popular and typically Dutch institution is the *kroegje* or *bruine kroeg* ("brown bar"), a cosy and unpretentious street-corner establishment which is a cross between an English pub and a café.

Kroegje, bruine kroeg

Similar to the kroegjes are the *bruine cafés* ("brown cafés"; so called because of their nicotine-stained walls), in which there may be facilities for billiards, pinball and darts.

Bruine cafés

Many cafés have a "happy hour" during which drinks are half price.

"Happy hour"

Mealtimes

In restaurants and hotels continental breakfast (*ontbijt),* with bread, rolls, jam, sausage, cheese and an egg, is served until about 10am Between 9 and 12 the Dutch always drink a *kopje koffie* with milk.

Breakfast

Lunch, between 12 and 2, normally consists of bread with cheese, sausage, etc., or a light hot dish. Popular items for lunch are an *uitsmijter* (see below) and *koffietafel* (like breakfast, but with soup and/or croquettes).

Lunch

429

Food and Drink

Afternoon tea	Between 3 and 5pm tea or coffee is drunk, with biscuits (*koekjes; koektrommel* = "biscuit barrel") or other titbits (*hapjes*) such as crackers, peanuts, etc.
Dinner	The main meal of the day is in the evening. It usually consists of meat, vegetables and potatoes, often preceded by soup and followed by a sweet.
	Since most restaurants close about 10pm (supper after the theatre is not a Dutch habit), those who want something more to eat must look for a late-opening restaurant or a bar.

Dutch Specialities

Fish	A favourite Dutch delicacy is herring, which can be bought – with or without onions – at the numerous herring stalls. During the early weeks of the fishing season, in May, it is sold under the name of "green" or "new" herring.
	At almost every street corner in the seaside resorts there are booths selling a wide variety of fish. Popular kinds of fish are sole, eel, mackerel, cod and plaice, cooked in many different ways.
Shellfish and crustaceans	From May to September there are oysters and mussels from the province of Zeeland, lobsters and prawns.
Meat	The Netherlands have a great variety of meat and meat dishes. Steaks are usually grilled only lightly on both sides (*biefstuk*): those who prefer their meat well done should ask for it to be *doorbakken.* "Duitse biefstuk" means hamburger.
	Another Dutch speciality is *rolpens* – brawn in vinegar marinade, sliced and grilled, with apple sauce and roast potatoes. *Huzarensalade* is a salad with meat.
Vegetables	Fresh vegetables grown in greenhouses are available throughout the year. In May and June there is excellent asparagus.
Fruit	Dutch strawberries, grapes, apples and pears are of high quality.
Casserole dishes (*stamppot*)	Simple and substantial dishes are sauerkraut with bacon, brown beans with bacon, cabbage with smoked sausage and *hutspot* (sirloin with carrots, onions and potatoes: see recipe below). In winter *erwtensoep* (pea soup: recipe below) is a favourite and very nourishing dish.
Pancakes (*pannekoeken*)	There are special pancake restaurants which serve pancakes in endless variety, with sweet (with syrup, apples, liqueur, etc.) or savoury (with bacon, salami, ham, cheese, mushrooms, etc.) fillings. *Flensjes* are a kind of thin pancake. *Poffertjes* are a kind of fritter, served with icing sugar and a piece of butter.
Open sandwiches	The popular *uitsmijter* (pronounced "outsmiter") is a slice of bread with cold meat topped by a fried egg. A great variety of open sandwiches can be had in *broodjeszaken* ("sandwich shops").
Sweets	*Hagelslag* (chocolate crumble), spread on bread, is popular with children. *Haagse hopjes* (caramels) and liquorice (*drop*) are other favourite sweets. *Boerenmeisjes* ("country girls": apricots in brandy), with cream, are sometimes served as a dessert.
Cheese	Popular kinds of cheese include Gouda, Edam, Maaslander, Texelaer, Leerdamer, cheese with caraway seeds and cheese with cloves. See Cheese Factories

Recipes

Ingredients:
2½ litres water, 400 grams peas, shelled or in pods, 500 grams leeks, 250 grams celeriac, a leaf of celery, 1 onion, 350 grams pork chop, 300 grams lean bacon, salt and pepper.

Erwtensoep
(pea soup)

Wash the peas (which if in pods should have been soaked in water for 24 hours and should be cooked in the same water). Chop up the celeriac (peeled), the leeks and the onion, and simmer with the peas, the meat and the bacon simmer for about 2 hours, until the soup has thickened and is thoroughly cooked. Then add the celery leaf, chopped up. If desired any left-over meat stock can be added at this stage. Take the bacon out of the soup, allow it to cool and serve it on a slice of coarse wholemeal bread together with the soup.

Ingredients:
3 pounds large carrots, 3 pounds potatoes, 1 pound large onions, 1½ pounds loin of beef (boned), 3 cups water, salt, pepper and 2 teaspoonfuls lard.

Hutspot met
klapstuk
(Leiden
hotchpotch
with loin of beef)

Wash the meat and soak it for an hour in salt water. Wash the carrots, chop them up and add them to the meat. Peel the potatoes, cut them into quarters and, after the carrots have simmered for a quarter of an hour, add the potatoes and the onions.
When the meat is done add the lard. Then simmer for an hour, until almost all the water has evaporated. If the vegetables are not completely done add a little water, taking care not to add too much. Take the meat out of the pot and keep it warm; mash the contents of the pot and add salt and pepper to taste.
Cut the meat into thick slices and add to the contents of the pot.

Drinks

The famous Heineken breweries are the world's largest exporter of beer.

Beer

In addition to light-coloured beers (Pilsener: e.g. Edel-Pils from Limburg, Hengelo Pilsener, Trappist beer) there is a sweet, dark-coloured beer known as Oud Bruin, ordered in the Netherlands as lager. Particularly popular is Grolsch, a light, clean beer of great delicacy, brewed in the state-owned Grolsche brewery.

Other favourite drinks are *jenever* (Hollands gin, made from juniper; various kinds), often drunk before a glass of beer; *beerenburger,* a schnaps from Friesland, incorporating herbs; and various liqueurs, including the well-known *advocaat,* a thick egg liqueur.

Schnaps
(*borrel*),
liqueurs

Spirits are often drunk during the so-called *borreluurtje,* the "schnaps hour", before the evening meal.

Borreluurtje

An Amsterdam speciality is the *proeflokaal* ("tasting bar"), in which the main drinks are brandy and liqueurs.

Increasingly popular are *frisdranks* ("refreshing drinks"), either sweet or bitter, and soda water.

Frisdranks

An old and traditional Dutch drink is *kandeel,* a kind of mulled wine formerly drunk, in special glasses or small porcelain cups, to celebrate the birth of a child.

Kandeel

Ingredients:
5 grams stick cinnamon, 10 grams cloves, the peel of a lemon, 2 decilitres water, 6 egg yolks, 100 grams white sugar, 1 bottle of Rhine wine.

Simmer the cloves, the cinnamon and the lemon peel in the water for an hour; then strain through a sieve and allow to cool. Whip the egg yolks with the sugar, and then add, stirring all the time, the herb liquor and the wine. Heat in a bain-marie, continuing to whip, until it thickens.

The Menu

English	Dutch
Menu	Spijskaart, menu
Wine list	Wijnkaart
Soup	Soep
Bouillon	Bouillon
Hors d'oeuvre	Voorspijzen, voorgerechten
Meat dishes	Vleesspijzen
Roast	Gebraden vlees
Roast lamb	Lamsvlees
Roast veal	Kalfsvlees
Roast pork	Varkensvlees
Stew	Gestoofd vlees
Veal cutlet, escalope	Kalfsoester
Kidneys	Nieren
Poultry	Gevogelte
Goose	Gans
Chicken	Kip
Turkey	Kalkoen
Game	Wild
Hare	Haas
Roedeer	Ree
Sausage	Worst
Ham	Ham
Fish	Vis
Fried	Gebakken
Boiled	Gekookt
Carp	Karper
Cod	Kabeljauw
Eel	Aal
Flounder	Bot
Herring	Haring
Perch	Baars
Pike	Snoek
Salmon	Zalm
Sole	Tong
Trout	Forel
Vegetables	Groente, bijlage
Beans	Boenen
Brussels sprouts	Spruitjes
Cabbage	Kool

Cauliflower	Bloemkool
Cucumber	Komkommer
Kohlrabi	Koolraap
Noodles	Macaroni
Peas	Erwten
Potatoes	Aardappelen
Red cabbage	Rodekool
Rice	Rijs
Salad	Sla, salade
Sauerkraut	Zuurkool
Spinach	Spinazie
Tomatoes	Tomaten

Dessert	Dessert
Cheese	Kaas
Custard pie	Pudding
Fruit salad	Compote
Ice cream	Ijs
Whipped cream	Slagroom

Fruit	Fruit
Apple	Appel
Banana	Banaan
Cherry	Kers
Grapes	Druifen
Lemon	Citroen
Orange	Sinaasappel
Peach	Perzik
Pear	Peer
Pineapple	Ananas
Plum	Pruim
Strawberry	Aardbei

Drinks	Dranken
Beer	Bier
Coffee	Koffie
Cream	Room
Milk	Melk
Mineral water	Mineraalwater
Tee	Thee
Water	Water
Wine	Wijn
Red wine	Rode wijn
White wine	Witte wijn

Bread	Brood
White bread	Wittebrood
Coarse wholemeal bread	Volkorenbrood
Roll	Broodje
Cake	Koek
Tart	Taart
Butter	Boter
Jam	Jam
Honey	Honing, honig

Egg	Ei
Hard boiled	Hard
Soft boiled	Week
Fried egg	Spiegelei
Scrambled eggs	Roerei
Omelette	Omelet

Salt	Zout
Pepper	Peper
Sugar	Suiker
Oil	Olie
Vinegar	Azijn

Getting to the Netherlands

By air

Amsterdam–Schiphol Airport is one of the great hubs of international air traffic, providing connections with cities all over the world. There are many flights daily (British Airways and KLM) to and from London Heathrow, and also frequent flights to and from other British airports (Belfast, Birmingham, Edinburgh, Glasgow, Manchester and Newcastle).

There are fast trains on the Schiphollijn from Schiphol to Amsterdam, The Hague and Rotterdam, and shuttle bus services to various hotels in Amsterdam (see Airports).

By sea

There are daily ferry services (passengers and cars) from Harwich to Hoek van Holland, from Hull to Rotterdam/Europoort and from Sheerness to Vlissingen (see Ferries).

Golf

There are eleven public golf courses in the Netherlands, open to anyone with a modicum of skill in the game. In addition there are a number of courses open only to members of clubs (either Dutch or foreign).

Information

Nederlandse Golf Federatie
(Dutch Golf Federation)
Soestdijkerstraatweg 172,
NL–1213 XJ Hilversum
tel. (035) 83 05 65

The National Board of Tourism publishes a brochure, "Golf and Tennis", which gives full details of both public and club golf courses in the Netherlands.

Since a golf course may sometimes be closed for a championship match, it is advisable to confirm in advance that it is available for play. In some golf clubs there are special rules applying to visitors.

Public Golf Courses

The following are the eleven public golf courses, listed in alphabetical order of provinces.

Drenthe
Roden

Golfclub Roden (9 holes), Oosteinde 7A, tel. (05908) 1 51 03

Gelderland
Wijchen

Golfclub Berendonk (9 holes), Panhuysweg 39, tel. (08894) 2 00 39

Limburg
Brunssum

Golfclub Brunssummerheide (9 holes), Rimburgerweg 50
tel. (045) 27 09 68 and 27 18 92

Noord-Brabant
Welschap

Golfclub Welschap (9 holes), Welschapse Dijk 164
tel. (040) 51 57 97

Noord-Holland
Velsen/
IJjmuiden

Openbare Golfbaan Spaarnwoude (9 and 18 holes), Recreatieschap Spaarnwoude, Hogeland 6 (near Lateral Canal C, in Velsen area)
tel. (023) 37 43 92 (administration), 38 48 72 (shop; professional), 38 37 39 (restaurant)

Golfclub Benson Lodge (9 holes), Blokhoeve 7
tel. (03402) 4 07 69

Utrecht
Nieuwegein

Golfclub Zeegersloot (9 holes), Kromme Aarweg 5
tel. (01720) 9 46 60

Zuid-Holland
Alphen
aan den Rijn

Golfclub Kleiburg (18 holes), Krabbeweg
tel. (01810) 1 42 25 (clubhouse) and 1 24 11

Brielle

Golfclub Oude Maas (two 9-hole courses), Veerweg 2A
tel. (01890) 1 80 58 and (01857) 23 66

Rhoon

Openbare Golfbaan Kralingen (9 holes), Kralingseweg 200
tel. (010) 4 52 76 46

Rotterdam

Golfclub Rozenstein (9 holes), Hoge Klei 1
tel. (01751) 1 78 46

Wassenaar

Golf Courses Open only to Members of Clubs

Golfclub De Gelpenberg (9 holes), Gebbeveenseweg 1
tel. (05917) 17 84

Drenthe
Zweeloo

Golfclub Almeerderhout (18 holes), Watersnipweg 19–21
tel. (03240) 2 18 18

Flevoland
Almere

Golfclub Zeewolde (9 holes), Golflaan 1
tel. (03242) 21 03, 20 68 (shop), 20 73 (buffet)

Zeewolde

Lauswolt Golf and Country Club (9 holes), Van Harinxmaweg 8A
tel. (05126) 25 94

Friesland
Beetsterzwaag

Edese Golf Club (9 holes), Nat. Sport Centrum Papendal,
Amsterdamseweg, tel. (08308) 19 85

Gelderland
Arnhem

Rosendaelsche Golf Club (18 holes), Apeldoornseweg 450
tel. (085) 42 14 38

Golfclub Het Rijk van Nijmegen (9 and 18 holes),
Postweg 17, tel. (08891) 7 66 44

Groesbeek

Hattemse Golf and Country Club (9 holes),
Veenwal 11, tel. (05206) 4 19 09

Hattem

Veluwse Golf Club (9 holes), Hoog Soeren 57
tel. (05769) 2 75

Hoog Soeren

Keppelse Golf Club (9 holes), Zutphenseweg 15
Hoog Keppel, tel. (08348) 14 16

Laag Keppel

Noord-Nederlandse Golf and Country Club (18 holes)
Pollselaan 5, tel. (05906) 12 75

Groningen
Glimmen

Geijsteren Golf and Country Club (18 holes), Aan de Blauwe Steen
tel. (04784) 18 09, 18 29 (shop) and 25 91 (buffet)

Limburg
Meerlo-Wanssum

Hoenshuis Golf and Country Club (18 holes)
Hoensweg 1, tel. (045) 75 33 00

Voerendaal

Crossmoor Golf and Country Club (9 holes)
Laurabosweg 8, tel. (04950) 1 84 38

Weert

Golf

Wittem	Wittem Golf and Country Club (9 holes) Dal Bissenweg 22, tel. 04455) 13 97
Noord-Brabant Eindhoven	De Tongelreep Golf and Country Club (9 holes) Velddoornwetg 2, tel. (040) 52 09 62
Leende	Golfclub Haviksoord (9 holes), Maarheezenweg Noord 11 tel. (040) 81 31 86
Molenschot	Noordbrabantsche Golf Club Toxandria (18 holes) Veenstraat 89, tel. (01611) 12 00
Sint Michielsgestel	Golfclub De Dommel (12 holes), Zegenwerp 12 tel. (04105) 23 16
Sint Oedenrode	Golf Baan De Schoot (9 holes), Schootsedijk 18 tel. (04138) 7 30 11
Valkenswaard	Eindhovensche Golf Club (18 holes), Eindhovenscheweg 300 tel. (04902) 1 27 13
Drenthe Wouw	Golf Wouwse Plantage (9 holes), Zoomvlietweg 66 tel. (01657) 5 93
Noord-Holland Alkmaar	Noord-Hollandse Golf Club (9 holes), Sluispolderweg 6 tel. (072) 15 61 77 and 165 61 75 (shop)
Duivendrecht	Amsterdamse Golfclub (9 holes), Zwartelaantje 4 tel. (020) 94 36 50 (secretary) and 94 74 09 (caddie-master)
Hilversum	Hilversumsche Golf Club (18 holes), Soestdijkerstraatweg 172 tel. (035) 85 70 60 (secretary), 85 86 88 (clubhouse) and 85 71 40 (shop)
Zandvoort	Kennemer Golf and Country Club (three 9-hole courses) Kennemerweg 78–80, tel. (02507) 1 28 36 (secretary), 1 84 56 (caddie-master) and 1 31 89 (members and buffet)
Overijssel Diepenveen	Sallandse Golf Club De Hoek (9 holes) Golfweg 2, tel. (05709) 27 05
Hengelo	Twentsche Golf Club (9 holes), Enschedesestraat 381 (entrance Morshoekweg), tel. (074) 91 27 73
Wierden	Golfclub De Koepel (9 holes), Rijssensestraat 142A tel. (05496) 7 61 50
Utrecht Bosch en Duin	Utrechtse Golf Club De Pan (18 holes) Amersfoortseweg 1, tel. (03404) 5 52 23 (secretary), 5 64 27 (caddie-master) and 5 62 25 (buffet)
Haarzuilens	Golfclub De Haar (9 holes), Parkweg 5, tel. (03407) 28 60
Maarsbergen	Golfclub Anderstein (9 holes), Woudenbergseweg 13A tel. (03433) 17 49 (clubhouse) and 13 30 (secretary)
Zeeland Axel	De Woeste Kop (9 holes), Justaas 4 tel. (01155) 44 67 (clubhouse)
Domburg	Domburgsche Golf Club (9 holes), Schelpweg 26 tel. (01188) 15 73
Zuid-Holland Noordwijk	Noordwijkse Golf Club (18 holes), Randweg 25 tel. (02523) 7 37 61 (manager), 7 37 63 (caddie-master) and 7 37 64 (buffet)

Golfclub Broekpolder (18 holes), Watersportweg 100
tel. (010) 4 74 81 40 (secretary and administration), 4 75 00 11 (caddie-master) and 4 74 81 42 (buffet)

Vlaardingen

Haagsche Golf and Country Club (18 holes)
Groot Haesebroekseweg 2, tel. (01751) 7 96 07 (secretary), 1 92 51 (caddie-master) and 7 98 07 (buffet)

Wassenaar

Help for the Disabled

Before Leaving Home

The Netherlands Bureau of Tourism can supply a free brochure, "The Handicapped", listing hotels, restaurants and places of interest with facilities for the disabled.

Information

In Britain the main sources of information on disabled travel are the Royal Association for Disability and Rehabilitation (RADAR), 25 Mortimer Street, London W1N 8AB, tel. (071) 637 5400; the Spinal Injuries Association, 76 St James's Lane, London N10 3DF, tel. (081) 444 2121; and Mobility International, 62 Union Street, London SE1, tel. (071) 403 5688.

"Holiday and Travel Abroad – A Guide for Disabled People", published by RADAR.

Useful publications

"The World Wheelchair Traveller", published by the AA for the Spinal Injuries Association.

"Low Cost Travel Tips for People Using Wheelchairs", published by Mobility International.

The AA also publishes a "Guide for the Disabled Traveller" (free to members).

Major sources of information in the United States are Louise Weiss's "Access to the World: A Travel Guide for the Handicapped" (available from Facts on File, 460 Park Avenue South, New York NY 10016) and the Society for the Advancement of Travel by the Handicapped, 26 Court Street, Penthouse Suite, Brooklyn NY 11242.

In the Netherlands

Mobility International Nederland
Postbus 165, NL–6560 AD Groesbeek
tel. (08891) 7 17 44

General information

Stichting Nederlandse Gehandicaptenraad
Postbus 169, NL–3500 AD Utrecht
tel. (030) 31 34 54

In many Dutch railway stations (as in many museums, zoos, etc.) wheelchairs are available free of charge. Many telephones, lavatories, etc., in stations are adapted for use by disabled people. Physically disabled persons, certified by a Netherlands Railways doctor as unable to travel without an attendant, can obtain a pass providing free travel for the person accompanying them on Netherlands Railways and municipal and regional public transport services. Detailed information and application forms can be obtained from any railway station in the Netherlands. (Advance application is necessary to allow time for processing).

Rail travel

Blind persons can obtain the application form from the Vereniging Het Nederlandse Blinden en Slechtziendenwezen, Postbus 13165, NL–3507 LD Utrecht, tel. (030) 73 22 44.

437

Passengers who need help in changing trains should apply in advance to Nederlandse Spoorwegen, Dienst van Exploitatie Afd. 6, Postbus 2025, NL–3500 HA Utrecht, tel. (030) 33 12 53.

Hotels

The annual guide to hotels in the Netherlands, obtainable from tourist information offices, indicates which hotels have facilities for disabled people.

Water sports

The Stichting Watersport met Gehandicapten (Water Sports for the Handicapped Foundation) has a special island named Robinson Crusoe in the Loosdrecht Lakes, near Utrecht, with a wide range of facilities for practising water sports (surfing, canoeing, sailing, etc.) by physically and mentally handicapped people.
Information: Stichting Watersport met Gehandicapten
Postbus 157, NL–1600 AD Enkhuizen
tel. (02280) 1 28 28.

Guided walks for the blind

There are guided walks for the blind and partly sighted in the Blijdorp Zoo in Rotterdam. Information about times and prices: Diergaarde Blijdorp in Rotterdam, Van Aerssenlaan 49, tel. (010) 4 65 43 33, ext. 122.

Banknotes for the blind

The value of a Dutch banknote is indicated by a pattern in relief (dots or a triangle).

Holidays with Children

Thanks to the bracing climate on the Dutch North Sea coast parents are offered wide scope for healthy and varied holidays for their children (and for themselves).

Playgrounds

Most Dutch towns have playgrounds for children. Information from local VVV offices.

Baby-sitters

Baby-sitters can be obtained through VVV offices. Charges during the evening and night are double the day rates.

Hotels

Hotels in the Netherlands are officially classified (on the Benelux hotel classification system) according to their equipment and amenities. The range extends from luxury five-star hotels to modest one-star hotels. There are considerable qualitative differences within the various categories.

In the larger towns and tourist resorts the hotels are, in general, fully up to international standards; but even in medium-sized and small towns visitors can usually rely on finding good accommodation and catering. In addition to the hotels there are numerous motels and pensions (guesthouses).

Hotel categories

In this guide luxury hotels are indicated by the letter L, the other categories by the letters A to D. The following are the standards of provision in the various categories:

L: every room with its own bath or shower
A: 80% of rooms with their own bath or shower
B: 50% of rooms with their own bath or shower
C: 25% of rooms with their own bath or shower
D: at least one bath or shower for every ten rooms

For further details see the official list of hotels issued annually by the Netherlands Bureau of Tourism (for address, see Information).

Hotel rooms can be booked through the Nederlands Reserverings Centrum (NRC), Postbus 404, NL–2260 AK Leidschendam, tel. (070) 3 20 25 00, fax (070) 3 20 26 11, telex 44+ 33755+, and VVV offices in all the larger towns. During the main holiday season it is advisable to make a booking by telephone well in advance.
A booking form can be obtained from the Netherlands Bureau of Tourism. Bookings can also be made by letter by telex, fax or telephone (the NRC has English-speaking staff); payment can be made by credit card.

Reservation

Hotel rates are inclusive of value-added tax and service; any rounding-up of the amount by way of a tip is at the guest's discretion. In some popular tourist centres, particularly seaside resorts, a tourist tax is levied in addition. In some establishments tariffs are higher during the main season. There is no direct relationship between the category of a hotel and its tariffs.

Tariffs

Guests' special diet requirements can be catered for. They should preferably be made known when booking.

Diets

The following list gives the name of the hotel, the type of establishment, its address and post code, its category and the number of beds (b.). The types of establishment are identified as follows:

List of hotels

AH	apartment hotel
HCR	hotel with café and restaurant
HR	hotel with restaurant
NR	hotel without restaurant
HP	pension (guesthouse)
M	motel

Kodde (HCR), Bosselaarstraat 14, 4363 AW, C, 18 b.

Aagtekerke

't Schouwsehof (HCR), Raadhuisplein 16, 1431 EH, B, 36 b.; Aalsmeer (HCR), Dorpsstraat 15, 1431 CA, A, 108 b.

Aalsmeer

De Kroon (HCR), Dijkstraat 62, 7121 EW, C, 22 b.; Herbergh d'Olde Marckt, Markt 10, 7121 CS, C, 22 b.; Nieuw Rensink (HP), Sondernweg 11, 7122 LH, D, 10 b.

Aalten

Herberg De Hoeve (HR), Zijlsterweg 5–7, 9892 TE, D, 34 b.

Aduarderzijl

D'Aertsche Burcht (HCR), Groenestraat 1, 6913 AE, 10 b.

Aerdt

Auberge de Papenberg (HR), Hengeland 1A, 5851 EA, A, 30 b.

Afferden

Akersloot (M), Geesterweg 1A, 1921 NV, A, 320 b.

Akersloot

De Oude Schouw (HCR), Oude Schouw 6, 8491 MP, A, 33 b.; Goerres (HCR), Kanadesestraat 45, 8491 BC, D, 22 b.

Akkrum

Het Wapen van Alblasserdam (HCR), Dam 24, 2952 AB, B, 50 b.; Kinderdijk (HCR), W. Kinderdijk 361, 2951 XV, C, 28 b.

Alblasserdam

Alkmaar (M), Arcadialaan 2, 1813 KN, B, 132 b.

Alkmaar

Ida Margaretha (HP), Kanaaldijk 186, 1831 BC, 18 b.

Alkmaar/Koedijk

Postiljon Almelo (HCR), Aalderinkssingel 2, 7604 EG, B, 98 b.

Almelo

Den Brouwer (HCR), Raadhuisstraat 1, 5131 AK, D, 22 b.

Alphen (NB)

Toor (HCR), Stationsplein 2, 2405 BK, B, 60 b.

Alphen a/d Rijn

Hotels

Ameland-Ballum   Nobel (HCR), G. Kosterweg 11, 9164 KL, A, 50 b.

Ameland-Buren   De Klok (HCR), Hoofdweg 11, 9164 KL, D, 52 b.

Ameland-Hollum   D'Amelander Kaap (HCR), Oosterhiemweg 1, 9161 CZ, A, 792 b.; 't Honk (HCR), J.W. Burgerstraat 4, 9161 BH, 15 b.; De Jong (HP), Westerlaan 33A, 9161 BH, 15 b.

Ameland-Nes   Hofker (AH), J. Hofkerweg 1, 9163 GW, B, 75 b.; Ameland (HR), Strandweg 48, 9163 GN, C, 41 b.; Huize Domingo (HP), Worteltuin 3, 9163 HL, D, 17 b.; Refugio (HP), Strandweg 49, 9163 GL, D, 28 b.; 't Wapen van Ameland (HR), Reeweg 29, 9163 GT, 29 b.; Zeewinde (HR), Torenstraat 22, 9163 HE, C, 41 b.

Amerongen   Vonk (HP), Pr. Bernardlaan 14, 3958 VM, D, 10 b.

Amersfoort   Berghotel Amersfoort (HCR), Utrechtseweg 225, 3818 EG, A, 52 b.; Euroase Hotel (HCR), Stichtse Rotonde 11, 3818 GV, C, 152 b.

Amstelveen   De Veenen (HCR), Ouderkerkerlaan 19, 1185 AC, C, 30 b.

Amsterdam   Luxury hotels:
Amstel Inter-Continental (HCR), Prof. Tulpplein 1, 1018 GX, 220 b.; Apollo (HCR), Apollolaan 2, 1077 BA, 424 b.; Golden Tulip Barbizon Centre (HCR), Stadhouderskade 7, 1054 ES, 397 b.; Golden Tulip Barbizon Palace (HCR), Pr. Hendrikkade 59–72, 1012 AD, 314 b.; Crest Hotel Amsterdam (HCR), De Boelelaan 2, 1083 HJ, 522 b.; Holiday Inn Crown Plaza (HCR), Nieuwezijds Voorburgwal 5, 1012 RC, 358 b.; De l'Europe (HR), Nieuwe Doelenstraat 2–8, 1012 CP, 188 b.; Garden Hotel (HCR), Dijsselhofplantsoen 7, 1077 BJ, 194 b.; Hilton Amsterdam (HCR), Apollolaan 138–140, 1077 BG, 274 b.; Marriott (HCR), Stadhouderskade 19–21, 1054 ES, 400 b.; Okura Amsterdam (HCR), F. Bolsstraat 333, 1072 LH, 535 b.; Pulitzer (HCR), Prinsengracht 315–331, 1016 GZ, 420 b.; Sonesta Hotel Amsterdam (HCR), Kattengat 1, 1012 SZ, 700 b.

Category A:
Acca International (NR), van de Veldestraat 3, 1071 CW, 55 b.; American (HCR), Leidsekade 97, 1017 PN, 332 b.; Apollofirst (HCR), Apollolaan 123–125, 1077 AP, 72 b.; Amsterdam Ascot (HCR), Damrak 95–98, 1012 LP, 210 b.; Atlas (HR), van Eeghenstraat 64, 1071 GK, 46 b.; AMS Hotel Beethoven (HR), Beethovenstraat 43, 1077 HN, 110 b.; Pullman Hotel Capitool (HCR), N.Z. Voorburgwal 167, 1012 RE, 281 b.; Caransa Crest Hotel (HCR), Rembrandtsplein 19, 1017 CT, 132 b.; Jolly Carlton (NR), Vijzelstraat 2–18, 1017 HK, 275 b.; Cok First Class Hotel (HR), Koninginneweg 28–32, 1075 CZ, 160 b.; Damrak (HCR), Damrak 49, 1012 LL, 52 b.; Delphi (NR), Apollolaan 101–105, 1077 AN, 86 b.; Dikker en Thijs (HCR), Prinsengracht 444, 1017 KE, 53 b.; Doelen Karena (HCR), Nw. Doelenstraat 24, 1012 CP, 160 b.; Grand Hotel Krasnapolsky (HCR), Dam 9, 1012 JS, 600 b.; De Roode Leeuw (HCR), Damrak 93–94, 1012 LP, 135 b.; Jan Luyken (HR), J. Luykenstraat 54–58, 1071 CS, 130 b.; Memphis (HR), De Lairessestraat 87, 1071 NX, 150 b.; Novotel Amsterdam (HCR), Europaboulevard 10, 1083 AD, 1093 b.; Parkhotel (HCR), Stadhouderskade 25, 1071 ZD, 361 b.; Die Port van Cleve (HCR), N.Z. Voorburgwal 178, 1012 SJ, 193 b.; Rembrandt Crest Hotel (NR), Herengracht 255, 1016 BJ, 195 b.; Sander (NR), J. Obrechtstraat 69, 1071 KJ, 36 b.; Schiller Crest Hotel (HCR), Rembrandtsplein 26–36, 1017 CV, 164 b.; Pullman Hotel Schiphotel (HCR), Oude Haagseweg 20, 1066 BW, 311 b.; Victoria (HCR), Damrak 1–6, 1012 LG, 291 b.; Nicolaas Witsen (NR), N. Witsenstraat 4–8, 1017 ZH, 58 b.

Category B:
Aalborg (NR), Sarphatipark 106–108, 1073 EC, 74 b.; Aalders (NR), J. Luykenstraat 13–15, 1071 CJ, 53 b.; Ambassade (NR), Herengracht 341, 1016 AZ, 96 b.; Bastion (HCR), Rode Kruisstraat 28, 1025 KN, 90 b.; Borgman

(NR), Koningslaan 48, 1075 AE, 32 b.; Canal House (NR), Keizersgracht 148, 1015 CX, 50 b.; Casa 400 (HCR), J. Wattstraat 75, 1097 DL, 800 b.; Cok Superior Tourist Class Hotel (HR), Koninginneweg 36, 1075 CZ, 100 b.; Cok Tourist Class Hotel (HR), Koninginneweg 34, 1075 CZ, 100 b.; Concert Inn (NR), De Lairessestraat 11, 1071 NR, 32 b.; Cordial (HCR), Rokin 62–64, 1012 KW, 90 b.; Delta (HCR), Damrak 42–43, 100 b.; Eden (HR), Amstel 144, 1017 AE, 210 b.; Estherea (HCR), Singel 303–309, 1012 WJ, 153 b.; Eureka (NR), Gravenlandseveer 4, 1011 KM, 34 b.; Flipper (HR), Borssenburgstraat 1–5, 1078 VA, 32 b.; Arthur Frommer (HCR), Noorderstraat 46, 1017 BJ, 185 b.; Heemskerk (NR), J.W. Brouwersstraat 25, 1071 LH, 19 b.; Prins Hendrik (HR), Pr. Hendrikkade 53, 1012 AC, 50 b.; Hestia (NR), R. Visscherstraat 7, 1054 EV, 35 b.; AMS Hotel Holland (NR), P.C. Hooftstraat 162, 1071 CH, 140 b.; Lancaster (HR), Pl. Middenlaan 48, 1018 DH, 100 b.; De Looier (NR), 3e Looiersdwarsstraat 15, 1016 VD, 51 b.; Maas (NR), Leidsekade 91, 1017 PN, 65 b.; Marianne (NR), N. Maesstraat 107, 107 b.; Mikado (NR), Amstel 107–111, 1018 EM, 73 b.; AMS Museum Hotel (HCR), P.C. Hooftstraat 2, 1071 BX, 230 b.; Nes (HR), Kloveniersburgwal 137, 1011 KE, 60 b.; Nova (NR), N.Z. Voorburgwal 276, 1012 RS, 140 b.; Owl (NR), R. Visscherstraat 1–3, 1054 EV, 63 b.; De Paris (NR), Marnixstraat 372, 1016 XX, 47 b.; San Francisco (NR), Nieuwendijk 100, 1012 MR, 60 b.; Singelhotel (NR), Singel 13, 1012 VC, 33 b.; Slotania (HCR), Slotermeerlaan 133, 1063 JN, 176 b.; AMS Hotel Terdam (HR), Tesselschadestraat 23, 1054 ET, 120 b.; Terminus (HCR), Beursstraat 11–19, 1012 JT, 177 b.; Toren (HCR), Keizersgracht 164, 1015 CZ, 100 b.; Torohotel (NR), Koningslaan 64, 1075 AG, 20 b.; AMS Hotel Trianon (HCR), J.W. Brouwersstraat 3–7, 1071 LH, 96 b.; Euromotel Utrecht-sebrug (M), J. Muyskenweg 10, 1096 CJ, 216 b.; Roemer Visscher (HCR), R. Visscherstraat 10, 1054 EX, 98 b.; Westropa 1 (NR), 1e Con. Huygensstraat 105, 1054 BV, 35 b.; Westropa 2 (NR), Nassaukade 389–390, 1054 AE, 86 b.; Zandbergen (NR), Willemsparkweg 205, 1071 HB, 32 b.

Categories C and D:
Abba en Cristal (AH), Overtoom 122, 1054 HM, 45 b.; Acacia (NR), Linden-gracht 251, 1015 KH, 26 b.; Van Acker (NR), J.W. Brouwersstraat 14, 1071 LJ, 24 b.; Acro (HR), J. Luykenstraat 40–44, 1071 CR, 120 b.; De Admiraal (NR), Herengracht 563, 1017 CD, D, 25 b.; Adolesce (NR), Nieuwe Keizers-gracht 26, 1018 DS, D, 50 b.; Agora (NR), A Singel 462, 1017 AW, C, 27 b.; Albert (NR), Sarphatipark 58, 1073 CZ, D, 12 b.; Amstelzicht (NR), Amstel 104, 1017 AD, C, 21 b.; Amsterdam Wiechmann (NR), Prinsengracht 328–330, 1016 HX, C, 63 b.; Armada (NR), Keizersgracht 713–715, 1017 DX, C, 53 b.; Arsenal (NR), F. van Mierisstraat 97, 1071 RN, 27 b.; Asterisk (NR), Den Texstraat 14–16, 1017 ZA, D, 47 b.; Atlanta (NR), Rembrandtsplein 8–10, 1017 CV, D, 70 b.; Barbacan (NR), Pl. Muidergr. 87–91, 1018 TN, D, 40 b.; Belga (NR), Hartenstraat 8, 1016 CB, D, 22 b.; Bema (HP), Concertgebouw-plein 19B, 1071 LM, D, 18 b.; Biervliet (NR), Nassaukade 368, 1054 AB, D, 18 b.; Bodeman (NR), Rokin 154–156, 1012 LE, C, 34 b.; Seven Bridges (NR), Reguliersgracht 31, 1017 LK, D, 21 b.; Casa Cara (NR), Emmastraat 24, 1075 HV, C, 26 b.; Centralpark West (NR), R. Visscherstraat 27, 1054 EW, D, 22 b.; City Hotel Amsterdam (HCR), Pr. Hendrikkade 130, 1011 AO, C, 49 b.; Clemens (NR), Raadhuisstraat 39, 1016 DC, D, 15 b.; Crown (HC), O.Z. Voorburgwal 5, 1012 EH, D, 32 b.; Cynthia (HCR), Vondelstraat 44, 1054 GE, C, 82 b.; Destine (NR), Sarphatikade 17, 1017 WV, C, 24 b.; Engeland (NR), R. Visscherstraat 30A, 1054 EZ, C, 60 b.; L'Espérance (NR), Stadhouderskade 49B, 1072 AA, D, 15 b.; Fantasia (NR), Nw. Keizersgracht 16, 1018 DR, D, 38 b.; Fita (NR), J. Luykenstraat 37, 1071 CL, C, 39 b.; De Gerstekorrel (HCR), Damstraat 22, 1012 JM, D, 65 b.; Vincent van Gogh (HP), V. d. Veldestraat 5, 1071 CW, D, 34 b.; Groenhof (NR), Vondelstraat 74–78, 1054 GN, C, 52 b.; Van Haalen (NR), Prinsengracht 520, 1017 KJ, D, 38 b.; De Harmonie (NR), Prinsengracht 816, 1017 JL, D, 22 b.; Hegra (NR), Herengracht 269, 1016 BJ, D, 23 b.; Piet Hein (NR), Vossiusstraat 53, 1071 AK, C, 51 b.; Hoksbergen (NR), Singel 301, 1012 WH, D, 29 b.; Holbein (NR), Holbeinstraat 5, 1077 VB, D, 15 b.; P.C. Hooft (NR), P.C. Hooftstraat 63, 1071 BN, D, 34 b.; Impala (NR), Leidsekade 77, 1017 PM, D, 38 b.; Imperial (NR), Thorbeckeplein 9, 1017 CS,

C, 35 b.; Interland (NR), Vossiusstraat 46, 1071 AJ, D, 60 b.; ITC (HP), Prinsengracht 1051, 1017 JE, D, 18 b.; Jupiter (NR), 2e Helmersstraat 14, 1054 CJ, C, 39 b.; Kabul (HCR), Warmoesstraat 38–42, 1012 JE, D, 265 b.; De Gouden Ketting (NR), Keizersgracht 268, 1016 EV, C, 342 b.; King Hotel (NR), Leidsekade 85–86, 1017 PN, D, 49 b.; Kooyk (NR), Leidsekade 85–86, 1017 PN, D, 49 b.; De Korenaer (HCR), Damrak 50, 1012 LL, C, 23 b.; De Lantaerne/Brabant (NR), Leidsegracht 111, 1017 ND, D, 39 b.; Leidse Plein (NR), K. Leidsedwarsstraat 79, 1017 PW, D, 24 b.; Linda (NR), Stadhouder-skade 131, 1074 AW, D, 40 b.; Middelberg (HP), Koninginneweg 149, 1075 CM, C, 33 b.; De Moor (NR), Prinsengracht 1015–1017, 1017 KN, D, 75 b.; Museumzicht (NR), J. Luykenstraat 22, 1071 CN, D, 27 b.; Sint Nicolaas (NR), Spuistraat 1A, 1012 SP, D, 42 b.; Omega (AH), J. Obrechtstraat 31, 1071 KG, C, 45 b.; Van Onna (NR), Bloemgracht 102–108, 1015 TN, D, 37 b.; Van Ostade (NR), v. Ostadestraat 123, 1072 SV, D, 37 b.; Parklane (NR), Pl. Parklaan 16, 1018 ST, C, 22 b.; Parkzicht (NR), R. Visscherstraat 33, 1054 EW, C, 28 b.; Pax (NR), Raadhuisstraat 37, 1016 DC, D, 20 b.; Perseverance (NR), Overtoom 78-80, 1054 HL, D, 28 b.; Peters (NR), N. Maesstraat 72, 1071 RC, D, 7 b.; De la Poste (NR), Reguliersgracht 3, 1017 LJ, C, 38 b.; Prinsen (NR), Vondelstraat 36–38, 1054 GE, C, 94 b.; Prinsenhof (NR), Prinsengracht 810, 1017 JL, D, 20 b.; Rembrandt (NR), Plantage Middenlaan 17, 1018 DA, C, 25 b.; Rokin (NR), Rokin 73, 1012 KL, C, 69 b.; Savoy (NR), Michelangelostraat 39, 1077 BR, C, 50 b.; Sipermann (HC), R. Visscherstraat 35, 1054 EW, C, 20 b.; Smit (NR), P.C. Hooftstraat 24–28, 1071 BX, C, 130 b.; Sphinx (NR), Weteringschans 82, 1017 XR, D, 36 b.; De Stadhouder (NR), Stadhouder-skade 76, 1072 AE, C, 48 b.; Tabu (NR), Marnixstraat 386, 1017 PL, C, 45 b.; International Travel (NR), Beursstraat 23, 1012 JV, D, 51 b.; Verdi (NR), Wanningstraat 9, 1071 LA, C, 30 b.; Victorie (NR), Victorieplein 42, 1078 PH, D, 38 b.; Village (HCR), Kerkstraat 25, 1017 GA, C, 20 b.; Vondel (NR), Vondelstraat 28–30, 1054 GD, C, 48 b.; Vondelhof (NR), Vondelstraat 24, 1054 GE, C, 22 b.; Vullings (NR), P.C. Hooftstraat 78, 1071 CB, C, 25 b.; Vijaya (NR), Oudezijds Voorburgwal 44, 1012 GE, 36 b.; Washington (NR), F. v. Mierisstraat 10, 1071 RS, D, 34 b.; Weber (AH), Marnixstraat 397, 1017 PJ, D, 20 b.; Wennekes Amsterdam (NR), 2e Helmersstraat 4, 1054 CH, 30 b.; Westertoren (NR), F. v. Mierisstraat 10, 1071 RS, D, 15 b.; De Wilde (NR), Koninginneweg 93, 1075 CJ, D, 40 b.; Wilhelmina (NR), Koninginneweg 167–169, 1075 CN, C, 40 b.; Wijnobel, Vossiusstraat 9, 1071 AB, D, 28 b.; De Zwaan (NR), Dorpsweg 70, 1028 BR, D, 16 b.

Anjum

Lauwersmeer (HCR), Singel 5, 9133 BN, D, 12 b.

Apeldoorn

De Keizerskroon (HCR), Koningsstraat 7, 7315 HR, L, 109 b.; Bloemink (HCR), Loolaan 56, 7315 AG, A, 150 b.; Astra (HP), B. Backerlaan 12–14, 7316 DZ, B, 53 b.; Berg en Bosch (HP), Aquamarijnstraat 58, 7314 HZ, B, 31 b.; Nieland (HCR), Soerenseweg 73, 7313 EH, A, 80 b.; De Parken (HP), Regentesselaan 42, 7316 AG, A, 30 b.; Abbekerk (HP), Canadalaan 26, 7316 BX, C, 28 b.; Apeldoorn, J.C. Wilslaan 200, 7313 CK, C, 75 b.; Suisse (HCR), Stationsplein 15, 7311 NX, C, 16 b.

Appingedam

Landgoed Ekenstein (HCR), Alberdaweg 70, 9901 TA, A, 54 b.; Het Wapen van Leiden (HCR), Wijkstraat 44, 9901 AJ, B, 54 b.; Koppel Paarden (HCR), Woldweg 2, 9902 AG, C, 28 b.

Arcen

Maashotel (HCR), Schans 18, 5944 AG, B, 25 b.; De Oude Hoeve (HR), Raadhuisplein 6, 5944 AH, C, 26 b.; Rooland (HR), Roobeekweg 1, 5944 EZ, 70 b.

Arnhem

Haarhuis (HCR), Stationsplein 1, 6811 KG, A, 200 b.; Golden Tulip Rijnhotel (HCR), Onderlangs 10, 6812 CG, A, 92 b.; Postiljon Hotel Arnhem (HCR), Europaweg 25, 6816 SL, B, 180 b.; Groot Warnsborn (HR), Bakenbergseweg 277, 6816 VP, B, 46 b.; Parkzicht (HP), Apeldoornsestraat 16, 6828 AB, D, 38 b.; Rembrandt (NR), Paterstraat 1–3, 6828 AG, D, 25 b.

Assen

De Jonge (HCR), Brinkstraat 85, 9401 HZ, B, 75 b.; Overcingel (HCR), Stationsplein 10, 9401 LB, A, 85 b.; Christerus (HP), Stationsstraat 17, 9401 KV, D, 18 b.

Assumburg (HCR), Dorpsstraat 375, 1566 BD, D, 56 b.; Sans Souci (HP),   **Assendelft**
Vaartdijk 6, 1566 PL, D, 28 b.

Hen Wapen van Zeeland (HCR), Markt 15, 4571 BG, D, 18 b.   **Axel**

Den Engel (HCR), Singel 3, 5111 CD, B, 14 b.   **Baarle-Nassau**

Kasteel De Hooge Vuursche (HR), Hilversumsestraatweg 14, 3744 KC, A, 40   **Baarn**
b.; Royal (HCR), Hoofdstraat 21, 3741 AC, B, 18 b.

Ibis (HCR), Schipholweg 181, 1171 PK, A, 1000 b.   **Badhoevedorp**

Jan Els (HP), Dalestraat 9, 6262 NP, D, 17 b.   **Banholt**

De Lochemse Berg (HP), Lochemseweg 42, 7244 RS, B, 32 b.; Herberg De   **Barchem**
Dolle Hoed (HCR), Lochemseweg 35, 7244 RR, D, 8 b.

Heidepark (HCR), Stationsweg 185, 3771 VG, C, 14 b.   **Barneveld**

't Gemeentehuis (HCR), Grootestraat 2, 9781 HC, B, 22 b.   **Bedum**

't Heuveltje (HCR), St Jansgildestraat 27, 7037 CA, C, 27 b.; Uitzicht (HCR),   **Beek (Bergh)**
Peeskesweg 1, 7037 CH, C, 38 b.

Spijker (HCR), Rijksstraatweg 191, 6573 CP, C, 62 b.   **Beek (Nijmegen)**

Altea Hotel Limburg, Vliegveldweg 19, 6191 SB, B, 124 b.; Kempener (HR),   **Beek (Limburg)**
Pr. Mauritslaan 22, 6191 EG, C, 14 b.; De Lindenboom (HCR), Burg. Jans-
senstraat 13, 6191 JB, C, 8 b.

Landgoed De Wipselberg (AH), Wipselbergweg 30, 7361 TK, A, 180 b.; De   **Beekbergen**
Smittenberg (HCR), Arnhemseweg 537, 7361 CJ, B, 65 b.; De Zwaan (HCR),
Arnhemseweg 520, 7361 CN, B, 60 b.; Euroase Hotel Beekbergen (HCR),
Loenenseweg 1, 7361 TK, C, 180 b.; Klein Canada (HCR), Ruitermolenweg
15, 7361 CB, C, 58 b.; Het Liederholt (HCR), Spoekweg 49, 7361 TM, C, 10 b.

Gemeentehuis (HR), Hoofdstraat 271, 9686 PD, C, 32 b.   **Beerta**

Beerzerveld (HCR), Westerweg 33, 7385 PL, D, 8 b.   **Beerzerveld**

Lauswolt (HR), Harinxmaweg 10, 9244 CJ, A, 64 b.   **Beetsterzwaag**

Praekken (HR), Brinkstraat 63, 9411 KL, B, 16 b.   **Beeilen**

Krekelberg (M), Parallelweg 11, 5951 AP, A, 14 b.   **Belfeld**

Twee Karspelen (HCR), Hoofdweg 12, 9695 AS, C, 16 b.   **Bellingwolde**

Bergrust (HCR), Bemelerberg 6, 6268 NA, D, 27 b.   **Bemelen**

Erica (HCR), Molenbosweg 17, 6571 BA, A, 110 b.; Golden Tulip Val-Monte   **Berg en Dal**
(HCR), Oude Holleweg 5, 6572 AA, A, 207 b.; Hamer (HCR), Oude Kleefse
Baan 82, 6571 BJ, A, 41 b.

Kasteel Geulzicht (HR), Vogelzangweg 2, 6325 PN, B, 26 b.; Holland (HCR),   **Berg en Terblijt**
Rijksweg 65, 6325 AB, B, 38 b.; Vue de Montagnes (HP), Wolfdriesweg 7,
6325 PM, B, 87 b.; De Lange Akker (HCR), Langen Akker 33, 6325 CK, C, 26
b.; Huis aan de Rots (HCR), Geulhemmerweg 32, 6325 PK, D, 25 b.; Schoon-
zicht (HCR), Wolfdriesweg 10, 6325 PM, D, 30 b.

Bergen (HP), Bergerweg 25, 1862 JT, D, 17 b.; Boschlust (HP), Kruisweg 60,   **Bergen**
1861 LB, C, 45 b.; Breeburg (HP), Breelaan 22, 1861 LB, C, 20 b.; Duinpost

(HP), Kerkelaan 5, 1861 EA, C, 32 b.; Edelweisz (HP), Breelaan 6, 1861 GE, D, 25 b.; Eikenhof (HP), Guurtjeslaan 1, 1861 EV, C, 22 b.; Holland (NR), S. v. Surcklaan 2, 1861 MA, 9 b.; Het Witte Huis (HCR), Ruinelan 13–15, 1861 LK, C, 60 b.; Marijke (HCR), Dorpsstraat 23–25, 1861 KT, A, 104 b.; De Meidoorn (NR), Russenweg 1, 1861 JN, 17 b.; De Nachtegaal (AH), Gasweg 4, 1861 TH, D, 25 b.; Parkhotel (HCR), Breelaan 19, 1861 GC, A, 55 b.; Pargzicht (NR), Breelaan 24, 1861 GE, C, 15 b.; Rozenoord (HP), Guurtjeslaan 3, 1861 EV, C, 50 b.; Sans Souci (NR), Hoflaan 7, 1861 CP, B, 14 b.; Simmerwille (HP), Vinkenbaan 8, 1861 GJ, D, 18 b.; Sylvester (HP), Ruinelaan 31, 1861 LK, D, 20 b.; La Vie en Rose (HP), Ruinelaan 34, 1861 LL, D, 17 b.; De Viersprong (HCR), Prinsesselaan 50, 1861 EP, B, 24 b.; De Waag (HP), Beemsterlaan 2, 1861 LH, D, 27 b.; Het Wapen van Bergen (HCR), Breelaan 35, 1861 GC, C, 23 b.; Wilma (HP), Loudelsweg 33, 1861 TC, C, 23 b.; Zee Bergen (HR), Wilhelminalaan 11, 1861 LR, B, 42 b.; De Zilveren Spar (HCR), Breelaan 21, 1861 GC, B, 15 b.

Bergen aan Zee   De Horizon (HP), C. F. Zeilverboulevard 1, 1865 BB, D, 14 b.; Meijer (HCR), J. Kalffweg 4, 1865 AR, B, 55 b.; Monsmarem (HCR), Zeeweg 31, 1865 AB, C, 70 b.; Nassau Bergen (HCR), v.d. Wyckplein 4, 1865 AP, B, 84 b.; Prins Maurits (HCR), v. Hasseltweg 7, 1865 BB, B, 14 b.; Rondom Zon (HR), Julianalaan 3, 1865 BG, D, 50 b.; De Stormvogel (NR), J. Kalffweg 12, 1865 AR, D, 25 b.; Victoria (HCR), Zeeweg 33–35, 1865 AB, C, 60 b.

Bergen op Zoom   De Draak (HCR), Grote Markt 36–38, 4611 NT, A, 74 b.; De Gouden Leeuw (NR), Fortuinstraat 14, 4611 NP, B, 40 b.; La Bonne Auberge (HCR), Grote Markt 3, 4611 NR, C, 16 b.; Old Dutch (HCR), Stationsstraat 31, 4611 CB, D, 14 b.; De Lantaarn (HP), Bredasestraat 8, 4611 CG, D, 14 b.; De Schelde (HC), Antwerpsestraat 56, 4611 AK, D, 50 b.; De Blauwe Vogel (HCR), Stationsstraat 33, 4611 CB, D, 15 b.

Bergeijk   De Kempenaer (HCR), Eerselsedijk 28, 5571 CM, B, 9 b.; De Beukenhof (HR), Hof 154, 5571 CA, C, 15 b.; De Eyckelbergh (HCR), Hof 20, 5571 CC, D, 16 b.

Berkel-Enschot   De Druiventros (HCR), Boscheweg 11, 5056 PP, C, 66 b.

Best   Best (HR), De Maas 2, 5684 PL, A, 137 b.; Heidelust (HCR), Oirschotweg 108, 5684 NL, C, 20 b.; Quatre Bras ((HR), Nieuwstraat 79, 5683 KB, C, 20 b.

Bilthoven   Heidepark (HCR), J. Steenlaan 22–24, 3723 BV, A, 35 b.; Gaudeamus (HP), G. Doulaan 21, 3723 GW, C, 18 b.

Bladel   Royal (HCR), Europalaan 75–77, 5531 BE, B, 24 b.

De Blesse   Spoorzicht (HCR), Spoorlaan 45, 8397 GJ, D, 14 b.

Blokzijl   Kaatje bij de Sluis (HR), Zuiderstraat 1, 8356 DZ, A, 16 b.

Boekel   De Beurs (HCR), Kerkstraat 4, 5427 BC, D, 17 b.

Bolsward   De Wijnberg (HCR), Marktplein 5, 8701 KG, B, 68 b.

Borculo   Het Wapen van Borculo (HCR), Lochemseweg 3, 7271 WB, D, 10 b.

Borger   Bieze (HCR), Hoofdstraat 21, 9531 AA, B, 51 b.

Born   Bilderberg Hotel Born (HR), Langereweg 21, 6121 SB, A, 98 b.

Borne   Jachtlust (HCR), Weerselosestraat 306, 7626 LJ, B, 32 b.

Boskoop   Neuf (HR), Barendstraat 10, 2771 DJ, B, 28 b.

Bovenkarspel   De Halve Maan (HCR), Hoofdstraat 254, 1611 AN, C, 62 b.

Van Diepen (HCR), Spoorstraat 74, 5831 CM, B, 21 b. **Boxmeer**

Van Boxtel (HCR), Stationsplein 2, 5281 GH, B, 15 b. **Boxtel**

Eldorado (HP), Gr. Hendrikstraat 2, 7047 AE, D, 10 b. **Braamt**

Brabant (HCR), Heerbaan 4–6, 4817 NL, A, 156 b.; Mastbosch (HCR), Burg. **Breda**
Kerstenslaan 20, 4837 BM. A, 80 b.; Mercury Hotel Breda (HCR), Stations-
plein 14, 4811 BB, A, 77 b.; Novotel Breda (HR), Dr Batenburglaan 74, 4837
BR, A, 250 b.; Breda (HCR), Roskam 20, 4813 GZ, B, 157 b.; Huis den Deyl
(HR), Marellenweg 8, 4836 BH, 11 b.; Van Ham, Coothplein 23, 4811 NC, D,
28 b.; Huis van Negotie (HCR), Haagweg 68, 4814 GG, D, 9 b.; Verbaan
(HCR), Teteringenstraat 42, 4817 MP, 15 b.

De Milliano (AH), Promenade 4, 4511 RB, A, 100 b.; 't Wapen van Breskens **Breskens**
(HR), Grote Kade 33, 4511 AT, C, 40 b.

Faroeta (HCR), Herenweg 41A, 3625 AB, C, 32 b. **Breukeleveen**

De Zalm (HCR), Voorstraat 6, 3231 BJ, B, 60 b.; Atlas (HCR), Nobelstraat 20, **Brielle**
3231 BC, B, 50 b.

Herberg De Gouden Leeuw (HCR), Bovenstraat 2, 7226 LM, D, 12 b. **Bronckhorst**

Schuddebeurs (HR), Donkereweg 35, 4317 NL, A, 50 b. **Brouwershaven**

Edenpark (NR), Vijverlaan 10, 6433 BB, 20 b.; Schikan (HCR), Allee 11, 6446 **Brunssum**
RA, D, 15 b.

Triente (HP), Molenstraat 25, 9428 RA, D, 15 b. **Buinen**

Postiljon Hotel Utrecht Bunnik (HCR), Kosterisland 8, 3981 AJ, B, 183 b. **Bunnik**

Haamstede (HCR), Hogezoom 1, 4328 EE, B, 10 b.; Bom (HCR), Noordstraat **Burgh-**
2, 4328 AL, D, 27 b. **Haamstede**

Golden Tulip Jan Tabak (HCR), Amersfoortsestraatweg 27, 1401 CV, L, **Bussum**
180 b.; Gooiland-Bussum (HCR), Stationsweg 16–22, 1404 AN, C, 29 b.

Residence Aparthotel Noordzee (AH), Noordzeestraat 2, 4506 KM, A, 98 b.; **Cadzand**
Strandhotel (HCR), Boul. v.d. Wieling 49, 4506 JK, A, 85 b.; Du Commerce
(HCR), Mariastraat 22, 4506 AE, C, 20 b.; Panta Rhei (HP), Boul. v.d. Wieling
29, 4506 JJ, D, 20 b.

De Blanke Top (HCR), Boul. v.d. Wieling 1, 4506 JH, A, 44 b.; De Wielingen **Cadzand-Bad**
(HCR), Noordzeestraat 1, 4506 KM, A, 100 b.; De Schelde (HCR), Schelde-
straat 1, 4506 KL, 50 b.; Vof 't Cazant (HP), Hennequinlaan 16, 4506 JR, D,
29 b.

Callantsoog, Abbestederweg 26, 1759 NB, B, 80 b.; De Horn (HP), Duin- **Callantsoog**
rooseweg 36, 1759 HJ, D, 25 b.

Golden Tulip Barbizon Capelle (HCR), Barbizonlaan 2, 2908 MA, A, 181 b. **Capelle a/d IJssel**

Talens (HR), Sallandsestraat 51, 7741 RM, B, 35 b.; Marktzicht (HCR), Markt **Coevorden**
3, 7741 JM, D, 24 b.

Cottage Casa Blanca (HR), W. Pyrmontdreef 2, 4104 KJ, C, 15 b. **Culemborg**

Van Geenhuizen (HCR), Haersolteweg 3, 7722 SE, C, 34 b. **Dalfsen**

Carelshaven (HCR), Hengelosestraat 30, 7491 BR, A, 38 b.; Recreatie Cen- **Delden**
trum Delden (AH), Sportlaan 7, 7491 DG, A, 200 b.; Het Wapen van Delden

Hotels

(HCR), Langestraat 242, 7491 AN, B, 90 b.; In de Drost van Twente (HR), Hengelosestraat 8, 7491 BR, A, 12 b.; De Zwaan (HCR), Langestraat 2, 7491 AE, A, 23 b.; De Groene Brug (HR), Vossenbrinkweg 78, 7491 DE, C, 10 b.

Delft
De Ark (HR), Koornmarkt 59–65, 2311 EC, A, 50 b.; Museum Hotel (HCR), Oude Delft 189, 2611 HD, A, 54 b.; Dish (NR), Kanaalweg 3, 2628 EB, B, 60 b.; De Vlaming (NR), Vlamingstraat 52, 2611 KZ, B, 14 b.; Centraal (HCR), Wijnhaven 6–8, 2611 CR, C, 70 b.; Coen (NR), Kanaalweg 3, 2628 EB, C, 60 b.; Juliana (NR), M. Trompstraat 33, 2628 RC, C, 60 b.; 't Raedhuys (HCR), Markt 38–40, 2611 GV, 28 b.

Delfzijl
Du Bastion (HR), Waterstraat 78, 9934 AX, B, 72 b.; Eemshotel (HCR), Zeebadweg 2, 9933 AV, A, 40 b.

Denekamp
Dinkeloord (HCR), Denekamperstraat 48, 7588 PW, A, 110 b.; Bekhuis (HCR), Nordhornsestraat 137, 7591 NN, D, 14 b.; Kampbeek (HCR), Olden-zaalsestraat 53, 7591 GL, D, 8 b.; Knippers (HCR), Vledderstraat 11, 7591 DH, D, 20 b.

Deurne
Goossens (HCR), Stationsplein 30, 5751 JN, D, 20 b.

Deventer
Postiljon Deventer (HCR), Deventerweg 121, 7418 DA, B, 99 b.; Royal (HCR), Brink 94, 7411 BZ, D, 31 b.

Diepenheim
Roelofsen (HCR), Goorseweg 22, 7478 BD, D, 14 b.

Diever
De Walhof (HR), Hezenes 6, 7981 LC, C, 30 b.

Doetinchem
De Graafschap (HCR), Markt 10, 7001 BJ, B, 60 b.

Dokkum
De Posthoorn (HCR), Diepswal 21, 9101 LA, B, 65 b.; 't Raedhuis (HCR), Koningstraat 1, 9101 LP, C, 15 b.

Doldersum
De Bosrand (HR), Huenderweg 11, 8386 XB, C, 45 b.

Domburg
Duinheuvel (HP), Badhuisweg 2, 4357 AV, A, 47 b.; Wigwam (HR), Heren-straat 12, 4357 AL, B, 58 b.; Zomerlust (HCR), Domburgseweg 11, 4357 BA, D, 30 b.; Astoria (HCR), Weststraat 13–22, 4357 BM, C, 26 b.; Bos en Zee (HP), Nehalenniaweg 8, 4357 BM, C, 26 b.; Brouwerij (NR), Brouwerijweg 6, 4357 CE, C, 40 b.; De Burg (HR), Ooststraat 5, 4357 BE, C, 35 b.; Centrum (HCR), Zuidstraat 2, 4357 BH, C, 21 b.; Golfzicht (HR), Badstraat 4, 4357 AT, 32 b.; Kijkduin (HP), Brouwerijweg 24, 4357 CE, C, 38 b.

Donderen
Hoving (HCR), Dorpsweg 8, 9497 PN, D, 14 b.

Doorn
Rodestein (HCR), Sitiopark 10, 3941 PP, D, 17 b.

Doorwerth
Parkhotel De Branding (HCR), Kabeljauwallee 35, 6865 BL, B, 134 b.; Kie-vitsdel (HCR), Utrechtseweg 454, 6865 CP, C, 36 b.

Dordrecht
Dordrecht (HCR), Achterhakkers 12, 3311 JA, B, 40 b.; Postiljon Dordrecht (HCR), Rijksstraatweg 30, 3316 EB, B, 145 b.; Klarenbeek (HR), J. de Wit-straat 35–37, 3311 KG, B, 46 b.

Dorst
De Roskam (HCR), Rijksweg 112, 4849 BR, D, 10 b.

Drachten
Drachten (HR), Zonnedauw 1, 9202 PE, B, 90 b.; Servotel (NR), Haverstuk 75, 9203 JD, B, 20 b.

Driebergen
De Koperen Ketel (HP), Welgelegenlaan 26–28, 3971 HN, C, 26 b.

Driel
Driessen (HCR), Kerkstraat 29, 6665 CE, D, 20 b.

Het Galjoen (HCR), De Rede 50, 8251 EW, C, 24 b.   **Dronten**

Royal (HCR), Raadhuisplein 13, 5151 JH, C, 35 b.   **Drunen**

Boer Goossens (HCR), Heilig Hartplein, 5275 BM, C, 26 b.   **Den Dungen**

De Koppelpaarden (HCR), Oude Kerkstraat 1, 4271 BB, D, 12 b.   **Dussen**

De Borken (HR), Lhee 76, 7991 PJ, A, 80 b.; De Brink (HCR), Brink 30–31, 7991 CH, B, 22 b.; Wesseling (HCR), Brink 26, 7991 CH, B, 46 b.; De Drift (HCR), 7991 AA, C, 34 b.   **Dwingeloo**

De Vos (HCR), Stationsstraat 4, 6101 HK, D, 11 b.   **Echt**

De Oude Duikenburg (HP), Voorstraat 30, 4054 MX, D, 16 b.   **Echteld**

Damhotel (HCR), Keizersgracht 1, 1135 AZ, D, 25 b.; Fortuna (NR), Spuistraat 3, 1135 AV, C, 72 b.; Harmonie (HP), Voorhaven 92–94, 10 b.   **Edam**

De Paasberg (HCR), Arnhemseweg 20, 6711 HA, B, 130 b.; Mon Rêve (HR), Oude Bennekomseweg 2–4, 6717 LL, D, 18 b.   **Ede**

Motel De Witte Bergen (HCR), Rijksweg 2, 3755 MV, A, 125 b.   **Eemnes**

D'Ouverture (HCR), Loensenseweg 140, 6961 HL, D, 32 b.   **Eerbeek**

Princenhof (HCR), P. Miedemaweg 15, 9264 TJ, B, 74 b.   **Eernewoude**

Het Gildehuis (HCR), Hint 10, 5521 AH, D, 18 b.   **Eersel**

Herberg De Aanhouder Wint (HP), Dorpsstraat 2, 9537 TC, D, 20 b.   **Eesergroen**

De Rustende Jager (HCR), Hoofdstraat 20, 9463 PC, D, 20 b.   **Eext**

Bellevue (HR), Boulevard A-7, 1931 CJ, A, 110 b.; De Boei (HCR), Westeinde 2, 1931 AB, B, 82 b.; De Dennen (HP), Pans. v. Kleefstraat 11, 1931 BL, B, 48 b.; Crishotel (HR), Voorstraat 66, 1931 AM, D, 32 b.; Golfzang (HP), Boul. Ir. de Vassy 19, 1931 CN, C, 39 b.; 't Noordlob (HCR), Dr W. Beckmanlaan 8, 1931 BX, D, 16 b.; Sonnevanck (HP), Wilhelminastraat 116, 1931 BT, B, 35 b.; Sunny Home (HCR), Parallelweg 2–4, 1931 EW, B, 48 b.; 't Suyderduin (AH), Trompenbergstraat 3, 1931 AC, C, 350 b.; De Vassy (HP), Boul. Ir. de Vassy, 1931 CN, C, 48 b.; Zeezicht (HCR), Boulevard Noord 2, 1931 EV, C, 18 b.   **Egmond aan Zee**

Anrero (HP), Grotestraat 81, 7151 BB, D, 10 b.; De Greune Weide (AH), Lutterweg 1, 7152 CC, B, 40 b.   **Eibergen**

Cocagne (HCR), Vestdijk 47, 5611 EC, L, 235 b.; Motel Eindhoven (HCR), Aalsterweg 322, 5644 RL, A, 400 b.; Holiday Inn (HCR), Veldm. Montgomerylaan 1, 5612 BA, A, 347 b.; Mandarin (HCR), Geldropseweg 17, 5611 SC, A, 178 b.; AMS Hotel Pierre (HCR), Leenderweg 80, 5615 AB, A, 93 b.; De Bijenkorf (HCR), Markt 35, 5611 EC, B, 80 b.; Parkhotel (HCR), A. Thymlaan 18, 5615 EB, B, 95 b.; Corso (HC), Vestdijk 17, 5611 CA, D, 25 b.; Eikenburg (HCR), Aalsterweg 281, C, 32 b.; De Ridder (NR), Hertogstraat 15, 5611 PA, D, 20 b.   **Eindhoven**

Het Smeede (NR), Smedestraat 5, 8081 EG, C, 30 b.   **Elburg**

Heuvelzicht (HP), Zutphensestraatweg 26, 6855 AH, D, 13 b.   **Ellecom**

Speelman (HCR), Hoofdstraat 1, 9442 PA, C, 26 b.   **Elp**

Kasteel Elsloo (HR), Maasberg 1, 6181 GV, B, 46 b.   **Elsloo**

Hotels

Elspeet
De Zwaan (HCR), Uddelerweg 8, 8075 CJ, C, 30 b.

Elst (Gld)
In de Ommelanden (HC), Rijksweg N 19, 6661 KA, D, 8 b.; Het Wapen van Elst (HCR), Dorpsstraat 28, 6661 EL, C, 50 b.

Emmeloord
't Voorhuis (HCR), De Deel 20, 8302 EK, B, 52 b.

Emmen
Boerland (NR), Hoofdstraat 57, 7811 ED, B, 22 b.; Ten Cate (HR), Noordbergerstraat 44–46, 7812 AB, B, 65 b.; Hunebed (HP), Ermerweg 90, 7812 BG, D, 23 b.

Enkhuizen
De Port van Cleve (HCR), Dijk 74–76, 1601 GK, B, 40 b.; Du Passage (HCR), Paktuinen 8, 1601 GD, C, 48 b.; Het Wapen van Enkhuizen (HCR), Breedstraat 59, 1601 KB, C, 47 b.

Enschede
Memphis (HR), M.H. Tromplaan 55, 7513 AB, A, 70 b.; Dish Hotel Schermerhorn Hall (HR), Boulevard 1945 2, 7511 AE, B, 600 b.; Internationaal Congres en Studiecentrum (HCR), O. Drienerlooweg 6, 7511 AE, B, 83 b.; Atlanta (HR), Markt 12, 7511 GA, D, 36 b.; Dolphia (HCR), Gronausestraat 664, 7534 AM, D, 12 b.; Holterhof (HC), Holterhofweg 325, 7534 PT, D, 57 b.

Epe
Dennenheuvel (HR), Heerderweg 27, 8161 BK, B, 32 b.; De Witte Berken (HR), Oost Ravenweg 8, 8162 DJ, C, 22 b.; Euroase Hotel Dellenhove (HP), Dellenweg 115, 8161 PW, B, 224 b.; Heidebad (HP), Molenweg 15–17, 8162 PE, C, 38 b.

Epen
Alkema (HR), Kap. Houbenstraat 12, 6285 AB, A, 38 b.; Creusen (HP), Wilhelminastraat 50, 6285 AW, A, 40 b.; Os Heem (HR), Wilhelminastraat 19, 6285 AS, A, 45 b.; Ons Krijtland (HCR), Julianastraat 22, 6285 AJ, B, 60 b.; Golden Tulip Zuid-Limburg (HCR), Julianastraat 23A, 6285 AH, A, 144 b.; De Berghoeve (HCR), Julianastraat 20, 6285 AJ, B, 38 b.; Berg en Dal (HCR), Roodweg 18, 6285 AA, B, 64 b.; Geuldal (HP), Wilhelminastraat 21, 6285 AS, B, 17 b.; Inkelshoes (HP), Terzieter 12, 6285 NE, B, 33 b.; Peerboom (HC), Wilhelminastraat 11, 6285 AS, B, 10 b.; Edelweiss (HC), Krekelstraat 4, 6285 AR, 20 b.; Ons Epen (AH), Wilhelminastraat 1, 6285 AS, C, 42 b.; Eureka (HR), Kap. 4, 6285 AB, 30 b.; Gerardushoeve (HCR), Julianastraat 23, 6285 AH, 12 b.; De Vier Jaargetijden (HR), Wilhelminastraat 43, 6285 AT, 10 b.

Ermelo
Zonnedauw (HP), Dr Holtropstraat 37, 3851 JG, 17 b.; Zwarte Boer (HCR), Dr C.J. Sandbergweg 67, 3852 PT, D, 20 b.

Erp
Tramstation (HCR), Molentiend 12, 5469 EK, C, 11 b.

Exel
De Exelse Molen (HCR), Oude Lochemseweg 4, 7245 VJ, D, 16 b.

Exloo
Bussemaker (HCR), Zuiderhoofdstraat 1, 7875 BW, C, 16 b.; Dorpshotel Swart (HCR), Hoofdstraat 8, 7875 AC, C, 20 b.

Eygelshoven
Posthoorn (HCR), Laurastraat 39, 6471 JH, D, 13 b.

Fluitenberg–Ruinen
De Spaarbankhoeve (HCR), Hoogeveenseweg 5, 7931 TD, D, 12 b.

Franeker
De Valk (M), Htg v. Saxenlaan 78, 8802 PP, A, 77 b.

Frederiksoord
Frederiksoord (HCR), Maj. v. Swietenlaan 20, 8382 CG, 21 b.

Garderen
Het Speulderbos (HR), Speulderbosweg 54, 3886 AP, A, 200 b.; Anastasius (HR), Speulderweg 40, 3886 LB, B, 32 b.

Gasselte
't Gasselterveld (M), Bosweg 2, 9462 TA, B, 120 b.; D'Olde Hof (HCR), Dorpsstraat 35, 9462 PK, C, 40 b.

Gasselternijveen
Adolfs (HCR), Vaart 13, 9514 AA, C, 45 b.

Lucianne (HP), Julianaweg 19, 6265 AH, C, 20 b.   **St Geertruid**

De Munt (HP), Brandestraat 18, 4931 AW, C, 14 b.   **Geertruidenberg**

De Gentel (HCR), Genteldijk 34, 4191 LE, 21 b.   **Geldermalsen**

Golden Tulip Geldrop (HCR), Bogardeind 219, 5664 EG, A, 222 b.   **Geldrop**

Golden Tulip Geleen (HCR), Geleenbeeklaan 100, 6166 GR, A, 100 b.; Normandie (HC), Wolfstraat 5–7, 6162 BB, B, 40 b.; Skal (HC), Mauritslaan 113–115, 6161 HT, C, 48 b.; Stadion (NR), Mauritslaan 2, 6161 HV, D, 15 b.   **Geleen**

Handelia (HCR), P. Castrelinjstraat 1, 5423 SP, C, 22 b.   **Gemert**

Het Zwarte Water (HCR), Westerkade 48, 8280 AB, D, 15 b.   **Genemuiden**

Van Arensbergen (HC), Spoorstraat 101–105, 6591 GS, D, 12 b.; De Kroon (HCR), Markt 11, 6591 BZ, C, 50 b.   **Gennep**

Braams (HCR), Brink 9, 9461 AR, A, 100 b.; Het Zwanemeer (HCR), Oude Groningerweg 1, 9461 BP, D, 12 b.   **Gieten**

De Jonge (HCR), Beulakerweg 30, 8355 AH, D, 30 b.   **Giethoorn**

Gilze-Rijen (M), Kl. Zwitserlandweg 8, 5126 TA, A, 270 b.; Gilze (HCR), Molenakkersweg 15, 5126 NV, C, 22 b.   **Gilze**

Oostduin (AH), Oostdijkseweg 47–51, 3252 LL, D, 21 b.   **Goedereede**

Goes (HCR), A. Fokkerstraat 100, 4462 ET, A, 84 b.; Terminus (HCR), Stationsplein 1, 4461 HP, B, 60 b.   **Goes**

Gorinchem (HCR), v. Hogendorpweg 8–10, 4204 XW, B, 35 b.; Metropole (HCR), Melkpad 3–5, 4201 HN, D, 14 b.; 't Spinnewiel (HCR), Eind 18, 4201 CR, C, 18 b.   **Gorinchem**

De Vries (HCR), Hoofdstraat 35, 8401 BV, D, 22 b.   **Gorredijk**

De Roskam, Hoofdstraat 26, 7213 CW, D, 22 b.   **Gorssel**

De Utrechtse Dom (NR), Geuzenstraat 6, 2801 XV, D, 27 b.; Keizerskroon (HCR), Keizerstraat 11–13, 2801 NJ, D, 26 b.   **Gouda**

De Hampoort (HCR), St Elisabethstraat 27–29, 5361 HJ, C, 14 b.   **Grave**

Het Wapen van Amsterdam (HR), Noorderwinde 129, 1243 JL, C, 22 b.   **'s-Graveland**

Het Vlaemsche Duijn (HCR), G. de Moorsweg 4, 4503 PD, B, 32 b.   **Groede**

De Oude Molen (HCR), Molenweg 48, 6562 AA, B, 35 b.; De Wolfsberg (HCR), Mooksebaan 12, 6562 KB, B, 40 b.; De Korenbloem (HCR), Hoge Horst 97, 6562 LC, 12 b.; In de Locomotief (HC), Dorpsstraat 25–29, 6562 AA, C, 35 b.   **Groesbeek**

Altea Hotel Groningen (HCR), Expositielaan 7, 9727 KA, A, 278 b.; De Doelen (HCR), Grote Markt 26, 9711 LV, B, 182 b.; Enter Hotel Groningen (HCR), Donderslaan 156, 9728 KX, B, 115 b.; Friesland (NR), Kl. Pelsterstraat 4, 9711 KN, D, 38 b.; Tivoli (HC), Ged. Zuiderdiep 67, 9711 HC, D, 29 b.; Weeva (HCR), Ged. Zuiderdiep 8, 9711 HG, C, 140 b.   **Groningen**

Breidenbach (HCR), Past. Vullinghsplein 14, 5971 CB, D, 18 b.   **Grubbenvorst**

Gysens-Zenden (HP), Pr. Ireneweg 28, 6271 JB, D, 20 b.; Troisfontaine (HP), Kienegracht 22, 6271 BN, C, 27 b.   **Gulpen**

Hotels

Den Haag

Des Indes (HR), L. Voorhout 54–56, 2514 EG, L, 136 b.; Sofitel Den Haag (HR), Kon. Julianaplein 35, 2595 AA, L, 144 b.; Atlantic (AH), Deltaplein 200, 2554 EJ, A, 360 b.; Bel Air (HR), J. de Wittlaan 30, 2517 JR, A, 700 b.; Carlton Beach Hotel (HCR), G. Deynootweg 201, 2587 HZ, A, 538 b.; Pullmann Hotel Central (HCR), Spui 180, 2511 BW, A, 310 b.; Corona (HR), Buitenhof 39–42, 2513 AH, A, 46 b.; Europa Hotel Scheveningen (HCR), Zwolsestraat 2–4, 2587 VJ, A, 338 b.; Flora Beach Hotel (HCR), G. Deynootweg 63, 2586 BJ, A, 150 b.; Paleishotel (NR), Molenstraat 26, 2513 BL, A, 40 b.; Parkhotel Den Haag (NR), Molenstraat 53, 2513 BJ, A, 198 b.; Aquarius (HR), Zeekand 107–110, 2586 JJ, B, 48 b.; Badhotel (HCR), G. Deynootweg 15, 2586 BB, B, 184 b.; Belgisch Park (NR), Belgischeplein 38, 2587 AT, B, 28 b.; Boulevard (HP), Seinpostduin 1, 2586 EA, B, 82 b.; Carmel 't Witte Huis (HCR), Bosschestraat 2–6, 2587 HE, B, 37 b.; Cattenburch (NR), Laan C. v. Cattenburch 38, 2585 GB, B, 12 b.; City Hotel (HR), Renbaan 1–3, 2586 EW, B, 55 b.; Esquire (NR), v. Aerssenstraat 59–61, 2582 JG, B, 47 b.; Meerbeek (NR), D. Hoogenraadtstraat 214, 2586 TR, B, 21 b.; Minosa (HCR), Renbaanstraat 18–24, 2586 BG, B, 46 b.; Petit (HC), Groot Hertoginnelaan 42, 2517 EH, 30 b.; Zeehaghe (NR), Deltaplein 675, 2554 GK, B, 175 b.; Zonnester (NR), G. Deynootweg 1302, 2586 HP, B, 16 b.; Albion (HP), G. Deynootweg 120, 2586 BP, C, 35 b.; Astoria (NR), Stationsweg 139, 2515 BM, D, 18 b.; Bali (HR), Badhuisweg 1, 2587 CA, C, 68 b.; Bristol (HCR), 126–130 Stationsweg, 2515 BR, C, 60 b.; Burgia (NR), Harstenhoekweg 4, 2587 SL, D, 14 b.; Clavan (HP), Badhuiskade 8, 2586 EM, D, 17 b.; Du Commerce (HCR), Stationsplein 64, 2515 BW, C, 30 b.; Corel (HCR), Badhuisweg 54–56, 2587 CJ, C, 40 b.; New Corner (HCR), v. Merlenstraat 132, 2518 TJ, C, 23 b.; Duinhorst (HP), Alkmaarsestraat 12, 2587 RN, C, 24 b.; Duinroos (HP), Alkmaarsestraat 27, 2587 RN, D, 17 b.; Lansink (HCR), Badhuisweg 7, 2587 CA, D, 12 b.; Luna Mare (HCR), Badhuisweg 9, 2587 CA, D, 13 b.; De Minstreel (HP), Badhuiskade 5, 2586 EM, 30 b.; Mont Blanc (HP), Stevinstraat 66, 2587 EN, D, 12 b.; Ockenburgh (NR), Monsterweg 4, 2553 RL, 56 b.; Rosa (HP), Badhuisweg 41, 2587 CB, D, 13 b.; Savion (NR), Prinsestraat 86, 2513 CG, C, 17

Hotels in The Hague . . .   *. . . and in Utrecht*

b.; Sebel (HCR), Zoutmanstraat 38, 2518 GR, C, 40 b.; Seinduin, Seinpostduin 15, 2586 EA, C, 36 b.; Het Spinnewiel (NR), Laan v. Nw. Oost-Indie 279,
2593 BS, 19 b.; Sweelinck (NR), Sweelinckplein 78, 2517 GL, C, 24 b.

Morssinkhof (HCR), Molenstraat 51, 7481 GK, B, 51 b.   Haaksbergen

De Torenhoeve (AH), Torenweg 38, 4328 KB, B, 84 b.; Vliegveld Haamstede   Haamstede
(HCR), Torenweg 1, 4328 JC, C, 32 b.

De Haarlerberg (HCR), Kerkweg 18, 7448 AD, B, 35 b.   Haarle

Golden Tulip Lion d'Or (HCR), Kruisweg 34–36, 2011 LC, A, 70 b.; Waldor   Haarlem
(HCR), Jansweg 40, 2011 VA, C, 40 b.

Burgers (HCR), Eibergseweg 49, 7273 SP, D, 15 b.   Haarlo

Over de Brug (HP), Veerlaan 1, 2821 BV, D, 10 b.   Haastrecht

See Den Haag   The Hague

De Keizerskroon (HCR), Amsterdamsestraatweg 38, 1165 MA, D, 60 b.   Halfweg

De Ram (HCR), Steenberghseweg 1, 4661 RJ, D, 13 b.   Halsteren

Hardegarijp (HCR), Rijksstraatweg 36A, 9254 DJ, B, 57 b.   Hardegarijp

Baars (HCR), Smeepoortstraat 52, 3841 EJ, B, 70 b.; De Koningshof (HR),   Harderwijk
Smeepoortstraat 2, 3841 EH, B, 30 b.; Klomp (HCR), Markt 8, 3841 CE, C, 60
b.; Marktzicht (HCR), Markt 6, 3841 CE, 26 b.; Conferentieoord De Stads-
dennen (HP), Leuvenumseweg 7, 3847 LA, C, 32 b.

De Horst (HCR), Rijksstraatweg 127, 9752 BC, B, 23 b.; Postiljon Haren   Haren
(HCR), Emmalaan 33, 9752 KS, B, 180 b.

Anna Casparii (HCR), Noorderhaven 67–69, 8861 AL, B, 35 b.; Zeezicht   Harlingen
(HCR), Zuiderhaven 1, 8861 CJ, C, 48 b.

Het Wapen van Harmelen (HCR), Dorpsstraat 14, 3481 EK, B, 85 b.   Harmelen

Molecaten (HR), Molencaten, 8051 PN, B, 13 b.   Hattem

Hoffmann's Vertellingen (HCR), Dorpsstraat 16, 7971 CR, B, 21 b.   Havelte

Groenendijk (HCR), Rijndijk 96, 2394 AJ, B, 100 b.   Hazerswoude

De Watersport (HCR), De Skatting 44, 8621 BW, D, 18 b.   Heeg

Klein Zwitserland, Klein Zwitserlandlaan 5, 6866 DS, A, 120 b.   Heelsum

Château Marquette, Marquettelaan 34, 1960 AD, A, 131 b.   Heemskerk

Heitkamp (HCR), Oudste Poortstraat 2, 7041 AR, C, 19 b.; Hofke (HP), Dr J.H.   's-Heerenberg
v. Heeklaan 17, 7041 CE, D, 10 b.

Grand Hotel Heerlen (HCR), Groene Boord 23, 6411 GE, L, 220 b.; Heerlen   Heerlen
(M), Ter Worm 10, 6411 RV, A, 320 b.; Baron Hotel Heerlen (HCR), Wilhelminaplein 17, 6411 KW, B, 109 b.; Sporthotel (HCR), Spoorsingel 10,
6412 AC, B, 49 b.; Baron Hotel de la Station (HCR), Stationsstraat 16, 6411
NH, B, 64 b.; Ora Hotel Auberge de Limbourg (HCR), Ganzeweide 125, 6413
GD, D, 64 b.; Marmi (NR), Leenkampsweg 51, 6415 RP, D, 15 b.; 't Spinnewiel (HCR), Spoorsingel 10, 6412 AA, 40 b.

Du Château (HCR), Kapelstraat 48, 5591 HE, A, 28 b.   Heeze

Hotels

Heilig Land Stichting Sionshof (HCR), Nijmeegsebaan 63, 6564 CC, A, 44 b.

Helden Antiek (HR), Mariaplein 1, 5988 CH, D, 12 b.

Den Helder Den Helder (M), Marsdiep 2, 1784 AP, B, 144 b.; Het Wapen van Den Helder (HCR), Spoorgracht 43–44, 1781 CD, D, 35 b.; Wienerhof (HR), Parallelweg 7, 1781 EA, C, 10 b.

Hellendoorn De Uitkijk (HCR), Hellendoornsebergweg 7, 7447 PA, C, 42 b.

Helmond Het Beugeltje (HP), Beugelsplein 10, 5701 PK, D, 15 b.; Wilhelmina (HC), Bakelsedijk 6, 5701 MC, D, 11 b.

Hengelo 't Tuindorp (HCR), Tuindorpsstraat 132, 7555 CS, D, 25 b.

Hengevelde Pierik (HCR), Goorstraat 25, 7496 AB, C, 22 b.

's-Hertogenbosch Golden Tulip Central (HCR), Burg. Loeffplein 98, 5211 RX, A, 240 b.; Eurohotel (NR), Hinthamerstraat 63–65, 5211 MG, B, 72 b.

Heusden In de Verdwaalde Koogel (HCR), Vismarkt 1, 5256 BC, B, 25 b.

Hierden Bosch en Lommer (HP), Molenweg 34, 3849 RN, D, 100 b.

Hilvarenbeek De Oude Kuyp (HCR), Gelderstraat 1, 5081 AA, C, 19 b.

Hilversum Het Hof van Holland (HCR), Kerkbrink 1–7, 1211 BW, A, 100 b.; Lapershoek (HCR), Utrechtsestraatweg 16, 1213 TS, A, 78 b.; Hilfertsom (HR), Koninginneweg 28–30, 1217 LA, B, 65 b.; De Waag (HC), Groest 17, 1211 CX, C, 24 b.

Hindeloopen De Hoefslag (HC), Nieuwe Weide 16, 8713 JE, D, 18 b.

Hipplytushoef De Harmonie (HCR), Kerkplein 1, 1771 CD, B, 11 b.

Hoedekenskerke Westerschelde (HCR), Havenstraat 22, 4433 AM, D, 10 b.

Hoek De Instuif (HCR), Langestraat 43, 4542 AH, D, 7 b.

Hoek van Holland America (HCR), Rietdijkstraat 94–96, 3151 GK, D, 52 b.; Ingemar (NR), Pr. Hendrikstraat 193, 3151 AH, C, 18 b.

Hoenderloo De Boer'nkinkel (HCR), Middenweg 7, 7351 BA, D, 16 b.; Buitenlust (HCR), Apeldoornseweg 30, 7351 AB, C, 32 b.; Residence Victoria (AH), Woeste Hoefweg 80, 7351 TP, C, 164 b.

Hoensbroek Amicitia (HC), Markt 9–10, 6431 LG, 19 b.

Hoevelaken De Klepperman (HCR), Oosterdorpsstraat 11, 3871 AA, L, 73 b.

Hollandscheveld Fieten (HP), Carstendijk 64, 7916 TS, D, 20 b.

Holten 't Losse Hoes (HR), Holterbergweg 14, 7451 JL, C, 60 b.

Hoofddorp Golden Tulip Barbizon Schiphol (HCR), Kruisweg 495, 2132 NA, A, 344 b.

Hoog Soeren Oranjeoord (HCR), Hoog Soeren 134, 7346 AH, 47 b.

Hoogerheide Het Pannenhuis (HCR), Antwerpsestraatweg 100, 4631 RB, B, 40 b.

Hoogeveen Motel Hoogeveen (HCR), Mathijsenstraat 1, 9707 AP, B, 80 b.; De Beurs (HCR), Grote Kerkstraat 26–28, 7902 CJ, D, 22 b.; Toldiek (HCR), Toldijk 23, 7901 TA, D, 17 b.

Faber (HCR), Meint Veningastraat 123, 9601 KE, B, 32 b.	**Hoogezand**
Rijnland Hoogmade (HCR), Kerkstraat 37, 2355 AE, B, 100 b.	**Hoogmade**
Petit Nord (HCR), Klein Noord 53–55, 1621 JE, B, 71 b.; Koegelwieck (HP), Dorpsstraat 35, 8896 JA, B, 12 b.; De Magneet, Klein Oost 5–7, 1621 GR, D, 30 b.	**Hoorn**
Beatrix (HCR), Badhuisstraat 2–10, 1783 AK, A, 80 b.	**Huisduinen**
De Betuwe (HCR), Markt 1, 6851 AG, D, 9 b.	**Huissen**
De Beyaerd (HR), Harderwijkerweg 497, 8077 RJ, B, 136 b.	**Hulshorst**
Korenbeurs (HCR), Grote Markt 10, 4561 EB, B, 11 b.	**Hulst**
De Gouden Karper (HCR), Dorpsstraat 9, 6999 AA, C, 26 b.	**Hummelo**
Augusta (HCR), Oranjestraat 98, 1975 DD, C, 24 b.; Kennemerhof (HCR), Kennemerlaan 116–118, 1972 ES, D, 28 b.	**IJmuiden**
Epping (HR), Utrechtsestraat 44, 3401 CW, C, 48 b.	**IJsselstein**
Joure (HCR), Klokmakkerij 1, 8501 ZS, C, 34 b.	**Joure**
De Kroon (HCR), Gasthuisstraat 140, 5171 GJ, C, 40 b.	**Kaatsheuvel**
De Rietlanden (HCR), Kalenbergerpad 7, 8377 HL, D, 24 b.	**Kalenberg**
D'Olde Brugge (NR), IJsselkade 48, 8216 AE, C, 32 b.; Van Dijk (NR), IJsselkade 30–31, 8261 AC, B, 38 b.	**Kampen**
Holland Hotel Kamperduin (HCR), Patrijzenlaan 1, 4493 RA, B, 48 b.	**Kamperland**
De Zwaan (HCR), Kerkeplein 47, 4421 AB, C, 19 b.	**Kapelle**
Van Beelen (NR), Kon. Wilhelminastraat 10–12, 2225 BA, B, 25 b.; Katanze (HP), Tooropstraat 2, 2225 XT, B, 20 b.; Parlevliet (HP), Boulevard 50, 2225 AD, B, 50 b.; Zee en Duin (HCR), Boulevard 5, 2225 AA, B, 30 b.; Het Anker (HP), Boulevard 129, 2225 HC, D, 16 b.; Boot (HP), Wilhelminastraat 4, 2225 BA, D, 23 b.; Van de Horst (HP), Andreasplein 3, 2225 GR, D, 12 b.; Lindehof (HCR), Boulevard 67, 2225 AE, C, 29 b.; Van der Perk (G), Boulevard 60–62, 2225 AE, C, 24 b.; Riche (HCR), Boulevard 73, 2225 HA, C, 40 b.; Witteveen (HP), Kon. Emmastraat 17, 2225 AW, D, 48 b.	**Katwijk aan Zee**
Katwoude (M), Wagenweg 1, 1145 PW, A, 180 b.	**Katwoude**
Erenstein (HR), Kerkradersteenweg 4, 6488 PC, B, 59 b.; Herpers (HC), Markt 56, 6461 ED, C, 14 b.; Dutch Inn, Heerlenersteenweg 115, 6466 KS, D, 16 b.	**Kerkrade**
De Post (HCR), Klimmenderstraat 24, 6343 AC, B, 13 b.	**Klimmen**
De Linde (HCR), Hulsterweg 47, 4587 EA, B, 10 b.	**Kloosterzande**
Het Veerse Meer (HP), Weststraat 2, 4484 AA, B, 20 b.	**Kortgene**
Golden Tulip Westduin Hotel (HR), Westduin 1, 4371 AE, A, 170 b.; Dorpszicht (HCR), Dorpsplein 6, 4371 AA, D, 12 b.; Duinlust (HCR), Dishoek 18, 4371 NS, C, 16 b.; De Wijde Landen (HR), Verl. Dishoekseweg 13, 4371 NV, C, 55 b.; Randduin (HCR), Kaapduinseweg 13, 4371 NP, C, 25 b.; Zeeduin (AH), Dishoek 22, 4371 NR, C, 150 b.	**Koudekerke**
Galamadammen (HCR), Galamadammen 1–4, 8723 CE, B, 25 b.; De Jister (HP), Beukenlaan 62, 8723 AX, D, 20 b.	**Koudum**

Hotels

Kraggenburg	Saaze (HCR), Dam 16, 8317 AV, D, 20 b.
De Krim	Horstra (HCR), Hoofdweg 18–19, 7782 PL, D, 20 b.
Krimpen a/d IJssel	De Stuw (HCR), Nieuwe Tiendweg 2, 2923 AE, B, 68 b.
Laag Keppel	De Gouden Leeuw (HCR), Rijksweg 91, 6998 AG, A, 40 b.
Lage-Vuursche	De Kastanjehof (HR), Kloosterlaan 1, 3749 AJ, B, 20 b.
Langweer	De Wielen (HCR), Stevenshoek 23, 8525 EK, C, 36 b.
Lattrop	Herbergh De Holtweyde (HR), Speikweg 7, 7635 LP, B, 100 b.
Leek	Leek (HCR), Euroweg 1, 9351 EM, B, 70 b.
Leerdam	Lucullus (HCR), Vlietskant 46, 4141 CM, C, 27 b.
Leeuwarden	Oranje Hotel (HCR), Stationsweg 4, 8901 BL, A, 150 b.; Eurohotel (HCR), Europaplein 20, 8915 CL, B, 87 b.; 't Anker, Eewal 69–73, 8911 GS, D, 29 b.; De Pauw (HCR), Stationsweg 10, 8911 AH, D, 65 b.
Leiden	Holiday Inn (HCR), Haagse Schouwweg 10, 2332 KG, A, 340 b.; Bastion Hotel Leiden (HCR), Voorschoterweg 8, 2324 NE, B, 90 b.; De Doelen (HR), Rapenburg 2, 2311 EV, B, 22 b.; Hotel Bik (HP), Witte Singel 92, 2311 BR, D, 16 b.; De Ceder (NR), Rijnsburgerweg 80, 2333 AD, D, 14 b.; Nieuw Minerva (HR), Boommarkt 23, 2311 EA, C, 90 b.
Leiderdorp	Ibis (HCR), Elisabethhof 4, 2353 EZ, B, 115 b.
Leidschendam	Golden Tulip Green Park (HCR), Weigelia 22, 2262 AB, A, 188 b.
Lekkerkerk	De Witte Brug (HCR), Kerkweg 138, 2941 BP, B, 60 b.
Lelystad	Lelystad (HCR), Agoraweg 11, 8224 BZ, A, 228 b.
Lemmer	De Wildeman (HCR), Schulpen 6, 8531 HR, C, 40 b.
Lettele	De Koerkamp, Bathmenseweg 18, 7434 PV, D, 11 b.
Leusden	Den Treek (HCR), Trekerweg 23, 3832 RS, B, 32 b.
Lichtenvoorde	't Zwaantje (HCR), Zieuwentseweg 1, 7131 LA, D, 14 b.
Limmen	De Pook (HC), Rijksweg 97, 1906 BG, D, 15 b.
Lisse	De Nachtegaal van Lisse (HCR), Heereweg 10, 2161 AG, A, 266 b.; De Duif (HR), Westerdreef 17, 2161 EN, B, 65 b.; Duif (HCR), Heerenweg 200, 2161 BP, D, 32 b.
Lochem	Hof Van Geire (HR), Nieuweweg 38, 7241 EW, A, 100 b.; Alpha (HCR), Paaschberg 2, 7241 JR, B, 70 b.; Ruighenrode (HCR), Vordenseweg 6–8, 7241 SB, B, 160 b.; De Scheperskamp (HCR), Paaschberg 3, 7241 JR, B, 73 b.; Hoog Landen (HR), Barchemseweg 85, 7241 JC, C, 22 b.; Vijverhof (HCR), M. Naefflaan 11, 7241 GC, C, 36 b.
Loenen (Gl)	Bosoord (HCR), Hoofdweg 109, 7371 GE, C, 115 b.; Eikenboom (HCR), Beekbergerweg 2, 7371 ET, D, 20 b.; 't Zonnehuis (HP), Beekbergerweg 25, 7371 EV, C, 40 b.
Loenen a/d Vecht	Motel Nieuwebrug (HCR), Mijdensedijk 1, 3632 NT, A, 30 b.
Loon op Zand	Castellanie (HR), Kasteellaan 20, 5175 BD, C, 21 b.

454

Jachthaven 't Kompas (HCR), O. Loosdrechtsedijk 203, 1231 LW, A, 42 b.; **Loosdrecht**
Loosdrecht (HCR), O. Loosdrechtsedijk 253, 1231 LZ, B, 160 b.; West End
(HCR), Veendijk 21, 1231 PD, D, 12 b.

Spoorzicht (HCR), Molenweg 11, 9919 AE, C, 31 b. **Loppersum**

De Lunterse Boer (HCR), Boslaan 85–87, 6741 KD, A, 31 b.; Hoge de Vries **Lunteren**
(HP), Dorpsstraat 13, 6741 AA, B, 55 b.; De Blije Werelt (HR), Westhofflaan 2,
6741 KH, C, 256 b.; Scheleberg (HP), Immenweg 15, 6741 KP, C, 40 b.; De
Wormshoef (HCR), Dorpsstraat 192, 6741 AS, C, 72 b.

Bloemenbeek (HR), Beuningerstraat 6, 7587 LD, A, 110 b.; 't Kruisselt (HCR), **De Lutte**
Kruisseltlaan 3–5, 7587 NM, B, 73 b.; De Lutt (HCR), Beuningerstraat 20,
7587 LD, B, 40 b.; Marktzicht (HCR), Martinusplein 25, 7581 AK, D, 25 b.

De Drie Linden (HCR), Rijt 1, 5575 CD, B, 10 b. **Luyksgestel**

Maarsbergen (M), Woudenbergseweg 44, 3953 MH, C, 75 b. **Maarsbergen**

President (HCR), Floraweg 25, 3608 BW, A, 344 b.; De Nonnerie (HR), Lange **Maarssen**
Gracht 51, 3601 AK, C, 13 b.

Taverne (HCR), Dorpsweg 12, 3738 CE, D, 10 b. **Maartensdijk**

De Hoogt (HR), Raadhuisstraat 3, 3299 AP, A, 20 b. **Maasdam**

Golden Tulip Maastricht (HCR), De Ruiterij 1, 6221 EW, L, 259 b.; Golden **Maastricht**
Tulip Barbizon Maastricht (HCR), Forum 110, 6229 GV, A, 174 b.; Beaumont
(HCR), Wycker Brugstraat 2, 6221 EC, A, 130 b.; Golden Tulip Derlon (HCR),
O.L. Vrouweplein 6, 6211 HD, A, 81 b.; De l'Empereur (HCR), Stationsstraat
2, 6221 BP, A, 188 b.; Du Casque (NR), Helmstraat 14, 6211 TA, B, 81 b.; Old
Hickory (HR), Meerssenweg 372, 6224 AL, B, 17 b.; In den Hoof (HR),
Akersteenweg 218, 6227 AE, B, 38 b.; Novotel Maastricht (HCR), Sibema-
weg 10, 6227 AH, B, 205 b.; Vroemen (NR), St Maartenslaan 1, 6221 AV, B,
31 b.; De la Bourse (HCR), Markt 37, 6211 CK, C, 70 b.; Du Chêne (HCR),
Boschstraat 104–106, 6211 AS, C, 28 b.; De Posthoorn (HC), Stationsstraat
47, 6221 BN, C, 24 b.; Stijns (NR), Stationsstraat 40, 6221 BR, C, 31 b.

De Korenbeurs (HCR), Kerkstraat 13, 4921 BA, B, 100 b. **Made**

Oer de Tsjonger (HP), Oosterhuisweg 23, 8423 VK, C, 10 b. **Makkinga**

Recretel Vigilante (HCR), Workummerdijk 14, 8754 EZ, 76 b.; De Waag **Makkum**
(HCR), Kerkstraat 4, 8754 CS, D, 30 b.

Wippelsdaal (HCR), Gr. Welsden 13, 6269 LB, B, 24 b.; De Boemerang (HC), **Margraten**
Rijksweg 49, 6269 AB, C, 16 b.; Frints (HP), Gr. Welsden 27, 6269 ET, D, 46 b.

De Haverkamp (HCR), Stationsstraat 28, 7475 AM, D, 13 b. **Markelo**

Eperhof (HP), Schweibergerweg 53, 6281 NE, D, 21 b.; De Oude Hamer (HP), **Mechelen**
Bommerigerweg 28, 6281 BS, D, 44 b.; Le Paradou (HP), Bommerigerweg
10, 6281 BS, C, 20 b.; Hoeve De Plei (HCR), Overgeul 1, 6281 BG, C, 45 b.;
Vouwere (HP), Schweibergerweg 46, 6281 NH, D, 28 b.

Het Wapen van Medemblik (HCR), Oosterhaven 1, 1671 AA, B, 52 b.; De Rivi **Medemblik**
(HP), Vooreiland 14A, 1671 HN, D, 8 b.; De Zilvermeeuw (NR), Oostersingel
5, 1671 HA, C, 18 b.

Koningin Gerberga (HCR), Volderstraat 31, 6231 LA, C, 21 b.; De Proosdij **Meerssen**
(HCR), Beekstraat 52, 6231 LH, D, 10 b.; Regina (HP), Beekstraat 40, 6231 LG,
D, 25 b.

Hotels

Merkelbeek Kleuters (HCR), Haagstraat 5, 6447 CH, C, 16 b.

Meijel Ketels (HCR), Raadhuisplein 4–6, 5768 AR, C, 32 b.; Oranjehotel (HCR), Raadhuisplein 11, 5768 AR, C, 24 b.

Middelburg Arneville (HCR), Buitenruststraat 22, 4337 EH, A, 59 b.; Du Commerce (HCR), Loskade 1, 4331 HV, A, 119 b.; De Huifkar (HCR), Markt 19, 4331 LJ, C, 10 b.; Het Wapen van Middelburg (HC), Pottenmarkt 12–20, 4331 LM, D, 16 b.

Middelharnis Parel van de Delta (HR), Vingerling 51–53, 3241 EB, C, 59 b.

Mierlo De Brug (HCR), Arkweg 3, 5713 PD, A, 300 b.

Mijdrecht Mijdrecht (HCR), Provincialeweg 3–1, 3641 RS, B, 29 b.

Mill Het Centrum (HCR), Kerkstraat 4, 5451 BM, D, 10 b.

Millingen a/d Rijn Millings Centrum (HCR), Heerbaan 186, 6566 EW, B, 24 b.

Moddergat Meinsma, Meinsmawei 5, 9142 DL, D, 16 b.

Monnickendam Lake Land Hotel (HCR), Jachthaven 1, 1141 AZ, B, 256 b.

Muiderberg Nooit Gedacht (HR), Dorpsstraat 29, 1399 CT, D, 14 b.; Het Rechthuis (HCR), Googweg 1, 1399 EP, C, 33 b.

Musselkanaal Platen (HCR), Kruisstraat 1, 9581 EA, D, 10 b.

Neer De Lindeboom (HCR), Napoleonseweg 128, 6086 AJ, D, 10 b.

Nibbixwoud Entius (HCR), Dorpsstraat 57, 1688 CC, C, 48 b.

Nieuwegein Mercury (HCR), Buizerdlaan 10, 3435 SB, A, 160 b.

Nieuweschans De Kanonnier (HCR), Achterweg 9, 9693 CS, B, 20 b.; Leeuwerik (HCR), Oude Zijl 2, 9692 PA, C, 12 b.; Routiers Nieuweschans (HR), Hamdijk 5, 9693 TB, D, 14 b.

Nieuwvliet Place Saint Pierre (HCR), Zouterik 2, 4504 RX, A, 84 b.

Nijemirdum Hoogervoorst (HP), Lyklamaweg 91, 8566 JK, D, 10 b.

Nijmegen AMS Hotel Belvoir (HCR), Gr. v. Roggenstraat 101, 6522 AX, A, 94 b.; Altea Hotel Nijmegen (HCR), Stationsplein 19, 6512 AB, B, 191 b.; Atlanta (HCR), Grote Markt 39–40, 6511 KB, B, 28 b.; Wienerhof (HCR), Hertogstraat 1, 6511 RV, B, 30 b.

Nijverdal Dalzicht (HR), Grotestraat 285, 7441 GS, C, 40 b.

Noorbeek Bon Repos (HR), Bovenstraat 17, 6255 AT, B, 70 b.; De Posthoorn (HR), Schilberg 19, 6255 NR, C, 18 b.

Noordwijk-Binnen Royal (HCR), Voorstraat 76, 2201 HZ, A, 16 b.; Het Hof van Holland (HCR), Voorstraat 79, 2201 HP, B, 40 b.; De Beurs (HR), Voorstraat 123–129, 2201 HS, D, 9 b.; Pirombo (HP), Oude Zeeweg 22, 2201 TB, C, 28 b.; De Poort van Kleef (HR), Douzastraat 5, 2201 JB, D, 15 b.

Noordwijk aan Zee Grand Hotel Huis ter Duin (HCR), Kon. Astridboulevard 5, 2202 BK, L, 544 b.; De Admiraal (HR), Q. v. Uffordstraat 81, 2202 ND, A, 48 b.; Alexander (HR), Oude Zeeweg 63, 2202 CJ, A, 125 b.; De Baak (HCR), Kon. Astridboulevard 23, 2202 BJ, A, 200 b.; De Witte Raaf (HCR), Duinweg 117–119, 2204 AT, A,

A seafront hotel in Noordwijk aan Zee

72 b.; Ladbroke Hotel Noordzee, Wilhelmina Boulevard 8, 2202 GS, A, 166 b.; Oranje (HCR), Wilhelmina Boulevard 20, 2202 GV, A, 400 b.; Astoria (HP), Emmaweg 13, 2202 CP, B, 54 b.; Golden Tulip Boulevard Hotel (HR), Wilhelmina Boulevard 24, 2202 GV, B, 200 b.; Duinmotel (AH), Duindamseweg 12, 2204 AT, B, 100 b.; Fiankema (HR), Julianastraat 32, 2202 KD, B, 60 b.; De Graaf van het Hoogveen (HR), Q. v. Uffordstraat 103, 2202 NE, B, 65 b.; Marie-Rose (HR), Emmaweg 25, 2202 AR, B, 556 b.; Noordwijk (HR), Parallelboulevard 7, 2202 NJ, B, 23 b.; Strandhotel (HP), Parallelboulevard 300, 2202 HV, B, 54 b.; Zeezicht (AH), Erasmusweg 20, 2202 CC, B, 110 b.; Zonne (HCR), Rembrandtweg 17, 2202 CC, B, 110 b.; Belvedere (HP), Beethovenweg 5, 2202 AE, C, 66 b.; Huize Bernadette (HP), Q. v. Uffordstraat 92, 2202 NK, C, 15 b.; De Branding (HP), Rembrandtweg 26, 2202 AZ, D, 110 b.; Driesprong (NR), Q. v. Uffordstraat 4, 2202 NG, C, 21 b.; De Duinkabouter (HP), Golfbaan 6, 2202 TC, D, 26 b.; Duinlust (HCR), Koepelweg 1, 2202 AJ, D, 40 b.; Eikenloof (HP), Koepelweg 26, 2202 AL, 20 b.; De Golf (HR), Q. v. Uffordstraat 120, 2202 NK, C, 36 b.; Golfzicht (HP), Golfweg 15, 2202 JG, C, 53 b.; Hotel Aan Zee (HP), Parallelboulevard 206, 2202 HT, C, 140 b.; De Instuif (HP), Duinweg 14, 2202 ZN, C, 85 b.; Het Keerpunkt (HP), Q. v. Uffordstraat 94, 2202 NK, D, 14 b.; De Laiterie (AH), Oude Zeeweg 88, 2202 CE, C, 32 b.; Mariatta (HP), Rembrandtweg 7, 2202 AR, D, 35 b.; Mitchbi (HP), Q. v. Uffordstraat 82–84, 2202 NJ, C, 23 b.; Opduin (HP), Rembrandtweg 12, 2202 AX, C, 54 b.; 't Reddertje (HCR), Schoolstraat 51, 2202 HE, 10 b.; Huize Schoonoord (HP), v. Hardenbroekweg 10, 2202 EE, 25 b.; Waikiki (HP), Katenblankweg 2, 2202 CN, C, 100 b.

Noordwijkerhout

Congres Center Leeuwenhorst (GCR), Langelaan 3, 2211 XT, B, 72 b.

Norg

Karsten (HCR), Brink 6, 9331 AA, B, 34 b.; Klokbeker (HCR), Westeind 7, 9331 CA, B, 20 b.

Nuenen

Collse Hoeve (HCR), Collse Hoefdijk 24, 5673 VK, B, 41 b.; Schafrath (HCR), Park 35, 5671 GB, C, 10 b.

Hotels

Nuland Nuland (M), Rijksweg 25, 5391 LH, A, 180 b.

Nunspeet Het Roode Wold (HCR), Elspeterweg 24, 8071 PA, B, 34 b.; Dennenhoeve (HP), Elspeterweg 14–16, 8071 PA, B, 134 b.; Veld en Boszicht (HCR), Spoorlaan 42, 8071 BR, C, 76 b.; Aparthotel 't Vennendal (AH), Vennenpad 5, 8072 PX, C, 140 b.

Nuth Smeijsterhoek (HP), Dorpsstraat 13, 6361 EJ, 20 b.

Odoorn Oringer Marke (HCR), Hoofdstraat 9, 7873 BB, B, 83 b.; De Stee (HCR), Hoofdstraat 24, 7873 BC, C, 24 b.

Oegstgeest Bastion Hotel Oegstgeest (HCR), Rijnzichtweg 97, 2342 AX, B, 90 b.; Het Witte Huis (HCR), Wilhelminapark 33, 2342 AE, C, 50 b.

Den Oever De Haan (HCR), Oeverdijk 4, 1779 AA, 10 b.; Wiron (HCR), Voorstraat 20–24, 1779 AD, 34 b.; Zomerdijk (HCR), Zwinstraat 65, 1779 BE, 26 b.

Oirschot De Kroon (HCR), Rijkeluisstraat 6, 5688 ED, B, 24 b.; Korteland (HP), Spordonkseweg 11, 5688 KB, D, 10 b.

Oisterwijk De Rosep (HR), Oirschotsebaan 15A, 5062 TE, A, 86 b.; De Swaen (HR), De Lind 47, 5061 HT, A, 37 b.; Belverts Hoeve (HP), Scheibaan 13, 5062 TM, C, 47 b.; De Blauwe Kei (HCR), Rosepdreef 4, 5062 TB, C, 19 b.; De Paddestoel (HP), Scheibaan 5, 5062 TM, C, 48 b.; De Waterput (HCR), Scheibaan 9, 5062 TM, D, 52 b.; De Stille Wilde (HP), Scheibaan 11, 5062 TM, 28 b.

Oldeboorn Goerres (HCR), Doelhof 3, 8495 KD, D, 10 b.

Oldebroek Herkert (HCR), Zuiderzeestraatweg 135, 8096 BE, D, 11 b.

Oldenzaal De Kroon (HCR), Steenstraat 17, 7571 BH, B, 57 b.; Ter Stege (HCR), Marktstraat 1, 7571 ED, B, 17 b.; Muller (HCR), Markt 14, 7571 EC, 18 b.; De Zon (HCR), Bentheimerstraat 1, 7573 CW, D, 20 b.

Olterterp Het Witte Huis (HR), v. Haerinxmaweg 20, 9246 TL, B, 17 b.

Ommen De Zon, Voorbrug 1, 7731 BB, A, 47 b.; Paping (HCR), Stationsweg 29, 7731 AX, B, 72 b.; Euroase Hotel 't Reggehuus (HP), Hammerweg 40, 7731 AK, A, 37 b.; Stegeman (HCR), Voorbrug 11, 7731 BB, C, 23 b.

Oostburg Du Commerce (HCR), Markt 24, 4501 CK, D, 50 b.

Oosteinde Ekamper (HCR), Radsweg 12, 9983 RC, B, 45 b.

Oosterbeek De Bilderberg (HCR), Utrechtseweg 261, 6862 AK, A, 275 b.; Dreijeroord (HR), Gr. v. Rechterenweg 12, 6861 BR, B, 55 b.; Johanna (HP), Pieterbergseweg 34, 6862 BV, B, 33 b.; Best Western Hotel Strijland (HCR), Stationsweg 6–8, 6861 EG, B, 65 b.; Margarita (HP), Backerstraat 18, 6874 ZG, D, 10 b.

Oosterhesselen Schepers (HCR), B. de Kockstraat 33, 7861 AA, D, 12 b.

Oosterhout Golden Tulip Oosterhout (HCR), Waterlooplein 50, 4901 EN, A, 80 b.

Oostkapelle De Moerbei (HP), Dorpsstraat 52, 4356 AK, D, 30 b.; Zeelandia (HCR), Dorpsstraat 39–41, 4356 AH, C, 34 b.

Oostvoorne 't Wapen van Marion (HCR), Zeeweg 60, 3233 CV, B, 147 b.; Centraal (HCR), Stationsweg 2, 3233 CT, D, 8 b.

Ootmarsum Vos (HR), Almelosestraat 1, 7631 CC, A, 24 b.; De Wiemsel (HR), Winhofflaan 2, 7631 HX, A, 96 b.; Kuiperberg (HR), Almelosestraat 63, 7631 CD,

B, 44 b.; Van der Maas (HCR), Grotestraat 7, 7631 BT, B, 40 b.; Twents Gastenhoes (HR), Molenstraat 22, 7631 AZ, B, 53 b.; Jolanda (HC), Westwal 1, 7631 BM, C, 68 b.; Jolanda II (HR), Marktstraat 15, 7631 BX, C, 14 b.; Oald Oatmoske (HCR), Laagsestraat 56, 7637 PC, C, 16 b.; De Rozenstruik (HP), Denekamperstraat 15, 7631 AA, C, 10 b.; Het Wapen van Ootmarsum (HR), Almelosestraat 20, 7631 CG, 40 b.

City Hotel (HCR), Raadhuislaan 43, 5341 GL, A, 60 b.   **Oss**

Dekkers (HCR), Z.M. Adolphinestraat 2–6, 4641 CP, B, 102 b.; De Boulevard   **Ossendrecht**
(HCR), Wilhelminastraat 1, 4641 GP, 6 b.; The Kettle (HCR), Aanwas 21, 4641
JE, D, 16 b.; De Prins (HCR), Dorpsstraat 2, 4641 HW, 21 b.; Rosita, Molen-
dreef 21, 4641 CS, D, 25 b.

Stuitje (HCR), Hoofdstraat 23, 8376 HC, C, 10 b.   **Ossenzijl**

Jagersrust (HR), Dorpsstraat 19–21, 6731 AS, B, 41 b.; 't Witte Hoes (HR),   **Otterlo**
Dorpsstraat 35, 6731 AS, D, 26 b.; De Wever (HP), Onderlangs 35, 6731 BK,
D, 26 b.

Boschlust (HR), De Brink 3, 8567 JD, C, 28 b.   **Oudemirdum**

De Kroon (HCR), Markt 35, 4731 HM, C, 10 b.   **Oudenbosch**

't Jagershuis (HCR), Amstelzijde 2–4, 1184 VA, B, 50 b.   **Ouderkerk
a/d Amstel**

Wilhelmina (HCR), Irenestraat 8, 5825 CB, D, 13 b.   **Overloon**

De Zonnehoek (HCR), Zeeweg 98, 2051 EC, D, 14 b.   **Overveen**

Crest Hotel Papendrecht (HCR), Lange Tiendweg 2, 3353 CW, A, 160 b.   **Papendrecht**

Golden Tulip Groningen 't Familiehotel (HCR), Groningerweg 19, 9765 TA,   **Paterswolde**
L, 160 b.

Dimar (HR), Singel 33, 1755 NS, B, 25 b.   **Petten**

Au-Port (HCR), Waterpoortstraat 1, 4553 BG, B, 15 b.   **Philippine**

De Plasmolen (HCR), Rijksweg 170, 6585 AB, A, 55 b.; De Heuvel (HCR),   **Plasmolen**
Rijksweg 199, 6586 AA, D, 10 b.

't Trefpunt, Groningerstraat 163, 9493 PA, D, 32 b.   **De Punt**

Waterland (NR), Herengracht 1, 1441 EV, C, 20 b.   **Purmerend**

Beemsterpolder (HR), Purmerenderweg 232, 1461 DN, B, 40 b.   **Purmerend/
Beemster**

Kasteel De Vanenburg (HCR), Vanenburgerallee 13, 3882 RH, A, 140 b.;   **Putten**
Postiljon Nulde-Putten (HCR), Strandboulevard, 3882 RN, B, 75 b.

Sallandia (HCR), Grote Markt 19, 8102 CR, B, 52 b.; De Zwaan (HCR),   **Raalte**
Kerkstraat 2, 8102 EA, B, 40 b.

Stadsherberg·De Keurvorst (HCR), Marktstraat 14, 5371 AD, D, 12 b.; 't   **Ravenstein**
Veerhuis (HCR), Maasdijk 33, 5371 PE, D, 14 b.

Apollo (HR), Laone 2–4, 4325 EK, A, 88 b.; De Zeeuwse Stromen (HCR),   **Renesse**
Duinwekken 5, 4325 GL, A, 200 b.; Delta Inn (M), Hogenboomlaan 3, 4325
DB, B, 100 b.; Am-Re (NR), Laone 23, 4325 EG, D, 16 b.; 't Klokje (HP),
Rampweg 16–18, 4326 LK, C, 17 b.; Renesse (M), Kromme Reke 5–6, 4325
AL, D, 36 b.

Hotels

Reusel Het Centrum (HCR), Wilhelminalaan 55, 5541 CT, C, 16 b.

Rheden Erica (HP), Groenestraat 8, 6991 GE, D, 20 b.; De Roskam (HCR), Arnhemsestraatweg 62, 6991 JG, C, 33 b.

Rhenen 't Paviljoen (HCR), Grebbeweg 103–105, 3911 AV, A, 65 b.; De Eekhoorn (HR), Utrechtsestraatweg 3–5, 3911 TR, 14 b.; Rhenen, Herenstraat 75, 3911 JC, 20 b.

Ridderkerk Sport (HCR), Raadhuisplein 41–43, 2981 ER, R, 43 b.

Riethoven De Sleutel (HCR), Dorpsstraat 1A, 5561 AS, D, 12 b.

Rijen De Herbergh (HCR), Rijksweg 202, 5121 RC, C, 60 b.

Rijperkerk E10 Zwartewegsend (HR), Rijkstraatweg 17, 9254 ZG, B, 56 b.

Rijs Jans (HR), Mientwei 1, 8572 WB, B, 20 b.; Gaasterland (HCR), Manderleane 21, 8572 WG, 100 b.

Rijssen De Rijsserberg (HR), Knottenbeltlaan 77, 7461 PA, A, 114 b.; Koenderink (HCR), Schild 3, 7461 DD, C, 24 b.

Rijswijk Piet van der Valk (HB), Geestbrugweg 18, 2281 CL, D, 21 b.

Rockanje Badhotel (HCR), Twee Slag 1, 3235 CR, A, 128 b.

Roden Het Wapen van Drenthe (HCR), Heerestraat 1, 9301 AC, C, 32 b.

Roden-Steenbergen Jachtlust (HCR), Hoofdweg 22, 9307 PB, C, 52 b.

Roelofarendsveen Huis ter Veen (HP), Westeinde 81, 2371 AE, C, 19 b.

Roermond Cox (HCR), Maalbroek 102, 6042 KN, B, 45 b.; De Roodververij (NR), Hertenerweg 2, 6041 NT, B, 24 b.; De la Station (HCR), Stationsplein 9, 6041 NT, B, 54 b.; De Pauw (HCR), Roerkade 2, 6041 KZ, C, 24 b.

Roermond-Leeuwen De Herberg (HCR), Borgeind 48, 6041 AP, D, 14 b.

Rolde D'Olde Schuur (HCR), Grolloerstraat 1, 9451 KA, A, 55 b.; Asselhorst (HP), Hoofdstraat 6, 9451 BB, D, 20 b.

Roosendaal Goderie (HCR), Stationsplein 5A–B, 4702 VX, A, 26 b.; Poort van Kleef (HCR), Molenstraat 70, 4701 JV, B, 16 b.; De Klomp (HCR), Kade 48, 4703 GH, D, 11 b.; Merks (HCR), Brugstraat 55–57, 4701 LC, C, 38 b.

Roosteren Roosterhoeve (HCR), Hoekstraat 29, 6116 AW, A, 86 b.

Rosmalen Postiljon Rosmalen (HCR), Burg. Burgerslaan 50, 5245 NH, B, 140 b.

Rossum Laanzicht (HCR), Kerkstraat 9, 5328 AA, D, 11 b.

Rotterdam Hilton (HCR), Weena 10, 3012 CM, L, 344 b.; Atlanta (HR), A. v. Nesstraat 4, 3012 CA, A, 350 b.; Central (HCR), Kruiskade 12, 3012 EH, A, 120 b.; Parkhotel (HCR), Westersingel 70, 3015 LB, A, 267 b.; Rijnhotel (HCR), Schouwburgplein 1, 3012 CK, A, 200 b.; Scandiahotel (HCR), Willemsplein 1, 3016 DN, A, 77 b.; Zuiderparkhotel (HCR), Dordtsestraatweg 285, 3083 AJ, A, 191 b.; De Beer Europoort (HR), Europaweg 210, 3198 LD, B, 116 b.; Breitner (NR), Breitnerstraat 23, 3015 XA, B, 39 b.; Commerce (HCR), Henegouwerplein 56–58, 3021 PN, B, 72 b.; Emma (NR), Nieuwe Binnenweg 6, 3015 BA, B, 50 b.; Pax (HG), Schiekade 658, 3032 AK, B, 115 b.; Savoy (HR), Hoogstraat 81, 3011 PJ, B, 200 b.; Traverse (HG), 's Gravendijkwal 70–72,

3014 EG, B, 35 b.; Van Walsum (HCR), Mathenesserlaan 199–201, 3014 HC,
B, 48 b.; Wilgenhof (HCR), Heemraadsingel 92–94, 3021 DE, B, 75 b.; Baan
(NR), Rochussenstraat 345, 3023 DH, 26 b.; Bienvenue (NR), Spoorsingel
24, 3033 GL, C, 23 b.; Floris (HCR), Gr. Florisstraat 68–70, 3021 CJ, C, 60 b.;
Gare du Nord (HC), Villapark 7, 3051 BP, C, 22 b.; De Gunst (HC), Brielselaan
190–192, 3081 LL, D, 34 b.; Heemraad (NR), Heemraadsingel 90, 3021 DE, C,
20 b.; Holland (NR), Provenierssingel 7, 3033 ED, D, 53 b.; Mathenesser
(HR), Mathenesserlaan 399, 3023 GG, D, 34 b.; Orion (NR), Zwaerdecroon-
straat 40, 3021 WV, D, 28 b.; Roxin (NR), 's Gravendijkwal 14, 3014 EA, D, 45
b.; Simone (NR), Nieuwe Binnenweg 162A, 3015 BH, D, 15 b.; Waldor (NR),
Heemraadsingel 334, 3021 ND, D, 25 b.

Kuik (HCR), Brink 15, 7963 AA, B, 25 b.; De Stobbe (HCR), Westerstraat 84, **Ruinen**
7963 BE, B, 42 b.

Herberg (HP), Hengeloseweg 1, 7261 LS, B, 24 b.; Lievestro (HC), Groenlo- **Ruurlo**
seweg 42, 7261 RN, C, 19 b.

De Weyman (HC), Hoofdstraat 248, 2071 EP, B, 38 b. **Santpoort**

Motel Sassenheim (HCR), Warmonderweg 8, 2171 AH, B, 122 b. **Sassenheim**

Royal (HCR), Gentsestraat 11–14, 4551 CC, B, 57 b.; De la Bourse (HCR), **Sas van Gent**
Westkade 67, 4551 CD, C, 21 b.

De Roode Leeuw (HCR), Markt 15, 1741 BS, C, 29 b. **Schagen**

De Brug (HP), Schagerweg 31, 1751 CA, D, 12 b. **Schagerbrug**

Scherpenzeel (HCR), Holevoetplein 282, 3925 CA, B, 24 b. **Scherpenzeel**

Novotel Rotterdam/Schiedam (HCR), Hargalaan 2, 3118 JA, A, 276 b.; **Schiedam**
Rijnmond (HCR), Nieuwlandplein 12–13, 3119 AH, B, 47 b.

Schiermonnikoog (AH), Reeweg 1, 9166 PW, B, 60 b.; Strandhotel (HCR), **Schiermonnikog**
Badweg 32, 9166 ND, C, 60 b.; Van der Werff (HCR), Reeweg 2, 9166 PX, C,
80 b.; Zonneweelde (HP), Langestreek 94, 9166 LG, C, 50 b.

Op de Beek (HP), Hoogbeek 12, 6305 BH, C, 45 b.; Funcken (HP), Strucht 22, **Schin op Geul**
6305 AH, B, 43 b.; Berg Bemelmans (HP), Grachtstraat 90, 6305 AP, C, 36 b.;
Heuvelzicht (HP), Vinkenbergstraat 22, 6305 PJ, C, 40 b.; Janssen Bastings
(HCR), Strucht 21, 6305 AE, D, 35 b.; Liere (HP), Strucht 70, 6305 AJ, C, 30 b.;
Ostara (HP), Hoogbeek 28, 6305 BH, C, 37 b.; Rosita (HP), Panhuis 3, 6305
AR, C, 18 b.; Salden (HR), Kerkplein 7, 6305 BB, C, 43 b.; Uitzicht (HC), Oud
Valkenburg 18, 6305 AB, D, 32 b.; Vinkenberg (HP), Vinkenbergstraat 2,
6305 PJ, C, 20 b.; De Waterval (HP), Graafstraat 41, 6305 BD, 25 b.

Hilton International Schiphol (HCR), Herbergierstraat 1, 1118 ZK, L, 379 b. **Schiphol**

West (HCR), Weststraat 9–11, 4507 AX, C, 37 b. **Schoondijke**

De Wolfshoeve (HCR), Europaweg 132, 7761 AL, C, 32 b. **Schoonebeek**

Roos (NR), Voorhaven 21, 2071 CH, D, 19 b. **Schoonhoven**

De Hoek (HCR), Sienerweg 1, 7848 AD, C, 28 b. **Schoonoord**

Merlet (HR), Duinweg 15, 1871 AC, A, 36 b.; De Viersprong (HCR), Laanweg **Schoorl**
1, 1871 BH, B, 10 b.; Hartland (HP), Voorweg 55, 1871 CL, D, 24 b.; Schoorl
(HCR), Laanweg 24, 1871 BH, C, 48 b.; Snow Goose Inn (HP), Duinweg
123, 1871 AH, D, 20 b.; D'Oude Voetpomp (HCR), Heereweg 269, 1873 GB,
D, 19 b.

Hotels

Sellingen   Homan (HCR), Dorpsstraat 8, 9551 AE, B, 20 b.

Sevenum   Kronenbergerhof (HP), Kronenbergerweg 19, 5976 NV, D, 10 b.

Silvolde   De Phoenix, Markt 1, 7064 AZ, D, 17 b.

Simpelveld   Bellevue (HCR), Deus 1, 6369 GA, C, 17 b.; Maxime (HCR), Vroenhofstraat 1, 6369 AR, C, 12 b.; Oud Simpelveld (HC), Irmstraat 23, 6369 VL, D, 12 b.

Sinderen   Tichelhoven (HP), Nibbelinklaan 4, 7065 AE, C, 40 b.

St Annaland   De Gouden Leeuw (HCR), Voorstraat 50, 4697 EL, B, 18 b.

St Maarten   Hier is't (HP), Dorpsstraat 17, 1744 KJ, D, 17 b.

St Nicolaasga   Het Witte Huis (HCR), Gaastweg 2, 8521 JC, D, 8 b.

Sittard   Nationaal Sportcentrum (HCR), Sportcentrumlaan 5, 6136 KX, A, 96 b.; Auveleberch (HCR), Wielewaalstraat 2, 6135 EN, B, 18 b.; De Limbourg (HC), Markt 22, 6131 EK, B, 20 b.; De Prins (HCR), Rijksweg Zuid 23, 6131 AK, C, 18 b.

Slagharen   De Bonte Wever (HR), Pr. Marijkelaan 36, 7776 XG, B, 520 b.

Slenaken   La Bonne Auberge (HCR), Waterstraat 7, 6277 NH, A, 38 b.; Het Gulpdal (HP), Dorpsstraat 33–35, 6277 NC, B, 33 b.; Klein Zwitserland (HP), Grensweg 10, 6277 NA, B, 38 b.; Alberts (HP), Heyenrath 24A, 6276 NB, C, 28 b.; Antoniushoeve (HP), Heyenrath 1, 6276 NA, C, 12 b.; Berg en Dal (HCR), Dorpsstraat 18, 6277 NE, D, 38 b.; Euroase Op den Dries (HCR), Heyenrath 22, 6276 NB, 110 b.; Eldorado (HP), Grensweg 2, 6277 NA, C, 16 b.; De Kleine Flap (HCR), Heyenrath 3, 6276 NA, 20 b.; De la Frontière (HCR), Dorpsstraat 7, 6277 NC, C, 19 b.; Van Houtem (HP), Heyenrath 40, 6276 NC, C, 16 b.; Kreutzer (HC), Heyenrath 19, 6276 NA, C, 20 b.; Slenakerhof (NR), Waterstraat 8, 6277 NH, C, 40 b.

Sluis   De Dikke van Dale (HCR), St Annastraat 46, 4524 JE, A, 43 b.; 't Hof van Brussel (HCR), Kaai 6, 4524 CK, D, 12 b.; Sanders De Paauw (HCR), Kade 42, 4524 CK, C, 24 b.

Sluiskil   Dallinga (HCR), Nieuwe Kerkstraat 5, 4541 EB, D, 40 b.

Smilde   De Jonkershof (HP), 9422 TA, D, 16 b.

Sneek   Bonnema en Van Beek (HCR), Stationsstraat 62–66, 8601 GG, B, 27 b.; Hanenburg (HCR), W. Noorderhorne 2, 8601 EB, B, 25 b.; De Wijnberg (HCR), Marktstraat 23, 8601 CS, C, 42 b.

Soest   Het Witte Huis (HCR), Birkstraat 138, 3768 HN, B, 130 b.; Buitenplaats (HP), Burg. Grothestraat 53, 3761 CL, C, 29 b.

Someren   Centraal (HCR), Wilhelminaplein 3, 5711 EK, B, 20 b.; De Zeuve Meeren (HP), Wilhelminaplein 14, 5711 EK, B, 14 b.

Son en Breugel   De Gouden Leeuw (HCR), Nieuwstraat 30, 5691 AD, D, 12 b.

Spier   De Woudzoom (HCR), Oude Postweg 2, 9417 TG, B, 50 b.

Sprang-Capelle   Herberg in het Gareel (HCR), Kerkstraat 63, 5161 EB, D, 22 b.

Spijkenisse   Carlton Oasis (HCR), Curieweg 1, 3208 KJ, A, 158 b.

Stadskanaal   Dopper (HCR), Hoofdstraat 33, 9501 CM, B, 15 b.

Waanders (HCR), Rijksweg 12, 7951 DH, A, 36 b. **Staphorst**

Van Tilburg (HCR), Burg. v. Loonstraat 87, 4651 CC, C, 20 b. **Steenbergen**

De Gouden Engel (HCR), Tukseweg 1–3, 8331 KZ, B, 40 b.; 't Posthuis (HCR), **Steenwijk**
Paardenmarkt 4, 8331 JW, D, 15 b.

't Aod Kloaster (HCR), Markt 6, 6107 AT, D, 24 b. **Stevensweert**

De Drie Musketiers (HR), Wolweg 57, 3776 LN, D, 12 b. **Stroe**

Graeterhof (HR), Graeterweg 23, 6071 ND, A, 20 b. **Swalmen**

Boschhuis (HCR), Boslaan 6, 9561 LH, D, 20 b. **Ter Apel**

De Roode Leeuw (HCR), St Jorisplein 14, 7061 CN, D, 20 b. **Terborg**

't Schippershuis (HCR), Zandvliet 69, 8439 LD, B, 26 b. **Terhorne**

Churchill Terneuzen (HCR), Churchilllaan 700, 4532 JB, A, 100 b.; L'Escaut **Terneuzen**
(HR), Scheldekade 65, 4531 EJ, A, 46 b.

De Walvisvaarder (HP), Lies 23, 8895 KP, B, 45 b.; Aletha (HP), Trompstraat **Terschelling**
6, 8881 AV, D, 26 b.; Nap (HC), Torenstraat 55, 8881 BH, B, 57 b.; De Berg
(HP), Zuidmidslandsweg 6, 8891 GH, R, 14 b.; Bornholm (HC), Hoofdweg 6,
8881 HA, C, 72 b.; Dellewal (HP), Burg. v. Heusdenweg 42A, 8881 EE, C, 46
b.; De Haerdstee (HP), Midslanderhoofdweg 11, 8891 GG, D, 20 b.; De
Holland (HP), Molenstraat 5–7, 8881 BR, D, 30 b.; Lutine (HCR), Boomstraat
1, 8881 BS, D, 21 b.; Oepkes (HCR), De Ruyterstraat 3, 8881 AM, C, 40 b.;
Paal 8 (HCR), Badweg 4, 8881 HB, C, 85 b.; Stormvogel (HR), Baaiduinen 32,
8884 HJ, 27 b.; Thalassa (HCR), Heerweg 5, 8891 HS, C, 46 b.; Het Wapen
van Terschelling (HC), Oosterburen 25, 8891 GA, D, 35 b.; De Westerkeijn
(HCR), T. Smitweg 5, 8890 AA, D, 30 b.; De Horper Wielen (HP), Kaart 4, 8883
HD, C, 30 b.

De Lindeboom (HCR), Groeneplaats 14, 1791 CC, B, 37 b.; 't Koogerend **Texel/Den Burg**
(HP), Kogerstraat 94, 1791 EV, B, 29 b.; Den Burg (HP), Emmalaan 2–4, 1791
AV, C, 38 b.; Huizinga ((HCR), Binnenburg 5–7, 1791 CG, D, 16 b.

Nieuw Breda (HR), Postweg 134, 1795 JS, B, 50 b.; Molenbos (HCR), Post- **Texel/**
weg 224–226, 1795 JT, B, 32 b.; 't Anker (HP), Kikkerstraat 24, 1795 AD, D, **De Cocksdorp**
15 b.

Op Diek (HR), Diek 10, 1797 AB, C, 39 b.; Bos en Duin (HCR), Bakkenweg 16, **Texel/Den Hoorn**
1797 RJ, C, 130 b.

Opduin (HR), Ruyslaan 22, 1796 AD, A, 160 b.; Alpha (NR), Boodtlaan 54, **Texel/De Koog**
1796 BG, B, 24 b.; Beatrix (HG), Kamerstraat 5, 1796 AM, C, 36 b.; Het
Gouden Boltje (NR), Dorpsstraat 44, 1796 BC, C, 24 b.; Boschrand (HP),
Bosrandweg 225, 1796 NA, D, 20 b.; De Branding (HR), Boodtlaan 6, 1796
BE, 19 b.; Brinkzicht (HCR), Dorpsstraat 40, 1796 BL, C, 19 b.; Dijkstra (HCR),
Nikadel 3, 1796 BP, D, 30 b.; Euroase Hotel De Kooger Hoop (HP), Kamer-
straat 23, 1796 AM, D, 160 b.; 't Jachthuis (HP), Boordtlaan 38, 1796 BG, C,
35 b.; De Strandplevier (HP), Dorpsstraat 39, 1796 BA, C, 38 b.; Tatenhove
(HP), Bosrandweg 202, 1796 NH, D, 65 b.; Zeerust (HP), Boodtlaan 5, 1796
BD, D, 25 b.; De Zwaluw (HP), Kamperfoelieweg 1, 1796 MT, C, 56 b.

Prins Hendrik (HR), Stuifweg 13, 1794 HA, C, 12 b. **Texel/Oosterend**

Hof van Holland (HCR), Kaay 1, 4691 EE, D, 12 b. **Tholen**

Golden Tulip Thorn (HCR), Hoogstraat 2, 6017 AR, B, 46 b.; Crasborn (HCR), **Thorn**
Hoogstraat 6, 6017 AR, C, 28 b.

Hotels

Tiel	Tiel (M), Laan v. West Royen 10, 4003 AZ, A, 250 b.
Tilburg	Altea Hotel Heuvelpoort (HCR), Heuvelpoort 300, 5038 DT, A, 126 b.; De Postelse Hoeve (HCR), Dr Deelenlaan 10, 5042 AD, B, 47 b.; Ibis (HCR), Dr. H. v. Doorneweg 105, 5026 RA, B, 156 b.; Stationsherberg (NR), Spoorlaan 422 bov., 5038 CG, D, 36 b.
Tubbergen	Droste (HCR), Uelserweg 95, 7651 KV, A, 28 b.; Nijhuis (HCR), Grotestraat 34, 7651 CJ, B, 33 b.
Twello	Taverne (HCR), H.W. Lordensweg 3, 7391 KA, D, 16 b.
Tynaarlo	De Vriezerbrug (HCR), Vriezerweg 20, 9482 TB, D, 17 b.
Uden	Arrows (HR), St Jansstraat 14, 5401 BB, A, 64 b.
Ugchelen	Motel De Cantharel (HR), v, Golsteinlaan 20, 7339 GT, A, 200 b.
Uithoorn	Uithoorn (HCR), Thamerhorn 1, 1421 CE, A, 53 b.
Uitwellingerga	Watersportcentrum Hart van Friesland (AH), Oostweg 8, 8624 TG, C, 80 b.
Utrecht	Holiday Inn (HCR), Jaarbeursplein 24, 3521 AR, A, 500 b.; Des Pays Bas, Janskerkhof 10, 3512 BL, A, 80 b.; Scandic Crown Utrecht (HCR), Westplein 50, 3531 BL, A, 260 b.; Ibis (HCR), Bizetlaan 1, 3533 KC, B, 159 b.; Malie (NR), Maliestraat 2, 3581 SL, B, 65 b.; Mitland (HCR), Arienslaan 1, 3573 PT, B, 90 b.; Smits (NR), Vredenburg 14, 3511 BA, B, 75 b.; De Admiraal (NR), Adm. v. Gentstraat 11, 3572 XE, C, 12 b.; Domstad (NR), Parkstraat 5, 3581 PA, D, 19 b.; Ouwi (NR), F.C. Dondersstraat 12, 3521 JA, D, 44 b.; Parkhotel (HP), Tolsteegsingel 34–34B, 3582 AH, 15 b.
Vaals	Sneeuwberg (HCR), Lemierserberg 33, 6291 NM, B, 25 b.; Het Witte Huis (HP), Mamelis 5, 6295 AN, C, 26 b.; Mergelland (HR), Holset 100, 6295 ND, C, 13 b.; Piethaan (HCR), Mamelis 6, 6295 NB, C, 77 b.
Valburg	Zwartkruis (HCR), Reethsestraat 1, 6675 CE, D, 15 b.
Valkenburg	Atlanta (HCR), Neerhem 20, 6301 CH, A, 68 b.; Grand Hotel Berg en Dal (HCR), Plenkertstraat 50, 6301 GM, A, 54 b.; Prinses Juliana (HCR), Broekhem 11, 6301 HD, A, 51 b.; Riche (HR), Neerhem 26–28, 6301 CH, A, 101 b.; Parkhotel Rooding (HCR), Neerhem 68, 6301 CJ, A, 180 b.; Tummers (HCR), Stationsstraat 21, 6301 EZ, A, 45 b.; Grand Hotel Voncken (HCR), Walramplein 1, 6301 DC, A, 80 b.; Walram (HCR), Walramplein 37, 6301 DC, A, 142 b.; Apollo (HCR), Nieuweweg 7, 6301 ES, B, 78 b.; Bel Air (HCR), Onderstestraat 66, 6301 KC, B, 120 b.; Continental (HCR), Oranjelaan 8, 6301 GW, B, 42 b.; Floriade (HCR), Neerhem 107, 6301 CG, B, 30 b.; Gelders (HR), Boschstraat 4–6, 6301 HM, B, 60 b.; 't Heinekenhoek (HCR), Grotestraat 5–13, 6301 CV, B, 80 b.; Heijnen ((HCR), Broekhem 40, 6301 HJ, 26 b.; Hermens (HR), Neerhem 61, 6301 CE, B, 70 b.; Lennards (HR), Walramplein 31–33, 6301 DC, B, 120 b.; La Résidence, Nieuweweg 40–44, 6301 EV, B, 60 b.; Schaepkens van Sint Fijt (HCR), Nieuweweg 40–44, 6301 EV, B, 198 b.; Spronck (HP), Spoorlaan 39–41, 6301 GB, B, 57 b.; Stevens (HCR); Broekhem 33–35, 6301 HD, B, 70 b.; Stijnen (HP), Vroenhof 40, 6301 KG, B, 52 b.; Huize Strabeek (HCR), Broekhem 134, 6301 HL, B, 65 b.; De Toerist (HCR), Hovetstraat 3, 6301 CR, B, 70 b.; Tourotel (HCR), Wilhelminalaan 30–34, 6301 GJ, B, 105 b.; Vermeulen (HR), Strabeek 18, 6301 HS, B, 50 b.; Wilgenhof (HCR), Broekhem 71, 6301 HE, B, 110 b.; Adler (HR), Neerhem 13, 6301 CA, C, 34 b.; All Good (HR), Neerhem 10, 6301 CH, C, 17 b.; Angelique (HP), Cremerstraat 11, 6301 GD, D, 15 b.; Oad Austen (HR), Wilhelminalaan 63, 6301 GH, C, 48 b.; Bergrust (HP), Emmaberg 8, 6301 ER, C, 45 b.; Botterweck (HCR), Bogaardlaan 4, 6301 CZ, C, 44 b.; Op de Boud (HR), Parallelweg 5, 6301 XX, D, 80 b.; Oud Broekhem (HP), Koningswinkelstraat 38, 6301 WJ, D,

12 b.; 't Centrum (HCR), Grendelplein 12–14, 6301 BS, C, 63 b.; Clementine (HCR), Broekhem 63–65, 6301 HE, C, 16 b.; Dorial (HP), Daelhemerweg 16, 6301 BK, D, 42 b.; Dupuis (HCR), Lindenlaan 5, 6301 HA, C, 72 b.; De Dwingelhof (HP), Daelhemerweg 22, 6301 BK, C, 29 b.; L'Empereur (HR), Grotestraat 32, 6301 CX, C, 85 b.; Eurlings (HCR), De Guascostraat 16, 6301 CT, C, 65 b.; Huis Ter Geul (HCR), Neerhem 87–89, 6301 CG, C, 33 b.; Geuldal (AH), Sint Gerlach 19, 6301 JA, C, 20 b.; De Goudsberg (HR), Herkenbroekerweg 14, 6301 EH, C, 60 b.; De Heek (AH), Hekerweg 5, 6301 RJ, D, 60 b.; Hof van Broekhem (HC), Broekhem 87, 6301 HE, D, 32 b.; Konertz (HCR), Grotestraat 3, 6301 CV, C, 24 b.; Lahaye (HC), Sint Gerlach 5, 6301 JA, C, 40 b.; Laheije (HP), Nieuweweg 76, 6301 EW, C, 22 b.; Lahey (HCR), Grotestraat 25, 6301 CW, D, 40 b.; Lechanteur (HCR), Daelhemerweg 140, 6301 BM, D, 28 b.; Limburgia (HCR), Grendelplein 19, 6301 BS, C, 50 b.; Lobelia (HP), Neerhem 17, 6301 CD, D, 45 b.; Villa Martine (NR), Broekhem 18, 6301 HH, D, 25 b.; Mieno (HP), Daelhemerweg 48, 6301 BK, D, 32 b.; Mimosa (HP), Parallelweg 65, 6301 XZ, D, 45 b.; Neerlandia (HCR), Plenkertstraat 1–3, 6301 GK, C, 58 b.; Nottem Scheyen (NR), Neerhem 67, 6301 CE, D, 28 b.; Palanka (HCR), Walramplein 9, 6301 DC, D, 65 b.; De Postkoets (HC), Grotestraat 29, 6301 CV, C, 22 b.; De la Ruine (HR), Neerhem 2, 6301 CH, D, 19 b.; De Ruiter (HP), Sint Gerlach 43, 6301 JA, D, 22 b.; Union (HP), De Guascostraat 14, 6301 CT, D, 28 b.; De Drie Valken (HC), Koningswinkelstraat 29, 6301 WH, D, 40 b.; Oud Valkenburg (HP), Oud Valkenburg 24–26, 6305 AB, D, 29 b.; Prinses Wilhelmina (HCR), Wilhelminalaan 39–41, 6301 GG, C, 111 b.

Du Commerce (HCR), Fr. v. Beststraat 7A, 5554 EA, D, 24 b.; De Valk (HCR), **Valkenswaard** Fr. v. Beststraat 1, 5554 EA, C, 50 b.; Warande (HCR), Wolbergstraat 99, 5555 KD, C, 30 b.

De Kroon (HCR), Kerkplein 6, 7051 CX, C, 10 b. **Varsseveld**

Tante Sien (HCR), Denekamperweg 210, 7661 RM, B, 29 b.; Mosbeek (HR), **Vasse** Hooidijk 15, 7661 RA, C, 45 b.

Parkzicht (HCR), Winkler Prinsstraat 3, 9641 AD, B, 70 b. **Veendam**

Ibis (HCR), Vendelier 8, 3907 PA, C, 80 b. **Veenendaal**

Popma (HCR), Stationsweg 1, 9269 PG, D, 14 b. **Veenwouden**

De Campveerse Toren (HCR), Kade 2, 4351 AA, C, 35 b.; 't Wapen van Veere **Veere** (HCR), Markt 23–27, 4351 AG, C, 28 b.

Van den Homberg (HCR), Rijksweg 104, 5941 AH, B, 20 b.; Bascule (HC), **Velden** Markt 7, 5941 GA, D, 7 b.

Koningshof (HCR), Locht 117, 5504 RM, A, 374 b. **Veldhoven**

Velp (HCR), Pr. Kennedylaan 102, 6883 AX, A, 156 b.; Rozenhoek (HCR), **Velp** Roozendaalselaan 60, 6881 LE, C, 22 b.; Theresia (HP), Pinkenbergseweg 7, 6881 BB, D, 20 b.

American (HCR), Keulsepoort 14, 5911 BZ, A, 31 b.; De Bovenste Molen **Venlo** (HCR), Bovenste Molenweg 12, 5912 TV, A, 165 b.; Novotel Venlo (HCR), Nijmeegseweg 90, 5916 PT, A, 264 b.; Valuas (HR), Urbanusweg 9–11, 5914 CA, A, 24 b.; Wilhelmina (HCR), Kaldenkerkerweg 1, 5913 AB, A, 67 b.; Stationshotel (HCR), Keulsepoort 16, 5911 BZ, C, 45 b.

Juliana (HCR), Julianasingel 7, 5802 AS, B, 56 b.; Wieenhof (HCR), Leunse- **Venray** weg 20, 5802 CH, B, 55 b.

Vianen (HCR), Pr. Bernhardtstraat 75, 4132 XE, B, 164 b. **Vianen**

Hotels

Vierhouten   De Mallejan (HCR), Nunspeterweg 70, 8076 PD, A, 80 b.; De Vier Foreesten (HP), Gortelseweg 8, 8076 PS, C, 90 b.

Vierhouten   De Mallejan (HCR), Nunspeterweg 70, 8076 PD, A, 80 b.; De Vier Foreesten (HP), Gortelseweg 8, 8076 PS, C, 90 b.

Vinkeveen   Residence Vinkeveen (HCR), Groenlandsekade 1, 3645 BA, A, 180 b.; De Lokeend (HR), Groenlandsekade 71, 3645 BB, B, 14 b.; De Plashoeve (HCR), Baambrugse Zuwe 167, 3645 AG, B, 40 b.

Vlaardingen   Delta (HCR), Maasboulevard 15, 3133 AK, A, 154 b.

Vlieland   Geertzen (HR), Berkenlaan 18, 8899 BP, A, 42 b.; Altea Hotel Seeduyn (HCR), Badeweg, 8898 ZN, A, 244 b.; Zeezicht (HCR), Havenweg 1, 8899 BB, C, 16 b.; Badhotel Bruin (HCR), Dorpsstraat 88, 8899 AL, C, 65 b.; Golfzang (HR), Dorpsstraat 3, 8899 AA, C, 49 b.; Sporthotel Rispens (HR), Dorpsstraat 11, 8899 AA, C, 40 b.; Strandhotel Vlieland (HCR), Badweg 3, 8899 BVM C, 225 b.; De Veerman (HP), Dorpsstraat 173, 8899 AG, D, 32 b.

Prinsen (HCR), Julianastraat 21, 5251 EC, B, 56 b.

Vlissingen   Britannia-Watertoren (HCR), Boulevard Evertsen 244, 4382 AG, A, 84 b.; Piccard (HR), Badhuisstraat 178–182, 4382 AR, A, 90 b.; Strandhotel Vlissingen (HCR), Boulevard Evertsen 4, 4382 AD, A, 68 b.; Elisabeth (HCR), Singel 2–4, 4382 LA, C, 30 b.; Garuda (HR), Nieuwendijk 23–25, 4381 BW, C, 16 b.; Royal (HCR), Badhuisstraat 3–13, 4381 LM, C, 36 b.; Schouten (NR), Boulevard de Ruyter 416, 4381 KP, D, 26 b.; Huize Truida (HP), Boulevard Blankert 108, 4382 AC, D, 40 b.; De Waterman (HP), Boulevard Evertsen 34, 4382 AE, D, 22 b.

Vlodrop   Boshotel Vlodrop (HR), Stationsweg 1, 6063 NN, A, 50 b.; Etsberg (HC), Etsberg 7, 6063 NG, D, 9 b.

Volendam   Spaander (HCR), Haven 15–19, 1131 EP, C, 106 b.; Van Diepen (HCR), Haven 35, 1131 EP, C, 37 b.; Van den Hogen (HCR), Haven 106, 1131 EV, D, 13 b.

Vollenhove   Saantje (HP), Kerkstraat 1, 8325 BH, D, 12 b.

Voorschoten   De Gouden Leeuw (M), Veurseweg 180, 2252 AG, A, 64 b.; Boerhave (HR), Herenstraat 57, 2215 KE, D, 10 b.; Het Wapen van Voorschoten (HCR), Voorstraat 16, 2251 BN, D, 28 b.

Voorthuizen   De Kamphorst (AH), Apeldoornsestraat 131, 3781 PM, A, 117 b.

Vorden   Bloemendaal (HCR), Stationsweg 24, 7251 EM, B, 34 b.

Vries   Sint Nicolaas (HCR), Brinkstraat 1, 9481 BJ, D, 16 b.

Vrouwenpolder   Duinoord (HCR), Breezand 65, 4354 NL, C, 16 b.; De Palster (HP), Dorpsdijk 22, 4353 AC, C, 29 b.

Vught   St Joris (HCR), Taalstraat 217, 5261 BD, D, 18 b.

Vijlen   Vijlerhof (HCR), Hilleshagerweg 2, 6294 AP, A, 130 b.

Waddinxveen   De Unie (HCR), Kerkweg Oost 226, 2741 HA, B, 20 b.

Wageningen   Nol in 't Bosch (HR), Hartenseweg 60, 6704 PA, A, 60 b.; Congresgebouw IAC (HP), Lawickse Allee 11, 6701 AN, B, 176 b.

Wanneperveen   Meerzicht (HCR), Beulakerweg 2, 7946 LX, D, 15 b.

Wanssum   Verstraelen (HR), Geijsterseweg 7, 5861 BK, B, 35 b.

Onder de Linden (HCR), Midden 202, 8351 HM, C, 19 b.

Bijhorst (M), Zijdeweg 54, 2245 BZ, A, 200 b.; Auberge De Kievit (HR), **Wassenaar**
Stoeplaan 27, 2243 CX, A, 43 b.; Wassenaar (HCR), Katwijkseweg 33, 2242
PC, A, 120 b.; Duinoord (HCR), Wassenaarse Slag 226, 2242 PJ, B, 36 b.

Jan van der Croon (HCR), Driesveldlaan 51, 6001 KB, B, 76 b.; Juliana (HCR), **Weert**
Wilhelminasingel 76, 6001 GV, B, 22 b.

Auberge De Grote Waay (HCR), Kevenaarsedijk 1, 5855 GC, B, 18 b. **Well**

De Hamert (HCR), Hamert 2, 5856 CL, 8 b. **Wellerlooi**

Vredebest (HR), N. Achterweg 62, 4424 EG, C, 50 b. **Wemeldinge**

Maasdam (HCR), Nieuweweg 2, 4251 AG, D, 11 b. **Werkendam**

't Helje (HC), Onderdijk 175, 1693 CE, 12 b.; Het Nes (HCR), Onderdijk 189, **Wervershoof**
1693 CE, C, 43 b.

Het Roode Hert (HCR), Raalterweg 28, 8124 AE, D, 12 b. **Wesepe**

Ruyghe Venne (HR), Beilerstraat 24A, 9431 TA, B, 12 b.; Meursinge (HR), **Westerbork**
Hoofdstraat 48, 9431 AE, C, 40 b.; De Westerburcht (HCR), Hoofdstraat 7,
9431 AB, C, 18 b.

Westerbroek (M), Rijksweg W. 11, 9608 PA, A, 89 b. **Westerbroek**

Zuiderduin (HR), De Bucksweg 2, 4361 SM, A, 185 b.; Badmotel Westkapelle **Westkapelle**
(AH), Grindweg 2, 4360 AA, C, 288 b.

De Prins (HCR), Kerkbuurt 31, 1551 AB, B, 27 b. **Westzaan**

Hegen, Wezuperstraat 15, 7582 TG, D, 8 b. **Wezup**

De Drie Mispelbloemen (HCR), Markt 19, 6602 AN, D, 10 b. **Wijchen**

Het Wapen van Wijdenes (HR), Kerkbuurt 71, 1608 EL, D, 12 b. **Wijdenes**

De Halve Maan (HCR), Dijk 5, 8131 VA, D, 6 b. **Wijhe**

Het Hoge Duin (HCR), R. Aertsweg 50, 1949 BD, A, 48 b.; Kennemerduin **Wijk aan Zee**
(HCR), Verl. Voorstraat 8–10, 1949 CM, B, 130 b.; Mare Sanat (NR), R.
Aertsweg 8, 1949 BD, B, 31 b.; De Wijck (HCR), v. Ogtropweg 12, 1949 BA, B,
30 b.; De Klughte (NR), v. Ogtropweg 2, 1949 BA, 32 b.; Sonnevanck (HCR),
R. Aertsweg 2, 1949 BD, 24 b.; Zeecroft (HP), Zeecroft 19–21, 1949 BA, C,
36 b.

De Oude Lantaarn (HR), Markt 1–2, 3961 BC, B, 54 b. **Wijk bij**
Duurstede

Bemelmans (HC), Wielderdorpsstraat 18, 6321 AD, C, 25 b.; Heiligers Bind- **Wijlre**
sels (HCR), Wielderdorpsstraat 19, 6321 AD, D, 35 b.; De Pelikaan (HP),
Kapolder 8, 6321 PV, D, 25 b.

De Veenkoloniën (HR), K. J. de Vriezestraat 1, 9643 HA, C, 22 b. **Wildervank**

Royal York (HCR), Stationsweg 21, 9671 AL, B, 90 b.; De Nederlanden (HCR), **Winschoten**
Torenstraat 2, 9671 EE, D, 12 b.

De Frerikshof (HCR), Frerikshof 2, 7103 CA, A, 181 b.; Stad Munster (HCR), **Winterswijk**
Markt 11, 7101 DA, A, 36 b.; Bulten (HCR), Parallelweg 72, 7102 DH, C, 16 b.

Winterswijk/ Meddo	Onland (HP), Goorweg 9, 7111 RE, C, 20 b.
Wirdum	Duhoux de Grand Cour (HCR), Greate Buorren 4–8, 9088 AE, D, 56 b.
Wittem	Brull (HP), Hoofdstraat, 6281 BD, B, 53 b.; In den Roden Leeuw van Limburg (HCR), Wittemerallee 28, 6286 AB, B, 20 b.; Kasteel Wittem, Wittemerallee 3, 6286 AA, B, 24 b.; Alpenzicht (HCR), Schweibergerweg 49, 6281 NE, 42 b.; Beukenhorst (HP), Rijksweg 8, 6286 AG, C, 12 b.; Posthotel (HCR), Wittemerallee 20, 6286 AB, D, 21 b.; Zinzelbeek (HP), Rijksweg 12, 6286 AG, D, 32 b.
Woerden	Baron Hotel Woerden (HR), Utrechtsestraatweg 33, 3445 AM, B, 142 b.
Wolfheze	De Buunderkamp (HR), Buunderkamp 8, 6874 NC, A, 166 b.; Wolfheze (HR), Wolfhezerweg 17, 6874 AA, A, 125 b.
Wolphaartsdijk	Royal (HCR), Lepelstraat 9, 4471 AW, D, 16 b.
Woubrugge	De Weger (HCR), B. Hosangweg 86, 2481 LA, A, 24 b.
Woudenberg	Schimmel (AH), Stationsweg 243, 3931 EP, B, 24 b.; De Nieuwe Poort (HCR), Dorpsstraat 4, 4931 EG, 20 b.
Wouw	Wouwse Tol (HCR), Bergsebaan 85, 4726 SH, A, 58 b.
Zaandam	Inntel Amsterdam Zaanstad (HR), Provincialeweg 15, 1506 MA, A, 154 b.
Zaandijk	De Saense Schans (HR), Lagedijk 32, 1544 BG, A, 32 b.
Zaltbommel	Tivoli (HCR), Steenweg 2, 5301 HL, C, 28 b.
Zandvoort	Palace (HCR), Burg. v. Fenemaplein 2, 2042 TA, A, 200 b.; Bad Zandvoort (HCR), Thorbeckestraat 23, 2042 GL, B, 38 b.; Bell (HCR), Hogeweg 7, 2042 GD, B, 18 b.; Hoogland (HR), Westerparkstraat 5, 2042 AV, B, 50 b.; Interlaken (HP), v. Speykstraat 20, 2041 KM, B, 35 b.; Van der Aar (NR), Brederodestraat 44, 2042 BG, D, 49 b.; Amare (NR), Hogeweg 70, 2042 GJ, C, 35 b.; Astoria (HCR), Dr Gerkestraat 155–159, 2042 ER, C, 27 b.; Centraal (NR), Grote Krocht 16, 2042 LW, C, 17 b.; Charlotte (HP), Haarlemmerstraat 17, 2042 NA, D, 20 b.; Cocarde (NR), Hogeweg 39, 2042 GE, C, 22 b.; Esplanade (HCR), Badhuisplein 2–6, 2042 JB, D, 60 b.; Faber (HCR), Kostverlorenstraat 16, 2042 PA, C, 70 b.; Fawlty Towers (HC), Dr Smitstraat 5, 2031 KJ, C, 39 b.; Feikje (HP), Haltestraat 77–79, 2042 LL, C, 28 b.; Noordzee (HCR), Hogeweg 15, 2042 GD, D, 27 b.; Odijssee (HCR), Hogeweg 5, 2042 GD, C, 25 b.; 't Oude Posthuis (HC), Poststraat 11, 2042 HA, C, 33 b.; Triton (HR), Zuiderstraat 3, 2042 GA, C. 44 b.
Zeddam	Centraal (HR), Benedendorpsstraat 11, 7038 BA, B, 60 b.; De Bascule (HCR), Terborgseweg 2, 7038 EW, B, 18 b.; Engelbarts (HP), 's Heerenbergseweg 9, 7038 CB, B, 57 b.; Montferland (HCR), Montferland 1, 7038 EB, B, 15 b.; Moors (HCR), Benedendorpsstraat 15–19, 7038 BA, B, 68 b.; Aaldering (HCR), 's Heerenbergseweg 1, 7038 CA, C, 54 b.; Euroeke (HP), Kilderseweg 2, 7038 BW, C, 26 b.; Ruimzicht (HCR), Kilderseweg 19, 7038 EH, C, 92 b.; Het Wapen van Zeddam (HCR), 's Heerenbergseweg 3, 7038 CA, C, 30 b.
Zeegse	Duinoord (HCR), Schipborgerweg 8, 9483 TL, B, 110 b.
Zeist	Golden Tulip Figi (HCR), Het Rond 3, 3701 HS, A, 102 b.; Oud London (HR), Woudenbergseweg 52, 3707 HX, A, 120 b.; Hermitage (HCR), Het Rond 7, 3701 HS, B, 25 b.; 't Kerkebosch (HCR), Arnhemse Bovenweg 31, 3708 AA, B, 60 b.; Cornelis Jetses (NR), Bergweg 37, 3707 AA, 12 b.; Spoorzicht (HC), Slotlaan 301–303, 3701 GJ, 32 b.
Zenderen	Haarhuis (HR), Hoofdstraat 16, 7625 PD, D, 18 b.

Mondragon (HCR), Havenpark 21, 4301 JG, B, 23 b.; Monique (HR), Drie-koningenlaan 7, 4301 HK, C, 36 b. **Zierikzee**

't Witte Paard (HCR), Dorpsstraat 49, 7136 LG, C, 28 b. **Ziewent**

Baron Hotel Zoutermeer (HCR), Boerhanvelaan 1, 2713 HB, A, 126 b. **Zoetermeer**

De Distel (HCR), Westkapelseweg 1, 4373 BA, A, 69 b.; Beach Hotel Zonne-wende (HCR), Duinweg 97, 4374 EC, B, 60 b.; Willebrord (HR), Smidsstraat 17, 4374 AT, B, 40 b.; Coranjo (HCR), Willebrordusplein 18, 4374 AX, D, 20 b.; Oase (HP), Noordendolfer 6, 4374 EJ, D, 30 b.; Het Streefkerkse-huis (HCR), Duinweg 48, 4374 EG, C, 10 b.; Valkenhof (HCR), Zuidstraat 9–11, 4374 AJ, C, 60 b. **Zoutelande**

De Zeearend (HCR), Dorpsplein 1, 9974 PM, D, 14 b. **Zoutkamp**

Hulsebos (HCR), Stationsstraat 4, 9636 BA, C, 35 b. **Zuidbroek**

Brinkhotel (HCR), Brink Z.O. 6, 9471 AE, B, 82 b.

De Zwaan (HCR), Dorpsplein 10, 4505 AR, D, 24 b. **Zuidzande**

Ossekop (HC), Molenstraat 63, 4881 GR, D, 13 b. **Zundert**

Inntel Zutphen (HCR), De Stoven 37, 7206 AZ, A, 134 b. **Zutphen**

Zwartewater (M), De Vlakte 20, 8064 PC, A, 120 b.; Roskam, Stationsweg 1, 8064 DD, B, 18 b. **Zwartsluis**

Kniephof (HP), Hoofdstraat 14, 7851 AA, C, 14 b. **Zweeloo**

Grand Hotel Wientjes (HCR), Stationsweg 7, 8011 CZ, A, 91 b.; Postiljon Zwolle (HCR), Hertsenbergweg 1, 8041 BA, B, 144 b.; Fidder (HP), Wil-helminastraat 6, 8019 AM, C, 30 b.; Weenink (HR), Rode Torenplein 10–11, 8011 MJ, D, 30 b. **Zwolle**

Information

Netherlands Board of Tourism (NBT)

Nederlands Bureau voor Toerisme
Vlietweg 15
NL–2266 KA Leidschendam
tel. (0703) 70 57 05

Head office

25–28 Buckingham Gate
London SW1E 6LD
tel. (071) 630 0451

United Kingdom

355 Lexington Avenue, 21st floor
New York NY 10017
tel. (212) 370 7367

USA

225 N. Michigan Avenue, Suite 326
Chicago IL 60601
tel. (312) 819 0300

90 New Montgomery Street, Suite 305
San Francisco CA 94105
tel. (415) 543 6772

Information

Netherlands Reservation Centre (NRC)

Information
Nederlands Reserverings Centrum
(Accommodation Centre)
Postbus 404
NL–2260 AK Leidschendam
tel. (070) 3 20 25 00

Services
The NRC is the largest organisation in the Netherlands through which accommodation can be booked in hotels, self-catering apartments and houses, and log cabins on camping sites; it can also arrange group bookings in restaurants. The NRC can also provide the services of guides, and it works closely with the Amsterdam VVV (see below): for example it can obtain tickets for all cultural events in Amsterdam.

Tourist Information Offices (VVV)

In all towns of any size in the Netherlands there are offices of the Vereniging voor Vreemdelingenverkeer, or VVV for short, which provide help and information for visitors. For their opening times see Business Hours.

Provincial VVV Offices

For information about any of the twelve provinces of the Netherlands you should apply in writing to the following addresses:

Drenthe   Postbus 10012, NL–9400 CA Assen

Flevoland   Postbus 548, NL–8200 AM Lelystad

Friesland   Stationsplein 1, NL–8911 AC Leeuwarden

Gelderland   Postbus 988, NL–6800 AZ Arnhem

Groningen   Naberpassage 3, NL–9712 JV Groningen

Limburg   Postbus 811, NL–6300 AV Valkenburg

Noord-Brabant Postbus 90, NL–5260 AB Vught

Noord-Holland Florapark 6, NL–2012 HK Haarlem

Overijssel   Postbus 500, NL–7600 AM Almelo

Utrecht   Maliesingel 38, NL–3581 BK Utrecht

Zeeland   Postbus 123, NL–4330 AC Middelburg

Zuid-Holland   Markt 85, NL–2611 GS Delft

Local VVV Offices

There are some 400 local VVV offices throughout the Netherlands.

Room booking
service
In addition to providing information, VVV offices displaying the sign "i-Nederland" will also book accommodation for visitors, either locally or elsewhere in the country. Application must be made in person; bookings cannot be made by telephone.

Alkmaar   Waagplein 3, NL–1811 JP Alkmaar, tel. (072) 11 42 84

Rixt van Doniaweg 2, NL–9163 GR Nes, tel. (05191) 20 20	**Ameland**
Stationsplein 27, NL–3818 LE Amersfoort, tel. (033) 63 5151	**Amersfoort**
Postal address: Postbus 3901, NL–1001 AS Amsterdam tel. (020) 6 26 64 44 (Mon.–Sat. 9am–5pm) Information office: Stationsplein 10 Open October 1st to Easter, Mon.–Fri. 9am–6pm, Sat. 9am–5pm; Easter to June and in September, Mon.–Sat. 9am–11pm, Sun. 9am–9pm; July and August, Mon.–Sun. 9am–11pm There is also a VVV office (open daily) at Leidsestraat 106.	**Amsterdam** Office opposite Central Station
Stationsplein 45, NL–6811 KL Arnhem, tel. (085) 42 03 30	**Arnhem**
Plein 1, NL–1861 JX Bergen (N.H.), tel. (02208) 1 21 24 and 1 31 00	**Bergen**
Van der Wijckplein 8, NL–1865 AP Bergen aan Zee tel. (02208) 1 31 73 and 1 24 00	**Bergen aan Zee**
Hoogstraat 2, NL–4611 MT Bergen op Zoom tel. (01640) 6 60 00	**Bergen op Zoom**
Willemstraat 17–19, NL–4811 AJ Breda, tel. (076) 22 24 44	**Breda**
Boulevard 14, NL–4511 AC Breskens, tel. (01172) 18 88	**Breskens**
Noordstraat 45A, NL–4328 AK Haamstede, tel. (01115) 15 13	**Burgh- Haamstede**
Boulevard de Wielingen 17A, NL–4506 JH Cadzand, tel. (01179) 12 98	**Cadzand**
Jewelweg 8, Postbus 10, NL–1759 ZG Callantsoog tel. (02248) 15 41	**Callantsoog**
Stationsweg 46, NL–1901 AA Castricum, tel. (02518) 5 20 09	**Castricum/ Bakkum**
Markt 85, NL–2611 GS Delft, tel. (015) 12 61 00	**Delft**
See Texel, below	**Den Burg**
Julianaplein 30, NL–1781 HA Den Helder, tel. (02230) 2 55 44 In Julianadorp during the summer: Van Foreestweg tel. (02230) 4 56 62	**Den Helder– Julianadorp**
Brink 55, NL–7411 BV Deventer, tel. (05700) 1 62 00	**Deventer**
Schuitvlotstraat 32, NL–4357 EB Domburg, tel. (01188) 13 42	**Domburg**
Stationsweg 1, NL–3311 JW Dordrecht, tel. (078) 13 28 00	**Dordrecht**
Damplein 1, NL–1135 BK Edam, tel. (02993) 7 17 27	**Edam**
Herenweg 207, NL–1934 BA Egmond aan den Hoef, tel. (02206) 10 15	**Egmond aan den Hoef**
Voorstraat 82A, NL–1931 AN Egmond aan Zee, tel. (02206) 13 62/23 71	**Egmond aan Zee**
Herenweg 60, NL–1935 AG Egmond Binnen, tel. (02206) 13 10	**Egmond Binnen**
Stationsplein 17, NL–5611 AC Eindhoven, tel. (040) 44 92 31	**Eindhoven**
Stationsplein 1, NL–1601 EN Enkhuizen, tel. (02280) 1 31 64	**Enkhuizen**

Information

Enschede	Oude Markt 31, NL–7511 GB Enschede, tel. (053) 32 32 00
Gouda	Markt 27, NL–2801 JJ Gouda, tel. (01820) 1 36 66
Groote Keeten	See Callantsoog, above
Groede	See Breskens, above
Groet-Camperduin	Heereweg 252A, NL–1873 GE Groet, tel. (02209) 14 23
Haamstede	See Burgh-Haamstede, above
Haarlem	Stationsplein 1, NL–2011 LR Haarlem, tel. (023) 31 90 59
The Hague	Postal address: Postbus 17224, NL–2502 CE Den Haag tel. (0703) 3 54 62 00 Groot Hertoginnelaan 41, NL–2517 EC Den Haag, tel. (0703) 3 54 62 00 VVV Babylon (shopping centre), The Hague Open mid April to mid September, Mon.–Sat. 9am–9pm, Sun. 10am–5pm; mid September to mid April, Mon.–Sat. 9am–8pm, Sun. 10am–5pm (closed Dec. 25th and Jan. 1st)
Harlingen	Voorstraat 34, NL–8861 BL Harlingen, tel. (05178) 1 72 22
Hellevoet-sluis	Oostzanddijk 26 (Vesting), NL–3221 AL Hellevoetsluis, tel. (01883) 1 23 18
's-Hertogen-bosch	Markt 77, NL–5211 JX Den Bosch, tel. (073) 12 30 71
Hilversum	Emmastraat 2, NL–1211 NG Hilversum, tel. (035) 21 16 51
Hoek van Holland	Hoekse Brink 23, NL–3151 GB Hoek van Holland tel. (01747) 24 56 See also Rotterdam, below
IJmuiden-Velsen	Marktplein 42, NL–1972 IJmuiden, tel. (02550) 1 56 11
Kampen	Oudestraat 85, NL–8261 CH Kampen, tel. (05202) 1 35 00
Kamperland	VVV Noord-Beveland, Voorstraat 36, NL–4491 EW Wissenkerke tel. (01107) 15 95
Katwijk aan Zee	Vuurbaakplein 11, NL–2225 JB Katwijk aan Zee, tel. (01718) 7 54 44
Kijkduin	See The Hague, above
Koudekerke	Postbus 7, NL–4370 AA Koudekerke, tel. (01185) 14 44
Leiden	Stationsplein 210, NL–2312 AR Leiden, tel. (071) 14 68 46
Leeuwarden	Stationsplein 1, NL–8911 AC Leeuwarden, tel. (058) 13 22 24
Lelystad	Agorahof 2, NL–8224 BX Lelystad, tel. (03200) 4 34 44
Maastricht	Kleine Staat 1, NL–6211 ED Maastricht, tel. (043) 25 21 21
Middelburg	Markt 65A, NL–4331 KL Middelburg, tel. (01180) 1 68 51
Monnickendam	De Zarken 2, NL–1141 BG Monnickendam, tel. (02995) 19 98
Monster	Lijsterbesstraat 1, NL–2681 CT Monster, tel. (01749) 1 25 71
Naarden	A. Dorstmanplein 1B, NL–1411 RC Naarden, tel. (02159) 4 28 36

See Ameland, above	**Nes**
June to September: Molenweg 5, NL–5504 AP Nieuwvliet tel. (01171) 13 25 At other times information from VVV Breskens, above	**Nieuwvliet**
Sint Jorisstraat 72, NL–6511 TD Nijmegen, tel. (080) 22 54 40	**Nijmegen**
De Grent 8, NL–2202 EK Noordwijk, tel. (01719) 1 93 21	**Noordwijk**
Herenweg 14, NL–2211 CC Noordwijkerhout, tel. (02523) 7 20 96	**Noordwijker- hout**
Duinweg 2A, Postbus 21, NL–4356 ZG Oostkapelle, tel. (01188) 29 10	**Oostkapelle**
Stationsweg 55, NL–3233 CS Oostvoorne, tel. (01815) 27 49	**Oostvoorne**
Hofdijkseweg 30A, NL–3253 KB, tel. (01878) 17 89	**Ouddorp**
Plein 1945, No. 3, NL–1755 NH Petten, tel. (02268) 13 52	**Petten**
De Zoom 17, Postbus 41, NL–4325 BG Renesse, tel. (01116) 21 20	**Renesse**
Molenstraat 12, NL–4525 AE Retranchement tel. (01179) 16 24 or (01178) 12 00	**Retranchement**
Dorpsplein 16A, NL–3235 AD Rockanje, tel. (01814) 16 00	**Rockanje**
Markt 24, NL–6041 Roermond, tel. (04750) 3 32 05	**Roermond**
Coolsingel 67 (corner of Stadhuisplein), NL–3012 AC Rotterdam, tel. (010) 4 13 60 00 Open April to September, Mon.–Thu. 9am–6pm, Fri. 9am–9pm, Sat. 9am–5pm, Sun. 10am–6pm; October to March, Mon.–Thu. 9am–6pm, Fri. 9am–9pm, Sat. 9am–5pm, closed Sun. There is another information office in the concourse of the Central Station, tel. (010) 4 13 60 00. Open throughout the year Mon.–Sat. 9am–midnight, Sun. 10am–midnight (earlier closing on public holidays).	**Rotterdam**
Gevers Deynootweg 126, NL–2586 BP Scheveningen/Den Haag tel. (070) 3 54 62 00 Open mid April to mid September, Mon.–Sat. 9am–9pm, Sun. 10am–5pm; mid September to mid April, Mon.–Sat. 9am–8pm, closed Sun., Dec. 25th and Jan. 1st.	**Scheveningen**
Reeweg 5, NL–9166 PW Schiermonnikoog, tel. (05195) 12 33 and 19 00 (reservations)	**Schiermonni- koog**
Duinvoetweg 1, NL–1871 EA Schoorl, tel. (02209) 15 04	**Schoorl**
Naaldwijkseweg 24, NL–2691 RH 's-Gravenzande, tel. (01748) 1 73 15	**'s-Graven- zande**
Zeeweg 9A, NL–1753 BB Sint Maartensvlotburg, tel. (02246) 13 07	**Sint Maartens- zee**
Leeuwenburg 21, NL–8601 CG Sneek, tel. (05150) 1 40 96	**Sneek**
See Monster, above	**Ter Heijde**
Willem Barentszkade 19A, Postbus 20, NL–8880 ZN AA West-Terschelling, tel. (05620) 30 00	**Terschelling**
Groeneplaats 9, NL–1791 CC Den Burg, tel. (02220) 1 47 41	**Texel**

Language

Tilburg	Stadhuisplein 128, NL–5038 TC Tilburg, tel. (013) 35 11 35
Utrecht	Vredenburg 90, NL–3511 BD Utrecht, tel. (030) 31 41 32
Valkenburg	Th. Dorrenplein 5, NL–6301 DV Valkenburg, tel. (04406) 1 33 64
Venlo	Koninginneplein 2, NL–5911 KK Venlo, tel. (077) 54 38 00
Vlieland	Havenweg 10, Postbus 1, NL–8899 ZN Oost-Vlieland, tel. (05621) 13 57
Vlissingen	Nieuwendijk 15, NL–4381 BV Vlissingen, tel. (01184) 1 23 45 and 1 92 75
Vrouwen-polder	Dorpsdijk 19, NL–4353 AA Vrouwenpolder, tel. (01189) 15 77
Wassenaar	See Scheveningen, above
Westkapelle	Markt 69A, NL–4361 AE Westkapelle, tel. (01187) 12 81
Wijk aan Zee (Beverwijk)	Stationsplein 46, NL–1949 AT Wijk aan Zee, tel. (02517) 42 53
Wissenkerke	See Kamperland, above
Zandvoort	Schoolplein 1, NL–2042 Zandvoort, tel. (02507) 1 79 47
Zierikzee	Havenpark 29, NL–4301 JG Zierikzee, tel. (01110) 24 50
Zoutelande	Ooststraat 19, NL–4374 AE Zoutelande, tel. (01186) 13 64
Zutphen	Groenmarkt 40, NL–7201 HZ Zutphen, tel. (05750) 1 93 55
Zwolle	Grote Kerkplein 14, NL–8011 PK Zwolle, tel. (038) 21 39 00

Language

Dutch	The official language of the Netherlands, and the ordinary spoken and written language, is Dutch. Dutch is also spoken in northern Belgium, under the name of Flemish. There are various dialects of the language, but these are not written except in specifically dialect literature.
Frisian	A related Germanic language, Frisian, is spoken in the northern province of Friesland. It is used in many schools and is increasingly being used in local administration.
English	Visitors without any knowledge of Dutch will have no difficulty in finding their way about in the Netherlands, since English is widely spoken and understood.

The Dutch Language

Dutch is a West Germanic language closely related to the Low German dialects of northern Germany. As early as the 12th century there was a written language (Middle Dutch), which later – particularly after the struggle for independence in the 17th century – developed into modern Dutch. This was the period when political and economic power moved to the northern part of what is now the Netherlands, and the modern literary language is strongly influenced by northern (Amsterdam) usage.

Dutch is strongly Germanic in vocabulary, though there are some borrowings from French.

Pronunciation	Vowels: All vowels are pronounced in the "continental" fashion, without the diphthongisation found in English. The vowels *a, e, i* and *o* may be

either short or long; the corresponding vowels *aa, ee, ie* and *oo* are long; long *u* or *uu* is pronounced like the vowel in French "lune", short *u* something like the vowel in French "peur"; *oe* is pronounced *oo*.

Diphthongs: The diphthongs *au* and *ou* have the sound of the diphthong in English "cow"; *ei* and *ij* (sometimes spelt *y*) are similar to the diphthong in English "by"; *ui* is pronounced like the short Dutch *u* followed by an *i* or *y* sound; *uw* is like a long Dutch *u* followed by a short *oo* sound; the combinations *aai, ooi* and *oei* are like the Dutch vowels *aa, oo* and *oe* followed by a short *i*; and *ieuw* and *eeuw* are like long *i* and *e* followed by a short *oo* sound.

Consonants: The consonants *p, t* and *k* are pronounced as in English, though without the slight puff of breath which follows them in English; similarly with *b* and *d*, which are unvoiced (i.e. pronounced like *p* and *t*) at the end of a word; *w* is pronounced something like English *v; ch* as in Scottish "loch"; *g* a guttural *gh*, or at the end of a word like *ch; j* like consonantal *y; r* is always trilled; *sj* is pronounced *sh*. In the combination *sch* the *ch* sound must be pronounced separately from the *s*, not combined (as in German) to make *sh*; in the combination *schr* the three consonants (*s/ch/r*) should similarly be pronounced separately, though the *ch* is frequently omitted, simplifying the pronunciation to *sr*.

There are two forms of the definite article: *de* (common gender and in plural) and *het* (neuter singular). The singular indefinite article is *een*.

Articles

When addressing strangers the formal *U* should be used for "you" rather than the familiar *jij* or *je*. *U*, derived from a term meaning "your honour", is used with the third person singular of the verb. A man is addressed as *mijnheer*, pronounced *meneer*, a married woman as *mevrouw*, an unmarried woman as *juffrouw*. Waitresses, etc., are addressed as *juffrouw* even if they are married.

Forms of address

Cardinal numbers

	English	Dutch
0	zero	nul
1	one	een
2	two	twee
3	three	drie
4	four	vier
5	five	vijf
6	six	zes
7	seven	zeven
8	eight	acht
9	nine	negen
10	ten	tien
11	eleven	elf
12	twelve	twaalf
13	thirteen	dertien
14	fourteen	veertien
15	fifteen	vijftien
16	sixteen	zestien
17	seventeen	zeventien
18	eighteen	achttien
19	nineteen	negentien
20	twenty	twintig
21	twenty-one	eenentwintig
22	twenty-two	tweëntwintig
30	thirty	dertig
31	thirty-one	eenendertig
40	forty	veertig
50	fifty	vijftig

Language

60	sixty	zestig
70	seventy	zeventig
80	eighty	tachtig
90	ninety	negentig
91	ninety-one	eenenhegentig
100	one hundred	honderd
101	one hundred and one	honderd een
200	two hundred	tweehonderd
1000	one thousand	duizend

Ordinal numbers	1st	first	eerste
	2nd	second	tweede
	3rd	third	derde

Fractions	½	a half	een half
	⅓	a third	een derde
	¼	a quarter	een kwart

Common expressions	**English**	Dutch
	America	Amerika
	American	Amerikaan
	Britain	Groot-Brittannië
	British	Brits
	England	Engeland
	English	Engels
	Scotland	Schotland
	Scottish	Schots
	Wales	Wales
	Welsh	van Wales
	Ireland	Ierland
	Irish	Iers
	Netherlands	Nederland
	Dutch	Nederlands
	Do you speak . . .?	Spreekt U . . .?
	I do not understand	Ik versta niet
	Yes	Ja
	No	Neen
	Please	Alstublieft
	Thank you (very much)	Dank U (zeer)
	Excuse me; I beg your pardon	Pardon
	Good morning	Goedemorgen
	Good afternoon	Goedendag
	Good evening	Goedenavond
	Goodnight	Goedenacht
	Goodbye	Tot ziens
	Where is . . .?	Waar is . . .?
	. . . Street	De . . . straat
	. . . Square	De . . . plaats, het plein
	A travel agency	Een reisbureau
	The church	De kerk
	The museum	Het museum
	When?	Wanneer?
	When is . . . open?	Wanneer is . . . open?
	The Town Hall	Het Stadhuis
	A bank	Een bank
	The station	Het station
	A hotel	Een hotel

Have you a room free?	Heeft U een kamer voor mij?	
Single room	Met een bed	
Double room	Met twee bedden	
With bath	Met een badkamer	
The key	De sleutel	
The lavatory	Het toilet	
A doctor	Een arts, een dokter	
Right	Rechts	
Left	Links	
Straight ahead	Rechtuit	
Above	Boven	
Below	Beneden	
Old	Oud	
New	Nieuw	
What does . . . cost?	Hoeveel kost . . .?, wat kost . . .?	
Expensive	Duur	
Restaurant	Restaurant	
Breakfast	Ontbijt	
Lunch	Middagmaal	
Dinner	Avondeten	
Eat	Eten	
Drink	Drinken	
Much, many	Veel	
Little, few	Weinig	
Bill	Rekening	
Pay	Betalen	
At once	Dadelijk	
Stop	Halt	Traffic signs
Customs	Tol	and warnings
Caution	Pas op	
	Opgelet	
	Waarschuwing	
Slow	Langzaam rijden	
Danger	Levensgevaar	
One-way street	Straat met eenrichtings-verkeer	
No through road	Afgesloten rijweg	
Road works	Bestratingswerkzaam-heden	
Dangerous curve	Gevaarlijke bocht	
Accelerator	Gaspedaal	Car terms
Air	Lucht	
Axle	As	
Battery	Accu	
Bolt	Schroef	
Brake	Rem	
Breakdown	Defect (motor)	
Car	Auto	
Carburettor	Carburateur	
Clutch	Koppeling	
Cylinder	Cilinder	
Direction indicator	Richtingaanwijzer	
Driving licence	Rijbewijs	
Exhaust	Uitlatpijp	
Fuse	Sekering	
Garage	Garage	
Gasket	Pakking	
Gear	Versnelling	
Grease	Smeerolie	
Headlight	Koplamp	
Horn	Claxon	
Ignition	Ontsteking	

Language

Jack	Crick
Key	Sleutel
Motorcycle	Motorijwiel
Nut	Moer
Oil	Olie
Oil change	Olie verversen
Parking place	Parkeerplaats
Petrol	Benzine
Petrol station	Tankstation
Petrol tank	Benzinetank
Piston	Zuiger
Radiator	Radiator
Repair garage	Reparatie-inrichting
Spanner	Moersleutel
Spare part	Onderdeel
Sparking plug	Bougie
Speedometer	Snelheidsmeter
Spring	Veer
Tyre	Band
Valve	Ventiel
Wash	Wassen
Wheel	Wiel
Windscreen	Voorruit
Windscreen wiper	Ruitewisser

Months	January	Januari
	February	Februari
	March	Maart
	April	April
	May	Mei
	June	Juni
	July	Juli
	August	Augustus
	September	September
	October	Oktober
	November	November
	December	December

Days of week	Sunday	Zondag
	Monday	Maandag
	Tuesday	Dinsdag
	Wednesday	Woensdag
	Thursday	Donderdag
	Friday	Vrijdag
	Saturday	Zaterdag
	Day	Dag
	Holiday	Feestdag, rustdag

Public holidays	New Year	Nieuwjaar
	Easter	Pasen
	Ascension	Hemelvaart
	Whitsun	Pinksteren
	Corpus Christi	Sacramentsdag
	Assumption	Maria-ten-Hemelopneming
	All Saints	Allerheiligen
	Christmas	Kerstmis
	New Year's Eve	Oudejaarsavond

At the post office	Post office	Postkantoor
	Head post office	Hoofdpostkantoor
	Stamp	Postzegel
	Letter	Brief

Postcard	Briefkaart
Postman	Postbode
Registered	Aangetekend
Printed paper	Drukwerk
Express	Expres
Air mail	Luchtpost
Telegram	Telegram
Telephone	Telefoon

Language Courses

For those who want to learn Dutch there are courses at the study centres mentioned below. They must make their own arrangements for accommodation during the course; or alternatively apply to ISOK, which can make arrangements for them to stay in a Dutch family as a paying guest.

ISOK, De Zeeuw
Jan Tooropstraat 4, NL–2225 XT Katwijk aan Zee
tel. (01718) 1 35 33

There are study centres in Amsterdam, The Hague, Rotterdam and Utrecht.

Leisure Parks, Theme Parks and Zoos

There are many leisure and theme parks in the Netherlands (amusement parks, fairytale parks, miniature cities, fun pools, etc.) offering a wide variety of facilities for relaxation and entertainment. In addition there are numerous zoos, safari parks, aquariums, dolphinariums, etc., which also attract many visitors.

The opening times of the various parks, etc., are shown below; but since changes are always possible it is as well to check by telephone.

There is normally a charge for admission, usually with reduced rates for children.

Leisure and Theme Parks

The leisure and theme parks usually have special facilities for children – dodgem cars, merry-go-rounds, play areas, children's farms, etc. There may also be more instructive features such as collections of birds, fossils and insects and butterfly gardens.

The following list mentions some of the special features of each park. More detailed information can be obtained from local tourist information offices.

Koningin Julianatoren Recreation park — Apeldoorn
Amerfoortseweg 35, tel. (055) 55 32 65
Open: mid April to September and during the autumn holidays, daily 10am–6pm.
Features: outlook tower, Bengali Cave, maze, motorboats.

Appelscha Miniature Town — Appelscha
Boerestreek 7A, tel. (05162) 22 00
Open: end of March to October, daily 9.30am–6pm.

Duinenzathe Recreation park
Boerestreek 13, tel. (05162) 22 03/19 60
Open: April to September and in the autumn holidays, daily 9.30am–6pm.
Features: amusement arcade, motor scooters, cakewalk, haunted house, etc.

Leisure Parks, Theme Parks and Zoos

Huis Arcen Gardens (see A to Z, Venlo)
Lingsforterweg 25, NL–5944 Arcen, tel. (04703) 18 82
Open: May to end of October, daily 9.30am–6pm.
Features: flower garden (32 hectares/80 acres; rhododendrons, azaleas, hydrangeas; rosarium; 150,000 plants); 900 tons of rock from the Ardennes; artificial canyon and rock garden, with watercourses.

Arnhem

Sculpture Park of the Kröller-Müller Museum (20 hectares/50 acres: see A to Z, Veluwe)
North of Arnhem in the Hoge Veluwe National Park.
Information: VVV Zuidwest-Veluwe, Achterdoelen 36, NL–6711 AV Ede, tel. (08380) 1 44 44.

Bennebroek

Linnaeushof Recreation Park (see A to Z, Bollenstreek)
Rijksstraatweg 4, tel. (02502) 76 24
Open: end of March to September, daily 10am–6pm.
Features: wide range of games, pedalos, mini-golf, play garden, railway.

Biddinghuizen

Flevohof (see A to Z, Dronten)
Spijkweg 30, tel. (03211) 15 14
Open: April to mid October, daily 10am–6pm.
Features: agricultural and gardening shows, with stock farm; Adventure Island (in a lake, reached only by boat); Indian Village; Luna Park; Children's Village (supervised); Butterfly Centres: Flevo Train; Coach Museum (farm carts and coaches).

Drouwen

Het Drouwenerzand Recreation Park
Gasselterstraat 7, tel. (05999) 6 43 60
Open: March to September, daily 9am–9.30pm.
Features: museum of nature and the underwater world, collections of birds, butterflies, fossils and insects.

**Drunen/
Vlijmen**

Kasteelpark Het Land van Ooit (Never-Never Land)
Parklaan 40, tel. (04163) 7 77 75
Open: mid April to mid October, daily 10am–6pm.
Features: Theatre Park (performances in Manege Theatre, Baroque Theatre, Puppet Theatre and, in summer, open-air theatre) in grounds of Oultremont Castle; Giants' World and World of Fable; Children's Land; sculpture garden, horses.

The Hague

Omniversum (see A to Z, The Hague)
Pres. Kennedylaan 5, NL–2517 JK Den Haag, tel. (070) 3 54 54 54
Presentations: Tue.–Thur. hourly from 11am to 4pm; Fri., Sat., Sun. and pub. hols. also at 5pm and from 7 to 9pm.
Features: shows illustrating discovery and science.

Madurodam Miniature Town (see A to Z, The Hague)
Haringkade 175, tel. (070) 3 55 39 00
Open: end of March to May, daily 9am–10.30pm; May 4th 9am–6pm; June to August, 9am–11pm; September 9am–9.30pm, October to early January 9am–6pm.
A miniature Dutch town on the scale 1:25; *son et lumière* show.

Hellendoorn

Hellendoorn Recreation, Adventure and Fairytale Park
Luttenbergerweg 22, tel. (05486) 5 55 55
Open: mid April to mid September, September 22nd, 23rd, 29th and 30th, and October 6th, 7th and 13th–21st, 9.30am–6pm.
Features: parrot and sealion shows; roller-coaster, monorail; water chute with fall of 12m/40ft; Magical Monkey Show.

Hengelo

De Waarbeek Recreation Park
Twekkelerweg 327, tel. (074) 91 34 17
Open: end of April to beginning of September, daily 9.30am–5.45pm; September 10th to October 7th, Sat. and Sun. 9.30am–5.45pm; at other times in April by arrangement.

Bosbad Hoeven Recreation Park
Oude Antwerpsepopstbaan 81a, tel. (01659) 23 66
Open: End of March to end of April, Sat., Sun, and in Easter holidays,
1–5pm; beginning of May to beginning of September, Mon.–Fri.
10am–8pm, Sat. and Sun. 10am–6.30pm; at other times by arrangement.
Features: equipment for games, play garden, electric motorboats; open-air
pool with water chute.

De Efteling (see A to Z, Tilburg)   Kaatsheuvel
Europalaan 1, Postbus 18, tel. (04167) 8 81 11
Open: mid April to mid October, daily 10am–6pm.
Features: Fairytale Forest, Haunted Castle, Dwarfs' Village, bobsleigh run
(560m/610yds), ponds for rowing and canoeing, beautiful flower gardens.

Nienoord Youth Park   Leek
Nienoord 9, tel. (05945) 1 22 60
Open: end of March to October, Mon.–Sat. 9am–6pm, Sun. 1–5pm.

Walcheren in Miniature (see A to Z, Middelburg)   Middelburg
Koepoortlaan 1, tel. (01180) 1 25 25
Open: end March to June and September to October, daily 9.30am–5pm;
July and August, daily 9.30am–6pm.
A model of the Walcheren peninsula and the town of Middelburg on a scale
of 1:20.

Sybrandy's Recreation Park   Oudemirdum
tel. (05147) 12 24
Open: April to September, Tue.–Sun. 10am–6pm.

Drievliet Recreation Park   Rijswijk
Jan Thijssenweg 16, tel. (070) 3 99 93 05
Open: end of April to August, daily 10am–6pm (at other times by
arrangement).
Features: pirate ship, wild water rafting, "Old 99" railway.

Tropicana   Rotterdam
Maasboulevard 100, tel. (010) 4 02 07 00
Open: Mon.–Fri. 10am–10pm, Sat. and Sun. 10am–7pm.
Features: Subtropical Swimming Paradise, wild water rapids.

Gouden Handen Recreation Centre   's Heerenberg
Emmerikseweg 13, tel. (08346) 6 23 43
Open: beginning of April to mid October, daily 10am–6pm.
Features: puppet show, "Magical Wonderland".

Slagharen Recreation Park and Pony Park   Slagharen
Zwarte Dijk 39, tel. (05231) 30 00
Open: end March to beginning of September and in autumn holidays, daily
10am–5.30pm; September 9th to October 11th, Sat. and Sun.
10am–5.30pm.

Steinerbos Recreation Park   Stein
Dieterenstraat 19, tel. (04490) 3 25 25
Open: end April to mid September, daily 10am–6pm.
Features: mini-cars, mini-train; swimming pool with water chute.

Valkenburg Fairytale Park   Valkenburg
Sibbegrubbe 1, tel. (04406) 1 29 85
Open: mid April to June, 10am–5pm; in July and August 10am–6pm;
September 10am–5pm.
Features: moving fairytale figures; water organ; water chute.

Leisure Parks, Theme Parks and Zoos

Thermae 2000 (see A to Z, Valkenburg)
Cauberg 27, tel. (04406) 1 46 00
Open: daily 9am–11pm.
Features: extensive bathing facilities (hot mineral bath opened 1989), with several whirlpools; Lotus Bath in a beautiful botanical garden, with luxuriant tropical plants; yoga and meditation cells.

De Valkenier Recreation Park
Koningswinkelstraat 53, tel. (04406) 1 26 82
Open: end of March to end of September, daily 10am–6pm.
Features: roller-coaster, Rodeo Hall, Haunted House.

Wanroij   De Bergen Recreation Park
Campinglaan 1, tel. (08859) 7 89 00
Open: April to September, daily 9am–6pm.
Features: play garden, mini-car track, helter-skelter; indoor sports complex.

Wassenaar   Duinrell Leisure Park
Duinrell 1, tel. (01751) 1 92 12 and 1 93 14
Open: April to October, daily 10am–5pm.
Features: the largest amusement park in the western Netherlands, with summer bobsleigh run and theatre shows; Tikibad (tel. (01751) 1 93 14), a tropical pool with artificial waves and flumes.

Zoos (Aquariums, Bird Parks)

Alphen aan den Rijn   Avifauna Bird Park
Hoorn 65, tel. (01720) 8 75 05
Open: April to September, daily 9am–9pm; October to March, daily 9am–6pm.

Amersfoort   Amersfoort Zoo
Barchman Wuytierslaan 224, tel. (033) 61 66 58
Open: mid May to September, daily 9am–6pm; October to mid May, daily 9am–5pm.

Amsterdam   Artis Zoo
Plantage Kerklaan 40, tel. (020) 5 23 34 00
Open: daily 9am–5pm.
Features: over 6000 animals; reptile house, nocturnal animal house.

Apeldoorn   Apenheul/Park Berg en Bos (see A to Z, Apeldoorn)
J. C. Wilslaan 21–31, tel. (055) 55 25 56
Open: April to June, 9.30am–5pm; July and August, 9.30am–6pm; September and October, 10am–5pm.
More than 250 monkeys roam free in the forest among the visitors.

Arnhem   Burger's Zoo (animal and safari park) and Burger's Bush (tropical forest): see A to Z, Arnhem
Schelmseweg 85, tel. (085) 42 45 34 and 45 03 73
Open: daily 9am–7pm.
Burger's Bush (roofed) is a faithful copy of a real jungle, with plants and animals (including crocodiles, tapirs and monkeys) from Africa, Asia and South America. A train trip through the safari park is included in the admission charge.

Bergen aan Zee   Underwater Marine Aquarium
Van der Wijckplein 16, tel. (02208) 1 29 28
Open: April to October, daily 10 a.m–6pm; November to March, Sat. and Sun. 11am–5pm.

Ecomare Marine Aquarium
De Koog (Texel)
Ruyslaan 92, tel. (02220) 1 77 41
Open: daily 9am–5pm (from November to March closed on Sun. and on December 25th and January 1st).
Features: Natural History Museum; ornithological station; large colony of seals.

Noorder Dierenpark (Animal Park: see A to Z, Emmen)
Emmen
Hoofdstraat 18, tel. (05910) 1 88 00
Open: daily 9am–5pm; June to August 9am–6pm.
Features: "The Farm of Today" (greenhouses with tropical and other plants; beautiful gardens; laboratory); zoo, with tropical butterfly garden.

Harderwijk Marine Animal Park
Harderwijk
Strandboulevard Oost 1, tel. (03410) 1 60 41
Open: end of February to beginning of November, daily 10am–6pm (last ticket 4pm).
Feature: a large collection of marine animals, with dolphin, walrus and sealion shows.

Beekse Bergen Safari Park
Hilvarenbeek
Beekse Bergen 1, tel. (013) 36 00 32
Open: December, January and February, 10am–3.30pm; March, October and November, 10am–4pm; April to June and September, 10am–5pm; July and August 10am–6pm.
Features: a 100 hectare/250 acre park with lions, tigers, giraffes, rhinoceroses, elephants and rhesus monkeys; dodgem boats, cycle-cross track, Europe's longest funicular.

Oisterwijk Bird Park
Oisterwijk
Gemullehoekenweg 147, tel. (04242) 8 34 49
Open: April to October, daily 9am–6pm.

Ouwehand's Animal Park
Rhenen
Grebbeweg 109, tel. (08376) 1 91 10
Open: April to September, 9am–6pm; October to March, 9am–5pm.
Features: parrot show, train trip by monorail.

Blijdorp Zoo (see A to Z, Rotterdam)
Rotterdam
Van Aerssenlaan 49, tel. (010) 4 65 43 33
Open: November to April, daily 9am–5pm; May to October, 9am–6pm.

Aquadome
Scharendijke
Randweg 13, tel. (01117) 20 38 and 16 39
Open: end of March to mid July, in September and autumn holidays, daily 10am–6pm; mid July to August, 10am–8pm.
An aquarium, lying half under water, with North Sea flora and fauna.

Maps

In addition to the general map of the Netherlands it is helpful, particularly for motorists, to have additional maps on a larger scale. The following is a selection.

Michelin map 408: Netherlands
1:400,000
BV map of Waterways in the Netherlands

Bartholomew–RV Euromap: Netherlands
1:300,000
Kümmerly & Frey: Netherlands

AA/Baedeker: Netherlands
1:250,000
Roger Lascelles: Netherlands

Markers

Hallwag: Netherlands
Bartholomew, Easy Fold Map: Netherlands

1:200,000   ANWB: three sheets covering northern, central and southern Netherlands
              Michelin: maps 210, 211 and 212

1:100,000   ANWB: Toeristenkaart, 14 sheets (showing cycle tracks):
              Sheet 1: Noord-Holland, with the island of Texel
              Sheet 2: Friesland West, Midden (Central) and Noordoostpolder,
                       with the islands of Ameland, Terschelling and Vlieland
              Sheet 3: Groningen and Drenthe Noord, with the island of
                       Schiermonnikoog
              Sheet 4: Drenthe Midden (Central) and Zuid (South)
              Sheet 5: Randstad Noord and the Gooi, with Amsterdam, Haarlem
                       and Hilversum
              Sheet 6: Randstad Midden (Central) and Zuid (South), with The
                       Hague, Delft and Rotterdam
              Sheet 7: Veluwe, with Zwolle, Apeldoorn, Arnhem and Nijmegen
              Sheet 8: Salland and Twente, with Enschede and Zwolle
              Sheet 9: Achterhoek and Münsterland West
              Sheet 10: Zeeland Noord, Midden (Central) and Noord-Brabant West
              Sheet 11: Noord-Brabant Midden (Central), Oost (East) and Limburg
                        Noord, with Eindhoven
              Sheet 12: Zeeuws en Belgisch Vlaanderen (Dutch and Belgian
                        Flanders)
              Sheet 13: Limburg Midden (Central) and Belgian Kempen
              Sheet 14: Limburg Zuid (South), Liège and the northern Eifel

ANWB   ANWB Waterkaarten (water sports maps) of the Netherlands: 18 sheets at
Waterkaarten various scales from 1:125,000 to 1:10,000.

Leisure maps Various tourist information offices (VVV) publish leisure maps and water
and water sports sports guides for their area. Thus a leisure map of the Frisian lakes can be
guides   obtained from the Friesland VVV office, and a water sports guide to the
              Delta area of Zuid-Holland and Zeeland from the VVV office for either of
              these provinces.

Sailing guide The ANWB publishes a sailing guide (in Dutch), the "Almanak voor Water-
              toerisme", in two volumes. Volume 1 contains sailing regulations and
              general information, and volume 2 lists towns and sailing waters in alpha-
              betical order.

Markets

In addition to the regular markets held weekly, or sometimes more than
once a week, there are numerous special markets held at particular times,
all offering colourful scenes which attract many visitors. The following is
merely a selection.

Alkmaar   Kaasmarkt (cheese market), Waagplein
              Mid April to mid September, Fri. 10am–12 noon

Amsterdam   Market in Albert Cuypstraat (foodstuffs and textiles)
              Mon.–Sat. 9am–5pm

              Antiekmarkt de Looier (antiques), Elandsgracht 109
              Mon.–Thur. and Sat. 11am–5pm

              Art market, Thorbeckeplein
              April to mid October, Sun. 12 noon–6pm (in July, August and September
              also on Sat.)

Flower market

Cheese market (Alkmaar)

Boerenmarkt (farm market), Noordermarkt
Sat. 10am–3pm

Book market, Oudemanhuispoort
Mon.–Sat. 10am–4pm

Flea market (new products as well as junk), Waterlooplein
Mon.–Sat. 10am–4pm

Stamp market, Nieuwezijds Voorburgwal
Wed. and Sat. 1–4pm

Lamb market   Den Burg
Mon. (usually combined with the weekly market)   (Texel)

Market in Grote Markt and Scheffersplein   Dordrecht
Fri. 8.30am–12.30pm, Sat. 8.30am–4pm

Cheese market   Edam
Mid July to mid August, usually Wed. 10am–12 noon.
(The famous Edam cheeses are brought to market in boats of traditional
type and carried to the weigh-house, which dates from 1778, by porters in
period costume).

Cheese market (combined with auction of art, antiques and traditional   Gouda
handicrafts), Marktplein
Last week in June to last week in August, Thur. 9.30am–12.30pm

In addition to the weekly market and the flower market (see below) there   Groningen
are a flea market, a fruit and vegetable market and livestock markets.

Folk market   Haarlem
Whit Sunday. The market begins at night, and in accordance with an old
tradition children buy a small pot plant for their parents during the night.

Cheese-porters, Alkmaar

The Hague	Market of antiques, curios and books (including antiquarian books, old pictures, mirrors, furniture and crockery), Lange Voorhout Mid May to end of September, Thur. and Sun. 9am–9pm
	Stamp market, Amicitia Building, Westeinde 15 Sat. 12 noon–5pm Also in Paleisstraat/Noordeinde, Wed. afternoon and Sat. morning
	Fish auction Mon.–Sat. 7–10am
Hoorn	Hartje Hoorn Markten July to mid August, every Wed. (A folk market, with dance groups and demonstrations of traditional crafts)
Leiden	Market along the Nieuwe Rijn canal Wed. and Sat. 9am–5pm
Maastricht	Wednesday market, Markt Wed. 8am–1pm
	Friday market, Markt Fri. 8am–1pm
	Junk market, Stationsstraat (opposite station) Sat. 10am–4pm
Purmerend	Cheese market First week in July to end of August, Thur. 11am–1pm
Rotterdam	Market of antiques, curios and general goods, in and around Mariniersweg Tue. and Sat. 9am–5pm

Stamp, coin and book market, Grotekerkplein
Tue. and Sat. 9.30am–4pm

Sunday market (art, books and antiques), Schiedamsedijk
End of April to end of September, Sun. 11am–5pm

West Frisian folk market (folk dancing, old-style carts)   Schagen
End of June to end of August, Thur. 9am–2pm

Markets in Stevinstraat, Thur. 9am–4.30pm; Leyweg, Tue. 8am–5pm; and   Scheveningen
Loosduinse Hoofdstraat, Wed. 9am–4.30pm

Antiques market in Ossekop, Voorstraat 19   Utrecht
Fri. and Sat. 9am–5pm
Cloth market, Breedstraat
Sat. 8am–1pm

Horse market, Stock Market Hall, Sartreweg
Mon. 7am–12 noon

Junk market, Willemstraat
Sat. 8am–2pm

Livestock and poultry market, Stock Market Hall, Sartreweg
Thur. 7am–1pm

Stamp market and exchange, Vismarkt
Sat. 12 noon–5pm

Zuidlaardermarkt (the largest horse market in western Europe), Brink   Zuidlaren
Mid October

Livestock market, Grote Markt   Zwolle
Fri.
(Many countrypeople in traditional costume).

Flower Markets

In many Dutch towns there are flower and plant markets, held weekly or
oftener throughout the year. The following is a selection.

Havik, Fri. 7am–1pm   Amersfoort

Amstelveld, Mon. 10am–12 noon   Amsterdam
(plants and herbs for gardens and balconies; house plants)

Singel, Mon.–Sat. 9am–5pm
Some of the flower-sellers are on houseboats (a "floating flower market").

Hippolytusbuurt, Thur. 8am–5pm   Delft

Tue.–Sat. 8am–5pm (in October only until 4pm)   Groningen

During the summer, Sat. 9am–5pm   Haarlem

Janskerkhof (flower and plant market), Sat. 7am–4pm   Utrecht

Oude Gracht (flower market), Sat. 8am–5pm

Christmas Markets in Limburg Province

Of the traditional Christmas markets in the province of Limburg the one in   Heerlen
Heerlen is the largest. Large numbers of wooden booths offer a variety of

wares for sale, and many Christmas cribs (Nativity scenes) are set up in squares in the town as well as in churches.

A leaflet can be obtained from the Limburg VVV office or from the local VVV office in Valkenburg indicating where these cribs can be seen.

See also Events

Military Cemeteries

Information about British and Commonwealth military cemeteries of the Second World War in the Netherlands can be obtained from the Commonwealth War Graves Commission, 2 Marlow Road, Maidenhead, Berks SL6 7DX, tel. (0628) 34221. The Commission will be glad to help in tracing particular graves, and help and advice can also be obtained from the Commission's office in Belgium: Elverdingsestraat 82, B–8900 Ieper, tel. (057) 20 01 18 and 20 57 18.

Motoring in the Netherlands

Roads

The road network of the Netherlands is modern and comprehensive, bringing all destinations throughout the country within easy reach. Even minor country roads are in excellent condition.

Motorways

Much of the road system is now of motorway (*autosnelweg*) standard, and almost all the major towns are linked by motorways. Almost the whole of the motorway system has hard shoulders.

Motorways are designated by red A numbers. Those which form part of the European highways network also have green E numbers.

When entering a motorway priority must be given to traffic on the motorway. Where the motorway is entered by a short filter lane there is a blue sign with the legend "Korte invoegstrook" below the "Give way" sign.

Trunk roads

The main national highways (*autowegen*) have yellow N numbers.

Road conditions

Information about road conditions (weather, traffic hold-ups) can be obtained by telephoning the ANWB (see below) in the Hague: tel. (070) 3 31 31 31 (24-hour service).

Traffic Regulations

N.B.

Drivers contravening the road traffic regulations can expect heavy fines.

General

As in the rest of continental Europe, traffic travels on the right, with overtaking on the left. At the intersection of roads of equal status trams have priority. Fast traffic has priority over slow traffic (mopeds, cyclists) except on main roads.

Parking

Parking on yellow lines is prohibited. Cars must not park overnight in public car parking places; for motor caravans and mobile homes permission must be obtained from the police or the municipal authorities.

Children

Children under 12 must sit in the rear seats of a car.

Alcohol

The blood alcohol limit is 0.50%.

Warning triangle

All vehicles must carry a warning triangle.

Belts must be worn by drivers and front seat passengers. | Seat belts

Full or dipped headlights must be used between half an hour after sunset and an hour before sunrise. They must also be switched on during the day when weather conditions make this necessary. | Lights

Speed limits

Built-up areas: usually 50km p.h./31 m.p.h.
Motorways: 120km p.h./75 m.p.h. unless otherwise indicated (cars with trailers 80km p.h./50 m.p.h.)
Expressways (blue sign with white car): 100km p.h./62 m.p.h. (cars with trailers 80km p.h./50 m.p.h.)
Other roads: 80 m.p.h./50 m.p.h.

In "quiet traffic areas" (marked by a sign showing a white house on a blue ground) vehicles must travel at walking speed.

Particular care is required at the numerous bascule bridges. Canals are frequently spanned by humpbacked bridges which may be difficult for mobile homes and trailer caravans to negotiate. | Bridges

Tolls are payable at certain bridges and tunnels (e.g. the Zeeland Bridge, the Kil Tunnel, the Prins Willem Alexander Bridge). Drivers should make sure that they have the necessary small change. | Bridge and tunnel tolls

Cycles and mopeds are not allowed on motorways. They must use either the (N-numbered) national highways or specially marked cycleways. | Cycles and mopeds

In view of the large numbers of cyclists using the roads in the Netherlands motorists must drive with particular care.

Motorcyclists and their passengers must wear helmets. | Helmets

Fuel

Petrol stations all over the country sell lead-free petrol (*loodvrije benzine*) in two grades, Super-Plus (98 octane) and Euro-Super (95 octane). | Lead-free petrol

Standard-grade leaded petrol is no longer sold; only Super grade (98 octane), diesel fuel and LPG (liquefied petroleum gas). | Leaded petrol

Motorists can take in, duty-free, a spare can of petrol containing up to 10 litres (just over 2 gallons). | Spare cans

Note-operated petrol pumps in the Netherlands accept 10-guilder and sometimes 25-guilder notes. | Note-operated petrol pumps

Dutch Motoring Organisations

The Royal Dutch Touring Club (Koninklijke Nederlandse Toeristenbond) was originally a cycling association, the Algemene Nederlandse Wielrijdersbond: hence the initials ANWB by which it is always known. | ANWB

Head office in The Hague:
Wassenaarseweg 220,
NL–2596 EC, tel. (0703) 14 71 47

The ANWB has offices in over 40 towns in the Netherlands, in Alkmaar, Amersfoort, Amstelveen, Amsterdam, Apeldoorn, Arnhem, Assen, Bergen op Zoom, Beverwijk, Breda, Den Helder, Deventer, Doetinchem, Dordrecht, Ede, Eindhoven, Emmen, Enschede, Gouda, Groningen, Haarlem, Heerlen, 's-Hertogenbosch, Hilversum, Hoogeveen, Hoogvliet, IJmuiden, Leeuwarden, Leiden, Lelystad, Maastricht, Middelburg, Nieuwegein, Nijmegen, Roermond, Rotterdam, Schiedam, Terneuzen, Tilburg, Utrecht, Venlo, Zaandam, Zeist and Zwolle.

ANWB offices supply tourist information and sell a wide range of maps and plans.

KNAC

Koninklijke Nederlandse Automobielclub (KNAC)
Westvlietweg 118
NL–2260 AK Leidschendam
tel. (0703) 99 74 51

Breakdown Assistance

ANWB road patrols (the Wegenwacht, "Road Watch"), operate throughout most of the Netherlands. In the event of a breakdown the driver should get the car to the edge of the road, or off it, and place a warning triangle a short distance to the rear. A Wegenwacht patrol should then be stopped or a telephone call made to the nearest ANWB office.

Breakdown assistance is provided free on production of the AA 5-Star Service voucher booklet. However in certain parts of the country (Eindhoven, Enschede, Nijmegen, Oss, Rotterdam, Terneuzen, Zeeuws-Vlaanderen, Zwolle and the islands of Texel, Terschelling and Ameland), where service is provided by contract garages, the assistance must be paid for, either by AIT credit vouchers or in cash, and a claim for the cost made against the 5-Star Service.

Museums

The most important museums in the Netherlands are referred to in the various entries in the A to Z section of this guide. Information about opening times (see Business Hours) and admission charges can be obtained from local tourist information offices (VVV).

Museum guide

A useful guide to museums in the Netherlands is "Nederland Museumland", published by the Stichting Museumjaarkaart (for address see below), which can be bought in the larger museums, in VVV offices and in bookshops.

Museum card

If you intend to visit many museums it is worth while buying a museum card (*museumkaart, museumjaarkart;* reduced rates for young people and senior citizens), valid for the calendar year, which gives free admission to some 350 museums in the Netherlands (with small additional charges for special exhibitions).

The card can be obtained on application to the Netherlands Bureau of Tourism. A passport photograph is required.

Further information can be obtained from the Stichting Museumjaarkaart, Groenhazengracht 2C, NL–2311 VT Leiden, tel. (071), 13 32 65, 13 30 68 and 14 13 04.

Principal museums

Altogether there are over 800 museums in the Netherlands, covering a very wide range of interests. The most important museums are the Rijksmuseum (with famous paintings by Rembrandt), the Van Gogh Museum and the Jewish Historical Museum in Amsterdam; the Paleis Het Loo (once a favourite residence of Kings William I and II and Queen Wilhelmina) at Apeldoorn; the Municipal Museum (large collection of works by Mondriaan) and the Mauritshuis (17th century Dutch masters, etc.) in The Hague; the Frans Hals Museum in Haarlem; and the Kröller-Müller Museum (sculpture park) at Otterlo.

Specialised Museums

See Railways

See Postal, etc., Services

There are also museums in a number of castles and palaces (see Castles and Palaces).

There are numerous other interesting – and sometimes surprising – specialised museums, for example:
Amsterdam: Tropical Museum, Madame Tussaud's Waxworks;
Rotterdam: Maritime Museum, Toy Museum;
St Oedenrode, near Eindhoven: Jukebox Museum;
Doesburg, east of Arnhem: Mustard Museum
Alkmaar: Cheese Museum;
Delden (Overijssel): Salt and Saltcellar Museum;
Hellendoorn, between Enschede and Zwolle: Ice Museum;
Utrecht: Musical Box and Barrel Organ Museum;
Bunschoten (Utrecht province): Costume Museum.

The loss of so many old buildings, particularly in country areas, has stimulated a movement for the preservation of these relics of the past, and there are now many open-air museums bringing together characteristic old houses and farms, well restored, in addition to furniture, domestic equipment and craft tools and implements.

Particularly popular are the Netherlands Open-Air Museum (Nederlands Openluchtmuseum) at Arnhem; the Zuiderzee Museum (which also includes a 6 hectare/15 acre nature reserve: meadowland, with wild orchids; birds of prey; duck trap, etc.) at Enkhuizen; and the Biblical Open-Air Museum (Heilig Land Stichting) near Nijmegen.

Bonnefanten Museum, Maastricht

491

Nature Reserves and National Parks

Some 350,000 hectares/865,000 acres of the Netherlands are occupied by forest and woodland and over 150,000 hectares/370,000 acres by natural landscapes including dunes, beaches, heathland and bog country.

Much of this natural landscape is controlled by the Staatsbosbeheer (Forestry Commission). Information about the Commission's visitor centres and maps for walkers (*voetspoorkaarten*) can be obtained from the following addresses:

Staatsbosbeheer
Griffioenlaan 2,
Postbus 20020
NL–3502 LA Utrecht
tel. (030) 85 24 02 and 85 91 11

Educatief Centrum Staatsbosbeheer
Kasteel Groeneveld
Groeneveld 2
NL–3744 ML Baarn
tel. (02154) 2 04 46

In addition to this government body there are some 600 private organisations concerned with the protection of nature, which acquire areas of unspoiled natural country and run them as protected nature reserves. The oldest of these organisations is:

Vereniging tot Behoud van Natuurmonumenten
(Association for the Protection of Natural Monuments)
Noordereinde 60
NL–1243 JJ 's-Graveland
tel. (035) 6 20 04

Visitor centres

For information about the topography, flora and fauna of a particular area application should be made to the visitor centre for the area, which can also supply walking and cycling maps showing paths and trails (signposted by the white mushroom sign). Information can also be obtained from local VVV and ANWB offices.

Long-distance trails

There are also waymarked long-distance trails (*lange-afstands-wandelpaden*, LAW). Maps showing these routes can be obtained from:

Stichting Lange-Afstands-Wandelpaden
Buxtehudelaan 1
Postbus 433
NL–3430 AK Nieuewegein
tel. (03402) 4 70 73

Regulations

Notices at the entrances to National Parks and nature reserves draw attention to the regulations for the protection of nature which must be observed by visitors.

Opening times

National Parks and nature reserves are closed at night.

National Parks

The National Parks are large areas of land (minimum 1000 hectares/2500 acres) which are of particular interest for their topography and of importance for the preservation of the native flora and fauna. They are listed below in geographical order from north to south.

Area: *c.* 5000 hectares/12,500 acres; dunes, heath, woodland; birds
Bezoekerscentrum (visitor centre) "De Centrale"
NL–9166 LK Schiermonnikoog
tel. (05195) 61

**Schier-
monnikoog**
(island in the
Waddenzee,
Friesland)

Area: *c.* 1200 hectares/3000 acres; heathland
Informatiecentrum (information centre) "De Schaapskooi Dwingelose Heide"
Bendersee 38, NL–7963 RA Ruinen
tel. (05221) 14 78

**Het Dwin-
gelderveld**
(Drenthe)

Kennemerduinen (west of Bloemendaal-Santpoort, near Haarlem)
Area: 1250 hectares/3125 acres; dunes, dune lagoon, deciduous and coniferous woodland, game and birds
Nationaal Park De Kennemerduinen
Bezoekerscentrum "Van Floedlijn tot Binnenduin", Zeeweg
Militairenweg 4, NL–2051 EV Overveen
tel. (023) 25 76 53
Information also from VVV offices in Haarlem, IJmuiden and Zandvoort

**De Kennemer-
duinen**
(Noord-Holland)

Area: *c.* 3000 hectares/7500 acres; lakes and bogs; water birds
Bezoekerscentrum "Weerribben"
Hogeweg 26, NL–8376 EM Ossenzijl
tel. (05617) 2 72

Area: *c.* 6000 hectares/15,000 acres; forest, heathland, drift sand; game
preserve
Nationaal Park De Hoge Veluwe
Bezoekerscentrum "De Aanschouw"
Houtkampweg, NL–6731 AV Otterlo
tel. (08382) 16 27

De Hoge Veluwe
(Gelderland)

Bezoekerscentrum "Zandenbos"
Eperweg 132, NL–8072 PL Nunspeet
tel. (03412) 29 96

Information also from VVV offices in Arnhem, Apeldoorn, Ede and Otterlo

Area: *c.* 4800 hectares/12,000 acres; sand, woodland, heath; game preserve (part of Deelerwoud)
Nationaal Park De Veluwezoom
Bezoekerscentrum "De Hoerne"
Heuvenseweg 5A, NL–6991 JE Rheden
tel. (08309) 5 10 23
Information also from VVV offices in Dieren, Velp and Loenen

De Veluwezoom
(Gelderland)

Only part of the Biesbosch, in the west of Noord-Brabant, has been declared a National Park.
Area: *c.* 2000 hectares/5000 acres; a landscape of lagoons traversed by innumerable watercourses; water birds
Information in the province of Noord-Brabant:
Bezoekerscentrum "Drimmelen"
Dorpsstraat 14, NL–4924 BE Drimmelen
tel. (01626) 29 91

De Biesbosch
(Noord-Brabant
and Zuid-
Holland)

Information about the recreation centre and water sports paradise De Hollandse Biesbosch in the province of Zuid-Holland:
Bezoekerscentrum "Merwelanden"
Baanhoekweg 53, NL–3313 LP Dordrecht
tel. (078) 21 13 11
Information also from VVV Dordrecht

De Groote Peel (Noord-Brabant)	Area: *c.* 1000 hectares/2500 acres; bog and marshland Moostijk 28, NL–6035 RB Ospel tel. (04951) 4 14 97 Information also from VVV Eindhoven

Other Nature Reserves

Of the numerous other nature reserves in the Netherlands only a selection of the most interesting ones along the Dutch coast can be listed here.

Boswachterij Terschelling	Some 10,000 hectares/25,000 acres (five nature reserves) Dunes, coniferous woodland, heathland; many water birds Information from VVV in West-Terschelling
Boswachterij Vlieland	Some 1500 hectares/3750 acres (three nature reserves) Dunes, coniferous woodland, heathland; ducks and black-winged stilts Bezoekerscentrum Vlieland Dorpsstraat 150, NL–8899 AN Vlieland tel. (05621) 7 00
Boswachterij Texel	Some 4000 hectares/10,000 acres (three nature reserves) Dunes, heathland, woodland, lakes; sandpipers, meadow birds Ecomare (Waddenzee and North Sea ecological centre) Ruyslaan 92, NL–1796 AZ De Koog (Texel) tel. (02228) 7 41
Boswachterij Schoorl	2000 hectares/5000 acres (seven nature reserves) Dunes, coniferous woodland, heathland, sand-drifts, lakes; many species of birds Bezoekerscentrum "Het Zandspoor" Oorsprongsweg 1, NL–1871 HA Schoorl tel. (02209) 33 52
Noordhollands Duinreservat	5000 hectares/12,500 acres between Wijk aan Zee and Bergen Dunes, deciduous and coniferous woodland, heathland, orchids; birds Information from VVV in Bergen and Wijk aan Zee
Amsterdamse Waterleiding- duinen	Some 4000 hectares/10,000 acres between Noordwijk and Zandfoort Dunes, deciduous and coniferous woodland, orchids; game and many species of birds Bezoekerscentrum "De Oranjekom" Teneover Vogelenzangseweg 21B, NL–2114 BA Vogelenzang tel. (023) 28 80 50
Hollands Duin, Boswachterij Wassenaar	Some 1700 hectares/4250 acres extending from north of The Hague to Katwijk Dunes and dune lakes Bezoekerscentrum "Meijendel" Meijendelseweg 36, NL–2243 GN Wassenaar tel. (01751) 1 72 76
German–Dutch Nature Park	See A to Z, Duits Nederlandse Natuurpark

Newspapers and Periodicals

Foreign newspapers	British and other foreign newspapers are readily available in the Netherlands, and at least in the larger towns can usually be bought on the day of publication.
Dutch newspapers	Het Parool, De Telegraaf, Trouw, De Volkskrant (Amsterdam) Haagsche Courant/Het Binnenhof (The Hague) Eindhovens Dagblad/Helmonds Dagblad (Eindhoven) Nieuwsblad van het Noorden (Groningen)

Dutch and foreign newspapers

Utrechts Nieuwsblad (Houten)
Leeuwarder Courant (Leeuwarden)
De Limburger (Maastricht)
De Gelderlander/De Nieuwe Krant (Nijmegen)
Algemeen Dagblad, NRC Handelsblad, Rotterdams Nieuwsblad/Het Vrije
Volk (Rotterdam)

On a recent estimate some 4000 periodicals are published in the
Netherlands.
    Periodicals

The monthly English-language "Holland Herald" gives information about
what's on throughout the Netherlands.

Algemeen Nederlands Persbureau (ANP)
    News agency

Night Life

See Casinos

Opening Times

See Business Hours

Postal and Telephone Services

Postal Services

Post Office Headquarters
Postbus 30000
NL–2500 GA Den Haag
    Information

Postal and Telephone Services

Post office signs

Telephone kiosk

Opening times

Post offices in the larger towns are usually open Mon.–Fri. 8.30am–5pm, and frequently also on Sat. 8.30am–12 noon. In smaller places they are closed between 12.30 and 1.30pm. Some post offices stay open later on the late shopping evening (see Business Hours).

Postage rates (Jan.1992)

Post box

Letters up to 20 grams:
75 cents within the Netherlands and to Britain, Ireland, Austria, Belgium, Cyprus, Denmark, Finland, France (including overseas territories), Germany, Greece, Iceland, Italy, Liechtenstein, Luxembourg, Malta, Monaco, Norway, Portugal, San Marino, Spain, Sweden, Switzerland, Turkey, the Vatican and Yugoslavia; 1 fl to other European countries; and 1.50 fl to all other countries.

Postcards: 55 cents to the countries named in the previous paragraph, 75 cents to all other countries.

Information about other rates can be obtained in post offices or by dialling 00 17.

Telegrams

Telegrams are accepted in post offices.

Telephone

Trunk calls from the Netherlands to other countries can be made either from a post office or a public telephone kiosk. When dialling from a telephone kiosk insert a coin (at least 25 cents), wait for the dialling tone, dial the international code 09, wait for a further dialling tone and then dial the country code, the area code (omitting a prefixed zero) and the subscriber's number.

International dialling codes

To the Netherlands:
from the United Kingdom: 010 31
from the United States or Canada: 011 31

Street scene in The Hague on National Day

From the Netherlands:
to the United Kingdom: 09 44
to the United States or Canada: 09 1

A call to the United Kingdom costs 1.10 fl a minute; to the United States or   Charges
Canada 2.60 fl a minute between 10am amd 7pm, 2.30 fl a minute between
7pm and 10am.
Calls from a hotel may cost up to three times as much.

Calls via the operator. Dial 06 04 10

Information (international calls). Dial 00 18

Public Holidays

Official public holidays in the Netherlands are January 1st (New Year's
Day), Good Friday, Easter Monday, April 30th (National Day), Ascension
Day, Whit Monday, December 25th and 26th (Christmas).

National Day, Koninginnendag (Queen's Day), is on April 30th.   National Day
The present queen, Beatrix, was crowned on April 30th 1980, the birthday
of her mother Queen Juliana, and the anniversary is celebrated in towns
and villages throughout the country with processions, concerts, military
parades and fairs or markets. A special feature of the celebrations in
Amsterdam is the Vrijmarkt (Free Market), when anyone can set up a stall
anywhere in the city and sell his wares; the market offers a particularly
lively spectacle in the Jordaan district in the old town.
In the larger towns National Day ends with a firework display.

On public holidays (except Good Friday) most shops are closed. On days of
public commemoration such as May 4th (remembering those who died in

497

the Second World War) and May 5th (liberation from German occupation) they remain open.

Public Transport

In the course of a year the various forms of public transport in the Netherlands carry some 1000 million passengers. The country is served by a dense network of local and regional systems which provide frequent bus and tram services.
In small places with populations between 1000 and 2000 the government subsidises "neighbourhood bus services".
There are usually bus stops close to railway stations.

GVB Amsterdam

Public transport in Amsterdam is provided by the municipal transport system:
Gemeentevervoerbedrijf Amsterdam (GVB)
Stationsplein, tel. (020) 6 27 27 27
(information by telephone Mon.–Fri. 7am–10.30pm, Sat. and Sun. 8am–10.30pm)

Underground

There are underground systems (Metros) in Amsterdam and Rotterdam.

Timetables

Public transport systems in towns operate from 6am to 11pm or midnight, in smaller places until about 10pm. Information about local timetables can be obtained from VVV offices.

Transport zones

Public transport systems in the Netherlands (including the large towns) are divided into zones, and the same zonal fares apply throughout the country. A plan showing the division into zones is displayed at bus and tram stops.

"Strip tickets" (*strippenkaarten*)

Tickets for public transport in the Netherlands are sold in the form of *strippenkaarten* ("strip tickets", each consisting of 15 strips) valid on buses, trams, metros and trains (2nd class) within the cities of Amsterdam, The Hague, Rotterdam, Utrecht and Zoetermeer.
Strip tickets can be bought at railway stations, public transport offices, post offices and some VVV offices, and from tobacconists. They can also be bought from the driver of a bus or tram, but at a rather higher price. (Drivers also sell packs of 2, 3 or 10 strip tickets.)
The strips must be cancelled by the driver or by the passenger in a yellow cancelling machine. The number of strips required depends on the number of zones travelled through: one strip as the basic fare, plus an additional strip for each zone (e.g. 3 strips if the journey covers two zones).

National day ticket

A national day ticket, covering travel on all tram, bus (except KLM buses) and metro systems can also be obtained.

See also Air Travel, Railways

Radio and Television

Radio and television services in the Netherlands are provided by a number of independent broadcasting companies, which put on a wide variety of programmes. A government Commissioner for Broadcasting is responsible for the distribution of finance and the allocation of transmission times (including cable services), and also promotes co-operation between the supra-regional broadcasting companies and the Dutch Broadcasting Production Company (Nederlandse Omroepproduktie Bedrijf, NOB).

Nederlandse Omroep Stichting

The various broadcasting companies are members of the Dutch Broadcasting Foundation (Nederlandse Omroep Stichting, NOS), with headquarters in Hilversum, which represents all the Dutch broadcasting companies in dealings with broadcasting systems in other countries and also produces its own radio and television programmes.

There are five radio transmitters in the Netherlands. They can all be received throughout the country on VHF and medium waves (in some areas on only one of these frequencies).

Radio 3 transmits mainly pop music, Radio 4 mainly classical music.

Netherlands World Radio (Radio Nederland Wereldomroep) beams programmes on short waves throughout the world in Dutch, English, French, Spanish, Portuguese and other languages.
Detailed information and programmes can be obtained from:
Radio Nederland Wereldomroep
Postbus 222, NL-1200 JG Hilversum

In cases of extreme emergency Dutch radio will transmit messages for visitors travelling in the Netherlands. Information from motoring organisations (see Motoring) or the police (see Emergency Calls).

There are three television channels – Nederland 1, 2 and 3. Colour television (PAL system) started in 1967.

Almost all households in the Netherlands have access to cable television, enabling them to receive foreign as well as Dutch programmes.

Satellite television is also available in the Netherlands.

Radio

Dutch
World Radio

Emergency calls
for tourists

Television

Cable television

Satellite
television

Railways

The first railway line in the Netherlands ran between Amsterdam and Haarlem in 1839. The Dutch railway system, operated by Netherlands Railways (Nederlandse Spoorwegen, NS) now has 3000km/1865 miles of line, travelled by more than 4000 passenger trains daily.

The most important railway junction in the country is Utrecht, with connections in all directions.

Netherlands Railways
25–28 Buckingham Gate
London SW1E 6LD
tel. (071) 630 1735

A useful brochure, "Travelling by Rail in Holland", can be obtained from Netherlands Railways.

There are direct connections between the main towns in the Netherlands by Intercity and express trains.
There are also local services in the Intercity network, stopping at every station.
On main lines there are between four and eight trains (in both directions) every hour throughout the day; on branch lines there are usually at least two trains every hour (in both directions).

The Schiphollijn (Schiphol Line) runs fast services from Schiphol Airport to Amsterdam, The Hague and Rotterdam. See Airports.
On weekdays the trains run at 15 minute intervals from 5am to 1am on the following morning, on public holidays from 7am. During the night they run at hourly intervals.

Yellow timetables, showing the time of departure and platform number, are displayed at all railway stations in the Netherlands (more than 300 in number).

**Netherlands
Railways**

**Nederlandse
Spoorwegen**

Information
in Britain

Services

Schiphollijn

Railways in the Netherlands

—— **Main lines**
— **Branch lines**

Waddenzee

North Sea

IJsselmeer

© Baedeker

NETHERLANDS

Leeuwarden
Groningen
Sneek
Assen
Den Helder
Meppel
Alkmaar
Zwolle
Haarlem
Deventer
AMSTERDAM
Enschede
Leiden
DEN HAAG
Utrecht
Arnhem
Rotterdam
Nijmegen
's-Hertogenbosch
Breda
Eindhoven
Middelburg
Maastricht

An annual timetable (running from the end of May) can be bought at most railway stations, and can also be obtained from the Netherlands Railways office in London. A free booklet (in Dutch and English) giving the timetables of Intercity trains is available at railway stations.

Fares

There are tickets for 1st and 2nd class. A day return ticket is cheaper than two separate tickets for the outward and inward journeys. See also Reduced Fares, below.

All types of ticket can be ordered from the Netherlands Railways office in London or through a travel agent.

Transport of bicycles

Bicycles can be hired at railway stations and transported by rail. For full details ask Netherlands Railways for their "Bicycle Fact Sheet".

Art on the railway line

Along the railway line between Zwolle and Emmen is a kind of open-air art gallery, initiated by Netherlands Railways and the Kunstlijn (Art Line) Foundation. The works of art are displayed at more than ten stations or in their immediate vicinity; in some cases they can be reached on a short footpath or cycleway.

The Netherlands Railway Museum (Nederlandse Spoorwegmuseum) is housed in the old Maliebaan Station in Utrecht.

Railway Museum

The Train–Taxi project, which under present plans is due to continue until 1993, provides taxi services to and from railway stations for the exclusive use of rail passengers. It operates in all provincial capitals with Intercity stations, except in Amsterdam, The Hague, Rotterdam and Utrecht, which have comprehensive public transport services.
Passengers who want a taxi from the station must obtain a Train-Taxi voucher from the ticket office of the station on presentation of a valid railway ticket; there is a flat-rate charge of 5 fl, covering the whole area within the town's boundaries. It is also possible to book a train-taxi to the station if you have purchased a voucher.

Train–Taxi

Package air tours and "camping flights" can be booked at the Netherlands Railways desk at Schiphol Airport: tel. (020) 6 01 94 94 (24-hour service).

"Last-minute flights"

Trips on steam railways are becoming increasingly popular in the Netherlands. Information: Netherlands Railways (address above). The following are examples of the trips on offer:

Steam railways

Through the Veluwe forests (Gelderland province). Information: Veluwsche Stoomtrein Maatschaapij, Dorpsstraat 140, Apeldoorn, tel. (08338) 5 13 14.

From Hoorn to Medemblik (Noord-Holland). Information: Museum Stoomtram Hoorn–Medemblik, tel. (02290) 1 48 62.

Through Zuid-Beveland (Zeeland). Information: Stoomtrein Goes–Oudelande, tel. (01100) 2 83 07.

Reduced Fares

Leaflets giving the fares for rail travel within the Netherlands, and reduced rates for senior citizens, families, groups and the disabled, can be obtained at ticket offices in railway stations.

Children under 4 travel free. For children between 4 and 11 travelling unaccompanied there is a reduction of 40% on the adult fare. There are also flat-rate Railrunner tickets which allow up to three children between 4 and 11 accompanied by an adult to travel at token fares equivalent to about 30 pence.

Children

Passengers with a British Railcard for senior citizens can buy a Rail Europ Senior card (obtainable through British Rail) entitling them to a 50% reduction on ordinary single fares and 40% off return fares.

Senior citizens

One-day and seven-day Rovers (beginning on any day) cover unlimited travel on the whole Dutch railway network. A passport photograph, or the number of the passenger's passport, is required.

One-day and seven-day Rovers

This ticket, issued in conjunction with a one-day or seven-day Rover, allows unlimited travel on all buses, trams and metros.

Public Transport Link Rover

The Teenage Rover ticket, for young people up to 18, covers unlimited rail travel on any four days within a period of ten days, during June, July and August. The Teenage Rover Plus also includes buses, trams and metros.

Teenage Rover

The Holland Summer Tour Rail Pass covers unrestricted rail travel on any three days within a period of ten days, during July and August only.

Holland Summer Tour

A Benelux Tourrail Card covers travel on any five days within a period of seventeen days in the three Benelux countries (Belgium, the Netherlands

Benelux Tourrail Card

	and Luxembourg). There are two categories, junior (4–25 years) and senior (26 and over).
Return tickets	Day return tickets: see above. Weekend return tickets (valid Friday to Sunday) offer a 40% reduction on the normal fare. They are available for travel to and from Alkmaar, Amsterdam, Apeldoorn, Breda, Castricum, Eindhoven, Groningen, The Hague, Den Helder, Harlingen, 's-Hertogenbosch, Hoek van Holland, Leeuwarden, Maastricht, Rotterdam, Utrecht and Zandvoort.
Group tickets	There are reductions for groups of ten or more people travelling together, and also Multi-Rover tickets covering one day's unlimited travel over the whole rail network for groups of two to six people.
Day trips	Netherlands Railways offer a range of more than 75 day rail trips (*dagtochten*). Tickets (*dagtochtkaartjes*) can be bought at any Dutch railway station.
Keukenhof, Lisse	During the flower season (March–May) combined rail/bus tickets, with admission tickets for Keukenhof, can be bought at many railway stations.

Restaurants

General	The Netherlands offer a wide and very varied range of restaurants. Most hotels have restaurants. In the larger establishments in the main tourist centres the cuisine is of standard international type. See also Food and Drink
Prices	Prices in restaurants, snack bars, etc., include a service charge (see also Tipping) and value-added tax.
Alliance Gastronomique Néerlandaise ALLIANCE GASTRONOMIQUE NÉERLANDAISE	Restaurants which are members of the Alliance Gastronomique Néerlandaise (AGN) meet the highest culinary standards, with cooking of outstanding quality and fine wines. Such restaurants are indicated in the following list with a red star. A booklet listing AGN restaurants is obtainable from: Secretariaat, Alliance Gastronomique Néerlandaise Postbus 237, 5600 AE–Eindhoven tel. (040) 63 11 53
Tourist menu  TOURIST MENU	More than 400 restaurants offer a tourist menu of good quality at a reasonable price. The best of these restaurants are annually awarded a prize, the Silver Fork (De zilveren Vork), by the Netherlands Bureau of Tourism and the Nestlé Food Service. The tourist menu, at present priced at 19.50 fl, comprises a first course, a main dish and a dessert. The price is the same at all restaurants serving a tourist menu (indicated by a sign with the legend "Tourist Menu" and a white fork on a dark blue ground), though the composition of the meal varies. Many of these restaurants will also serve, on request, a "children's menu". A booklet listing restaurants which serve a tourist menu can be obtained from branches of the Netherlands Bureau of Tourism, VVV offices and ANWB offices.

Typical Dutch dishes (Neerlands dis) are served in more than 200 restaurants which display the symbol of a red, white and blue soup tureen. First, second and third prizes (Neerlands Dis Pokal) are awarded annually to such establishments on the basis of quality and service.

A brochure listing Neerlands Dis restaurants can be obtained from branches of the Netherlands Bureau of Tourism, VVV offices and ANWB offices.

In many towns in the Netherlands there are Eastern restaurants specialising in Far Eastern, particularly Chinese, cuisine. It is well known, that nowhere outside Indonesia will you find a better *rijstafel* than in the Netherlands.

There are also many restaurants serving French, Greek, Spanish, Italian and other national cuisines.

The sandy heathland in northern and central Limburg is particularly suited to the growing of asparagus, and about 80% of the asparagus grown in the Netherlands comes from this region. A brochure, "Asparagus Land", with two suggested routes through the asparagus-growing area, hints on serving and eating asparagus and lists of asparagus restaurants can be obtained from local VVV offices.

Restaurants (a Selection)

TM = restaurant serving a tourist menu
ND = Neerlands Dis restaurant
AGN = member of Alliance Gastronomique Néerlandaise

Restaurants of particular quality are distinguished by a star.

De Zijlsterhoeve (TM), Zijlsterweg 5–7.

*Rotisserie Rue Du Bois, Van den Boschstraat 3; De Nachtegaal (TM), Langestraat 100; 't Gulden Vlies (TM), Koorstraat 30.

In Alkmaar–St Pancras: Spoorzicht (TM), Bovenweg 316.

De Stadsherberg (TM), Kerkstraat 2; Postiljon Almelo (TM), Aalderinkssingel 2.

De Aanleg (TM), Scheggertdijk 10; De Hoofdige Boer (ND), Dorpsstraat 38.

Bunga Melati (Indonesian cuisine), Oude Rielseweg 2; Den Brouwer (TM), Raadhuisstraat 1.

Umberto (TM), Graafseweg 699.

Boeddha (Chinese cuisine), Utrechtseweg 2; Dorloté, Bloemendalsestraat 24; Torenrestaurant Sportfondsenbad (TM), Bisschopsweg 175.

*Molen De Dikkert (AGN), Amsterdamseweg 104A; Abina (TM), Amsterdamseweg 193.

*Excelsior (AGN), in Hotel de l'Europe, Nieuwe Doelenstraat 2–8; *De Kersentuin, Dijsselhofplantsoen 7; *Dikker en Thijs, Prinsengracht 444; *Halvemaan, Van Leyenberglaan 20 (Gijsbrecht van Aemstelpark); *Parkrestaurant Rosarium, Amstelpark 1, Europaboulevard; Bodega Keyzer (ND), vam Baerlestraat 96; Bon Appétit (TM), Ceintuurbaan 350; Cajun (Creole cuisine), Ceintuurbaan 260; Chinees-Indisch Restaurant Ling Nam

Restaurants

(TM), Binnen Bantammerstraat 3; David en Goliath (TM), Kalverstraat 92; De Oesterbar (seafood), Leidseplein 10; De Roode Leeuw (ND), Damrak 93–94; Die Port van Cleve (ND), N.Z. Voorburgwal 178; D'Vijff Vlieghen, Spuistraat 298–302; Haesje Claes (ND, TM), N.Z. Voorburgwal 320; Heineken Hoek (TM), Kleine Gartmanplantsoen 1–3; Het Koepelcafé (TM), in Hotel Sonesta, Kattengat 1; Indonesia (Indonesian cuisine), Singel 550; Jacquet (TM), Raadhuisstraat 6; Jama (TM), Jan van Galenstraat 103; Julia (ND), Amstelveenseweg 160; Kopenhagen (Danish cuisine), Rokin 84; Le Pêcheur (fish restaurant), Reguliersdwarsstraat 32; Manchurian (Chinese cuisine), Leidseplein 10A; Norway Inn (TM), Kalverstraat 65–69; Oud Holland (TM), N.Z. Voorburgwal 105; Petit Restaurant Simon (TM), Spuistraat 299; Pier 10, De Ruyterkade, Steiger 10 (at Central Station); Radèn Mas (Indonesian cuisine), Stadhouderskade 6; Rhapsody (TM), Rembrandtsplein 7; Sea Palace (floating restaurant, with fine view of city; Asiatic cuisine), Oosterdokskade 8; 't Swarte Schaep, Korte Leidsewarsstraat 24; Vivaldi's, van Baerlestraat 49.
De Wildeman (Pijlsteg 3, near the Dam) has a "tasting bar".

In Schiphol: Aviorama, Schipholweg 1.

Apeldoorn	*De Echoput (AGN), Amersfoortseweg 86; *De Wilde Pieters, Hoofdstraat 175; De Passage (ND), Arnhemseweg 341; Mandarin (Chinese cuisine), Stationsplein 7; Motel Apeldoorn (ND), J. S. Wilslaan 200.
Appingedam	Passe Partout (ND), Opwierderweg 19.
Arcen	Alt Arce (TM), Raadhuisplein 16.
Arnhem	*Rijzenburg, Koningsweg 17; Carnegie (ND), Stationsplein 39; De Boerderij, Parkweg 2; De Dorsvlegel, Hoogstraat 1; De Menthenberg (ND), Schelmseweg 1A; De Pan (ND), Koningsstraat 67; De Thermiekbel (TM), Zweefvliegcentrum Terlet, Apeldoornseweg 203; Haarhuis (TM), Stationsplein 1; Postiljon Arnhem (TM), Europaweg 25.
Assen	La Belle Epoque, Markt 6; De Nieuwe Brink (ND), Brink 13.
Axel	Sol (ND), Noordstraat 12
Baarle-Nassau	La Gare (TM), Stationsstraat 2–4; Landgoed Schaluinen (TM), Schaluinen 11.
Baarn	De Generaal (ND), Lt. Gen. van Heutzlaan 5; Prins van Oranje, Stationsweg 65.
Balk	Aan de Luts (ND), van Swinderenstraat 42.
Barchem	In de Groene Jager (ND), Ruurloseweg 2.
Beek (Gem. Bergh)	't Heuveltje (TM), St Jansgildestraat 27.
Beek (Limburg)	Pension Traiteur Modern (TM), Stationsstraat 7; restaurant in Altea Hotel Limburg (TM), Vliegveldweg 19.
Beekbergen	Het Lierder Holt (TM), Spoekweg 49; Taveerne Heideheuvel (ND), Hoge Bergweg 30.
Beek en Donk	De Hommel (TM), Oranjelaan 55.
Beetsterzwaag	*Landgoed Lauswolt (AGN), v. Harinxmaweg 10; Boschlust (TM), Beetsterweg 1.
Bennebroek	*De Geleerde Man (AGN), Rijksstraatweg 51.

Palace (TM), Barrier 7.	Bergeijk
De Zilverspar (ND), Breelaan 21.	Bergen
Bergs Koffiehuis De Moyses (TM), Molstraat 1; Eethuis De Koperen Ketel (TM), Bosstraat 9; La Bonne Auberge, Grote Markt 3; Napoli (Italian cuisine), Kerkstraat 10; Old Dutch (TM), Stationsstraat 31.	Bergen op Zoom
De Potkachel (ND), Rijksweg 65.	Berg en Terblijt
't Roodhert (TM), Schoolstraat 3.	Bergum
De Lekpot (ND), Bosscheweg 72.	Berkel-Enschot
*Kaatje bij de Sluis (AGN), Brouwerstraat 20.	Blokzijl
An d'r Plei (ND), Wilhelminastraat 3.	Bocholtz
De Beurs (TM), Kerkstraat 4; Nia Domo (ND, TM), St Agathaplein 2.	Boekel
Bolsward (TM), Kloosterlaan 24; De Wijnberg (TM), Marktplein 5; De Doele (TM), Nieuwmarkt 22.	Bolsward
Bleze (TM), Hoofdstraat 21; Harbarg (ND), Hoofdstraat 10.	Borger
't Maatveld (ND, TM), Tusveld 31–33.	Bornerbroek
*De Hoefslag (AGN), Vossenlaan 28.	Bosch en Duin (Zeist)
Auberge De Arent, Schoolstraat 2; D'Oude Vest (TM), Oude Vest 21; Mastbosch (ND), Burg. Kerstenslaan 20; Mirabelle, Dr Batenburglaan 76; Stationsrestauratie (TM), Stationsplein 16; Van Ham (ND), van Coothplein 23; Walliser Stube, Grote Markt 44.	Breda
Wegrestaurant De Lucht (TM), Rijksweg A 2.	Bruchem
Kerkeveld (TM), Kerkeveldstraat 7.	Brunssum
Postiljon Utrecht-Bunnik (TM), Kosterijland 8.	Bunnik
*Gravin van Buren (AGN), Kerkstraat 4.	Buren
Het Grote Zwijn (TM), Achterweg 9.	Burgh-Haamstede
Beekzicht (TM), Broekheurnerweg 27.	Buurse
Kornman (ND), Mient 1.	Castricum
De Baander, Hoofdstraat 23,	Dalen
De Daalfser Poort (ND), Prinsenstraat 2; Het Boskamp (TM), Terrebosweg 2.	Dalfsen
De Buteriggel (TM), Badweg 13; 't Pruttelhuis (TM), Parnassiastraat 1.	De Koog
*Carelshaven (AGN), Hengelosestraat 30; Het Wapen van Delden (TM), Langestraat 242; Vossenhoek (TM), Vossenbrinkweg 40.	Delden
*De Zwethheul (AGN), Rotterdamseweg 480; Bodega De Keyser (ND), Markt 17A; Het Straatje van Vermeer, Molslaan 18; Monopole (TM), Markt 48A.	Delft
Du Bastion (ND), Waterstraat 74–78.	Delfzijl

Restaurants

De Lutte/ Losser	Bistro 't Delleke (ND), Dorpsstraat 3; De Lutt (ND), Beuningerstraat 20.
De Meern	De Oude Bakkerij (ND), Zandweg 103.
Den Bosch	*Châlet Royal, Wilhelminaplein 1; Central (TM), Mr Loeffplein 98; De Pette-laar, Pettelaarseschans 1; De Veste (Japanese cuisine), Uilenburg 2; In den Vergulden Hoed (ND), Markt 34–36; Metropole (TM), Orthenseweg 58–60.
Denekamp	Van Blanken (TM), Grotestraat 16.
Den Ham	Harwig (ND), Ommerweg 1.
Den Helder	Restaurant in Hotel Beatrix, Badhuisstraat 2.
Den Oever	Zomerdijk (TM), Zwinstraat 65.
Deurne	Den Vergulden Helm (ND), Stationsstraat 76.
Deurningen	Golbach (TM), Hengelosestraat 17; Luttikhuis (NDM, TM), Hengelosestraat 13.
Deventer	Postiljon Deventer (TM), Deventerweg 121; Royal (ND), Brink 94; 't Diek-huus, Bandijk 2.
Didam	De Harmonie (TM), Kerkstraat 2.
Diepenheim	Boonk (TM), Grotestraat 94; Roelofsen (TM), Goorseweg 22.
Diever	De Lange (TM), Kruisstraat 7; De Walhof (ND, TM), Hezenes 6; Meina (TM), Achterstraat 7.
Diffelen	Boerderij De Gloepe (ND), Rheezerweg 84A.
Dinteloord	De Beurs (ND), Westvoorstraat 6.
Dokkum	De Posthoorn (ND), Diepswal 21.
Domburg	Zomerlust (TM), Domburgseweg 11.
Doornenburg	Rijnzicht (ND), Sterreschans 15.
Dordrecht	Au Bon Coin, Groenmarkt 1; De Merwelanden (ND), De Bekramming 13; De Stroper (seafood), Wijnbrug 1; Herberg De Hellebaard (ND), In de Groot-hoofdspoort; Merwehal Westergoot (ND), Baanhoekweg 1; Postiljon Dor-drecht–'s Gravendeel (TM), Rijksstraatweg 30.
Drimmelen	De Biesbosch (TM), Biesboschkade 1.
Drouwen	Het Drouwenerzand (ND), Gasseltestraat 7.
Dussen	De Koppelpaarden (TM), Oude Kerkstraat 1.
Dwingeloo	De Brink (TM), Brink 30–31.
Ede	De Reehorst (TM), Bennekomseweg 24; Gea (TM), Stationsweg 2; Het Boterlam, Stationsweg 117.
Eerbeek	Heideroos (ND), Harderwijkerweg 28.
Eernewoude	Jeen Wester (ND), Wiidswei 32.
Eersel	*De Acht Zaligheden, Markt 3; Eethuis 't Menneke (TM), Markt 6; Het Gilde Huis (TM), Hint 10.

Barbecue De Bikkerij (ND), Egmonderstraatweg 34. — Egmond aan den Hoef

De Boei (TM), Westeinde 2; De Klok (TM), Pompplein 1. — Egmond aan Zee

*De Karpendonkse Hoeve (AGN), Sumatralaan 3; De Blauwe Lotus (Chinese cuisine), Limburglaan 20; De Volder (ND), Nieuwstraat 40; Ravensdonck, Ten Hagestraat 2; Trocadero (ND, TM), Stationsplein 15. — Eindhoven

Het Wapen van Elst (ND, TM), Dorpsstraat 28. — Elst

De Luifel (TM), Lange Nering 39; 't Prinsenhof (TM), Zuiderkade 6C; 't Voorhuys (ND), De Deel 20. — Emmeloord

Van Veenen (TM), Weerdingerstraat 84. — Emmen

Schaveren (ND), Oranjeweg 72. — Emst

Die Port can Cleve (ND, TM), Dijk 74–76; Die Drie Haringhe, Dijk 28; Het Wapen van Enkhuizen (TM), Breedstraat 59. — Enkhuizen

Museumsrestaurant Schokland (ND, TM), Middelbuurt 3. — Ens

*Het Koekshuis, Hengelosestraat 111; Bistro de Graaff (ND), Korte Haaksbergerstraat 3; Dish Hotel (ND), Boulevard 1945 2; Hoge Boekel (TM), Hogeboekelerweg 410. — Enschede

*De Twentsche Hoeve (AGN), Langevoortsweg 12. — Enter

De Witte Berken (ND, TM), Oost Ravenweg 8; 't Hof van Gelre (TM), Hoofdstraat 46. — Epe

Berg en Dal (ND, TM), Roodweg 18; De Kroon (TM), Wilhelminastraat 8; Ons Krijtland (TM), Julianastraat 22. — Epen

Moorman (ND), Oosterlangen 2. — Erm

*De Zwaan (AGN), Markt 7. — Etten-Leur

Bussemaker (ND), Zuiderhooftstraat 1; De Meulenhoek (ND, TM), Hoofdstraat 61; Café Het Witte Peert (TM), Hoofdstraat 65. — Exloo

De Stadsherberg (TM), Oud Kaatsveld 8; De Valk (ND, TM), Hertog van Saxenlaan 78. — Franeker

Frederiksoord (ND), Majoor van Swietenlaan 20. — Frederiksoord

Wegrestaurant De Lucht (TM), Rijksweg 19. — Geffen

Bistro Bonaparte (ND), Markt 124. — Geleen

De Keizer (ND, TM), Ridderplein 3. — Gemert

Adolfs (TM), Stationsstraat 2; Bistro La Cabriole (TM), Schoolstraat 5. — Gieten

De Rietstulp (ND, TM), Ds. T.O. Hylkemaweg 15; 't Achterhuis, Ds. T.O. Hylkemaweg 43. — Giethoorn

De Gouden Leeuw (TM), Markt 9–11. — Goedereede

Goes (TM), Anthony Fokkerstraat 100. — Goes

An d'Olde Putte (TM), Voorstraat 8. — Goor

Restaurants

Gorinchem	't Spinnewiel (TM), Eind 18.
Gorredijk	De Vergulde Turf (TM), Hoofdstraat 37.
Gouda	Brunel, Hoge Gouw 23; De Mallemolen (traditional Dutch interior), Oosthaven 72; La Grenouille, Oosthaven 20; Rotisserie l'Etoile, Blekerssingel 1; Zes Sterren (in Municipal Museum; traditional Dutch interior), Achter de Kerk 14.
	In Reeuwijk: D'Ouwe Stee (traditional Dutch interior; terrace), 's-Gravenbroekseweg 80.
Grave-Velp	De Nieuwe Nachtegaal (ND), Bosschebaan 10.
Groede	Het Vlaemsche Duyn (ND), Gerard de Moorsweg 4.
Groenlo	Wissink (ND, TM), Markt 3.
Groningen	*Le Mérinos d'Or (AGN), A-Straat 1; De Pauw, Gelkingestraat 52; Eetcafé De Stadlander (TM), Poelestraat 35; Hollands Restaurant De Koperen Pan (ND), Oosterstraat 30; Naberhof (TM), Naberpassage 8; Restaurant-Grill In den Helperhoeck (TM), Verl. Hereweg 81; 't Pannekoekschip (TM), Schuiterdiep t.o. No. 41; 't Wad (fish restaurant; TM), A-Kerkhof 27.
Haaksbergen	't Hoogeland (TM), Eibergsestraat 157.
Haarle	De Haarlerberg (TM), Kerkweg 18.
Haarlem	De Componist, Korte Veerstraat 1; De Karmeliet (ND), Spekstraat 6; Peter Cuyper, Kleine Houtstraat 70.
The Hague	*Corona (AGN), Buitenhof 39–42; Da Roberto (Italian cuisine), Noordeinde 196; De Hoogwerf, Zijdelaan 20; Royal Dynasty (Asian cuisine), Noordeinde 123; Salle à Manger La Spore (TM), Javastraat 138A; Shirasagi (Japanese cuisine), Spui 170; 't Goude Hooft (ND, TM), Groenmarkt 13.
	In Scheveningen: City (TM), Renbaanstraat 1–3; De Mosselman (TM), Keizerstraat 55; Lansink (TM), Badhuisweg 7l Radèn Mas (Indonesian cuisine), Gevers Deynootplein 125; Seinpost (seafood), Zeekant 60; Strandpaviljoen Zeezicht (TM), Boulevard 49.
Halsteren	De Ram (TM), Steenbergseweg 1.
Hardenberg	Koffiehuis Heemse (TM), Haardijk 2.
Harderwijk	Baars (ND), Smeepoortstraat 52; Marktzicht (TM), Markt 6.
Haren	De Horst (TM), Rijksstraatweg 127; Postiljon Haren (TM), Emmalaan 33.
Harlingen	De Gastronoom (ND, TM), Voorstraat 38; 't Heerenlogement (TM), Franekereind 23–25.
Harmelen	Restaurant-Partycentrum De Putkop (ND, TM), Leidsestraatweg 46.
Havelte	De Linthorst (TM), Rijksweg NZ 22; Hoffmann's Vertellingen (ND), Dorpsstraat 16.
Hazerswoude	De Hazershof (ND, TM), Rijndijk 177.
Heeg	De Watersport (ND, TM), De Skatting 44; T & T (TM), Harinxmastraat 57–59.
Heerde	De Keet (TM), Eperweg 57.

De Grieteneije (ND), Achter de Kerk 4–6; Postiljon Heerenveen (TM), Schans 65. Heerenveen

De Heer van Jericho (TM), Middenweg 247; De Zandhorst (TM), Gildestraat 2. Heerhugowaard

Heerlen (ND), Groene Boord 23. Heerlen

De Toren (ND, TM), Torenstraat 12. Heeswijk-Dinther

*Du Château (AGN), Kapelstraat 48. Heeze

De Paddestoel (TM), Sanatoriumlaan 6. Hellendoorn

De Roef (TM), Sportlaan 2. Hellevoetsluis

*De Hoefslag (AGN), Warande 2–4; De Smickelerie (TM), Veestraat 28. Helmond

De Appel (TM), Enschedestraat 34; Le Grand Café (TM), Pastoriestraat 33. Hengelo

De Witte (TM), Goorsestraat 1. Hengevelde

Havenzicht (TM), Vismarkt 2. Heusden

Nusantara (Indonesian cuisine), Vaartweg 15A; Spandershoeve (Indonesian cuisine), Bussumergrintweg 46. Hilversum

Boulevard (TM), Badweg 8. Hoek van Holland

Rust een Weinig (ND, TM), Apeldoornseweg 20. Hoenderloo

Schep (ND), Amerfoortsestraat 10. Hoevelaken

Fieten (TM), Carstensdijk 64. Hollandscheveld

't Zeepaardje (ND), Westerlaan 7. Hollum

De Molenbelt (TM), Burg. van de Borchstraat 8; De Witte (ND), Deventerweg 61. Holten

Motel Hoogeveen (TM), Mathijsenstraat 1. Hoogeveen

In Hoogezand-Foxhol: De Boer (TM, ND), Korte Groningerweg 47. Hoogezand

Hoog Soeren (ND, TM), Hoog Soeren 15. Hoog Soeren

De Oude Rosmolen, Duinsteeg 1; L'Oasis de la Digue, De Hulk 16; Pejo (TM), Keern 203. Hoorn (Noord-Holland)

Hornerheide (TM), Heythuyserweg 13. Horn

Coppus (TM), Jacobmerlostraat 1. Horst

De Engel (ND), Burg. Wallerweg 2. Houten

Lunchroom Malpertuus (TM), Gentsestraat 1. Hulst

Wegrestaurant Stad Parijs (TM), Rijksweg 6. Hulten

IJmond (ND), Seinpostweg 40. IJmuiden

Restaurants

Kaatsheuvel	Smit (TM), Peperstraat 25.
Kampen	De Buitenwacht (TM), Stationsplein 2; D'Olde Vismark (ND), Ysselkade 45; Zuiderzee Lido, Flevoweg 85.
Kamperland	Kamperduin (TM), Patrijzenlaan 1.
Kapelle	De Caisson (ND), Smokkelhoekweg 10–12.
Katwijk aan Zee	Bistro Le Cornet (ND), Zuid Boulevard 145; Riche (ND), Boulevard 73.
Klarenbeek	Pijnappel (TM), Hoofdweg 55.
Kloosterzande	De Linde (ND), Hulsterweg 47.
Kruiningen	*Inter Scaldes, Zandweg 2.
Langweer	De Wielen (ND), Stevenshoek 23.
Leeuwarden	De Mulderij, Baljeestraat 19; De Waag (ND, TM), Nieuwestad 148B; Onder de Luifel (ND, TM), Stationsweg 5.
Leiden	Bernsen (TM), Breestraat 157; Lunchroom Hendriks (TM), Donkersteeg 7; Surakarta (Indonesian cuisine; TM), Noordeinde 51; La Cloche, Klocksteeg 3; Nieuw Minerva (TM), Boommarkt 23. In Oegstgeest, 3km/2 miles N: *De Beukenhof, Terweeweg 12.
Leidschendam	*Chagall (AGN), in Hotel Green Park, Weigelia 20–22; *Villa Rozenrust (AGN), Veursestraatweg 104.
Lekkerkerk	De Witte Brug (farm restaurant and hotel), Kerkweg 138.
Lemelerveld	Wim Reimink (ND), Dorpsstraat 2.
Lemmer	De Wildeman (ND), Schulpen 6.
Lisse	De Beurs (ND), Haven 4; De Engel (TM), Heereweg 386.
Lochem	Bousema (TM), Zutphenseweg 35; De Pepermolen (TM), Noorderwal 40; Jan Patat (TM), Zutphenseweg 11; La Forêt (ND), Walsteeg 37.
Loenen	De Marshoeve (TM), Reuweg 51.
Lonneker	Savenije (TM), Dorpsstraat 149.
Lunteren	De Wormshoef (TM), Dorpsstraat 192.
Maarsbergen	Motel Maarsbergen (TM), Woudenbergseweg 44.
Maarssen	*De Wilgenplas (AGN), Marsseveensevaart 7A.
Maasbommel	De Mulder (ND, TM), Bovendijk 6.
Maasbree	Boszicht (TM), Provincialeweg 2.
Maasdam	De Hoogt (ND), Raadhuisstraat 3.
Maashees	Op den Berg (ND, TM), Op den Berg 1.
Maastricht	*Grand Hotel de l'Empereur (TM), Stationsstraat 2; Au Coin des Bons Enfants, Ezelmarkt 4; Old Hickory, Meerssenerweg 372; Panaché (ND), Vrijthof 14. 5km/3 miles SW: *Château Neercanne, Cannerweg 800.

't Trefpunkt (TM), Raadhuisplein 1. — Made

In de Kop'ren Smorre (romantic restaurant), Holterweg 20. — Markelo

De Kruisweg (ND, TM), Kruisweg 1. — Marum

Het Wapen van Medemblik (ND, TM), Oosterhaven 1. — Medemblik

Ketels (TM), Raadhuisplein 4–6; Oranjehotel (TM), Raadhuisplein 11. — Meijel

Kleuters (TM), Haagstraat 5. — Merkelbeek

Den Tol (ND, TM), Rijksstraatweg 80. — Meteren

De Huifkar (TM), Markt 19; Het Groot Paradijs, Damplein 13; Stations-restauratie (TM), Kanalweg 24. — Middelburg

*De Hooge Heerlykheid (AGN), Voorstraat 19–23. — Middelharnis

De Hunebedden (ND), Groningerstraat 31. — Midlaren

Petit Restaurant 39 (TM), Markstraat 39. — Mierlo

Relais (ND), Steenweg 2. — Moerdijk

De Posthoorn (traditional Dutch interior), Noordeinde 41. — Monnickendam

De Gouden Leeuw (TM), Hoogstraat 41; Het Gouden Hoofd (ND), Hoog-straat 37. — Montfoort

In Naarden-Vesting: Auberge Le Bastion, St Annastraat 3; De Oude Smidse, Marktstraat 30. — Naarden

Schepers (TM), Oude Deldenseweg 3. — Neede

De Lindeboom (TM), Napoleonseweg 128. — Neer

De Jong (ND, TM), Reeweg 29. — Nes (Ameland)

Het Wapen van Nibbixwoud (ND), Dorpsstraat 57. — Nibbixwoud

De Witte Wimpel (TM), Weijland 13A. — Nieuwebrug aan den Rijn

De Kanonnier (TM), Achterweg 9. — Nieuweschans

De Lichtmis (TM), Rijksstraatweg 3. — Nieuw-Leusden

Belvédère, Kelkensbos 60; De Gans (TM), Stikke Hezelstraat 54; Fong Shou (Chinese cuisine), Van Schaeck Mathonsingel 16; Wienerhof (TM), Hertog-straat 1. — Nijmegen

Dalzicht (ND, TM), Grotestraat 285; Mulder (TM), Grotestraat 154. — Nijverdal

Restaurant in Beach Hotel Noordwijk (TM), Kon. Wilhelminaboulevard 31; Blauwe Gans (ND, TM), Kon. Wilhelminaboulevard 4; De Beurs (TM), Voor-straat 123–129; De Poort van Kleef (TM), Douzastraat 5; De Ruiter (TM), Hoofdstraat 100. — Noordwijk

Motel-Restaurant De Duinvos (TM), Duinschooten 12; Zegers (TM), Heren-weg 78. — Noordwijker-hout

Karsten (TM), Brink 6. — Norg

Restaurants

Belvedere restaurant, Nijmegen

Nunspeet	Les Routiers Nunspeet (TM), Rijksweg A 28; Resto (TM), Stationslaan 81; 't Centrum (ND, TM), Dorpsstraat 8; 't Vosje (TM), Stationsplein 4.
Odoorn	Oring (TM), Hoofdstraat 49.
Oegstgeest	Alexander (ND), Lange Voort 11.
Oene	De Riefstulp (ND), Eperweg 66.
Oirschot	Eethuys Den Gevel (TM), Markt 18; De Zwaan (TM), Markt 4.
Oisterwijk	*De Swaen, De Lind 47; Camping De Boskant (TM), Oirschotsebaan 8A.
Oldeberkoop	't Hof van Oldeberkoop (ND), Oosterwoldseweg 3.
Oldemarkt	Hof van Holland (ND), Hoofdstraat 2.
Oldenbroek	Herkert (TM), Zuiderzeestraatweg 135.
Oldenzaal	Frits Muller (TM), Markt 10–14.
Ommen	De Hongerige Wolf (ND), Coevorderweg 27B.
Oosteinde	Ekamper (ND), Radsweg 12.
Oosterhout	't Arendsnest (TM), Arendshof 104.
Oostkapelle	Zeelandia (TM), Dorpsstraat 39–41.
Oostrum	Bowling Restaurant Venray (ND), Mgr Hanssenstraat 10.

*De Wanne (AGN), Stobbenkamp 2; *De Wiemsel (AGN), Winhofflaan 2; Ootmarsum
De la Poste (TM), Marktstraat 5; Van der Maas (TM), Grotestraat 7.

Tjaarda (ND, TM), Kon. Julianaweg 98. Oranjewoud

De Naaldhof (TM), Docfalaan 22. Oss

Dekkers (TM), Zr. M. Adolphinenstraat 2–6. Ossendrecht

Partyboerderij La Mère Anne (ND), Dorpsweg 110. Oudendijk

De Holle Boom (ND, TL), Dwarsweg 63. Overberg

't Hof van Loon (TM), Museumlaan 33. Overloon

*De Bokkedoorns (AGN), Wethouder van Gelukpark, Zeeweg 53. Overveen
(Bloemendaal)

Dimar (ND, TM), Singel 33. Petten

Blankendaal (TM), Neckerdijk 2. Purmerend

De Heerdt (ND), Kerkplein 1; Postiljon Nulde-Putten (TM), Strandboulevard Putten
3; 't Puttertje (TM), Poststraat 17–19.

De Kroon (TM), Grotestraat 28. Raalte

De Horizon (TM), Hoogenboomlaan 44. Renesse

De Dennen (TM), Utrechtseweg 34. Renswoude

Rustoord (TM), Ootmarsumseweg 303. Reutum

Pannekoekhuis Strijland (TM), Groenestraat 1. Rheden

La Montagne (TM), Kerksewijk 115; Stichtse Oever (TM), Veerplein 1. Rhenen

De Vechtstreek (TM), Groete Beltenweg 17. Rheeze

Boerderij Frouckje State (ND), Binnendijk 74. Rijperkerk

Sterrenhotel Gaasterland (TM), Manderlaene 21. Rijs

Het Rechthuis (ND), Rechthuisstraat 1. Rinsumageest

Het Wapen van Drenthe (TM), Heerestraat 1. Roden
In Roden-Steenbergen: Jachtlust (TM), Hoofdweg 22.

De Beurs (ND), Markt 25; La Cascade, Koolstraat 3. Roermond

Finders (TM), Brugstraat 20; Restauratie Het Station (TM), Stationsplein 1; Roosendaal
Zeelandia (ND, TM), Bloemenmarkt 17–19.

Postiljon Rosmalen (TM), Burg. Burgerslaan 50. Rosmalen

*La Vilette (AGN), Westblaak 160; *Parkheuvel (AGN), Heuvellaan 21; Eet- Rotterdam
café The Broker (TM), Blaak 329; Hong Kong (Chinese cuisine), Westersingel 15; Old Dutch (traditional Dutch interior), Rochussenstraat 20; Party-
en Congrescentrum Engels (TM), Stationsplein 45; Radèn Mas (Indonesian
cuisine), Kruiskade 72; 't Schubbejak (TM), Meent 98; World Trade Center,
Beursplein 37 (27th floor; *view over city).

Het Wapen van Smallingerland (ND), Muldersplein 2. Rottevalle

Restaurants

Ruinen	Kuik (ND), Brink 15.
Ruurlo	De Luifel (TM), Dorpsstraat 11.
St Nicolaasga	Hjir is't (ND), Huisterheide 6.
Sas van Gent	De la Bourse (ND, TM), Westkade 67.
Schagen	Igesz (ND, TM), Markt 22.
Schalkhaar	De Cräddenburg (TM), Kanaaldijk, Oost 16; De Lindeboom (TM), Lindeboomseweg 1.
Scharwoude	De Karperput (ND), IJsselmeerdijk 16.
Schayk	Nieuw Schayk (TM), Rijksweg 46.
Schelluinen	Eethuis 't Centrum (TM), Kerkplein 6.
Scheveningen	See The Hague, above
Schin op Geul	Salden (TM), Tolhuisstraat 1A.
Schoonebeek	De Wolfshoeve (TM), Europaweg 132.
Schoonoord	De Hoek (ND), Slenerweg 1.
Schoorl	De Rustende Jager (TM), Heereweg 18; De Viersprong (TM), Laanweg 1; Schoorl (ND), Laanweg 24.
Schuddebeurs/ Zierikzee	Hostellerie Schuddebeurs (romantic hotel with restaurant), Donkereweg 35, Schuddebeurs/Zierikzee.
Sellingen	Homan (TM), Dorpsstraat 8.
Sevenum	Hofstee De Turfhoeve (ND, TM), Middenpeelweg 1.
's-Heerenberg	Knoek (ND, TM), Molenstraat 7.
Sittard	Het Wapen van Sittard (ND), Paardestraat 14.
Sloten	Bolwerk (ND), Voorstreek 116–117; De Zeven Wouden (TM), Voorstreek 120.
Sneek	Bonnema en Van Beek (TM), Stationsstraat 62–66; De Kriel (TM), Prins Hendrikkade 29; De Stolp (TM), Smidsstraat 6; De Wijnberg (TM), Marktstraat 23; Hanenburg, Wijde Noorderhorne 2; Onder de Linden (ND, TM), Marktstraat 30; 't Grootzand (TM), Grootzand 4; 't Hoffy (TM), Leeuwenburg 4; Van de Wal (TM), Leeuwenburg 7–11.
Soest	De Korte Duinen (TM), Birkstraat 108.
Someren	Centraal (TM), Wilhelminaplein 3; 't Weekend (ND), Provincialeweg 1.
Son en Breugel	De Zwaan (ND), Markt 9.
Spakenburg	De Mandemaaker (TM), Kerkstraat 103.
Spier	De Woudzoom (TM), Oude Postweg 2.
Stadskanaal	Dopper (ND), Hoofdstraat 33.
Staphorst	Waanders (TM), Rijksweg 12.

It Hearehus (ND), Hellingpad 2.   Stavoren

Boei 12 (TM), Roegeweg 3.   Steendam

Restaria Oost (TM), Oosterstraat 69; 't Geveltien (ND), Markt 76.   Steenwijk

François (ND), Mauritsweg 96.   Stein

Den Hook (TM), Markt 19.   Swalmen

De Kombuis (ND), De Poort 23–25.   Swifterbant

Buitenlust (ND), Moerdijkseweg 10.   Terheijden

Monopole (ND), Korte Kerkstraat 14–16.   Terneuzen

Crasborn (TM), Hoogstraat 6.   Thorn

Restaria De Schouw (TM), Hoogeindsestraat 13–15.   Tiel

*De Gouden Zwaan, Monumentstraat 6; Central (TM), Spoorlaan 422; De   Tilburg
Korenbeurs (ND), Heuvel 24; De Leijhoek (TM), Hilvarenbeekseweg 60;
Partycentrum Old Factory (ND), Veldhovenring 88; Petit Restaurant De
Katterug (TM), Stadhuisplein 321; Petit Restaurant Het Station (TM),
Spoorlaan 45.

Stationskoffiehuis (TM), Stationsstraat 31; Taverne (ND), H.W. Iordensweg   Twello
3.

Prinsen (TM), Hoenderloseweg 44.   Ugchelen

Ruimzicht (ND), Mennonietenbuurt 1.   Uithoorn/
                                                                         Amstelhoek

Havenzicht (TM), Bootstraat 65.   Urk

*Juliana, Amsterdamsestraatweg 464; Eethuis Het Draeckje (ND), K. Oude   Utrecht
Gracht 114–116; Graaf Floris (ND), Vismarkt 13; Herberg Bij de Molen (ND),
Adelaarstraat 23; Het Snackhouse (TM), Godenbaldkwartier 69; Tantes
Bistro (ND), Oudegracht 61.

Du Limbourg (TM), Maastrichterlaan 16–18.   Vaals

*Prinses Juliana (AGN), Broekhem 11; *Lindenhorst, Broekhem 130; De   Valkenburg
Kei (TM), Th. Dorrenplein 4; De L'Empereur (TM), Grotestraat 32; Gouden   aan de Geul
Leeuw (TM), Grotestraat 49; La Brasserie (ND), Passage 1–3; Mommers
(TM), Plenkertstraat 32–36; Monument (TM), Grendelplein 20; Prinses Wil-
helmina (TM), Wilhelminalaan 39–41; 't Heekerhöfke (ND), Hekerweg 40.

Mosbeek, Hooidijk 15; Tante Sien (ND), Denekamperweg 210.   Vasse

Warande (TM), Wolbergstraat 99.   Valkenswaard

De Kroon (TM), Kerkplein 6; De Ploeg (TM), Kerkplein 17.   Varsseveld

Parkzicht (ND, TM), Winkler Prinsstraat 3.   Veendam

Van den Hombergh (ND), Rijksweg 104.   Velden

Brasserie Born (ND), Parade 42; Valuas, St Urbanusweg 9.   Venlo

Quick Inn (TM), Grote Markt 11.   Venray

Restaurants

Restaurant in Hoog Catharijne shopping centre, Utrecht

Vlaardingen	De Gasterij (TM), Westhavenkade 35–36.
Vlissingen	Boulevard (ND), Bellamypark 4; De Gevangentoren, Boulevard de Ruyter 1A; restaurant in Strandhotel Vlissingen (TM), Boulevard Evertsen 4; Station Vlissingen (fish restaurant; TM), Stationsplein 5.
Volendam	Spaander (ND), Haven 15–19.
Voorburg	*Vreugd en Rust (AGN), Oosteinde 14.
Voorthuizen	Edda Huzid (ND), Hunneweg 16.
Vriescheloo	De Oude Witte School (TM), Dorpsstraat 88.
Vrouwenpolder	Vrouwenpolder, Veersegatdam 81.
Vught	De Vier Kolommen (TM), Helvoirtseweg 166.
Waardenburg	Wegrestaurant De Nieuwe Brug (ND), Afslag A 2.
Wageningen	Nol in het Bosch (TM), Hartenseweg 60.
Wartena	De Brigantijn (ND), Hoofdstraat 29–31.
Wassenaar	*Auberge de Kieviet (AGN), Stoeplaan 27; De Schulpwei (ND), Katwijkseweg 7; Duinrell (TM), Duinrell 9; Huize den Deyl (TM), Rijksstraatweg 390; Sport (TM), Rijksstraatweg 344C.
Weert	De Brookhut (ND), Heugterbroekdijk 2; Jan van der Croon (ND), Driesveldlaan 99.
Weesp	De Kromme Elleboog (ND), Nieuwstad 32.

De Vijf Sinnen (ND), Hegedijk 2.	Weidum
't Wellse Veerhuis (TM), Wellsedijk 29.	Well (nr Ammerzoden)
*De Hamert (AGN), Hamert 2.	Wellerlooi
De Brabantse Biesbosch, in Biesbosch Museum, Spieringsluis 6.	Werkendam
Meursinge (ND), Hoofdstraat 48.	Westerbork
Nap (TM), Torenstraat 55.	West-Terschelling
*Duurstede (AGN), Maleborduurstraat 7.	Wijk bij Duurstede
In den Stallen (TM), Oostereinde 10; Vrijheid (ND, TM), Blijhamsterstraat 60.	Winschoten
Bulten (ND), Parallelweg 72; De Zwaan (TM), Wooldstraat 6.	Winterswijk
*Kasteel Wittem (AGN), Wittemerallee 3.	Wittem
't Oude Raedthuis (ND), Heerenveenseweg 1.	Wolvega
De Petiele (TM), Noord 13–15.	Workum
De Weger (TM), Boddens Hosangweg 86.	Woubrugge
Bellevue (TM), Stationsweg 33; Schimmel (ND), Stationsweg 243.	Woudenberg
De Nieuwe Rakken (ND), Midstraat 2.	Woudsend
*Nolet/Het Reymerswale (AGN), Jachthaven 5.	Yerseke
*De Hoop op d'Swarte Walvis (AGN), Kalverringdijk 15, Zaanse Schans.	Zaandam
Den Boogerd (ND), Kon. Wilhelminaweg 85.	Zaltbommel
De Zeeuwse Herberg (TM), Havenpark 2; Mondragon, Oude Haven 13.	Zierikzee
Brinkhotel (TM), Brink O.Z. 6.	Zuidlaren
De Roskam (TM), Molenstraat 1.	Zundert
Wegrestaurant Zurich (TM), Viaduct 3, Kop Afsluitdijk.	Zurich
De Poort van Kleef (TM), Turfstraat 28; Galentijn, Stationsstraat 9; IJsselpaviljoen (ND), IJsselkade 1.	Zutphen
Roskam (TM), Stationsweg 1; Motel Zwarte Water (TM), De Vlakte 20.	Zwartsluis
Warners (TM), Hoofdstraat 15.	Zweeloo
Develpaviljoen (ND), Parklaan 1.	Zwijndrecht
De Handschoen, Nieuwe Deventerweg 103; Eethuisje De Sassenpoort (TM), Sassenstraat 54; Postiljon Zwolle (TM), Hertsenbergweg 1; Urbana (ND), Wipstrikkerallee 213.	Zwolle

Riding

See Sport

Sailing

See Sport

Safety and Security

Safety on the Road

Seat-belts

The driver must ensure that all occupants of the car wear seat belts. The belts should be properly adjusted – taut and not twisted. A loosely fitting belt can cause additional injury in an accident.

Seat-belts are most effective when used with properly adjusted head-restraints. These should have their upper edge at least as high as the level of the eyes: only then do they give protection to the cervical vertebrae.

Obligatory equipment

Obligatory requirements are a warning triangle, a first aid kit and, if the view through the rear window is blocked by luggage or you are trailing a caravan, an additional external mirror.

Such items as the first aid kit should be carefully stowed and not left loose, for example on the rear shelf, since they might become dangerous projectiles if you have to brake sharply.

Other useful equipment

Other items that it is advisable to have:
tow rope; spare light bulbs, fuses and fan-belt; tools; jump leads; woollen rug; gloves; torch.

Fire extinguisher

A fire extinguisher of at least 2 kilograms capacity should be carried.

In the case of a car fire there is usually time to get the passengers and luggage out: experiments have shown that when a fire starts in the carburettor it takes between five and ten minutes to spread to the interior of the car. Extreme caution is required, however, if the petrol tank is damaged and there is a leak of petrol: when this happens fire can rapidly envelop the whole car.

Camera

It is useful to have a camera (with flash) to record the circumstances of an accident. What is important is not the damage to the vehicles involved but the general situation. In particular photographs should be taken from some distance away in the direction of travel (in both directions).

Laminated windscreen

A laminated windscreen is an important safety precaution. When hit by a stone, for example, it will not break into dangerous fragments: the outer skin will shatter but will remain in place, and you will still be able to see through the windscreen.

Spare fuel

A spare can of fuel is a useful precaution in some countries, though hardly necessary in the Netherlands, which are well supplied with petrol stations. Fuel can be saved on the motorway by not putting your foot fully down on the accelerator. A little less pressure on the pedal will significantly reduce petrol consumption without much reduction in speed.

Brakes

The effectiveness of brake fluid is reduced over time by dust, water condensation and chemical decomposition: it should, therefore, be renewed at least every two years. It is advisable before going on a long journey to check the whole braking system: when you go on holiday – with a heavily laden car, and perhaps driving in hilly country – the brakes have more work to do.

Tyres should have at least 2 millimetres of tread to hold the road properly and maintain their grip even in wet weather. Wide sports tyres should have 3 millimetres, winter tyres at least 4 millimetres.   Tyres

Tyres at the proper pressure hold the road better and save fuel. Pressures should be checked when the tyres are cold, not when they are hot after driving.

All tyres are required by law to be of the same type (i.e. either radial or cross-ply). For maximum safety all tyres should have the same depth of tread.

Drivers who alternate between summer and winter tyres should store the tyres not in use on their rims. This lengthens their life and saves time and money when fitting them to the car.

Lights should be regularly checked. If your lights are working properly you not only see better but are seen better by other drivers.   Lights

When driving at night or on wet roads you should wipe your headlights and rear lights every 50–100km/30–60 miles. Even a thin layer of dirt on the headlights can reduce their strength by half; if they are very dirty they can lose anything up to 90% of their power.

With increasing age lights decline markedly in efficiency, as tungsten from the coil is deposited on the glass. Bulbs which are defective should be replaced in pairs, so that they are equally bright on both sides.

Spectacle-wearers drive more safely at night if they have special non-reflective glasses. Tinted glasses should not be worn after dark. Since all glass reflects part of the light reaching it, even a clear windscreen lets through only some 90% of the available light; and spectacle-wearers lose another 10%. Tinted windscreens and tinted glasses allow only about half the available light to reach the eye, and safe driving is no longer possible.   Spectacle-wearers

Fog-lights should be mounted symmetrically, in pairs and at the same height. The best place for them is on the front bumper: at that height they give best visibility without dazzling oncoming drivers.   Fog-lights

It is illegal to use fog-lights except when visibility is seriously reduced by fog, rain or snow.

Up to two rear fog-lights may be mounted, not less than 10cm/4 in. from the brake-lights and no higher than 100cm/40 in. above the road. They may be used only when visibility is reduced to 50m/55yds.

When driving in fog: Driving in fog

Rear fog-lights should be switched off when you see the outline of a vehicle following you in your rear mirror.

If, during the day, you encounter oncoming cars with their lights switched on, be prepared for fog and switch on your own lights.

Adjust your speed according to the visibility.

Keep a safe distance behind the vehicle in front of you. Do not overtake.

Use your windscreen-wipers: heavy fog deposits a film of water on the windscreen.

Organising your Trip

Good organisation, starting before you leave home, is important. If you know that everything is in order at home this will allow you to enjoy a relaxed holiday.

It is helpful to draw up a check list of what requires to be done and thought of, ticking off each item as it is dealt with.

Decide in plenty of time who is going to water your plants, look after your pets and ensure that mail is not left protruding from your letter-box as an indication that you are away from home. Leave objects of value, photocopies of important papers and your holiday addresses with some suitable person or in your bank.

Don't forget:
passports;
driving licence and car registration document;
green card;
AA membership card and 5-Star Service documents;
tickets (air, rail, ferry) and confirmation of bookings;
photocopies of important documents (in luggage);
traveller's cheques, Eurocheques, credit and cheque cards, cash; road maps; first aid kit, and any medicine which you take regularly;
spare glasses if worn, and sun-glasses.

Insurance

Make sure that you have adequate insurance cover (car insurance, health insurance, insurance against loss and theft of property). Full cover matched to your requirements is provided by the AA 5-Star service (which is available also to non-members).

If you have an accident in the Netherlands

However carefully you drive, accidents can happen. If you are involved in an accident, the first rules are: whatever the provocation, don't get angry; be polite; and keep calm. Then take the following action:

1. Warn oncoming traffic by switching on your car's warning lights if you have them and setting your warning triangle (and, if you have one, a flashing light) some distance before the scene of the accident.

2. Look after anyone who has been injured, calling an ambulance if necessary.

3. The Dutch police take particulars and make a report only in case of a severe accident. Otherwise the police need be brought in only if you cannot reach agreement with the other driver involved.

4. Record full particulars of the accident. These should include:
a names and addresses of witnesses (independent witnesses are particularly important);
b damage to the vehicles involved;
c name and address of the other driver, and of the owner if different; name and address of the other party's insurance company and, if possible, the number of the insurance certificate; registration number of the other vehicle; damage or injury to yourself or other persons; number of policeman or address of police station if involved; date, time and location of the accident; speed of the vehicles involved; width of the road, any road signs and the condition of the road surface; any marks on the road relevant to the accident; the weather and the manner of the other driver's driving.

5. Draw a sketch of the accident, showing the layout of the road, the direction in which the vehicles were travelling and their position at the time of impact, any road signs and the names of streets or roads. If you have a camera, take photographs of the scene.

6. Fill in a European Accident Statement if you have one (it is supplied by most insurers and is included in the AA 5-Star Service pack), have it signed by the other driver and give him a copy.

Make no admission of responsibility for the accident, and above all do not sign any document in a language you do not understand.

On your return home you should of course report the accident to your insurance company and send them the European Accident Statement together with the form which they will ask you to complete.

Self-Catering

In recent years there has been a considerable increase in the provision of self-catering accommodation in the Netherlands, and there are now large numbers of holiday apartments, studios (in effect bed-sitters) and bungalows (chalets) available for rent.
There are also numerous apartments and studios in the larger cities such as Amsterdam, Rotterdam and The Hague, either in or attached to hotels or in separate blocks.

The Netherlands Reservation Centre (for address, see Information) can book self-catering accommodation as well as hotels. It is open Mon.–Fri. 8am–8pm, Sat. 8am–2pm Bookings are confirmed in writing. *Netherlands Reservation Centre*

During the main holiday season it is advisable to book well in advance.

Rates vary according to equipment and facilities, classification and time of year. The more luxurious types of accommodation (e.g. holiday apartments with cable television, heated indoor swimming pool, restaurant, etc.) are correspondingly more expensive. Prices tend to be higher at Easter, Whitsun and Christmas and during the main summer holiday season.
Visitors are usually expected to bring their own bed-linen and towels.

Bungalows (chalets) and holiday houses are let only by the week, or sometimes for the weekend. Particularly popular are the bungalow parks, mainly situated along the Dutch coast, which provide a wide range of amenities as well as accommodation – shops, restaurants, sports facilities, swimming pools, etc. *Bungalows*
A brochure, "Bungalow", listing bungalow parks in the Netherlands, can be obtained from the Netherlands Bureau of Tourism.

Shipping Services

Ferries (see entry) are an important form of transport, particularly for connections with the West Frisian islands and Zeeland. *Ferries*

Cruises on lakes and canals, in the large ports of Amsterdam and Rotterdam and through the Biesbosch nature reserve (see Nature Reserves and National Parks) and canal trips in Amsterdam are a very popular and enjoyable form of sightseeing. **Cruises**

Rederij Woltheus, Ark "Dia"
Kanaalkade t/o 60, NL–1811 LT Alkmaar, tel. (072) 11 48 40
Cruises in and from Alkmaar *Alkmaar*

Alg. Amsterdamse Rederij Noord-Zuid   Amsterdam
Stadhouderskade 25 (nr Rijksmuseum and Leidseplein)
NL–1071 ZD Amsterdam, tel. (020) 6 79 13 70, 6 73 56 46 and 6 71 61 27
Canal trips and harbour cruises

Holland International Canalcruises
Rokin 54, NL–1012 KV Amsterdam, tel. (020) 6 22 77 88
Canal trips

Rederij Lovers
Prins Hendrikkade, Postbus 802, NL–1000 AV Amsterdam
tel. (020) 6 25 64 64, 6 22 21 81 and 6 25 93 23
Canal trips and harbour cruises

Meyers Rondvaarten
Reservations: Damrak, Steiger 4–5, NL–1012 JX Amsterdam
tel. (020) 6 23 42 08
Canal trips

Rederij Plas
Damrak, Steiger 3, NL–1012 JX Amsterdam, tel. (020) 6 24 54 06
Canal trips and harbour tours

Pedalo trips on the Amsterdam canals: landing-stages in Leidseplein, between the Rijksmuseum and the Heineken Brewery, between the Westerkerk and the Anne Frank House and on the Keizersgracht (corner of
Leidsestraat), tel. (020) 6 26 55 74.

Other forms of water transport are the Canal Bus (between the Central
Station and the Rijksmuseum, with three stops) and the Canal Bike. Information: Amsterdam VVV office.

Heymen Holland Cruises   Arnhem
Rijnkade, NL–6811 HD Arnhem, tel. (085) 51 51 81
Cruises in the Netherlands (and in Germany)

Biesbosch Tours   Biesbosch
Biesboschweg 7, NL–4926 SJ Lage Zwaluwe, tel. (01648) 22 50
Cruises through the Biesbosch
(See Nature Reserves and National Parks)

Rondvaart Bedrijf Zilvermeeuw
Weitjes 3, NL–4924 BJ Drimmelen, tel. (01626) 8 26 09 and 44 23

Rederij Brands   Delft
Sumatrastraat 27, NL–2612 AL Delft, tel. (015) 12 63 85 and 61 97 45
Cruises in Delft

Rederij Flevo   Harderwijk
Strandboulevard 1, NL–3841 AB Harderwijk, tel. (03410) 1 25 98   (IJsselmeer)
Trips in the IJsselmeer

Rederij Wolthuis   's-Hertogen-
Erik de Rodestraat 19, NL–5223 RT 's-Hertogenbosch, tel. (073) 21 83 37   bosch
Cruises in and from 's-Hertogenbosch

Rederij Triton   Katwijk
Rijnmond 137, NL–2225 VR Katwijk, tel. (01718) 1 32 28
Canal cruises, windmill cruises

Rederij Stiphout   Maastricht
Maaspromenade 27, NL–6211 HS Maastricht, tel. (043) 25 41 51
Cruises on the Maas in the Netherlands and Belgium

◄ *Bascule bridge, Middelburg*

Shopping, Souvenirs

Marcken, Monnickendam	See Volendam, below
Nijmegen	Rederij Tonissen Waalkade, NL–6511 XR Nijmegen, tel. (080) 23 32 85 Boat trips from Nijmegen
	Rederij Mississippi Queen Oude Haven 47, NL–6511 XR Nijmegen, tel. (080) 22 06 17 Boat trips from Nijmegen
Rotterdam	Spido Willemsplein 20, NL–3016 DR Rotterdam, tel. (010) 4 13 54 00 Harbour tours and trips to the Deltawerken; hire of luxurious motor launches
Utrecht	Utrechts Rondvaartbedrijf Vogelaarsweide 2, NL–3437 DE Nieuwegein tel. (03402) 4 13 76 and (030) 31 93 77 Cruises in and from Utrecht
Volendam	Marken-Express Schoklandstraat 111, NL–1131 LB Volendam, tel. (02993) 6 33 31 Cruises from Volendam, Marken and Monnickendam
Warmond (nr Leiden)	Rederij van Hulst Sweiland 47A, NL–2361 JB Warmond, tel. (01711) 1 01 33 Cruises on the Kaager Plassen (Kaager Meer)
Willemstad	Rederij Otter Groenstraat 50, NL–4797 BC Willemstad, tel. (01687) 28 14 and 24 64 Cruises from Willemstad
Zaandam	Rederij De Schans Jan van Goyenkade 15, NL–1506 JN Zaandam, tel. (075) 17 29 20 Cruise through Zaanse Schans

---

Shopping, Souvenirs

Visitors looking for worthwhile souvenirs of a visit to the Netherlands will find a wide choice, both in the luxury shops in the larger towns and in the famous art and antique markets and fairs held during the season in many Dutch towns (see Markets, Events). Second to Amsterdam as a town of antique shops is Hoorn.

There are also picturesque weekly and other markets in many towns in the Netherlands. Information about times and places from local VVV offices.

Souvenirs

Clogs, etc.	Dutch clogs (*klompen*) can be bought all over the country. Other favourite souvenirs are beautifully produced illustrated books, colour slides, records, cassettes and CDs, old prints with views of Dutch towns, reproductions (posters) of pictures by famous Dutch masters, dolls in traditional costumes, decorative plates and tiles.
Clog factories	Havenrak 21, Broek in Waterland, tel. (02903) 14 32 Open daily 8am–6pm (admission free)
	Irenehoeve Hogedijk 1, Katwoude, tel. (02995) 22 91 Open daily 9am–6pm (admission free)

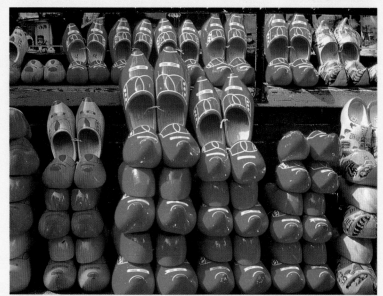

Clogs, an ever popular souvenir

Also very popular as souvenirs is the beautifully painted peasant furniture made in Hindeloopen (Friesland).

Peasant furniture

Among the most celebrated examples of Dutch craftsmanship are Delft porcelain and tiles (usually blue on a white ground) and hand-painted porcelain and tiles from Friesland's Royal Porcelain and Tile Manufactory in Makkum.

Delfter Blauw Tiles and porcelain

De Delftse Pauw Porcelain Manufactory
Delftweg 133, Delft, tel. (015) 12 49 20 (presentation)
Open: April to mid October, daily 9am–4pm; mid October to March, Mon.–Fri. 9am–4pm, Sat. and Sun. 11am–1pm Admission free.

De Porceleyne Fles
Rotterdamseweg 169, Delft, tel. (015) 56 02 34
Open: April to November, Mon.–Sat. 9am–5pm, Sun. and pub. hols. 10am–4pm; December to March, Mon.–Fri. 9am–5pm, Sat. 10am–4pm Admission free.

Royal Dutch Porcelain and Tile Manufactory
Turfmarkt 63, Makkum, tel. (05158) 1 41
Conducted tours: Mon.–Fri. 10am–4pm, Sat. 9am–4pm (video show).

Beautiful goldsmith's work can be found in the province of Zeeland, silver in the town of Schoonhoven.

Gold and silver

The little red cheeses of Edam are famed throughout the world (cheese market: see Markets, Edam).
As well as its famous cheese (see Markets, Gouda) Gouda produces beautiful candles and long clay pipes.

Cheese, candles, clay pipes

Also popular as souvenirs are pieces of crystal, for example from Leerdam or Maastricht.

Crystal

Delfter Blauw

A fashionable shop in Maastricht

Sweets
: A speciality of The Hague are the coffee caramels known as *Haagse hopjes.* Dutch coffee is of outstanding quality, as is Dutch cocoa. Other favourite sweets are *kinderköppkes, grameerkes* and *steerkes.* Deventer's speciality is spiced cakes, and Gouda is famed for its waffles and short-crust pastry (*sprits*).

Diamonds
: Visitors with more spending money might think of diamonds. Amsterdam is one of the world's leading diamond-cutting centres.

Duty-Free Shopping Centres

Amsterdam-Schiphol
: Schiphol Airport has a large duty-free shopping centre in which departing passengers (except those travelling to an airport in one of the Benelux countries) can buy a wide range of goods (drinks, tobacco goods, perfume, cosmetics, cameras, films, watches, blouses, scarves, radios, television sets, etc.) at tax-free prices.

Rotterdam-Zestienhoven
: There is a smaller duty-free shopping centre at Rotterdam-Zestienhoven Airport.

International ferries
: There are also duty-free shops on the ferries sailing to and from Britain and Scandinavia.

Recovery of Value-Added Tax

The Dutch equivalent of VAT is BTW.
Visitors from European Community countries can recover value-added tax on articles bought in the Netherlands of a minimum value of 910 fl per item; for visitors from Ireland the minimum value is 200 fl, for visitors from

non-Community countries 300 fl. They should obtain from the shop an export certificate as well as a receipt and have it stamped by the Dutch customs when leaving the country; the customs officer will explain the procedure for recovery of tax.

Some shops are affiliated to Holland Tax-Free Shopping, an organisation which arranges for repayment of the tax. In this case the shop gives the purchaser a cheque for the amount to be repaid (which after allowing for administrative charges will be rather less than the tax paid), and this, after being stamped by Dutch customs, can be cashed by the holder at the frontier exchange office (GWK: see Currency). At Schiphol Airport the cheques can be left in a "mail-box" at the customs office, with an address for repayment.

Holland Tax-Free Shopping

Sightseeing Tours

Sightseeing tours in coaches, with commentaries by guides (frequently multilingual), can be booked in VVV offices. These range from city tours to tours in the immediately surrounding area, tours of the whole province or the whole country, and sometimes of neighbouring countries as well.

The services of guides can also be obtained through the Nederlands Reserverings Centrum (see Information).

Many bus companies and tour operators run coach tours with multilingual guides. Following is a selection of such firms:

International Tours Center (ITC)
Postbus 7527, NL–1117 ZG Schiphol Airport–Oost
tel. (020) 6 04 10 11

Euroworld
Bexuidenhoutseweg 117, NL–2594 Den Haag
tel. (070) 3 85 97 00

Keytours Holland
Dam 19, NL–1012 JS Amsterdam
tel. (020) 6 23 50 51 and 6 24 73 10

NBBS Travel
Schipholweg 101, Postbus 360
NL–2300 AJ Leiden
tel. (071) 25 33 72

In some VVV offices (e.g. in Dordrecht, Gouda, The Hague, Middelburg, Utrecht and Zutphen) visitors can hire a portable cassette recorder with headphones. The commentary on the cassette, which is regularly brought up to date, guides the visitor on a tour of the town.
A cassette guide does not, of course, replace a good guidebook with its more detailed information and its maps and plans.

Cassette guides

Some museums also have cassette guides to introduce visitors to their collections.

Sport

Among the most popular sports in summer are all kinds of water sports (swimming, sailing, wind-surfing), cycling, golf, riding and tennis.

In addition to individual sports holidays it is possible to take part in holidays organised by various clubs and organisations. For sailing camps and organised sailing holidays, see Water Sports, below. Apart from the arrangements for practising the sport which is the main object of the holiday there

Organised sports holidays

are recreational programmes (e.g. fishing, cycling, walking) and opportunities for playing with local sports clubs.

Sporting events

In the various provinces there are sporting events of traditional character, like *fierljeppen* (pole vaulting over a canal) in Friesland.

Sport for
the disabled

See Disabled, Aid for

Information

Information about facilities for the various kinds of sport can be obtained from the Netherlands Bureau of Tourism, VVV offices and the sports associations and organisations listed below.

Fishing

There are some 350,000 hectares/875,000 acres of fishing waters (in lakes, canals, rivers, ponds and the IJsselmeer) in the Netherlands, as well as the waters of the North Sea. There are two angling organisations, NVVS and CNHV.
Information about fishing waters, types of fishing permitted, fishing licences and permits, species of fish, close seasons and minimum sizes, as well as about angling clubs in the Netherlands, can be obtained from the Dutch Association of Angling Federations:
Nederlandse Vereniging van Sportvisserfederaties (NVVS)
Postbus 288, NL–3800 AG Amersfoort
tel. (033) 63 49 24

A brochure, "Holland – the Ideal Angling Country", can be obtained from the Netherlands Board of Tourism or from VVV offices.

To fish in the Netherlands it is necessary to have a fishing licence (*sport-visakte),* valid for a calendar year, which can be obtained in any post office, and a permit (also valid for a year) which is obtained by becoming a member of a fishing club belonging to the national association.
For sea angling, either in the North Sea or in the Waddenzee, no licence or permit is required, but the statutory regulations on minimum sizes must be observed.
Throughout the year there are organised fishing trips in the North Sea, the waters round Zeeland and the Waddenzee, starting from various fishing ports (e.g. Scheveningen, Den Helder, Den Oever, IJmuiden). They usually leave around 8am and return in the afternoon; the boats have facilities for supplying light meals and drinks.

Fishing gear can be hired.

Land Sports

Football

The Royal Dutch Football Association is the largest sports organisation in the Netherlands. There are large football stadiums in Amsterdam, Rotterdam, Eindhoven and other towns.

Golf

See entry

Motor racing

Information:
Koninklijke Nederlandse Toeristenbond (ANWB)
Wassenaarseweg 220, NL–2596 EC Den Haag
tel. (0703) 14 71 47

Parachute jumping

There are facilities for parachute jumping (in tandem with an instructor), for example on the West Frisian island of Texel.

Riding

There are facilities for riding in many places throughout the Netherlands – among dunes, in forest country or on the beach. There are both waymarked bridle paths and areas in which riders can go as they please. The Dutch Forestry Commission (for address see Nature Reserves and National Parks) publishes footpath maps (*voetspoorkaarten*) on which bridle paths are specially marked.

Riding lessons are available in various riding schools and riding centres; some hotels also have a riding ring. Some riding schools and nature reserves require riders to produce a *ruiterbewijs* (certificate of competence); but even without this it is possible to ride in many areas provided that you are accompanied by an experienced rider.

Information:
Nederlandsche Hippische Sportbond (NHS)
Postbus 456, NL–3740 AL Baarn
tel. (02154) 2 18 41

A brochure, "Horse Riding in Holland", which in addition to general information about riding gives a list of riding schools, can be obtained from the Netherlands Bureau of Tourism.

There are a number of ice rinks in the Netherlands with a 400-metre track for skating races (e.g. at Heerenveen) and a pitch for ice hockey or figure skating. | Skating

Also very popular is long-distance skating on the frozen canals.

In cold winters the Eleven Cities Race is a great event in the province of Friesland. This is a 100km/125 mile long skating race in which up to 17,000 skaters take part. The race starts from the Friesland Halls in Leeuwarden.

Information: | Skittles
Koninklijke Nederlandse Kegelbond
Buurerstraat 39, NL–7481 EG Haaksbergen
tel. (05427) 1 17 72

Hotels in almost all the larger tourist centres have tennis courts, either outdoor or indoor. | Tennis

Information:
Koninklijke Nederlandse Lawntennis Bond
Postbus 107, NL–1200 AC Hilversum
tel. (035) 4 69 41

A brochure published by the National Board of Tourism, "Golf and Tennis", lists hotels which have their own tennis courts.

Tennis tournaments are held in many towns in the Netherlands, e.g. at Het Melkhuisje in Hilversum, the Metsbanen in Scheveningen and Ahoy in Rotterdam.

Walking

There are beautiful walking and jogging areas in the Netherlands, for example in the forests, in heathland and the polders, past fields of flowers or through orchards, along the coast and through the dunes.

In summer there are guided walks at low tide in the Waddenzee. The walks, which take several hours, start for example from Pieterburen in Groningen province and from various places in Friesland. | *Wadlopen*

There is a dense network of waymarked paths and trails, for example in nature reserves and National Parks (see entry). The routes are marked by | Waymarked paths small posts in various colours, so that it is usually not necessary to have a map or route description.

Walking maps

The Forestry Commission (Staatsbosbeheer: for address see Nature Reserves and National Parks) publishes walking maps (*voetspoorkaarten*) for over 30 areas, with directions for getting to the area and information about its history and flora and fauna.
Maps for walkers can also be obtained from local VVV and ANWB offices and from the Vereniging tot Behoud van Natuurmonumenten (for address see Nature Reserves and National Parks).

Trekkershutten
(log cabins)

Accommodation for walkers is available from April to October in *trekkershutten* (simple log cabins accommodating up to four people; no heating; bring a sleeping bag and cooking equipment; maximum stay three nights).
It is advisable to book in advance through the Netherlands Reservation Centre (see Information).

See also Camping and Caravanning

Events

In July there are International Four-Day Walks (30, 40 and 50km), starting from Apeldoorn and Nijmegen.

Water Sports

Information

Koninklijk Nederlands Watersport Verbond
(Royal Dutch Water Sports Union)
Postbus 53034, NL–1007 RA Amsterdam
tel. (020) 6 64 26 11

A brochure issued by the Netherlands Bureau of Tourism, "Holland: Land of Water", contains much useful information on the various water sports that can be practised in the Netherlands.

Information on all kinds of water sports is also available from ANWB offices. Head office: tel. (070) 3 14 71 47.

Weather reports
and shipping news

The Dutch Meteorological Institute (KNM) supplies weather reports (in Dutch) by telephone:
Frisian lakes, IJsselmeer and Waddenzee: tel. (06911) 2 23 52
Delta area (Ooster- and Westerschelde), Biesbosch and Zuid-Holland: tel. (06911) 2 23 53
Rhine estuary (weather report and shipping news): tel. (06911) 2 23 27

Swimming

Many holiday resorts have swimming pools (indoor and/or outdoor), and many hotels have their own indoor pools.
There are also facilities for swimming in the sea (see Bathing Beaches), on inland lakes and in the IJsselmeer. Prudence is advisable in waters with unknown currents and in tidal waters.

Surfing

The Netherlands offer ideal conditions for wind-surfing in all grades of difficulty. Information from the wind-surfing section of the Koninklijk Nederlands Watersport Verbond (see above).
Since surfing is prohibited in certain areas prospective surfers should enquire locally about possible restrictions or obtain the ANWB wind-surfing map (telephone number for information: see above).

There are many surfing schools which run courses and hire out surfboards. A list can be obtained from the Netherlands Bureau of Tourism.

Favourite surfing areas (with good surfing conditions and facilities, reliable wind, clean water and reasonable prices) are the Veerse Meer (province of

Wind-surfers in the Ijsselmeer

Zeeland), the IJsselmeer and the Brouwersdam. Other good surfing waters are the Maas area around Roermond in Limburg province, the lakes of Noord- and Zuid-Holland and the large lakes round the Flevopolder.

Only experienced surfers should go in for surf-boarding in the North Sea.

Two surfing competitions are held in Friesland – the Eleven Towns Surfing Tour (the most difficult surfing contest in the world) in March and the Eleven Lakes Surfing Tour at the beginning of October.

In some areas water-skiing can be practised only with special permission. Water-skiers must not start from the beach, and speed must not exceed 6km/3¾ miles an hour within 100m/110yds of the shore.
See also Motorboating, below.

Water-skiing

Boating

There is endless scope for boating holidays in the Netherlands, either in your own boat or in a hired one. A wide range of boats in all sizes and categories, with or without sleeping accommodation, are available for hire, at rates which vary according to the season as well as to the size and equipment of the boat.

Information about canoeing in the Netherlands and a list of canoe hirers can be obtained from:
Nederlandse Kano Bond
Postbus 3800, NL–3818 BD Amersfoort
tel. (033) 62 23 41

Canoeing

Information also from:
Toeristische Kano Verbond Nederland
Poststraat 35, NL–2613 PE Delft
tel. (015) 13 92 22

Books and maps for canoeists:
Jacob van Wijngaarden
Overtoom 13, NL–1054 HN Amsterdam
tel. (020) 6 12 19 01

A brochure, ''Canoeing in Holland'', is published by the Netherlands Bureau of Tourism.

Modern canoes have room for a certain amount of luggage, like a tent and clothing. For those who like a little more comfort there are packages combining canoeing and hotel accommodation. Information from VVV offices, particularly in the provinces of Friesland, Gelderland, Groningen, Noord-Holland, Overijssel and Noord-Brabant.

Motorboating

It is easier for beginners to master the operation of a motorboat than a sailing boat, and motorboats offer more room than sailing dinghies or yachts. A driving licence is required only for boats over 15m/49ft in length and with a speed of over 20km/12½ miles an hour, and most of the boats available for hire fall below these limits. The hiring firm gives a quick course of instruction before handing over the boat.
It is important to have good maps and charts. There is a speed limit of 6km/3¾ miles an hour within 100m/110yds of the shore and beyond this usually a limit of 16km/10 miles an hour. In certain areas motorboats with a speed of over 20km/12½ miles an hour are required – even if they do not exceed these speed limits – to have a special permit, obtainable from the local VVV office.

Reservations of motorboats can be arranged, for example, through the Friesland VVV office.

Sailing

Sailing enthusiasts will find ideal sailing conditions in the Netherlands and a wide range of facilities, from small jetties to large and well equipped marinas.

Types of
sailing boat

Botter (fishing smack): flat bottom, high, full head, slender stern, open deck area behind mast, narrow on the beam.
Galjas: trading ship; mast fore and aft.
Klipper (clipper): trading ship; S-shaped prow, slim underwater line, one or two tall masts.
Klipperaak (clipper barge): a cross between a clipper and a spritsail barge.
Kotter (cutter): a fast sailing ship; mast fore and aft.
Logger (lugger): originally a seagoing fishing vessel; straight stem.
Schoener (schooner): a fast sailing ship; fore-and-aft rig, two or three masts.
Schokker: fishing boat; flat or round bottom, heavy and straight bow, open deck area behind mast.
Tjalk (spritsail barge): freighter for inland waters; flat bottom, rounded bow and stern, large hold.

Classification

A brochure available from the Netherlands Bureau of Tourism, ''Traditional Sailing'', lists boat hire firms and classifies boats available for hire on a ''star'' system, from five stars for a luxury boat with every amenity to one star for the most modest type of craft.
Yacht harbours and charter boats are in future to be classified on the same system.

To be accepted for a sailing course the applicant must have a swimming badge.
There is a difference between sailing schools and sailing camps. Sailing schools concentrate on the theory and practice of sailing, while sailing camps also provide facilities for sport and recreation.

Organised sailing holidays are run by the following bodies among others:

Algemene Kampcommissie voor Doopsgezinde Kampen
Kerkstraat 54, NL–3581 RE Utrecht, tel. (030) 31 25 33

Buro Intersail Groepsreizen
Postbus 119, NL–8600 AC Sneek, tel. (05150) 2 30 62

Nederlands Instituut voor Volksontwikkeling en Natuurvriendenwerk
Nieuwe Herengracht 119, NL–SB 1011 Amsterdam, tel. (020) 6 26 93 11

Stichting Watersport met Gehandicapten
(water sports for the handicapped)
Postbus 157, NL–1600 AD Enkhuizen, tel. (02280) 1 28 28

Zeilvloot Stavoren
(sailing on restored historic ships)
Dwinger 19, NL–8715 HV Stavoren, tel. (05149) 18 18
For a day, a weekend or one or more weeks

Zon en Vrijheid Vakantiecentra
't Frusselt 30, NL–8076 EE Vierhouten
Postal address: Postbus 268, NL–8070 AG Nunspeet, tel. (05771) 5 56

A list of sailing schools can be obtained from the Netherlands Bureau of Tourism.

There are a number of major sailing events throughout the year. The best known is Sail Amsterdam, in which some 1000 sailing vessels of all sizes take part.
Skûtjesilen (July): races with old cargo yachts and market boats on the Frisian lakes.

Boat Hire

Sailing boats, motorboats and surf-boards can be hired from numerous charter firms and from some VVV offices. The following is a selection of hire firms in the various provinces.

Zeil- en Surfschool Zuidlaarder Meer
Emmalaan 30, NL–9471 KR Zuidlaren, tel. (06905) 23 79

Aqua Centrum Bremerbergsehoek
Bremerbergdijk 35, NL–8256 RD Biddinghuizen, tel. (03211) 16 35

Firma Roukema
Polsleatwei 11, NL–8491 EK Akkrum, tel. (05665) 18 88

Beekema's Jachtverhuur
Jachthavenkade 21, NL–8560 AB Balk, tel. (05140) 26 87

Zeilcentrum Allemansend
Mardijk 7, NL–8581 KG Elahuizen, tel. (05140) 40 80

Botenverhuurbedrijf Grouw
NL–9000 AA Grouw, tel. (05662) 38 10 and 16 85

Watersportbedrijf Anja
Meersweg 9A, NL–9001 BG Grouw, tel. (05662) 13 73 and (05105) 15 85

Sport

Harlingen	Bijko Jachtservice Koningsweg 4, NL–8861 KN Harlingen, tel. (05178) 1 51 16
Heeg	Yachtcharters Jan de Vries De Drael 33, NL–8621 CZ Heeg, tel. (05154) 25 67
Sneek	Abma's Jachtwerf De Domp Groenedijk 9A, NL–8607 CJ Sneek, tel. (05150) 1 90 65
	Aquanaut Yachtcharter Selfhelpweg 9, NL–8607 AB Sneek, tel. (05150) 1 22 53
	Frisia Yachtcharter Oude Oppenhuizerweg 79, NL–8606 JC Sneek, tel. (05150) 1 28 14
Warns	Sail Service Holland Ymedaem 1, NL–8722 Warns, tel. (05142) 23 00
Ylst	Skipper Club Charter Sneekerpad 8–14, NL–05155 15 99
Gelderland Harderwijk	Watersportcentrum Harderwijk Lorentzhaven 1, NL–3846 BR Harderwijk, tel. (03410) 1 76 54
Groningen Groningen	VVV Groningen Naberpassage 3, NL–9712 JV Groningen, NL–050) 13 97 00
Limburg Roermond	Watersportbedrijf K. Hermus Hatenboer, NL–6041 TP Roermond, tel. (04758) 15 89
Noord-Brabant Eindhoven	Zeil- en Vaarschool Nautilus De Vriesstraat 43, NL–5612 KG Eindhoven tel. (040) 43 58 47 and (04183) 28 87
Noord-Holland Purmerend	Waterland Yacht Charter Boekweitstraat 81, NL–1442 CM Purmerend tel. (02990) 4 00 89 and (02995) 10 58
Overijssel Ossenzijl	Jacht-Charter Fluvius Opdyk 12, NL–8376 HH Ossenzijl, tel. (05617) 6 o3 and 6 76
Utrecht Loosdrecht	De Vier Windstreken NL–1230 AC Loosdrecht, tel. (02158) 33 70
Nieuwegein	Hatenboer Yachting Marconibaan 26, NL–3439 MS Nieuwegein and Israelslaan 15, NL–3582 HH Nieuwegein, tel. (030) 51 03 81
Oud Loosdrecht	Ottenhome Loosdrecht Oud Loosdrechtsedijk 207, NL–1231 LW Oud Loosdrecht tel. (02158) 33 31 and 55 44
Maarssen	OCC-Yachting Nederland Bloemstede 46, NL–3608 TJ Maarssen tel. (03465) 6 79 91 and (02159) 5 02 44
Zeeland Arnemuiden	Watersport Bedrijf De Arne Jachthaven Oranjeplaat, NL–4341 PZ Arnemuiden, tel. 01182) 14 19
Noordwijkerhout	VW Charters Postbus 83, NL–2210 AB Noordwijkerhout, tel. (02523) 7 41 14
Vlissingen	Beaver Ships, J.A. van Fraasen-Jongman Pres. Rooseveltlaan 770, NL–4382 NB Vlissingen, tel. (01184) 1 76 10

Jachthaven J. van Asselt
Julianalaan 55, NL–2159 LD De Kaag, tel. (02524) 42 33

Jachtwerf Olympia Charters
Veerpolder 61–67, NL–2361 KZ Warmond
tel. (01711) 1 00 43 and 1 19 20

Environmental Standards

Beaches and pleasure harbours in European Community countries are awarded a blue "Europe flag" if they meet certain criteria on water and beach quality, are free from noise and objectionable odours and have proper sewage disposal arrangements.

Telephones

See Postal and Telephone Services

Television

See Radio and Television

Time

The Netherlands observe Central European Time, which is one hour ahead of Greenwich Mean Time.
From the end of March or beginning of April to the end of September – the exact times are published in the press – Summer Time (two hours ahead of GMT) is in force.

Tipping

Hotels, restaurants, cafés, etc., include a service charge in the bill, but it is usual to round up the sum to the nearest guilder; similarly with taxis. An additional tip (*fooi*) may be given for any special service.

Women attendants in public lavatories are usually given 25 or 50 cents.

Trade Fairs

Information about trade fairs can be obtained from the Netherlands Bureau of Tourism.   Information

Among the best known trade fairs, with reputations extending well beyond the bounds of the Netherlands, are those held in Amsterdam, Maastricht, Rotterdam and Utrecht.

See also Conferences and Congresses, Events and Markets

Travel Documents

Visitors from Britain, the United States, Canada and most other Commonwealth and European countries require only a passport for a visit to the   Passport

Netherlands of less than three months. For a stay of over three months a visa is required.

Car papers
National driving licences and car registration documents are accepted (and should of course be taken).
Cars must have an oval nationality plaque.
No special documents are required for trailers, bicycles or mopeds.

Motorboats
Motorboats capable of a speed of over 16km/10 miles an hour must be registered with the Dutch authorities (which can be done at the larger post offices) and must have insurance cover.

Long sporting and pleasure boats
Sporting and pleasure boats (canoes, rowing boats, etc.) over 5.50m/18ft in length must be reported to the Dutch customs, which will issue a certificate (*verklaring*) permitting them to be used for a maximum period of twelve months without payment of duty. In the case of boats of substantial value the customs may ask for a deposit of 20% value-added tax.

Car Telephones, Radio Transmitters, etc.

For information on the regulations governing the import and use in the Netherlands of car telephones, CD band radios and radio transmitters in boats, apply to the telecommunications authorities:
Telecommunicatie en Post Operationele Zaken (HDTP/OZ)
Postbus 450, NL–9700 AL Groningen
tel. (050) 22 21 11

Water Sports

See Sport

Weather

See Facts and Figures, Climate; When to Go

When to Go

Spring
Cities such as Amsterdam, of course, with their treasures of art and culture, can be visited at any time of year; but for the Netherlands in general the best time for a visit is spring, when the parks and fields of flowers are in their full glory of blossom.

Summer
The main season for the seaside resorts on the Dutch coast and on the islands is from June/July to the end of August. Since hotels tend to be full during this period it is advisable to book well in advance.

Autumn
Autumn (from the end of August onwards) can also be very beautiful, when the country is bathed in the luminous light which inspired the great Dutch painters of the golden age. In the coastal areas, however, this is the rainiest season.

Winter
The Dutch winter is relatively mild. This is also the season for skating and ice hockey enthusiasts, who can practise their sport in more than twenty ice rinks or, in a severe winter, on the frozen canals, rivers and lakes.
See also Sport.

Reminder
It should be remembered that west winds predominate in the Netherlands and that the summer can be relatively cool and sometimes wet. It is

advisable, therefore, to have protection from wind and rain, including a pullover or other warm woollen garment, as well as stout footwear.

See also Facts and Figures, Climate

Windmills

The Netherlands once had something like 10,000 windmills; now there are barely 1000. Some are situated close together, as at Kinderdijk (see A to Z, Kinderdijk); others stand by themselves in the landscape; and some can be seen in various open-air museums.

Some 200 windmills are still working, and some of these are open to visitors during the summer. A flag or pennant displayed on a mill indicates that visitors are welcome.
On the first Saturday in the month, from May to September, hundreds of windmill sails are set in motion.

The following is a selection of windmills open to the public.

Wolzigt oil and flour mill (1852)
Hoofdstraat 60, tel. (05908) 3 21 98
May to Sept., Tue.–Sat. 1.30–5pm

Drenthe
Roderwolde

De Eendracht flour and hulling mill (1889); still in use
Mounebuorren 18, tel. (05193) 19 26
Apr. to Sept., Mon. 1–5pm, Tue.–Sat. 10am–5pm

Friesland
Anjum

De Witte Molen (15th c.); a drainage mill still in use as a flour mill
Zijpendaalseweg 24, tel. (085) 42 40 95
Tue.–Fri. 9.30am–4.30pm, Sat. 11am–4pm (admission free)

Gelderland
Arnhem

De Doornenboom flour mill (1830)
Doelenstraat 53, tel. (04255) 31 24 and 32 20
May to Sept., Sat. and Sun. 2–5pm (by appointment outside these hours; admission free for children under 7)

Noord-Brabant
Hilvarenbeek

Den Deen flour mill (1839)
Kapellerweg 13
By appointment, tel. (04974) 13 14

Luyksgestel

Assumburg flour mill (1778); Dutch Windmill Museum
Veerweg 1, tel. (01676) 27 24 and 23 50
Mid May to Aug., Sat. and Sun. 2–5pm

Nieuw-
Vossemeer

Het Pink oil mill (1620); in use during the summer
Pinkstraat 12; seen by appointment, tel. (075) 21 51 48

Noord-Holland
Koog aan de Zaan

Museum mill (1635)
Noordervaart 2, tel. (02202) 15 19
Apr. to Sept., Tue.–Sun. 10am–5pm; Oct. to Mar., Sun. 10am–4.30pm (guided tour)

Schermerhorn

De Schoolmeester paper-mill (1695); the only wind-paper-mill still in use
Guisweg, tel. (075) 21 51 48
July to mid Aug., Tue.–Sat. 9.30am–5pm

Westzaan

De Zoeker oil mill (1673); still in use
Klaverringdijk, tel. (075) 28 58 22
Apr. to Oct., Mon. 10am–5pm

Zaandam

De Kat paint mill (1784)
Klaverringdijk, tel. (075) 21 04 77
Apr. to Oct., Tue.–Sun. 9am–5pm; Nov. to Mar., Sat. and Sun. 9am–5pm

Windmills in the Netherlands

Types of windmill
see Facts and Figures, Culture

Waddenzee

North Sea

Dokkum

Leeuwarden

GRONINGEN

Groningen

Harlingen

Sneek

Assen

FRIESLAND

Den Helder

Hoorn

Meppel

Alk-
maar

IJsselmeer

Zaan-
dam

Haarlem

Zwolle

© Baedeker

Heemstede

AMSTERDAM

Deventer

ZUID-
HOLLAND

UTRECHT

Enschede

Leiden

Utrecht

GELDERLAND

DEN HAAG

Wijk
bij
Duurstede

NOM Arnhem

Gouda

Rotterdam

Kinder-
dijk

Arnhem

Zeddam

Schiedam

Gorinchem

Nijmegen

Dordrecht

s'Hertogenbosch

NOORD-

Veere

Breda

Tilburg

BRABANT

ZEELAND

Eindhoven

Sluis

LIMBURG

IJzendijke
Biervliet

Roermond

Maastricht

Kinderdijk — Place with one or more windmills

GELDERLAND — Province with mills at various places

Overijssel Denekamp	Singraven drainage mill (1448); still in use as a flour mill and sawmill Tel. (05413) 13 72 Tue.–Sat. 10.30–11.30am and 2–4pm
Diepenheim	De Haller flour mill (13th c. watermill); still in use Watermolenweg 32 By appointment, tel. (05475) 1 28 07, Tue.–Thur. 2–5pm
Ommen	Den Oordt flour mill and sawmill (1824) Den Oordt 6, tel. (05291) 16 38 Mid June to Aug., Mon.–Fri. 10am–12 noon and 2–5pm, Sat. 2–4pm; Sept. 1st–15th, Mon.–Fri. 2–4pm

Windmills, Kinderdijk

Nineteen polder mills (1740) along Molenkade Apr. to Sept., Mon.–Sat. 9.30am–5.30pm or by appointment, tel. (01859) 1 41 18	**Zuid-Holland** Kinderdijk
De Valk flour mill (1743) 2e Binnenvestgracht 1, tel. (071) 25 46 39 Tue.–Sat. 10am–5pm, Sun. and pub. hols. 1–5pm (closed Oct. 3rd, Dec. 25th and Jan. 1st)	Leiden
De Veijheid flour mill (1785); still in use Noordvest 40, tel. (010) 4 73 30 00 Sat. 10.30am–4.30pm (admission free; no children under 8)	Schiedam

De Noord flour mill (1794); in operation every Saturday
Noordvest 38

See also Facts and Figures, Windmills

Youth Hostels

There are more than forty youth hostels (*jeugdherbergen*) in the Netherlands, now open to people of all ages. They offer very reasonably priced
accommodation to holders of membership cards of youth hostel associations affiliated to the International Youth Hostel Federation. There are
special rates for families and groups.
Rates are higher for those without a membership card.

Advance reservation is advisable, and in July and August is essential. For
information about facilities for the disabled at a particular youth hostel
enquire at the hostel concerned.

Youth Travel

At some youth hostels bicycles can be hired.

Dutch
Youth Hostel
Association

Nederlandse Jeugdherberg Centrale (NJHC)
Prof. Tulpplein 4, NL–1018 GX Amsterdam
tel. (020) 5 51 31 33

NJHC Handbook

The NJHC Handbook, with a list of Dutch youth hostels, can be obtained from the NJHC office (free to holders of youth hostel membership cards; otherwise a small charge) or from national youth hostel associations.

Budget
accommodation

Budget accommodation is also available in family rooms, apartments, bungalows (chalets) and log cabins (see Camping and Caravanning).
The "Guide to Budget Accommodation" published by the International Youth Hostel Federation has a chapter on the Netherlands in Vol. 1.

Youth Travel

The Netherlands Bureau of Tourism publishes a brochure, "Holland: Land for the Young", which contains a variety of information and suggestions for holidays for young people in the Netherlands, including the addresses of organisations which arrange exchanges or provide help and advice, work camps, university courses, teaching in Dutch schools, etc.

Index

Index

Source of Illustrations

Beermann: 4; Bildagentur Schuster: 2; Brinks: 101; De Efteling: 2; Diamond Center: 1; Feltes: 83; Frans Hals Museum: 3; Gesellschaft für Länder und Völkerkunde: 1; Heineken Brewery: 1; Helga Lade: 4; Historia: 9; Kröller-Müller Museum: 1; Netherlands Bureau of Dairy Products: 3; Netherlands Bureau of Tourism: 38; Stichting Het Nationale Park De Hoge Veluwe: 1; Vergeer/Reitzig: 5.